Thinking Biblically

Thinking Biblically

Exegetical and Hermeneutical Studies

André LaCocque and Paul Ricoeur

Translated by David Pellauer

The University of Chicago Press
Chicago and London

The University of Chicago Press, Chicago 60637
The University of Chicago Press, Ltd., London
© 1998 by The University of Chicago
All rights reserved. Published 1998
Printed in the United States of America
23 22 21 20 19 18 17 16 15 14   2 3 4 5 6

ISBN-13: 978-0-226-71337-3 (cloth)
ISBN-13: 978-0-226-71343-4 (paper)

Library of Congress Cataloging-in-Publication Data

LaCocque, André
    Thinking biblically: Exegetical and hermeneutical studies / André LaCocque and
    Paul Ricoeur; translated by David Pellauer.
        p. cm.
    Includes bibliographical references and index.
    ISBN 0-226-71337-7 (cloth: alk. paper)
    1. Bible.   O.T.—Criticism, interpretation, etc.   2. Bible.   O.T.—Hermeneu-
    tics.   I. Ricœur, Paul.   II. Title.
    BS511.2.L24   1998
    221.6—dc21   97-44091
                                                                                 CIP

To Simone Ricoeur
of blessed memory
6 January 1998

I will put my Spirit in you and ye shall live!
—Ezekiel 37:14

Contents

Preface

The volume you are about to read is the result of an unusual collaboration. It brings together an exegete, who is a specialist in the Hebrew Bible, and a philosopher, who identifies himself with the so-called hermeneutic school of thought. Both authors decided to read and comment on the same texts taken from the Hebrew Bible. The exegete first wrote out his contribution, then the philosopher responded to it. Next, they both revised their respective contributions in such a way that the final redaction would yield a book in which each author's work took account of that of the other. Our working field is deliberately circumscribed by "strong" texts of the First Testament, representative of the various biblical literary genres: *mythic; narrative; prescriptive; oracular; apocalyptic; hymnic; sapiential;* plus a sui-generis text from Exodus 3 on the *Name* of God.

For the sake of completeness with literary genres, André LaCocque is the sole author of two complementary essays, one on the Joseph narrative in the book of Genesis, the other on a most controversial prophetic oracle in Zechariah 12:10. In these monologues of sorts, no less than in the dialogical parts of this book, the reader will find the same kind of trajectory movement that characterizes the other essays.

In what follows in this preface, we shall speak with one voice and explain the basis of our collaboration.

At first glance, our approaches may appear different to the point of standing in opposition to each other. The exegete makes use of the historical-critical method, modified in light of the methodological considerations we discuss below that have made possible our collaboration in this volume. Yet the historical-critical method makes precise demands that one might even qualify as scientific without abusing the term.

These are sufficiently well known so that there is no need for us to list them here. We prefer instead to speak about the inflections and complements we have added that go beyond them.

From his side, the philosopher takes into account the reception of the biblical text by thinkers initially marked by Greek philosophy, then by modern philosophy. It is not so much the diversity among these modes of thought that took up the Bible that causes problems as it is the introduction into the commentary on biblical texts of tools of thought—concepts, arguments, theories—that were forged outside the biblical field of thought, from the Greeks up to the present.

From this initial opposition, indicated only sketchily here, one might conclude that there is a radical heterogeneity between the two exercises in reading presented in each section of this book. Does not the one seek to be scholarly, even scientific, and the other to be philosophic? Is not the one turned toward what lies behind the text, toward its archaeology, while the other looks toward what comes afterward, toward its teleology (as if in fact all the successive readings are united by a unique telos, something that is far from being true)? It is this apparent antinomy between retrospection and prospection, between the production of the text and its reception, that we want to refute in the following pages.

On the one hand, the exegete does not overlook the role of reading in the elaboration of the meaning of a text, which one might think the sole concern of the philosopher. He too takes account of the act of reading in his methodology, in a way we shall speak of below. On the other hand, the philosopher does not ignore the specificity of the texts found within the biblical *corpus,* anymore than he denies the originality of the Hebrew, then the Christian way of thinking. He is so aware of this, in fact, that the very concept of a Christian philosophy, or even of a "biblical metaphysics," once put forward by Etienne Gilson, appear completely inadequate to him.

It is in terms of this double movement by which we have taken up each other's work that we should like now to briefly discuss and justify the title *Thinking Biblically,* which seemed to us to characterize each of the sections of the voyage we each made through these texts.

I

Beginning from the side of the exegete, we want to indicate in what ways, proper to his discipline, we have been able to integrate into the method of historical-criticism one of the most interesting recent developments in biblical studies, which we may call attending to the *Wirkungsgeschichte* or even the *Nachgeschichte* of sacred texts. In English, we could say their foreground or their traditional history, in the sense of a history that is at the same time a tradition, where tradition is to be understood in a dynamic rather than a static sense. Thanks to this addition, the exegetical approach is open to considering the ways in which a text has been received, to which the philosopher seeks to add still another dimension. What considerations governed this expansion of the historical-critical method?

The first factor exegesis takes into account has to do with the role writing played in the formation of the biblical *corpus*. Reading is a response to this writing, in a multitude of ways of which we shall speak further below. Here, let us simply note that the first effect of reading is to confer an autonomy, an independent existence on a text, which thereby opens it to subsequent developments and subsequent enrichments, all of which affect its very meaning. In light of this, we would like to recall the wonderful saying of Gregory the Great, whom Pier Cesare Bori cites in his book significantly entitled *L'Interpretazione infinita:* "Scripture grows with its readers."

The first corollary of this thesis regarding the autonomy of the text is the abandonment of the concern, so characteristic of Romanticist hermeneutics and associated with the name of Friedrich Schleiermacher, to recover the author's intentions and to set them up as governing all interpretation. Without claiming that investigations having to do with the author or the date and place of production of a text have nothing to do with making sense of a text—the studies that make up this volume will bear this out—we do hold that the meaning of a text is in each instance an event that is born at the intersection between, on the one hand, those constraints that the text bears within itself and that have to do in large part with its *Sitz im Leben* and, on the other hand, the different expectations of a series of communities of reading and interpretation that the presumed authors of the text under consideration could not have anticipated.

The second factor that pushes the critical exegete to consider subsequent history, what above we called the foreground or traditional history, is the inscription of the text, which is contemporary with the formation of this foreground, in terms of one or several traditions, which in return have left their stamp on the text in question. This is especially evident at the literary level when it is a question of following the track of the formation and accumulation of these different traditional readings within the very canon of Scripture. What then becomes evident is that the interpretive process is not limited to restoring the source text all along this sequence or sequences of repeated actualizations, rather this process re-invents, re-figures, and re-orients the model. This second phenomenon distances us a bit more from the hermeneutical principle of the authority attached to the author's presumed intention. In this sense, the phenomenon we are indicating might well be termed a "trajectory" that has its origin in the text itself. Indeed, at one point we even considered using *Trajectories* as the title for this volume.

The third factor, the one that the exegete most takes into account, has to do with the connection between the text and a living community. This factor follows from the preceding ones concerning the history of the tradition or traditions incorporated into the biblical *corpus*. In this respect, the original orientation toward the act of reading, which is constitutive of the first form of the reception of a text, can be observed on the level of the Hebrew Bible with regard to its relationship with the people of Israel. Here, reception is not just reading, even a scholarly reading, it is a new word spoken with regard to the text and starting from the text.

In fact, it is from this perspective that the later Jewish tradition speaks of a "written Torah" accompanied by an "orally transmitted Torah." There is no separation between the two; the second constitutes the extension of the first, of its vitality and its capacity to fill the temporal horizon. In this regard, the hermeneutical principle of the sixteenth-century Reformers—summed up in the phrase, *sola scriptura*—turns out to be untenable on the hermeneutical plane. It was, in fact, partly responsible for the divorce Christian exegesis of the Hebrew Bible brought about between the text and the people of Israel. Cut off from its ties to a living community, the text gets reduced to a cadaver handed over for autopsy. Despite its many merits, modern exegesis is largely vitiated by this conception of a fixed text, reduced once and for all to its current form. Recent "canonical" criticism contributes—in spite of itself, it is true—to this erroneous conception of a sacred text. And historical-critical method in its broad form all the more readily tends in this direction. In an artificial manner, it considers the development of Scripture as complete with the establishment of its final redaction. It is almost as though one were to give the funeral eulogy of someone yet alive. The eulogy might be accurate and appropriate, but it is nonetheless "premature," as Mark Twain might have put it.

As for the Hebrew Scriptures, the literary stage of their redaction was never conceived of as a way of cutting off their life span. For example, the oracles were not consigned to writing by the disciples of the prophets with the idea that, the page having been turned, one could now occupy oneself with other things. Quite the contrary. During their oral stage, these oracles were endowed with an existence marked by expectation, itself open to a horizon that had no other limit than their accomplishment. Once written down, these oracles took on another mode of existence that transformed them but that did not finish them. History gave flesh to the prophetic vision, thanks to which this vision was considered worthy of inscription in that collective memory that is assured through the mediation of the written text. The project of confiding a text to writing, thus, far from being encased in retrospection, turns out to be primordially prospective. Historical confirmation is always taken to be a merely *partial* fulfillment. Events, whose course was anticipated, become paradigmatic, thanks to their prophetic interpretation. They point in a certain direction. They determine a historical orientation. In short, they participate in the nature of the Torah. Hence textual redaction does not close a chapter, even if historical criticism limits itself to an analysis of the initially oral phase of the existence of a text, cut off from its subsequent development. This is why the exegetical part of the present work has been conceived of as an expansion of the historical-critical method, completed by an exploration of the "foreground" of the text under consideration. It is treated as a *written* text, the one that the tradition of reading set to work, re-affected, and re-animated. The dynamism of the text is taken into account, its course, and its trajectory is retraced on this basis.

This textual dynamism is found in almost every one of the genres represented in biblical literature. The very anonymity of the biblical texts can be interpreted from this point of view, the "original authors" being aware from the beginning of the irremediable incompleteness of their work, which seeks to be "remembered"; in other words, taking into account the biblical understanding of the term "memory," their work asks to be re-modeled, to be re-actualized by the community that is the only agent of these texts. These remarks give us a chance to add one other detail concerning the notion of a "text." We spoke above of the autonomy of a text. This feature applies to the text's author, not to its audience. The text exists, in the final analysis, thanks to the community, for the use of the community, with a view to giving shape to the community. In other words, if we take the relation to its author as the background of a text, the relation to the reader or readers constitutes the foreground. We must therefore say emphatically that the foreground outruns the background.

What we have said regarding the relation between the Hebrew texts and the community of the people of Israel has to be repeated with regard to the texts of the Second Testament. It was again in response to the needs and expectations of a living community that these texts were drawn up. It is these needs and expectations that have to be restored if we are to make sense of these texts in terms of their contemporary composition and redaction. Thus, the trajectory traced by the texts of the First Testament continues its course beyond this first *corpus* and inside a second *corpus*. One of our shared convictions is that it is the same trajectory, considerably ramified, it is true, that unfolds from one textual ensemble to the other. The First Testament is not abolished by the Second, but reinterpreted and, in this sense, "fulfilled." This fulfillment presupposes the consistency of a tradition and of already constituted traditions, without the support of which the new faith would remain a passing cry. One can say in this regard that the reinterpretation of already existing Scriptures by a new proclamation constitutes a hermeneutic model—sometimes placed under the heading "typology" or "allegory"—that governs several of the subsequent phases of the reappropriation of the canonical texts in communities of interpretation that in turn burst the limits attached to the needs and expectations of the primitive Christian community. In this regard, the practical exercise of hermeneutics offered by this volume can be characterized as Judeo-Christian to the extent that the Christian reading is not taken as a substitute but, rather, as an alternative to the traditional Jewish reading. The exegete will forbid himself from saying that the reading carried out in the New Testament is a "good" or a "bad" reading of the Hebrew texts. He will even confine himself to emphasizing the fundamentally Jewish aspect more than the various methods of interpretation might suggest. The trajectory of the text thus runs from one pole to the other, or, perhaps, to others, once the trajectory splits in two directions, with one of its branches leading to Christian "orthodoxy" and the other to Jewish "orthopraxis."

A final consideration opens the work of the exegete toward that of the philosopher. It has to do with the plurivocity of the text. This phenomenon too is closely linked to the opening of the text on the side of its readers and, more generally, the side of its subsequent reception. A hermeneutics that places the principal accent on the author's intention tends to claim a univocal status for the meaning of the text, if it is the case that what the author meant to say can in fact be reduced to a single intention. A hermeneutics that is attentive to the history of reception will be respectful of the irreducible plurivocity of the text. This feature holds from the first relation of a text with a variety of communities that interpret themselves in interpreting the text. Indeed, it is rare that several communities not be engendered by one and the same text. In this sense, the plurivocity of the text and a plurality of readings are connected phenomena. Hence the text is not something unilinear—something it could be in virtue of the finality instituted by the presumed intention of the author—but multidimensional, as soon as it is not taken as something to be read on just one level but on several levels at the same time by a historical community marked by heterogeneous interests. Just as a work of art solicits several interpretations whose cumulative effects are meant both to do justice to the work and to contribute to its subsequent life, the ways in which the interpreting community proposes a historical reading and interpretation contributes to the pluridimensionality of the text. These become part of the text. In this regard, there is no more striking indication of this process than the case of the Semitic form of writing where there are only consonants and where the reader has to supply the appropriate vocalization in reading it.

These are the developments that exegesis brings to the historical-critical method. They are also the ones that open the commentary to being taken up by a deliberately philosophical approach. The time has come to give the philosophical counterpart to what has been said about the exegetical side.

II

The philosopher takes up the other half of the path leading to the encounter with the exegete by putting himself in the school of exegesis, which means that the philosopher who is not a specialist in exegesis becomes a reader of exegesis.

This apprenticeship itself involves a number of requirements. To be more precise, the philosopher most disposed to a dialogue with an exegete is undoubtedly one who more readily reads works of exegesis than theological treatises. Theology, in fact, is a very complex and highly speculative form of discourse, eminently respectable in its place. But it is a mixed or composite form of discourse where philosophical speculation is already inextricably intermingled with what deserves to be called "biblical thought," even when it does not assume the specific form of

Wisdom, but also that of narrative, law, prophecy, or the hymn. Our working hypothesis here is that there are modes of thought other than those based on Greek, Cartesian, Kantian, Hegelian, etc. philosophy. Is it not the case, for example, with the great religious texts of India or the metaphysical traditions of Buddhism? Hence the initial philosophical wager here is that the literary genres we shall speak of below are forms of discourse that give rise to philosophical thinking.

The second presupposition that guides the hermeneutical philosopher is that this kind of thinking is linked to a corpus of texts not reducible to those one usually turns to when one "does philosophy" in the academic and professional sense. To read Genesis, Deuteronomy, Isaiah, a Psalm, a Gospel, or one of the Epistles in the New Testament is to enter into a wholly novel group of texts as compared with, say, a Socratic dialogue, or Descartes' *Meditations*, or Kant's *Critique of Pure Reason*. The kind of deliberate change of scenery advocated by Northrop Frye in his *The Great Code* is the rule here. This great literary critic from Toronto is correct when he says that, in order to make contact with this kind of discourse, it is necessary to turn back to a discourse that is not scientifically descriptive or explanatory, one that is not even apologetic, argumentative, or dogmatic, it is a world of discourse where the metaphorical language of poetry is the closest secular equivalent. Greek tragedy alone perhaps comes closest to the language of the Wisdom sayings and the hymns of the psalmist.

A third presupposition, thanks to which the work of the philosopher hermeneut moves toward that of the exegete hermeneut, has to do with the relation between the texts of the biblical *corpus* and those historical communities that we can here call communities of reading and interpretation. There is something completely unique here in relation to the reading of philosophical texts which, even within the setting of established schools, knows nothing comparable to the reception of a religious text by a historical community like that of the Jewish and Christian communities. A veritable hermeneutical circle imposes itself here, which remains a source of astonishment, even of perplexity, for the philosopher, particularly when criticism carries the day over conviction. This circle runs as follows. It is in interpreting the Scriptures in question that the community in question interprets itself. A kind of mutual election takes place here between those texts taken as foundational and the community we have deliberately called a community of reading and interpretation. If this circle is not vicious to the eyes of the faithful belonging to such communities, it is because the founding role attached to the sacred texts and the founded condition of the historical community do not designate interchangeable places. The founding text *teaches*—this is what the word *torah* means. And the community *receives* instruction. Even when this relation surpasses that between authority and obedience to become one of love, the difference in altitude between the word that teaches with authority and the one that responds with acknowledgment cannot be abolished. In this regard, faith is nothing other than the confession of this asymmetry between the word of the teacher and that of the disciple, and between the writings in which these two types of words are inscribed.

The fact that the same texts could have engendered several historical communities and given rise to the phenomenon of plurivocity discussed above does not alter the circular relation we refer to here between the elected text and the elected community. Even less does it attenuate this relationship; it makes it even more complex. Let us add, in passing, that these reflections concerning the mutual election between a *corpus* of texts and a historical community suggest that we take the closing of the canon for the cause as much as the effect of this elective affinity between founding texts and founded communities. And it is into this circle that the hermeneut philosopher has to enter if he wants to listen to something like biblical thinking. To enter this circle is to participate at least by way of imagination and sympathy in the act of adhesion by which the historical community recognizes itself as founded and, if we can put it this way, as comprised, in every sense of the word, in and by this particular *body* of texts. Yet we need also immediately to add: readers do not have to "believe-with," to share the faith of those members of communities that declare themselves to be grounded in the biblical texts. It is with these "outside" readers in mind that we have spoken of a participation in the relation of mutual election between founding texts and founded communities of reading and interpretation through imagination and sympathy, as the minimum condition for access to the meaning of these texts. The same request can be addressed to *every* reader by the members of any historical community whatsoever that bases itself on any sacred *corpus* whatsoever.

It is under the sign of this threefold presupposition that perhaps we can make sense of the mixed mode of thought that stems from the intersection of biblical thought with other modes of thought coming from other cultures than those of Jews and Christians. The preeminence of Greek philosophies in the reception of the biblical heritage is a major fact that merits our concluding with it. The conviction shared by both authors of this book is that this encounter and the intersections that resulted from it constituted neither a misfortune that ought to be deplored nor a perversion that ought to be eradicated. This was the major risk run by the experience of reading that assured the perenniality of the biblical texts. The event of this encounter, once it took place, has become the constitutive destiny of our culture. If it is neither to be deplored nor deconstructed, this destiny indicates a task against which our reflections must measure themselves with total honesty and total responsibility. Yet it is also a conviction common to us as authors that the trajectory of reading of the texts we have selected has a much broader range and that it indeed embraces the whole history of reception. A part of the singular destiny of biblical texts is their having been received in an astonishing variety of cultures different from their original *Sitz im Wort*. In fact, philosophy too, with Locke and Descartes, Kant and Hegel, Nietzsche and Heidegger, has moved away from the conceptual paradigms that presided over the great theological syntheses of the Trinitarian and Christological Councils.

To indicate in a few words the path of our trajectory, we may end with the following remarks. The exegetical part of our undertaking opens the path to our interpretive work in two ways. First, beyond the reconstruction of the background of an even older text, it makes room for a re-reading brought about by a "younger" version found in the New Testament or in the Midrash. In this way, the dialectic between retrospection and prospection at work in "one and the other testament" is brought to light. Next, the typological exegesis grafted to the historical-critical method opens the way to a philosophical reflection that goes beyond the boundaries of the canon and links up with contemporary forms of thought, be they philosophical or not.

To briefly illustrate this: the sagas and the novella of the book of Genesis pose the problem of the permanence of the narrative function with regard to an individual or collective self-understanding. Similarly, the exegesis of the "Ten Words," in passing through the Golden Rule, finds its conceptual counterpoint in a contemporary reflection on law and justice. Parallel to this, in a century such as ours, marked by so much cruelty, how are we to read a Wisdom writing without once again raising the overwhelming problem of evil? This leads to the song of love in the two testaments: does it not give rise to a meditation on the dialectic of love and justice? And a reflection sharpened by oracular texts will raise a supplementary warning for a hermeneutics of religious language that gets too quickly caught up in the narrative cycle, even when this cycle is set in relation to the prescriptive cycle. Finally, the fragment from Exodus 3:14, which we take as a high point, will lead us to the moment where the audacious act of "naming God" simultaneously escapes all the literary genres considered and any conceptual *hubris*.

Genesis 2–3

Cracks in the Wall

ANDRÉ LaCOCQUE

In 1936, Gerhard von Rad published an important study on the doctrine of creation in the Hebrew Bible. In it, he forcefully argued that in Israel this was a secondary development to the primordial soteriological affirmation focusing on the great acts of salvation of Yhwh. This essay has been translated into English under the title "The Theological Problem of the Old Testament Doctrine of Creation."[1] It will be worth our while to begin by briefly summarizing its argument.

The doctrine of creation appears in Psalms (for example, Psalms 89 and 136) and in Second Isaiah, as an act of Yhwh's favor (*ḥasdei Yhwh*). Psalm 74, in particular, calls creation *yešuôt* (acts of salvation). "The belief finds expression almost exclusively in the mythological conception of the struggle against the dragon of chaos" (p. 138). In this regard, the Priestly tradition followed the Psalms and Second Isaiah. In P as well, creation is conditioned by the divine purpose of redemption; "in genuinely Yahwistic belief the doctrine of creation never attained to the stature of a relevant, independent doctrine. We found it invariably related, and indeed subordinated, to soteriological considerations" (p. 142). "The doctrine of redemption had first to be fully safeguarded, in order that the doctrine that nature, too, is a means of divine self-revelation might not encroach upon or distort the doctrine of redemption but rather broaden and enrich it" (p. 143). From there the doctrine of creation was adopted by Wisdom but through a "wholly unmythological, materialistic analysis of the created order" (pp. 162–63), as exemplified by Job 28; Proverbs 8; Sirach 24. "These passages are con-

---

1. Published in Gerhard von Rad, *The Problem of the Hexateuch and Other Essays*, translated by E. W. Trueman Dicken (New York: McGraw-Hill, 1965), pp. 131–43.

cerned to show that [the] two manifestations of deity, in creation and in history, are identical" (p. 163).

This analysis by von Rad proved very influential despite its evident tendentiousness (which some have attributed to a polemical stance against German political doctrine during the Nazi times). His conclusions have been vigorously criticized, however. For example, Richard J. Clifford takes exception to von Rad's thesis in a recent essay, "The Hebrew Scriptures and the Theology of Creation."[2] Clifford's main point is that there are deep differences in defining creation between modern and ancient views that von Rad did not sufficiently take into consideration. They may be summed up in relation to the following terms: process, emergence, description, and criterion for truth.

> 1. Process: the ancient cosmogony presents itself as a conflict of wills between clashing parties eventuating in the victory of one of them.
>
> 2. Emergence: what emerges is a human society organized in a particular place (cf. *Enuma elish;* Psalm 77; 78:41–45); in other words, creation is a passage "from a state of social disorganization . . . to structure and security in Yhwh's land" (p. 510).
>
> 3. Description: through the form of drama, for process meant wills in conflict, hence plot.
>
> 4. Criterion for truth: entirely geared toward the story's plausibility.

On this basis, Clifford questions von Rad's distinction between creation and soteriology. The creation story is soteriological in that it purports to show organized life emerging from disorganized chaos. What is more, none of the Communal Laments (Psalms 77, 74, 89, 44, 78, 135, 136, 19, 104) distinguishes between the creation of the world and the creation of Israel or between the redemption of the one and of the other. In Second Isaiah, the situation is comparable as regards the re-creation/redemption of Israel. Here, however, "the perspective differs from Genesis, where the creation of the world took place once and for all" (p. 519).

Clifford next turns to the classic reports on creation at the beginning of the book of Genesis. The first creation narrative in Genesis 1–2:4 is P's preface to the whole (p. 521). Now "the Priestly redaction intends

---

2. Richard J. Clifford, "The Hebrew Scriptures and the Theology of Creation," *Theological Studies* 46 (1985): 507–53.

Genesis 2:4–11:26 . . . to be a single cosmogony," so that here again, creation and history are not distinguished. Genesis 1–11 points in the direction of the call of Abraham and the election of Israel against the background of the care of God for the whole world. It is therefore a mistake to contrast Genesis 1–3 with Romans 5:12–21 and 1 Corinthians 15:21, 28, 45–47, thus resulting in a scheme of creation—fall—redemption (see p. 520).

We have begun with von Rad's and Clifford's studies because they both contribute in their differing ways to making the most important point, namely, that creation is the beginning of history, its initial event. In P, for example, this concept is indicated by the term *tôldôt* (2:4a). Similarly, the historical narrative of Exodus is built on the model of God's conquest over the sea.[3] Creation is the first of God's saving deeds (see Psalm 74:12–17). As Jon Levenson writes about Genesis 1, this chapter is to be seen "as a point on the trajectory that runs from the ancient Near Eastern combat myth to the developed creation theology of the Abrahamic faiths."[4] There is indeed a traditio-historical development of Israel's doctrine of creation, but not one culminating with the bringing together of creation and the divine acts in history. The end-product found, for example, in Isaiah 40:27–28, 44:24–28, is already present, at least *in nuce,* in the most ancient Israelite expression of faith implying a connection between Israel and the gift of a land, or in the development of a hymnic, nondidactic doctrine of creation, as in Psalms 136 and 148.

So the theme of creation and the theme of redemption belong to the same composite structure. "The miracle of creation is a miracle of redemption," says Paul Ricoeur.[5] True, but there is a trajectory within the Hebrew Scripture, and it culminates with the Wisdom genre. Von Rad, for instance, calls attention to the non-Israelite, Egyptian and nonmythological origin of that tradition.[6] In the sapiential Psalms 19, 150, or 8, the cosmos is the showcase of divine wisdom and power; see also Proverbs 3:19, 8:22, 14:31, 20:12; Job 28. But even in this textual group, the close connection between creation and history shows that the goodness of creation is not "natural," that is, innate and intrinsic to

---

3. See, for instance, Jon D. Levenson, *Creation and the Persistence of Evil: The Jewish Drama of Divine Omnipotence* (San Francisco: Harper and Row, 1988).

4. Ibid., p. 53.

5. Paul Ricoeur, "Sur l'exégèse de Genèsis 1.1–2.4a," in *Exégèse et herméneutique* (Paris: Seuil, 1971), p. 69.

6. Von Rad, "The Theological Problem of the Old Testament Doctrine of Creation," p. 142.

creatures. It is a dynamic force operating within history. That much was, of course, demonstrated in P by the use of the word *tob* (good) to express the great satisfaction of the Creator. As is well known, *tob* is no declaration of aesthetic beauty or inner efficiency. It expresses the vocational capacity of the creature to fulfill the expectation of its Creator. Hence, goodness is characterized by order within disorder (or "order-lessness"), an order brought about by God that is to be made operational, so to speak, by God's human partner. As I shall stress below, according to Genesis 3, it is an order threatened and even destroyed by the so-called Fall.

This is why it is not correct to call the universe a *cosmos,* because this term translates a harmony grounded upon reason, whereas the harmony of the world according to Genesis is by decree, by Law, and an equation is established between harmony and obedience.[7] Even the produce of the soil grows by order, by commandment (Genesis 1:11f., 24f.). This is true to such an extent that, according to Leviticus, the earth at some point can decide to take the sabbaths that Israel did not grant her; she may refuse to produce. The world created by God by commandment is kept in an uncertain equilibrium—with the hope that *adam* will obey.[8] Thus, reflecting upon the "paradox of created helplessness and created responsibility" being threatened on all sides in the Garden, Phyllis Trible writes, "Against such threats, the only 'security' of the man and the woman is obedience to Yhwh God."[9]

As the unfolding story shows, it suffices that *adam* disobey the commandment to reintroduce into the world the chaos from which it emerged in the first place. If, however, death and annihilation do not immediately prevail—despite the divine warning that they would in case of transgression: *môt tamut,* Genesis 2:17—it is due to sheer divine grace. History started with the endless gift of life, while death was on

---

7. Cf. von Rad: "Israel did not think of the world as a 'cosmos' at all . . . as a self-contained structure ordered by eternal laws" (ibid., p. 152).

8. A Talmudic text places in God's mouth the prayer *haleway we-yaʿamod* (may it [the world] stand).

9. Phyllis Trible, *God and the Rhetoric of Sexuality* (Philadelphia: Fortress Press, 1978), pp. 107–8. Louis Ginzberg writes, "The whole of creation was conditional. God said to the things He made on the first six days: 'If Israel accepts the Torah, you will continue and endure; otherwise I shall turn everything back into chaos again.' The whole world was thus kept in suspense and dread until the day of the revelation on Sinai, when Israel received and accepted the Torah, and so fulfilled the condition made by God at the time when He created the universe" (*Shabbath* 88a, see *The Legends of the Jews,* vol. 1, p. 52). In the same vein, the Talmudic tractate *Aboth* I.2 says, "The stability of the world rests on three things, on the Law, on worship, and on deeds of personal kindness."

an ever-receding horizon. Now death and dust are before and ahead. Existence is a respite, a reprieve of the sentence of condemnation. During that time, however, although chaos surrounds creation from all sides, it is contained by the "rebuke" of God (Psalm 104:7; cf. Job 9:13; Psalm 74:13f., 89:10f.; Amos 9:3; Isaiah 51:9–11, 44:27). As B. W. Anderson writes, "Creation is fundamentally an eschatological doctrine."[10]

It is, therefore a grave misunderstanding to think that the story told by J in Genesis 2–3 ends by drawing a line, called the "Fall," thus definitely closing a chapter of prehistory totally abstracted from the human history "on earth." The nonexistent versus the existent, nonlife versus life, "no plant/no tiller" versus *adamah/adam* are as much the ingredients of history here and now as they are of "prehistory" there and then. It is the ongoing sin of the human that returns the earth to chaos (Jeremiah 4:23f.; Hosea 4:3). As Claus Westermann has eloquently shown in his magnum opus on Genesis, the first chapters of Scripture take the reader through an aggravation of disorder starting in the "prehistory" and pursued throughout human history. Genesis 3 describes the break in the relationship between man and woman; chapter 4 between brothers; chapter 9:20–27 within the family; chapter 11:1–9 among peoples.[11]

The great narrator in Genesis 2–11 is the Yahwist (J). It is now time to look closer at the contribution of that inspired storyteller. According to Martin Noth, "[J] theologically contains the most important testimony found in the Pentateuchal narrative as a whole."[12] This is so, adds Werner H. Schmidt, because of J's "radical insight into human sinfulness (Genesis 6:5, 8:21)" and also because of "the promise of a blessing upon 'all the families of the earth' (12:3)."[13] In fact, J's rare insight into human evil reaches a depth that will be plumbed again only by Jeremiah (see 13:13) and Psalm 51:5. On the other hand, J's purpose is

10. "Creation," *Interpreter's Dictionary of the Bible* (New York: Abingdon, 1962), vol. 1, p. 730. The trajectory of our text, as mentioned above, starts with the ancient Near Eastern combat myth (cf. the Akitu, New Year festival in Babylon); cf. Hermann Gunkel: from *Götterkampfmythus* to *Völkerkampfmythus* (from the myth of the war among the gods, to the myth of the war among the nations), in *Schöpfung und Chaos in Urzeit und Endzeit. Eine religions-geschichtliche Untersuchung über Genesis 1 und Ap Joh 12* (Göttingen: Vandenhoeck and Ruprecht, 1921).

11. Claus Westermann, *Genesis 1–11: A Commentary,* translated by John J. Scullion (Minneapolis: Augsburg, 1984).

12. Martin Noth, *A History of Pentateuchal Traditions,* translated by Bernard W. Anderson (Engelwood Cliffs, NJ: Prentice Hall, 1972), p. 236.

13. Werner H. Schmidt, *Old Testament Introduction,* translated by Matthew J. O'Connell (New York: Crossroad, 1984), p. 74.

to introduce the history of redemption, which he immediately sets within a *universal* scope, both through the "preface" of Genesis 2–11 and with the indication that Abraham's call involves not only his descendants but the whole of humanity (Genesis 12:3). True, there is a growing power of sin in the world and with it harm is done to the wonderful creation of God. But, as Paul will say in a brilliant formula, "where sin has abounded, grace abounded all the more" (Romans 5:20). That is why J envisages humanity's history, and Israel's in particular, as entirely structured in terms of the scheme of promise and fulfillment. Progeny and land are promised to Abraham; all the nations shall be blessed in him.

Written around 950, the J narrative does not hesitate to use the name "Yhwh" from the time of creation on. As Genesis 4:26 makes clear, such a daring step is a statement that the God of Israel is the God of humanity. J used material, especially as regards primeval history, that had mainly a mythological, cultic origin, but now those moorings have been severed. The interests of J, focused as they are upon history and politics, are almost unique in Scripture—with the exception of the *Thronnachfolge* of David in 2 Samuel 9 and 1 Kings 2, which was composed around the same time as J, namely during the days of Solomon, when the age more and more took its distance from the sacral institutions. David's successes were claiming the spiritual warrant of the ancient amphictyonic ordinances. In fact, the events were so formidable, and the royal claim was so exorbitant in terms of election and appointed destiny, that a clash with the cultic sphere was inevitable. For the latter, divine guidance was embedded in the liturgy and celebrated as a theophany—the encounter with God occurred in a certain locus and according to a given ritual. But now, it was claimed, ever-changing history itself was carrier of revelation, a revelation whose continuity was dialectically qualified by unpredictable versatility! J faced the challenge of interpreting history up to his own time both as kerygmatic and entirely oriented toward the tenth century BCE. His presupposition was that there is no better vehicle for "theology" than narration. With J, storytelling takes the place of cultic liturgy. Hence, J had a second powerful reason to make humanity from the origins call upon Yhwh. The purpose was to state that the God of creation/history and the God of worship are the same Yhwh. As von Rad says, it was up to "P" to bring back and to shift backward the whole tradition within the ambit of the cultus.[14]

---

14. Von Rad, "The Theological Problem of the Old Testament Doctrine of Creation," p. 77.

As in the P fresco of Genesis 1, J presents the created *adam* as the apex of God's works. But J is a great deal more dramatic in his conception of the human; the latter's creation combines disparate elements: clay and divine breath (Genesis 3)—that is, one might well say, water and fire! This conception, which is not to be confused with any dualistic conception of body contrasted with soul, is another way for J to prepare the reader for the unfolding of a history whose ingredients are the good divine creation and the evil human inclination. By the same token, a caveat is indicated that what can be seen of the *adam* does not exhaust his being. Clay and divine breath serve as criteria for a distinction between the measurable and the imponderable, which has a "special origin." There is here a close parallel with Genesis 1:26f. (on the *imago Dei*). What Paul Ricoeur writes in his reflection upon Genesis 1–2:4 applies to J's conception as well: "Man is created in the form of the Elohim, that is, according to a celestial model that uproots him from the sphere of the visible. So, if God is anthropomorphic, man is theomorphic."[15]

Our interest in the trajectory of our texts invites us to look into a much older version of the myth at the basis of Genesis 2f., namely Ezekiel 28:11ff. (on the King of Tyre). Here too the central figure is the primeval man (28:13, 15); strikingly, the verb *bara'* is used only here in Ezekiel (as in P, but not in J).[16] Let us also note in passing that cherubs are posted at the paradise's entrance, as in Genesis 3. When the two texts of Genesis 2–3 and Ezekiel 28 are compared, it becomes clear that the creation of Adam was originally that of a royal figure (cf. Ezekiel 28:12–13). Genesis 2f., however, proceeded to a "deletion of all royal characteristics"[17] for the sake of universalizing the event. Ezekiel 28 also shows that the crime of the king of Tyre (greed, pride, highhandedness) is in fact the crime of "primeval man . . . of man pure and simple."[18]

15. Ricoeur, "Sur l'exégèse de Genèsis 1.1–2.4a," p. 72. Cf. Joseph Blenkinsopp, *Ezekiel* (Louisville: John Knox, 1990), pp. 22f., on Ezekiel 1 where the divine figure emerges in all its splendor: "comforting is that the profile, the outline, is like that of a human being. . . . Here God appears in the likeness of humanity (*demut kemar'eh 'adam*). Humanity is in God's image, God is in the humanity's image—a mysterious connaturality. . . . [Paul] spoke of the Christian reflecting the effulgence (*doxa*) of the Lord and being changed in his likeness from one degree to another (II Cor 3:18)."

16. Ezekiel 21:35 is a secondary addition; in 23:47 the verb is in the *piel* with another meaning.

17. Walther Zimmerli, *Ezekiel 2: A Commentary on the Book of the Prophet Ezekiel, Chapters 25–48*, translated by James D. Martin (Philadelphia: Fortress, 1983), p. 95.

18. Ibid., p. 95. Zimmerli adds that this is *the* human crime according to Ezekiel and, probably, according to J as well. Man is "homo incurvatus in se." To such an arrogance, the only counter-

Be that as it may, while all nations in antiquity attempted to find an escape from the circularity of time—by magic or by (pseudo-)philosophical reflection—J invites his readers to confront time, world, and reality, as they actually are. This world has been produced by divine will. Although not divine, the universe is the outcome of divine fiat and *adam* breathes the divine breath. Between God and world there is dialogue instead of an ontological dualism as in many religious speculations. In fact, there is creation because God loves someone else, or perhaps we should say that God loves himself in someone else. We shall return below to this point.

It is thus proclaimed, from the very first pages of the Bible, that love consists in creating someone from the inner self, and in return in being created by this someone. God is anthropomorphic, and humanity is theomorphous. It is an exchange of goodness. God is good and declares his creature also good (*tob*). The creature's goodness is its capability to respond to the Creator's goodness. Psalm 94:7–9 shows incisively that the essence of being human is to be in communication with others, to be turned *ad extra*. This is the human responsibility.

This is why, according to Genesis 1:28, the first words of God to the human couple are commandments, commandments to proliferate and to rule over the universe; that is, to relate most closely to each other and to the world, something that J had already intimated before P. In that sense, there is within the human a veritable divine incarnation. Human being is *imago Dei* because everything in him/her is meant to come into communication with the divine model, itself totally "extroverted." God is the ultimate reference of the human reaching out toward the Other. That is why the *imago* is put in relation to sexual life ("male and female he created them" 1:27; see 2:7, 21), that is, with communication par excellence. The same calls for the same. The divine speaker calls for someone able to speak; someone compassionate for someone able to have compassion. Immanuel Kant expressed this very well when he said that the *analogia fidei* "does not signify . . . an imperfect similarity of two things, but a perfect similarity of relations between two quite dissimilar things."[19]

On purpose, we have gone from J to P and back in what precedes. As a matter of fact, it is a mistake to oppose the two "versions" of creation in the first chapters of Genesis. P, to whom we owe the Penta-

---

action is what Philippians 2:5–11 describes (cf. Isaiah 5:15, 21; 10:13, 33; 13:1; 2:12–17; Jeremiah 9:22f.).

19. Immanuel Kant, *Prolegomena to Any Future Metaphysics*, §58.

teuch as actually transmitted, prefaced it with Genesis 1–2:4 in full knowledge of the J version in Genesis 2ff. We have seen above what P had in mind. The myth of Genesis 1 is meant to relate narrative to ritual, in parallel with the old Mesopotamian *Enuma elish*, for example. By contrast, Genesis 2–3 is simply a narrative, a story. Its role is pedagogical and explanatory, rather than restorative as in myth and ritual. With J's etiology of creation, we are still formally close to myth, but generically the distance from myth is considerable. If Jon Levenson is correct when he says that Genesis 1 must have appeared in "moments in which Yhwh and his promises to the nation seemed discredited," with the aim of "serving to counter the persistence of the dark forces identified with the chaos monster,"[20] such conditions do not obtain for Genesis 2–3. Here the ambiance has a sapiential quality. True, J's interest is equally universalistic, but the atmosphere is more idyllic than in P, and the political ideas are more democratic. J's depiction, we said, is far more dramatic. God is creator, incomparably powerful, a king of kings—but he is vulnerable. And this side of his divinity emphasizes his anthropomorphism.[21] Similarly, vulnerability is also a mark of *adam*. Human relations, especially sexual relations, are problematic, as are also those with animal nature. Finally, the human problem is one of wisdom, of discernment between "good" and "evil."

The sapiential character of Genesis 2–3 has been stressed by Luis Alonso-Schökel.[22] Adam is a sage (cf. Ezekiel 28 and Job 15:6–7); he names all the animals of creation. The text's discussion of the four rivers that water the earth is another wisdom feature. With these major streams of life spanning the expanse of the world, J's scope again characteristically appears as universal. It is also significant that at the center is the hearth (as in wisdom in general).

Alonso-Schökel speaks of a pattern of "triangular ascent" to "the single original fact which effected" a given situation, called here "the horizon." This triangle appears in Genesis 2:16f. where we are presented with an apodictic precept marked by a threat. Then love comes to the fore as a second force. Finally, there is the appearance of temptation as a third force, in mutual relation with the former two. In Genesis

---

20. Levenson, *Creation and the Persistence of Evil,* p. 132.

21. J's anthropomorphism of God is vastly different from "pagan" divine anthropomorphism as it stresses not the erotic but the "pathetic" in God.

22. Luis Alonso-Schökel, "Sapiential and Covenant Themes in Genesis 1–3," *Modern Biblical Studies* (1965): 49–61; reprinted in J. L. Crenshaw, ed., *Studies in Ancient Israelite Wisdom* (New York: KTAV, 1976).

2–3, "the triangular ascent [applies] to the origins of all humanity" (p. 58). J is not projecting "a subsequent event back into the past, nor does he project back in allegory the experience of all men. He really returns to the original event" as a historian. He applies the historical pattern of disobedience to the commandment resulting in punishment and, later, in divine mercy. Of importance is the realization that "the point of departure for reflection is not the abstract nature of man, but the concrete experience of man in salvation history" (p. 59).

Thus, wisdom, history, story, and myth, converge here. Genesis 2–3 has a quasi-mythical tonality because of the back and forth movement between experience/history and myth/metahistory necessitated by conflicting but complementary imperatives. On the other hand, a process of demythologization is also evident. The ancient Near Eastern material has been drastically reinterpreted by J along nonmythological (and to a certain extent sapiential) lines. But the reverse is also true in that there is here, as in general in Israelite narrative literature, a "tendency to mythologize historical episodes to reveal their transcendent meaning," as Frank M. Cross notes.[23]

A clear example of this "contact" with mythology is provided by the intervention in the narrative of the serpent. Most of its uncanny character in the history of religion has been suppressed by J, but not all of it. Primarily and fundamentally, the serpent here is said to be created by Yhwh (3:1), so that the accent is on its created-ness, not on the mythic symbolism found in other texts, such as Wisdom of Solomon 2:24 or Revelation 12:9, where the serpent is identified with Satan. The serpent in Genesis 3 is first envisaged in its status of animal before its choice makes it a monster of sorts. In this respect, the serpent's evolution is paralleled by the human fall into disgrace. We are indeed within the stream of J's demythologization. The serpent is just a snake—but with a characteristic that mythology, and hence the "natural science" of the time, attributed to the serpent, namely, cunningness, slyness.[24] These attributes are not unambiguously pejorative. They sometimes belong to the panoply of the wise. The serpent is "shrewd" (which can mean "perverse . . . or tactful" says Alonso-Schökel). The word is used in a highly

---

23. Frank M. Cross, *Canaanite Myth and Hebrew Epic: Essays in the History of Religion of Israel* (Cambridge: Harvard University Press, 1973), p. 144. Compare again Genesis 2f. with Ezekiel 28:12–19 (on Tyre). Both texts "incorporate . . . mythical motifs," says Alonso-Schökel. We could also adduce a text like Isaiah 24–27, which presents numerous close parallels with Ugaritic mythology.

24. Cf. Matthew 10:16.

positive sense in Proverbs 14:15, 18; 22:3 and repeated in 27:12. But there also remain, in the narrative, echoes of the association of the serpent with phallic symbols that tie it to the whole realm of sexuality.[25] In fact, the Hebrew has in Genesis 2:25 and 3:1, 7, a wordplay on 'arum, "shrewd," and 'arom, "naked." We shall return to this below.

In Genesis 3:6, man cancels the gap with animal nature. It is important to notice that the serpent is first presented as "more crafty than any other wild animal" (3:1, NRSV). We have already seen that the term "crafty" (or shrewd, cunning, etc.) is used with a positive connotation in Proverbs. In the Genesis myth, however, cunningness and subtlety are nothing more nor less than the means of enticement to another alternative in the relationship. Thus, 'arum is amphibological. It emphasizes in Genesis 3 that the serpent is the animal par excellence, the leader in the animal realm, its representative. Speaking with the snake, Eve speaks with *the* animal. Similarly, woman here represents more than herself; as mother of humanity as well as the "tender" side of the androgyne, she represents *the* human. The human is turning toward the animal. Again here, J inherited a crucial mythological motif: the human confrontation with the animal genus. In the Mesopotamian *Enuma elish*, the myth dramatically describes how the hero Enkidu, the future faithful companion of Gilgamesh, leaves behind the animal realm, as a "prerequisite to the development of culture and the mastery of nature." Thus the serpent's intervention (both in the myth of Gilgamesh and in the Genesis myth) appears as a "revenge by the animal kingdom against its defecting kin."[26] Between Eve and the serpent, there is much in common; so much indeed that animal nature is, like evil, as much within as without.[27]

Edmond Jacob calls attention to this by stressing the similarities between humanity and animal nature in Genesis: the animal is also *nepheš hayyah* (1:20). There is a dangerous proximity between human and animal evinced, for instance, by the naming in Genesis 2:19. Both are *basar* (6:13, 17; 7:15; 9:11; Psalm 36:25). God can withdraw the *ruach* from both of them (Psalm 104:9; Job 34:14). Their destinies are intertwined,

25. See Flemming Hvidberg, "The Canaanite Background of Genesis I–III," *Vetus Testamentum* 10 (1960): 285–94.

26. Cf. Joel Rosenberg, *King and Kin* (Bloomington: Indiana University Press, 1986), pp. 52ff. (the passages quoted are from p. 54).

27. Westermann says that woman is facing both her humanity (naked = availability, openness, offering), and her animal nature (canniness = capability of associating ideas). See Westermann, *Genesis 1–11*, pp. 234ff.

as is made clear by the Flood (cf. esp. Genesis 6:7, 9.15; see Qohelet 3:9; 12:28). But the human must dominate over the animal (Genesis 1:28; 9:2–4). There is curse on the sexual crime of bestiality (Exodus 22:18f.; Leviticus 18:23; Deuteronomy 27:21). Above all, the human can eat the animal; thus is erected the unsurpassable barrier between the two.[28]

The serpent in ancient Israel is associated with knowledge and sorcery (strikingly it can slough off its skin and thus be born again indefinitely). Another sign of its knowledge is its capacity of speech.[29] Although there seems to be no parallel in the ancient Near East to the serpent symbolizing the apex of science, there is, however, in the Bible a firm tradition making the serpent a magical animal, a source of hidden wisdom: Numbers 21:99; 2 Kings 18:4.[30] In Mesopotamia, Syria, Palestine, and Egypt, the serpent represents the god of fertility and fecundity. Not so in J, who treats the topic in a polemical way: God at no point dialogues with the serpent. This idol that is worshipped by some is here a humiliated (*humus-ligare*) animal that crawls on its belly and eats dirt.[31]

In summary, despite the radical demotion of the serpent in Genesis, something of its mythological dimension has not been totally obliterated by J. It remains a symbol of infernal wisdom. In fact, the serpent in J's version of creation plays the role of chaos in P's version. This did not escape later symbolists (and apocalypticists). They equated the serpent with the chaotic monster called Leviathan (Isaiah 27:1; cf. Job 26:18). The serpent has the distinct advantage of moving on the ground while coming from the sea (under the form of Leviathan). It is at any rate an infernal creature that ends up eating dust, a symbol of sterility and lifelessness, there where Adam returns after death (Genesis 3:14).

---

28. Edmond Jacob, *Theology of the Old Testament*, Part 2, translated by Arthur W. Heathcote and Philip A. Allock (London: Hodder & Stoughton, 1958), chap. 3 ("Nature and Destiny of Man"). There is more on this confrontation with the animal below, in my discussion of the serpent and sexuality.

29. The Rabbis of old contrast this natural capacity with the miracle of Balaam's ass speaking with the prophet.

30. Telluric wisdom? In Crete and Greece, the serpent is chthonic and represents the fertility of the underworld. Cf. Th. Vriezen, *Onderzoek naar de paradijsvoorstelling der oude Semitische Volken* (Wageningen, 1937), pp. 177f. Note that Hugo Gressmann (*Festsch. Harnack* [Tübingen, 1921], pp. 32f.) saw the serpent in tradition as a god of the netherworld. Hvidberg reminds us that Baal is often represented as a serpent ("The Canaanite Background of Genesis I–III").

31. Hermann Gunkel, *Genesis, übersetzt und erklärt* (Göttingen: Vandenhoeck & Ruprecht, 1901), p. 15, stresses that the serpent as an evil demon is reduced by Israel to the rank of an animal.

Since the world as a whole is threatened by chaos on all sides according to a long-standing tradition in Israel (cf. Psalm 74:10f., 18–20; 89:26; 104:6–9; Job 38:8–11; Isaiah 51:9f.; 54:9f.), so, on an anthropological level, Adam, according to J, feels existentially insecure in the world.[32] Even in the sexual realm, that is, the realm of life and of perpetuation of the species, Adam is menaced (Genesis 3:16).

At first, the threat is subtle and seemingly insignificant. After the indication that the man and the woman were both naked, J uses a sharp traveling shot and zooms in upon a strange scene where the woman and the serpent are talking. The normal dialogical partner of the woman is here conspicuously absent. So is also the primary partner, God, who will reappear only after the consummation of the conversation with the snake and its outcome (3:8ff.). As for Adam, the Rabbis of old intimate that he had "known" his wife and was sleeping; an interesting idea in that it stresses the separation that follows an intimate union. Clearly, the Rabbis thought of this because of the sexual connotation in the text,[33] to which we shall return. We can note, however, that there is communication between the animal and only one side of the human. The absence of the other side at this point is remarkable. It is not meant to exonerate the latter from the "Fall" (see 3:6); on the contrary, it emphasizes the breach between male and female.

The use of the same term *'arom/'arum* in the two consecutive verses of 2:25 about the human couple, and in 3:1 about the serpent, has been called by Karl Barth, "a stroke of genius."[34] Claus Westermann picks up on this and takes exception with Northrop Frye's statement that "[man] is the world's only naked animal, [a feature] indicating a uniquely alienated relation to his environment."[35] In Genesis, says Westermann, there is kinship between human and ophidian, between their nakedness and their cleverness. Even alienation from the environment makes sense for both. They are different from the "natural," and thus belong to another category than the rest of the animals.[36] But there is also contrast be-

32. As Rosenberg puts it, in J there is "a single consistent theme: the development of human identity against the backdrop of nonhuman factors" (*King and Kin*, p. 55).

33. Genesis Rabba 9:16a.

34. Karl Barth, *Church Dogmatics*, vol. 3, part 2, translated by Harold Knight et al. (Edinburgh: T. & T. Clark, 1960).

35. Northrup Frye, *The Great Code* (New York: Harcourt, Brace, Jovanovich, 1982), p. 109.

36. *Aboth de-Rabbi Nathan*, A 1.10 says, in the name of R. Shimeon ben Mansia that the serpent used to be "a great servant." It could have been the most precious help to humanity, even more than the camel, or the ass, for all kinds of chores.

tween them. "Nakedness" does not mean the same thing for both. The humans are naked but not empty (they have no shame, which is not a sign of naiveté but of holy simplicity), while the nakedness of the serpent means emptiness. It has no companion of its kind, no "helping mate" (*'ezer ke-negdô*, Genesis 2:18) unlike Adam and Eve. It is alone and alien, already an "enemy" (Genesis 3:15), before becoming one by being cursed. Feeling alienated from creation, it breaks the boundary set by the Creator between species; it literally transgresses the difference and brings about confusion. It invades another genus, only to corrupt it and pull it down to its own isolation. Its cunningness, potentially its wisdom, is of a bitter kind; worse, it is deadly. The serpent's nakedness is a parody of that of the humans.

Nudity points not only to weakness, but to availability, to "virginity." That both the serpent and the human are naked means that they are open to any possibility; that is, to adopt the Hebrew parlance, which is keen to embrace the whole spectrum of ethical options in a single expression, they are open to *tob* as well as to *ra'*. Among the possibilities discovered by the three who are said to be *'arom/'arum*, there is evidently the one of mating. Eve's nudity in particular is like an invitation (the serpent, like Adam, is a phallic being). Her nakedness was not shameful when facing Adam's nudity, and vice versa. But when there is another nudity interfering, then all nudity becomes an occasion for shame. The third party holds, so to speak, a mirror for each to look at him/herself, and what was formerly openness toward the other becomes withdrawal within the self.

Shame, Frye tells us, is used semantically in connection with barrenness (Genesis 30:23; Isaiah 4:1; Luke 1:25); with widowhood (Isaiah 54:4); with mutilation (Judges 1:6f.; 1 Samuel 11:2; 2 Samuel 10:4f.); with exposure (Leviticus 20:17; Judges 3:25; 2 Kings 2:17; Ezekiel 36:30; Luke 14:9). From this perspective, the serpent's punishment fits its character: it must crawl, which is an etiological explanation for the "mutilation" of its paws. It must eat dust, that is, feed on death itself, on nothingness, emptiness; and it must remain alone as if it were "widowed" and barren. From *'arum mikkôl ayyat ha-sadeh* (v.1), it becomes (v. 14) *'arur mikkol hayyat ha-sadeh* (which should be translated as "more cursed than any other wild animal"—the serpent is throughout the representative of animal nature, like Behemoth in Job 40).

Animal nature and sexuality are closely associated. Sensuality brings out the animal in man, says popular wisdom. It is so because rationality soon leaves room for untamed, uncontrolled desire.[37] At that point, the human "*arum*-ness" changes its meaning and becomes the serpent's "*arum*-ness," an animal "heat" unworthy of human mastery over those instincts that are called "lower."[38] The discourse of the serpent to Eve need not be overtly sexual. It suffices that the serpent be *the* animal, in contrast to Eve, a being breathing the divine breath. That is why the sexual connotations in the encounter could hardly pass unnoticed. Already the Rabbis of old discerned in the interposition of the snake between husband and wife an attempt of the animal to take the place of Adam.[39]

The alluring is extraordinary. Adam can only offer what he has himself received from Another to be human, but the serpent renders Adam's gift so microscopic as to be worthless. Rather, the serpent's gift will substitute for it as a formidable alternative. There is exciting magic involved in eating a fruit that makes you like God (or gods) in knowledge (the term used here is *yada'*, an intimate, existential knowledge, like the one experienced in the commerce between man and woman, cf. Genesis 4:1). The serpent then appears in its total phallic nudity. It is not just *the* animal; it is *the* penis. The serpent is symbolic of lovemaking without love, of the mating between animals. Here again there is a contrast between what is seen and what is unseen—just as the human is not only form and shape, but *nephes hayyah* (2:7). But what is a positive hiddenness in *adam*, is negative hiddenness in the serpent. For it stands as a force in opposition to the commandment to be the Image of God. It is disrespect of difference, distraction from the humanization of creation.

Before the "Fall," the sexual problem does not bother the humans, precisely because there is no problem. When the original science is perverted, however, reality is dismantled into two irreconcilable aspects. The aspect of difference gets separated from the aspect of sameness. In no domain more than in the sexual is the divorce more clearly experienced, for the sexual is paradigmatic of the existential in its entirety. More than in any other realm, the humans come close to the animal nature within them. Ironically, those who opted for rebellion against God in order to become like gods are locked into the realm of animals;

37. 4 Maccabees 2:1–4 emphasizes Joseph's mental effort in his successful resistance to sexual desire in Potiphar's house.

38. Paul Ricoeur writes, "The serpent [of Genesis] is . . . our animal nature" in *The Symbolism of Evil*, translated by Emerson Buchanan (New York: Harper and Row, 1957), p. 257.

39. See *Aboth de Rabbi Nathan*, A 1.9.

"qui veut faire l'ange fait la bête" (who wants to play the angel, ends up playing the beast), says Pascal.

In another study on our text that is highly interesting but also fraught with unevenly warranted extrapolations, Mieke Bal has also seen in the divine order not to eat from a particular tree the teaching of difference.[40] She continues with the idea that the serpent's argument is gamelike. Indeed sexual knowledge makes you die and not die (God had emphasized the former aspect, 2:17), she says. So, there is no lie in the serpent's promise and God acknowledges that much in Genesis 3:22! Wisdom here is acceptance of the human condition, including death, and the continuity of history. But Phyllis Trible is closer to the mark when she insists that now that, indeed, "the eyes of both are opened," "ironically they know the opposite of what the serpent promised. They know their helplessness, insecurity, and defenselessness. . . . The before and the after of disobedience contrast unselfconscious naked existence . . . [with] the knowledge of defenselessness."[41]

Let us stress that such knowledge of a situation that antedates their consciousness of it, was, before they ate the forbidden fruit, totally unnecessary because they were under the protection of the Almighty. Now for the first time, so to speak, they *are* naked; they themselves have manifested their nudity.[42] A weakness becomes a liability only when it is exposed by experience or by revelation.[43] The serpent's discourse is deceptive and in itself can be called a lie, as says John 8:44. The serpent is the liar, not God (*pace* Bal).

It is true that when the humans ate the fruit of knowledge something happened that resembles true science: their eyes opened (*pqḥ*), a verb that is used to describe the opening of the eyes of a blind (Psalm 146:8; Isaiah 35:5). But what they saw happens to be only a shameful reality, the very contrary of the *tob* of divine proclamation in Genesis 1. It is thus made clear that reality is our interpretation (vision) of reality. The humans' vision is a desire to reshape the world; they have the illusory feeling that they can do better than the Creator. What they obtain is the distortion of the given by an interpretation that itself is blurred. As

---

40. Mieke Bal, *Lethal Love: Feminist Readings of Biblical Love Stories* (Bloomington: Indiana University Press, 1987).

41. Trible, *God and the Rhetoric of Sexuality*, p. 114.

42. Again, it is clear that, for J, the phenomenon is opportunity, not fate. "Nakedness" is what Adam makes of it.

43. This principle is at the basis of Paul's argument about the "curse" of the Law, which reveals to me my indignity (Romans 3:20).

the Creator's vision of reality was from the standpoint of *tob*, it remains only for the humans cut off from God to share in the other vision, from the standpoint of *ra'; tertium non datur.* It will take no less than the coming of an Anointed One to open the eyes of the blind (Isaiah 42:7; cf. John 9:1–41). Meanwhile, far from mastering creation, as the humans thought they would, they are incapable of distinguishing what is good for them; their alleged "clear-sightedness" is myopia (or, on another level, nakedness). Blindness is alienation from the self as well as from the other, so that they may even entertain the illusion of not being seen by anyone else, of being hidden (3:8) from the eyes of the One who surrounds them (Psalm 139:5). Yes, now they *know* something they did not know—that they are naked, in the proper and the figurative sense. What they know is the surface of things, their *bare* materiality, not the inside of things or their meaning, not their reference. They are self-centered, incapable from now on of true communication. Their senses created for reaching out have become superfluous. Adam and Eve are now the "foolish and senseless people" of Jeremiah 5:21, "they have eyes but see not; they have ears but hear not." They have lost the relation of communion with God that allowed them to see as he sees, to share in his vision/interpretation (cf. Psalm 7:10; Job 34:21). Something that has lost its reference to God is indeed senseless and disgruntling.

So, the "eating of the forbidden fruit" consists in shunning the life received, for the sake of an existence earned, deserved, built "from scratch," by human efforts. The newly obtained situation shifts from Genesis 2:15 (tilling the garden of Eden) to 3:17 ("cursed is the ground because of you"). But each "poison," according to Israel's worldview, also has its antidote. Human eyes will not forever open to discover shame. Exodus 14:30–31 (J) says that after crossing the Reed Sea, the Israelites "*saw* Egypt dead on the seashore [and] *saw* the great work which the Lord did against the Egyptians. So the people *feared* [a wordplay in Hebrew with *saw*] the Lord . . ." The result of such a regenerated vision is that Israel "inherits" a land that is cured of its "sickness unto death." It is "a land flowing with milk and honey" (Exodus 3:8),[44] a compliment that serves as a springboard for developments in eschatologically oriented texts that tell us about the restoration of the tree of life for the saints. Reference can be made here to Revelation 2:7; 22:2; 4 Esdras 8:52 ("for you was the tree of life planted and the future eon prepared"); Testament of Levi 18:10f. (the Messiah will feed the saints

---

44. A very old expression of Canaanite (?) origin.

with the fruit of the tree of life); in Psalms of Solomon 14:2–3 and 1 QHod 8:5–6 from Qumran, "trees of life" designates the saints themselves.

"Eating" in its negative connotation means shunning the received wisdom, the one that granted life, for the sake of an acquired wisdom, the outcome of a process of trial and error, from which arises the consciousness of death (cf. Proverbs 3:19–22, 4:13, 9:6; Qohelet, *passim*). Then we shift from Genesis 2:19–23 (the whole creation as man's companions, even helpmates) to 3:19 (alienation of the whole universe). For J, the antidote lies in the election of Abraham and the promise made to him of an innumerable progeny in a Promised Land, and of the blessing for the whole family of nations (Genesis 12:1–2, 15:5–7, etc.).[45] The Deuteronomist, later, summarizes the Abrahamic and Mosaic option by exhorting Israel to choose good and life through the fulfillment of God's will, as says Deuteronomy 30:19.

What is more, the "eating"—that is now of the same order as snapping away, plundering—leaves behind the original innocence, which meant living within the purview of the commandment based on trust in the commander. Now, innocence makes room for ruse, for cunning: the cunning of the serpent, and soon for the cunning of the humans. This consists in living according to norms set by the self, in separation from the Other and from any other, that is, in adopting a criterion of judgment centered entirely on the ego. The shift is from Genesis 2:25 (innocent nakedness) to 3:7 (shameful nudity, shame over one's former innocence). The antidote, of course, is love; a love demonstrated again by Abraham, in his interceding for Sodom in Genesis 18:22f. (J). Love, in Israel's conception, is also, as paradoxical as it may seem, commanded. For if it is true, with Maimonides, that "we have received the commandment to be free," it is also true that we have received the commandment to love God and our fellow humans (Deuteronomy 6:5; Leviticus 19:18).

---

45. Cf. Michael Fishbane, *Text and Texture: Close Readings of Selected Biblical Texts* (New York: Schocken, 1979), p. 112: "the threefold promise of land, fertility, and blessing given to Abraham effectively reverses the curses of the expulsion and so establishes him as a new Adam." Within the framework of covenant, the language of the origins of the world must be taken up anew and redefined. Before God, there is a wisdom that is *ḥayim* (life) in contradistinction with the false wisdom acquired in Eden (see Proverbs 4:13, 3:19–22, 9:6, 16:22, 10:17, etc.). The "goodness" that it yields is not deceptive like the latter form, for now *tob* (good) is identified with *ḥayim* (see Deuteronomy 30:15–20, 4:1, 4, 10, 6:24, 16:20; Psalm 34:13; Ezekiel 18). So, the terms "wisdom," "good," and "life," become synonymous, for the finality of wisdom is no longer to become like gods but rather to fulfill God's will as revealed in the fabric of Creation and in the Torah, the map of the Covenant.

Meanwhile, however, everyone is on his/her guard, including God! The latter half of the mysterious text of Genesis 3:22 is translated by the NRSV as: "See, the man has become like one of us, knowing good and evil, now he might reach out his hand and take also from the tree of life, and eat, and live for ever . . ." The Jewish traditional reading of this text discovers irony here and invites the reader to supply phrases like "so man thinks" or "according to the tempter." Therefore, God decides, "let's show him how wrong he is." Another interesting interpretation by the Rabbis reads *mimennô* (not "like us" but "from himself," the Masoretic text [MT] remains unaltered), so that Adam is described as "one who knows good and evil of himself" (says *Yefê Tô'ar*). Rashi reads [man is] "like the Unique One (*êḥad*) among his kind in his capacity to discriminate between good and evil." And the Targum Onkelos mixes the two: "unique in the world by himself." According to Jewish tradition, therefore, God here expresses no fear and no jealousy.

However, the translation of *hayah* in 3:22 remains problematic. The NRSV translates, "the man *has become* . . ." This reading is almost consensual, but it is not the only one possible. *Hayah* can also mean here: "[the man] was [like one of us]"; it refers to a state before the eating of the fruit; God would then add something like, "now let us not allow him to perpetuate that confusion eternally." In that case, there is a terrible irony in the fact that the humans *were* wise, that their eyes *were* open in the first place, but they decided that there existed a magical way to be still more "divine," to surpass God in His divinity. This reading of *hayah* seems to be retrospectively and clearly confirmed by the contrasting "but now" (*we-'attah*) in the second part of the verse.[46] The expulsion from the Garden means that Adam does not belong anymore with the divine beings (cf. Ezekiel 28:2 and passim).

The irony continues with the serpent's promise that they will not die if they eat the fruit, for there has been so far no allusion whatsoever to any divine intention to let them die in the first place. On the contrary, the warning that eating the forbidden fruit would eventuate in *môt tamut* (2:17) clearly implies that death is not among the "normal" possibilities in Eden. Death had no place in paradise, and if need be there was a tree with fruits of life to keep humans alive for ever. Its presence in Eden indicates that death there, although threatening, like the chaos of chapter 1, was kept in check by the free gift of God—who is able to

---

46. Cf. "It is written, 'God made man upright' (Ecclesiastes 7:29). Now, 'man *was* upright' as it is written, 'behold man was like one of us' (3:22), meaning that he was upright like one of the serving angels" (*Tanḥumah Berešêth*, par. 7, f. 10a).

withdraw it at will, as the end of the episode shows. J is here again influenced by the ancient myths where the gods themselves are kept immortal by similar means of a tree of life and a fountain of youth.[47] It served J's dramatic purpose to show that even in paradise, life was not to be taken for granted. The divine warning to the humans not to eat of the forbidden fruit lest *môt tamut* (2:17) emphasizes the actualization of a possibility available since the beginning (cf. Psalm 82:6–7, 74:12–17, to be compared with Isaiah 25:8 where Leviathan is replaced by Death). Jon Levenson writes, "The truth is that Judaism [here inclusive of biblical religion] is not optimistic but *redemptive,* and the creation of humanity without their powerful, innate and persistent will to evil is part of its vision of redemption, not part of its description of present reality."[48] In his turn, Paul Ricoeur says, "a wholly relational approach is required . . . to think, simultaneously, creation *and* the persistence of evil. . . . Creation continues to be a drama where the initial vulnerability to chaos allows us to anticipate the fragility of the created order."[49]

It may be that in the sources used by J, the fruit of the tree of knowledge was supposed to open the eyes and reveal the existence of the tree of life. But if so, this idea was not retained by J, for he says explicitly that the fruits of all trees with the exception of the tree of knowledge are to be eaten freely. After the rebellion against the will of God, it is precisely the fruit of life that the humans must now be prevented from eating; this is certainly another way of saying, ironically, that now that they thought of being assured of living like a god, they will die like beasts. Moreover, the whole affair appears still more as an ironical paradox when we realize that the human condition before the eating of the forbidden fruit was not one of an absence of knowledge as regards good and evil, for then the divine commandments given earlier would make no sense.[50] What is at stake here, therefore, is the passage to another

---

47. See Geo Widengren, *The King and the Tree of Life in Ancient Eastern Religion* (Uppsala: Otto Harassowitz, 1951).

48. Levenson, *Creation and the Persistence of Evil,* p. 39 and passim.

49. Paul Ricoeur, "Fides quaerens intellectum: Antécédents bibliques?" *Archivio di Filosofia* 68 (1990): pp. 36–37. Ricoeur has shown in *The Symbolism of Evil* that evil is concomitantly "already there" and a human choice. Or, in the words of Michael Fishbane, "Evil enters the world through man and his choices as a creature of free will. . . . Such a perspective constitutes an anthropology of evil. . . . [But from a] second perspective the origin of evil is considered . . . as lying deep within the 'nature' of things despite the created 'order.'. . . The temptation is already there, from the beginning, mysteriously" (*Text and Texture,* pp. 22 and 25).

50. Good is what God wants, evil is what God abhors. The only basis for the discrimination between good and evil is the divine commandment and prohibition. It is no innate or acquired skill (here represented by the fruit of a tree). What is acquired by eating the forbidden fruit is the "profound interconnection between knowledge and death. The promised punishment of death . . .

understanding of realities already known beforehand, as we have insisted above, not the new discovery of things kept secret by a jealous god.

Creation is through separation,[51] through discrimination between one term and another, ultimately between opposites in the spectrum: good and evil (see Genesis 24:50; cf. 31:24–29; 2 Samuel 13:22, 14:17; Numbers 24:12). The humans wanted to be able to master these two terms because a fortiori they would also master every term in-between them, for all things in the universe are created in polarity. But opposition in human eyes is coincidence in divine governance. "Good and evil" together belong to God, as says Numbers 24:13, and they are thus kept in harmony, in mutual but contrasting complementarity, like light and darkness (see Genesis 1). It is at the moment when the humans seize for themselves the criteria of the "ethical," that this structure of polarity/complementarity becomes one of adversity/exclusivity. *Tob* (good) finds itself curtailed by the presence of *ra'* (evil), and *ra'* is made conscious and accountable for by the presence of *tob.* J thus is dealing with a mutual alienation of terms that used to be complementary and also with the tension introduced by human rebellion between terms that now receive reversed meanings opposite of the ones they had before. The new life is death and the new wisdom is shame. Eating the fruit of the forbidden tree means fleeing the commandment to choose good and neutralizing the fundamental trust on which it rested.

In that respect, the Genesis text shows incisively the astounding reduction imposed by the newly discovered human "wisdom" on the notion of *tob.* Now, ruefully, three domains of knowledge are assumed by the humans as covering all reality (3:6): "good to eat" = sensual pleasure (or the physical); "nice to see" = aesthetical delight (or the psychological); "desirable to be intelligent" = intellectual gratification (or the spiritual).[52] As says 1 John 2:16, "all that is in the world—the lust of the flesh and the lust of the eyes and the pride of life, is not of the Father but is of the world."[53]

---

is not only mortality but also the human awareness of mortality" (Fishbane, *Text and Texture*, p. 21).

51. Cf. Paul Beauchamp, *Création et séparation. Etude exégétique du chapitre premier de la Genèse* (Paris: DDB, 1969).

52. I owe this development to von Rad: see his commentary on *Genesis*, translated by John Marks (Philadelphia, Westminster, 1972), *ad* 3:6.

53. It is true that there is here seemingly a repetition of the description made by Yhwh himself in 2:9 of the trees he created "pleasing to the sight and good for food." The profound difference, however, lies in the delights of the trees not being combined with intelligence or knowledge; the two realms are left separated without confusion. Beside those trees, says 2:9, there were also the tree of life and the tree of knowledge of good and evil. That natural aesthetical beauty be mentioned at all beside the sensual pleasure of eating is one way to emphasize human transcendence

The sexual realm is specifically envisaged in the curse that punishes human rebellion. It is thus emphasized that the human perverted choice has an instantaneous effect on precisely the means of "knowledge" par excellence. God strikes the woman's womb, which is, as says Thierry Maertens, "the organ that all along the elect people's history shall be the privileged locus of divine benedictions" (cf. Deuteronomy 28:2–11; Isaiah 49:21; Genesis 22:17). He continues, "God has decided that benediction blossoms only within suffering and woe" (cf. Isaiah 26:16–19; Revelation 21:4; John 16:20–22).[54]

The modern reader finds it difficult to understand why the narrative makes the female undergo the brunt of the punishment. We shall return to this point. But it is important to recall that, according to the myth at the basis of J's composition, the woman was branded as the weaker member of the human couple. She was the first to "fall" into temptation. As Hartmut Gese says, "The Old Testament adopted the being and consciousness of early cultures but redirected them in their essential elements." In the myth at the basis of the Genesis narrative, he adds, the woman acted "in ignorance of the order of creation." She gave the forbidden fruit to her husband who thereby gained consciousness. It was his fall, because "it is only in respect to self-consciousness that humans experience death." For in Genesis, the woman is not naive. She knows the prohibition, and succumbs to "a temptation at the center of . . . [her] being." Death here is no "tragic event . . . but a human decision . . . to participate in the world of divine consciousness . . ." (cf. Genesis 6). We discover here death as guilt.[55]

Thus, Genesis 2ff. bridges the distance between myth ("then") and history ("now"). Between the two, there is no discontinuity, even if there is a scandalous empirical disjunction. In other words, Genesis 2ff. is more prototypal than archetypal. Paul Ricoeur says, "Every woman and every man are Adam; every man and every woman are Eve; every woman sins 'in' Adam, every man is seduced 'in' Eve. . . . The serpent . . . would be part of ourselves which we do not recognize . . . the seduc-

over animal nature. In Genesis 2:9, the adjectives are at the service of the idea of the density of bliss that the Song of Songs, for instance, echoes in its praise of love. By contrast, in Genesis 3:6, the bliss is perverted into temptation to leave love behind and adopt an attitude of hostility and revolt. In the tenth century BCE, J had already made clear that nothing is closer to virtue than vice (cf. the [otherwise wanting] notions of *privatio boni* and *amissio boni* of St. Augustine).

54. Thierry Maertens, *La mort a régné depuis Adam (Genesis. II.4b–III.24)* (Bruges: Abbaye de St. André), pp. 82, 81.

55. Hartmut Gese, *Essays on Biblical Theology,* translated by Keith Crim (Minneapolis: Augsburg, 1981), pp. 40f. on "Death in the Old Testament."

tion of ourselves by ourselves, projected into the seductive object. Temptation would be a sort of seduction from without; it would develop into compliance with the apparition that lays siege to the 'heart'; and, finally, to sin would be to *yield*" (see James 1:13–14).[56] "Likewise, St. Paul identified the quasi-externality of desire with the 'flesh,' with the law of sin that is in my members. The serpent, then, represents this passive aspect of temptation, hovering on the border between the outer and the inner. . . . [But] the serpent is not only the projection of man's seduction by himself, not only our animal nature. . . . The serpent is also 'outside' in a more radical fashion and in various ways. . . . Every individual finds evil *already there.*"[57]

Therefore, there is no more reason to blame Eve alone for "eating the fruit" than there would be to limit to Adam alone the saying that *he*[58] is taken from dust and returns to dust (3:19). With the motif of the apparent absence of Adam while Eve is eating the fruit, the author of our text wants to show the separation and alienation within the human unity. But as far as culpability is concerned, both are to blame as both do eat. Similarly, when it is stated to *Adam* alone that he is taken from and returns to dust, it is again to stress the division in the couple and to give a kind of priority to the dissolving process and eradication that hits especially one of the two, since he is no "life-bearer" as is Eve (Genesis 3:20).

The curse on the male parallels the one upon the female. Man must toil in pain, *'eseb*, the same word used for Eve's future predicament. To the *'akhal* (eating) of transgression corresponds the *'akhal* in pain of the punishment. To both the implicit *tešukah* (desire) at the basis of the human temptation and the *mašal* (dominion) under which the female human put herself, correspond now the *tešukah* and the *mašal* of Genesis 3:16. The initial *tešukah* first appeared in analogues such as *tob*, *ta'a-wah*, *nehmad*, that described the attraction of the forbidden tree. And the *mašal* is also first implied in the acceptance of the authority of someone else than God over Eve and in the acquisition of dominion for herself by the eating of the fruit (*dei eritis*). The shift from one "desire" to

56. Ricoeur, *The Symbolism of Evil*, pp. 255–57.

57. Ibid. Michael Fishbane, *Text and Texture*, speaks rather of the presence of the serpent as showing evil lying deep within the "nature" of things (see p. 22). In Genesis 4, at any rate, there is internalization of the serpent (sin recoils like the snake at the door, 4:7). J's reflection on human sin leads him to the conclusion that *sin has always been there* in time and in space. But, with Luis Alonso-Schökel, we must realize that the author places that ever-present and ubiquitous sin within the framework of the history of salvation (cf. p. 61).

58. The text has *'attah*, "thou" in the masculine.

the other, and from one "dominion" to the other, describes twisted and abnormal relationships. Only the *eschaton* shall restore the normal conditions that prevailed before rebellion. Ezekiel 28, a text that we have repeatedly mentioned above in parallel with the J version of creation, announces: "For the house of Israel there shall be no more a brier to prick or a thorn to hurt them" (v. 24, see also the *locus classicus* of Isaiah 11).

The human couple is now standing on a soil upon which they depend for their subsistence but which is cursed. To this soil from which they were taken, they also return. As regards these far-reaching texts, we must keep in mind that it is not a question here of the passage from one reality to another, or, for that matter, from one world to another.[59] As Paul Beauchamp says, "heaven and earth" are orientations and limits.[60] Human rebellion alters both, so that the "orient" is disoriented and the "limit" is transgressed. This does not prevent the orient and the limit from remaining forever the norms in the world created by God. As is true for Genesis 3:22, where I have read the verb *hayah* as referring to a human state before the rebellion, so too 3:16 indicates a change of value, not of nature. This is made absolutely evident as far as the earth is concerned: it remains the earth it was before, but instead of cooperating with man's efforts, it has now become hostile (3:18). It produces as before plants of all kinds, but now those plants are "thorns and thistles"; man tills the ground as before and this demands his efforts (2:15), but now the effort takes toil and sweat and appears as almost fruitless.

The words addressed to woman and man by God must be read with the utmost care, as displayed, for instance, by Carol Meyers, whose methodology will serve here as a model, although with somewhat different results.[61] With Meyers, I translate the first Hebrew words in 3:16 by "greatly increase." The term indicates the enhancement or worsening of a preexisting situation, not the emergence of an original reality (cf. Genesis 16:10). "Something cannot be multiplied unless it is already there" (Meyers, p. 103, cf. p. 105). What is increased is the *hêrôn* of the woman, the period of her pregnancy (envisaged exclusively in terms of giving birth; cf. Jeremiah 20:14–18). This is "pain" (more mental perhaps than physical, see Meyers p. 104, but certainly not exclusive

59. Despite the rabbinic *ha-ʿolam ha-zeh* (this world) versus *ha-ʿolam ha-baʿ* (the world to come) where, besides, the word *ʿolam* should be understood as "economy," not as "world."

60. Beauchamp, *Création et séparation.*

61. Carole Meyers, *Discovering Eve: Ancient Israelite Women in Context* (New York: Oxford University Press, 1988).

of the latter if only because of its long duration).[62] That the question in the text of Genesis is not one of the number of pregnancies (inadvertently inserting a modern problem into an ancient text for which many offspring would not in itself constitute a problem but rather a blessing) is also demonstrated by the use of singular for the word *hêrôn* in the text.

The text continues by saying, *be-'eṣeb têledî banîm* ("in pain you shall bring forth children," NRSV). Meyers's argument is here circumvoluted. She attempts to shift the bearing of the text from the pangs of giving birth, and the result is a tour de force of sorts. However it is simpler to understand that God says to woman, (You were created to beget children with ease, but now) "you shall beget children in travail." Or even, on account of the dynamic thrust in the preposition *be,* "[now] it is *for* pain/toil that you shall beget children."[63]

In a similar vein, it is to be noted that female "desire" is "an attraction that already exists" (Meyers, p. 110). It will continue to prevail in the new economy inaugurated by human rebellion, despite the evil outcome of it in long pregnancies and in the travail of childbirth. The socioeconomical conditions in the ancient world[64] emphasize still more the understandable fear of woman to beget children in such "pain" and for such an uncertain future. Against that background, the rest of the sentence makes sense. Such dire conditions imposed on "mothering" could perhaps end up in a standstill of sexual relationships, but then one disregards the female *tešukah* (of course, woman does not have the exclusivity of sexual desire, but the male *tešukah* need not be mentioned here because the outcome of lovemaking for him is not comparable with the outcome for the female. The "pain/toil" for him is situated elsewhere, as is indicated in the next verse. There is, therefore, no restraint on the male to go in with the female.) Woman's *tešukah* shall prevail over her fears, thus giving to her male companion a "power" over her in the realm of sexuality (cf. Genesis 30:1). In this context, it must be remembered that the pivotal term *yada'* (to know; or to have sexual intercourse) has also the meaning of "to have power over" someone. Something of this

62. If we contrast this description of Genesis with eschatological expectations—as we already did earlier when dealing with the acquired "blindness" of the human couple—it is striking that the sages of old envisioned the Messianic age as providing conditions for giving birth the very day of conception (see *Shabbath* 30b, teaching of Rabban Gamliel).

63. According to the eschatological promise of Isaiah 65:23, "they shall not bear children for terror."

64. Meyers (pp. 112–13) explains this well (and in more detail in "The Roots of Restriction: Women in Early Israel," in Norman K. Gottwald, ed., *The Bible and Liberation: Political and Social Hermeneutics* [Maryknoll: Orbis, 1983], pp. 189ff.).

meaning is evident in the moving text of Amos 3:2 ("only you have 'known' among all the families of the earth . . ."). It is still clearer in Genesis 19 or Judges 19 (the Sodomites and the Benjaminites of Gibeah want to 'know' carnally, and overpower, the newcomer[s] in their city). It is thus paradoxical that the woman allows her male companion to exercise, within the sexual realm, dominion over her for the sake of the perpetuation of the species. It is now the price to pay after shunning the gracious immortality granted by God within the dialogue in Eden. This individual immortality is now replaced by a collective one through the succession of generations.

Genesis 3:16d is thus no general and sweeping statement about male rule (and still less "superiority") over the female. Rather, it is a statement to be read within the immediate context provided by the preceding lines. Of prime importance is that the "dominion" of the male is granted by the female herself in the sexual relationship. Not that it would just be good will on her part, however, for he exercises upon her (as she upon him, but with vastly different results) an irrepressible attraction, while she is aware of the unwelcome possible physical and moral/emotional consequences accompanying (blessed) pregnancy and birth-giving. There is nothing here of a "natural" superiority of the male that would be chauvinistically affirmed as divine right by a patriarchal society. The "rule" in question is here described as highly paradoxical, but it is the only explanation—the only sapiential etiology—that can account for the assumed risk taken by females in intercourse. One should, therefore, understand the biblical phrase as saying, "but *he* [and the dangers his commerce represents] will predominate[65] over you [and your fears]."

The Creation narrative presents a scene from which the addressee is conspicuously absent. This strange situation is found elsewhere in the Bible: "Where were you?" God asks Job (38:4).[66] This in itself is already a lesson in humility. No reader of the sacred text can boast having an immediate and firsthand knowledge of primeval history, that is, of the origin, raison d'être, and objective, of all that exists. All the reader

---

65. Cf. Meyers, *Discovering Eve,* p. 117.

66. The divine question, "where are you?" is not only defiance. Jacob Neusner quotes the Rabbis on Genesis 3:9, who say that the interrogative adverb means also "How has this happened to you?" The Hebrew word is *'eikhah,* which also begins the book of Lamentations, and hence stands for a lament. The Rabbis paraphrase: "I mourned for him (Adam) saying, 'How . . .'" (Jacob Neusner and Andrew M. Greeley, *The Bible and Us: A Priest and a Rabbi Read Scripture Together* [New York: Warner Books, 1990], p. 61).

knows is what the author cares to tell and how he cares to tell it. Here, more than ever, knowledge is trust in, and acceptance of, another's authority. But here the situation is uniquely compounded by the understood acknowledgment of the author's absence from the scene he is describing. When God created heaven and earth, no one was there to witness it.[67] There is, on the part of the author, and hence on the part of the recipient, reliance upon the credibility of tradition and history. The distance from myth is immense. For the author J operates as a sage contemplating the universe and as a prophet "reading" history and discovering its past and its future. His interest is less in what was than in what is and is to be.[68] "Adam and Eve" are every man and every woman, here and now. This is the bedrock of J's authority and credibility. This is what can be called "inspiration," or *theopneustia* (2 Timothy 3:16). Had J wanted to report a myth about paradisiacal bliss, there would be no "cracks in the wall." On the contrary, J's "story" is bursting with power because, in spite of her or his supposed absence as addressee, the reader is actually present in the whole and in each detail. She recognizes herself in Eve, he recognizes himself in Adam. S/he acknowledges that chaos is never far away; the enemy is ever "like a roaring lion . . . looking for someone to devour" (1 Peter 5:8).

The struggle is particularly fierce between the serpent (signifying sterility and death) and the woman (whose name is *ḥawwah*, Eve, "the living one, for she is the mother of all living," Genesis 3:20). In the connected realm of food,[69] Adam finds life highly precarious. The humans are surrounded by "thorns and thistles," that is, by the vegetation of the desert, a remnant of primordial chaos. The situation is thus utterly dismal; but, steadily faithful to his project, J raises hope here as he introduces a clear eschatological dimension. In the same way that, in other streams of tradition, chaos is destined to be once and for all overcome, and Leviathan to be slain (Isaiah 27:1), so here the serpent's head shall be crushed by the woman's offspring (Genesis 3:15). Children of the "Living One" shall be able to triumph over the "Dead One." The ancient serpent, who is the Devil and Satan, shall be seized and bound forever and shall deceive people no more (cf. Revelation 20:2–3).

67. "However the narrative is of a unique type when the element of authority it carries is brought to its highest point, the object of the narrative being what no one could have seen, what was there before man was there" (Beauchamp, *Création et séparation*, p. 381).

68. Similarly, with the "splitting" of Adam into two beings (male and female), the unity of man and woman is *to be*, to become. It is the passage from myth to history.

69. In Hebrew, as so often in other cultures, "to eat" is used metaphorically for sexual intercourse (cf. Exodus 2:20–22; Proverbs 30:20; 9:5; etc.).

Thinking Creation

PAUL RICOEUR

For the past few decades, one problem has dominated the exegesis and theology of the Old Testament: what degree of independence is to be accorded the doctrine of creation in relation to the fundamental soteriological affirmation that is assumed to run through both testaments of the Bible. This problem is of interest to more than just specialists in the thought of ancient Israel within the setting of ancient Near Eastern cultures. It concerns contemporary theology and the preaching influenced by it to the degree that the resolutely Christocentric reading of the two testaments, influenced by Karl Barth, is warranted by an exegesis of the Old Testament that takes as its guiding thread the theme of *Heilsgeschichte*, the history of salvation. Within Christian communities, then, the stakes of this discussion are high. I hope to show that it also affects all those for whom the enigma of beginnings or of origins gives rise to anxiety, perplexity, or simply to curiosity and a quest for knowledge.

André LaCocque recalls, from the very first pages of his essay, the role played in this discussion by Gerhard von Rad's well-known essay from 1936, "The Theological Problem of the Old Testament Doctrine of Creation."[1] This German exegete was one of the first to maintain that even though the doctrine of creation is in fact inseparable from that of salvation, its categories still call for a distinct treatment. André LaCocque adopts the thesis upon which I too will base my comments, namely, that the Creation arises out of a prehistory whose reported events set into movement a broad dynamism operating at the very heart

---

1. Gerhard von Rad, *The Problem of the Hexateuch and Other Essays,* translated by E. W. Trueman Dicken (Edinburgh and London: Oliver & Boyd, 1966), pp. 131–43.

of history.[2] The references to prehistory and history throughout his presentation of the contemporary exegetical debate leads me to think that it is at the level of the relations between pre- or proto-history (or even better: primordial history) and history that we must approach this discussion. If it is the sense or meaning of history that is in question for the soteriological thesis, in the texts relative to Creation it is those events arising from this primordial history that are dealt with. Therefore we must first be clear about the use of these two terms and their relation, as much on the literary plane as on the level of meanings capable of nourishing a biblical theology worthy of this name.

The working hypothesis guiding the following analyses can be broadly stated as follows. The bond that unites the primordial history and dated (or datable) history has still to be thought through. I shall call it the relation of *precedence,* out of prudence, for reasons I will explain without further delay. What is paradoxical in this relation is that it has to be thought of in terms of the intersection of two lines of interpretation. The first emphasizes the *caesura* between primordial and historical time. By "caesura," I mean more than just a discontinuity in a succession. It also includes the fact that the time of the primordial events in relation to the time of those of history cannot be fully coordinated in terms of some temporal succession, even if we begin the latter with the time of the ancestors, inaugurated by the call addressed to Abraham in Genesis 12, and by the unheard-of promises that accompany the call to leave Ur. It is, more fundamentally, in terms of chronology that these two times, which we might better call two temporal qualities, cannot be coordinated. Hence there is no sense in asking if the history of Abraham succeeds that of Adam and the other characters presented in Genesis 2:4–11:22. Still less is there any sense in asking if the history of Abraham is situated after that of the Creation in seven days, which, we know, belongs to a later redaction than that of Genesis 2–11, which belongs to the sequence upon which André LaCocque and I are concentrating here. Whatever the term "precedence" may signify, it does not mean chronological anteriority.

This initial comment is relevant not only to the exegesis of the biblical text, it also affects the use that has been made and still is sometimes made of the Creation narratives, particularly by fundamentalists. Just as

2. André LaCocque shows the different ways in which this solidarity between creation and history is expressed. First, the order instituted by the act of Creation remains threatened by a disorder that has its counterpart in the tribulations within the history of Israel. Next, the close kinship between the cosmic order and the Law has its echo in the theology of the covenant. Finally, both Creation and history have the same eschatological horizon.

the events of the primordial history cannot be coordinated with what the ancient Hebrews took as the time of history—and in this they were in agreement with ancient Near Eastern cultures in general—neither can we today, as the heirs of the physical science of Galileo and Newton, the Darwinian theory of evolution, and scientific research into the origins of humanity, do so. All these inquiries—cosmological, biological, anthropological, and so on—proceed in terms of one homogeneous time, whose time periods are parts of a sequence pointing back toward a beginning that I shall later say is ungraspable.[3] Thus it is not just within the bounds of the exegesis and theology of the Old Testament, even when enlarged to include the broader horizon of ancient Near Eastern cultures, that the caesura between primordial and historical time imposes itself. To affirm this in recognition of scientific inquiry into beginnings and origins (and I am not yet distinguishing between these two terms) is a question both of intellectual honesty and, if I may put it this way, of sound thinking. It is liberating to admit that there is no call for trying to date the creation of Adam in relation to Pithecanthropus or Neanderthal man.

Still, this first stance, which we may call disjunctive, does not do justice to the other idea contained within the idea of precedence: that the events that occurred in the time of origins have an inaugural value as regards the history that, on the literary plane of narration, follows the primordial events. At the very beginning of his study, André LaCocque approaches this founding relation from an important angle: the histories recounted in Genesis 2–3 serve to *universalize* the description made there of the human condition. Beyond—or, rather, before—the Jewish people, what we have are human beings apart from the ethnic qualification that already clothes the figure of Abraham as well as those of the other protagonists in the saga of the ancestors. And this foundational relation takes on other forms than just that of an archetype. Exegetes readily emphasize the etiologic function of certain of these narratives that explain things happen as they do today because that is how they happened at the origin. This applies particularly to the punishments at the end of the great narrative of Genesis 2–3. However, neither the universalizing/archetypal function nor the etiologic/causal function exhausts the founding role of the primordial events, as we shall see below in "The Foundation."

Whatever may be the case as regards this notion of founding events,

---

3. Cf. J. T. Fraser, *The Genesis and Evolution of Time* (Amherst: University of Massachusetts Press, 1982).

the insurmountable difficulty is to combine within the idea of precedence the noncoordinatable character of primordial and historical time in terms of chronology and the founding function assigned to the primordial events. This is why I shall deal in succession with these two dimensions of the idea of precedence, which will still remain to be thought beyond any simple juxtaposition of these two points of view.

Separation

Before taking up the question of what these narratives and the other relations that may be drawn from the primordial history pose for thought, we need to be more precise about some formal characteristics of the *Urgeschichte* that undercut the expectations forged by centuries, even millennia, of use of the Bible.

In the first place, before the Hellenistic era, the notion of Creation *ex nihilo* was unknown. Or, rather, the question to which this answer corresponds had not yet been posed. This is clear as regards the oldest narrative of Creation in Genesis, that of Genesis 2:3, which is introduced by a remarkable formula: "*when* no plant of the earth and no herb of the field had *yet. . . . then* the Lord God formed man from the dust of the ground" (2:5–7). This formula, "when . . . not yet . . . then" determines an unprecedented starting point for the creative act. (The elements that did not yet exist—plants of the field, grasses of the field, rain, man the tiller of the soil—are not, properly speaking, described. They are simply named as what was not yet there, when . . .) So long as we do not pose the question of what could have preceded the divine activity, we do not ask from where came the dust from which man is drawn, nor what the materials were that made up the trees of the garden or the rivers that watered it, nor whence came the ground from which God made the animals. To create is to form, to give a shape and a consistency. The same thing applies to the account of the creation of the world in Genesis 1: the deep is there, as is the darkness and the primordial waters. God's word does not create out of nothing and the successive separations that mark the six days of work constitute the creative act itself. The notion of Creation *ex nihilo* is a response to a subsequent speculation concerning what G. W. Leibniz will much later call "the radical origin of things."

A second expectation belied by our texts has to do with the idea of a single, total Creation. This strict criterion applies to Genesis 1 alone. Properly speaking, Genesis 2:5–3:26 recounts the creation of man, of the animals, of woman, and the irruption of evil with its train of punishments. We might, following some scholars, distinguish between an "absolute" and a "relative" beginning.[4] But this distinction between absolute and relative is foreign to Hebraic culture as it also is to other ancient Near Eastern cultures. What counts is the creation by a god—here by the Lord God, Yahweh God—of something important, when the scene of the creative act did not yet exist. The notion of multiple beginnings that is involved here will play a large role in our section entitled "The Foundation."

Another expectation that our texts derail is the much more modern idea of a beginning as a pointlike event. This idea is clearly dependent on the representation of time as a line and of events themselves as linear series, the beginning constituting the first term of the series, like a starting point. With the refutation of this expectation, we enter the heart of the notion of a primordial history. "History" is just the word that fits here, if we do not assimilate it to the sense of documentary history, which is elsewhere represented in the Bible by those narratives, manifestly inspired by royal archives, that have to do with the peripeteia of the Davidic and Solomonic monarchies. The primordial history is a history in the sense that it sets in order a multiplicity of events upon which it imprints the unity of an intelligible sequence. Claus Westermann uses the apt expression in this regard of a *Geschehensbogen*—an arch giving unity to a course of events.[5] In this respect, the narrative form is particularly appropriate for this ordering relation. Genesis 2:4b–3:24 constitutes a narrative in the best sense of the term. In this sequence, whose internal complexity I shall return to, primordial history and primordial narrative overlap. As for the narrative notion of an event, we may apply this in turn to the peripeteia taken one by one and to the whole sequence inasmuch as it intends the unity of the coming into existence, let us say, in the case of Genesis 2–3, of the human condition with all its ambiguities. It is this condition that is in a way put forth as a whole by an act whose details are spelled out by the narrative. Below, we shall need this notion of a totalizing event in order to correct the perverse effects that the narration itself introduces as soon as it recounts in succession what, in a way, was produced in one single outburst.[6]

4. For example, P. Gibert, *Bible, mythes et récits de commencement* (Paris: Seuil, 1986), p. 29.

5. Cf. Claus Westermann, *Genesis. Biblischer Kommentar, Altes Testament* (Neukirchen-Vluyn: Neukirchener Verlag, 1966), pp. 259–67.

6. The constraints imposed by narrative succession are largely responsible for the leveling of all the recounted histories to a single line of time, as well as for the deplorable confusions referred to

However, narration is not the only way we can relate ourselves to primordial time. Genesis 1 is not a narrative, but a didactic poem. It is only in an improper sense, owing to the succession of the words and acts of division, that we can say that Genesis 1 recounts the Creation of the world. In any case, this quasi-narrative lacks the dramatic character of the events reported in Genesis 2–3, which stem from its being a narrative in the strong sense of this term.[7] Nor ought we lose sight of the references to Creation in the Psalms, where the chorus of praise reduces to the form of a "narrative clause" the brief narrative sequences having a form such as "Glory to You *who* once did [this . . .]." We shall have to take into account these proclamations with their overall hymnic character when we refer to the diversity of models of Creation.

Finally, we must make a place for a confession of faith as denuded of any narrative character as that found in II Maccabees 7:25–29, where the Hellenic influence is quite evident.[8] Pierre Gibert's, at first sight disconcerting, remark that no privileged literary form captures Creation follows from this diversity of genres.[9] Even if the narrative form best fits the most dramatic sequences, such as those in Genesis 2–3, we can call in a broader sense "primordial narratives of creation" all the other

---

above regarding the noncoordinatable character of the primordial time in relation to historical time.

7. Iconography will restore its dramatic dimension to the representation of the Creation. I have in mind such examples as the ceiling of the Sistine Chapel painted by Michelangelo, Hayden's "Creation," and the first movement of Beethoven's Ninth Symphony. We shall account for this redramatization below in terms of the persistence of the themes of combat which continue even into the most free representations of the Creation.

8. As her youngest son is being tortured—the episode takes place during the persecution of the Jews in 167 BCE—the mother exhorts him in these words: "I beg you, my child, to look at the heaven and the earth and see everything that is in them, and recognize that God did not make them out of things that existed. And in the same way the human race came into being. . . . Accept death . . ." Cf. Gibert, *Bible, mythes et récits de commencement,* p. 142, and note 38 below.

9. "In my opinion, the *theme* of creation and therefore of an absolute beginning does not postulate some particular literary genre. . . . It can be taken up in different possible genres: narratives, poems (cf. Psalms), creeds, wisdom discourse, etc." Gibert, *Bible, mythes et récits de commencement,* p. 246. André LaCocque arrives at the same conclusion: "Thus, wisdom, history, story, and myths converge here" (above, p. 11). He is correct in placing wisdom at the head of this list, following the insightful analysis of Luis Alonzo-Schökel, "Motivos sapienciales y de alianza en Gn 2–3," *Biblien* 4 (1962): 295–315, translated as "Sapiential and Covenant Themes in Genesis 2–3," in *Modern Biblical Studies* (Milwaukee: The Bruce Publishing Company, 1967). The knowledge of good and evil, the "cunning" of the serpent, Adam's wisdom in naming the animals and the woman, and in falling only out of love, not through trickery, the detailed discussion of the "four rivers," and quite clearly, the whole discussion about the enigma of evil are all wisdom motifs. Schökel calls the way in which a whole of series of horizontal lines of explanation are transformed by being linked to a single point of view (the origin of humanity): a "triangular ascent." This is the mark of wisdom.

"references to creation" in order to take into account the succession of events reported in them.[10] This broad use of the expression "primordial narratives" can be justified by the character of the events that are recounted, whether it be a question of the episodes and incidents that constitute the elementary components of these narratives, poems, or hymns, or even if we have in mind the configurational unity through which is expressed the multiple unity of an act that posits the "thing" created as a meaningful whole: world, humanity, even evil (although it is a question here of something like a decreation, as in the case of the Flood). This characteristic of a global event, which I shall return to below in "Trajectories: Thinking Creation?," is what imposes the literary form of narrative, whether in the strict sense or in the broad sense, as being the most adequate one for telling what once happened, at the beginning. In this sense, everything that has to do with what can be considered an event can be called a narrative. Finally, the expression "primordial history" is most obviously justified inasmuch as in several languages the word "history" designates both the events that actually occurred and the account of them that is given on the plane of literary forms. I shall speak, therefore, of primordial histories in order to characterize the narrative or quasi-narrative accounts that are made about events that happened *in illo tempore*.

Let me add one last remark before turning to the meanings attached to the notion of a primordial history. Creation admits several operative models, if I may put it this way. Claus Westermann proposes a simple typology for them: creation by generation, creation through combat, creation by fabrication, creation through a word.[11] Psalms 40 and 79, as well as various references to Creation in the book of Job, relate to the second type. Our narrative in Genesis 2–3 belongs to the third type. Genesis 1 falls under the fourth one. Only the first type is strictly excluded from the Hebrew Bible. In a theory based on a concept of progress, which the history of religions has a difficult time avoiding, there

10. Here I am drawing on the careful typology of literary categories having generally to do with the narrative genre proposed by George W. Coats in his *Genesis, with an Introduction to Narrative Literature* (Grand Rapids, MI: W. B. Eerdmans, 1983). He distinguishes saga, tale, novella, legend, history, report, fable, etiology, and myth. The Creation narratives are part of the genre saga—"a saga is a long prose, traditional narrative"—owing to its episodic structure. The "primitive" saga is to be classed along with the "familial" and "heroic" forms. I would place the emphasis here more on the word "primordial" than on saga. On the other hand, I agree with the elimination of the term myth, which is borrowed from other literary domains, whether Hellenic or North American Indian, which only adds to the confusion.

11. Cf. Westermann, *Genesis. Biblischer Kommentar,* pp. 36–65.

would be a progression from one type to another, and our text from Genesis 2 would leave us at the midway point. We can, however, pose the problem in a different way, even as regards exegesis, and, more importantly, on the theological level. We can ask instead, with Jon D. Levenson,[12] to whose work I shall return, what traces the combat model, common to Israel and other cultures of the ancient Near East, has left on the other models, inasmuch as it is never a question of Creation *ex nihilo* before the speculations inspired by Hellenism. I think this question is of theological as well as of exegetical interest inasmuch as the Hebrew Bible never stopped confronting the good will of the Creator and the Redeemer with the persistence of evil. If this is the most encompassing theme of the Hebrew Bible and perhaps as well of the New Testament writings, is the most encompassing hypothesis then not that Creation remains a drama, in what ever way it is recounted or reported?

Following this discussion of the formal aspects that, on the literary plane, make the primordial history a "separated" history, let us consider the events themselves, as they are recounted or reported, and ask whether the formal aspect of separation is not reflected, on the plane of these contents, in a structure of separation, substantially bound to the very notion of a beginning. By stating this hypothesis for our reading, I am returning to my earlier remarks concerning the two sides of the idea of antecedence, which seem to me to constitute what is ultimately at stake in the relations between primordial history and dated or datable history. On the one hand, the beginning does not belong to the sequence of things recounted; on the other hand, it inaugurates and grounds this sequence. The hypothesis that we must now put to the test is whether we must push further the aspect of separation attracted to the idea of a beginning if we wish eventually to give its full meaning to the notion of founding events.

I shall concentrate on the sequence in Genesis 2:4b–3:24, where we find two histories recounted, that of the Creation of humanity and that which Claus Westermann places under the heading "Crime and Punishment." I propose reading these two histories as those of one progressive separation, where the recounted content is the homologue of its literary form.

When I speak of separation, I am not talking about dereliction or alienation. Separation is fundamentally what distinguishes the Creator and the creature and thereby simultaneously indicates the "withdrawal"

---

12. Jon D. Levenson, *Creation and the Persistence of Evil: The Jewish Drama of Divine Omnipotence* (San Francisco: Harper and Row, 1985).

of God and the consistency belonging to the creature. The properly human aspects of this separation are certainly the loss of proximity to God symbolized by the expulsion from the garden but, also, as I shall attempt to demonstrate, access to responsibility as regards oneself and others. Guilty and punished, humanity is not cursed.[13]

What I propose, therefore, is a second-degree reading of the narratives in Genesis 2, based on André LaCocque's and other scholars' exegesis of this material (especially Claus Westermann and Paul Beauchamp) and guided by the idea of a progression in separation, culminating in the "withdrawal" of God and the expulsion of the humans from the wonderful garden.

I shall not discuss Genesis 1 here. However, it is impossible, given a theological perspective based on a canonical exegesis, not to give some heading to our narrative in order to restore the whole trajectory of the theme of separation. If the Creation of the world signifies something, it is, at least in a negative sense, that the creature is not the creator. In externalizing himself, as Franz Rosenzweig puts it, using a language that recalls that of the later Schelling, God set up in exteriority a nature that henceforth exists, if not for itself, at least in itself. The first meaning the creature has owing to the fact of having been created is to exist at a distance from God, as a distinct work. In this regard, we recall what force and breadth Jewish thought has given to this theme where the Creator distances himself from those he distances from himself.[14] Just as the "successive" stages, which together make up the unique event of Creation as a complete whole, are distinguished from one another as so many separations,[15] so too Creation as a whole is placed under the sign of separation, which we can call "originary," through which the world

13. Frank Crüsemann, in "Die Eigenständigkeit der Urgeschichte: Ein Beitrag zur Diskussion um den 'Jahwisten,'" in *Die Botschaft und die Boten: Festschrift für Hans Walter Wolff* (Neukirchen-Vluyn: Neukirchener Verlag, 1981), protests against the dominant tendency among Old Testament exegetes to see in Genesis 2–11 a systematically "negative" picture of the human condition, destined to serve as a contrast to the blessing that accompanies the call of Abraham in Genesis 12. We need to stop reading Genesis 2–11 in light of Genesis 12:1–3, he claims. Once freed of this handicap, the description of the human condition in Genesis 2–11 shows "ambiguous" rather than exclusively "negative" features of the human condition. Crüsemann concludes, following a careful analysis of the vocabulary used here and the anthropological references that Genesis 2–11 was not written by the same hand as was Genesis 12ff. This contribution to the current dismantling of the *sogennante Jahwist* is not our concern here so much as its recognition of the thematic specificity of Genesis 2–11.

14. Pierre Gisel, "Reprises du thème de la création," in *La Création* (Geneva: Labor et Fides, 1987), pp. 79–91. Cf. J. Eisenberg and A. Abecassis, *A Bible ouverte* (Paris: Albin Michel, 1978); *Et Dieu créa Eve* (Paris: Albin Michel, 1979).

15. Paul Beauchamp, *Création et séparation. Etude exégétique du chapitre premier de la Genèse* (Paris: Aubier/Cerf, 1969).

exists as a manifold reality, hierarchically organized and closed-in on itself. It is true that this separation is not known or reflected upon, owing to the lack of any witness who could internalize it or its meaning. Nonetheless, "when God created the heavens and the earth," this multiplicity started to exist "in itself" without yet being "for itself."

It is the "for itself" of separation that comes about with the Creation of humanity recounted in Genesis 2:4b–3:24.[16] This sequence, which is clearly marked from a literary point of view, recounts "successively" two histories that each present a certain narrative unity, but which overlap. We may thus read them together by stitching the one to the other. An effect of superposing is thereby created that somewhat annuls the illusion of succession, which I said above stems from the constraints of the narrative genre. The narrative of the Creation of humanity extends from Genesis 2:7 to Genesis 2:25, including one incident related to the cycle of "numberings" having to do with the "four rivers" of the garden.[17] The second narrative is tied to the preceding one by the theme of the "garden" and the "two trees" (2:9). Moreover, it is anticipated by the posing of the prohibition in 2:16–17. It unfolds without interruption from the temptation to the expulsion from the garden. Properly speaking, the second narrative recounts not so much a Creation as a breech in Creation (which justifies André LaCocque's title: "Cracks in the Wall"). In any case, as a narrative of the beginning of evil, it does stem from the primordial history.

If we reread each of these two half-narratives, first separately, then as superimposed, guided by the idea of separation, we are struck by the strong sense this theme illuminates concerning certain details in each of these two half-narratives and even more so by the effect of entanglement resulting from their superimposition.

First, one "man" is created, but in two times, or rather two acts. There is the formation of man from the dust of the earth and the insufflation into his nostrils of a breath of life. The man is not yet a living being but is already dependent. His task of cultivating and overseeing the garden (2:15) begins to render him responsible for something fragile confided

---

16. The cosmos is not lost from sight, in the sense that at the time "Yahweh made the earth and the heavens," there were no bushes *on the earth*, no plant *of the fields*, no rain to fall *on the earth*, and no "man to till the soil." The triad—world-life-man—is implicitly posited along with the creation of humanity.

17. Claus Westermann distinguishes in his General Introduction between "numbering" (*Aufzählende*) and "narrative" (*Erzählende*) texts (p. 24). See also his discussion of verses 2:10–14 (pp. 292–98). The *Toldoth* "genealogies" belong to the former ground, as does Genesis 1–2:4a.

to him. A major separation is indicated by the uttering of a command-ment that itself consists of a general permission (to eat any of the fruit) and a precise prohibition (to eat of all but one). "Before" any fault, the commandment is a structure of the created order for man. The Law implies a Limit, and the limit is constitutive of man in his finitude, distinct from the divine Unlimited. Yhwh thus figures as beyond the limit, the inaccessible, at the same time that he is presented as the au-thor of a commandment not motivated by its content (do not eat the fruit of the tree) but, instead, secured by the authority of the one who posits the limit. In this sense, it is not this or that that is forbidden, but, if I may put it this way, that *there is* originarily a limit. Someone may object that it is only under the reign of sin that the Law is perceived as traumatizing and mutilating. This is how Paul understood the relation between the Law and sin. The Law, aroused by sin, gives death. But, apart from sin, the limit would have been only a limit and not a mutila-tion of the human, hostile to life, as, for example, Nietzsche understood it, drawing here upon Paul and not upon Genesis 2. Between the Law and Life, the relationship is what is stated in Deuteronomy: choose the good and you will live. In this sense, the primordial limit, in the setting of an innocent Creation, is constitutive of a distance that, far from ex-cluding proximity, constitutes it. As will have been observed, the ut-tering of the limit is immediate; that is, apart from any institutional mediation, even apart from the tables of the Law. God still speaks di-rectly to the man. This intimacy in terms of distance defines "proxim-ity," an unknown relation between God and the rest of Creation.

To continue in the same vein, under the guidance of the theme of separation, does not the naming of the animals, a major act of division and classification, testify to an initiative that is in some ways emanci-pated? And does not the search for a "helper," which the Creation of the animals in a way misleads, lead to the Creation of a partner who is not God, but the woman? Does not the man, in his cry of jubilation, celebrate the woman without naming God? In this manner, humanity, twofold yet one, arises like a complete event indicating the advent of a separated humanity, which lives for all that in proximity to God.

The second half-narrative can also be read from the point of view of a progression in separation in terms of a qualitative change affecting the very meaning of separation. From the point of view of the narrative composition, this half-narrative includes three episodes: the tempta-tion, the transgression of the prohibition, and the trial (which itself is divided into three sequences: concealment, discovery, and the sentences passed). Finally comes the expulsion from the garden. We must be very attentive to the composition of the narrative configuration if we are correctly to designate what counts as the primordial history. It would be an error and a grave mistake for the theological comprehension of this whole sequence to consider the transgression as an event separating two successive "states," a state of innocence that alone would be primordial and a fallen state, which would henceforth be part of history. The break between the primordial and the historical does not occur in the middle of the narrative, rather it separates the *Geschehensbogen* as a whole,[18] including the prohibition, the temptation, the transgression, and the trial from all the histories of disobedience attributed to Israel or the nations. This large-scale configuration designates one complex, integral event, namely, the positing overall of the originary human condition. But, if there are not two successive "states," one of which, the state of innocence, would be primordial, the narrative does suggest the idea of a progression in the separation, within the single primordial history, a separation that culminates in the impoverished condition represented by the episode of the expulsion from the garden.

Considered from this angle, the temptation episode takes on a noteworthy significance. It stems from the questioning of the prohibition as a structuring component of the created order. Did God say? Posing this question ends the unquestioned confidence in this prohibition, as one of life's conditions, that had made it seem as self-evident as the plants of the garden. The era of suspicion is opened,[19] a fault line is introduced into the most fundamental condition of language, namely, the relation of trust, what linguists call the sincerity clause. In this respect, the serpent must not be considered just from the point of view of its narrative role, whatever mythical features lie behind it.[20] These features are in

18. As regards the inseparable unity of the *Geschehenablauf,* excluding a break between two "states" separated by the fault, see Westermann, *Genesis. Biblischer Kommentar,* pp. 374–80. "The goal of Genesis 2–3," he observes, "is not to recount the substitution of one 'state' for another but the expulsion from the garden and separation from God that goes with it" (ibid., p. 377).

19. Cf. Paul Beauchamp, "Le serpent herméneute," in *L'Un et L'Autre Testament,* vol. 2: *Accomplir les Ecritures* (Paris: Seuil, 1990), pp. 137–58.

20. I agree completely with what André LaCocque says about the demythologization/remythologization of the motif of the serpent and about the humanity/animality dialectic at work here. Indeed, even if we say with Claus Westermann that the serpent is demythologized due to the narrative reduction that goes with its role in this story, whatever its mythical antecedents, its role is such that it cannot be entirely demythologized. There is the need, if I may put it this way, for a mythic residue in order to convey the unfathomable aspect of the power that perverts language and desire and thereby "inclines" us toward evil. This partial remythologization of the serpent as the other of the human calls into question the boundary between humanity and animality established in the episode of the naming of the animals. A fabulous character, an animal who talks, was required as a basis for the narrative of a human—all too human—drama.

fact demythologized by the narrative reduction of this tempter who comes from who knows where.[21] As the only other one the woman talks to, the serpent represents the inscrutable dramatization of evil as always already there. Whoever—or whatever—the serpent may be, what is important for the progress of the total narrative is the sudden mutation in human desire: "So when the woman saw that the tree was good for food, and that it was a delight to the eyes [there is nothing condemnable about either this 'goodness' or this 'seductive' delight], and that the tree was to be desired to make one wise . . ." (3:6). Here we have the exact moment of temptation: the desire for infinity, which implies a transgression of all limits. We may admire here how in this composition the narrator has joined suspicion at the level of language and subversion at the level of desire. When the limit is suspect as a structure, the desire for unlimitedness flows through the breech thereby opened.

Whatever may be said about the riddle of the tempter, the narrative does not orient thinking in quest of meaning toward the idea of a necessary implication between temptation and the violation of the prohibition. Instead, the narrative presents this violation as a distinct and unexplained act (3:6b). The force of the narrative connection in its specificity is irreducible to a logical or physical connection. This is why this happened "one time." The event is thereby shrunk down to its pointlike dimension as the climax of the whole arc of what is to come.

For our reflection, centered on the theme of separation, we may take the expulsion from Eden as the sufficient as well as the actual conclusion of this narrative.[22] The three sentences of punishment are certainly meaningful to the extent that they tend to give a punitive sense to the arduous, vulnerable, and mortal aspects of the human condition such as a Palestinian peasant might experience them.[23] The expulsion from Eden is the true conclusion of the narrative as a whole, however. It indi-

---

21. "The extraordinarily important affirmation for J that *there is no aetiology for the provenance of evil* would be destroyed by an interpretation in terms of myth where a precise provenance was stated" (Westermann, *Genesis. Biblischer Kommentar,* p. 324). Westermann agrees with Zimmerli that "the seduction suddenly takes place like something absolutely inexplicable within God's good creation. It remains as an enigma" (Walther Zimmerli, *Die Urgeschichte Mose 1–11* [Zurich/Stuttgart: Zwingli Verlag, 1967], p. 163).

22. Here I am in agreement with Westermann that the actual conclusion of the whole story is the expulsion from the garden. The punishments have such a pronounced etiologic character that it is difficult to see in them the intention to depict a primordial humanity. Nevertheless, we shall have to return to these punishments when we take up the question whether Genesis 2–3 conveys an exclusively negative judgment on the human condition.

23. André LaCocque's comments on the three sentences interpolated between the trial and the expulsion from the garden are noteworthy for taking into account the analyses and discussions of them that have been proposed by feminist theology.

cates the end of that proximity in separation that characterizes the creature's condition.

Is this to say that Genesis 2:3 depicts the fundamental human condition in entirely negative terms? One might be tempted to say so, especially if one reads the whole sequence starting from its conclusion, the expulsion from Eden. It is certainly true that this peripeteia marks a reversal of the initial condition depicted in 2:8, that of a humanity living in proximity to God in a garden planted by God. From now on, the primordial history will unfold "outside Eden." Perhaps we should also interpret the narratives that run from the Creation narratives in Genesis 2 to Genesis 11 in terms of this setting of a condition cast out from Eden. Yet, however far we may push our interpretation in this direction, there is one limit we cannot cross: the expulsion from Eden does not make human beings cursed.[24]

To comprehend the gap that remains between separation and condemnation, we have only to superimpose the episode of the Creation of the humans and that of their dereliction and read them in terms of each other. It then can be seen that the humans do not stop being creatures and, as such, good creatures. The same fundamental capacities that make up human beings' humanity remain, albeit as affected with a negative sign. In this respect, two features of the human condition are expressly referred to: nakedness and death. Within the realm of the good Creation, nakedness is exempt from shame (2:25); shame at being naked only arises under the reign of the Fall.[25] But shame is far from being a curse. This feeling, studied by anthropologists and insightfully analyzed by Max Scheler,[26] constitutes a considerable cultural acquisition. And does not the joy of shared nakedness not remain in the loving embrace celebrated in the Song of Songs? As for death, the hesitations found in the narrative are instructive. On the one hand, the threat of death in Genesis 2 is not carried out. (The narrator has Adam die outside Eden, with no word of commentary, in Genesis 5.) On the other

24. Setting Genesis 2 in parallel with Genesis 12:1–3 introduces a false opposition between curse and blessing. In this regard, Frank Crüsemann's warning, referred to in note 13, is worth recalling. "The original gifts of God linked to creation are not entirely abolished. In each life, they combine with the infirmities bound to the fall and together make up the ambivalence of the human condition" (p. 23). It is also worth recalling that the word "sin" is only used regarding Cain in Genesis 4:7.

25. Regarding the relationship between nakedness and shame, see André LaCocque's comments on p. 16.

26. Max Scheler, *Ressentiment,* translated by William W. Holdheim (New York: The Free Press of Glencoe, 1961).

hand, the return to dust mentioned in the closing sentences indicates the end of suffering rather than a further punishment: By the sweat of your face / you shall eat bread / until you return to the ground, / for out of it you were taken; / you are dust, / and to dust you shall return (3:19). Should we not then say of death what we have said about nakedness, that the Fall does not create a new experience, which would be that of mortality, but that it inverts the sense of this fundamental sign of finitude. Death, which ought to have been an "easy" death, has become a source of anxiety and of terror—what the apostle Paul will subsequently speak of as the "wages of sin." Furthermore, is death beyond all hope, when Saint Francis of Assisi received the grace to greet it as a sister, alongside brother sun?

And what are we to say about the knowledge of good and evil? Does it not sum up all the ambiguities of the human condition? Yes, this knowledge was obtained through a fall, but it designates a henceforth irrevocable dimension of the human condition. It is no surprise that, in the Enlightenment tradition and even beyond it, this knowledge was hailed as a "happy fall." This sort of challenge to the divine was required for humanity to attain its proper status, even at the price of the torments attached to this discernment, and deplored by many sages. I am tempted to put it this way: that is how it is! Henceforth, human beings are confronted with making sense of this unhappy condition. Did not even God, in this narrative of origins, play a part? "Then the Lord God said, 'See, the man has become like one of us, knowing good and evil'" (3:22).

Things become more obscure, and the ambivalence increases, if we move backward from this conquest to the earlier insinuations of the serpent and to the hermeneutics of suspicion that it began.[27] Distinguishing good and evil, as a consequence, henceforth will be bound to the prior subverting of the confidence on which is based the institution of language. In one sense, the serpent spoke the truth: "your eyes will be opened, and you will be like God, knowing good and evil" (3:5).[28]

27. See the observations of Paul Beauchamp regarding the "hermeneut serpent" referred to in note 19. Beauchamp refers to Hans Robert Jauss's interpretation in *Question and Answer: Forms of Dialogic Understanding*, translated by Michael Hayes (Minneapolis: University of Minnesota Press, 1989), pp. 51–94. God's goal was to lead the first human couple along the ways of history by means of the detour through an "original fall," concerning which man would have nothing to be ashamed of in the eyes of his descendants (p. 151, n. 31).

28. We need to recall a feature to which our attention had already been drawn: the tree was not just "good for food" and "a delight to the eyes," it was "to be desired to make one wise" (3:6). The quest for discernment arises out of the depths of desire, seduced, bewitched, and led astray by a "bad infinity."

The shadows thicken even more if, in following the slope of the text, we come upon the theme of being sent far away from the Tree of Life (3:22 and 24). It is true that the majority of exegetes tend to see in the final episode of the Tree of Life (prepared by the allusion to the two trees standing in the garden in 2:9) a discordant theme, stemming from another tradition, that of God being jealous of human beings. Still, this episode belongs to the final redaction and a canonical reading has to take account of it.[29] May we not risk saying that in order to cap off a reflection on the human condition as separated, it was perhaps necessary to open the possibility, projected into God himself, of a feeling of jealousy as regards human accomplishments? For reflective human beings, it is perhaps difficult to make a fair distinction between the just condemnation of a desire not to be bound by limits and the suggestion that the gods did not want human beings to be like them. Once human beings become responsible for themselves and for others, the image of God we are has to appear as the possible place for a rivalry with the divine. This rivalry is perhaps merely a fantasy, but the fantasy is real. It is the culmination of the ambiguity of the human condition within the realm of separation.

The Foundation

In privileging the theme of separation—separation between the creator and the creature, separation of the human within what is created, separation of evil humans from their good creaturely depths—we have illumined only one aspect of the idea of antecedence. We have yet to discuss in what sense the constitutive events of the primordial history

---

29. The difficult question posed by the role of the "Tree of Life" in this whole narrative has given rise to an immense literature relating it to other texts of the ancient Near East. Cf. Claus Westermann, *Genesis. Biblischer Kommentar,* pp. 288ff. It is clear that only the Tree of Knowledge of good and evil plays a role in the drama of the temptation and the Fall, so it is plausible that the final reference to the Tree of Life in Genesis 3:22 does stem from another tradition. Still, that it should have some theological significance, for a canonical reading, seems equally legitimate. André LaCocque recalls the traditional Jewish interpretation according to which the text ironically connotes something left unsaid such as "so thought the man" or "according to the tempter." The interpretation I am proposing is not so far removed from this tradition as it might at first seem. Part of the confrontation between the man and God is that the former should attribute jealousy to the latter, as is attested to by, among numerous myths from the ancient Orient, the Greek myth of Prometheus. It may be another ironic paradox that from the very moment that man thinks he can live like a god, he has to die like an animal. This fantasy-laden play of desire is related to the hermeneutics of suspicion articulated by the serpent.

inaugurate history itself, first of all as the legendary history of the ancestors, then as the traditional history of Israel among the nations.[30]

This second line of interpretation is imposed by the Bible as it is laid
out in its final redaction. The question arises what intention could have
presided over that obstinate imposition of continuity that most exegetes
attribute to the Jahwhist, which continues to raise problems for a canonical reading of the Bible as regards every historical-critical hypothesis.

We are provided with one transition between the discontinuous approach, imposed by the literary status of the narratives about the beginning, which sets them apart from the historical narratives, even the legendary ones, and the continuous approach imposed by the canonical
order of the book of Genesis, which makes these narratives the prehistory of history, by two remarks arising from the former approach. In
the first place, it has been observed that as concerns the redactional aspect of Genesis 3, three beginnings are mentioned, which we can represent graphically by three concentric circles: the creation of the world,
the creation of humanity, and the creation/discreation of evil. These are
three beginnings in the sense that in each case something is recounted
as coming to be that nothing precedes. Someone may reply that these
three beginnings all belong to what we ordinarily call the Creation, but
what are we then to say about all those other beginnings reported in
Genesis 4 through Genesis 11, which, despite the generational tie that
covers over the breaks, do concern the appearance of hitherto unknown
realities, situations, relations, and even institutions? As we have already
noted, the break brought about by the expulsion from the "garden" does
not prevent the first pair from pursuing their existence elsewhere. (The
narrative does not announce the death of Adam until Genesis 5:4–5.)
And Eve's exclamation in Genesis 4:1—"I have produced a man with
the help of Yhwh"—makes the first birth of a child an event comparable to the appearance of the first woman, one greeted with a similar cry
of jubilation. The narratives that follow recount other beginnings. For
example, the murder of Abel certainly counts as "the first crime between

---

30. Here I rejoin André LaCocque's central affirmation that the Jahwist, by placing the primordial history on a plane of universality, made this narrative a "preface" to the particular history of
Israel. This thesis is true even if Genesis 2–11 comes from another hand than does Genesis 12
and even if the redactor of these chapters had in mind nothing more than the opposition between
curse and blessing. The Creation remains the beginning of history, a dynamic force operating
within history.

brothers," completing in its way humanity's initial experiences. Under the sign of the five ancestors, the genealogies that follow make inventions appear that were not predicted in Eden: the town, the pastoral life, musical instruments, the forge, and even the cultus. It is said of Enosh, son of Seth, "he was the first to invoke the name of Yhwh" (Genesis 4:26).[31] There is no need to list all the new things linked to the Flood narrative or to that of the tower of Babel. Yes, it is a question of narratives of diverse origins expressing distinct intentions. But from the point of view we are adopting here, they all tend to constitute, at least at the level of the final redaction, a chain of beginnings that taken together make up the picture of humanity in its beginnings.

This stream of beginnings continues beyond the broadened circle of the primordial times to the very heart of those times we can call, in a broad sense, historical time, in contrast to these primordial times. Pierre Gibert speaks of "relative beginnings" in order to characterize two large categories of things coming to be that follow those we have just mentioned. The first of these categories has to do with the narratives relative to the birth of Israel as a people; the second has to do with the call narratives pertaining to individuals, to which Gibert links the narratives of annunciation. Let us note that the narratives relative to the coming to be of Israel themselves are distributed into several different narratives of origins: the individual and collective call of Abraham, the passage through the Reed Sea during the escape from Egypt, the crossing of the Jordan at the threshold of the Promised Land. The call narratives, too, are multiple by their very nature.

Despite their multiplicity, these reported events should be called primordial. They have no precedent, in the strong sense of this term, among all that has preceded them. What is more, they depict a face-to-face encounter between God and a human partner: Abraham or Moses, with no third party involved, therefore without any witness! The event is proclaimed as having occurred in just this way and not differently, without any justification offered that would be capable of discussion. Finally, these narratives of relative beginnings make use of the symbolism of the absolute beginning, as two narratives in particular, two symmetrical narratives, attest: the passage through the Reed Sea and the crossing of the Jordan. The waters of the Reed Sea are threatening as were the primitive waters, and they are set apart just as were the

---

31. As André LaCocque puts it in his essay "Cracks in the Wall," Yahweh is named "the God of humanity."

waters below and those above at the time of the Creation. For the Egyptians, the disaster is equivalent to the decreation of the Flood.

In this way, a relation is set up between what we can call the intersignification between relative and absolute beginnings.[32] It is even a matter of a circular relation between beginnings, one that tends to wipe out the distinction between absolute and relative beginning, a distinction that was foreign, as already noted, to the culture of the ancient Near East. Every beginning is ab-solute, in the most basic sense of not being bound to what preceded it. Thus the beginnings of Israel and those of the prophetic calls appear as so many uprootings from the course of history and from its continuity. This circular relation assures the transference of features attached to the first Creation to every founding event and raises them all to the status of Creation events.

This paradox of a multiplicity of founding events confirms my initial comment concerning the prejudices belied by the biblical Creation narratives. It is never a question of a Creation *ex nihilo*, the beginning is not unique by definition, and a first event cannot be represented by a point on a line. These events have a temporal thickness that calls for the unfolding of a narrative.[33] In sum, the very idea of Creation emerges enriched from this kind of proliferation of originary events. Thus an initial sense can be attached to the notion of a founding event, namely, that in it is expressed what we can call the energy of beginning. What circulates among all the beginnings, thanks to the relation of intersignification, and thanks to the circular relation brought about by the initial events, is the initiating, inaugural, founding power of *a* beginning. The continuity assured by this circular relation among founding events can be compared with that of a line that runs in the mountains from peak to peak, the energy of beginning circulating along this chain of high points.

The idea of a founding event is not exhausted by this representation of a chain of events, all founding in their own ways. Added to it is the idea of a continuation, of something following, that allows us to say that the founding event begins a history. This is what is at stake from the very beginning of the exegesis proposed by André LaCocque. Even if it is true that the founding event is set apart from the history that it

---

32. Pierre Gibert speaks here of "a complex interplay of fusion, of exchanges" (*Bible, mythes et récits de commencement*, p. 36).

33. Where Westermann speaks of *Geschehensbogen* (*Genesis. Biblischer Kommentar*, pp. 259–67), Gibert speaks of the "enduring of the beginning" (*Bible, mythes et récits de commencement*, pp. 103–13).

inaugurates by a specific word, the beginning is not one unless it propagates what I have just called the energy of beginning, not just to other, homologous beginnings, but to the history inaugurated by these founding events.

Here is where a reflection on the pair "to begin" and "to continue" can take place. This reflection is called for here all the more because in the Bible beginning is always to some degree the promise[34] or at least the demand for a continuation: the promise of an orderly world, or a responsible humanity, of many descendants, of a common identity, of a land in which to dwell; a demand in the form of a mission, in the call narratives, the call inaugurating the tests of an often overwhelming destiny. This promise and this demand for a continuation are redoubled by the assurance that what God has begun will be continued through his grace. What the Bible calls God's faithfulness constitutes the veritable principle of continuity for the history inaugurated by the founding events.

In fact, the connection between beginning and continuing—however familiar it may have become to us over the course of our individual or collective experience—is even more subtle than it might appear at first sight; indeed, it is filled with paradoxes and enigmas.

The paradox is presented in the following terms by Pierre Gibert in the work to which I have already referred. For a reflective subject situated in life, in the history of his people, even at the end of the chain of living beings, "the beginning is the place that cannot be grasped, a place that is radically impossible to perceive or experience as such a beginning" (p. 8). The origin does not even belong to the memory that plumbs the past depths of experience. In this sense, it is immemorial. How, then, rejoin the origin starting from the midst of historical experience otherwise than by recognizing *after the fact* the inaugural force of the origin in what continues and perpetuates its initial energy? In this sense, the continuation attests to the beginning, but only after the fact, in the absence of any witness to the beginning. If we adopt the point of view of present consciousness, the paradox of the after the fact gets caught in the aporia of an unlocatable beginning. This beginning is intended on the horizon of a regressive movement that retraces time and gets lost in a maze of relative beginnings that in turn lead back to a first beginning, which is, as I have said, ungraspable. This way of ap-

---

34. Jon Levenson (*Creation and the Persistence of Evil*, p. 17) gives great importance to the promise that God makes to Noah in Genesis 8:21 to never again curse the earth because of man.

proaching the problem, starting from lived experience, which is at once psychological and philosophical, is legitimate on the condition that we complete it with a consideration oriented in the opposite direction. The former is the approach of the scientist, whether he be the psychoanalyst returning toward the origin of psychic life (from whom, by the way, comes the notion of "after the fact" I am using here), or the historian inquiring into the birth of this or that nation, or of the anthropologist seeking the beginnings of humankind, or the biologist asking about the beginnings of life, or of the cosmologist who dares to speak, in terms of the image of a "big bang," of the explosion held to have taken place at the "beginning."[35] It is not unreasonable to attribute to the narrator of the Creation narratives a kind of behavior comparable with that of such scientists seeking to return to an origin starting from experiences belonging to their own sphere of observation.[36] This way of reading the history of beginnings backwards is plausible in at least two ways. In the first place, it makes sense of the kinship, which is not negligible, that relates the allegedly "mythic" point of view and the scientific one.[37] Next, and for our inquiry this is perhaps the more important of the two, this return toward the origin starting from present experience clarifies in a certain way the dialectic between beginning and continuing, which we are focusing on here. We do not speak of beginning except after the fact of continuing. The inaugural function of the beginning is recognized in this "after the fact"-ness.

We cannot, however, simply stop with this parallel between the biblical intending of origins and the return toward origins of a psychoanalytic, historical, anthropological, biological, or cosmological perspective. This parallel between what the biblical narrator seeks to do and what scientists seek to do makes sense only if we attribute to the biblical narrator an operation of "projecting the origins" from the experience he shares with his contemporaries. However, how would he form the very idea of an origin, if it were not already familiar to him from the myths, hymns, and wisdom writings that, for him, are already there and that speak of a human condition and a cosmic situation that themselves were

35. Gibert (*Bible, mythes et récits de commencement*, p. 58) refers to S. Weinberg, *The First Three Minutes: A Modern View of the Origin of the Universe* (New York: Basic Books, 1977).

36. Thus Gibert sees a significant parallel between the story of Adam and Eve and that of the rape of Tamar by Amnon, a narrative that stems from the historiography of the monarchic period, hence a contemporary experience of the narrator.

37. Gibert gives a lively criticism of the use and abuse of the term "myth" in the comparative history of religions (*Bible, mythes et récits de commencement*, pp. 92ff.). Cf. the rejection of this term in Jean-Paul Vernant, *Le Temps de la réflexion* (Paris: Gallimard, 1980), pp. 21ff.

already there before they were recounted? The idea of this double "already there" says more than does "after the fact," which confirms the primacy of a questioning rooted in the present. It requires a radical de-centering of the subject. Whereas the present thinker returns to the origin starting from his experience, the narratives about the origins exercise their inaugural and foundational function only by positing events "after which" there is a subsequent history. They do this, of course, by exploiting resources, which themselves are immemorial, of transmitted representations that so to speak schematize the idea of an origin. Thanks to this preparation, which we can call "mythic," in a broad and in many ways improper sense of the term, the origin narratives speak of the beginning as that "starting from which" there is a subsequent history.

We are thus confronted with the paradox of two versions of the "starting from which": starting from present experience and starting from talking about the origin. This double paradox is inevitable. On the one hand, apart from speaking of the origin, there would be no sense in speaking of a present experience of "projecting the origins," whether individual or collective, psychological, historical, anthropological, biological, or cosmological. It is because the origin has always already been recounted that we can, after the fact, form the plan of returning toward it. It is true that this conjunction between two versions of starting from gives rise to an internal conflict that explains the tumultuous character of the founding events. Talk about the origin, as we have seen, makes use of anthropomorphic representations (engendering, struggle, making, commanding) inherited from unfathomable traditions. Even more important, talk about an origin without any witnesses is authorized only by itself. It posits itself in positing the beginning that it recounts. This self-referentiality indicates the unsurpassable kerygmatic aspect of such speech. Which is why talk about the origin exercises an initiating, an inaugural, a founding function.

On the other hand, the return to origins starting from present experience, even when guided in its quest by the attestation of an origin that precedes it, has to exercise a critical function in regard to all the representations that schematize any talk about the origin, and it must do so to the extent that the narrator's experience offers more and more refined models capable of guiding the "projecting of origins" and of conjecturing "how" they took place.

This accounts for the truth of the answer Pierre Gibert gives to the question why there are several narratives about the same beginning, which is not the same question as the one we considered above concerning the multiplicity of beginnings. Taking up in sequence Genesis 2–3, Genesis 1, and 2 Maccabees 7:25–29,[38] he sees a process of increasing demythologization, first affecting the Canaanite myths that lie on the horizon of Genesis 2–3, then the protoscientific knowledge of the Babylonians at the horizon of Genesis 1, then the complete erosion of every representation of the beginning under the pressure of Hellenistic culture at the horizon of 2 Maccabees. The projecting of origins starting from the narrator's contemporary experience would be responsible then for the progressive purging of the narratives of the beginning in the direction of a vanishing point where the recognition of Creation of everything by God would no longer be borne by any representation and would thus be reduced to the status of a pure confession of faith.

I think we need to follow Pierre Gibert here. But his critical reflection takes on its full meaning only if we situate the report of the origin in each instance at the crossing point of two postulations: that of an origin that asks to be spoken of as that "starting from which" there is a subsequent history, and that of the experience of a narrator as that "starting from which" this narrator attempts to represent the beginning in terms of a model known to him.[39] What is important for any thought or language relative to the beginning, to the origin, is the conflict between these two movements arising at this crossing point. The one speaks of the origin in an emphatic, preemptory, kerygmatic fashion, the other seeks it and, at the limit, leads to the admission that the origin is ungraspable. This latter movement starts from a present, self-centered awareness, seeking its own beginning; the former starts from

38. "The king [Antiochus] called the mother to him and urged her to advise the youth to save himself. After much urging on his part, she undertook to persuade her son. But, leaning close to him, she spoke in their native language as follows, deriding the cruel tyrant: 'My son, have pity on me. I carried you nine months in my womb, and nursed you for three years, and have reared you and brought you up to this point in your life, and have taken care of you. I beg you, my child, to look at the heaven and the earth and see everything that is in them, and recognize that God did not make them out of things that existed. And in the same way the human race came into being. Do not fear the butcher, but prove worthy of your brothers. Accept death, so that in God's mercy I may get you back again along with your brothers'" (2 Maccabees 7:25–29). The rest of this chapter tells how the son and his mother died from "horrible tortures" (see Gibert, *Bible, mythes et récits de commencement*, p. 142).

39. We might ask whether the intersection of these two "starting from which" is not to be found in an attenuated fashion even in contemporary scientific forms of a quest for the origin. Our anxiety concerning our origin, underlined by psychoanalysis, presupposes, at a minimum, the certitude that I was born, already born, that I descend from my parents, from my ancestors; in short, that my own beginning did occur and, inasmuch as it did happen, it precedes any consciousness I have of it. We ask in the same way about the origins of humanity, of life, of the world.

the beginning itself, which decenters consciousness and imposes itself as being there already before consciousness starts to look for it.[40] The religious presupposition here is that the origin itself speaks in letting itself be spoken of. The origin of things and that of speech coincide at this point. This coincidence has to be taken as a gift: a gift of being and of speaking of being.[41] Starting from this gift, every return toward the origin is possible, allowed, required, even if they do end up at the ungraspable.[42]

Trajectories: Thinking Creation?

In this section, which carries the same title as this essay, I would like to explore several pathways along which I shall endeavor to think what might have been signified by way of the representations through which Genesis and the other texts of the Hebrew Bible speak of Creation. There is not really a break between this new inquiry and the two preceding ones, which were closer to exegesis, inasmuch as the Creation narratives, even the most archaic ones in appearance, all bear the mark of the reflection of the sages of the ancient Near East, of which Israel was an integral part. If these sages think differently than do the Greeks, they testify to the same curiosity, the same astonishment, the same wonder, the same will to understand as do the Greeks, from the Pre-Socratics to Plotinus.

---

40. The phenomenon of coming after the fact, which Gibert speaks of, is situated at the intersection of the two "starting from which." Otherwise Gibert could not speak of the "bedrock of the event," using an expression borrowed from psychoanalysis, which finds itself confronted with the "primal scene." Cf. Jean Laplanche, *Vocabulaire de la Psychanalyse* (Paris: PUF, 1973), pp. 432–33.

41. There is also the capacity of the readers to recognize that they were created with an inclination toward evil. This, as André LaCocque says, is the key to the authority and credibility of J. Following Timothy 3:16, we might call it "inspiration" or *theopneustia*. Also LaCocque quite rightly brings together the absence of the audience of the inquisitory words, the "where are you" in Genesis 3:9, and the situation of the reader of the Creation narratives. "What the reader knows is limited to what the author cares to tell, and how he cares to tell it." It is true that he compensates for this declaration with the following comment. "J's 'story' is bursting with power because the reader is, despite her or his supposed absence as addressee, actually present in the whole and in each detail. She recognizes herself in Eve, he recognizes himself in Adam." This recognition is the requisite reply to the narratives of those events concerning which Beauchamp and Gibert point out that they had no witnesses in that they preceded us.

42. It will be useful to conclude this discussion with a remark touching on the discussion Gibert opens about how theology and science are related as regards the question of the origin. If the biblical narrator is close to the scientist in his quest for the origin starting from his knowledge of present reality, he stands alone at the intersection of the already said about the origin and a quest oriented toward a finally ungraspable origin. The resulting discourse has the paradoxical status of a broken discourse, one already spoken and always inadequate.

Our exploration can take two directions.[43] We may first ask about the status of reality—whether cosmic or human—as a creature. Next, moving back from the creature as a given fact to the creative act, we may pose anew the question of the meaning of the idea of precedence that dominated our first two sections.

Along the first line of thought, our distance from the ancient texts will be speculative and critical. It is only along the second way that we shall take into account the important changes that the New Testament and the Patristic period introduced into the idea of a beginning and or an origin.

Our first cycle of reflections finds its starting point in the question posed at the beginning of this essay, whether a theology of Creation can be autonomous despite its close ties to a theology of salvation. Recently this question has received a wholly affirmative answer from the German exegete-theologian Hans Heinrich Schmid, to whom we also owe a serious investigation of the question of the contribution of the Jahwhist to the composition of the Pentateuch. However, it is not his *Der Sogennante Jahwist* that I am going to consider but, rather, his 1974 book *The World of the Ancient Orient in Old Testament Theology*.[44] His thesis there is both exegetical and theological. On the exegetical plane, Schmid emphasizes the solidarity of Hebraic thought with its cultural setting in the ancient Near East. On the theological plane, he affirms that the theological theme of Creation is just a partial expression of a "cosmic kind of thinking," which has to be taken as the *Gesamthorizont* of biblical theology.[45] Whence the subtitle of his book: *Schöpfung, Recht, Heil*, creation, law, salvation. To think of Creation as a work that has been done and received is to think through the profound unity that binds together three orders or orderings (*Ordnungen*), on the cosmic, political, and juridical planes, with salvation being envisaged as the return to order in each one of these different registers.

I turn to this work at this stage of my inquiry because Schmid thinks that our contemporary aspirations for justice stem from the same kind

43. The bifurcation of my meditation is almost parallel to the one proposed by Pierre Gisel in his work *La Création*. On the one side, there is the question of a beginning; on the other, that of the consistency of the real. I am making use of his term "precedence" as a way of speaking of these two faces of the great riddle of Creation.

44. Hans-Heinrich Schmid, *Altorientalische Welt in der alttestamentlichen Theologie* (Zurich: Theologische Verlag, 1974).

45. Schmid goes so far as to say that the Paulinian theme of the "righteousness of God" belongs to the same "overall horizon," which allows us to call the new cosmic and historic order inaugurated by the resurrection a "new creation."

of thinking about order, which, despite its archaism, ought to be able to find a current application precisely by way of these aspirations.[46]

But can an eventual theology of creation be thought through solely by means of the idea of order, even if this idea is taken in the sense of ordering? I would like to propose three correctives to this idea of creation as an ordered reality.

First, we need to speak of the contingency of order.[47] In brief, to think of the real as a whole—as encompassing humanity and the world—as a creature is to think of it as a work, as something made. This implies a paradox. On the one hand, we have to emphasize the already instituted aspect of Creation as a whole, and this runs against two tendencies characteristic of modernity (as Pierre Gisel points out in *La Création*). The first of these characteristics, which appeared at the time of Galileo and Descartes with the mathematization of physical reality, leads to removing all opacity from the real and to reducing it to a mathematical model, homogeneous to certain operations of thinking characteristic of the human mind; the second characteristic leads to making the thinking subject the center of the universe of meaning.[48] Thinking in terms of the order of the world, to return to Schmid, is a plea, on the cosmic plane, for the irreducibility of the real to the representations the human mind gives to it, and, on the anthropological plane, for a place for a passivity and receptivity that denies the *hubris* of the sovereign subject, returning it to its place, that of a human being situated within a creation that precedes it. This twofold plea finds strong echoes in many contemporary critics of modernity.[49]

However, the other side of this paradox regarding Creation must not

46. Rather than there being a exact fit between the "righteousness of God" and that of the world, the former term alone "authorizes us to speak *coram deo* of the world's righteousness" (Schmid, *Altorientalische Welt*, p. 29). "All human thinking has . . . to do with the question of the correct understanding of the world and its orders, hence with the question of right and of justice in the broadest sense of these terms" (ibid.). In a note, Schmid concedes it is true that this *Ordnungsthematik* is a "second degree abstraction of the interpreter" (n. 45).

47. I come back here to the central thesis of Pierre Gisel's *La Création*. Speaking of the biblical texts and how they were taken up during the Patristic and Medieval periods, he declares: "We have discovered that what happens there, in every instance, is the interplay of a genesis and of something positive, and we must think through the irreducibility of these two terms to each other and their reciprocal need for each other" (p. 241).

48. This double plea finds a strong echo in any number of contemporary critiques of modernity—in Husserl, Heidegger, and Gadamer, for example—that aim at rediscovering the concrete values of an experience of the world that would resist the complete mathematization of nature.

49. Pierre Gisel finds a theological and philosophical approximation of the meaning intended by the biblical doctrine of creation in the Thomist concept of an "act of existing" and in the primacy that this entails of existing over essence (cf. *La Création*, pp. 148–67). I shall return to this problem below in my remarks regarding Exodus 3:14: "I am who I am."

be lost from sight, otherwise we will turn such thinking about order into an idol. To think in terms of the idea of Creation is not the same thing as thinking in terms of the idea of order. It is, more fundamentally, to think of Creation as a genesis; that is, to conceive of order itself as an *event*. In the language of the ancient Near East as in that of the Hebrew Bible, the idea of such an irruption without precedent of the cosmic and human order is conveyed through such diverse representations as the struggle against chaos, as quasi artisanal fabrication, as the efficacity of a word that calls forth, orders, that brings into existence. The meaning that runs through these representations is the same: a doing, an act is at the origin of what is. This idea is difficult for reason to accept and maintain. It requires interweaving the ideas of contingency and necessity and saying, in a quasi mythic way, that necessity is the work of a contingent act, hence not necessary, an act without reason or precedent. If, however, we do join the ideas of necessity and contingency under that of "ordering," we may ask whether the idea of order itself does not take on a more dynamic than static sense, particularly when we pass from the cosmic to the human plane of right and justice. Even if, following Schmid, we rightly hold that it is still the idea of order that demands justice, this order no longer designates a completed work but rather a work still in process, one confronted with the injustice of the world.

Here a second cycle of problems and difficulties comes to light.

In an article on the theology of creation, Schmid refers to the discordance (*Diskrepanz*) between the order of Creation and the historical experience of evil. This discordance takes on the form of open conflict if, within the field of a presumed theology of creation, we extend the idea of order on the cosmic plane to the ethical-juridical plane, and if thereby we include the idea of justice within that of order. What then opens is the gap between the "justice" or "righteousness of God" and the injustice of the world. We may then ask whether, by the very fact of adding the notion of justice to that of Creation in the narrow cosmic sense of the term, we do not introduce, within the very heart of the idea of order, an aspect of fragility, an aspect that alters the initially reassuring character of the idea of order, and which does so to a greater extent than does the mere idea of the contingency of order, where only the origin of this order seems to be in question. Here it is the very occurrence of order, its efficacity, that is called into question, as though a threatening element were originarily implied in Schmid's "thinking through the cosmic order."

What is more, whereas the idea of discordance seems to imply a challenge coming from the outside, the idea of fragility suggests a vulnerability intrinsic to order itself.

Several features of what the Bible says about Creation suggest this. First, the final redactors of the Pentateuch preserved Genesis 2–3 and they placed this narrative immediately following Genesis 1, whose reassuring, not to say triumphal, tone it discretely challenges. Genesis 2–3 only recounts the Creation of man in order to set the scene for an exemplary tale, the one that Claus Westermann has entitled "crime and punishment." Next, as a number of commentators have indicated, the shadow of Genesis 3 is projected retrospectively on Genesis 2. For example, the prohibition, at first presented as a structure of the created order, which provides a reason for Schmid's bringing together "creation, justice, and salvation," appears retrospectively, from the point of view of Genesis 3, as the occasion for the Fall. And the narrative passes gradually, by means of the trickery assigned to the serpent, from obedience to temptation and from temptation to fault. Schmid may well say that the retribution still arises from the thinking of order, which, having been upset, is restored, but the possibility remains that evil appears as inscribed in the ethical structure of Creation. For what is a prohibition that does not entail an alternative between obedience and disobedience? And is not the Tree of Knowledge the tree of this alternative, however we translated the knowledge of good and evil?[50]

This vulnerability of order in its ethical form invites us in turn to ask whether, among all the models of Creation that a careful typology might distinguish, it is not Creation conceived of as a battle with adverse forces that has the greatest affinities with the kind of fragility that the originary fault transforms into actual misdeeds. There is here, at first sight, a troubling paradox: What, would be the most "archaic" representations, the most "mythical," the most "barbaric" ones that would best give an account of the strange, subterranean solidarity there seems to be between the already-there aspect of evil and the dramatic aspect of Creation?

This is what, to me, gives such force to Jon Levenson's book *Creation and the Persistence of Evil*, which takes the theme of "mastery" rather than that of order, even than that of order as ordering, as its central

---

50. Cf. the discussion introduced by Claus Westermann concerning the biblical sense of the expression "knowledge of good and evil" (*Genesis. Biblischer Kommentar*, pp. 328–38). Is it a question of moral discernment in the precise sense of Deuteronomy or, rather, of a practical wisdom based on an evasive phrase for what is at issue? As regards my own thesis, either interpretation reflects the fragility of order.

theme. Resistance to order is not then reduced from the very beginning to an idea of a secondary, extrinsic rebellion, finally reducible to human misdoing, to sin. This resistance, expressed in the phrase "the persistence of evil," appears on the contrary inherent to a Creation that is in essence vulnerable and fragile.

The exegetical basis for this profoundly dialectic conception of Creation runs as follows. Instead of distributing the models of Creation as Westermann does, that is, as creation by generation, by combat, by fabrication, by the word, Levenson sets them out in terms of a scale of the degrees and modalities of resistance of those forces hostile to a well-ordered and beneficial Creation for human beings. The first result of this investigation is that the diverse theologies of the Bible can be arranged between those conceptions where the forces of chaos remain unconquered and always threatening—even after the victory over chaos, as we see in Psalm 104:6–9, Job 38:8–11, Psalm 74:12–17—and the conception of a victory without resistance, as in Genesis 1, and even there the traces of the myth of a combat with chaos are not completely effaced.[51]

Levenson's second lesson is that in periods of distress the omnipotence of God is evoked, as testified to by the psalms of lamentation. Unhappy times are experienced as those where God is sleeping, as times of latency, of a withdrawal of God as we might say today. Sometimes the psalmist implores, recalling "other days," that God should awake. Sometimes God's victory is projected into eschatological times. As Levenson puts it, we do not find "absolute faith in God's *ultimate* goodness, but rather qualified faith in his *proximate* goodness" (*Creation and the Persistence of Evil*, p. 45).

A third theme is the assurance that the originary and final goodness of Creation rests upon confidence in God's faithfulness; that is, upon a divine oath, which finds its model in the oath God made, following the Flood, to never again unmake his Creation.[52]

The final lesson is that the Creation without resistance, illustrated in Genesis 1, finds its meaning in an essentially liturgical context, as the

51. The formless void of Genesis 1:2 certainly does not appear to have been created, nor do the waters that are set apart, nor especially do the shadows which are contained within the light. However none of these theologies refers to a Creation *ex nihilo*.

52. The oath and the faithfulness that follows from it indicate the extreme closeness of the theology of Creation and that of the Covenant, which mutually reinforce each other. According to the former, God overcomes chaos; according to the latter, God's faithfulness is the only assurance that chaos will be finally conquered, as it was at the origin, and that the time of affliction is transitory.

reference to the Sabbath, which seems indeed to be the organizing pole of this inaugural text, bears witness. Conflict is not abolished, however. It now insinuates itself between our liturgical confidence in God's omnipotence and our daily experience of the persistence of evil.

There is one last point to note, one that is no less significant. If the faithfulness of God to the Covenant is the sole guarantee that God will finally carry the day against the forces of evil, the contribution of human beings to this final victory is the *mitzvah*—good, right action. The whole of Jewish ethics thus finds itself mobilized as a kind of mediation between the fragility of Creation and the persistence of evil.

We next need to consider the kinship that is thereby suggested between the hostile forces inherent to the process of Creation and human evil. The lesson of Genesis 2–3 is certainly not that we ought to confuse fragility and evil doing, finitude and guilt. The origin of evil is instead presented there as distinct and, finally, as enigmatic. This is why we have spoken about a third circle of founding events, distinct from those that concern the Creation of humanity and those that have to do with the Creation of the world.

But then if the origin of evil is something other than the fragility constitutive of Creation, another perplexity assails us concerning the assimilation Schmid proposes between creation and order. It has to do with the consistency of the very sequence that his exegesis proposes as creation, justice, salvation.

A theology of creation that wants to reunite in one thought, the thought about the cosmic order, the three terms creation, justice, and salvation is overthrown by the forces that lead to dissociating the Creation as the coming to be of the world from the justice required of human beings and the salvation projected on the eschatological horizon of history. In this regard, Creation may remain the "surrounding horizon" of the theological field, but it cannot become encompassing as regards its various themes. Why not? Because the theological field cannot be totalized. Our most basic experiences in the three domains that Schmid would like to unify—that of physics, that of the law and ethics, and that of the expectation of salvation—in fact lead to the breaking apart of any attempt to forge some totalizing concept.

The critical point is as follows. We no longer know how to think the "justice of God" both as a structure of the Creation of the world and as a demand organizing the practical field, that is, the field of human action. Of all the concepts to which Schmid refers, and with which he ends his essay, it is assuredly the "justice of God" that has become the most enigmatic to us. If the justice of God belongs to the same kind of thinking as does Creation and Salvation, then we must say that we have left the field where that connection is still conceivable. But are we alone in having become strangers to this kind of totalizing thinking? Did not ancient Near Eastern and Jewish wisdom strike the first blow against this kind of totalizing thinking? And were not these first blows not delivered in the very domain where the cosmic order revealed its fragility, the experience and the enigma of evil? The irreducibility of the lesson of Genesis 2 to the totalizing ambitions of Genesis 1 already bears witness to this. Yes, thought about the cosmic order must preserve its totalizing intention. But it can do so only by placing the problematic of evil under the sign of retribution, where all suffering must discharge some sin. This is, it is true, the conception that the prophets of Israel tried to convey to the Jewish people. In fact, the doctrine of retribution is that conception that governs to the point of nausea deuteronomist historiography, where the rulers of Israel are always judged and condemned for a single infraction, that of the first commandment. But if this totalizing theology is to take over, what sense can we make of the psalms of lamentation or of Job's protest? And even if Job finally bows before God, resigned to an order that surpasses him, his question remains, stronger than his final response. This question indicates the breaking apart of the idea of order as encompassing creation, justice, and salvation. The injustice of the world constitutes such a massive fact that the presumed tie between the idea of justice and that of creation loses almost all its pertinence. Creation may remain the surrounding horizon, but it ceases to be the encompassing idea that would constitute its identification with the idea of order.

In the final analysis, we speak of creation, justice, and salvation in terms of different modes of thought. This split between cosmological thought, ethical and political thought, and eschatological thought is perhaps one of those features by means of which the historical experience of Israel stands out against the background of "thought about the cosmic order" that it continued to share with its ancient Near Eastern neighbors.

I want now to indicate two important points along the long road that leads to the arguments in classical and modern philosophy concerning the ideas of a beginning or an origin. I speak of beginning *or* origin in order to take into account a discussion that will play a considerable role in philosophy having to do with the distinction between the idea of a beginning, taken in the limited sense of a temporal beginning (that is, the first term in a successive series of events, states, or systems), and that of an origin, taken in the sense of a foundation, in an atemporal sense of the term. As can be seen, this discussion prolongs the bifurcation we have taken into account on the exegetical plane between the separated aspect of the originary history and founding function of the events that comprise it.

Let us recall the formula of Genesis 2:4b: "When (there was not) yet (this or that) then God created . . ." Nothing is decided here as regards the temporal or atemporal sense of the event in question. And the same thing seems to apply to the formula in Genesis 1:1: "In the beginning God created," which leading Jewish interpreters such as Rashi, Buber, and Rosenzweig read in terms of Genesis 2:4b as "[When] in the beginning God created the heavens and the earth, the earth was empty and without form." The Greek lexicon provided a concept, that of *arkhe*, that tended to subordinate the notion of beginning in a temporal sense to that of origin in the atemporal sense of foundation. In turn, the Greek *arkhe* became the Latin *principium*, as can be seen in the first translations of the Bible into Latin and in Jerome's Vulgate: "in principio Deus . . ." What ought we to understand by *en arkhe* or *in principio?* The sense in Genesis 1 of what comes first, *berešhith*, what is principle or primordial, excellent, "prime." The sense of the preposition is dynamic: "toward/for excellence, God created . . ."

Here is where the most important theological decision intervenes, that of assimilating this "principle" to the Word. The prologue to John naturally comes to mind, which is meant as an explicit replica of Genesis: "In the beginning was the Word / and the Word was with God / and the Word was God. / In the beginning the Word was with God. / Everything was made through it / and without it nothing was made."[53] This assimilation of the beginning and the Word of course has Hebraic antecedents in the wisdom writings, where quasi personified wisdom is associated with a mediatrice in the work of Creation,[54] and the idea of a beginning is compounded with that of an origin thanks to the works assigned to wisdom, elevated in this way to the rank of a co-creator. The text of the epistle of the Colossians is especially noteworthy in this regard: "He is before all things [a temporal indication of the beginning]

---

53. We must not lose sight of the proclamations that accompany this hymn in the letter to the Colossians. "He is the image of the invisible God, the first born of all creatures, for all things were created in him" (1:15).

54. "Yahweh created me at the beginning of his plans, / before his oldest works. / From eternity, I was founded, / from the beginning, before the origin of the earth . . ." (Proverbs 8:22f.).

and everything subsists through him [an atemporal indication of the origin]" (1:15). The hesitation, or if you will, the overdetermination owing to which it is possible to write "beginning and/or origin" was perhaps already present in the *beth* of the *berešhith* of Genesis 1:1. However, whatever the case may be regarding the background of this latent polysemy of "in the beginning," the decision to assimilate the two expressions "in the beginning" and "in Christ" (or "through" Christ) was a crucial one for the future of Christian theology. The temporal sense of beginning was not completely excluded, but it was virtually subordinated to the atemporal sense of origin understood as foundation.

Yet the concurrence between the temporal sense of "beginning" and the atemporal sense of "origin" was to be emphasized once again during the Patristic period on the occasion of the quarrel with Greek philosophers, who were tenacious advocates of the eternity of the world. The thesis of the eternity of the world appeared to be incompatible with the doctrine of creation inasmuch as it seemed to imply the self-sufficiency of the world. In these circumstances, Christian apologists and the founders of patristic theology were led to link the idea of creation to that of a temporal beginning, as a kind of counterpoint, so to speak, to the idea of a foundation/origin. In affirming that the world had not always existed, these Christian thinkers confirmed that it had been created at some time, one day. But what of the time prior to this initial event? Their opponents mocked them, asking, "what was God doing before creating the world? Was he lazy, this all powerful God? And why did he decide at one moment rather than another to create the world, this all wise God? What was he lacking, this God who needs nothing?" This is the debate Augustine inherited when he took up the first verses of Genesis in Books X and XI of the *Confessions*.

It is important that his first point was the identification already referred to between beginning and *principe*. "May I hear and understand how in the beginning [*in principio*] you made [*fecisti*] heaven and earth" (XI.iii[5]). To speak of the beginning is to speak of the "word": "Therefore you spoke *and they were made*, and by your word you made them" (XI.v[7]).[55] In this way, we have from the start the idea of a temporal beginning solidly attached to that of a foundation/origin. The first opposition that then imposes itself is between things that pass away, including our own words, and the eternal Word. This is not to say that

55. Augustine, *Confessions*, translated by Henry Chadwick (New York: Oxford University Press, 1992), pp. 223 and 225.

the question of a temporal beginning is brushed aside, rather it is hence-forth open to an intelligible solution: the first answer to be given to the adversary who demands to know what God was doing before making the heavens and the earth, which is directed at the Manicheans and which remains on the formal plane of contradiction, is: "he was not making anything" (XI.xii[14]). In effect, if he was making something, this would mean creating something. Augustine's second answer, which is addressed more to the Neoplatonists, touches the heart of our prob-lem, for it is the very notion of "before" that is set aside, inasmuch as time as a whole was created along with all other created things. "You have made time itself. Time could not elapse before you made time. . . . There was no 'then' [*tunc*] when there was not time" (XI.xiii[15]).

In this way, a definite meaning is given to the notion of precedence that set our inquiry in motion. But this is no longer the precedence of a primordial history but the precedence of eternity, the eternity of God and his Word, in relation to time. "It is not in time that you precede [*praecedis*] times. . . . In the sublimity of an eternity which is always in the present, you are before all things past" (XI.xiii[16]). The stamp of temporal succession, which narrative constraints still imposed on the biblical and Ancient Near Eastern notion of a primordial history, has disappeared. The vocabulary of anteriority may be preserved—"You created all times and you exist before all times" (ibid.)—but anteriority signifies antecedence, that is, the transcendence of eternity in relation to time. More precisely, eternity's transcendence of time receives from Augustine the precise signification of an opposition between a sub-sisting present—that is, a present without past or future—and a human present, which, as the continuation of Book XI.14–29 shows, suffers from the "distention" between a present of the past, which is memory, and a present of the future, which is expectation, and the present of the present, which is intuition or attention.

The need to make a place for a temporal beginning of the world still remains, however. Augustine could not avoid doing so given the exis-tence of those who upheld the eternity of the world. This is why among the various interpretations of the expression "in the beginning God made heaven and earth" for which Augustine makes a place, he ends with "'In the beginning God made heaven and earth' means that at the very start [*in ipso exordio*] of his making and working, God made . . ." (XII.xx[29]). We can understand why he speaks in this way. If created things are changing and mutable, they are finite, as is their total time span. Therefore the world has a beginning, but a beginning within created time. This beginning, then, is no longer a subject of perplexity since it is identical with the beginning *of* time, which, taken as a whole, is one dimension of Creation, hence itself a creature. The question of the beginning is not thereby abolished, it is simply exorcised. And it is exorcised because the *principe* is an origin in the sense of a foundation for temporal things, themselves derived from eternal things, namely God and his Word.

We owe to this discussion one of the more forceful and perspicacious attempts to set in order the various accepted senses of "antecedence": priority through eternity (as in the case of God in relation to things); through time (as in the case of the flower over the fruit); through preference (as in the case of the fruit over the flower); and through origin (as in the case of the sound over the song) (XII.xxix[40]). As Augustine admits, with great candor, the first and the last of these four orders of priority are the most difficult ones to understand. Why the first one? Because it is necessary to take an exact measure of the paradox of a God immutably creating mutable things. And why the last sense? Because the idea of an origin expresses a merely logical priority, whereas our words, those of the *enarratio* of the *Confessions,* unfold themselves in succession. Hence, to conclude, Augustine says, "In this diversity of true views, may truth itself engender concord, and may our God have mercy upon us that we may 'use the law lawfully,' for the 'end of the precept, pure love'" (XII.xxx[41]). An admirable lesson of hermeneutic generosity![56]

To conclude these exegetical, theological, and philosophical considerations, I would like to call on the testimony of a Jewish thinker of our time, Franz Rosenzweig, in his *The Star of Redemption.*[57] This work is applicable in two ways. First, it begins with a thorough critique of every idea of totality, of every system where God, the world, and humankind—the three distinct "objects" of classical metaphysics—become separate elements. In this regard, Hegel is the paradigm of such a totalizing kind of thinking. I do not mean to say that with Hegel it is

---

56. Cf. *Confessions* XII.xxiii(32) and xxvi(36) regarding the plurality of current interpretations. Seeking to make sense of the intention of Moses, to whom the whole Torah was attributed, Augustine concedes, "When he wrote 'In the beginning,' he could have been thinking of the initial start of the making process [*in ipso faciendi exordio*]" (XII.xxiv[33]). This is the place for him to recall that the true is inseparable from charity.

57. Franz Rosenzweig, *The Star of Redemption,* translated by William W. Hallo (New York: Holt, Rinehart and Winston, 1970).

a matter of the same kind of totality as that attributed by H. H. Schmid to the thought of the ancient Near East and, from it, to ancient Israel. However, to the extent that this archaic thought is reconstructed by the exegetes and theologians of our century, they have to rethink the thought of the cosmic order of the Babylonians and the Hebrews with the help of the conceptuality available in their own time. This is where the Hegelian thinking of totality becomes an obligatory passage for whoever attempts to restore a conception, even an archaic conception, of totality. And it is here that Rosenzweig's demolition of such thinking proves exemplary. After this effort, the thinker is left with the disjoint members of a broken totality: an unknown God, a self-explanatory world, humankind delivered over to the tragedy of evil and of death. And it is upon these ruins that Rosenzweig reconstructs, not a system, but a network, one whose nodes are called Creation, Revelation, and Redemption. Through Creation, God externalizes himself in a world, but he is spoken of then only in the third person and in the language of narrative. Through Revelation, God addresses himself to an individual soul and says, "you, love me!" Dialogue is born from being so addressed. Through Redemption, an expectation is opened for us, which is a historical community.

Is this a new system, constructed on some obscure totality? No, for Rosenzweig's second important idea, upon which I would like to concentrate my final reflections in this essay, runs as follows. A few years before the publication of Heidegger's *Being and Time*, Rosenzweig had understood that the tie between Creation, Revelation, and Redemption was not that of some logical mode of thought but that of a profound temporality, one irreducible to any chronology or to any linear representation. If it were to be a question of a time of succession, we would have to say that Creation, Revelation, and Redemption do not succeed one another along the same line. Rather it is a matter of a sequence of strata. Redemption—utopia, if one prefers—constitutes the highest level; Revelation, the middle level; and Creation the lowest level. The "new thinking" that Rosenzweig calls for has something of the allure of an archeology of biblical time. This profound temporality does justice to the discontinuities that mark the passage from one thematics to the next one. Between the beginning, which is the theme of the externalization of God as well as of the words that speak of this, and the continual call by which God sets up the dialogue with the rebellious and obedient soul, and again between the dialogue with the single human being and the advent of the historical events indicating the growth of the Kingdom, there is not totality.

The temporal bond does not abolish these breaks; instead, it incorporates them into a truth that has no other expression than the three figures of Creation, Revelation, and Redemption. There is a time of Creation, that of the immemorial past; a time of Revelation, that of the colloquy of the lover and the beloved; and a time of the Kingdom, that which is always coming. Rosenzweig is careful to make use of subtitles that indicate this: "Creation or the Perpetual Foundation of Things." Creation, in this sense, is always behind us. The beginning is not a passed past, but an unceasingly continued beginning. As for the present of Revelation, the today of the joy of the lover and the beloved, this is not a present that passes, simply a transition between the future of expectation and the past of memory. As Rosenzweig's subtitle indicates: Revelation or "the ceaselessly renewed birth of the soul." This "ceaselessly renewed" prolongs the "perpetual" of the foundation of things. As for the future of the Kingdom, the subtitle again informs us: "Redemption or the Eternal Future of the Kingdom."

In this way, Rosenzweig can help us to think both the fracture of order, as it was perhaps thought by the sages of the ancient Near East and, in their wake, by the sages of Israel, and the recomposition of what no longer merits being called order, or even "ordering," but rather something like a rhythmic unity, more accessible to an existential mediation than to philosophical-theological speculation. The place of Creation in this rhythmic unity is that of the "always already there." With this title we can do justice to the antagonistic interpretations we have been considering: separation from the origin in those narratives having to do with a time that is not coordinatible with the time of any history; the irruption of multiple beginnings that inaugurate a history or histories, which give a continuation and a meaning to these founding beginnings. What is more, the idea of an immemorial past helps us make sense of our two approaches to the "origin": the one that starts from the origin in the name of a word that itself lacks witnesses, and the one that starts from experience and moves back, after the fact, in the direction of an ungraspable beginning.

Finally, to link our endpoint to our starting point, which was also that of André LaCocque, we can affirm that the theology of Creation constitutes neither an appendix to the theology of Redemption nor a separate theme. The always-already-there of Creation does not make sense independently of the perpetual futurity of Redemption. Between these two is intercalated the eternal now of the "you, love me!" Perhaps it is in this eternal now that the proclamation arises "I am the one who is," which will be the object of another of our joint ventures.

Exodus 20:13

Thou Shalt Not Kill

ANDRÉ LaCOCQUE

A Study of Israel's Apodictic Law, Its Span, and Its Limits in Light of Genesis 22

The origin of law in Israel is a much disputed point. There is clearly a prehistory to the early development as described by Rolf Knierim:

> In formulating the laws and collecting them in written corpora, the community by consensus seems . . . to consent to *law* as the future basis *for* the courts, and no longer on the ongoing transmission of decisions by the courts. . . . [It] becomes a legally prescribing community, a community based on law instead of and/or in addition to being a community based on customary adjudication only.[1]

In principle, the community has an absolute authority. It reflects upon the absolute or relative authority of a decision, the latter dependent upon the case, either being arbitrated or adjudicated. So, from the onset, it must be made clear that the laws called by Albrecht Alt and Martin Noth "casuistic" are not by their nature relative, in contrast to other laws called apodictic or absolute; rather, their focus is on one case in distinction from other cases.

Two routes seem to be open to track down the origins of law in Israel. One has become a *via regalia* with its insistence on the notions of covenants and treaties. In opposition to this, Erhard Gerstenberger has suggested with great vigor another path: Law would have an original setting in clan Wisdom. It is worth our while to successively review, however briefly, these two proposals.

---

1. Rolf Knierim, "Thinking Biblical Law," *Semeia* 45 (1989): 17.

Law and Treaties

The original treaty form comes probably from Mesopotamia, for the non-Semitic Hittites—the other candidates as originators of the treaty pattern—use Semitic terms such as *riksu*, covenant, and *mamitu*, oath. The first extant treaty is found on the "Stele of the Vultures" (before 2500) in Sumer. The second is the treaty of Naram-Sin (ca. 2280) in Akkad. These ancient treaties display two forms and belong to two types. The treaty may be between partners on an equal footing; it is then a "parity treaty"—for instance, the famous one concluded between Hattusilis III and Rameses II (ca. 1280). But the compact more generally is between a suzerain and a vassal.

The structure of the "Sumerian" or "Hittite" treaty is recognizable in biblical legal texts, most often in a fragmented form. In the Decalogue, for example, there are only three of the six parts present. The other three are found elsewhere (the deposition in the sanctuary in Exodus 25:16; the reading at regular intervals in Deuteronomy 31:10–13, cf. Exodus 24:7; the call to witnesses in Deuteronomy 4:26, 30:19, 32:1; the curses and blessings in Leviticus 26 and Deuteronomy 28). One can, of course, explain away the absence of one or more elements of the treaty by considering them as implicit in a given Israelite document. Thus, for Walter Beyerlin, the apodictic form of the Decalogue does imply curses and benedictions.[2] Such a stance is far-reaching. It squarely states the *Sitz im Leben* of the Decalogue to be the Sinai complex. So, despite the skepticism of previous German scholarship (especially Gerhard von Rad) as regards an alleged disunity between Exodus and Sinai traditions, Beyerlin insists that, on the basis of the treaty structure, as well as on the evidence of a common designation of Yhwh as the God of the Exodus, Sinai and Exodus cannot be separated. The Exodus is the narrative-recitation, and the Sinai complex provides the covenantal expression of the event. We might compare this with Walther Zimmerli's opinion that the Law is derived from the Covenant, of which it is the proclamation embedded in liturgical celebration.[3] Hence, the prophets preached on that basis. In reaction to this, Dennis McCarthy believes that Zimmerli's understanding is too unilateral. He thinks, with Gerstenberger (see below), that family and school tradi-

2. Walter Beyerlin, *Origins and History of the Oldest Sinaitic Traditions*, translated by S. Rudman (Oxford: Basil Blackwell, 1965).

3. Walther Zimmerli, *The Law and the Prophets: A Study on the Meaning of the Old Testament*, translated by R. E. Clements (New York: Harper and Row, 1965).

tions as well were at work here, not just sacral imperatives. D. J. Mc-Carthy also reacts against the implicitness of elements suggested by Beyerlin, for these things are never implied in the extant treaties.[4]

For his part, Jon D. Levenson is also impressed with the biblical parallels provided by the "Hittite" kind of treaties.[5] He writes:

> The theology of the Pentateuch is deeply imbued with the idiom of the Near Eastern suzerain treaty: Yhwh . . . elicits from [Israel] a sworn commitment to observe the stipulations he imposes. . . . Much the same pattern can be detected in mythic literature, such as the *Enuma Elish* . . . the gods willingly and gladly accept the kingship of their heroic savior.

Besides, he adds, there is a "curious dialectic of autonomy and heteronomy" (p. 143), on the model of the suzerain treaty into which the vassal enters freely. Not entering it, however, is nothing short of suicide. There is no real alternative. All the same, the suzerain must woo his vassal (p. 144). But precisely, "the element of courtship mediates between autonomy and heteronomy" (p. 144). In summary, "those who stand under covenantal obligation by nature and necessity are continually called upon to adopt that relationship by free decision" (p. 148). The Bible emphasizes the "need for a *continual* surrender of autonomy." But, "one can never achieve heteronomy of the will by an act of will alone; the will cannot effect its own extinction." On the other hand, as says Michael Wyschogrod, "a slave who is totally enslaved is an inanimate object."[6]

Law and Clan Wisdom

In my opinion, Levenson's dialectical stance states the issue correctly. Whatever may be said about the historical origins of law in Israel, the concept of Covenant is central and it is unique in the ancient Near East. Gerstenberger, as already noted, takes his distance from the Hittite

4. D. J. McCarthy, *Treaty and Covenant: A Study in Form in the Ancient Oriental Documents and the Old Testament* (Rome: Analecta Biblica, 1963).

5. Jon D. Levenson, *Creation and the Persistence of Evil: The Jewish Drama of Divine Omnipotence,* (San Francisco: Harper and Row, 1988), chap. 11: "The Dialectic of Covenantal Theonomy" (pp. 140ff.).

6. Cf. *Shir ha-shirim R.* 8, 2 (obedience but not slavery); Mishnah Aboth 6, 2, about Exodus 32:16: R. Yehoshua b. Levi says, do not read ḥarut (engraved) but ḥerut (freedom). Cf. David Banon: "la loi gravée est chemin de liberté" in *La lecture infinie* (Paris: Seuil, 1987), p. 33, n.2. Michael Wyschogrod: personal communication; see also *The Body of Faith, God in the People Israel* (San Francisco: Harper and Row, 1989).

treaty paradigm, however.[7] He recalls that each treaty document is but the result of the agreement between the parties, and each document is drafted by only *one* of the parties. Therefore, we should not deal with those documents in isolation. The treaty expresses the mutual dependence and obligation between the partners; they call themselves "brothers" even when the stations of the two are unequal. Such brotherhood is directed against a common enemy: "My enemy (friend) is your enemy (friend), and your enemy (friend) is my enemy (friend)." As to the stipulations in the treaty, they seem to be there for the sake of "particularizing demands, wishes, obligations within the established friendship" (p. 42). Here the conditional phrases far outnumber any other form (a rare occurrence). They envisage cases of emergency and they provide for such future possibility. They are, however, to be distinguished from case law, which would look back to a potentially committed crime. In other words and most importantly, the stipulations are there to protect the covenant that always comes first. They are "nothing by their own right . . . they fill the span between initiation and termination of an alliance" (p. 46).

By contrast with this model, the Decalogue's apodictic utterances are not Covenant stipulations.[8] In the treaties' stipulations, there are no third persons or groups (like the neighbor in the Decalogue). Commandments, on the contrary, are there for correct social behavior. They are concentrated in the Hebrew Bible in a few collections, Exodus 20:7–17, 22:17–23:9; Leviticus 18, 19; Deuteronomy 22:1–12, 23:1, 16–26, 24:8–22, 25:13–15.[9] They are not cultic. Even in the case of cult-centered exhortations,[10] such as in Exodus 20:2–6, the use of the first-person singular for designating God is secondary; they are not cultic either, but "reflect the life of civil bodies" (p. 48), cf. Exodus 20:7ff.; Leviticus 19.

7. Erhard Gerstenberger, "Covenant and Commandment," *Journal of Biblical Literature* (1965): 38–51.

8. Cf. D. J. McCarthy, *Treaty and Covenant*, pp. 32ff. and 158ff. Further, in *Old Testament Covenant: A Survey of Current Opinions* (Richmond: John Knox, 1974), p. 57, he writes, "the origins of apodictic law and so of the Decalogue are to be sought elsewhere than in the treaties."

9. Walter Harrelson complains (in *The Ten Commandments and Human Rights*, [Philadelphia: Fortress Press, 1980], p. 21) that "Gerstenberger has underestimated the significance of the Ten Commandments as a collection." This is a unique list of ten commandments without parallel in the ancient Near East, he says. His criticism is addressed to Gerstenberger's primary thesis that the original setting of Israelite law is to be found in Wisdom.

10. For instance, the reminder that the inappropriate use of the Name endangers the whole community.

Gerstenberger continues by denying that apodictic law must be of a unified style. What brings apodictic laws together is their "prohibitive" style, but this is not unique to Israel and is not at home in a cultic/covenantal ceremony. He proceeds by filling the gap he has just created and argues for a "clan ethic" (*Sippenethos*). "The commandments point to an order given to man, not created by contract. . . . The commandments presuppose a social order which antedates all historical beginnings and therefore is not made a subject of reflection. . . . [With the commandments man] accepts the inherited rules for his society. . . . They are universal and timeless" (p. 49).

In other words, the original setting of law is in family Wisdom and is reflected in Wisdom literature. The ethical exhortations of Proverbs 3:27–30 ("Do not diminish. . . . Do not plot evil. . . . Do not quarrel. . .") are not "apodictic laws," but they are, on the model provided by the whole of the ancient Near East, moral prescriptions to protect society (cf. the teachings of Amenemope and Ani, or those to Merikare).[11] "Not priests or prophets but fathers, tribal heads, wise men" decreed them (p. 50). Some of those prescriptions and prohibitions received a secondary cultic setting and were adopted as standards of the social good conduct demanded by entrance liturgies. But this did not become a general condition. "Only a representative sample of the commandments were elevated to this position" (p. 51). That is why (in spite of Beyerlin's opinion reviewed above) they are not guarded by oath or curse. The commandments are given to man. Oaths, as a matter of fact, envisage a possible breach of trust, and are, therefore, accompanied by curses. Gerstenberger writes, "The terms for curse or oath can stand for the whole covenant relationship" (p. 45).

In agreement with Gerstenberger, Jacques Leclercq and Pierre Buis insist on the existing parallel with negative confessions in Mesopotamia and Egypt (cf. 2nd Tablet Shurpu and The Book of the Dead 125:[12] "The Decalogue draws on the whole of Oriental Wisdom, especially that of Egypt, as well as upon the traditions of the nomads").[13]

Perhaps the last word should be left to Moshe Weinfeld, for whom the use by Deuteronomy of the vassal treaty form comes from sophisticated official circles, that is, scribes of the entourage of Hezekiah and

11. James B. Pritchard, ed., *Ancient Near Eastern Texts Relating to the Old Testament* (Princeton: Princeton University Press, 1969), pp. 34ff. Cited hereafter as *ANET*.
12. Ibid.
13. Pierre Buis and Jacques Leclercq, *Le Deutéronome* (Paris: Gabalda Salutis, 1963), p. 65.

Josiah, a sapiential-didactic milieu. "They freed Israelite faith from its mythical character, religious worship from its ritual stress, and the laws of the Torah from their strict legalistic character."[14]

Law and Covenant

We must, however, go further. All that precedes concerns only the remote origins of the Law in Israel. No light is thereby shed upon the Decalogue's astonishing originality within the framework of covenantal relationship between God and Israel. First, the negative form of most of the Ten Words does not make them a "negative confession." Between the alleged Egyptian model and the Decalogue the comparison seems at times to be between apples and oranges. Gerstenberger, for example, quotes Isaiah 33 and calls upon that text from verse 13ff. in support of his Wisdom theory, but verse 8 speaks specifically of the Covenant with its stipulations. Similarly, he does not refer to Psalm 50, despite its evident interest regarding the "correct" understanding of Law and sacrifice against the cultic background.[15] It is true that, according to Hartmut Gese, for instance, Psalm 50 dates from the 4th century, BCE,[16] but even as a late example of the shift from wisdom to cult, the evolution in legal settings is important. In the present textual setting (*Sitz im Wort*), the relationship between Law and Covenant is unmistakable. There is, for instance, an uncanny relation in the texts between promise and commandment. The best example is offered by the Promised Land that need also be conquered. For that matter, even sexuality, according to P, is the accomplishment of a divine command that is concurrently a promise to humanity.

That is why Walther Zimmerli insists on the dialectical "close encounter with the 'God of Israel' that is totally unique. But the solidarity . . . is based on an unequivocal appeal to concrete obedience to the commandments of Yhwh."[17] Zimmerli refers to Exodus 34:27f. where we

14. Moshe Weinfeld, "Deuteronomy: The Present State of Inquiry," *Journal of Biblical Literature* 86 (1967): 262.

15. Gerhard von Rad, *The Problem of the Hexateuch*, pp. 22–25, calls attention to the clear parallels between Psalm 50:7 and Exodus 20:2 (cf. Psalm 50:17: discipline of the covenant partner); Psalm 50:17–20 and the whole Decalogue (v. 18 // Exodus 20:15, v. 18b // Exodus 20:14; v. 20 // Exodus 20:16). See also Psalm 81 (v. 8–9 // Exodus 20:3–4; v. 10 // Ex 20:2).

16. Hartmut Gese, "Psalm 50 und das Altestestmentliche Gesetzesverständnis," in Johannes Friedrich, Wolfgang Pöhlmann, and Peter Stuhlmacher, eds., *Rechtfertigung. Festscrift für Ernst Käseman* (Tübingen: J. C. B. Mohr, 1976), pp. 52–77.

17. Walther Zimmerli, *Old Testament Theology in Outline*, translated by David E. Green (Atlanta: John Knox Press, 1978), pp. 53ff.

are specifically told that the concept of Covenant is on the basis of the "[Ten] Words"; and also to Joshua 24, which exhibits a clear association between Covenant and Law. Zimmerli, therefore, concludes that one must reject the view "that covenant and law are fundamentally separate concepts (Gerstenberger)" (p. 55). "Joshua drew up for them *ḥôq u-mišpat* (statutes and ordinances)" (Joshua 24:25, cf. Exodus 15:25) at the culmination of the Conquest. Now, "every gift implies an element of duty."[18] The dialectical relation of those two terms is confirmed in that freedom is envisaged within a "Covenant," *berit,* a word that can mean also commandment, especially in the Deuteronomistic work (see below). "In a late phase of redaction, the Decalogue in Exodus 20:2–17 was deliberately placed at the beginning of the commandments" so that all "responsibility" in Israel be a "response" to God (p. 110).

By contrast, but within the same perspective, "Deuteronomy switches the entire proclamation of the law from the beginning of the desert period to its end," thus associating Law with the gift of land. Law is thereby boldly made part of the great blessings that conclude the treaties of the ancient Near East. Commandment presupposes promise for the future. The work of the Deuteronomist exemplifies this principle. It is an alternation of what God promises and how the promise is fulfilled by the combination of the grace of God and the obedience of Israel.[19] The verbal modes of the Decalogue emphasize this point. They are less in the imperative than in the indicative, at the nexus of a conditional and unconditional promise. Israel's fidelity to the Covenant corresponds to God's grace. When such a correspondence transpires, the divine gracious design is unthwarted, so to speak, and it succeeds. Thus, "Thou shalt not" is the assurance that indeed "we shall not," provided—as says D—that we play our part in the I-Thou relationship that the Covenant establishes between the two parties. From that perspective, the historical *telos* is reached not just by the act of either God (grace) or humans (performance), but by the conjugation of both—and this is still a manifestation of God's grace.

Thus von Rad's stance remains at least in part accurate; he says, "On the basis of this legal foundation, a relationship [developed] in matters affecting their common life."[20] In this way, Covenant and Law are so

---

18. As Dietrich Bonhöffer puts it, "Gabe ist Aufgabe."

19. See Robert Polzin, *Moses and the Deuteronomist* (New York: The Seabury Press, 1980), passim.

20. Gerhard von Rad, *Old Testament Theology,* vol. 1, translated by D. M. G. Stalker (New York: Harper and Row, 1962), p. 130. "Tout ce qui ne peut se ramener à une relation interhumaine

closely related that, in Deuteronomy and the Deuteronomist, "Covenant," as said above, means also the Commandments (von Rad, *Old Testament Theology*, vol. 1, p. 147). But now the "matters affecting common life" need to be specified, and we can already discern a tight relation between Law and Narrative in Israel's consciousness. It dictates to Calum Carmichael the title of his book.[21] He warns, "The laws in both Deuteronomy and the Decalogue arise not as a direct, practical response to the conditions of life and worship in Israel's past, as is almost universally held, but from a scrutiny of historical records about these conditions. The link is between law and literary account, not between law and actual life" (p. 17). Such a link is not surprising, he continues. The Decalogue is embedded in a narrative, so are the Noachian laws (p. 18). The episode of Jacob wrestling with the angel ends with a dietary rule in Genesis 32:32. The Deuteronomic school responsible for the Deuteronomic laws is also the composer on the Deuteronomic history; and so on.

The importance of Carmichael's thesis resides in his emphasis on the literary character of the relationship between two literary genres, the narrative and the prescriptive. So the *Sitz im Wort* is respected. And so also is the intertextuality between telling and commanding (cf. Genesis 1:3, 28, 2:16, etc.). I would only insist on the mutuality of the relationship. The movement is not one-way from narrative to prescriptive. The narrative does not just provide a historical (archaeological) background, which indicates the Law's application as historical praxis; it points also toward a teleology, as the Law is surrounded on all sides by the oriented process of God-human relationship. This point will prove decisive for the latter part of this study. What this means is that, although universally law is by definition atemporal, here paradoxically it leaves behind its atemporality and becomes a historical option. The narrative sends readers to the prescriptive and the prescriptive refers them back to the narrative. In this ping-pong match of sorts, the narrative exemplifies the rule and the rule brings the narrative to the level of paradigm. Not only is there in the canonical texts of the Bible a physical proximity of the two genres, but literary criticism attributes to the same literary sources J, E, D, P, the juridical documents and the narratives.

But it must be said with Carmichael that narrative comes first. Ethics precedes Law; first the commandment, then the law. The latter is never

---

représente, non pas la forme supérieure, mais à jamais primitive de la religion." Emmanuel Lévinas, *Totalité et Infini* (The Hague: Martinus Nijhoff, 1968), p. 52.

21. Calum Carmichael, *Law and Narrative in the Bible: The Evidence of the Deuteronomic Laws and the Decalogue* (Ithaca: Cornell University Press, 1985).

without historical-existential foundation. *Torah* means orientation, style of life, education, "pedagogy" (cf. Paul's use of the term in Galatians 3:24f.). As such, the Law is interpretation and susceptible to change by interpretation. As Mieke Bal puts it, "The law . . . [is a] paradoxical institution . . . *subject* to interpretations by *subjects* who are *subjected* to it. . . . It represents the performative acts of interdiction (of transgression) and of promise (of social inter-subjectivity), both turned toward the future; it also represents the constative act of *stating* (transgression in the past)."[22] We may also subscribe to Moses Mendelssohn's opinion that the state institutes laws, while religion utters commandments, as it is concerned with interiority and thought. But, no one has expressed more clearly the difference between commandment and law than Franz Rosenzweig. He says, "Judaism is *not* law; it creates law, but it *is not* identical with it; Judaism is *being* a Jew."[23] Thus, says Rosenzweig, "Law reckons with times, with a future, with duration. The commandment knows only the moment."[24] Elsewhere he continues, "God is not a Law-giver. But he commands. It is only by the manner of his observance that man in his inertia changes the commandments into Law, a legal system with paragraphs."[25] The essential project of Jewish faithfulness is not the fulfillment of the 613 commandments Rabbis computed in the whole Writ. "Therefore, whether much is done or little, or maybe nothing at all, is immaterial in the face of the one and unavoidable demand, that whatever is being done, shall come from that inner power [of the divine]. As the knowledge of everything knowable is not yet wisdom, so the doing of everything do-able is not yet deed. The deed is created at the boundary of the merely do-able, where the voice of commandment causes the spark to leap from 'I must do' to 'I can.'"[26] Ronald Miller puts it this way: "The interpretative third-person

---

22. Mieke Bal, *Lethal Love: Feminist Literary Readings of Biblical Love Stories* (Bloomington: Indiana University Press, 1987), p. 79. She continues by saying that, in the Law, "the present is lacking, the subject is alone." We will contrast this with what follows with reference to Franz Rosenzweig.

23. Franz Rosenzweig, *Briefe und Tagebücher*, edited by Edith Rosenzweig and Ernst Simon (Berlin: Schocken, 1935), vol. 1, p. 762.

24. Franz Rosenzweig, *The Star of Redemption*, translated by W. W. Hallo (Boston: Beacon Press, 1972), p. 177.

25. Franz Rosenzweig, *On Jewish Learning*, edited by Nathan Glatzer (New York: Schocken, 1965), p. 166.

26. Ibid., p. 86. Ronald H. Miller, *Dialogue and Disagreement: Franz Rosenzweig's Relevance to Contemporary Jewish–Christian Understanding* (Lanham, MD: University Press of America, 1989), p. 17, judiciously adds, "And yet, just as stored information can open the door to wisdom, so the wealth of Jewish observance can be the beginning of faithful living."

statement of law ('it is forbidden to . . .') can be transformed into the dialogical reality of commandment ('thou shalt . . .')."[27]

Law and Codes

Against this background, a comparison with the highly developed legal systems of the neighboring nations—as brief as such a comparison can be in this limited study—makes abundantly clear that biblical law is not a law code, if that term implies comprehensiveness and systematization. Especially strong was the Mesopotamian legal influence over the whole ancient Near East; it lasted some two thousand years and thus is comparable with Roman law in the Western world. Parallels do exist between the Mesopotamian and the Israelite types of legislation, but the difference in spirit is all the more arresting. In the famous code of Hammurabi, for instance, the application of the law varies according to social classes. But it is especially in the realm of chastisement that there is a yawning gap between the two conceptions of justice. According to penal provisions among the Assyrians, the death of someone's son is punished by the death of the murderer's son, a practice that contrasts with its express prohibition among the Israelites (cf. Deuteronomy 24:16). To be highlighted also in this respect in Mesopotamia are the mutilation of the body; the lack of concern for the disadvantaged in society; the capital punishment for violation of property rights. "Human life is cheap, but property is highly valued," says Nahum Sarna.[28] By contrast, the Torah never imposes death for those types of crimes. For it, the sacredness of human life is paramount.

This is what led Sarna to a characterization of what he emphatically calls the Israelite innovations.[29] First, nowhere but in Israel is there Covenant between God and an entire people; second, the Covenant is embedded in a narrative giving it meaning, and is inseparable from it. Third, the Decalogue's applicability is universal, unconditioned by temporal considerations. Fourth, and perhaps most important, "This picture is in striking contrast to the situation in the ancient world, where the legislators are kings, princes, and sages. The king and the state constitute the source of law, its sanction, and the authority behind it." To which point it must be added that, although the gods want humanity

---

27. Ibid., p. 67.
28. The present development is indebted to Nahum M. Sarna, *Exploring Exodus: The Heritage of Biblical Israel* (New York: Schocken, 1986), pp. 162ff. The sentence quoted is from p. 178.
29. Ibid., pp. 140ff.

to have good laws, "they themselves were not thought of as needing to behave according to moral norms" (p. 141).

In Israel, by contrast, there is the fundamental conviction that the Law is God's will and God's norm, not just for human justice, but for divine justice. The Law is reflection of God's being. That is why the Decalogue's demands are unqualified and apodictic. "The motivation for observing the law is not fear of punishment but the desire to conform to the will of God. The Decalogue thus becomes a self-enforcing code . . . not the threat of penalty that is imposed by the coercive power of the state. . . . This explains the total absence of specific penalties for the violation of the individual injunctions and prohibitions in the Ten Commandments." Consequently, there is here a need for the "popular and unanimous assent" before the laws can be put in writing; then the document is again read to the people.[30] "The written text becomes henceforth the permanent embodiment of the covenant and its stipulations for future generations."[31]

Finally, the specificity of Torah is in its very essence, for in it are interwoven the "religious" and the "social," both forming an entity that excludes any dichotomy and rejects the ancient Near East atomistic approach to life. Around Israel, it is characteristic to allot human liabilities to various realms ruled by discrete norms. Thus, civil obligations belong to the domain of law—a strictly secular body of prescriptions; moral demands belong to the domain of wisdom; and cultic responsibilities to the domain of priestly manuals. Israel, on the contrary, understands human existence as a whole, without compartments. The love of God is reflected in the love of the neighbor (Leviticus 19:18, 32, 34). "Religion" and "ethics" belong together, although the former precedes the latter, as human liability is first to God, before it is to fellow humans and to other creatures.[32]

That is why Israelite Law does not claim to exhaust all the legal aspects of life. None of the collections in the Bible claims to be a "law code." Vital spheres of legal practice are missing. Furthermore, although a great number of actual judgments are available, they do not often conform to what the "codes" prescribe. "Most decisive is the fact that not a single extant court record ever cites or refers to the royal collections by name in any manner or form," says Dale Patrick, who, therefore, insists on the "unwritten" character of Torah, during the period of

---

30. We thus return to the point made by Rolf Knierim with which I introduced this essay.

31. Sarna, *Exploring Exodus*, pp. 141, 142, 175.

32. A point that will prove crucial in the further development of this essay.

its formation.[33] It means that the codes are "not prescriptions with statutory force but testimony to God's just and righteous will." Their intent is "to inculcate the values, principles, concepts, and procedures of Israel's legal tradition, not to decree specific rulings for specific cases."[34] A case in point is the legal reasoning of Zelophehad's daughters in Numbers 27; or the securing of Absalom's pardon in 2 Samuel 14 (the king gives a ruling running counter to all laws on murder in the First Testament; cf. Numbers 35:31, 33). Similarly, the promise made to Rahab in Joshua 2 is contrary to the rules of the holy war in Deuteronomy 20:15–18 (cf. 7:1–5). The same judgment applies to the spoiling of Ai in Joshua 8:2. Joshua uses *epieikeia*, moderation, indulgence, refraining from applying the Law in its full rigor—as notes R. Polzin.[35] Above the letter of the Law,[36] there is *ḥèsèd weʾ-èmèt* in the words of the Israelite spies to Rahab (representing the Nations) in Joshua 2:14. This "continuing reinterpretation of the law of Moses" is the Deuteronomist's way of "appropriation of the law."[37]

The Decalogue

The *mise au point* that precedes is particularly important in understanding why the eighth-century prophets indict Israel on the basis of the *unwritten* Law (see, for instance, Micah 6:8). Amos, another eighth-century prophet scathes the nations all around Israel on that very basis.

This notion of law, however, applies better to one of its kinds, namely, the apodictic. I am here referring to the classical division of the Israelite laws by Albrecht Alt between casuistic and apodictic laws. The

33. Dale Patrick, *Old Testament Law* (Atlanta: John Knox, 1985), p. 69.

34. Ibid. p. 190. He continues, "Lawbooks were intended not for judicial application but for instruction in the values, principles, concepts, and procedures of the unwritten divine Law ... [they are] moral homilies [in] a mode of persuasive speech." They are *"exercises* in legal thinking" (pp. 198, 200).

35. Robert Polzin, *Moses and the Deuteronomist,* see p. 83 (where, incidentally, the word *epieikeia* is misspelled).

36. Below, I shall mention the Talmudic notion of *liphnim mi-šurat ha-din,* that, to a certain extent, can be understood as meaning "beyond the letter of the law."

37. Polzin, *Moses and the Deuteronomist,* p. 208. Harrelson adds: "According to Deuteronomy 4 God gave the commandments orally to Moses, so they are "essentially vocal, spoken. . . . They were words still having within and around them the heat of God's breath" (*The Ten Commandments,* pp. 159–60). Werner Schmidt calls the Commandments norms for the exercise of justice (*Old Testament Introduction,* translated by Matthew J. O'Connell [New York: Crossroad, 1990], p. 114). N. M. Sarna also affirms the existence of unwritten, orally transmitted laws; so that the legal collections in the Torah are "records of amendments, supplements, or annulments" (*Exploring Exodus,* p. 171).

casuistic laws are characterized by their impersonal style (as indicated by their use of the third person); they display no concern for what is morally right or wrong. Their structure is typical; it consists in a *protasis* (when . . . if . . .) followed by an *apodosis* (legal consequences). The *Sitz im Leben* of such jurisprudential laws is to be looked for in Canaan and the ancient Near East in general. The apodictic laws are unconditional and axiomatic; their application needs no stated ground. "Thou shalt not kill" ever and in any circumstance. Their *Sitz im Leben* is found by Alt to be in the periodic assembly of the tribes for renewing the Covenant.[38] Alt's cultic origins of the apodictic prescriptions did not remain unchallenged, however, as shown in our discussion of Gerstenberger's position. Also Alt's opinion that Israelite apodictic laws were unique and original in the ancient Near East and thus independent from Israel's environment has been shown to be incorrect. George E. Mendenhall, for example, has shown Hittite parallels to the Decalogue's structure and character. In both the Decalogue (of Exodus 20 and Deuteronomy 5) and Hittite compacts, he says, the king/god tells his name and titles and continues with all or part of the classic six-part alliance treaties of the ancient Near East. This, by the way, allows Mendenhall to predate the origin of the Decalogue. While Alt and Martin Noth balked at giving it a Mosaic authorship, Mendenhall says that its principle is to be traced back to Moses. The Hittite treaty form, both in its suzerain-vassal variant and its parity compact, first appeared in the eighteenth century BCE, well before the time of Moses.[39]

We may, however, wonder whether structure is a sufficient ground for passing judgment on the age and nature of the Decalogue. As the apodictic form of laws is found elsewhere in the ancient Near East, it is

---

38. Albrecht Alt, *Die Ursprünge des israelitischen Rechts* (1934), reprinted in *Kleine Schriften zur Geschichte des Volkes Israel*, vol. 1 (Munich: C. H. Beck, 1953), pp. 278–332. Casuistic laws are found in Exodus 20:22–23:19; Leviticus 17–26). As regards the apodictic laws (cf. Exodus 20:2–17; Deuteronomy 5, 27), they have their moorings in the festival of Sukkot and the renewal of the Covenant. They are read aloud by Levites, and the people respond "Amen." Other apodictic texts are Exodus 21:12, 15–17, 22:18–19, 31:14f. (plus scattered sentences in Leviticus; cf. 18:7–18, where the second person singular is used. So also Exodus 22:17, 21, 27, 23:1–3, 6–9; cf. Leviticus 19:15f.). The same *Sitz im Leben* in the festival of Sukkot is true for the Decalogue (its hymnic introduction behooves a festival). Sukkot was first celebrated at Shechem (cf. Deuteronomy 27; Joshua 24). Later, Sukkot was assimilated with the New Year celebration and thus bridges the past with the renewed reality. Through reading aloud apodictic laws, "the community returns to its ideal, original existence" (Alt, *Geschichte des Volkes Israel*, 1: 328). See Psalm 81.

39. Cf. George E. Mendenhall, "Ancient Oriental and Biblical Law," *Biblical Archeologist* 17 (1954): 26–46, 49–76; *Law and Covenant in Israel and the Ancient Near East* (Pittsburgh: The Biblical Colloquium, 1955).

probably preferable to focus our attention on its contents and see how they are indicative of the Decalogue's identity. Its insistence on the exclusivity of the relationship between God and people is readily apparent. This, says Rudolph Kilian, is what constitutes the veritable originality of the Israelite code, without parallel anywhere in the ancient Near East.[40] This, it could be argued, is not foreign to a cultic celebration of the intimacy between Yhwh and Israel (to the exclusion of other groups and nations). But this represents probably only one phase in the Decalogue's trajectory: there may have been a further evolutionary shift. Already Alt was led to make a distinction between the original setting of the Decalogue (which he thought was cultic), and its reworking, which eventually disregarded the original metric structure and gave it a new, noncultic form.[41] For Alt, the simple negative participle plus a predicate was designed to give the Decalogue the widest possible scope and application and the most absolute moral force.[42]

Scope, however, is not comprehensiveness. Von Rad rightly insists on the Decalogue's general orientation. It is concerned with laypeople and indicates a direction for their lives.[43] It is not a law (a wide field of action remains unregulated), and nowhere is it called so (it is "the Ten Words" in Exodus 34:28; Deuteronomy 4:13, 10:4). It is effective only in the most extreme marginal situations (murder, idolatry, adultery). It is content to establish "signposts on the margins of a wide sphere of life to which he who belongs to Yhwh has to give heed."[44] It is no condition for the Covenant, but it comes after the Covenant is established.[45]

On that ground, it becomes understandable that commandment is *promise.*[46] It is so because all arbitrariness of the commander and of what is commanded is absent. The commandment is an expression of love, as it compassionately spells out what constitutes the obstacles on the way to the fulfillment of the Covenant, hence its negative form. Thus, when Joshua "again" circumcised Israel, God declared, "Today I have

40. Rudolph Kilian, *Literarkritische und formgeschichtliche Untersuchung des Heiligkeitsgesetzes* (Bonn: Peter Hanstein, 1963).

41. Albrecht Alt, *Essays on Old Testament History and Religion,* translated by R. A. Wilson (Garden City: Doubleday, 1967), pp. 151–53.

42. Ibid., p. 157.

43. G. von Rad, *Old Testament Theology,* vol. 1, pp. 193–95.

44. Ibid., p. 194.

45. G. von Rad, *The Problem of the Hexateuch and Other Essays,* p. 24.

46. As Klaus Koch writes, "In the Hebrew th[e] construction [of the particle always preceding a verb in the imperfect] is the same as an indicative statement in the future: 'you will not do this or that'" (*The Growth of the Biblical Tradition: The Form-Critical Method,* translated by S. M. Lupitt [New York: Charles Scribner's Sons, 1969], p. 9).

rolled away from you the reproaches of the Egyptians" (Joshua 5:9b, cf. Deuteronomy 9:28: God's *grace*). The whole of the Deuteronomistic history is built on the structure anticipation-confirmation. The fulfillment described is of "prescriptive, predictive, or prefigurative statements in the text."[47]

In this respect, it is of utmost importance to emphasize again the contextual setting of the Decalogue. As the revelation of the Name in Exodus 3 must be read within the framework of the *Botenspruch* to Moses,[48] so here the Decalogue is deliberately put by tradition within a context of divine self-manifestation/revelation. God's being and God's will are one without hiatus. The divine self-revelatory prologue to the Decalogue is a "recapitulation and summary of . . . Exodus 6:2 (cf. 3:14) the revelation of God's name to Moses."[49] Brevard Childs traces the trajectory of the text as follows:

> [The prologue] points back to this history of redemption, but it also points forward to a new stage in the relation between God and his people. . . . In the act of creating a people for himself history and law are not antagonistic, but different sides of the one act of divine self-manifestation.[50]

Both history and law establish the divine right over Israel: "I am the Lord your God for the reason that I took you out from Egypt." This understanding by the French (*Traduction Œcuménique de l'Bible*) translation (in a footnote) has the extra merit of stressing the tie between Exodus 3:14 and 20:2. Within such a perspective, it is more understandable why the Decalogue is not in the imperative mode, "Do . . . Don't." There is here a plea to *remember* how good God has been and is to his people. Then, consistent with such a historical graciousness on his part, is described in the guise of "*therefore*," and in "Ten Words," the way God sees Israel accomplished. They *are* in his eyes as not having any other God, as honoring his Sabbaths, as not stealing, coveting, etc. For the fundamental verbal tense of the Decalogue is the indicative present, and the negation—that precedes most of the Ten Words— does not introduce a prohibition (*'al*), but an ordinary statement in the indicative (*lo'*). Israel is set before a task of honor, not before a tall order to fulfill. "Noblesse oblige." The realization that they are seen by God

47. Polzin, *Moses and the Deuteronomist*, p. 105.
48. See my essay "The Revelation of Revelations" in this volume.
49. Brevard S. Childs, *The Book of Exodus* (Philadelphia: Westminster, 1974), p. 401.
50. Ibid., pp. 401, 402.

as pure and spotless puts upon them the burden of responding to the divine expectation and of fitting the image the loving God has made of them. As Werner Schmidt writes, "Being for the most part negatively formulated, [the Ten Commandments] cannot even describe the relationship of humanity with God but can only assert the boundaries whose transgression breaks the relationship."[51] And Frank Michaéli adds, "We could almost translate by formulas such as 'You could not any longer [have any other god before me] . . .'"[52]

It is often said that the original Decalogue was entirely in the negative form. But Childs calls attention to "the juxtaposition of positive and negative laws in a series [a]s a characteristic feature of all Old Testament law (cf. Exodus 34:14ff.; Leviticus 19:14ff.; Deuteronomy 14:11ff.). . . . [There is even no evidence for] the historical priority of the negative."[53] The same applies to the shift in persons (in the Decalogue, from the first person to the third after verse 7. Cf. Exodus 34:19, 23, 22:26, 27; Leviticus 19:5, 8, 12, 19). The addressee is consistently in the second person singular (in contrast with most series presenting an alternation of singular and plural [see Exodus 34; Leviticus 19]). Thus, Childs reacts against von Rad's (and W. Schmidt's) assertion that the Decalogue "charts the outer limits of the covenant." The Decalogue also provides "positive content for life within the circle of the covenant" (p. 398).[54] I agree with Childs's position only to the extent that, indeed, the aim of the Decalogue is not the creation for God of a "static" human partner, whose expected response would be found in the abstention from doing this or that. The commandments' negativity is not predicative but differential, in opposition to other values or significations.[55] The negation preceding the expression of divine will leaves a margin of imprecision in meaning or bearing that is precisely protection of human liberty.[56] Before Israel was told what to do, she is told what to be, or even what she actually is: a free people. They are "taken out of the land

51. Schmidt, *Old Testament Introduction*, p. 115.

52. Frank Michaéli, *Le livre de l'Exode* (Neuchâtel: Delachaux et Niestlé, 1974), p. 223.

53. Childs, *Exodus*, p. 394.

54. Similarly, Ezekiel 18:5–8 lists twelve good deeds, seven in the negative and five in the positive.

55. Linguists will find here a striking parallel with *concepts* according to Ferdinand de Saussure. He says, "Their most precise characteristic is in being what the others are not" (*Course in General Linguistics*, translated by Wade Baskin [New York: McGraw-Hill, 1966], p. 88).

56. See the very interesting development by Paul in 1 Corinthians 15 where he constantly uses forms such as "it is not like . . ." to describe a resurrected state which cannot in fact be described with any kind of precision but only contrasted with what we know through our limited experience of reality.

of Egypt, of the house of bondage." Some critics have been particularly sensitive to this crucial point; Josef Schreiner, for instance, says, "Old Testament humanity is called to freedom to an ordered life, to answerability before God."[57] I have cited Bonhöffer already, "Gabe ist Aufgabe" (gift is task). Not that responsibility would be a price to pay for the gift of God (it would cease to be a gift), but here freedom is not license, it is a commandment. As Maimonides once said: "We have received the commandment to be free." It is a command because liberty does not consist in following our natural desires but in transcending them.[58] Freedom is not static, but the fruit of effort, the outcome of work. To my students, I often say that there is no better understanding of the Gift of Law by God to his people than what the Gospel tells of Jesus healing the paralytic. The healing-gift is entirely in the order: "Stand up, take your mat and walk!"[59] Human freedom is thus to be spelled out by God who gives the "Ten Words" in the present of the indicative, in the future tense, and in the imperative. That is why Scripture has little tolerance for anyone who refuses to see the obvious. Anyone who bypasses the Torah's program of liberty chooses death (Deuteronomy 30:15, 19).[60] Patrick Miller is thus right when he warns against a certain anomistic understanding that sometimes prevails in the movement called "Theology of Liberation." Once Israel is made free, she is under the commandment to obey.[61]

The order of the propositions is important. First comes freedom, then the obedient response to liberation. Just as the recognition event, of which Zimmerli eloquently speaks, cannot but follow Yhwh's act, so the commandment (to recognize) never comes first. There is here an

57. "The Old Testament person is called by the Ten Commandments to be free, to shape his life, and to respond to God." See Josef Schreiner, *Die zehn Gebote im Leben des Gottesvolkes* (Munich: Kösel, 1966), p. 44.

58. Hartmut Gese, speaking of the Law in the book of Ezekiel, says, "Cult corresponds to a transcendental reality. Just as the sabbaths are God's sabbaths . . . so the entire cult reflects the transcendental primeval pictures (*tabnit* Exodus 25:9, 40; 26:30 P)." The Law itself "is the transcendental basing of life in symbolic actions. Transcendental reality can be portrayed in human reality" (*Essays on Biblical Theology*, p. 73).

59. Mark 2:9 and parallels.

60. Jacob Neusner writes: "When you think of how Moses broke the tablets of the Ten Commandments, when you think of how Jesus Christ was crucified, you and I realize that is the only way revelation—Torah—can come to us: as a challenge to what we are." In Andrew M. Greeley and Jacob Neusner, *The Bible and Us* (New York: Warner Books, 1990), pp. 47–48.

61. Patrick Miller, *Deuteronomy* (Atlanta: John Knox, 1990), p. 75. Cf. W. Keszler: "Die literarische, historische und theologische Problematik des Dekalogs," *Vetus Testamentum* 7 (1957): 1–16. "Gott betrachtet das Leben Israels als Ganzes und fordet totalen Gehorsam in Kultus, Ritus und Ethos" (ibid., p. 14).

interesting parallel with Deuteronomic paraenesis. It is on the basis of Yhwh's intervention that people are invited to confess that he is God and to live accordingly. The imperative is an immediate component of the invitation, for the "lack of recognition is the same as disobedience."[62] The indicative mode in the formula of invitation to recognition ("you *shall* know") stresses the sovereign divine intention. But, adds Zimmerli, the indicative here and elsewhere includes as well a hint of the imperative. The recognition formula in the Decalogue is a case in point; in D, the recognition formula "includes keeping the commandments" (cf. 4:39f.). The formula "they shall know that I am Yhwh" implies that they *should;* it is both an imperative and an acknowledgment of human freedom. "In a fundamental sense, of course, both elements are always contained in the prophetic pronouncement."[63]

Thou Shalt Not Kill

At this point, I would like to turn to one example taken from the "Ten Words," namely, the commandment not to commit murder. This selection is deliberate. It corresponds to a grave problem that immediately emerges once the prohibition is expressed. As apodictic, it would seem that this prohibition is true and enforceable at any time and in any circumstance. As we saw above in considering the apodictic form of the Decalogue, this form of the Law indicates unconditionality and absoluteness. It is obvious, though, that historic Israel did not feel bound to such a formulation in that sense. Israel engaged in wars; and capital punishment seems to have been practiced (cf. Exodus 21:15, 17; 22:18f.; Leviticus 20, 24:17; etc.). On those two counts at least, the prohibition was certainly not understood as meaning sweepingly "Thou shalt not kill." Furthermore, one of the most striking narrative traditions of Israel tells us about the willingness of Abraham, "the father of faith," to sacrifice his son on the altar for God's sake. This latter text will serve in what follows as the litmus test for the extent and meaning of Torah in ancient Israel. But, before we turn to that text, more must be said about the philological bearing of Exodus 20:13 (= Deuteronomy 5:17).

The verb used in the prohibition is *razaḥ*, which in the piel (intensive) form means to assassinate. Here, however, the verb is in the qal

---

62. Walther Zimmerli, "Knowledge of God according to the Book of Ezekiel," in *I Am Yahweh*, translated by Douglas W. Stott (Atlanta: John Knox, 1982), p. 71.

63. Ibid., pp. 52 and 37.

(plain) and thus would include as well nonintentional, accidental man-slaughter (cf. Numbers 35; Deuteronomy 4:41–43; Joshua 20:3; etc.), were it not for the fact that, as says Dale Patrick, "It makes no sense to prohibit accidents."[64] *Razaḥ* appears relatively infrequently, some forty-six times and especially in the context of a personal enemy. It is used only once for capital execution (Numbers 35:30). As it generally covers also accidental killing, the Deuteronomic and the Priestly documents mention cities of refuge for the one guilty of *razaḥ* (Deuteronomy 4:41–43, 19:1–13; Numbers 35; Joshua 20, 21).[65] It seems, therefore, that we should follow the lead of modern scholars, like Ludwig Köhler, and see with him in the commandment, a condemnation of an abusive use of law entailing the death of the guilty party.[66] In a broader scope, J. J. Stamm suggests that *razaḥ* is used "when it is a case of the death or murder of a personal adversary."[67] Hence it is an act that is antisocial (in contrast to *harag* and *hêmith*, other frequent terms also translated by "killing"). Since, on the other hand, the large majority of cases are about blood vengeance, Henning Graf Reventlow thinks that the prohibition envisages both the initial killing and its retaliation.[68] The law would put a limit on vendetta. But, with Childs, it seems that we should broaden the definition to cover killing "out of enmity, deceit, or hatred" (= murder). Later, among prophets and sages, the verb describes intentional and evil violence (Isaiah 1:21; Hosea 6:9; Job 24:14; Proverbs 22:13; Psalm 94:6). It is this understanding that is envisaged by the Decalogue in its present form.[69]

64. Patrick, *Old Testament Law*, p. 53.

65. Cf. Johann J. Stamm, "Sprachliche Erwägungen zum Gebot: Du sollst nicht töten," *Theologische Zeitung* (1945): 81–90. The cities of refuge constitute "the only legal treatment of homicide in the Deuteronomic Law" (Patrick, *Old Testament Law*, p. 123). Those cities are named in different texts: Numbers 35:9–28 (Numbers 35:16–23 describes cases of intentional and unintentional homicide); Deuteronomy 4:41–43; Joshua 20:1–6, 9. Either the judges of the city of asylum rendered a judgment to keep the culprit in the city or to turn him in for execution, or again the judges of the city where the crime occurred conducted the judgment. Conviction required two or more witnesses, "evidence played a much smaller role" (cf. Patrick, *Old Testament Law*, p. 125). Machinations were perhaps neutralized by character witnesses (perhaps Exodus 23:1–3; Amos 5:10; cf. story of Susanna. Thus the witness who is found guilty of false charge is undergoing the punishment with which the accused was threatened; Deuteronomy 19:19).

66. Ludwig Köhler, "Der Dekalog," *Theologische Rundschau* 1 (1929): 161–84; cf. p. 182.

67. Stamm, "Sprachliche Erwägungen" ("when it is a question of killing or murdering a personal foe").

68. Henning Graf Reventlow, *Das Heiligkeitsgesetz formgeschichtich untersucht* (Neukirchen-Vluyn: Neukirchener Verlag, 1961). So also W. Keszler, "Die literarische, historische und theologische Problematik des Dekalogs."

69. Childs, *Exodus*, p. 421.

Although the division of the Decalogue into two tablets is problematic (Childs says that it did not occur in Exodus 20, but in Exodus 34 and Deuteronomy 5; see his *Exodus,* p. 395), this sixth commandment—first in the series of the "second table" regarding the relations with fellow human beings—does correspond to the first commandment on the "first table." The honor due to Yhwh and not taking a human life are put on a par.[70] The ground for this is certainly the acknowledged sanctity of human life, as both von Rad and Schreiner have emphasized.[71] This basic principle is time and again reiterated, whether expressly or implicitly, so that the commandment against murder becomes a showcase of the growth and development in meaning and force of the Decalogue within Scripture and beyond. It becomes even clearer in the ever broadening of the definition of *razaḥ,* until Jesus' full extension in Matthew 5:21–26 (love even of enemies).[72] Before that, and within biblical trajectory of the text, the Elohistic (E) version of Exodus 20:13 sees a striking extension of its meaning in the Yahwistic (J) text of Genesis 4, where Cain is a type. Whoever kills a human, kills his brother.[73] The evolution continues with the Priestly text of Genesis 9:6 and the "Code of Holiness" (H) formulation of Leviticus 19:17f. As Dale Patrick says, Leviticus 19:17–18 "can be interpreted as an expansion of the commandment against killing [as the commandment would] discourage any course of action that might end in killing . . . 'You shall not hate

70. See also Harrelson, *The Ten Commandments,* p. 112. Already the Jewish Midrash draws conclusions from the first and sixth commandments facing each other on the two tablets. *Mekhilta baḥodesh* 8 says that the commandments were written five on one table and five on the other. "On one was written '*I the Lord am your God*' and opposite it '*You shall not murder*'—Scripture thus teaches that whoever sheds blood is regarded by Torah as if he had diminished the image of the divine King." Then the text recalls the concept of the *imago Dei.*

71. J. Schreiner, *Die zehn Gebote;* G. von Rad, in *Theologisches Wörterbuch zum Neuen Testaments* (Stuttgart: W. Kohlhammer Verlag), vol. II, s.v. "*zaô,*" p. 844. That is why according to Rabbinic law, the Jew under duress may transgress minor prescriptions, but in no circumstance may he commit idolatry, fornication, or murder; see Roger Brooks, *The Spirit of the Ten Commandments: Shattering the Myth of Rabbinic Legalism,* (San Francisco: Harper and Row, 1990), pp. 142–43. In Job 24:14–16, murder comes with two other basic sins: theft and adultery. In Hosea 4:2, they are five: deception, swearing, murder, stealing, and adultery.

72. Sarna calls attention to the laws' concern for the unfortunates of society, including the enemy. Cf. Exodus 23:3–4 (help provided to the enemy who has an animal lost or down with a heavy burden.) "Such civilized conduct must inevitably disarm mutual hostility" (*Exploring Exodus,* p. 173). Cf. David Flusser, "A New Sensitivity in Judaism and the Christian Message," *Harvard Theological Review* 61 (1968): 126: "It is clear that Jesus' moral approach to God and man . . . is unique and incomparable. According to the teaching of Jesus you have to love the sinners, while according to Judaism you have not to hate the wicked . . . [but] love to the enemy is not prescribed."

73. Genesis 4:9 // 3:9; 4:11 // 3:17. On this, see W. Schmidt, *Old Testament Introduction,* p. 80.

... but you shall love your neighbor as yourself.'"[74] About this latter text, I cannot resist the urge to recall that for Franz Rosenzweig "as yourself" signifies the universal response to God's unconditional love for all His creatures; anyone, everyone is "like you," an "alter ego." The human reveals God to me in one of his manifestations. According to Emmanuel Levinas, the Other's *face* is the immediate carrier of the Sinai message. It tells me: "you, don't kill me!" Interestingly enough, Zimmerli translates Leviticus 19:34 as "you shall love him as a man like yourself."[75]

What is more, chances are that Exodus 20:13 had originally a more expansive phrasing and that the term "neighbor" appeared in the formulation. In his reconstruction of an older form of the Ten Words, Eduard Nielsen, for example, brings the sixth commandment close to Jeremiah 7:6 and 22:3 (which, indeed, allude to the Decalogue).[76] He is also sensitive to the recurrence of the word "your neighbor" in the seventh, ninth, and tenth commandments. On those grounds, he thinks that it should be present here as well: "Thou shalt not pour out the blood of thy neighbor" (*šaphakh dam*), which indicates a prohibition of homicide "committed in private," he says.

Paradoxically, the sacredness of human life and the "love of neighbor" demanded that the penalty for transgressing the law be capital punishment. Rabbinic literature intentionally quotes the sixth commandment in sequence after Leviticus 24:17 (capital penalty for murder, cf. Jerusalem Talmud, Tractate Baba Qoma 4:6). Jacob J. Finkelstein, in his influential essay "The Goring Ox,"[77] has shown that, in the instance under consideration, the death penalty is imposed on the owner of the ox because of the aversion of the lawgiver for a monetary compensation for human life (cf. Exodus 21:12, 16, 20, 22f., 29, 22:2f.; in the same respect, N. Sarna calls attention to Numbers 35:31–33).[78] By contrast,

74. Patrick, *Old Testament Law*, pp. 254f.

75. Zimmerli, *Old Testament Theology in Outline*, p. 137. Cf. Deuteronomy 10:19; Galatians 6:10.

76. Eduard Nielsen, *The Ten Commandments in New Perspective: A Traditio-Historical Approach*, translated by David J. Bourke (Naperville: Alec R. Allenson, Inc. 1968), pp. 85, 90–91. See also Genesis 9:6 (P). Cf. Karlheinz Rabast, *Das apodiktische Recht im Deuteronomium und im Heiligkeitsgesetz* (Berlin-Hermsdorf: Heimatdienstverlag, 1948).

77. Jacob J. Finkelstein, "The Goring Ox: Some Historical Perspectives on Deodands, Forfeitures, Wrongful Death, and the Western Notion of Sovereignty," *Temple Law Quarterly* 46 (1973): 169–290.

78. That the ethical is not just another aspect of the theological, but is in dependence upon the theological, as we shall insist below, explains why, for instance, the commandment not to kill reaches a limit in Genesis 9:6: blood must not be shed, "unless it should be at the express demand

"none of the laws governing property (except slaves) have penalties involving the execution or physical punishment of the culpable. The rule is restitution with compensation" (Finkelstein, "The Goring Ox," p. 256). In the words of Dale Patrick, "The biblical system of law elevated the human world above nature and accorded the individual human self an infinite value. By contrast, Mesopotamian law subjected human society to nature and the individual to society."[79]

The prohibition against murder is, according to unanimous Jewish tradition, one of the fundamental commandments to be obeyed always and everywhere.[80] When Genesis 3–11 reflects upon evil's invasion of the world, it starts by showing murder as a primordial sinful act, at the same time that it typically calls that act a fratricide. These chapters continue with the description of increasing violence on earth. In Genesis 9, one of the basic seven Noahide laws prohibits in no uncertain terms the shedding of human blood (verse 6; see also Exodus 21:12–14; Leviticus 24:17, 21b; Numbers 35:21, 25, 28; Deuteronomy 21:1–9, 27:24; etc.). The same text invokes the divinely granted quality to the human of being the *imago Dei*. But the *bearing* of the prohibition must be explored further.

In the words of Paul Ricoeur, "The process of justice is through conceptual reduction, the process of love is through poetic amplification."[81] Abraham Heschel would not have repudiated such an assertion. He says, "All observance is training in the art of love."[82] The "poetic amplification" has been brought to its ultimate development by Jesus, who evidently was more poet than lawyer. All the same, notes E. P. Sanders, when there is in the opinion of others transgression of the Law, Jesus offers a *legal* defense, thus displaying his respect for the Law. In the Sermon on the Mount, for instance, there is no opposition to the Law on the part of Jesus. But, as is shown already in the first antithetic terms

---

of God himself," as says W. Harrelson (*The Ten Commandments*, p. 113), a demand that takes the form of a full warrant given to the community to exercise the death penalty. The prohibition on taking a life is not due to an alleged sacrosanct nature of life but that life belongs to God, who has an exclusive claim on it. Similarly, the prohibition against stealing someone else's property is no consecration of the right of property, but property is acknowledged as a condition for free existence granted by God to humans. Hence, when the death penalty is exercised by the community, it can only be *on God's behalf* (cf. Harrelson, *The Ten Commandments*, p. 110).

79. Patrick, *Old Testament Law*, p. 250. N. Sarna, *Exploring Exodus:* The case of the goring ox is exemplified in the laws of Eshnunna (par. 54–55) and of Hammurabi (par. 250–52). Their concern is solely for the economic side of the affair.

80. I have already described the parameters of the word "murder" in the Decalogue.

81. Personal communication.

82. *The Wisdom of Heschel, selected by Ruth Marcus Goodhill* (New York: Farrar, Straus and Giroux, 1970), p. 256.

of the Sermon—which precisely concern the prohibition to kill—the whole matter is a question of interpretation. "But I say to you" in Jesus' mouth falls in parallel with the Qumran expression, "But regarding this we say" (4 QMMT). In legal debate, "to say" means "to interpret" (as also in Rabbinic literature). "If one compares the very minor disputes between Jesus and others with the major disagreements which separated Qumran from Jerusalem, one will see the point."[83] How Jesus of Nazareth understands the sixth commandment to include an immense territory of positiveness is well known. In Mark 12:28–34, he quotes Deuteronomy 6:4–5, in conjunction with Leviticus 19:18, as the very epitome of the divine will for all people at all times.[84] These two commands to love God and to love neighbor are, for him, inseparable in theory and in practice. Within that total love for Creator and creature, murder, rape, stealth, covetousness, adultery become as inconceivable as idolatry or taking the Name of God in vain. Reciprocally, any commandment, even the prohibition to commit murder, is but one facet of the same prism expressed in its totality in the "summary" of Deuteronomy 6 and Leviticus 19.

Before Jesus or contemporarily with him, such summaries were found in different places of the Jewish tradition, as, for instance, Tobias 4:15; Hillel in *Shabbath* 31a; Philo in *Hypothetica* 7.6; or again Jesus in Matthew 7:12. All these texts, according to Sanders, are based upon Leviticus 19:18 and 19:34.[85] In fact, as Exodus 20:13 "actually covers lesser crimes as well, that is, any act of violence against another person that might result in death," the step to "the positive formulation of Leviticus 19:17–18" is not a large one.[86] Not to take the life of anyone eventuates in loving each and all. Jesus' positive form of summary must be seen within that perspective and contrasted with (but, of course, not opposed to) the negative form used by Leviticus 19. Whereas the negative form of the Decalogue in general left a margin of free invention to the obedient Israelite, and thus called him or her to give form to personal obedience, the all-inclusive positive formulation stresses the illegitimacy of restricting that very imagination/invention.[87]

The shift from the negative to the positive already occurs in what

---

83. E. P. Sanders, *Jewish Law from Jesus to the Mishnah* (Philadelphia: Trinity Press International, 1990), p. 95.

84. Leviticus 19 is the P version of the Ten Commandments.

85. Sanders, *Jewish Law*, p. 70.

86. Patrick, *Old Testament Law*, p. 53.

87. "The Decalogue is the negative counterpart of the commandment to love God and the neighbor. . . . Given such a structure to ward off disobedience, one *is* free for the love of God and of neighbor in fresh ways" (W. Harrelson, *The Ten Commandments*, p. 186).

may perhaps be seen as a later redaction[88] of the Sabbath-command-ment and the parents-commandment. From a possibly negative formu-lation in accordance with the other "Words" of the Decalogue, the new wording is a step toward a broader interpretation of personal dedication to God. In the commandment to honor one's parents, in particular, there is a dramatic evolution toward *love* as expected by the legislator rather than a mere avoidance of disrespect (as in the three parallel texts, Exodus 21:15, 17; Deuteronomy 27:16). This line of broadening "as far as possible" the bearing of the Law through the Commandment of Love, is properly teleological.

Corresponding to the enlarged definition of the verbs of action in the Law, the definition of the object of love is also affected. In Judges 17:10, the master of wisdom, here a priest, is called "father," and so is the prophet in 2 Kings 2:12.[89] They are honored, even venerated, as such. The shift to the positive, says Nielsen, corresponds to the passage from one conception of Torah to another, through the influence of Wisdom upon the Law (cf. Psalm 19). First the function of the Law is one of "marking out the bounds laid down by the terms of the covenant, and of defining the sphere within which the life of the Israelites could take its normal course," but later, the Law becomes "a positive stimulus to undertake certain courses of action."[90] Thus Gerstenberger's insistence on the role of Wisdom upon the Decalogue is recuperated, but I would rather see that role, with Nielsen, at the end of the process, not at its beginning. With Wisdom, we reach a milepost on the way to the *telos* of the Law, but it is not yet the end of the process. The sixth "word" receives its fullest interpretation in the commandment to love one's en-emy, that is, when the definition of neighbor becomes all-inclusive, even embracing its antonym.

True, the love of enemy requires more than one can fulfill. But this "more than" is properly the scope of the commandment. Any definition, any delineation of the prohibition in terms of strict parameters never goes far enough and thus participates in the very murder that is here forbidden. The reader will, I believe, recognize here the argumentation of Paul when dealing with the "letter," that is, ultimately with the inter-pretation, of the Law.[91] In that respect, the early summary provided by

88. We have seen above that such is not the opinion of Childs and others.

89. Cf. Erhard Gerstenberger, *Wesen und Herkunft des "apodiktischen Rechts"* (Neukirchen-Vluyn: Neukirchener Verlag, 1965), pp. 95ff.

90. Nielsen, *The Ten Commandments*, p. 117.

91. The "letter" like the "saying" ("but I say to you," see above) is interpretive.

Deuteronomy 6 is already: "Now, this is the commandment. . . . You shall love . . ."

Genesis 22

The issue that I would like to explore at this point is internal to the Hebrew Scripture. Does the latter indicate how it understands the *nature* of the Law? Does the Law *reflect* on its own essence?

The importance of the historical framework of the Law in the First Testament cannot be overstated. It is a precious indication that the Law must be considered within an intertextual context. The Law sends us back to the history of the relationship between God and People, and history provides the ground for the commandment of God to the People.

But then, it is clear that Exodus 20:13 readily clashes with the history (or the historylike narrative) of the attempted murder of Isaac in Genesis 22. Although the chronological gap between the two is allegedly 430 years—a hiatus that Paul in the Second Testament uses for his argumentation that the justification by faith has precedence over justification by obedience to the Law (cf. Galatians 3:17)—it is not only fair but required that we put the two texts side by side, for both belong to *Torah.* It can even be said that Genesis 22 loses all of its meaning[92] if it is not put within the context of the prohibition of Exodus 20:13. Abraham is supposed to know the Law. Such is the unanimous opinion of Jewish literature which, across all sectarian boundaries, affirms that Torah was known by the Ancestors before it was finally collected at the time of Moses. Besides, laws against murder are found all over the ancient Near East and predate by far any period we would assign to Abraham (if such an exercise makes any sense). As already mentioned above, the prohibition against murder is already found in "Book of the Dead" A 14–15; B 5; and in Shurpu 49, where it is an act done by an individual, not a collectivity.[93] Finally and decisively, it is clear that Genesis 22 (attributed to J and P) was written centuries after the codification of the Decalogue by traditionalists sharing the same nonchronological views.

92. In fact a "surplus of meaning," as says Paul Ricoeur. William J. Peck, "Murder, Timing, and the Ram in the Sacrifice of Isaac," *Anglican Theological Review* 58 (1976): 25, speaks of "saturation with an overplus of meaning."

93. See Buis and Leclercq, *Le Deutéronome,* p. 71. Abraham "knew" the Law; cf. Sirach 44:19–21; 2 Baruch 57:1–2; Jubilees 16:20–23; 1 Maccabees 2:52; Damascus Document 3:1–3; Josephus, *Jewish Antiquities* 1.225, and the whole of Rabbinic literature. In my essay on Genesis 37ff., we see the same knowledge attributed to Joseph.

The Patriarchal stories are paradigmatic stories. The greatest injustice one can do to them is to see them as episodic and their teaching valid only for a time long past.[94] Whatever may be the *kerygma* of Genesis 22, it is certainly exemplary, and its lesson is prescriptive for future generations. In other words, there is a common purpose to the narrative and to the prescriptive in Israel. As Abraham Heschel once said, "*Halakhah* without *Agadah* is dead; *Agadah* without *Halakhah* is wild."[95] The narrative (*Agadah*) introduces, for instance, the custom/commandment of circumcision (Genesis 17:23); while the prescriptive (*Halakhah*) makes it a command (Leviticus 12:3, cf. Genesis 17:10f.). The narrative brings about the motive for not eating the hollow of thigh on the hip socket (Genesis 32:32), and its prescription, although not present in the *textus receptus,* is clearly understood. Similarly, in a first approximation, the narrative in Genesis 22 states in no uncertain terms that the firstborn son (or, for all practical purposes, the one with primogeniture rights) belongs to God, who owns him as a private property; the prescriptive repeatedly makes of this divine ownership a legal privilege and therefore prescribes the means by which the natural parents are to redeem their firstborn child from a sure death, which is the way of God to claim his own. The firstborn child is mysteriously a child of death (cf. Job 18:13), and, if living, it is as a survivor, a resurrected one (Exodus 13:12, 13, 15, 22:29; Numbers 3:13, 18:15; see Luke 2:13). In other words, "Thou shalt not murder" is, narratively and prescriptively, countermanded by the divine claim over the firstborn son, whom the father (here, Abraham) must by Law offer in sacrifice to God. We would thus reach an extra limit to the sixth commandment, besides capital punishment and acts of war! But the text of Genesis 22, as well as the texts already cited, show that this is *not* the case.

Now, the firstborn is the *rᵉ̄šît,* the prime, the most excellent, in the sense that the head is also the whole body (cf. Psalms 78:51, 105:36). The prime belongs to God as a sign that the whole belongs to him. Isaac is inclusive of all the existing and potential children of Abraham. Abraham takes his "son, only son, the beloved one, Isaac," as, *a fortiori,* he would take another son, a common son, not so much beloved, Ishmael, for example.[96] If Isaac, then any other one. If Isaac, then all the

---

94. Franz Rosenzweig, in his correspondence with Gertrude Oppenheim, states that "God's descent to the world is commandment and promise but not report and description" (*Briefe und Tagebücher,* I–1, p. 426).

95. In *The Wisdom of Heschel,* p. 260.

96. Let us note here that if Genesis 22 were a legend grounding the prohibition of child sacrifice, any son would do, certainly Ishmael who was born before Isaac to Abraham.

others. If the divine order is to murder this one, then it is to murder them all. The opposition between Exodus 20:13 and Genesis 22 cannot be starker. Exodus 20:13 *excludes* Genesis 22, as Genesis 22 *precludes* the proclamation of Exodus 20:13.

With Genesis 22 in the background, we can understand Rosenzweig's distinction between Law and Commandment. I already quoted his saying, "It is only by the manner of his observance that man in his inertia changes the commandments into Law, a legal system with paragraphs." As Søren Kierkegaard—whom I shall call to the witness stand below—would say, Law belongs to the general, the Commandment to the particular. Between the two there may occur not only hiatus, but even opposition. Rosenzweig says it is so because God must conceal his true purpose. If not, the least free, the most timid and fearful would be the most "pious." "[God] must make it difficult, yea, impossible [to understand his actions], so that man have the possibility of believing him and trusting him in truth, that is to say freedom" (*The Star*, p. 266). "God's first word to the soul that unlocks itself to him is '*love me!*'" (ibid., p. 177). "Yes, of course, love cannot be commanded. No third party can command it or extort it. No third party can, but the One can. The commandment of love can only proceed from the mouth of the lover. Only the lover can and does say: 'love me!'—and he really does so" (ibid., p. 176).

The "Teleological Suspension of The Ethical"

Rabbinic Judaism's tendency is to the universal, that is, intellectually to the ethical and socially to the collective. The Rabbis display a remarkable sense of pastoral care. Although the demands of the Torah are taken in all earnestness—so that Jesus already could speak of the burden that Pharisees put on the others' shoulders—it remains that Rabbinic law's basic quality is that it is put in the realm of the feasible. Anything unfeasible or unbecoming within the society familiar to the Rabbis was reinterpreted and updated in terms acceptable to their contemporaries. No death penalty, for instance, remains in force, but for stubborn blasphemy and murder. Financial compensations are substituted in most of the cases where the written Torah demanded death. In general, human weakness is at the center of Rabbinic concern.

Also the irrational is made rational. The subversive is aligned with the traditional (so, for instance, in the Targumic and Midrashic interpretation of the Song of Songs, or of the Suffering Servant). The extravagant is aligned with the providential and the normal (the traditional interpretation of the *Aqedah,* the "binding of Isaac" is a case in point). Maimonides significantly states that "a miracle cannot prove that which is impossible; it is useful only as a confirmation of that which is possible" (*Guide* III, chap. 24).

Here yawns one of the deepest chasms between Judaism and Christianity. Jesus of Nazareth displayed a low level of tolerance for what he considered the half-hearted, even hypocritical stance on the part of those who are called in the Gospel "Pharisees and doctors of the Law." In that respect, the insistence of Judaism on being "normative" is a most revealing phenomenon. For it is clear that Jesus' teaching can never become "normative," because it is essentially a scandal for some and a folly for others.

Thus, reflecting upon the *Aqedah,* Kierkegaard in *Fear and Trembling* adopted from early Church Fathers the categorical principle "*credo quia absurdum est.*" *Absurdum,* by the way, is not to be translated by "meaningless," but refers to logical contradictions the believer finds in his existence as a person of faith.[97] I believe because it is extravagant, said Kierkegaard, and he proposed the solitary hero of faith as the perfect Christian, "the knight of faith who in the solitude of the universe never hears any human voice but walks alone with his dreadful responsibility."[98]

Whatever may be our reaction to these points, and, most especially to the latter one, it is difficult to deem invalid the intuition of the Danish "lone wolf." There is indeed, and in spite of some Midrashic arguments to the contrary, a "teleological suspension of the ethical" in the Bible, and particularly in Genesis 22. When this is not acknowledged, the *Aqedah*—and in its foreground, Auschwitz—becomes a punishment. Notwithstanding this, a Midrash on Genesis 22 presents the sacrifice as in chastisement of Abraham who missed a sacrificial ceremony (*Genesis Rabba* 45). The vindictive God then demands the supreme sacrifice. Abraham complies "to justify himself," says Marvin Fox, unaware for a moment of the monstrosity of having Abraham justifying himself at the cost of his son's life. This is a case of fleeing from the lion or the bear (of the *absurdum*) and being bitten by the snake (of the *tremendum;* cf. Amos 5:19).

Another Midrashic attempt at rationalization is also found in *Genesis*

97. See the response of Jacob Halevi in "Kierkegaard and the Midrash," *Judaism* 4 (1955): 13–28, to Marvin Fox's article "Kierkegaard and Rabbinic Judaism," *Judaism* 2 (1953): 160–69.

98. Søren Kierkegaard, *Fear and Trembling and the Sickness unto Death,* translated by Walter Lowrie (Princeton: Princeton University Press, 1968), p. 90.

Rabba 46: Abraham weeps as a father but rejoices as he fulfills a divine commandment. This way, the Midrash is able to ferret out the *Aqedah* from the category of the extraordinary. But in the process, the person of Isaac is marginalized; what is to be imitated is not the sacrifice of one's child but the fortitude of Abraham under duress.

Before we turn to other and more powerful Midrashic reflections on the *Aqedah*, let us note at this point that modern Jewish studies, when they intend to prolong the traditional line of interpretation, are not any more convincing than their ancient models. If, for example, we were to follow Rabbi J. H. Gumbiner, Genesis 22 is the demonstration that God does *not* demand the sacrifice of a child.[99] But this demonstration *ab absurdo* would entail, it seems to me, that other stories show God commanding the perpetration of idolatry or adultery in order to prove a point. In short, one falls into some kind of Sabbatianism.

I have kept in reserve other Midrashic readings because they do not escape the Text's extravagance (*absurdum;* one could also speak of risk, remembering Kierkegaard saying that "without risk there is no faith"). The "absurdity" of God's demand to Abraham is very much present, veiled but with a fig leaf, when the Midrash imagines a debate between God and Satan, like in the Prologue of Job. It is on the instigation of Satan that God "did tempt Abraham" (*Sanhedrin* 89 b). Similarly, the extravagance of God's demand is not the least dampened when *Tanḥu-mah Vayera* 46 has God explain that the reason for tempting Abraham is "to let the peoples of the world know that I did not choose you [Abraham] arbitrarily." Was there no other way to show this than through the claim on Isaac's life? And if one possible response is that such a command is not absurd coming from an all-demanding God, what about Abraham lending himself to the performing of an infanticide? This is exactly what Kierkegaard was dealing with. J. Halevi comments, "It is not that Abraham has no reason [for doing this] but his reason is comprehensible to God and the angels and cannot be made clear in terms of the existing society, Abraham's family . . . [that is, it] cannot be made intelligible to the universal" ("Kierkegaard and the Midrash," p. 18).

But the Midrash goes deeper. There is a profound mutuality of effect of the *Aqedah* upon man and God. Abraham's trial, like the one of Job, is God's trial: "I have tried you with many trials and you have passed

---

99. J. H. Gumbiner, "Existentialism and Father Abraham," *Commentary* 5 (February 1948): 143–48.

them all successfully. Now, I beg of you, for my sake, withstand also this trial, so that people will not say that all the earlier ones were without true worth" (*Sanhedrin* 89 b). But then we are very much within a "Kierkegaardian" perspective. Between God and Abraham there is an exchange of extravagance. It is truly extravagant on the part of God to demand the supreme sacrifice from Abraham in order to win the approval of "people."[100]

It is still more extravagant that God would need such approval ("for my sake") and for that depend on his servant (Abraham or Job). It is correspondingly extravagant that Abraham would obey at the cost of his only son's life to save God's face. Abraham, by divine order becomes an infanticide, a murderer, he contravenes the express command not to commit murder, thus pitting God against God. That the story in Genesis 22 "ends well" does not change anything of the fact that Abraham is and remains a murderer (see *Fear and Trembling*, p. 41). Religionists and ethicists must now struggle with this fact. If this is not a "teleological suspension of the ethical," then what is? The Midrash draws a parallel with the leaving by Abraham of his father's house in Genesis 12, "I exempt you from the duty of honoring your parents, though I exempt no one from this duty" (*Genesis Rabba* 39:7). This is a veritable subversion, a counterpoint in history. At one level of the Covenant there is God's abhorrence of child sacrifice, or of contempt for father and mother. At another level, there is a "suspension of the ethical."

Thus we raise the question: even before the Torah is put in writing by the hand of Moses (Exodus 34), to what extent does the *Aqedah* set a limit of the Law? It will be argued that the ethical is not the ultimate but is conditioned by a transitory economy. The norm, the ethical, the Law, must be transcended. To follow the norm is only the minimum required. But Abraham, because he is the "knight of faith" is called to go *liphnim mi-šurat ha-din*—as say the Sages in the Talmud—above and beyond the line of duty.

This, I believe, is Jesus' understanding of the *miṣwah*. His radicalism brought him to dismiss as mediocrity the "measured" fulfillment of the Law and as hypocrisy when such "measurement" is calculated to satisfy a divine judge. The fulfillment within measure, that is, without infinite love, is no fulfillment at all, he thought. It becomes a self-imposed yoke when "You shall love your neighbor as yourself" is in need of a defini-

---

100. Let us, however, realize how non–Kierkegaardian this latter element of approval or disapproval sounds; it constitutes the reentry of the general within the exceptional and thus the destruction of extravagance.

tion for each word, in need of the tracing of precise limits around each term, so as to avoid guilt by not loving someone who does fit the definition of "neighbor," or by loving the latter more than I would love myself.[101] Kierkegaard brilliantly sharpens the issue when he writes, "in this case the temptation is itself the ethical ... which would keep [someone] from doing God's will" (*Fear and Trembling*, p. 70). A parallel with Paul's conception of the Law imposes itself here. As for Jesus, he radically transforms the problem by calling us to *be* the neighbor *of others*, of the hated Samaritan for instance. Love knows no limit and no restrictive definition; it takes the lover so far as to give up one's life for the other's sake. It goes *liphnim mi-šurat ha-din.*[102]

Of course, this is extravagant, *absurdum*, but the Kingdom of God is for the adventurers of the faith. It is not a reward for mediocrity. For the sake of the Kingdom of God (the "teleological"), one leaves behind spouse, parents, dead ones. For the sake of the Kingdom of God, one raises the knife to cut off in one stroke one's greatest treasure on earth, one's "Regina Olsen," one's raison d'être, one's everything, one's self. "Take your son, your only son, Isaac, your loved one," and also Abraham's only tie with the past and with the future.

In this study of the sixth commandment, Genesis 22 and its "teleological suspension of the ethical," as well as its Kierkegaardian and Midrashic understanding, interests us because it shows that the "ethical" or the Law must and can be transcended. Short of this, we remain on this side of history and never reach the *beyond* of "ha-'olam ha-ba'" (the Kingdom of God). This is why it is a grave mistake to believe that Genesis 22 is unique. Other cases of a "suspension of the ethical" occur in the Bible. Already above we saw that the Midrash draws a parallel with Abraham's leaving his father's house, thus being exempted from the common law to honor one's parents. The Rabbis tell us that Cain, by necessity, had to marry one of his sisters to propagate the race, despite Leviticus 20:17. This was permitted by the kindness of God, say the Rabbis on the basis of Psalm 89:3. The daughters of Lot are moved by the same rationale when having incestuous relations with their father to save the human race. The outcome, it is true, is ominously Edom and Moab, but the motivation of the protagonists is not refuted. The Rabbis again conclude, from the absence of Sipporah in Exodus 4 to

---

101. Or perhaps also, by loving someone who is *not* my neighbor?

102. Brooks, *The Spirit of the Ten Commandments*, calls us "to act above and beyond the call of the law" (p. 143). And Heschel states, "The goal is to live beyond the dictates of the law" (*The Wisdom of Heschel*, p. 255).

28, that Moses had separated from her so as to be always pure when God unexpectedly appeared to him. Despite the severe criticism of Miriam and Aaron as representatives of the ethical, it is clear that Moses was theologically right to set that exception in his person (cf. Rashi on Numbers 12:1). One thinks as well of the eschatologically motivated celibacy of the Qumran covenanters, or of Jesus and Paul. Already Jeremiah receives the astonishing command not to get married. Hosea, on the other hand, is ordered to marry the unfaithful Gomer, and Ezekiel not to mourn the death of his beloved wife.

The ancestry of David (and of the Messiah) is composed of highly surprising characters, the Canaanite prostitute Rahab, the promiscuous Canaanite Tamar, the Moabitess Ruth. The Gospel adds Bathsheba, the wife of Uriah, to the scandalous trio in the genealogy of Jesus (see Matthew 1). Moses is never blamed for murdering the Egyptian and hiding his body in the sand (Exodus 2:12).[103] Jacob steals his brother's birthright; he shamelessly tricks his father Isaac, taking advantage of his blindness, an act specifically prohibited by the Law (Leviticus 19:14; Deuteronomy 27:18). His whole life indeed is a "suspension of the ethical."

Manfred Vogel, however, takes exception to the Kierkegaardian principle,[104] and directs our glance instead toward "the classical prophetic approach" (p. 42). He states that "the classical prophetic approach" holds as axiomatic that God "will never suspend the ethical." But, we may ask, is this true, for instance, of Isaiah 53? of Zechariah 12:10? of Jeremiah's prophetic life (see, for example, chapter 12, or 16:1–13: Jeremiah's imposed celibacy; etc.)? of Hosea's compelled retrieval of a "slut"? Does not Ezekiel receive different orders that run counter to (priestly) propriety (Ezekiel 4–5)? He is to shave off the hair of his head and beard (in spite of Leviticus 21:5; see Ezekiel 44:20), to eat bread baked on human dung (as a later concession, on animal dung) despite Deuteronomy 23:14. And what says the *Torah* in Genesis 12:10ff., 16, 21:12? in Genesis 27 or Genesis 38 or again Exodus 2:12?

Although, in the string of biblical "holy" murderers, David's disposal of Uriah is certainly not to be put on a par with Abraham's or Moses's, it remains that David's dynasty is perpetuated through his impure union

---

103. This action of Moses is consistently considered by tradition as an exception to the rule against murder (cf. *Exodus Rabba* on 2:11, 12; Acts 7:24).

104. Manfred Vogel, "Kierkegaard's Teleological Suspension of the Ethical: Some Reflections from a Jewish Perspective," in *The Georgetown Symposium on Ethics* (Lanham, MD: University Press of America, 1984), pp. 19–48.

with Uriah's wife ("David was the father of Solomon by the wife of Uriah," says Matthew 1:6)! Elijah's murderous wrath against the "prophets of Baal" is perhaps exonerated by his zeal for God, but what about 2 Kings 1:9ff.?

For that matter, even among the Talmudic (and conservative) Sages, the "suspension of the ethical" is not unknown. It is said that the discrepancy between *'ehyeh aser 'ehyeh* in the first part of Exodus 3:14 and *'ehyeh* in the second part of the verse finds its explanation in the following: *'ehyeh* means "I shall be with you in the servitude of Egypt," while *'ehyeh aser 'ehyeh* means this *and* that God will be with Israel in further servitudes to come. Thus, in order to spare the Hebrews in Egypt, Moses was ordered to speak in the Name of *'ehyeh* only and to conceal the other servitudes to come. (So Jacob b. Abina in the name of Rabbi Huna of Sepphoris; *Exodus Rabba* 3:6; cf. Rashi on Exodus 3:14.)[105]

It is, therefore, rather surprising how much Kierkegaard irritates some modern Jewish commentators. Martin Buber made no great effort at understanding him in his works *Between Man and Man* and *Eclipse of God*. Rabbi Milton Steinberg has asserted that, "From the Jewish viewpoint—and this is one of its highest dignities—the ethical is never suspended, not under any circumstances and not for anyone, not even for God. Especially not for God!"[106] This impassioned but wrong statement is very puzzling. Another "rabbinic" Jew, Jacob Halevi, as we saw, is able to show the striking kinship between Kierkegaard's "suspension" and the Midrash. But one could say, in line with Steinberg, that to the extent that in "normative" Judaism the *Agadah* is superseded by the *Halakhah*, the "suspension of the ethical" found in the former belongs more to folklore than to paradigm. One generally cites a halakhic text with deep seriousness, however irrelevant it may be for contemporary times, but refers to an *Agadah* with a smile, with a wink that says, "those Rabbis of old were delightfully bold, but who can really take them seriously when they tell stories?"

In this sense, Steinberg is right. It is evident that halakhic Judaism knows of no "suspension" of itself. It is also evident that the subversive in the Bible or in Rabbinic literature will be absent from genres that are refractory to such extravagance: the legal (per definition) and the sapiential or paraenetic. It is, therefore, a veritable revolution or scandal

---

105. This compassionate dealing with the people amounts to a "teleological suspension of the ethical" à la Kierkegaard, says Jacob L. Halevi ("Kierkegaard's Teleological Suspension of the Ethical. Is It Jewish?" *Judaism* 8 [1959]: 291–302; see pp. 297f.).

106. Milton Steinberg, "Kierkegaard and Judaism," *Menorah Journal* 37:2 (1949): 176.

when the Nazarene forces the agadic spirit (at home in the narrative) into the halakhic. The penetration of the agadic into the halakhic is not novel, however. The Hebrew Bible presents numerous examples of the phenomenon, especially in the prophets but not exclusively there. The narrative transforms the prescriptive in the book of Ruth, for instance, where levirate marriage is conveniently reinterpreted to fit a highly unusual situation, indeed, a situation forbidden by law: the integration of a Moabite into the Community. Another example is provided by 1 Samuel 21: David and his men eat of the shewbread at the shrine of Nob. This particular episode of "suspension" of the legal and cultic is recalled by Jesus (Matthew 12; Mark 2; Luke 6).

In his 1984 article on Kierkegaard, Vogel contrasts Judaism with the Lutheranism of the Dane. For Judaism (= "type I"), he says, religion and ethics are inextricably intertwined and inseparable; while for Lutheranism (= "type II"), religion and ethics are separate and there is a clear superiority of the former over the latter. Kierkegaard in *Fear and Trembling* attributes "ultimacy to the religious even when the ethical is countermanded in its most fundamental signification" (p. 21). This, even for type II, "need not be viewed too seriously" (p. 22). But for type I, this is an impossibility. Here, instead of being a statement, the suspension of the ethical becomes problematic.

A response to Vogel's article can, I believe, clarify the issue at the center of the present discussion. His contrasting stance takes us to the dividing line between the two conceptions of Law that characterize Judaism and Christianity (not just Lutheranism).

First, it is to be noted that the typology which permeates his article, that is, the division made by the author between "type I" and "type II" religions, is flawed, or highly questionable. It is certainly most unfortunate to present Kierkegaard's suspension of the ethical as in no need of being viewed "too seriously" (p. 22). To present the whole existential tragedy of Kierkegaard's life as easy to bear because of his religious denomination is not to take him seriously.

Next, there is a contradiction in presenting religion and ethics as intertwined and of perfectly equal value, on the one hand, and then calling ethics the *expression* of the religious, on the other (cf. pp. 31, 32, 36). With the latter statement I do agree, not with the former. For if the religious is the message and the ethical its expression, it is possible to draw all kinds of parallels that explicate the relation between the two. One might say, for example, that fidelity is an expression of love, not the converse; the fidelity is clearly dependent upon love, and it is conceivable that the latter will one day demand a type of non-normative fidelity, as when St. Mary-the-Egyptian prostituted herself in Marseille to pay her fare to the Holy Land, or when, in a time of crisis, a woman offers herself to unscrupulous tyrants to obtain the liberation of her imprisoned husband.

Furthermore, Vogel himself mentions Buber's sharp criticism of equating an expression of the will of God with the will itself.[107] When one equates the theological and the ethical, God becomes inevitably the guarantor of morality. If anything, the guarantors of morality in Isaiah's time, king, prophets, priests, sages, come under his scathing attacks. What the son of Amots sees in the Temple is a God whose main characteristic is *holiness*. Now, holiness is no "moral irreproachableness, or the highest form of morality . . . the holy is at once *fascinosum* and *tremendum* [in R. Otto's words]," says K. Koch.[108] From that perspective, it is evident that even if Israel would be the most ethical of all human communities on earth, she would still remain "a people of unclean lips." Preaching to such a people may harden on purpose their hearts (Isaiah 6:10), a not very ethical divine move (*pace* M. Steinberg)!

The main object, the only object of Torah, is for Israel to discover *who* Yhwh is, or simply *that* he is Yhwh (see Ezekiel 20:26). Hence, Ezekiel may describe laws given to Israel by Yhwh as being "no good" (20:25–26)! Among them, precisely Yhwh's demand for the lives of the firstborn sons (see Micah 6:7; cf. Judges 11:13–40). However, such sacrifices occurred under King Ahaz (2 Kings 16:3) and King Manasseh (2 Kings 21:6). And the situation that obtained in some texts of the Torah is not that clear. According to Exodus 13:11–13 and 34:19–20 (cf. Numbers 3:11–13, 40–45, 8:17f., 18:15f.), the firstborn had to be redeemed, but such provision may be a later accretion on the basis of Exodus 22:28b–29. At any rate, Ezekiel does not argue against God giving the commandment to offer one's son to God; he only says that this particular law brought death, not life (20:25). He sees consistency

107. Vogel, "Kierkegaard's Teleological Suspension of the Ethical," p. 28. As is well known, for Buber no written code can be an authoritative statement of the will of God—although the human response to God may lead to the production of a legal code. As soon as the prophet formulates a code or a statement, it is the prophet's reflection on God. So, the reader's duty is to go beyond the formulation to the experience that inspired it, beyond the commandment to the One who commands. "An I–Thou knowledge that can be held fast, preserved, factually transmitted does not really exist." "Reply to my Critics," in Paul Schlipp, ed., *The Philosophy of Martin Buber* (LaSalle, IL: Open Court, 1967), p. 692.

108. Klaus Koch, *The Prophets*, vol. 1, translated by Margaret Kohl (Philadelphia: Fortress Press, 1983), p. 110.

in God leading the sinner to ever greater infractions so as to punish him ever more severely (Ezekiel 14:9; cf. Isaiah 63:13)—which again is not very ethical. The same judgment applies to God's making prophets disobey (Ezekiel 14:19) and the righteous run to disaster (3:20).

In fact, "the Torah teaches us that everything must be judged from the standpoint of the highest, the most 'inaccessible,' reference, from the level of the *infinite,* of the *absolute.* Only the religious sphere is capable of transcending dread and absurdity, that is, to elevate the absurd to the plane of the sublime."[109] In that respect, the parallel is perfect between Genesis 22's event and the crucifixion event.[110] If there is "typology" here, it is a typology of event, not of figure. Abraham represents himself, and Isaac represents himself. But what happens between them, that is, the "teleological suspension of the ethical," is no "lost star," it is a "guiding star." True, Abraham/Christ's event must be emulated, not imitated (despite the ill-inspired notion of *imitatio Dei/Christi*). As says Kierkegaard, "It is only by faith one attains likeness to Abraham, not by murder . . . if one would do the terrible thing which love has sanctified as an immortal exploit, then all is lost, including the exploit and the bewildered doer of it."[111] Yet Kierkegaard renounces marrying Regina Olsen, and, as unique as the sacrifice of one's life *"le-šém ha-šamayim"* (for heavens' sake) may be, it remains that Jesus tells his disciples "whoever does not take up the cross and follow me is not worthy of me. Those who find their life will lose it, and those who lose their life for my sake will find it" (Matthew 10:38f., see 16:24).

Finally, what is universal does not stand when opposed by the particular. For the particular demonstrates the oppression of what is considered as "universal" (a conclusion that may certainly be drawn from the judicious statements on page 28 in Manfred Vogel's article). God only can be the Absolute and Universal *qua living;* but when something, even God's expressed will, becomes absolute, the absolute becomes an It and is oppressive. This is demonstrated in a story toward which Rabbinic Judaism does not feel much attracted, namely the book of Job.[112] Here it is shown with utmost clarity that there is hiatus between the

109. Michel LaCocque, personal communication.
110. One suspects that the reaction of Buber and Vogel to the Kierkegaardian "suspension of the ethical" is "remote controlled" by their rejection of Christianity, conveniently categorized as another religious type than Judaism.
111. *Fear and Trembling,* p. 42.
112. According to ancient Rabbis, Job's sufferings were deserved because he did not take the correct position when consulted by the Exodus' Pharaoh: *Exodus Rabba* 1:12 and *Sotah* 11a.

ethical and the religious. Job is ethically without reproach. He, however, has relations with God that need to go through disorientation and re-orientation. True, in the address of Yhwh to Job (38ff.), there is no denunciation of any specific sin, but it is all the same evident that Job's sinlessness is only penultimate. Indeed, some New Testament texts go even further and claim that sinlessness might at times be the obstacle on the road to an encounter with God, as when Jesus says to the law-abiding rich young man, "Go, sell everything you have and follow me" (Luke 18.18ff.).

When one does not choose extravagance, one falls into the categories derided by Kierkegaard as the husband over against the lover, or the general over against the hero. Without the extravagance of the Dane renouncing Regina Olsen, there is no Kierkegaard—as there is no Abraham without the extravagance of Genesis 22, and no Jonah without his going to Nineveh. As Paul Ricoeur reminds us, whereas the Golden Rule, proposed by Jesus and Rabbi Hillel, belongs to a "logic of equivalence" (what you wish that others do to you, do also to them), the love of one's enemies is governed by a "logic of superabundance." The former is ethical, the latter is properly religious. The limits of the ethical are in its very generality (a Kierkegaardian concept). "Generality" must be distinguished from universality. The love of one's enemy pulls the ethical to the universal, not the general level. So Jesus says, "If you do good to those who do good to you . . . even sinners do the same" (Luke 6:33). Only the religious takes us *liphnim mi-šurat ha-din*, to the gratuitous, to the nonexpectation of reciprocity. Clearly, the ethical and the religious are not two discrete and independent areas of human action. The placing side by side by Jesus of the Golden Rule and the command to love the enemy shows how the former is to be interpreted in the light of the latter, so that the ethical is transformed (but not canceled) by the religious.[113] The eleventh-century *Kuzari* of Yehudah Ha-levi insists on the God of Israel being God by *hityaḥud*, through particularization. This alone allows God to have a proper name, Yhwh (*Kuzari* 4.1). God makes himself particular (*ya'had, 'ehad*) for the sake of and to the benefit of humans, as he becomes *together with* (*ya'had*) them. Halevi's insight cannot but evoke in our minds Genesis 22's accent on the particular. God demands from Abraham his *yaḥid*, his "only" son, Isaac.[114]

---

113. See the following contribution by Paul Ricoeur.
114. We found an echo of this in Genesis 37ff.: Jacob loves Joseph as an "only son."

The prescriptive before the Second Temple period is an expressed response to the saving acts of God by which he establishes a covenant with his people. As Martin Buber says of the prescriptive, it is an ethical response that can never take the place of the veritable will of God. The narrated Covenant demonstrates how important history is as the foundation of the prescriptive, not only in the past, but at all times. There is the prescriptive because there is narrative, and there is narrative to explicate the prescriptive.[115] But with Ezra and Nehemiah, the two became dissociated. The ethical took precedence over the theological and, consequently, over history. The "institution" swallowed up the "event." It was now assumed as an absolute certainty that history *cannot* any longer accompany the prescriptive. History has now become "sacred history," a *Heilsgeschichte* of ancestors.[116] Torah is understood as ethical prescription and as the condition for belonging to the covenantal community, itself understood as a constituted corpus that can be joined only through merit. In the fifth century BCE, the Torah became the Judean State's constitution, in the image of the *dath* in the Persian empire, and as such an institution de facto independent from an ever-renewable or revokable covenant. This reversal of priorities constituted a fundamental transformation to which neither Jesus nor Paul remained indifferent.

But once all this is said, and on the ground that, indeed, the ethical is only made relative but not canceled out by the religious, it must be allowed that for the people of God, there is room for both the Rabbinic and the Christian approaches. Abraham and Jesus do not send to hell those who do not rise to their own level. It is just that their passionate response to God brings shame upon us all, the mediocre of faith. This does not mean that there is a dichotomy between the knights of faith and the believing mass; for as there is for the knights a temptation to climb down the rungs and reenter generality, so there is for the individuals within the Qahal, the Community, the call to become "Abrahams" and "Jesuses" following their own vocations.[117]

---

115. For, in ancient Israel, theology is embedded in narrative creeds (Deuteronomy 26; 6; Joshua 24; etc.), as G. von Rad has emphasized (see his "The Form-Critical Problem of the Hexateuch" in *The Problem of the Hexateuch and Other Essays*, pp. 1ff.).

116. See Yosef H. Yerushalmi, *Zakhor: Jewish History and Jewish Memory* (Seattle: University of Washington Press, 1982).

117. The address of the apodictic laws in general in the second person singular is an indication that, if the community as a whole is by no means excluded, the intimacy of God with the individual is, however, stressed. "Each Israelite is to find the commandments binding, but the commandments fall upon the community of the covenant and thus upon all of its members" (Harrelson, *The Ten Commandments*, p. 51). Indeed, the second person singular emphasizes that all Israelites of all times are concerned and even "all individuals and all groups in all times and places" (ibid., p. 52).

In conclusion, we may speak of the span and limits of biblical Law. The sixth commandment, for example, is apodeictic; it is absolute in the sense of not being subject to particular circumstances for its validity. "Thou shalt not kill" is always true; it even takes the addressee to the ultimate realization that one must love the neighbor as being a person like oneself. The scope of the commandment is as broad as can be, with only the restriction—which does *not* belong to the ethical—that God can order the launching of a Holy War against enemies that are not just Israel's but God's, or that he may demand the life of a culprit, or, in the case of Isaac, of an innocent, for "reasons which reason does not know" (Pascal, *Pensées,* iv).

"Thou Shalt Not Kill": A Loving Obedience

PAUL RICOEUR

André LaCocque's inquiry, whose trajectory I propose to prolong to include our modernity, is centered on one commandment from the Decalogue stated in the apodictic form transmitted by the Hebrew Bible: "Thou shall not kill." My subtitle is meant to summarize the surprising thrust of his undertaking, namely, an assessment of both the import and the limits of the validity of the apodictic Law in Israel. This means that the style of André LaCocque's essay is essentially dialectical, and this calls for a prolongation of the same nature.

As a good exegete, he does not overlook the question of origins. However, the present state of that discussion leads him in two directions. The first, laid out by a long exegetical tradition, brings this question in contact with the idea of the Covenant, a notion itself rendered more specific through the example of suzerain/vassal treaties, well known to ancient Near East specialists. The second way, which is not as well traveled, leads in the direction of clan wisdom.

But, already with the first step, the dialectic of amplitude and limit is prefigured by the conjunction, in the canonical version of the Old Testament, between the recitative of the Exodus—hence something "narrative"—and the legislation given at Sinai—hence something "prescriptive." In this way, a polarity is indicated between the recounted event and the proclaimed Law; in fact, something more than a polarity, an intersection, is indicated as soon as the giving of the Law is itself a recounted event whose occurrence leads to the memory of the founding event that constitutes the Exodus. There is something more like a suture than a fault line between these two aspects. And the suture is all the more remarkable if we admit with many exegetes that these two aspects stem from two different traditions. This conjunction between the prescriptive and the narrative is traced out by André LaCocque, in the footsteps of Calum Carmichael, across the whole biblical corpus. In this interplay he shows both that the narrative exemplifies the Law and that the Law elevates the narrative to the rank of a paradigm. At first sight, no discordance is evident here, even if we redouble the narrative-prescriptive pair with the commandment-law one, which below will pose a completely different problem in that it suggests a distinction internal to the prescriptive per se. If, however, we remain for the moment within the circle indicated by the narrative-prescriptive pair, the very heterogeneity of the literary genres in question already bears the seed of a future dissociation within Jewish culture. It is no accident that in Judaism as it has perpetuated itself to the present a certain antagonism has arisen between the more free, more narrative and imaginative Hagada and the more strictly normative Halakha. André LaCocque refers to this point in that part of his inquiry devoted to the limits of the apodictic, illustrated by the stupefying episode of the binding of Isaac in Genesis 22.

Another indication of tension, within the biblical text itself, is provided by the way in which the Mosaic Law is situated in relation to the model of Hittite treaties. Jon Levenson speaks in this regard of "a curious dialectic of autonomy and heteronomy." The free decision of the person who enters into an unequal relation implies what is not yet an antinomy, but what will become one for modern thinkers who come after Kant. Briefly put, this antinomy can be stated as follows: Can we profess moral autonomy and religious heteronomy at one and the same time? Or, in order to avoid such a head-on collision, must we not formulate the relation between religion and ethics in other terms? This sticky question will occupy us at length, but it already arises with André LaCocque's energetic assertion that the apodictic prescriptions of the Decalogue are not "covenant stipulations," in the sense of a fraternal agreement directed against a common enemy, even one established between nonequals. It is the very idea of an apodictic regulation of social behavior that causes a problem, whether it comes from the sages, the prophets, or the priests. We may even say that the problem posed by the primacy of heteronomy over autonomy—if this language continues to apply—is rendered sharper by the comment of Moshe Weinfeld, cited by André LaCocque: "[Scribes of the entourage of Hezekiah and Josiah] freed Israelite faith from its mythical character, religious worship from its ritual stress, and the laws of the Torah from their strict legalistic character."[1] Nor is the difficulty attenuated by the addition of promises to the commandments, even the promise of the Promised Land. Spinoza and Kant—who are in agreement on this point—will see here a perversion. We may, instead, with André LaCocque, choose to follow Franz Rosenzweig's proposal to distinguish between commandment and law, especially if we place this, as I shall, within the framework of the vast philosophical-theological fresco that is his *Star of Redemption*. This proposal can already aid us, however, to resolve the problem posed by the apodictic status of the "Ten Words." Perhaps we shall also be able to return to it again at a more advanced stage of our meditation, one of a post-Kantian and post-Hegelian type; that is, a kind of thinking that will have passed through the test of the contradiction between heteronomy and autonomy. That Rosenzweig's proposal has more to do with an "I can" than an "I must," following a suggestion of R. H. Miller noted by André LaCocque, is a suggestion that we must hold in reserve for the time being.

Going further, we can, with Nahum Sarna, whom LaCocque also discusses, place a strong accent on the "Israelite innovations" in relation to the types of legislation known to the ancient Near East. These innovations are not negligible—the Covenant of God with a whole people, the inclusion of the Covenant within a narrative, its universal applicability, and, above all, the substitution for the fear of punishment of a desire to conform to God's will. We may also, with Dale Patrick, note that Israelite law does not cover every legal aspect but limits itself to setting the major directions of life, and with Robert Polzin, we can say that there is room left for interpretation, even for a more or less loose application. We may even go so far as to say, with Gerhard von Rad, that it is not just a question of "Ten Words," otherwise we would not talk about laws, especially since these sayings only apply to extreme situations (murder, idolatry, adultery). Yet, despite all these important distinctions, it remains true that Israel did not fundamentally distinguish itself from its cultural setting on the principal point, namely, the idea of a legislation given by God through the intermediary of a human legislator. This idea constitutes the very essence of heteronomy. The specificity of the Torah, which is rightly noted, does not remove it from the background of this widespread idea of a theonomy. And, once again, it is the way religion and ethics go together that today is a problem for us.

1. Moshe Weinfeld, "Deuteronomy: The Present State of Inquiry," *Journal of Biblical Literature* 86 (1967): 249–62, quoting p. 262.

Any analysis will trip over this as soon as it concerns itself with those laws that, following Albrecht Alt, are designated as apodictic so as to distinguish them from casuistic laws. Now the sixth commandment, which provides the title for my remarks, is one of these types of laws and while the question of the original setting along with that of successive elaborations is important on the exegetical plane, it cannot eclipse the question posed by the claim to a divine foundation. Hence it will be of greater importance, if we are to take up the accusation of heteronomy, to discover whether the connection between the Decalogue and the revelation of the Name in Exodus 3:14—that is, between the apodictic and the divine self-manifestation, grounded on the remembrance of deliverance—does not invite a reformulation of the problem posed by modern thinkers who make use of the Kantian vocabulary of autonomy. Does this connection designate, at the horizon of the theonomy, an economy of the gift capable of calling into question the very categories of autonomy and heteronomy, to the point of completely overthrowing their antagonism and with it the equation of theonomy and heteronomy? The possibility of seriously considering this question is why I shall reserve for the end of this essay any discussion of those pages where André LaCocque touches on the relation of the economy of the gift and the commandment.

For the moment, it is the strictness of the apodictic that we have to confront inasmuch as the whole modern discussion bears on the nature and ground of the apodictic or, if one prefers, of the categorical within the moral order. It is only after having exhausted the resources of the apparent equivalence between the biblical apodictic and the Kantian categorical that we shall be able to ask whether the very notion of the apodictic is not displaced in the case of a law of which we are told that it is not a code, that it unfolds a program of freedom on the basis of the proclamation of freedom.

Therefore we find ourselves confronted by the sixth commandment: "Thou shall not kill," chosen precisely because of its unconditionality, which immediately classes it among the apodictic laws, despite its prohibition not being applicable to war, nor to capital punishment, or that one has to limit the prohibition in the case of murder, that is, the illicit use of laws authorizing the use of violence, including death, for one's own profit. But does not the law, Kant will subsequently ask, in the *Doctrine of Law*, include the authorizing of constraint, in the sense of setting up an obstacle to an obstacle, in order to protect freedom? If so, what is absolutely prohibited is the use for personal ends of public violence, vengeance, the vendetta; in short, all violence that is not permitted. It is easy, we can see, in the very name of the presumed universality of the commandment, to rewrite it using the terms of a juridical ethics constructed on a small number of categorical imperatives. The divorce with modern thought would then apparently consist only in the manner of grounding an imperative that would be the same, up to its ultimate justification, and with this in the dissociation between the first commandment concerning God and the sixth commandment concerning the neighbor. But does the sixth commandment, if cut loose from the first commandment, preserve the same sense on the plane of utterance? At first sight, it seems to do so. For example, when the commandment is stated in its positive form in Leviticus 19:17–18 ("You shall love your neighbor as yourself"), it seems to lend itself to such a reconstruction in terms of an autonomous ethics, without losing its semantic identity. What is more, while the claim that the negative form of the prohibition opens a field more open to the invention of just forms of behavior than does the positive form of the Commandment of Love is an interesting one, albeit one that has often been disputed, this finally constitutes a secondary issue as regards the principal question, which is whether it is possible to dissociate the sixth from the first commandment in an ethics that seeks to free itself of any religious attachment and, in this sense, seeks to be autonomous. This is like asking if it is possible to dissociate the indissociable pair of commandments that Jesus cites, in Mark 12:28–34, following other "summaries" of the Law and the prophets familiar to the Jewish tradition.

Hence it is along the path of this really crucial question that I would like to set André LaCocque's exploration of the limits of the supposedly apodictic law. We have already seen how access to this critical moment was prepared by his comments concerning successively the conjunction of the prescriptive and the narrative, then the place for free consent to a properly unequal relation between a superior and an inferior, then by the suggestion from Franz Rosenzweig to distinguish between commandment and law (which is not really developed), and finally by the place left for interpretation in the utterance of the law and, especially, by the excursions in the direction of a special tie between gift and obligation, which may be premature at this exegetical stage.

LaCocque draws upon the evident discordance between the episode of the "binding of Isaac" in Genesis 22 and the apodictic law forbidding murder to pose the question whether within Hebrew Scripture itself there are not voices that plead in favor of a "supraethics," hence for a suspension of the apodictic demand. If this question is to preserve its full force, it is important to preserve the paradigmatic character of the recounted story, something that is justified by the insistence from the very beginning on the interweaving of narrative and prescription at the very heart of the Torah, which in turn calls for paying as much attention to the more narrative and imaginative Hagada as to the more prescriptive Halaka in subsequent Jewish tradition. The contrast between then must be maintained, however, if it is to remain significant.

LaCocque finds encouragement for moving in this direction in what I shall below call the rhetoric of excess and in what we both call the extravagant features, such as those found in the words and acts of Jesus. In order to preserve the vehemence of this approach, he fights against every attempt to rationalize Abraham's murderous gesture, whether it comes from the Midrash or elsewhere. The only Midrash that has any merit in his eyes is one that he finds Kierkegaardian and that draws the following exclamation from him: "Abraham's trial, like the one of Job, is God's trial." Abraham must be and remain a "murderer," as Kierkegaard puts it in *Fear and Trembling*.

To preserve the subversive force of Genesis 22, André LaCocque also looks for a series of parallels in the narrative parts of the Pentateuch and in narratives from the prophetic books for the aberrant behavior of other inspired individuals. Jesus recalls one of these episodes of suspending the rules in the synoptic passage found in Matthew 12, Mark 2, and Luke 6.

To what does such narration bear witness? To the limit of the Law, which only governs a measured realm, one that is mediocre in the literal sense of this word, a realm of generality? "The 'ethical' or the law can and must be transcended." To the "general" according to the law must be opposed the "particular," of Kierkegaard's vocabulary, or what Karl Jaspers calls "the exception."

I would like now, at my own risk and peril, to pose the question if and how it may still be possible to speak of the commandment "thou shall not kill" as a divine commandment, enjoined by God, once we admit as a cultural circumstance that in the practice of institutions and communities of all sorts, as well as of individuals, the reference to God has to be placed in parentheses, even totally eliminated. My enterprise could be called postmodern if this qualification can apply to reconstruction and not (or not only) to deconstruction. It will be a question of reconstruction to the extent that it will involve a recovery of resources of biblical faith that were either neglected or misunderstood, even overlooked, prior to the revolution of the Enlightenment.

Such reconstruction first depends on the correlation that has to be recognized between the first commandment, which defines our fundamental relation to God in a negative way, and the sixth commandment, which places the prohibition at the very heart of human coexistence. This is the same correlation that is affirmed in positive terms in the commandments to love both God and one's neighbor. However, it is only regarding these two commandments formulated in positive terms that we can say that they are "alike" or similar. What correlation, or difference, or similitude is really at issue here? Above all, in what way can this correlation be reconstructed within a moral, juridical, social, or political culture that has won for the law a space where it is autonomous and self-sufficient?

The first preliminary condition for any reconstruction is to give the first commandment its full scope, by locating the prescriptive genre within the whole network of literary forms that bear the naming of God: narratives, prescriptions, prophecies, hymns, wisdom sayings.[2] Human beings are not confronted with an artificially isolated prescriptive. This first point is important if we must be able to attribute to humanity's response a corresponding variety of forms, the obedience that corresponds to the prescription being just one among many dispositions, or as James M. Gustafson puts it, "affections," by which he means a way of being affected by one or another of the ways God is named.[3] In saying this, I do not mean to conceal the "leap" that is demanded by biblical faith, but I do mean to distance it from an overly narrow obedience that could be too rapidly identified with a heteronomy, which itself would stand over against autonomy in the modern sense. It we must propose a single name to characterize the set of affections constitutive of the human response to the naming of God, I would propose "dependence," whose different modes I shall unfold below as a function of the many different ways in which the correlation between the love of God and the love of neighbor gets expressed. We can, however, give this affection of dependence its full scope right away if we see in it the human correlate to the divine withdrawal signified by the "I am who I am" from Exodus 3:14 discussed elsewhere in this volume. If God is named in different ways, depending on the literary forms in which this naming takes place, there is not just a convergence among these modes of nam-

2. See Paul Ricoeur, "Naming God," *Union Theological Seminary Quarterly Review* 34 (1979): 215–27. Reprinted in *Figuring the Sacred: Religion, Narrative, and Imagination* (Minneapolis: Fortress Press, 1995), pp. 217–35.

3. James M. Gustafson, *Ethics from a Theocentric Perspective*, 2 vols. (Chicago: University of Chicago Press, 1981). Re the concept of affection, see, vol. 1, pp. 197–204.

ing but also, from the rhetorical point of view, an *excess* that the redundance of the Hebrew '*eyeh* ("I am") points to, as though the naming of God were not limited to circulating among the different genres but escaped all of them and indicated God something like a vanishing point on their common horizon. In this way, the greatest distance is indicated between an un-known, in-effable God and human beings caught up in the abyss opened by the question "Who am I?" Any relation between the two extremes can only be an interval that has been crossed, precisely by the other ways of naming that, in some way, bring God and human beings close together. Yet this proximity must be that of a distance overcome, on the basis of distance, as is conveyed by the German expression *Entfernung*, which etymologically suggests something like a de-distanciation.

The second preliminary consideration for our projected reconstruction is to make sense of the verb "love" in the expression "love of God." Besides the full scope of the naming having to be related to this verb, the attribution of love to God lends itself to an interpretation that I have discussed at length elsewhere.[4] This interpretation consists in setting side by side, and comparing and contrasting with each other, the affirmation of Deuteronomy 6 ("Hear, O Israel, Yhwh, our God, is the one Yhwh") and the New Testament affirmation from 1 John 4 that "God is love." To the second formula, I applied the resources of a theory of metaphor, based on the idea of an initial discordance that is overcome by a mutual overlapping of the two terms that confront each other in the utterance, resulting in an "iconic augmentation" of each of the terms.[5] In other words, what we may think of God prior to the metaphor is changed by the unexpected, even odd attribution of love, just as what we may have previously thought about love is also changed. On the one side, we have God "alone," according to the Hebraic *shema*, and, in this sense, a "jealous" God, a God who reduces any challenger to the rank of being absolute to the status of an idol and who condemns idolaters to the point of their destruction. On the other side, there is love among humans, which unfolds across the whole range of forms such love may assume, from the sexual and erotic plane to that of veneration and devotion, blending together the nuances of *eros*, *philia*, and *agape*.

4. Paul Ricoeur, "D'un Testament à l'autre: Essai d'herméneutique biblique," in *Collana "Dialogo di Filosofia*," no. 9 (Rome: Herder-Università Lateranense, 1992); reprinted in Paul Ricoeur, *Lectures III* (Paris: Seuil, 1994), pp. 255–66.

5. See my *The Rule of Metaphor: Multi-Disciplinary Studies of the Creation of Meaning*, translated by Robert Czerny et al. (Toronto: University of Toronto Press, 1977).

Now the metaphor suggests that we think of God *as* love with all the connotations of its various forms and of love *as* God, following the strict rule to exclude all idols. In this regard, I argue that the Johannine proposition is not to be substituted for that of Deuteronomy 6, rather it develops and enriches it "iconically."

The expected response on the part of humans is proportionate to the semantic richness of the name God itself, so "augmented" by the metaphor of love drawn from the ground of human experience. The feeling of dependence that we might at first have not included within the strictness of obedience takes on, correlatively, the paradoxical form of a "loving obedience"[6] where submission is "iconically" augmented" by the dilection of love. Thanks to the qualification "loving," the initial feeling of dependence receives the stamp of being-loved. The genitive of the expression "love of God" must thus be read in two ways: addressed to . . . and coming from . . . It should be written: love (of) God. The de-distanciation evoked by the first preliminary consideration, traversed distance, is this love.

The third preliminary condition is to make sense of the *commandment* to love. Freud was not alone, nor was he the first to rebel against the very idea of a commanded love. Nor do I believe that it suffices to reply that while it is true that one human being cannot require another to love him or her, God can do so. Or at least this response is insufficient insofar as it remains tributary to the anthropomorphism of one will that obligates another will. Things are different if we say that it is the love (of) God that commands. But what are we then to make of the formula that then comes to mind: "love obligates"? Franz Rosenzweig, whom we have already mentioned above, tried to answer by proposing to distinguish between the commandment and the law.[7] The formula of the commandment is just "love me!" That of the law is "do this, don't do that."

If we are to make sense of this startling proposition of a contemporary Jewish thinker, we have to set it within the framework and particularly within the movement of *The Star of Redemption*.[8] First of all, re-

---

6. I borrow the expression "obedient love" from Paul Ramsey, *Basic Christian Ethics* (Chicago: University of Chicago Press, 1950), p. 34, although I invert the terms.

7. Franz Rosenzweig, *The Star of Redemption*, translated by William W. Hallo (New York: Holt, Rinehart and Winston, 1971).

8. Cf. Stéphane Moses, *System and Revelation: The Philosophy of Franz Rosenzweig*, translated by Catherine Tihanyi (Detroit: Wayne State University Press, 1992); Paul Ricoeur, "The Figure in *The Star of Redemption*," in *Figuring the Sacred*, pp. 93–107.

garding the very project of this work, which we can classify as philosophical-theological, it is necessary to note that it is constructed on the ruins of absolute knowledge, knowledge that would include God, humanity, and the world in one unique system of a Hegelian style. This is succeeded by a threefold structure that is broken apart, including Creation, Revelation, and Redemption, a triad that is structured by a nonchronological temporality that unfolds a "Way." Creation occupies the place of an immemorial past and concerns "the ever-enduring base of things."[9] Creation has always already occurred and it continues to occur! Creation is the power of God outside of God. Revelation, whose stake is "the ever-renewed birth of the soul,"[10] occupies the plane of the present, just as Redemption occupies that of the future under the sign of the "eternal future of the Kingdom."[11] So it is in the median part of this work, in a position that recalls the Kierkegaardian instant, that the Commandment of Love arises, the "love me" that precedes and grounds the "love your neighbor," which sums up the Law.

Rosenzweig does not conceal the questionable aspect of what seems beyond question.

> All commandments which derive from that primeval "love me!" ultimately merge in the all-inclusive "love thy neighbor!" Now if this too is a commandment to love, how is that to be reconciled with the fact that this "love me!" commands the only kind of love which can be commanded? The answer to this objection could easily be anticipated in one brief word. Let us rather devote the entire concluding part of this book to it instead. For this answer, simple as it is, contains within itself all that the two preceding books still had to leave open.[12]

His complete answer will only be given in the section on Redemption and in terms of the dimension of futurity. The love of God remains "hidden" or, in Rosenzsweig's vocabulary, "figureless," unlike the visible hero in tragedy. The soul takes on a figure only in passing from Revelation to Redemption. And at the juncture of these two sections of the Way, the "hidden" love externalizes itself, just as God externalizes himself in creating. "From out of the depths of his own soul, it bursts ever anew upon the exterior. It is not fated but borne by volition."[13]

9. This is the title of Part II, Book 1 of *The Star of Redemption;* see ibid., p. 112.
10. Ibid., p. 156: the title of Part II, Book 2.
11. Ibid., p. 205; the title of Part II, Book 3.
12. Ibid.
13. Ibid., p. 213.

The force of expansion that spreads beyond the abandon demanded of the soul in the commandment to love God, is the love of neighbor.

> Love of neighbor is that which surmounts this mere dedication with every moment, while at the same time always presupposing it. . . . Man can express himself in the act of love only after he has first become a soul awakened by God. It is only in being loved by God that the soul can make of its act of love more than a mere act, can make of it, that is, the fulfillment of a—commandment to love.[14]

In short, "love cannot be commanded except by the lover himself. . . . The love of God is to express itself in love for one's neighbor."[15]

We can now say something about this distinction between commandment and law. At its origin is the love commanded by the lover. Next comes "the externalization in love for the neighbor." A commanded interhuman love cut off from its source would be scandalous. Yes, the love that love requires is surprising, but it is not scandalous. Perhaps we can make better sense of this if we think of a situation apparently quite distant from the idea of a supreme legislation coming from a cloud. This situation is the birth of a baby. From the mere fact that the baby is there, we are obligated by its fragility.[16] Perhaps the birth of an infant, but also that of everything that is subject to the law of being born, growing, and dying is the occasion par excellence where we humans can hear something like "love me!" The same experience is repeated, or rather recreated, in the maturity of an erotic love like that of the Song of Songs, which is in its own way a birth, one just as threatened as is the newborn child and just as exigent as regards what may help it to grow. Love me, help me.

Let us return to Rosenzweig. When he distinguishes between commandment and law, he sets himself immediately in opposition to what modernity has turned the Law into, namely, a formal imperative, empty of any content, rooted in human freedom alone, in autonomy. In this regard, the rediscovery of a love that obligates us is postmodern. It would be an error to seek in it a repetition of the Mosaic scene of the giving of the Law and, in truth, the condition for ethics before the Enlightenment and prior to the crowning of this latter in the self-sufficient totality of the Hegelian spirit. It is we, postmoderns, who have to dis-

14. Ibid., p. 214.
15. Ibid.
16. See Hans Jonas, *The Imperative of Responsibility: In Search of an Ethics for the Technological Age* (Chicago: University of Chicago Press, 1984).

tinguish the commandment issuing from the love (of) God from laws
that stem from the autonomy of a perfectly self-sufficient freedom. Modernity both discovered and constructed the universality of each and
every person, Revelation is what points beyond it—to the singularity
of being loved. Someone is enjoined to love. Enjoined by someone? I
would reply, no, if it were merely a question of getting beyond any form
of anthropomorphism. But I would also add an even stronger yes if
what we are meant to say is that the God-love of the great Johannine
metaphor can be nothing less than a person, inasmuch as he/she/it has
to give rise to a love in return that is capable of externalizing itself, to
use Rosenzweig's expression, in love for the neighbor, and in this way
to set itself on the Way of Redemption.

Rosenzweig does not deny this suggestion of a God who is at least
personal. Seen from the point of view of Revelation, Creation remains
a divine monologue. In the "let us make man" of Genesis the "I" is an
unmarked "I." "It is thus an I still concealed in the secret of the third
person and not yet a manifest I."[17] It looks as though it would not be
excessive to say that for Rosenzweig God only becomes an "I" when he
calls to a "you" and gives this you a proper name, a name that will be
proper to this you, that will be his or her name. As Rosenzweig puts it:
"The commandment to love can only proceed from the mouth of the
lover. Only the lover can and does say: love me!"[18] The imperative goes
with such an utterance because, unlike the indicative, its present is absolutely pure, nothing that could be said in the past tense prepares such a
statement. It lacks premeditation and makes no forecast that could be
stated in the future tense: "The imperative of the commandment makes
no provision for the future; it can only conceive the immediacy of obedience. If it were to think of a future or an Ever, it would be, not commandment nor order, but law. Law reckons with times, with a future,
with duration."[19] If something shameful gets bound up with all this, it
is not loving enough. The soul confesses at present, "I still do not love
nearly as much as I—know myself loved."[20] The reader will not be surprised that this chapter in Rosenzweig ends with the parable of the
Song of Songs, which he holds to be indivisibly erotic and spiritual.
Does he not begin, without mentioning the Song of Songs, with the
declaration from 8:6, "'Love is strong as death.' Strong in the same way

17. *The Star of Redemption*, p. 175.
18. Ibid., p. 176.
19. Ibid., p. 177.
20. Ibid., p. 181.

as death? But against whom does death display its strength? Against him whom it seizes."[21]

Before taking up the difficult task of indicating a place for the prohibition of murder within an ethics of autonomy, even one expanded to the dimensions of an ethics of communication and discussion, we have to consider, in light of the preliminary considerations we have just indicated, the meaning of the correlation between the prohibition of the first commandment and that of the sixth commandment—or, by implication, between the commandment to love God and the commandment to love our neighbor.

This first thing we have to consider is the asymmetry, the disproportion, between these two poles. The *shema*, reinforced by the "I am who I am," tends to exile the divinity as the unique unity of something in itself, whereas the love of neighbor tends to push human beings outside themselves toward an unlimited plurality of others who stand over against them. In this way, love finds itself caught between Height and Exteriority.[22]

Starting from this being caught between two poles, we can begin to think about the similitude of these two commandments. Similitude does not mean identity, and even less, fusion. Rather we must apply to the relation of similitude what was said above concerning proximity, proximity as distance that is both preserved and traversed. What both opens and crosses this interval is love itself in the effusion of the commandment that the one God addresses to the soul. This active mediation between Height and Exteriority provides one possible means of access to the well-known but little understood notion of the image of God. The divided expression that Genesis uses to characterize the status of the human creature, made "in the image and resemblance of God," proposes a dialectic close to that of Height and Exteriority, of distance and proximity.[23] Perhaps the disproportion and the similitude between the two loves help us to make sense of the notion of the image of God, rather than the other way around, in that this notion of an image, taken as our starting point, solely within the framework of a theology of Creation, is open to unlimited variations. This may be a good thing in that it conveys the price of any attempt to found the si-

21. Ibid., p. 156.

22. See Paul Ricoeur, "Emmanuel Levinas: Thinker of Testimony," in *Figuring the Sacred*, pp. 108–26. I am using these two terms to characterize the cardinal dimensions of bearing witness or testimony.

23. See Ramsey, *Basic Christian Ethics*, pp. 249–83.

militude of the two commandments, where love itself obligates us in terms of the difference and the community of its two objects, the Most High and the neighbor, upon the indeterminate idea of an *imago Dei*.

Now, having considered these preliminary matters, I would like to undertake the perilous exercise of a confrontation between what I would like to call the rediscovered paradigm of loving obedience and the principle of autonomy, as it is proclaimed by both classical and contemporary thinkers[24] and completed in an ethics of communication.[25] This confrontation will have to avoid two pitfalls, that of apologetics as much as that of refutation. On the one hand, I want to show that loving obedience, far from being opposed to an ethics of autonomy, helps it to reach its full extent. On the other hand, I do not mean to transform the services biblical faith renders to a moral philosophy that lacks coherence into some kind of indirect justification of such faith. I have not forgotten Bonhöffer's warning against any "God of the gaps" conception of biblical faith.[26] In a pluralistic culture such as our own, what is at issue is nothing more than a contribution to the public discussion to which Jews and Christians bring their convictions whose portrait I indicated above, convictions that, in light of discussion, they want to have recognized as "considered convictions," to use an expression favored by John Rawls.[27]

My starting point is close to the place reached by André LaCocque in his reflections on the limits of the apodictic, taking account of what I have already said.

In his Kierkegaardian reading of Genesis 22, André LaCocque accentuates the idea of the exception. Parallel to this, I want to consider that of "excess," that is, the excess of love in relation to justice. In a number of earlier works, I have opposed the logic of superabundance, characteristic of what I call an economy of the gift, to the logic of equivalence that reigns in the different spheres of justice.[28] For example, as

24. Kant's essay "What is Enlightenment?" can serve as a guide to the whole Enlightenment discussion.

25. See, for example, Karl-Otto Apel, *Transformation der Philosophie* (Frankfurt: Suhrkamp, 1973); Jürgen Habermas, *Moral Consciousness and Communicative Action*, translated by Christian Lehardt and Shierry Weber Nicholson (Cambridge: MIT Press, 1990). See also Apel, *Erläuterung zur Diskursethik* (Frankfurt: Suhrkamp, 1991).

26. Dietrich Bonhöffer, *Letters and Papers from Prison*, translated by R. H. Fuller (New York: Macmillan, 1962), pp. 217–20.

27. John Rawls, *A Theory of Justice* (Cambridge: Harvard University Press, 1971), p. 46.

28. Paul Ricoeur, "The Logic of Jesus" and "Love and Justice," in *Figuring the Sacred*, pp. 279–82 and 315–29.

Kant shows in his *Doctrine of the Law*,[29] commutative justice aims at making these spheres of justice "co-exist" despite the obstacles he himself places under the heading of the "unsocial sociability" of human beings.[30] Similarly, distributive justice aims at introducing the highest degree of equality compatible with productivity and, in general, with the efficacy of society into the unequal distribution of places, status, and roles. Then there is corrective justice, which is expressed directly on the plane of penal law, in an effort to make the punishment be proportional to the crime, and indirectly on the plane of social law in terms of various forms of redistribution all aimed at compensating for the failures of distributive justice, particularly when this latter form condemns whole groups to exclusion from social goods.

The excess of the logic of superabundance in relation to the logic of equivalence is expressed first of all by a disproportion that opens a space between the two poles for practical mediations capable of affirming the most basic moral project of justice.

This disproportion first announces itself through language. For love speaks, but through another kind of language than does justice. The discourse of love is first of all a discourse of praise. In praising, human beings rejoice at the view of their object, which reigns over every other object of their concern. Thus the language game that best fits with praise is the hymn, the acclamation: "Happy is the one who . . ." Setting this remark concerning the language of love next to what I said above concerning the odd character of the commandment to love, I shall speak of a poetic use of the imperative, which runs from the loving invitation to the anger of love betrayed, passing through supplication. What is more, it is under the aegis of the poetics of the hymn, broadened to include that of the commandment, that we may place the power of metaphorization that attaches to the expressions of love. This is why love engenders an ascending and descending spiral embracing the effects distinguished by the terms *eros*, *philia*, and *agape*. In this way, an analogy is "invented," that is, both discovered and created, between those affects that I believe it is wrong to oppose to one another in the manner of Anders Nygren in his influential book, *Agape and Eros*.[31]

29. Immanuel Kant, *Metaphysics of Morals*, translated by John Ladd (Indianapolis: Bobbs, Merrill, 1965), pp. 51–129.

30. Immanuel Kant, "Idea for a Universal History," in *Kant on History*, translated by Lewis White Beck (Indianapolis: Bobbs-Merrill, 1963), p. 15.

31. Anders Nygren, *Agape and Eros*, translated by Philip S. Watson (Philadelphia: Westminster, 1953).

Compared to that love which does not argue but rather declares itself, as we see in 1 Corinthians 13, justice is initially recognizable internal to communicative activity through the confrontation between claims and arguments in typical conflict situations and lawsuits, then by that decision that breaks off the debate and cuts off the conflict. The rationality of this process is assured by the procedural attitudes that govern each of its phases. These procedures, in turn, are governed by a formalism, which, far from indicating some lack, is the mark of the force of justice, joining the sword that cuts through the argument to the scale that weighs things in the balance. It is this formalism, within the dialectic of love and justice, that makes the logic of equivalence, whose primary expression is equality before the law carry the day. To treat similar cases in the same manner is the rule of justice as it applies in the judicial order. Distributive and commutative justice are also governed by procedural rules, just as formal as those that preside over the judicial order.[32]

It is at this level of formalism that love may have a role to play, at the very heart of those institutions that give justice the observable contours of positive law, which citizens live under and which they are called to obey.

My suggestion here is that the sense of justice underlying these formalisms does not have that univocal character that prevails within the laws characteristic of positive law. This sense, which we can call a reasonable emotion, moves back and forth between two levels that bear witness to its equivocity. At the lower level, the one that applies to the contractualist conceptions underlying the origin of the concept of law, illustrated by Hobbes, Rousseau, and Kant, right up through Rawls, in the manner illustrated by a hypothetical situation prior to any such contract, is a feeling of mutual disinterest, in the strong sense of an "interest," not marked by any sense of envy, that each of those entering into the contract seeks to promote. At the higher level, the ideal that marks our sense of justice and that reveals our indignation in the face of the injustices of the world that cry out to us, is expressed by a desire for mutual dependence, even for what we can called mutual indebtedness. Social cooperation, such as that which Rawls's principles of justice, for example, seek to reinforce, illustrates this oscillation between competition and solidarity insofar as the calculations that lead to the contract lay the basis for a higher feeling of mutual disinterestedness,

---

32. See Paul Ricoeur and Michel Rocard, "Justice and the Market," *Dissent* (1991): 505–10.

but one that is still less profound that the feeling of mutual indebtedness.[33]

Is it not then the function of love to help this sense of justice to reach the level of a veritable mutual recognition wherein each and everyone feels indebted to all the others? If so, a bridge has to be built between a love that is praised simply for itself, for its heights and its moral beauty, and a sense of justice that rightly is suspicious of any recourse to charity that seeks to substitute itself for justice, that may even seek to free men and women of good will from any such claim upon them. Between confusion and opposition, we need to explore a difficult path where the tension between the distinct and sometimes opposed claims of love and justice becomes the occasion for reasonable action. What I said above about the obligation love engenders can point us in the direction of such behavior. If, indeed, love obligates, it is first of all justice that it obligates us to, but a justice educated by the economy of the gift. It is as though the economy of the gift sought to infiltrate the economy of equivalence.

It is principally in the exercise of moral judgment in actual situations,[34] when we have to take a side in the conflicts among duties, or in the conflicts between respect for the rule and solicitude for the individuals involved, or in those difficult cases where the choice is not between good and bad but between the more and less worse, that love comes to plead in the name of compassion and generosity in favor of a justice that would openly place the sense of mutual indebtedness above that of the confrontation of disinterested interests. But it is also at the level of institutions that this compassion and generosity have to be expressed. Penal law recognizes extenuating circumstances, exemptions from punishment, amnesties. Over against social exclusion, corrective justice represents something like the way of love on the plane of distributive justice. Even international politics can be touched by love in the form of unexpected acts of pardon, as exemplified by German Chancellor Willy Brandt falling on his knees before the Holocaust monument in Warsaw or King Juan Carlos asking pardon from the Jews for their expulsion from Spain at the end of the fifteenth century.[35]

33. See Paul Ricoeur, "Le cercle de la démonstration," *Esprit* 2 (February 1988): 78–79.

34. See study 9 of my *Oneself as Another*, translated by Kathleen Blamey (Chicago: University of Chicago Press, 1994).

35. See my "Welches neue Ethos für Europa," in P. Koslowski, ed., *Europa imaginieren* (Berlin: Springer, 1992), pp. 108–20. There I consider three "models" for imagining a Europe that would not be merely that of business: translation, the exchange of memories, and forgiveness.

A second way in which love converts justice to its highest ideal is when it contributes to the effective universalization of moral rules through the exemplary force of the exception. This suggestion prolongs the Kierkegaardian style of interpretation that André LaCocque proposes concerning the binding of Isaac in Genesis 22. The "suspension" of ethics, as he says, marks the limit of the Law. My own proposal is slightly different, yet complementary. Might it not be that the exception serves to reveal another sort of limit than that to which the categorical per se has to submit? I have in mind those factual limits imposed on the categorical by historical experience.

The suggestion I am making here directly concerns the discussion that divides contemporary ethicists, divided over a formal universalism (for example, Karl-Otto Apel and Jürgen Habermas) or a concrete contextualism (for example, Michael Sandel, Michael Walzer, Charles Taylor, and Alasdair MacIntyre).[36] The former are close to the procedural conception of law, the latter put the accent on the cultural limitations that affect the juridical and political practices of communities whose internal consensus rests on some apprehension of what is good and obligatory that is always limited. Confronted with this apparently insurmountable antinomy, can we not say that the universalism, expressed in Kant by the idea of an obligation without exception and in Apel and Habermas by that of an ideal community of communication without limits or fetters, is never realized in actual practice except in the form of an "inchoate," even a merely alleged, universalism, which seeks to be recognized by other cultures? If so, the advocates of this universalism must learn to listen to these other cultures, which also make a claim to genuine universal values, but which are also caught within actual practices that bear the stamp of cultural limitations symmetrical to our own.[37]

Would it not then be the role of love to contribute to reducing this gap between an ideal universalism without restriction and the contextualism wherein cultural differences prevail? The biblical world, Jewish in the first instance, then also Christian, offers examples that have become paradigmatic of this extension of culturally limited spheres in the direction of an effectively universal recognition. The repeated call to ancient

36. Michael Sandel, *Liberalism and the Limits of Justice* (New York: Cambridge University Press, 1982); Michael Walzer, *Spheres of Justice* (New York: Basic Books, 1983); Charles Taylor, *The Sources of the Self: The Making of Modern Identity* (Cambridge: Harvard University Press, 1989); Alasdair MacIntyre, *After Virtue* (Notre Dame, IN: University of Notre Dame Press, 1981).

37. *Oneself as Another,* pp. 273–83.

Israel to include "the widow, the orphan, and the stranger at the gates"—in other words, the other, as the beneficiary of hospitality—is an initial exemplary illustration of the pressure exerted by love on justice, so that it may attack head-on those practices of exclusion that are perhaps the counterpart of any strong social bond.[38] The commandment to love our enemies, as found in the Sermon on the Mount, constitutes the strongest example of this. The imperative form given to the "new commandment" inscribes it within the ethical sphere. But its kinship with the commandment "love me," which Rosenzweig distinguishes from the Law, qualifies it as supra-ethical insofar as it stems from an economy of the gift as soon as it renounces any claim to reciprocity.[39] Furthermore, Jesus associates the commandment to love our enemies with other exceptional sorts of behavior that challenge the logic of equivalence of ordinary justice. However, the commandment to love our enemies occupies a preeminent place among these challenges to ordinary, good moral sense inasmuch as it directly affects the sixth commandment of the Decalogue. The commandment to love our enemies is "new" only through the extension it gives to the concept of the neighbor, which does not escape those cultural restrictions underscored by contextualist theories. The gravity of this injunction results from the fact that such restrictions seem constitutive to this day of the social bond. After all, did not Carl Schmitt make the category friend/enemy a criterion of the political?[40] The current state of international law confirms this diagnosis. And has not war, so horribly illustrated by the terrors of our twentieth century, always been the driving force of the history of nations and states? International law is not capable today of providing an appropriate institutional form to the universality without restrictions of the rule of justice. Hence the ideal of perpetual peace, to use the title of Kant's well-known opscule, must still for a long time to come find refuge in the idea of Utopia. But at least Kant had already argued in terms of justice and a law that would exclude war from the field of relations among states. In this sense, he demonstrated that peace is a requirement of the very idea of law and right.

Does it not fall upon the love of neighbor, then, to motivate the con-

38. Israel's prophets shot one arrow in the direction of this recognition of one's enemy as another human being: "Remember that you too were a stranger in Egypt."

39. Paul Ricoeur, "Ethical and Theological Reflections on the Golden Rule," in *Figuring the Sacred*, pp. 293–302.

40. Carl Schmitt, *Der Begriff des Politischen* (Berlin: Duncker und Humblot, 1987; originally published in 1932).

crete approaches of international politics in the direction of perpetual peace? The suffering that peoples inflict upon one another by itself does not not seem a sufficient reason for "making peace." Everything happens as though a desire for murder, stronger than the fear of death, from time to time arises among human beings and pushes them to disaster. Without such a collective death drive, how are we to explain the hate that seems to be consubstantial with the claims to identity of so many peoples? Would that we would, on the contrary, begin from the memory of sufferings inflicted on others before we reassess our past glory and misery. But this *metanoia* of memory only seems capable of proceeding from love, from that Eros, concerning which Freud, with his own death approaching and surrounded by the sobering events we are all aware of, asked if it could ever come to terms with Thanatos.[41]

I do not want to leave this theme of the contribution of excess to the historical realization of abstract universalism without referring to another example with a biblical origin, which may open a more promising era of actualization. I have in mind the words of the apostle: in Jesus Christ there is no longer Jew, nor Greek, nor male, nor female, nor free, nor slave. There is more than a secret kinship between this declaration, stated this time in terms of the indicative of "realized" eschatology, and the commandment to love our enemies, insofar as the Pauline enumeration is based on mutual ignorance, hate, even war. In particular, it has taken almost two thousand years to end slavery, at least legally; that is, the right of possession and therefore of commerce applied to human persons. In truth, we have always known that human persons where not things. But there were always human beings who did not count as persons. Love presses justice to enlarge the circle of mutual recognition. And it is often through the means of transgression of the established order, through the case of exemplary exceptions, that love pursues its work of conversion at the very level of the sense of justice.[42]

---

41. Sigmund Freud, *Civilization and Its Discontents*, translated by James Strachey (New York: W. W. Norton, 1961). This work ends with the perplexing question: "The fateful question for the human species seems to me to be whether and to what extent their cultural development will succeed in mastering the disturbance of their communal life by the human instinct of aggression and self-destruction. . . . Men have gained control over the forces of nature to such an extent that with their help they would have no difficulty in exterminating one another to the last man. They know this, and hence comes a large part of their current unrest, their unhappiness and their mood of anxiety. And now it is to be expected that the other of the two 'Heavenly Powers,' eternal Eros, will make an effort to assert himself in the struggle with his equally immortal adversary. But who can foresee with what success and with what result?" (p. 92).

42. One thinks here, of course, of Gandhi, Martin Luther King, Jr., and others. Juridical thought has dealt with this problem in terms of the problem of the right to regicide, in the case of tyranny, and more generally the relation between justice and civil disobedience. Besides Rawls's *A*

Another apparent effect of this pressure that love exercises on justice has to do with the singularity and nonsubstitutability of persons. It is not just in terms of extension but also through intensity that love acts. Here we should undoubtedly recall the "one God" of the monotheistic proclamation of the Hebrew Bible. Above, I tried to indicate that the Johannine formula "God is love" develops this proclamation metaphorically rather than abolishing it. Thus between the first and the sixth commandment there is a sort of mirroring relation. Indeed, Rosenzweig thinks of the commandment "love me" as addressed to the individual soul, thereby reserving the passage to the plurality of neighbors for what he calls Redemption. May we not then say that the profession of Israelite and Johannine faith reinforce the recognition of persons as always unique?

Why is this kind of assistance desirable? One reason is because there does not seem to exist a moral reason that is absolutely constraining for which the difference among persons would be, as such, an object of obligation. Yes, there is the practice of exchange of roles in conversation, the difference of position of social actors in every transaction, the irreducible difference among individual and collective memories, and finally the search for individual responsibility in the case where damages must be recompensed or punishments inflicted, but all these social situations seem to make of the difference among persons an irreducible component of the *humana conditio*. Yet all these considerations seem to be *de facto*, not *de jure*. We can already envisage at the horizon of recent work in genetic manipulation the possibility, which for the moment remains a fantasy, of fabricating an unlimited number of copies of a human being through cloning. Why should this be prohibited? Is it because in communal ethics difference is bound to otherness and otherness is a condition of mutual recognition? Undoubtedly. But what will prohibit making an exception to this conviction? And where does this conviction draw its force?

This need for reinforcement can also be felt in another way. Justice differs from friendship and in general from those interpersonal relations based on a face-to-face relation, hence from the forceful injunction that emanates from the face, from each face that says to me, according to Emmanuel Levinas's powerful expression, "thou shalt not kill me!"[43] The vis-à-vis of justice is faceless others, that is, all those others to

Theory of Justice, see Ronald Dworkin, *Taking Rights Seriously* (Cambridge: Harvard University Press, 1978).

43. Emmanuel Levinas, *Totality and Infinity: An Essay on Exteriority*, translated by Alphonso Lingus (Pittsburgh: Duquesne University Press, 1969).

whom I am bound by law through a multitude of institutions.[44] The vis-à-vis is no longer you, but each and all. But how is the each and all to be prevented from slipping into the "one," the "they"? Each and all is still distributive. To each his or her due, to each his or her fair share, even when the shares are not equal. The "one" is anonymous, it coagulates into an indistinct mass. But is it not then up to love's imagination and singularizing regard to extend the privilege of the face-to-face relation to include all those other relations with (faceless) others? The same thing applies here as in the case of loving our enemies, which negates the political difference between friends and enemies. In attending to the problematic of each and all, love means to overcome the gap between the thou and the third person. This is how it contributes to preserving the unsubstitutableness of persons in every exchange of roles.

Another reason for expecting that love will protect justice against its skids and swerves has to do with the contemporary discussion concerning the grounds of justice. Above I referred to the debate between universalization and contextualism. Another debate is opened by the objection addressed to Kant by his rebellious disciples—Habermas and Apel, among others—in the name of an ethics of communication. The test of the rule of universalization to which each subject must submit the maxim of his action leads to a monologue of the moral subject with himself.[45] This objection is probably ill-founded as regards Kant himself. His *Doctrine of Right* presupposes diverse typical situations where the coexistence of spheres of free action is threatened by the enmity and adversities to which the social bond is exposed. But whatever the case may be as regards Kant, the question is whether an ethics of communication really succeeds in placing its dialogical vocation safely apart from any falling back into the solitude of a monologue. If subjects invited to dispute among themselves must divest themselves of everything ethicists regard as mere conventions, what remains of the singularity and alterity of the partners in the discussion? If their convictions are only conventions, what distinguishes the participants from one another other than their interests? Only a lively sense of the alterity of persons can preserve the dialogical dimension against every reduction to a monologue carried out by an undifferentiated subject. Singularity, al-

44. See my *Oneself as Another*, pp. 194–202.

45. This objection is discussed in O. Höffe, *Kategorische Rechtsprinzipien. Ein Kontrapunkt der Moderne* (Frankfurt: Suhrkamp, 1990), chaps. 12–14. There is also a balanced evaluation of the terms of this debate in J. M. Ferry, *Les puissances de l'expérience. Essai sur l'identité contemporaine*, vol. 2, *Les ordres de la reconnaissance* (Paris: Cerf, 1991).

terity, and mutuality are the ultimate presuppositions of the dialogical structure of argumentation. Is there are better guarantor of these three than love?

In the preceding sections, the accent has been on the diverse ways in which love can aid justice by helping it raise itself and to maintain itself on the highest level of moral exigency. Now I would like to suggest the idea that love can also put justice on guard against excessive ambitions. The excess here is no longer on the side of love, in the form of the exception, but on that of justice, in the form of *hubris*. In this case, the dialectic of love and justice takes on a decidedly more polemical form.

I would like here to return to the sense of dependence through which I have characterized religious feeling. Left to itself, this sense of dependence leads to a theonomic realm that seems diametrically opposed to moral autonomy. However what I said next about the metaphorical identity between the one God of the Exodus and the apostle's God of love, then about the priority of the commandment to love in relation to every law, allows us to complete this feeling of dependence with one of *antecedence.* This involves what I am willing to recognize as a certain founding passivity: "Because you have been loved, love in turn." We ought not to hesitate to extend this feeling of antecedence to those laws called apodictic. We can say that they come from God, not in the mythical form of the Sinai narratives and the giving of the tablets of the Law to Moses, but in virtue of their proximity to the commandment to love, which proceeds from the love that is God. This, in my opinion, is the only acceptable sense of the notion of theonomy. Love obligates; what it obligates is a loving obedience.

It is this latter notion that now has to be set over against the autonomy of the Kantian imperative and the communicational theory form of this autonomy.

On the one hand, I want to emphasize that loving obedience gives rise to responsibility for the concerns of others, in the sense that Emmanuel Levinas speaks of this in terms of the face, whose injunction calls me to care for others, to the point of becoming their hostage and through the gesture of substitution.[46] In this sense, theonomy, understood as a summons to loving obedience, engenders autonomy, understood as the summons to responsibility. Here we touch upon a delicate point where a certain founding passivity links up with an active accep-

---

46. See Emmanuel Levinas, *Otherwise than Being, or Beyond Essence,* translated by Alphonso Lingus (Boston: Kluwer, 1991).

tance of responsibility, which has no other field of exercise than communication, the quest for recognition, and, at the limit, the commitment to and search for consensus. This connection between the antecedence of the Law and responsible spontaneity finds an echo in the depths of conscience. Under the figure of the "voice of conscience," the Law attests to its structuring character, which is not simply oppressive and repressive. Yes, we will not find a precise particular law that has not been instituted by human beings in the course of history. The theory of positive law is not completely nonsensical. But the legality of the law is as much instituting as instituted. In one sense, it is always already there, just like every symbolic order upon which all education, and perhaps every form of psychotherapy, rests.[47]

On the other hand, I want to guard against an over elevation of moral autonomy. Considered in terms of its rational core, it includes numerous propositions that take on their meaning only when unfolded in terms of an ethic of responsible spontaneity. Which propositions?[48] First of all, on the plane of a semantics of obligation, there is the assertion that the law is the *ratio cognoscendi* of freedom and that freedom is the *ratio existendi* of the law. In other words, there is law only for free beings, and there is no freedom without submission to an obligation. If this obligation takes place on the human plane of the imperative, this is owing to the fact of the recalcitrance of emotional inclinations. And if the imperative is categorical, it is so in the sense of an absence of restriction attached to the obligation. But how do we recognize the categorical character of an imperative? Through the capacity of certain maxims of our action to successfully pass the test of universalization. Having said this, we can situate with greater precision the points where moral autonomy seems to reveal itself as incompatible with theonomy, even when this is understood as loving obedience. Their confrontation takes place at two specific points. First, at the level of the connection between freedom and the Law, then at the level of the rule of universalization. In my opinion, this latter must not lead to conflict, inasmuch as it only constitutes a criterion, a test, a touchstone for recognizing the morality of an intention and for distinguishing it from a disguised interest. The responsibility to which a loving obedience summons us, not only is not incompatible with this criterion, it requires it if it is to be reasonable and not simply emotional.

---

47. Marie Balmary, *Le sacrifice interdit. Freud et la Bible* (Paris: Grasset, 1986).
48. See O. Höffe, *Introduction à la philosophie pratique de Kant* (Albeur, Switzerland: Castelfa, 1985), chap. 4.

There remains the critical point in the definition of autonomy as self-sufficient. We may well doubt whether Kant succeeded in founding this principle upon itself. Did he not characterize our consciousness of the synthetic a priori judgment that makes law and freedom solidary with each other as a "fact of reason," which comes down to taking morality as something given?[49] Certainly this given is practical reason itself, in other words the practical capacity of reason. However, beyond the obscurity of the notion of a "fact of reason," we may inquire whether human freedom is not open to something beyond itself, an other, when it investigates this very capacity on the plane of individual consciences. Human being can surely be defined as a "capable subject"—a subject capable of speaking, of acting, of narrating, of allowing responsibility for its acts to be attributed to it. But is this capacity itself really simply available to us? Does not evil consist in a radical incapacity? This is what Kant himself says in his *Religion within the Limits of Reason Alone*.[50] In this work, reflection on religion gets underway by a meditation on radical evil and continues through an examination of the conditions for the regeneration of a moral subject. Does this come about through this subject's own powers or with help from elsewhere? Here is where the antinomy, expelled from moral philosophy, reappears in the philosophy of religion.[51] What little Kant concedes here to the idea of a gracious assistance suffices to prevent practical philosophy from forbidding any opening to the quite unique dialectic between autonomy and what is called, strictly on the plane of morality, heteronomy. Of course, the philosophy of religion is not the same as moral philosophy. But can we preserve an airtight bulkhead between an ethics that separates the principle of obligation from any consideration of the capacity of a human being to obey the law and religion which has no other object, according to Kant, than the regeneration of the moral subject; in other words, the restoration or, even better, the founding of a subject capable of acting as a moral subject?

The question now will be to consider whether an ethics of communication succeeds any better in founding upon itself the obligation for discussion and argumentation, which is held to remove the difficulties connected with the idea of a "fact of reason," or in giving a straightaway

49. See ibid., pp. 136ff.

50. Immanuel Kant, *Religion within the Limits of Reason Alone*, translated by Theodore M. Greene and Hoyt H. Hudson (New York: Harper Torchbooks, 1960). Cf. my essay, "A Philosophical Hermeneutics of Religion: Kant," in *Figuring the Sacred*, pp. 75–92.

51. See *Religion within the Limits of Reason Alone*, parts 2 and 3.

dialogical form to the criteria for universalizing any ethical maxim. The self-founding character of the ethics of discussion seems to me to proceed from a kind of *hubris* of practical reason, a *hubris* against which Kant was able to guard himself.[52] But, even if we assume that Karl-Otto Apel—who is more of a target here than Habermas, who is more preoccupied with the question of the force of attraction that the theory of morality and the social sciences exercise on each other—is successful in convincing skeptics of the solidity of his transcendental pragmatics, he, like Kant, still needs to take into account the capacity and the good will of any protagonists in a public discussion. It is at this level, that of motivation, of disposition (which German philosophers speak of as *Gesinnung*), rather than at the level of argumentation properly speaking, that I would like to try to articulate what I am calling loving obedience, which we can also call the willingness to enter into discussion, our access to a capacity for conversation. To put it in the form of a question: why finally discourse rather than violence, using Eric Weil's well-known opposition at the beginning of his *Logique de la Philosophie*?[53] The problem is said no longer to exist once protagonists decide to appeal in their conflicts only to the better argument. Once they have crossed the threshold of argumentation, they no longer will succumb to the objection of a "performative contradiction."

These last comments link up with those I made earlier: must not the ethics of communication accept the supraethical assistance of a love that obligates if it is to be able to hold firmly to the distinction that in the final analysis is most dear to it, that between communicative and instrumental or strategic reason? What is stronger than the love for the neighbor when it comes to preserving the gap between these two levels of practical reason?

To conclude, allow me to open one more area of discussion. All the phases of what I have said so far have tacitly assumed that human beings are the sole target of moral obligation. When I spoke of the pressure that love exercises on the commandment, in particular in the cases of the exception and of excess, did I not impose another kind of restriction that we might call the "humanist" one? Every human being, all human beings, I said, but only human beings. This "only" ratifies the legitimate demarcation that the *logos*/discourse traces between humans and other living creatures. In this respect, a discursive ethics, more than any other,

52. O. Höffe, *Kategorische Rechtsprinzipien. Ein Kontrapunkt der Moderne*, pp. 346ff.
53. Eric Weil, *Logique de la philosophie* (Paris: Vrin, 1950), pp. 54–86.

tends to make sense of the *logos* solely in terms of discourse. Indeed, this is true of most philosophers following the "linguistic turn." But then we find human beings separated from other living creatures and especially from other animals. Is there some way to preserve a certain tension between "only human beings" and "also all animals"? Clearly, these animals do not enter directly into the sphere of the ethics of argumentation. But do language, and more particularly discourse and argumentation, express the whole of what it means to be a human being? Does not what in human beings is not expressed by discourse find itself clearly on the side of the animal? A reflection more attentive to the connections between a theology of the law and a theology of creation may be one way to respond to these perplexities.[54] This connection has too often been disregarded by the kind of fascination exercised by the history of salvation and the conception of justification attached to it. However, if we reestablish the connection between the theology of the Law and that of Creation, does not human being first of all appear as the existence of one creature among others? And, in this regard, is not humanity the beneficiary of a divine solicitude that extends to the whole of creation? I am not unaware of the difficulties that any attempt to reduce redemption to a mere figure of creation will run into.[55] But does the contemplation of creation not invite us to grant a cosmic dimension to redemption?

No doubt, we cannot conclude immediately from this that the animal has its rights even though it cannot make them prevail in a trial-like situation where the antagonists all have an equal right to be heard. But we can at least draw the implication that human beings have a duty to animals. Are these duties without any corresponding rights? Yes, in fact it is this dissymmetry between rights and duties that the theme of Creation institutes and protects. What is more, there is an aesthetic element mixed in at this point with the ethical-religious element. The beauty of Creation calls for a specific reverence that cannot lack some influence on the relations between humans and other animals. Thus there is a time for saying "only human beings" and another for "the other animals, too." A specific form of solicitude is required here, which runs from the prohibition of cruelty to the search for a kind of friendly companionship. When applied to other animals, the commandment "thou shall not kill" can undoubtedly be interpreted in different ways:

54. Cf. Pierre Gisel, *La Création* (Geneva: Labor et Fides, 1987).
55. See, for example, our essays on Genesis 2–3 in this volume.

kill without inflicting unnecessary suffering, kill according to certain ritual forms, or not kill at all? Whatever the answer may be, if the love of neighbor can be of assistance to the exercise of justice, might not the love of a St. Francis for the birds not in return be of aid to our love for our neighbor, by adding to it reverence and admiration for creation? And did not Jesus speak of the lilies of the field as a model of a supra-ethical carefreeness?

These divagations may seem to carry us far from the rigor of the Law. But is it really so?

Ezekiel 37:1–14

From Death to Life

ANDRÉ LaCOCQUE

"L'honneur du Dieu d'Israël est le plus sûr gage de la résurrection du peuple élu."

Robert Martin-Achard[1]

A man of extremes, fiery, meticulous, sublime, vulgar, attracted by the baroque (17:1–10; 32:1–8), says Walther Eichrodt; Ezekiel's harsh judgment upon his contemporaries and their past history is balanced by a message of renewal in which the prophet exploits all the resources of a visionary poet, harbinger of the apocalyptic genre. The style of Ezekiel is easily recognizable. Indeed, one word characterizes his style and diction: surrealism. He goes into dazzling details in the report of his initial vision (chap. 1). "The same habit of mind appears," says Jon Levenson, "in Ezekiel's account of the trade of Tyre (Ezekiel 27:12–24), where the almost pedantic detail is enough to drive the most dedicated topographer and gemmologist to insanity."[2] An identical judgment applies to the prophet's description of Jerusalem's past sin (chaps. 8–11) and, *a fortiori*, of Jerusalem's restoration to come (chaps. 40–48). In his programmatic final nine chapters, he plays the role of a High Priest, although the title never comes under his pen. He also brings about the only piece of legislation in Israel not put in Moses' mouth, thus making him, as it were, a new Moses. Like his model, Ezekiel sees the land only from afar and is not allowed to settle there (cf. Numbers 27:12f.; Deuteronomy 32:49–52; 34:1–4). In Ezekiel 40–42 (the great Temple vision), the parallel is striking with Moses' vision of the Tabernacle in

---

1. Robert Martin-Achard, *De la mort à la résurrection d'après l'Ancien Testament* (Neuchâtel: Delachaux et Niestlé, 1956), pp. 82–83.

2. Jon Levenson, *Theology of the Program of Restoration of Ezekiel 40–48* (Missoula, MT: Scholars Press, 1976), p. 111.

Exodus. In short, the prophet is personally called to play an active part in the events he announces, either in action or in suffering. He is instrumental in reviving the dry bones in the chapter that we have selected.[3]

Ezekiel is prophet of the exiles, and he himself lives in Babylonia. Jerusalem, however, is the object of his oracles as the fate of the city constitutes the burning problem for those who find themselves uprooted in Babylon. Of particular importance are his visions of the Lord's *kabôd* (glory), which he first saw in the exile (1:1ff.), then a second time in Jerusalem (chaps. 8–11), specifically in the Temple, at that point going out from the city (11:22f.). Finally, the *kabôd* returns to the Temple "from the east" (43:1ff.). But, before this divine move occurs, the Temple as well as the city must be utterly destroyed; for God knows no earthly limitation, he is not bound even by the people Israel (chaps. 7; 9–11). God, therefore, is described by Ezekiel as leaving his Temple (11:2–23). There has been a total failure on the part of the people to fulfill its share of the Covenant (according to chap. 8, idolatry is rampant in the very Temple of God). Ezekiel uses repeatedly the terms "horror, abomination," 5:9–11; 6:9; 16:22, 52; 23, and he denounces the root of all this appalling situation as arrogance (16:49f.; 28:2, 5, 17; 32:12; etc.). If God were not to respond with chastisement and even perhaps with the utter rejection of his people, this would mean that his Name would be dishonored and remain unknown among all nations. Thus, in opposition to priestly assertions of the inviolability of the Temple and the irrevocability of the Covenant with Israel, Ezekiel, in the first half of his career, announces the removal of the one and the other.

Furthermore, the prophet contrasts the exiles with those who are left behind in the land (11:14–21; 33:23–29), a contrast that "opens the way for the renewal of life in Jerusalem and in the land of Israel through those who returned from exile."[4] The future salvation includes a new Temple, and to a certain extent a new people, the seeds of which are in exile and constitute a Remnant (cf. 5:3–4; 9:4–8; 14:22; 11:13 [*še'ērit*]; 12:16; 6:8–10 [verb]). They are called to develop independently of the former people. Falling in line with the prophet's active participation in the fulfillment of the proclaimed evolution of events, this development first takes place in the prophet's own house (8:1; 14:1; 20:1; 24:19; 33:30ff.), a possible indication of a Babylonian birth of the Synagogue.

---

3. I shall take up Ezekiel's active participation in the accomplishment of his own oracles below.

4. Rolf Rendtorff, *The Old Testament: An Introduction* (Philadelphia: Fortress Press, 1986), p. 210.

There, the prophet announces the breaking of the hereditary chain of guilt and punishment (see Ezekiel 33:10–20; cf. 18:4–20).

Ezekiel is conscious of proclaiming the dawn of a new understanding of God; God will make himself known as never before through his actions both in Israel and among the nations. So the knowledge that he is the Lord will be shared by one and all. Ezekiel frequently uses the expression, "And they shall know that I am Yhwh" (*Erkenntnisformel*), already familiar to us from the Deuteronomist and from the Priestly writing.[5] The knowledge of God is based on God's saving acts, like the exodus; but now Ezekiel creates a type of speech that Walther Zimmerli calls a "word of proof-of-identity." He says that this turn of style is "a matter of recognition of Yhwh and of his unique activity."[6] This "proof-saying" occurs in Ezekiel in three contexts:

> 1. The context of judgment against Israel; 7:2–4, for instance, speaks of the "end (impending) upon the four corners of the land." After the punishment, the text concludes "you will know that I am Yhwh."
>
> 2. The second context is one of judgment against nations; 25:3–5 (against Ammon), reads, "then you will know that I am Yhwh."
>
> 3. Finally, and most importantly for us here, a "proof-saying" closes the vision of the Dry Bones in chapter 37: "'you shall live and I will place you on your own soil; then you shall know that I, the Lord, have spoken and will act,' says the Lord."

Zimmerli rightly insists that such a proof-of-identity formula never appeals to human (intellectual) speculation or effort but always comes as a human recognition after divine action. Structurally, it never occurs in an isolated position but frequently as a conclusion. It is, says Zimmerli, "Yhwh's goal in all his actions." These actions are meant to bring about human (not exclusively Israelite) knowledge (cf. 20:26; 38:16).[7]

---

5. Out of the ninety-nine occurrences of the verb *yd'* in Ezekiel, fifty are accompanied by the *Erkenntnisformel*. In post-Ezekiel traditions, cf. Isaiah 43:10; 45:3, 6; 49:23.

6. Walther Zimmerli, *I Am Yahweh*, translated by Douglas W. Scott (Atlanta: John Knox, 1982), p. 31. See Ezekiel 14:23.

7. Ibid., pp. 36f. The recognition formula in Ezekiel ("You will know that I am YHWH" appears some seventy-two times) is first found in a profane context; see Genesis 42:34, "that I may know that you are not spies." Benjamin is the proof-sign, Genesis 42:33, *be-z'ot éda'*. We are in the "sphere of legal examination," as Zimmerli says (ibid., p. 37). The same applies to the recognition formula used about the prophet himself instead of God in 2:5 and 33:33, "They will know that a prophet has been in their midst."

As regards the Vision of the Dry Bones, it is therefore of utmost importance that we read the text, not only prospectively, from its beginning to its end, but also retrospectively, from its end—the recognition formula—to its beginning. In other words, Ezekiel 37:1–14 is to be read "teleologically," and reread "archaeologically." Only the second reading is illumined by the crucial realization that the "resurrection of the dead" finds its apex and its justification in Israel recognizing that the Living God is the Lord. Already at this point we can dismiss the idea that "resurrection" would have its own raison d'être in, or would be a concession to, the human aspiration not to fall into nothingness with one's death. The text starts and ends with the concern that God's Name be honored through the formal and existential recognition that, indeed, "I, the Lord, have spoken and will act." Ezekiel 37 is theocentric, not anthropocentric.

Another dimension of Ezekiel 37 is its eschatological character. Beginning with chapter 33, Ezekiel has changed his tune. Before that *terminus,* he was adamant about the utter destruction of a people and a land that did not respect the terms of the Covenant. Once this destruction did occur (cf. 33:21ff.), however, he started preaching with a comparable radicalness the advent of a new covenant and of salvation. At the heart of that new message, Ezekiel 36:16–38 clearly corresponds to Jeremiah's eschatological oracle in 31:31–33. Ezekiel then introduces a typology—the term is here somewhat improper as we shall see—based on the exodus pattern. As the first exodus from Egypt was immediately followed by a period of wandering in the wilderness, so too must be the case for the second exodus. This goes, however, far beyond a mere repetition of the type. The necessity of a second exodus is due to the failure of the first one. History is not repeating itself with only a change in scenery from Egypt to Babylon. Ezekiel does not share the concept of the "eternal return" of time. According to that cyclical cadence, the golden age evolves inevitably toward the iron age, before turning again into a new golden age with the same further prospect of progressive degradation. But Ezekiel is not promoting this Hesiodic conception. In his opinion, already the first generation of Israelites who received the commandments readily transgressed them; the second generation (20:18–26) heard Yhwh swearing to drive the people into exile even before they entered the land. Repeatedly, in chapters 16, 20, 23, the prophet describes the sin of Israel starting already in Egypt,[8] from

---

8. Probably finding confirmation in a text like Joshua 24:14.

which point it was, as it were, transmitted from generation to generation. In fact, the whole of Israel's history is a series of increasingly sinful periods (20:4, 18, 24, 27, 30, 36, 42): such a patterning of Israel's backsliding announces the apocalyptic "periodization" of universal history as we find it in Daniel and elsewhere. Israel itself is characterized as "a rebellious house" (2:5) and Jerusalem as "the bloody city" (24:9). As a nation it is entirely guilty (16; 22:23ff; 23; etc.), so that Ezekiel envisages that only individuals will escape the collective judgment (9:4; 33:1–9). Even God's giving the Torah did not prevent the people from rebelling (20:13a). A second giving of the Law happened at the end of the wilderness period (20:18f.), to no avail. At that time, God decided to scatter Israel among nations (20:13), so that the exile in Babylon is the historical fulfillment of such an early divine resolve, and the settlement in the Land "was an irrelevant exercise," says Ralph Klein; its mention occupies only three verses in chapter 20 where they denounce a rampant idolatry.[9] The conquest of Canaan occurred only thanks to God's oath given earlier to the Ancestors (20:42). The whole of Israel's history, therefore, comes to its forecast determination in Babylon. Being born already crippled in Egypt, Israel dies in Babylon. All seems to be said with this finding, and the prophet can only conclude that the "valley" of their dereliction is filled with dry bones.

The exiles are metaphorically dry bones, as they themselves recognize (see the discussion of 37:14 below; cf. Lamentations 3:52–55; Isaiah 66:14; Job 21:24; in Ezekiel, see 24:1–14).[10] But death did not just occur unexpectedly in exile; Israel was moribund much earlier. In other words, and again in a preapocalyptic spirit, history is declared a total failure. Even the Torah, meant to make the people holy (20:12, 20) is interspersed with "laws that are not good" (20:25–26). The *Heilsgeschichte* is only a dream expressed in three verses, as we saw above (20:28–29). There is no hope that human achievement will ever redeem a history that, since its inception, brings humanity steadily closer to death in the image of existence itself. The end (the *telos*, the finality) of all this is "dry bones."

Thus the vision of Ezekiel 37 does not take us to the scene of an historical accident. The description of dry bones sweeps the whole of history; the latter is shown for what it actually is: sterile, meaningless,

9. Ralph W. Klein, *Ezekiel: The Prophet and His Message* (Columbia: University of South Carolina Press, 1988), p. 77.

10. The metaphor of desiccated bones occurs in poetry, cf. Isaiah 66:14; Job 21:24. Again, we hear an echo of Jeremiah's preaching (8:1–2).

absurd. What Israel has called history was from its beginning no-history. In this respect, Ezekiel is unique among the prophets. His pessimistic judgment is radical and unswerving. But his message is all the same consistent with the iconoclastic declaration of one of his predecessors, Hosea, declaring that Israel is *lo-'ammi* and *lo-ruḥamah* (Hosea 1:6, 9). It is echoed by a later prophet's declaration that Jerusalem is called "Forsaken" and "Desolate" (Isaiah 62:4). The last word like the first is nothingness, "vanity," a fleeting breath on a cold morning. True, exile brings vision; exile (*galut*) brings revelation (*galah*, see Ezekiel 13:14; cf. Daniel 2:12, and esp. Lamentations 4:22), the vision and revelation of an existence leading to death.

That is why "the Israelites have to go through the whole process again," as says Joseph Blenkinsopp.[11] They will be taken from the country of their exile and led through the "wilderness of the peoples" to the Land. In that new experience of the desert, Ezekiel 40ff. appears as prospectively describing a new Sinai, after a new exodus.

Ezekiel presents us with a new formation of Israel, not a resumption of the past. Chapter 37's imagery must be taken in all seriousness when it describes the nation as long dead, so long indeed that the bones are dry and about to turn to dust, that is, to the preformal, as if the long past had been for nought.[12] In the wake of the first part of his book (chaps. 1–32), Ezekiel does not begin chapter 37 with good news. The death of the nation in Babylon is no mere chastisement; the exile is no eclipse, no parenthetical time, no transient night before morning comes, and still less the feigned decease of an initiate. The exile is no sleep; it is death, death without morrow. That is why the sixth-century "prophets" who proclaimed "peace" were false prophets; they were guilty of reductionism: the exile in Babylon in their eyes was a mere episode, a historical mishap perhaps, or, using a linguistic trope, a rite of initiation (cf. the term *galah* which is open to such an optimistic interpretation). In that way, the tragic aspect of existence is denied. Religion itself is used as a bashful veiling of the obscene nakedness of life (cf. 13:21–23). "Here is the Temple, the Temple, the Temple!" they cry (cf. Jeremiah 7:4). False prophecy often is sheer demagoguery and self-delusion, a "denial of death" that paradoxically brings about death.

---

11. Joseph Blenkinsopp, *Ezekiel* (Louisville: John Knox, 1990), p. 91.

12. Note the agreement of Ezekiel with Jeremiah. The latter also proclaimed the cancellation of the Ancestors' history (cf. 23:7f.; 31:32, 31). See also the parallel between the two prophets on the restoration of the Davidic dynasty (Ezekiel 34:23f. [depending on Jeremiah 23:1–8]; Ezekiel 37:24, 25 and Jeremiah 23:5; 33:14f.; 30:8–9).

In Ezekiel 37, the prophet reverses the proposition. If the denial of death is the best way to grant it full sway, what will obtain from its acknowledgment as the finality of existence and of history? Nothing perhaps but the procurement of a space for hope. Where death is denied, there can be no room for a hope beyond meaninglessness. But where death is confronted face to face, the possibility is left open that the absoluteness of chaos might be transcended by the creative Word of the Beginning, which is also the Word of the End. The backdrop is constituted by the correspondence of *Endzeit* with *Urzeit*. The "dry bones" are another way of speaking of the primeval *tohu wa-bohu* of Genesis 1:2; and their revivification is hailed by Ezekiel as paradise recovered (chapter 47). The *tohu* is insufflated with the Spirit hovering over it, and the *bohu* becomes creation. In parallel to this, the dry bones are filled with the Spirit of life and they become a vast living multitude; the seed brings up the ear of wheat.[13]

Let us note, at this point, that the theme of the New Creation—which would be subsequently greatly expanded by Second Isaiah, Ezekiel's successor (cf. Isaiah 41:18; 51:3, 9–11)—is sketched in verse 14 and further developed in the sequel to our passage, verses 23–28. Also in Second Isaiah, the "return to the beginning" remains a historical phenomenon. In both Ezekiel and Second Isaiah, therefore, it is a new age after a period of history is over. In short, Second Isaiah shares with Ezekiel the "sense of an ending." Both see Creation as salvation; both see salvation transcending Israel's history and spilling over to benefit the whole of creation. After a universal desolation comes a universal restoration embracing the entire cosmos.

Meanwhile, the scandal and folly of recognizing that the bones are dry is a necessity before "perhaps" (cf. Jonah 3:9) they can be given the possibility of joining together and therefore be living again. It is for Ezekiel the *conditio sine qua non* of the new Israel's birth. It is the same

---

13. This point must be emphasized. Ezekiel 37, and the Ezekielian worldview in general, constitutes the seedbed of forthcoming apocalypticism. Ezekiel himself remains, however, within the historical register: the return to "chaos" is not mythological as it will be in Jewish apocalypse. The formal distinction between these two returns to chaos, the one historical and the other mythological, confirms J. Lindblom's assertion in *Die Jesaja-Apokalypse, Jes. 24–27* (Lund: Gleerup, 1938), p. 103, that "Eschatologisches hat es mit dem sachlichen Inhalt, nicht mit der Form und der Ursprung zu tun." At times, both conceptions are found side by side; so in Isaiah 27:1 and context; or with the "transferal of a mythological theme into the realm of the historical" in Isaiah 25:6–10a, as says Wallace March, "A Study of Two Prophetic Compositions in Isaiah 24.1–27.1," Th.D. Dissertation (Union Theological Seminary, 1966), p. 110, quoted by William R. Millar, *Isaiah 24–27 and the Origin of Apocalyptic* (Missoula, MT: Scholars Press, 1976), p. 14.

scandal and the same folly that obtained with the destruction of the Jerusalem Temple that are the condition for the latter to be at last erected in a city whose name is "Yhwh is There" (48:35). It is after it has been deprived of the divine presence altogether when God left the place (cp. Ezekiel 11:13 and 43:1–3) that it can fulfill its vocation. The old age must be buried in the grave of spiritlessness. The dead must bury their dead. False prophecy, as exemplified by Ezekiel's "colleagues," often is the result of fearful rejection of the dialectical.

Thus, the vision of the Prophet is about creation, not about the end of a period of testing. "Could these bones live?" is no rhetorical question; and Ezekiel's answer, "Lord God, (only) you know" is no perfunctory *Hofstil*. There is no way these bones could revive. They have never been really alive in the first place. Furthermore, God's question does not necessarily raise the problem of feasibility; "can those bones live?" is a common translation, but the text simply asks whether those bones *will* live. And the main verb in 37:3 may be translated by "be alive" rather than "be revived," as there is here no mention whatsoever of their previous existence. At any rate, if God's question really expects an answer, it should be a negative one: "No, Lord, those bones are returning to the dust from where they came. They illustrate the fundamental saying, 'you are dust and to dust you shall return.'" Ezekiel, though, raises himself to the level of faith and trust, and his response is an ultimate sign of deference, owing to the fact that God must have something in store if he evokes the impossible possibility that the very index of death become promise of life.[14] God's question amounts to asking, before the creation of the universe, whether a universe can come into existence at all. It is highly improbable, it is beyond all imagination, it is impossible. Until Creation makes of the impossible a reality, and *a posteriori*, makes the absence of the universe unimaginable. The divine question to the "mortal" ("son of man") Ezekiel touches him at the very nexus of this double impossibility: that those dry bones would live at all once more; that those dry bones would remain forever lifeless. Ezekiel wisely responds, you only, Lord, can untie the Gordian knot; "Lord God, (only) you know."

The rest of the vision will show that those bones, as dry as they may be, can indeed live. But, before we turn to that phase in the narrative, it has to be stressed that it is only through death that another people,

14. Cf. the commentary in the *Metsudot* in *Mikraoth Gedoloth*, vol. 2 (Warsaw, 1862) and Ezekiel 37:3: "Only you know whether it is your will that they should live."

an eschatological people, can be born. At their head will be a David-like Prince of Peace rendering harmless all the forces threatening life, even the wild beasts (34:24ff.). But there again, the term "David-like," although correct, must be taken cautiously. There is no word of a repetition of former events, of anything "déjà vu." True, the office envisaged by Ezekiel is in continuing fulfillment of the promise to David, and Ezekiel's term *nasi'* designates the Davidic head of state (7:27; 12:10, 12; 19:1; 21:30; 34:24, perhaps also 21:17; 22:6). But now the *nasi'*, the prince, that Ezekiel prefers to *melekh*, king, is in the words of Jon Levenson the "designation of a messianic individual shorn of the structural temptations to commit abuses. . . . [A title] severed from its politico-mythological matrix."[15] Ezekiel's "David" is more the messianic David than the historical David ever was. He is not just *David redivivus*, but he is, we may venture, a David made alive from the dry bones he used to be. David-the-dry-bones is such not just because he died some four hundred years earlier, but because historically he never went beyond that "skeleton" stage of the one he some time would become.

Space does not allow for a further development of this crucial point in the theology of Ezekiel. But it must be emphasized that what the prophet announces is not a restoration, but the eventual beginning at last of the *Heilsgeschichte*. In the prophet's judgment, there have only been attempts so far at fulfilling the divine promise. But all these attempts sunk into nothingness with the exile in Babylon. Now is the time for a new Creation, a new Covenant, a new David, a new Zion, a new Temple, a new liturgy. Even the Torah must be replaced by a new Torah. Ezekiel is definitely closer to apocalyptic than has been often conceded. The radicalness of the newness of time testifies to this. If, however, the book of Ezekiel cannot be ranged among the full-fledged apocalypses, it is because the prophet expects *history* to start for good with the return from exile. When the hope of Ezekiel for a transfigured relationship between God and Israel and/or God and humanity remained largely unfulfilled, then prophecy shifted to apocalyptic.

This point deserves fuller consideration, but let us first note that Ezekiel 37 is one of the four major visions in the book (the other three are: chapters 1-3 = vocation; chapters 8-11 = vision of judgment; chapters 40-48 = the new Jerusalem). All four visions are introduced by the phrase, "The hand of Yhwh was on me" (1:3; 3:14, 22; 8:1; 37:1; 40:1, for a total of six times in the book), which belongs to the *word-*

---

15. Levenson, *Theology of the Program*, p. 67.

event formula, as Zimmerli says (cf. "then the word of Yhwh came to me," 1:3; 3:16; 6:1; 7:1; etc.).[16] The hand of God pulls Ezekiel, so to speak, from one location to another,[17] that is, to the same location as in the first vision (3:22–27). There the *biq'ah* (valley) signified absence of prophetic inspiration and spelled out death. Similarly, the second vision in the valley (8:1, 4) heralded the destruction of the Temple. The third occurrence, in Ezekiel 37, although not bewailing the absence of prophetic inspiration or of the Temple, belongs again to the symbolism of the below, the netherworld, the dwelling of the dead, the place of chaos.[18] In the inaugural vision, Ezekiel was commanded to preach to the obtuse (2:3ff.), but now even to the dead.[19] This rhetorical progression in the negative betrays Ezekiel's sense of history's increased regression, another parallel with the apocalyptic conviction that the bottom must be reached before the new divine dispensation starts. The inner logic of the book dictated that the bones be in the valley (cf. also 3:22, 23; 8:4; a topographical-symbolic designation of Babylon, perhaps on the model of Genesis 11:2), and that the "Restoration" occur on the "lofty mountain of Israel" (cf. 40:2, 23; 34:14, that is, on Mt. Zion— seen as a cosmic mountain).[20] The tension between those two extremes, of the plain as the scene of condemnation and of the mountain as the scene of forgiveness, illustrates the dialectical relation, particularly well developed by Claus Westermann, between judgment and salvation. The judgment, says Westermann, is a necessary ingredient of the history between God and Israel. Thus, it is already inserted within the ancestral history of salvation in the Pentateuch, with the episode of the Golden Calf, Exodus 32–34. When it is again exercised with the exile, it is not yet the Final Judgment, but its inclusion between the initial salvation and the final redemption is noteworthy. The actual judgment comes after the prophecy of salvation; but, rhetorically, judgment and punish-

16. Also in Isaiah 8:11; Jeremiah 15:17; cf. Elijah, 1 Kings 18:46; Elisha, 2 Kings 3:15.

17. Translocation of the prophet: cf. 3:14; 8:3; 11:1, 24; 43:5. Roots in Elijah's story: 1 Kings 18:12; 2 Kings 2:16. In both cases, the idea, as Rashi emphasized, is of violence. Ezekiel is taken by force, "as though he were in a trance" (Commentary on Ezekiel 1:2).

18. Already Redaq identifies the valley in Ezekiel 37 with the one of 3:22. Ernst Haag thinks of a contrast between the Mesopotamian plain and Israel's mountains. Symbolically the plain is the place of the exile as a whole (cf. Ezekiel 3:22). See Ernst Haag, "Ezekiel 37 und der Glaube an die Auferstehung der Toten," *Trierer Theologische Zeitschrift* 82 (1973): 78–92; see p. 80.

19. On this, see Blenkinsopp, *Ezekiel*, pp. 155ff.

20. For Julian Morgenstern, the valley is located at the foot of the Mount of Olives where the resurrection traditionally takes place; cf. Zechariah 14:4f. and the Dura Europos paintings. "The King-God among the Western Semites and the Meaning of Epiphanes," *Vetus Testamentum* 10 (1960): 181.

ment are first meted out, and then a prophecy of salvation takes place that does not remove the former announcement of judgment. The divine compassion permeates the whole, for "God keeps it back until after the judgment when it blazes new paths."[21]

The compassion shown after the exile recalls the compassion expressed before the exodus from Egypt (cf. Exodus 2:24f.), but the two moves are to be distinguished since the former is predicated by forgiveness, which restores the broken communion. For Ezekiel, in contrast, the exile in Babylon is not inscribed within the process of redemption, as the exodus was according to Pentateuchal traditions. Exile is a breach, the interruption of history. However, Ezekiel 37 is paradoxically inserted between the announcement of the new Covenant with God and its gracious gift of a new heart, on the one hand (36:26ff.), and the resurrection of the dead Israel, on the other. For such is the compassion of God that it need no precondition. Its ground is not a positive attitude on the part of the recipients.

Above, it has been stressed that the vision of the Dry Bones is first a radical word of judgment upon a people that is dead, utterly dead. No hope is entertained that they could be revived, whether through a reform movement, through amending their ways, or through repentance. Hence, I said, the prophet sees in a vision the birth of a new people. Death blossoms into life; the index of death becomes the index of life. It is now time to emphasize the other side of the complex reality brought about by Ezekiel 37. The new people with a new heart about to return to a new land graced by a new Temple—is *Israel*. The old Israel is dead in the exile, but the new Israel is none else but the people of divine election since the beginning, the people under the promise made to the Ancestors of old. There is here no clue to any "supersessionism." No community takes the place reserved by God to Abraham's children. As Ernst Haag puts it, the question addressed to the prophet in verse 3, concerns less the divine capacity to revive dry bones than the issue of whether the God who committed himself to his people by electing them is giving up on his people or whether he is to give them life anew.[22] For none other than the Israelites dead and buried in exile does the summoning of the Spirit by the prophet change the minus sign before death into its opposite. "Would those bones live?" is not first a question of divine power, it is a question of justice. Will the sense of

21. Claus Westermann, *Theologie des Alten Testaments* (Göttingen: Vandenhoeck & Ruprecht, 1978), Part iv, B "The Divine Compassion."

22. Haag, "Ezekiel 37 und der Glaube," p. 84.

death be changed from being the outcome of sin to becoming an *ada-mah* for a new *adam* (a fertile earth for a new earthling)? Can the dry bones be interpreted in any other way than as the ultimate condemnation of the culprit? Can they be the sign of unjust suffering? The identity of the dead makes all the difference here; but also and above all the identity of the One who raises the question. By letting the elect stay in the grave, God's Name is exposed to profanation. There will be no witness any more in the world of the divine glory. The world will be deprived of the divine presence, becoming a creation without Creator! With the defeat of Israel, God is the great loser. We could even say that the dead bone Israel then has drawn God into the grave with it. That is why, reflecting on Christ's death, the Apostle Peter exclaims, "God raised him up, having freed him from death, because it was impossible (*ouk ên dunaton*) for him to be held in its power" (Acts 2:24). Ezekiel 37 concludes to the same impossibility as concerns "the whole house of Israel."

In one case as in the other, furthermore, the particular care of God for his own people is, paradoxically, the guarantee of its universality. Death has here nothing to do with annihilation. Israel alive in Jerusalem, or Israel dead in Babylon, is still Israel. If indeed from Zion comes the Torah and from Jerusalem the Word of God, then *sub specie universi*, from the compost of dead Israel spring still hope and life for the rest of the world.[23] That is why the imagery and the vocabulary of Ezekiel's vision are so closely akin with the texts of the creation of humanity. The connection between Resurrection and Creation (and also the miracle of generation) is perhaps nowhere better expressed than in a later text, namely, 2 Maccabees 7:23, where the mother says to her sons about to be tortured to death:

> The Creator of the world, who shaped the beginning of humankind and devised the origin of all things, wi'l in his mercy give life and breath back to you again . . .

The resurrection of Israel in the *biq'ah* spells out the universal return to life. The *ruaḥ* blows from the four corners of the world, thus stressing the cosmic dimension of the event.[24] There is, as it were, a universal concentration of energy "in the middle of the valley [where] there are very many bones lying . . . and they are very dry." It is the same *ruaḥ* as

---

23. As says St. Paul, "neither life nor death can separate us from the love of God . . ."
24. The reverse of Ezekiel 7:2–3.

in Genesis 2:7; Psalm 104:29f.; Job 34:14; Ecclesiastes 12:9. It corresponds to the *nepheš ḥayyah* of Genesis 2:7, which God breathes into the nostrils of the human formed from the dust of the ground. But as this wind comes from everywhere simultaneously in Ezekiel 37:8–9, the *ruaḥ* in question pervades the whole world.[25] Between the first part of the vision and the second, there has been an evolution in the identification of the *ruaḥ* from wind/breath to Spirit/breath, and from a cosmic occurrence to a personalized event (verse 14, see Ezekiel 36:27). This serves the prophet's purpose to show that the old history is not simply resumed. The text, therefore, says Haag ("Ezekiel 37 und der Glaube," p. 84), becomes *pre-eschatological*, although still *undifferenziert* (p. 91).

It is also, surprisingly enough, from a universal earthly perspective that we must examine the theme stressed in verse 12, which reads, "I will bring you back to the Land of Israel." This motif is strikingly emphasized in verse 14, where the prophet draws a parallel between being reanimated, "I will put my spirit within you and you shall live," and being resettled in the land, "I will place you on your own soil." It is a "new" people starting a "new" history in relation to God, marked by a vivifying relationship with the Land. Ontologically each term of the proposition remains what it used to be (spirit, land, soil, people, history), but existentially all terms have changed. Few books in the Bible insist as much as Ezekiel does on the central importance of the land. God dwells in the land (7:7; cf. 45:1; Isaiah 8:18), which is his own possession and he gives it to whom he pleases (11:5; 20:15), namely, to Israel's Ancestors (36:28; 47:14). Such a gift is no superfluity. From the beginning, as is demonstrated in the Patriarchal sagas, the land is the people's salvation from extinction, from nonexistence. In other words, the land is the *conditio sine qua non* for Israel's creation.[26] Already here, as developed later in Second Isaiah, the tie between history and geography is obvious, as is also the tie between Salvation and Creation.

The motif of the Dry Bones took us to the antipode of *Eretz*, the Land. For the Land is symbolically the locus of life and of "moisture" (cf. Genesis 2:5–7), whereas what lay outside the confines of the *Eretz*

---

25. Walther Zimmerli, *Ezekiel 2: A Commentary on the Book of the Prophet Ezekiel, Chapters 25–48* (Philadelphia: Fortress Press, 1979), p. 261. This conception, Haag notes ("Ezekiel 37 und der Glaube," p. 82), is of the divine spirit permeating Creation, thus giving it life and sustaining it; death is the withdrawal by God of his spirit. It is "intimately associated with God's breath of Genesis 2:7." (Note the presence here and there of the Hebrew verb *npš*). Christopher R. Seitz writes, "The biological reality is inherently a theological reality" ("Ezekiel 37:1–14," *Interpretation* 46 [1992]: 53).

26. As the land/soil is also necessary for the creation of humanity, according to Genesis 2:5, 7.

is the place of chaos, desiccation, and death. Ezekiel insists on the dryness of the bones, because, according to the ancient Near East mentality, as long as what looks dead is "moist," it still can constitute the seedbed for life, the earth being at that point like the uterus with its amniotic fluid. Archaic man saw the womb as a seat of darkness and chaos as well as a source of "sheer profuse abundance." At the other extreme, in the netherworld, the myth signals waters that may revive the dead. But Ezekiel leaves no ambiguity as regards the situation of the people in exile: they are dry as dust.[27] No life can possibly spring from them. If there is any reminiscence of Canaanite mythology in Ezekiel 37, it is mainly of the contrast between Moth (as in Isaiah 25:8) and Yamm.

This, by the way, may be of importance when one reflects on the conspicuous absence in Ezekiel 37 of the notion of impurity through contact with the dead. The prophet-priest is "set down in the midst of the valley full of bones" (37:1) and he is "led all around them" (v. 2 NRSV), but he does not even mention their contaminating impurity to the great surprise of students of the chapter. Jewish exegetical tradition, evidently aware of the problem, insists on the expression "all around" of verse 2: God led the prophet around, not through, the valley and among the bones, says Rashi.[28] Modern readers would concur with Redaq when he argues that Ezekiel 37 is a prophetic vision, not an actual occurrence. As Christopher R. Seitz says, the chapter blurs "the distinction between metaphor and reality . . . [but is] in reality a metaphor. [Dead] Israel speaks," etc.[29]

But let us return to the relation between land and life as we find it

---

27. Haag says, "das grosse Sterben."

28. The translation by the NRSV of 37:2 "around them" fits that understanding; but not the French text of the *TOB* which reads "parmi eux en tous sens."

29. Seitz, "Ezekiel 37:1–14," p. 54. He adds, "What remains, remains only to testify to all that is lost" (p. 55). Besides, the later Jewish distinction between what is impure and what is pure does not necessarily correspond in detail to the situation prevailing at the time of Ezekiel. In this respect, it may be suggested that what makes impure in the Bible is the liminal state between the "positive" and the "negative," so to speak. When leprosy has contaminated the whole body, for instance, the person is pure again (Leviticus 13:13); the same is true, of course, of someone who is cleansed from his/her skin disease (Leviticus 14, esp. v. 20; Matthew 11:5). "Dry bones" unambiguously belong to only one state. Another analogy can be found in the consumption of dry foodstuffs, which are *kašer*. The absence of moisture has canceled any ambiguity in the produce, as it were. By the same token, a corpse might have been considered as making impure (see Leviticus 5:2; 11:39; Numbers 19:11ff.; 31:19), but not dry bones. In that respect, the ashes of the burnt Red Cow (Numbers 19) not only do not make impure, but they purify anyone who has touched a dead body (Numbers 19:11ff.; see *Numbers Rabba*, Hukkat, 19:8). What precedes is, of course, purely speculative on my part.

once again stressed by Ezekiel 37:12, 14. Such a bond is not due to an intrinsic quality of the land of Israel. For, when considered from the point of view of its nature, the land used to belong to Canaanites and other impure and undeserving peoples (Ezekiel 16). If Eretz Israel becomes "the glory of all lands" (Ezekiel 20:6, 15; cf. 26:20), if it can be described as situated at "the navel of the earth" in 38:12 (cf. Judges 9:37), with Jerusalem "set in the midst of the nations" (5:5), it is owing to the divine presence there, signified by the Temple in Zion and manifested by Israel's presence in the Land. Now, in Ezekiel, the promise to the new people resettled in the Land is expressed in 37:25ff. In a striking concatenation, "they shall live in the land . . ."; "I will make a covenant of peace with them . . ."; "my dwelling place shall be with them; and I will be their God and they shall be my people"; "my sanctuary will be among them forevermore."

"The Holy Land" is a dialectic reality. Forever, the Land remains a Promised Land. For it is the event of the encounter that makes the land holy. In the image of the ground on which Moses was standing in Midian and which had no quality of its own before God started to speak, saying to Moses, "Remove your sandals from your feet for the ground on which you are standing is [now] holy" (Exodus 3:5); on that model, Eretz Israel *is* holy by divine choice and *becomes* holy by the synergetic action of God and People. Zion becomes the center of the world *because* of the events that happen there.[30] That is why Ezekiel dedicates one-fifth of his writings to the restoration of the Land after the exile (chaps. 40–48). The oversized description of the coming Jerusalem obviously takes us beyond a mere "restoration." The vision of the prophet is properly eschatological. The Land is transformed, but "such as in itself eternity transforms it," as Mallarmé would put it. For the Land has always been actualization of the *eschaton*. The first entry into the Land was for the people *menuḥah*, rest (Deuteronomy 12:9; 25:19; 28:65), and the final return to the Land inaugurates the ultimate *menuḥah* (Ezekiel 44:30, "that a blessing may rest on your house"; cf. Isaiah 11:2, "The Spirit of the Lord shall rest on him . . .").

With the exception of Jerome, early Christian and Rabbinic com-

---

30. Of course, numerous other places in the world have been claimed as central by different religious traditions. Even immense expanses of lands have been self-proclaimed as "the Middle Kingdom." What makes Israel's claim for Jerusalem outstanding is that there is here no calling to an intrinsic or naturally endowed quality of a land that, besides, used to belong to seven or more Canaanite nations, but rather to the central, the foundational quality of the history of the encounter between God and his people there.

mentators alike found in Ezekiel 37 a warrant for the belief in resurrection of the dead. So did also the artists who painted the walls of the Dura-Europos synagogue (between 245 and 256 CE).[31] But was individual resurrection already known to the prophet and his contemporaries? We must first stress that Ezekiel (like Job 14:14) knows nothing of a general eschatological resurrection of the dead. As Walther Zimmerli notes, in our text we are dealing with a unique event that concerns the people of Israel in exile. But, on the other hand, the notion itself of resurrection was hardly unknown in Israel, if only in terms of the seasonal revival of divinities among Israel's neighbors.[32] Beyond the possible recourse to foreign influence, the stories of individual revivification told by the prophets Elijah and Elisha demonstrate that the notion in earlier biblical texts need not be dubbed "Canaanite."

We must make a sharper distinction than has generally been made in the past between revivification and (final) resurrection. Revivals do occur in the Hebrew Scripture and this concept never died out completely. Not only are there such returns to life in the New Testament, as well as in Jewish and Christian hagiographies, but the matter continues to fascinate our contemporaries, as a recent symposium (1991) at the University of Chicago testifies. (Final) resurrection offers parallels with revivification, but the resemblance between the two is more external than substantial. In the latter case, it is a question of a divine reprieve granted to a (deserving) individual. Besides the already-mentioned cases in the time of Elijah and Elisha, reference should be made to King Hezekiah (Isaiah 38:5; 2 Kings 20:6). In contradistinction to this, the idea of a final resurrection is a late development in Israel. It is highly probable that it originated there under Iranian influence after the return from Exile, when Judea was under Persian suzerainty.[33]

31. Harald Riesenfeld calls attention to a Jewish tradition according to which the vision of the prophet Ezekiel occurred in the valley of *Dura,* cf. *Pirke de Rabin Eliezer* (= *PRE*) xxxii (G. Friedlander, p. 249); *Targum Exodus* 13:17. Note here the addition in some manuscripts of the mention: "YHWH revealed to Ezekiel . . . that he was destined to raise the dead." H. Riesenfeld, *The Resurrection in* Ezekiel *xxxvii and in the Dura Europos Paintings* (Uppsala: A.-R. Lundequistska Bokhandel, 1948). "The valley of Dura" is also mentioned in Daniel 3:1, but it is not Dura on the Euphrates.

32. One thinks of a text like Hosea 6:2 that is used, somewhat surprisingly, in later Christian traditions, from the time of Tertullian, as a prophetic attestation to the resurrection of Christ.

33. Albeit, as says Theodore Gaster in his article on "Resurrection" in the *Interpreter's Dictionary of the Bible* (New York: Abington, 1962), vol. 4—which incidentally does not mention Ezekiel 37—the foreign influence on the idea of resurrection in Israel may also come from other quarters. Egypt and Mesopotamia must be mentioned. But "similar ideas always obtained among the Greeks (cf. *Iliad* III.278–79; XIX.259; Aeschylus, *Eumenides* 267ff.; *Supplices* 414ff.; Democritus,

With Ezekiel 37, we reach a point of transition, not only chronologically but ideologically. The Vision of the Dry Bones is a most interesting phase in the doctrine of resurrection because it links the notion's past and future. On the one hand, the resurrection envisaged by the prophet is a temporary one.[34] The scene in chapter 37, as I said above, is not apocalyptic. It does not describe the end of history but its revival, or even its "beginning"—it is Genesis 1–2 *redivivum*! But, on the other hand, by virtue of its collective, historical, and theological dimensions, Ezekiel 37's vision is not about divine reprieve. The scope is now much broader. Not an individual but the people; not a "lengthening" of past history but the beginning of *Heilsgeschichte;* not a grant entirely centered on the human beneficiary but an operation to "rescue" God's Name within history. Here resurrection is a feat that belongs to eschatology, to *prophetic* eschatology.[35]

The next step in the evolution of the notion takes us to Daniel 12. The differences with Ezekiel 37 are considerable. Here the focus is clearly on human destiny, more specifically on the fate of the righteous after death. The vantage point of the visionary is still *sub specie Dei gloriae,* that is, here also resurrection belongs to theodicy, but the category of beneficiaries is situated between the individuals of Elijah's and Elisha's stories, on the one hand, and the crowd of Ezekiel 37, on the other hand. They are the just, the martyrs, the *maskilim* and *maḥdiqim* of the end-time. Furthermore, their resurrection is not a reprieve but

---

Frgmts 199, 297; Plato *Phaedrus* 248f; *Gorgias* 523; *Laws* IX.870; *Phaedo* 112e) and might thus have reached the Jews of the Hellenistic period from other than oriental sources" (ibid., p. 43).

34. Rabbi Moshe Eisemann, *Yechezkel: The Book of Ezekiel* (New York: Mesorah Publishing, 1988), p. 570, asks: "What happened to the people who were resurrected by Yechezkel? Three opinions are recorded in *Sanhedrin* 92b: Rabbi Eleazar said, '[They] stood up on their feet, said *širah,* [a song of jubilation to God] and immediately died.'—Rabbi Yose HaGallili said, '[They] went up to the Land of Israel, married, and bore children.' . . .—Rabbi Yehudah said, 'Truly the whole episode was a parable.' . . . [The] *Maharal* (*Hiddushei Aggadah* there) explains: The sole purpose of the resurrection was to demonstrate God's power. To accomplish this it was sufficient that they live for a short time only. . . . God sent a *niṣoṣ, spark,* of the true *teḥiat ha-mêtim,* resurrection, which will one day take place. . . . These people . . . said *širah,* thereby fulfilling the purpose of their creation." Interestingly enough, some early Christian texts also saw in the Ezekiel 37 revitalization a phenomenon of "former resurrection," that is, the return to life of the dead during the Messianic millennium (cf. Justin, *Dial.* 80,5; Methodius of Olympia, *Conv.* ix, 5, 253–55) presumably before returning to death and waiting for the final resurrection; see note 35.

35. Being a *mašal,* Ezekiel 37 is a parable of the ultimate redemption, albeit speaking of a temporal resurrection as we saw above. Because of the dual quality of that prophecy, Justin, for example, who gave in his *Dialogue* a millennialist interpretation of Ezekiel 37 (see note 34), sees however in *I Apology* the same text announcing the final resurrection (lii, 3–5; see also with the same understanding Cyprian, *Didasc.* v, 7, 5).

ultimate; history ends here. In other words, while Ezekiel 37 is theocentric and nonspeculative as regards the individual fate after death, Daniel 12 stands between the theocentric and the anthropocentric. It addresses the issue of justice for those who did not die on account of their sins but on account of their faith. Therefore their sacrifice must be compensated with eternal reward. Clearly, the focus shifts and the way is open toward doctrines of partial or general resurrection at the end-time.

Still another text comes under consideration. Unfortunately, Isaiah 24–27 is difficult to date with any precision. The texts of Isaiah 26:19 and 25:8 are central here; both speak of the defeat of death and of the revival of (some) dead. Scholars are most divided as to the time of composition of such passages and to their meaning. Isaiah 26:19 concludes a hymn to Yhwh with the words, "*Thy* (God's) dead shall live, their corpses shall rise. O dwellers in the dust, awake and sing for joy! For thy dew is radiant dew, and the earth shall give birth to those long dead." It is clear that such a paean would not be out of place in Ezekiel 37 as the prophet's response to the (re)creating God.[36] It is true that the Hebrew of Isaiah 26:19 can be understood as in the jussive mode, and therefore as a petition in the midst of a communal lament ("Let Thy dead live!"), unless it be a *Heilsorakel* in response to the lament.[37] At any rate, the proclamation said in whatever tone provides a ground for hope and praise. It must be noted that it is within a hymn, and as such the evocation of the resurrection cannot carry the same weight as in oracular Ezekiel 37. That is probably why Yehezkel Kaufmann has a minimizing reading of Isaiah 27:1 and other such texts. The Canaanite basis of such mythology, he says, proves, on the one hand, that the text of Isaiah can be ancient, and, on the other hand, that the "resurrection" here is nothing more than a healing-revival of the sick in body or soul (cf. Psalm 88:4ff.). Kaufmann is, however, in the wrong when he draws a parallel with Ezekiel 37. True, in Ezekiel 37 "resurrection" also means deliverance, not final resurrection at the Last Judgment,

36. Especially as the vision of Ezekiel is reported in the first person singular. Clement of Rome (50, 3–4), for example, combines the texts of Ezekiel 37 and Isaiah 26:20. Ezekiel 37 figures among the early *Testimonia* (and also in Matthew 27:52 and Revelation 11:11; see also Odes of Solomon 22:8–11) as a proof-text on the resurrection. See Jean Daniélou, *Etudes d'exégèse judéo-chrétienne (Les Testimonia)* (Paris: Beauchesne, 1966), pp. 111–21.

37. Joachim Begrich has advocated the existence of such "*Heilsorakel*" in the midst of the lament, before it turns to praise. See his "Das Priesterliche Heilsorakel," *Zeitschrift für alttestamentliche Wissenschaft* 52 (1934): 81–92.

but it is more than healing as in Psalms or, *per* Kaufmann's thesis, in Isaiah.[38]

Pursuing that Israeli scholar's line of thought, there is no reason to give a late date to Isaiah 25:8. "He (God) will swallow up Death forever" comes as a conclusion in the well-known hoary structure of the Warrior God Hymn (Threat/War/Victory/Feast) present in Isaiah 25:6–8. But Kaufmann's conservatism carries him too far. I would rather conclude with William R. Millar that "a sixth-century date is not unreasonable."[39] In other words, both the texts of Isaiah 24–27 and of Ezekiel 37 are probably contemporaneous compositions, although envisaging slightly different kinds of "resurrection."

Thus, that the image of the revivification of dry bones be at all used by Ezekiel is highly significant. As Riesenfeld writes, "If Ezekiel testifies to the thought of the resurrection of the dead as not having been entirely foreign to the religious belief of the Jews in the sixth century before Christ, this passage is not entirely alone. Is. xxvi.19 leads us to approximately the same period."[40]

Ezekiel chose to give to his pessimistic evaluation of the people's predicament a particular emphasis. Israel is actually defunct and the prophet's vantage point is *ex post facto*. The nation is not dying; it is dead. Hence, what is described in Ezekiel 37 is *lifelessness*, the *state* of being deceased. As stated above, we are exactly at the same point as with Genesis 1:2 speaking of the *tohu wa-bohu*. It is also on the model of the shift from Genesis 1:2 to Genesis 1:3 that there is also here a (new) creation.[41] But, a *non sequitur* occurs in the prophetic text, and in verse 12 the image shifts from battlefield to discrete graves, thus setting the stage for an individual resurrection interpretation. The prophetic image has become one of interred corpses. This may be a later commentary by the prophet himself or one of his disciples;[42] besides, as the poet is speaking of death and desolation, the logic of mentioning graves must be recog-

---

38. Yehezkel Kaufmann, *The Religion of Israel* (Chicago: University of Chicago Press, 1960), p. 385. Edward Kissane, *The Book of Isaiah* (Dublin: Browne and Nolin, 1941), with regard to those texts of Isaiah, also speaks of political revival, as in Ezekiel 37.

39. Millar, *Isaiah 24–27*, p. 115.

40. Riesenfeld, *The Resurrection in Ezekiel xxxvii and in the Dura-Europos Paintings*, pp. 3–4.

41. 2 Corinthians 5:17 says, in the same spirit, "if anyone is in Christ, there is a new creation, *kainè ktisis.*"

42. See Martin-Achard, *De la mort*, p. 82. On the other hand, the form adopted here is typically the one of the Ezekielian disputation (v. 11: complaint of the people; vv. 12–14: God's response). Furthermore, the dry bones scattered on a battlefield is a metaphor susceptible to variations.

nized. What is meant, however, is more than just the idea of a cemetery. Beyond it is the inner relationship of the grave with *hades*. As Johannes Pedersen writes, "All graves have certain common characteristics constituting the nature of the grave, and that is Sheol. The 'Ur-grave' we might call Sheol . . . manifests itself in every single grave, as *mo'ab* manifests itself in every single moabite."[43]

All this does not detract from the fact that Ezekiel 37 is less about the doctrine of resurrection from the dead than about the divine power of re-creation, of the creation of new beginnings. On the other hand, it is tied to the notion of a *people* and is comprehensible only within the framework of the Covenant with Israel. Ezekiel and Isaiah 24–27 not only chronologically precede Daniel 12, they afford the genuine origin of the notion of resurrection in Israel, before the focus shifted to the miraculous quickening of the dead.[44] At this point, however, resurrection is cut from its original moorings, namely the inauguration of the history of Salvation, and becomes, paradoxically, the end of such history and the beginning of another world, without history as we know it.[45] This is not the case with Ezekiel. As said above, *Heilsgeschichte* starts

43. Johannes Pedersen: *Israel: Its Life and Culture*, vol. 1 (London: Oxford University Press, 1926), p. 462.

44. In the mind of early Christians, Christ's resurrection combines the theocentric and the anthropocentric. The risen one is unique from all points of view. An individual, he, however, is the "first-born" of a new humanity (see Galatians 4). His resurrection is promise and guarantee of universal resurrection. An "unsuccessful" man, his fate conveys a universal consolation: human meekness, poverty, hunger, suffering will be vindicated and rewarded by no less than eternal life. Divine Presence in the world, he is also and primarily for early Christianity the vindication of God himself. Both acts of vindication are interrelated.

45. Also in Isaiah 25:6–8, the enemy that is overcome is not Leviathan or any such chaotic monster, but Death (*Mawet*). We are still, however, at the level of the mythopoetic. The same must be said of some Intertestamental parallels. Roughly contemporary with Daniel 12, Jubilees 23:22, in a context of promised bliss to come, says, "Their bones shall rest in the earth, and their spirits will have much joy," thus apparently endorsing the idea of a division of flesh and spirit at death, with a potential immortality of the righteous spirits. Later documents become more explicit about the resurrection of the righteous dead. Testament of Judah 25 reads, "And after this, Abraham and Isaac and Jacob will rise to life again. . . . And those who have died in grief will rise again in joy. . . . And those who have been put to death for the Lord's sake will awake to life" (verses 1 and 4). As for Testament of Moses 10, written in the first decades of the first century CE, it does not specifically mention the resurrection of the dead, but George Nickelsburg speculates that the exaltation of Israel in verse 9 presumes a resurrection of the righteous or at least their immediate assumption to heaven. *Resurrection, Immortality and Eternal Life in Intertestamental Judaism* (Cambridge: Harvard University Press, 1972), p. 31. Johannes Tromp has a somewhat minimizing reading of the same text from the Assumption of Moses. He mentions numerous parallels both in the Bible and the Pseudepigrapha, including already Isaiah 14:13; Jeremiah 51 (28):9; LXX Deuteronomy 26:15 and Psalm 33 (32):13–14. See his *The Assumption of Moses* (Leiden: Brill, 1993), p. 237.

with the return from exile, as the pre-exilic history was only failure. Resurrection here stands for redemption, of which it constitutes only one aspect. If death means separation from God, the recovery of life signifies reconciliation, renewal. The prophetic eschatology represented in Ezekiel 37 is about a new start. In other words, omega becomes a new alpha striving toward another omega. At each rebound of history, it can be said that the new era has only been adumbrated by the former one. A choice example is David who remains a *figure* until at last and ultimately he becomes the head of the messianic kingdom. I shall come back to this point.

The new and blessed era envisioned by Ezekiel starts with his own prophecy, indeed with his inspiration in the full sense of the word. Like Plato, who conceived an ideal Republic in which the Philosophers would rule, Ezekiel sees a new and blessed era where prophecy is triumphant. As Robert Martin-Achard has said, "Ezekiel is not just the witness of the resurrection, he is also its instrument."[46] Thus, as a *primus inter pares,* the prophet Ezekiel brings about his people's participation in divine activity (cf. 1:1ff.; 8–11; 40ff.). This is his commission, which he introduces with the messenger formula, that is, with the formula that identifies the ambassador with the one who sends him.[47] The synergy between God and people, with the effect of rendering a land already holy by divine election actually holy within history and geography, starts with the person of the herald. In chapter 37, Ezekiel sets himself, or rather is set by divine command, at the "midnight" point between death and life. No other text of the Hebrew Bible shows more dramatically the stake of prophetic discourse. Ezekiel 37 not only transmits such a discourse, but, in the background, it provides a reflection upon its nature.

After all, the divine question, "would these dry bones live?" was at the antipode of a rhetorical interrogation. It was a way to mobilize Ezekiel for the task of reviving the dead. He is the one to summon the Spirit from the four corners of the universe. He is the one to prophesy to the bones, as if they were able to hear the oracle, "O dry bones, hear the word of the Lord!" (v. 4), after which he tells them what will happen to and for them (vv. 5–6).

This active role of Ezekiel in the revivification of the bones was

---

46. Martin-Achard, *De la mort,* pp. 80–81. Cf. Augustine: "Without God we cannot, without us God will not."

47. Cf. Rolf Rendtorff, "Botenformel und Botenspruch," *Zeitschrift für alttestamentliche Wissenschaft* 74 (1962): 165–77.

picked up by Rabbinic literature. Together with Elijah and Elisha, Ezekiel is credited with the power of awakening the dead. He thus belongs to the time of the Messiah and he will actively take part in the raising of the dead.[48]

The central role of prophecy in the inauguration of the new age is all the more striking as it takes the place formerly occupied by the Divine Warrior mystique. This contrasting parallelism is equally justified by a theme common to both: the proclamation of creation as victory over chaos. One of the main functions of the Divine Warrior Hymn in the Jerusalem cult was to celebrate God's protection of his people from the ravages of chaos (cf. Psalm 118:15–18; 98:1–3; 144:9). In a mythopoetic form, the Hymn describes God's rebuke of cosmic hostile powers (cf. Exodus 15; Psalm 48 [*i. a.*]; Job 9:13; 26:12; 40:25). Ezekiel's shift to prophecy is highly unusual. Second Isaiah (as well as Isaiah 24–27), for instance, decidedly returns to the mythopoetic in several of his oracles (and so does Third Isaiah), see 42:10–13; 43:16f.; 51:9–11.[49] Only in Ezekiel do we find summoning the *ruaḥ* from the four corners of the world put on a par with the cultic "awakening" of the divine arm, the arousing of Yhwh to fight his enemies (cf. Isaiah 51:9). It is thus clear that what is happening in Ezekiel 37 is complex. On the one hand, the prophetic invocation is made liturgical and amounts to the priestly conjuration of the cultic theophany. On the other hand, this invocation displaces a central ingredient in the Jerusalem Festival liturgy (cf. Psalm 2; 9; 24; 29; 46; 47; 65; etc.) celebrating Zion as the impregnable stronghold against the forces of chaos and death. There is no need at this juncture to recall in detail how disastrous such an ideology proved to be for the Jerusalemites of the sixth century (cf. Jeremiah, *passim*).

Ezekiel's daring substitution of prophecy for the mythopoetic Hymn is consistent with his unequivocal condemnation of Israel's past, which is what led the people to become dry bones scattered in a *biq'ah*. Clearly, Ezekiel's move constitutes a definite return to the "insecurity" of the spoken word as opposed to the (false) security of institutionalized myth or ideology. This confirms what we saw above regarding his development of the *nasi'* figure in his theological programmatic chapters 40–48,

48. Cf. *Sanhedrin* 92 b; 98 b; *PRE* 32 (G. Friedlander, p. 249); etc. H. Riesenfeld, *The Resurrection*, p. 38, quotes this beautiful text from *Qohelet Rabba* 3.15 par. 1, "Rabbi Aha said in the name of Rabbi Halafta: 'Everything which the Holy One ... will do or renew in His world in the Messianic future He has already done in part through the medium of a prophet in this world.'"

49. Second Isaiah is well-known for reusing mythic patterns and images. See Paul Hanson, *The Dawn of Apocalyptic* (Philadelphia: Fortress Press, 1975), p. 300 in particular.

a title shorn from "its politico-mythological matrix." The *nasi'* in Eze-kiel's program is a liturgical figure, not a political one, and he functions like a High Priest. There is here a "depoliticization of the messianic office." Ezekiel rebukes the Judean theology of the Davidic dynasty and revives the old League's worldview. Chapter 37's emphasis on the pro-phetic word is harking back to the premonarchic time of the tribal League (cf. chap. 34). Along the same line, the tribal allotment of lands in chapters 47f. shuns the ideology of the Davidic empire and concen-trates solely on the territory west of the Jordan river, according to the promise made to the Patriarchs (see 47:14). "The covenant with David has become the corollary of the covenant of Mount Sinai."[50]

Within such perspective, something of the eerie and absurd nature of Ezekiel's harangue to skeletons starts to make sense. Consistent with the Sinai ideology—dubbed rightly or wrongly a conditional cove-nant—the participation of the beneficiaries is wanted: "and you shall know that I am the Lord." The dry bones must desire to be alive and they must work to the realization of their desire. The dead must want their resurrection; they must be open to the coming of the Spirit. The resurrection is thus not reduced to an extraneous divine action, inde-pendent from human partnership. It is only with the later concept of general resurrection that the dead are resurrected without their will and their acquiescence. The distinction established by both Jeremiah and Ezekiel between those of the Judeans who remained in the land and those who went into exile, is again maintained here. The dry bones are the exiles exclusively. Only these who went through death will also know resurrection. Only these who became impure in an impure land will come out of their impurity of corpses and accede to the purity of life. Later on, Daniel 12 as well speaks of a resurrection for the *maskilim* only, for the martyrs.[51]

True, the revival of the bones is not presented here as a compensation for the damage undergone, a recompense for the suffering of exile. But the free grant that the bones receive from the hand of God is preceded by a confession: "They say, 'Our bones are dried up, and our hope is

50. On all this, see Levenson, *Theology of the Program*, p. 94, and esp. pp. 121ff.

51. With time, the concept of resurrection evolved and became more and more inclusive until it became general. Paul Volz conveniently lists the different phases of the evolution: (*a*) some per-sonalities of ancient history (Moses; Elijah; David; Hezekiah; Daniel . . . Cf. Daniel 12:13); (*b*) martyrs from a more recent past (Daniel 12:1; 2 Maccabees 7:9; 1 Enoch 90:33); (*c*) the righteous in general (Psalm of Solomon 3:10ff.; 1 Enoch 91–92; etc.); (*d*) all of humanity (1 Enoch 22; esp. 51:1). See his *Die Eschatologie der jüdischen Gemeinde im Neutestamentlichen Zeitalter* (Tübingen, 1934), pp. 231–32.

lost, we are cut off completely.' Therefore prophesy [God tells Ezekiel] and say to them, Thus says the Lord God: I am going to open your graves, and bring you up from your graves, O my people; and I will bring you back to the land of Israel" (verses 11–12). The confession of their lifelessness is their participation in their own resurrection.

Strikingly, the word of life is uttered in a foreign land, even in a valley of death, viz., Babylon. Such a step was not made by Ezekiel's priestly colleagues; rather, they taught that God revealed his name only after they had left Egypt, that impure land (Exodus 6:2ff.). But Ezekiel's daringness is congruent with his vision of the divine presence being ex-iled with his people and returning from "the east" to Jerusalem at the time of the restoration (cf. 43:2; etc.). Within this perspective, it may be said that the new beginning springs from the grave, life from death, the ear from the rotten seed. We find in Ezekiel the feeling that the seed had to die (John 12:24).[52] For Ezekiel, the past history of infidelity had to be closed so that another economy might begin, like the ear from a dead grain, like the risen one from a tomb. The new economy has little in common with the previous economy, as little as the living has with the dead, or as a "vast multitude" with a heap of dry bones. For, in contradistinction to past unfaithfulness, now they know that God is the Lord (37:6), and the city where they at long last live is called "Yhwh is there."

52. In the resurrection of Christ, says Walther Zimmerli, the New Testament community "expe-rienced the validity of God's promise of life to his people. . . . [They] have seen expression given to what was promised by the prophet to his people and . . . made universally valid" (*Ezekiel II*, p. 265). He adds (in *I am YHWH*, p. 97): The event is not only accompanied by its emissary in Christ, but becomes itself "totally a word of proclamation. 'And the word became flesh and dwelt among us' (John 1:14)." The recognition event is bound with the Christ event in 1 Corinthians 12:3; cf. 1 John 4:2f.

Sentinel of Imminence

PAUL RICOEUR

The "trajectory" of Ezekiel 37:1–14 seems, at first glance, fixed by tradition in a univocal way. Early Judaism and the first Christians, often followed by the Fathers of the Church, saw in its vision of a return to life of the dry bones an anticipation, a still hesitant indication, of what, shortly thereafter, will become an express faith in the resurrection of the dead, understood in the bodily and individual sense of this phrase.

Let me say straightaway that it is not a question of throwing discredit on such an interpretation, at the price of violating our hermeneutical rule that recognizes the right of amplifying and innovative rereadings, which, based elsewhere than in the text under consideration, project after-the-fact meanings that contemporary scholarly exegesis will hold as contrary to the most probable intention of the text, even that of its presumed redactor.

My contribution is meant to be a plea in favor of the plurivocity of the parable proposed by the vision, a plurivocity that is not accidental but inherent to the "genre" from which this text springs. I will link this indecision to three factors. Considering first of all the intention common to every mode of expression of the prophetic message—words, symbolic actions, visions—we shall focus our attention on the idea of an "announcement," whether it be one of judgment or salvation, and propose to see in it the first source of indetermination. Next, focusing on the vision in Ezekiel 37, we shall seek in the parable it proposes the privileged setting of this indetermination. Finally, we shall look for the last and decisive reason for the openness of the prophetic message to a plurality of interpretations in the theme of "Life and Death." It will then be possible, at the end of this threefold investigation, to replace the traditional interpretation mentioned in opening within the range of possible readings of the parable of "resurrection."

The Prophetic Announcement: Structure and Meaning

That prophecy is in essence an "announcement" is the conclusion of exegetes attentive to its literary form.[1]

Three features of this form need to be recalled here: (1) the delimitation of the "prophetic genre" by what has been called the "messenger's formula": "Thus says Yhwh"; (2) the structure of the announcement, as an announcement of judgment or salvation, that the messenger authorizes; and (3) the formula of "recognition of God," which closes the cycle of divine acts opened by the messenger's formula.

Allow me to recall briefly what today is well known concerning the delimitation of the "prophetic genre," at least during the period of the writer prophets. If the so-called messenger formula "Thus says Yhwh" has the introductory value that generally assigns it its place at the beginning of the message to be delivered, this is because it authorizes—in the literal sense of the word—this message.[2] Someone speaks. In Ezekiel, he speaks in the first-person singular in a discourse that, from one end to the other, presents itself as an autobiography. But the one who speaks does not do so in his own name, but in the name of an Other, the true author of the message. Of course, taking a distance from the historian or phenomenologist, we could describe the "prophetic phenomenon" in the following way: a message (words, actions, visions) is taken up by someone who says "I," where this word "claims" to be a word of God. The message is thus that of a double subject. A divine "I" expresses itself by way of a human "I." Yet, between these two "I"s there is both identity and difference. It is precisely the status of the messenger to speak in the name of . . . This relation between the messenger and the sender of the message is unknown in traditional narratives in which God speaks directly to Adam and Eve, to Cain and Noah, to Moses. This indirect relation, emphasized by the messenger's formula, is im-

1. See, for example, Claus Westermann, *Grundformen prophetischer Rede* (Munich: C. Kaiser, 1960).

2. Besides Westermann, see Walther Zimmerli, *Ezechiel, Biblischer Kommentar Altes Testament* (Neukirchen, 1969, vol. 1, *Einleitung,* pp. 1–130; vol. 2, *Die Auferweckung des toten Israel,* pp. 885–902). Rolf Rendtorff, "Botenformel und Botenspruch," *Zeitschrift für die alttestamentliche Wissenschaft* 74 (1962): 165–77, argues that we ought not to confuse the concept of the *Botenspruch* (the messenger's mandate), insofar as it designates a genre of prophetic discourse, with the messenger's "formula," which is capable of introducing other acts of discourse than that consisting specifically in mandating the messenger. His inquiry, dealing principally with the historical books, concerning the prophets (Nathan, Elijah), but also messengers of every kind (for example, the story of Joseph in Genesis 45:9), allows the conclusion that the messenger's "formula" is not necessary in order to characterize the situation of being sent.

portant for the remainder of our investigation owing to the vocation of writing that this intermediary position includes. This does not exclude that the prophetic message was initially oral, as the formula "go and say" indicates. It is also clear that the first form of writing was that of the letter the messenger carries with him, crossing in this way the interval of space and time that separates the sender and the receiver. But already in the letter the very first literary fixation of a reputedly oral message finds expression. It is easy to understand that writing, transferred from the *Sitz im Leben* to a *Sitz in Schrift*, assures the destiny of the message as able to reach other receivers than those intended by the original speech act. This is particularly the case with Ezekiel, concerning whom scholars have given up trying to decide once and for all what relation the prophet might have borne to his words, his actions, and his visions apart from all the rewritings due to his school or to later scribes. In this sense, writing is not limited to fixing an immutable oral message, it contributes to concealing its origin. And once freed from its original setting, written prophecy will be able to become the fixed basis for its subsequent history of reception and, by way of this history, for rereadings that themselves will exceed the limits of those readings accredited by the canon.

No doubt, we ought not to go too far in the direction of this effacement of the voice by writing. The same thing applies here as does to Psalm 22: the elevation to a literary status does not abolish the expressive force of language. To the extent that the prophetic saying is the saying of another, its utterance, like that of a prayer, continues to bear the mark of a personal "event." Something "happens" to someone. He finds himself grasped by the word of an Other. There is no contradiction between this remark and what was said above concerning the literary destiny of speech acts. It is one of the effects produced by certain literary genres to recreate through writing the character of a speech act. Elsewhere I have discussed a similar phenomenon, that of the "narrative voice," where readers "hear" the narrator (who is not necessarily the author) speaking to them.[3] In the same way, the prayer of lamentation makes "heard" the cry, even though it is couched in writing, of the suppliant. Written prophecy deploys a comparable power of summoning. Readers not only read the words, they hear them. In this way, it is a matter of a genuine return to spoken word by way of the written word.

---

3. See Paul Ricoeur, *Time and Narrative*, vol. 2, translated by Kathleen McLaughlin and David Pellauer (Chicago: University of Chicago Press, 1985), pp. 88–99.

In turn, new interpretations, themselves perhaps heard, will have to guard something of the force—even the violence—of the initial message. The necessity for the perpetual reactualization of a personal event of human speech grasped by the divine word already expresses itself within the framework of the prophecy transmitted to us. The repetition of the "Thus says Yhwh," apart from its purely rhetorical function and beyond its stereotyped style, recalls that each summons of the prophet grasped by a "go and say" is a new event. André LaCocque strongly emphasizes that the prophet is implicated in his message. What is more, the prophet himself brings about the event of reanimation. It is paradoxically the repetition of the novelty of such an event that writing allows.

As for the messenger himself, the heart of what is at issue is his announcement (*Verkündigung*) of judgment or salvation.[4] In this regard, Claus Westermann has carried through a far-reaching discursive analysis of the prophetic message. He distinguishes from the announcement, properly speaking, the statements that often precede it: a recalling of earlier acts of salvation, a summary of transgressions presented in an accusatory fashion, or even a simple reference to the honor of Yhwh. These diverse declarations serve as "proofs," "justifications," "accreditations." Westermann speaks in this regard of an *Erweiswort*, a divine *Selbsterweis* (I shall return to this theme in terms of the more appropriate setting of the "recognition of God"). The announcement, properly speaking, is often linked to these "proofs" by an explicit "because."

As for the announcement itself, it constitutes the living, breathing heart of prophecy. Ezekiel, more plainly than any other of the writer prophets, knows just two types of announcements, one of judgment—that is, finally of condemnation, misfortune, destruction—and one of salvation, of restoration. We can already see dawning the symbolism of death and life that will occupy our attention.

What does announcing signify here? It is not a foreseeing, in the sense of seeing into the future. Rather it is a saying in advance what will be. The announcement, in this sense, bears on an apodictic future, halfway between the indicative and the imperative. This unique kind of link to the future holds in reserve the enigmas that will occupy us. But we can already note the strangeness of a future divested of that aspect of contingency that occupied Greek "logicians." In this respect, other

---

4. Westermann distinguishes, even within the historical books, among the announcements of judgment directed against individuals, against Israel, and against the enemies of Israel.

acts of discourse found in the Old Testament present the same relation to the future. Whether it be a promise, a benediction, or a curse, these are all acts with something like a delayed effect. A second aspect helps clarify this first one. The future announced in the name of God will be God's *doing*. It is God who will destroy, God who will deliver. It is the certitude that this action will come from God that gives the force of conviction to the prophet's voice, along with his certitude of being sent to make this announcement. But these two certitudes really go together as one. The prophet is a messenger certain of being sent by God to say what God most certainly will do.

Having said this, there does not seem to be any source of indetermination in the prophetic announcement, inasmuch as the two events so far discussed—that of the present message and that of future catastrophe or deliverance—are certain. What we need still to consider is the tenor of the announced event, the *quid* of what is announced. Here is where indetermination slips in, an indetermination that will be amplified in the case of the visions that up to now we have taken as just one expression among others of the prophetic announcement.

In order to take some measure of this margin of indetermination, we must give momentary consideration to the relation between the prophet and history. Here a twofold contrast imposes itself, a contrast with traditional history and a contrast with the apocalypse. Whereas the great narrators have a relation to a history that is not just past, but also reassuring, the prophet is confronted with a real, fundamentally dangerous and destabilizing history. Narrative theology, which von Rad so ably discussed, is a theology that gives the guarantee of the founding events to the identity of the people, events that give certitude to the lived experience of a communal existence. Prophetic theology, on the contrary, proceeds from a confrontation with a history that gives rise to anxiety, inasmuch as it includes the frightening alternative of destruction or salvation. We cannot overemphasize this opposition between the mythic and legendary history of the theology of traditions and the very real history that confronts the prophet. When Ezekiel thunders against Egypt, whose aid had helped protect the people against Mesopotamian oppression, it is contemporary Egypt and not the legendary Egypt of the Exodus that he has in view. We can see in this opposition the opposition between a traditional history that yields security and an imminent, traumatic history. This quite unique relation to a history that is in process governs the relation of the prophetic oracle to time. Considered from his point of view, the announcement, the core of the prophetic message, is above all else a relation to imminence. The position of the prophet himself as regards this imminence is defined, by the writer himself, as that of a "sentinel," a sentinel of imminence, we might say, in order to characterize in a brief phrase the quite particular relation of the prophet to history.

Let me add two points as corollaries to this definition. First, however "crazy" the prophet may appear, or, to put it in a more moderate way, however "ecstatic" or "enthusiastic," this madness, which does not exclude the vigilance of the sentinel, is set within a history that is happening now. Second, this relation to imminence can be found in all the expressions of the prophetic message—not just in the discourses, but also in the symbolic actions and the visions. We shall need to recall this when we come to the vision of Ezekiel 37. All these forms of expression are exercises of vigilance confided to the sentinel of imminence.

The second major contrast has to do with the fundamental difference between prophecy and eschatology as regards their respective relations to time. However true it may be that eschatology is the heir of prophecy, once this latter lost its spark in circumstances I shall discuss below, it is also important to oppose the relation of the oracle to imminence to the relation of eschatological discourse to the "end times." There are other differences between these two types of discourse as well, such as the hermeticism of what are held to be secret texts and the role of an intermediary figure who breaks the seals. But the relation to time alone makes for a considerable difference between them. The imminence that the prophet confronts is decidedly intrahistorical. This does not prevent Ezekiel's prophecy from lying on the way to eschatology as is indicated by those features that André LaCocque points out: the absolute newness of the time of the re-creation of the people, a new Exodus, a new Sinai, a new David, new relations to the land, and, most of all, the affirmation that past history is exhausted, as signified by the "dry" bones of the vision. The new history will not be a restoration, but a genuine inauguration. Prior to this there is only a non-history of a non-people, as in Hosea 1:6. And in this sense, we can indeed speak of Ezekiel's prophecy as a "prophetic eschatology."

However, it is in terms of the breadth of history that this renewal is projected. Hence the threshold of apocalyptic is not crossed, as LaCocque's comparison with Daniel confirms.

So prophecy, considered in terms of its relation to time, is opposed both to traditional, mythic, and legendary history, which is basically secure and comforting, and to the non-history of the "end times," which is what the apocalyptics scrutinize, in a posture that is not that of the sentinel but that of the person who deciphers enigmas, who solves riddles.

Having clarified this unique relation of prophecy to historical time, we can return to the question left in suspense, namely what margin of indetermination is included within this relation to imminent history? At first sight, none at all, inasmuch as the announced events—destruction or salvation—are held to be the irrevocable work of God. Although uncertain for human beings, the future is certain for God. And it is this certainly that drives the prophet. Yet . . .

Yet it is remarkable, as literary analysis confirms, that the announcement, constitutive of the prophetic message, is not followed by any development of a narrative character where the accomplishment of the prophecy would be recounted. It belongs to the genre of prophecy that it remains an announcement deprived of any narrative of its accomplishment. Exegetes, it is true, have legitimately tried to establish a correlation between this or that prophecy and a real course of events. And they are all the more inclined to pursue this investigation in that the writer-prophet took care to date a good number of his invectives. This exercise succeeds, as might be expected, in the case of prophecies *post eventum*, interpolated by Ezekiel's school into the text imputable with more or less certitude to the prophet himself. But these correlations are the result precisely of a historian's inquiry. They are not part of the meaning of prophecy as an "announcement." Everything unfolds as though the imminence remained imminent, the eventual fulfillment of the oracle belonging to other literary genres, principally narrative, but also the lamentation, which, it is true, is not absent from the book of Ezekiel. But a lamentation is another genre than prophecy insofar as it is distinguished from the announcement.

Two factors of indetermination result from this noteworthy character of prophecy. First, from a temporal point of view, the announcement includes an element of indetermination concerning the delay in execution, imminence consisting in a variable relation between proximity and distance. This is why, even if a prophecy is dated—and takes a date, as Paul Beauchamp puts it[5]—its accomplishment is not dated. The oracle is not a history of the future or a history in the future. Second, however precise the announcement may be, it leaves an important margin of in-

---

5. "Even though biblical law allows its time and date to be forgotten by constantly relating to an archetypal period, prophecy sets forth the precisely moment of its production." In Paul Beauchamp, *L'un et l'autre Testament, Essai de lecture* (Paris: Seuil, 1976), p. 75.

certitude as regards the exact nature of the anticipated catastrophes and, even more so, the announced deliverances. Just as the oracle is not a history of the future, it is not an account, comparable to a narration, of imminent events. In this regard, the allegories, metaphors, and parables that punctuate prophecies produce an effect similar to the one brought about by the poetry of the Psalms and the Song of Songs. Once again, with these figures of style, it is a question of variations in speaking. What do the symbolic actions and visions we are going to consider say? It is not by chance that for Hosea, Isaiah, Jeremiah, and Ezekiel these nonverbal forms of figuration get intertwined more and more frequently with verbal figures. Perhaps it is even a part of the literary genre of prophecy to anticipate the announced events in a nondescriptive yet figurative mode, if we include under this term verbal figures (allegories, metaphors, parables) and nonverbal figures (symbolic actions and visions). The prophetic oracle satisfies in its own way what Heraclitus said about the words of a god: "they neither affirm nor deny, but signify (*semainei*)." Or, leaping from one end to the other of the history of ideas, might we not say, in the vocabulary of Frege, that prophecy signifies without referring, without denoting? What we have is the whole distance between announcing and showing, making seen. A signifier with a floating referent, such would be the "logical" status of what is announced in prophecy.

This odd status of the imminent event is particularly appropriate to the announcements of salvation from which stems the vision in Ezekiel 37. The prophet better succeeds through these figurative images in making us quasi see the announced catastrophes and in creating the illusion of their presence, following the procedure that Roland Barthes described as a "reality effect." Events of blessing and salvation are, in essence, infinitely more difficult to figure and, for this reason, to make seen. The multiplication of figurations can thus be seen as a way of filling this lack. One draws on the tradition in order to borrow models that are newly projected toward the future. Hence one speaks of a new Exodus, a new David, a new Zion, a new temple (Ezekiel 40–48). And other figures get joined to this verbal ones: symbolic actions and visions. What is important here is that happiness is more difficult to depict, to visualize than unhappiness, and that the gap here is greater between signifying and showing. The figurations of restored life do not succeed either in filling or concealing this gap.

I do not want to end these general considerations about the prophetic genre—at least in terms of the privileged form it finds in Ezekiel—

without also considering the concluding formula ("And you will recognize that I am Yhwh") just as I did for the introductory formula ("Thus says Yhwh"). This knowing—or better, this recognizing—gives, in effect, a new occasion for reflection on the indetermination of the prophetic message as regards the coming about of the announced events that this "recognition" seems at first sight to exclude.

In a study Walther Zimmerli devoted to what he calls the "formula of recognition," two distinct questions are posed, each of which opens a new space of variation for the projection of the imminent future.[6] First, in what sense does this recognition count as a conclusion to the announcement? My question links up with one of André LaCocque's comments. As he says, the formula of recognition invites a retrospective rereading of the text. The obstinate insistence of the redactor to so mark the announcement of salvation as well as that of destruction, the visions as well as the symbolic actions and discourse, is striking. To know, to recognize God is the all-encompassing conclusion that the prophet gives to his prophecy. What is more, this conclusion does not constitute a marginal addition, it represents rather a crown with a teleological aspect. What knowing and recognizing complete and fulfill is always a divine act. This follows from the very character of the prophetic announcement: to judge or to save is in every case an act of God. It is this doing, this act that ends up in a kind of terminal event: the knowledge of God. A recipient is thus given to the divine intervention, a human recipient.

We still need to consider how this recognition comes about. As Zimmerli's study, which goes well beyond the prophetic writings, shows, the "recognition of God" is held to result from events taken as "signs"—whether we call them marvelous or miracles—for which Exodus 31:13 is a good illustration. These "signs," in the quasi-juridical sense of the term, have the value of a "proof," an accreditation. Thus we rediscover, under the idea of sign-proofs, the kind of "logical" tie we encountered above between the announcement of judgment and the accusation that underlies it. The same connection, which Zimmerli designates by the terms *Erweis* and *Erweiswort*, is brought about in this case by the events presupposed as having happened and by the event of recognition.[7] First among these will be the sign proving that it is God who has acted. Ob-

6. Walther Zimmerli, *Erkenntnis Gottes nach dem Buche Ezechiel* (Zurich: Zwingli Verlag, 1954).

7. See Walther Zimmerli, "Das Wort des göttlichen Selbsterweises (Erweiswort), eine prophetische Gattung," in *Mélanges bibliques rédigés en l'honneur d'André Robert* (Bloud et Gay, 1957), pp. 154–64.

viously, it is not a question here of some kind of argument from causality, as in the "Greek" proofs of the existence of God, but rather of a discernment of the "signative" value of noteworthy events. We might even speak in this regard of a divine semiology, to which the vanquished themselves, those who survived the great tribulation, and even all the nations of the earth are summoned. We see in what sense the formula of recognition is symmetrical with the messenger's formula. This latter formula only applies in the case of God's envoy; for the recognition, everyone is included, as though a cosmic clamor must one day ratify the claim of a messenger to have spoken in the name of the Other. Here is where Ezekiel's prophecy will be joined by that of Second Isaiah, which clearly opens to a truly universal history.

But what happens to this *Erweiswort,* as regards univocity, once it is in terms of signs that events are supposed to take on the force of "proof." Have we left the circle of signification in passing from the announcement to its presumed accomplishment? Certainly, it is not in the same sense of the word "sign" that the announcement, when separated from its accomplishment, was called an anticipated sign of an event yet to come, or that the event assumed to have happened is now taken for a sign of a divine act. Nonetheless, what remains common to both uses is the distance between signifying and showing. Into this gap slips the possibility of multiple and competing interpretations.

This suggestion finds support in the exegesis of the second part of the formula of recognition: "You will recognize that I am Yhwh." It is worth noting that the prophet or his school should have incorporated into the formula of recognition another formula that, itself, is to be found in numerous other contexts than just the prophetic writings, namely, the so-called formula of self-presentation that introduces God.[8] What theological meaning should be given to this conjunction? God, we said above, wants to be recognized through his works. But this recognition is a human act, even if it is grafted to a divine act. The danger

8. Here, Zimmerli incorporates into *Erkenntnis Gottes* the essence of the conclusions of his essay "Ich bin Yahve," published earlier in the Festschrift for Albrecht Alt: *Geschichte und Altes Testament* (Tübingen: J. C. B. Mohr, 1953), pp. 179–209. According to Zimmerli, this formula stems from the words accompanying a theophany during which God reveals himself through his name. Such words might really have been pronounced by the priests within the setting of extraordinary cultic festivals. In this sense, the prophet's use of this formula would be derived from its first appearance within a cultic setting. This problem of the *Sitz im Leben* is of more interest for a historical-critical approach. For a literary analysis, like our own, the significant fact is the reuse of this formula as a component of the formula of recognition. What theological meaning ought to be given to this conjunction? This is our principal question.

then is that the subject of this knowing will push itself to the forefront. It is this possibility that is barred by the formula "I am Yhwh," inasmuch as what must be recognized is not a *What* but a *Who*. The "who" of one who says of himself: I am. In this way, a limit is set up to the temptation to turn this knowing into a knowledge about a thing. Zimmerli puts it well: the reprise of "I am Yhwh" in the formula of recognition prevents the event of knowing from placing the one who knows in the position of the subject.[9] He already did not occupy this dominant position in the messenger's formula, nor will he occupy it in the announcement of judgment or of salvation. It is not a place he is permitted to occupy in the deciphering of signs. God, the subject of the act, remains the self-attested subject at the heart of the knowing/recognizing. Even there where the knowing/recognizing becomes an event, it is not the human subject of this act that affirms itself, but instead the divine subject presents himself without "becoming captive of this human knowing." "All knowing of God can only lead to the threshold where it is clearly indicated that here God says 'I am Yhwh.'" This is why we do not here encounter the opposite formula, which we might have expected to find: "Now I know that God is Yhwh." This can be said only by God himself: "You will recognize that I am Yhwh." Just as the formula of recognition concludes the prophetic message, the divine "I am" is pronounced at the end of the formula of recognition. This fusion of the formula of recognition and that of self-presentation thus has the double effect of uprooting the self-presentation of Yhwh from its cultic context and consequently from the temptation of taking hold of the Name through divination or magic, and of removing the knowledge of God from another misuse, that of objective knowledge. In other words, when removed from sacred space by its insertion into the prophetic word, the word of self-presentation is reoriented toward history, which remains its unique place for proof or disproof.[10]

However, at the same time, the conjunction between the formula of recognition ("you will recognize that . . .") and that of self-presentation ("I am Yhwh") has another unexpected effect that applies this time to the very nature of a test or proof of the truth. To the extent that what is attested is the divine "I," divested of every title, every qualification that might "objectify" it, the proof by signs, expected from historical

9. Zimmerli speaks here of a "belonging together," a *Zusammengehörigkeit* between the act (*Tat*) of Yhwh and its recognition by human beings. Nevertheless, it is the divine act that provides the basis and the occasion for this recognition and this knowing.

10. See Zimmerli, *Erkenntnis Gottes*, pp. 69f.

events themselves, does seem to be capable of providing a final point stripped of all equivocation to the *disputatio* that we find a good example of precisely in the exegesis proposed by the biblical writer for the vision of the dry bones recalled to life. The purity, the nakedness of the "I am Yhwh" consecrates in a way the irreducible indetermination of human judgment called to "recognize" God on the basis of faith in the "sign-proofs" exhibited by history.

From Death to Life: An Open-Ended Symbolism

Turning now to the sequence found in Ezekiel 37:1–14, we will seek in the vision itself those resources of equivocity that, added to the aspect of indetermination of prophecy considered apart from the ways its message is conveyed, open the way to a plurality of interpretations, of which the traditional theme of the bodily and individual resurrection of the dead is just one among many. It is not indifferent that it is within a vision, and more precisely in this vision, that such resources of equivocity are concentrated.

Let us first recall that the vision in Ezekiel 37 is inscribed within the prophetic genre with the same status as the discourses, thanks to the various distinctive indications upon which we built our preceding development: the presence of the messenger's formula in 37:5, 9, 12 (to which we can add the introductory expression: "The hand of Yhwh was upon me"); the command: "Prophesy to these bones. You will say to them . . ." (v. 4 and v. 12); the announcement of salvation: "Look, I make the Spirit enter and you will say . . ." (v. 5f.) and again, "Look, I am opening your tombs (vv. 12, 14); and, finally, the formula of recognition: "and you will know . . ." (v. 15).

But it is a vision and not a discourse.[11] It is a vision, concerning which we must not ask if it was experienced like a dream or as an hallucination: the prophet is transported by the spirit of Yhwh into the "valley full of bones," he looks at the field of "completely dry" bones; then he begins to carry out the command to prophesy; followed by the spectacle of the reanimation of the bones, brought about in two times, as in the creation narrative of Genesis 2: first to the bones that are put back together come sinews, muscles, and skin, then comes the spirit, from the four winds, breathed into the bodies.

To complete this examination of the vision on the formal plane, let

11. André LaCocque includes the vision of chapter 37 among the four great visions to be found in the book of Ezekiel.

us add the insertion of a fragment of *disputatio,* in which the expression of the survivors' doubt, even despair, is confided to the words of the Lord: "He said to me: 'son of man, will these bones live?'" In the name of those without hope, the prophet, who is here just a son of man, answers: "Lord Yhwh, you know." In this way the ground of impotence against which the prophet's call stands out is recalled, before he receives the force that alone the imperative can communicate to him: "Prophesy to these bones."

There is nothing, therefore, on the formal plane that adds to the vision in relation to the word, other than the fact that the vision leads to an announcement that goes beyond it. First, it is said that the prophet carried out the order to prophesy: "I prophesied as I had been commanded to do" (v. 7). Above all, the prophet sees accomplished the announcement of salvation that elsewhere discourse leaves in suspense: "And they returned to life and stood upright on their feet; a vast army of them" (v. 10). What above we called the "figuration" of the accomplishment has become, thanks to the vision, the spectacle of the accomplishment, which is recounted by a short narrative section, just as the order to prophesy had been narrated. And it is this spectacle of accomplishment that, by distinguishing the vision from the word on the formal plane, introduces the problem of interpretation on the plane of content. For what, in effect, happens in this figured accomplishment?

We have not yet said anything about one feature of this sequence that leads from the formal plane of composition to that of the contents, the plane of signification. Yet it is on this plane that the orientation of our interpretation is decided. This feature goes as follows. The sequence 37:1–14 contains two parts: the vision properly speaking (1–10), which we have been analyzing, and an interpretation that, at one and the same time, proposes a key to our reading and reiterates the prophesied order, but at the price of a displacement in the symbolism, and concludes with the formula of recognition, without the prophet reporting, however, the accomplishment of what is signified within the framework of the new symbolism. Let us begin from the end: "And you will know that I, Yhwh, I said and I do, oracle of Yhwh" (v. 14). This conclusion seals the theological meaning of the prophecy: the reanimation of the dry bones is not the result of some natural capacity of those the Greek poets call "mortals." Ezekiel himself is called "son of man," that is, mortal. The miracle is God's work, and this work is equivalent to a new creation.

As for the change in symbolism: the opening of the tombs and the rising up out of the tombs appears not to introduce anything, in relation to the spectacle of the dry bones, other than a simple variation on the figurative plane. Note however that this variation is what helps the reader to disengage the meaning common to the two scenes, namely, the passage from death to life. It is just this meaning that is at stake in the declarative phrase in which we can see the hermeneutical key to the whole sequence: "Then he said to me: 'son of man, these bones are the whole house of Israel'" (v. 11a). Is not this declaration the equivalent of an interpretation? And is it not oriented wholly toward a "historical" interpretation, namely, the announcement of the return of the "house of Israel" to its land? Indeed, it is to those of the "house of Israel" that the second *disputatio* is confided. It is they, this time, who breathe the sigh of despair: "Our bones are dried up, our hope is destroyed, we are cut off completely" (11b). Do not the tombs from which they rise figure, within the allegory of a wholly verbal allegory, substituted surreptitiously for the vision of the dry bones, the condition of these living-dead who are condemned to exile? And is it not the return to Palestine that is signified in the barely disguised terms: "See, I open your tombs and I make you rise from your tombs, my people, and I will guide you back to the land of Israel"? André LaCocque spells out in great detail the tie between Life and Land in Ezekiel. It is this promise of a return to the Land of Israel that he sees crowning chapters 40 through 48, rejoining in this way the insightful analyses of Jon Levenson concerning this long sequence that runs through no less than one-fifth of the book of Ezekiel.[12] In short, is it not to them and to them alone that the announcement of salvation is addressed?

Having reached this stage, it seems as though we should be constrained by the text itself to admit just one interpretation of the dry bones recalled to life by the Lord: it is only a question here of the return of the living-dead from the Babylonian exile. Besides the clear declaration of Ezekiel 37:11a, the predominant attitude of prophecy as regards history, which we emphasized above, and the role assumed by Ezekiel himself as a sentinel of imminence plead in favor of this interpretation.

I would like, however, to make a plea in favor of the thesis that the vision, as a vision, offers other resources that can be transposed into discourse. We can begin by observing that the interpretation given in Ezekiel 37:11a imposes a certain limit on the free play of the imagina-

---

12. Jon Levenson, *Theology of the Program of Restoration of Ezekiel 40–48* (Missoula, MT: Scholars Press, 1976).

tion, inasmuch as it only answers one question, who are these dry bones? "These bones are the whole house of Israel." But in locking in on the question "who are they?" the parable is also reduced to an allegory, closer to a discourse than a vision, even to an oxymoron: the living-dead.

Does this remark constitute a plea in favor of the interpretation current in early Judaism and early Christianity that Ezekiel 37:1–14 announces in a clumsy fashion the eschatological resurrection? Nothing prevents our saying this, especially if we take account of the conditions of production of this interpretation.

First of all, it attests to the substitution of eschatology for prophecy properly speaking. Above, I referred to the important gap that separates the former from the latter as regards the relation to history. The idea of a resurrection at the end of time presupposes that this gap has been crossed, once prophecy died out. Next, this interpretation underestimates the role played by new beliefs in the rereading of texts like this one from Ezekiel. These include an increasing concern for the destiny of the individual within the Hellenistic setting, Iranian influences, and controversies with Greek philosophers about immortality. Within the Christian setting, it is quite evident that the *kerygma* of the resurrection of Christ was the decisive factor. It is on this basis that Paul argues in I Corinthians 15. As has been said elsewhere, a innovative interpretation is born most often from the irruption of a new event within the order of belief. It is on the basis of this new event that a rereading of ancient texts becomes possible, which displaces, broadens, and augments their meaning.

Let us add that a certain de facto continuity had been introduced between Ezekiel and early Jewish interpretations and the Christian conception of a final resurrection by the habit of setting Old Testament texts relative to life and death in series, in taking the explicit belief in the resurrection of the dead as the point of reference, thereby setting it up as the telos of the whole development.[13] It would probably be more in conformity with the genius of the Hebrew Bible, as I have proposed elsewhere, to respect the diversity of ways open to interpretation by these venerable texts. The apocalypse of Isaiah 24–27 is quite different from Ezekiel 37, even if Isaiah 25:8 does make one think of Ezekiel 37. But the rehabilitation of the "servant of Yhwh" in the fourth song in

13. See Robert Martin-Achard, *De la mort à la résurrection d'après l'Ancien Testament* (Neuchâtel: Delachaux et Niestlé, 1956), pp. 82–86 (re Ezekiel).

Isaiah 53 is quite different, for this rehabilitation includes its own indeterminations concerning not only the identification of the personage
whose sufferings are promised redemption, but also the very nature of
this rehabilitation.[14] It seems to me, in this respect, that if we bring
together Isaiah 53 and Ezekiel 37, the indeterminations of the one text
reinforce those of the other and thereby liberate each one's potential for
interpretation. The mode of reading in terms of a series of biblical texts,
whose teleological character I have indicated, is certainly not forbidden.
The synchronic disposition of the Bible allows for a transversal reading.
It even produces a quite remarkable and unexpected effect of meaning,
namely the projection after the fact on prophecy of a note of a quest
and a presentiment. The Hebrews become the heralds of this tentative,
inchoate quest, of this clear-obscure presentiment. And this effect of
meaning does not do harm to the text, if we remain aware of the procedures of reading that make it possible. The harm begins if we claim that
the sacred author had this meaning in mind. We can say that an exegesis
that imposes a subsequent interpretation on an earlier text not recognizing the steps involved in such a reading is false. But we ought to take
as plausible an innovative exegesis that knows what it is doing, how it
does it, and in whose name it does it.

Having said this, it is permissible to ask what other interpretations
besides the historical interpretation accredited by Ezekiel 37:11b and
the subsequent eschatological interpretation are opened by the vision of
the dry bones recalled to life.

I would like here to return to a comment made above. The theme of
the return of the exiles only answers one partial question, that of the
identity of the dry bones thus recalled to life. In this regard, it is worth
noting that the interpretation that became traditional remains within
the limits of this quest for identity. It gets stated in the following way:
"Son of man, these bones are all of humanity that has died." The eschatological interpretation remains so obstinately within the limits of identification that it ends up fixating on the literal meaning of the vision by
simply shifting it to the end of time. In this sense, this is the interpretation that most overlooks the parabolic dimension and not just the allegorical dimension of the vision.

What we have to disengage from the concern to identify the address-
ees of the prophecy is the whole symbolism of the passage from death
to life, the symbolism of the resurrection.[15] This meaning of the vision

14. Ibid.
15. See Walther Zimmerli, "'Leben' und 'Tod' im Buche des Propheten Ezechiel," *Theologisches Zeitschrift* 13 (1957): 494–508.

is the one most strongly emphasized by André LaCocque throughout his essay. The announced Resurrection, he notes, is not the result of some human capacity, nor is it the end of an aspiration. Its meaning is theological, not anthropological. The adjective "dry" underscores the radical character of death, which excludes the return to life being inscribed within the cycle of a great circle. In this sense, the vision first works like a word on judgment on a dead people. Even God is caught in the tomb. Israel, born paralyzed, dies in Babylon. Death is thus the forgotten path of life as a new creation. This new creation finds no guarantee in prior existence, as is said in John 12:24: "The seed has to die in order to be reborn."

Here perhaps is where the vision goes most beyond the prophetic discourse, which alternates between the announcement of judgment and that of salvation. The vision of the dry bones recalled to life "figures" the passage from death to life and, in this sense, makes us "see" the turn from one announcement to the other.

But the confession of the absence of life is an integral part of the announcement of the resurrection as André LaCocque has indicated. The end of history is the pathway to the new history. This dialectical radicality, which ignores the balancing of the discourses of condemnation by those of salvation confers its whole gravity on the question in 37:3: "Son of man, all these bones, will they live?" along with the heartbroken response of the prophet: "Lord Yhwh, you know." This way of interrogating the vision is perhaps the one that best does justice to the vision as vision—that is, as irreducible to discourse. After all, does not the vision differ from the words of salvation in that it preserves a symbolic potential that even the poetic prose of these discourses does not transmit? A narrative of a vision can in this respect be taken as the equivalent in prose of a piece of poetry.

To explore the resources of the symbol "Death and Resurrection," we can remain within the limits of the canonical, Jewish and Christian, scriptures, but we can also make ourselves attentive to what the biblical symbolism shares with the symbolisms of other cultures and other literature.

In Ezekiel himself, the connection is strong between life and justice, and death and injustice in 33:10–20. Thus we might speak of a conversion from injustice to justice as like a passage from death to life. This model of a "return" is accompanied by a promise that is equivalent to repentance by the Lord in Ezekiel 18:1–3. In this way, it is attested that God himself is Life, the living God—"Seek me and you will live," we read in Amos 5:4. To turn away from evil is to go from death to life. Of course, we can also discern in these texts an indication of the symbolism of life and death opposite to the one that reduces the announcement of the resurrection to an oracle of life after death. The allusions to the "law of Yhwh" draw the symbol away from the ethical-juridical side, even from the cultic control of this law by the clergy of the Temple. In this regard, the New Testament reopens a whole range of significations, even while remaining within the horizon of a spiritual *metanoia*. Paul can write, in the manner of Hosea and Ezekiel: "You were dead through your sins, but now you live." The force of the symbol is even more plainly evoked in the rite of baptism, where the spiritual sense of conversion receives the reinforcement of the revivification of the old myths of the flood and of being swallowed by the waters. Having been so "swallowed up," the baptized person is "saved from the waters." His baptism signifies a rebirth. The Gospel of John confers a well-known vigor and splendor on this symbol of a second birth.

Thus the connection between the symbolism of resurrection and that of the originary creation is periodically reconstituted. No doubt this connection is very old. And we ought not to set aside in this regard the suggestion of a few exegetes that the Hebraic symbolism of the resurrection might have one of its sources in the ritual of Adonis or of Osiris and also in the ancient Near Eastern mythologies of nature that have come down to us from Ugarit and the Canaanite religions.[16] As we said above, the reanimation two times of the dry bones evokes a deep-lying kinship between the vision of Ezekiel 37 and the narratives of creation in Genesis 2. This rootedness in the creation myths lends its energy

16. In *The Resurrection in Ezekiel xxxvii and the Dura-Europos Paintings* (Uppsala: A. B. Lunde-quistska Bokhandeln/Leipzig: Otto Harrassowitz, 1948), Harald Riesenfeld attempts to demonstrate that the idea of resurrection already had roots in the piety of the annual liturgy of the New Year and its ritual celebrating the regeneration of life by Yhwh. The tendency to eschatologize the belief in the new creation, by removing it from its annual rhythm, is said to be included in the ritual itself; Hosea 6:2, Micah 7:8, as well as Psalm 17:15, and even the sublime chapter about the Suffering Servant in Isaiah 53 preserve a trace of this cultic root, as does the reference to the Spirit in Ezekiel 37. If we admit that archaic rites get perpetuated in the historicized myths and in metaphorical expressions, this hypothesis is just as plausible as any other explanation in terms of "sources" or "origins." The displacement of myth toward history, then of history toward eschatology seems no less noteworthy. It is the whole question of typological interpretation that arises here, in its double aspect of creation of a new meaning and the persistence of an old meaning. It is, by the way, under the sign of typology that Riesenfeld explains the reproduction of Ezekiel's vision on the walls of the synagogue at Dura-Europos. What is depicted are the "things to come" in the messianic age, history being taken as preforming eschatology. Might this not suggest that the typological interpretation, in the sense of the resurrection of the dead at the end of time, is to the prophetic announcement of the restoration of Israel what this latter was to the belief in the renewal of life within the cultic framework of the New Year festival?

to the symbolism of resuscitated life beyond the limitations that, in an opposite way, are applied to it by the physical conception of life after death and the moral concept of conversion. That the God who said "I am" is a living God is a confession that constitutes the vanishing point toward which converge, and from which proceed, the components of the great symbol of Life emerging from Death. In its widest extension, this symbol inverts the expected natural order that makes death succeed life. It is this reversal that is signified in many ways. In this regard, we may return to the notion of *Erweiswort*, elaborated by Walther Zimmerli with regard to the formula of recognition. God, it is proclaimed, makes himself known, recognized through his works. Life being reborn from death is the proof-sign par excellence of divine action. Among the multiple signs indicating a rebirth, there is no place for establishing a hierarchy. In this regard, life after death does not constitute a literal meaning, the proper meaning, in relation to which the *metanoia* would be a derived meaning, the figured meaning. It is the very distinction between proper and figured meaning, first and derived meaning, that has to be challenged. This distinction results from what we might have called a linguistic reduction of the symbolic amplitude, a reduction encouraged sometimes by the materialistic tendency, sometimes by the moralizing tendency of ordinary language.

Hence it is not surprising that the symbol overflows the religious register and unfolds its poetic force in all those registers where Life and Death signifies more and in another manner. There are so many ways to return from death to life! It is with regard to the word life that meaning in the end turns out to be inexhaustible.

Remaining within the biblical framework of these studies, it would be with the Song of Songs that I would like to compare the amplifying exegesis we have just practiced in regard to Ezekiel 37:1–14. Love seems to me to unfold, around the nuptial symbol, a comparable range of significations, unfolded in this case between sexuality and spiritual dilection. It seems as though death and life offer parallel metaphorical possibilities. What unites them is the idea of creation. There where the singer, in his "wisdom," declares love to be as strong as death, the prophet, in his "madness," proclaims life stronger than death. We need to listen to both voices.

Psalm 22

My God, My God,
Why Have You Forsaken Me?

ANDRÉ LaCOCQUE

Psalm 22 belongs to the category of "psalms of individual lament," that is, for the most part, psalms spoken by people suffering from illness, or loss, and some other mishap. As is well known, the biblical conception of illness sees it as a deprivation of *shalom*, and as a foretaste of death, concerning which the Israelites were much more conscious during their lives than we care to be. The sick person finds himself or herself already at the confines of Sheol. Conversely, relief means a return to the living, a resurrection of sorts.

Thus the Psalmist is engaged in Yhwh's struggle against the forces of evil and destruction. She begs for justice, which is not only a social notion. To bring about justice is to restore *shalom* in all its aspects; see Matthew 25 (see also Psalms 6; 38; 32:1–5). In contrast, the rich and the happy few are in no need of justice, therefore the "poor" look at them with mistrust, for they constantly skirt the danger of becoming complacent, callous, self-satisfied, and of eventually contributing to injustice by not fighting against it (see Mark 2:17). They need not ask for this day's bread. No wonder, then, that it is in the Lament Psalms that we find the terms "poor" and "foe/enemy," along with their cognates. The same terms are often used by the prophets to denounce God's foes and to place curses on them.

The most arresting feature of the Psalms of Lament is the abrupt shift from complaint to praise. In all the Laments of the Individual (LI), there is a polarity of petition and praise (Psalm 22:22, 25) and a progression from supplication to praise. It seems that from the LI, this motif passed over to the Collective Laments. Hermann Gunkel speaks of "an abrupt change of mood." Possibly there was an intervention with words of grace by a member of the Temple personnel; cf. Psalms 85:8f.;

12:5; 55:22; 91:14–16; 121:3–5. On the basis of Joachim Begrich's "Das priesterliche Heilsorakel," it is assumed that an oracle of salvation was given in the midst of the petition.[1] In Psalm 22, this would be verse 22. In this psalm, however, the "but clause" is already present in verse 4 and recurs in verse 20, while the actual turning point comes between verses 22 and 23. As Claus Westermann emphasizes, both God and man are affected by that change.[2]

Westermann discerns the following structure for the lament:

1. Address/cry for help;
2. Lament (the verbs have three possible subjects: God/I/foes),
cf. Psalms 79:1–3; 13:1–2;
3. Confession of trust (introduced by the *waw* adversative);
4. Petition;
5. Assurance of being heard;
6. Double wish: intervention for and against;
7. Vow of praise;
8. Praise of God.

It is worth noting that the lament's five basic motifs are the same as in the Babylonian psalms: address, praise, lament, petition, vow of praise.[3] But, in Israel, the praise comes after the suppliant is convinced that his petition has been answered. This makes the Israelite lament unique. Only here has one the "certainty that Yhwh in his heights (Psalm 22:3) has heard the one praying in the depths (28:6)."[4]

The vow of praise is common to both the Babylonian and the Egyptian psalms. It was probably originally connected with a promise to offer a sacrifice. Praise "belongs to the life of the god as much as does food. . . . [Similarly,] man cannot exist without food, but also not without some recognition, some 'honor,'" says Westermann.[5] Plea and praise

---

1. Joachim Begrich, "Das priesterliche Heilsorakel," *Zeitschrift für alttestamentliche Wissenschaft* 52 (1934): 83.

2. Claus Westermann, *Praise and Lament in the Psalms*, translated by Keith R. Crim and Richard N. Soulen (Atlanta: John Knox, 1981).

3. David Damrosch establishes a parallel with the Babylonian text *Lubdul bel Nemequi* (cf. W. G. Lambert, *Babylonian Wisdom Literature* [Oxford: Clarendon Press, 1960], pp. 21–62): "The first half of the text paints a powerful picture of widespread social injustice. . . . The second half of the text is a hymn of praise to Marduk, who has heard the speaker's prayers and saved him from all his enemies and miseries" (*The Narrative Covenant: Transformations of Genre in the Growth of Biblical Literature* [Ithaca: Cornell University Press, 1987], p. 133n. 35).

4. Westermann, *Praise and Lament in the Psalms*, p. 74.

5. Ibid., p. 77. Cf. the text of a lament to Ishtar cited in Bernard Anderson, *Out of the Depths: The Psalms Speak for Us Today* (Philadelphia: Westminster, 1983), p. 66f. (= *ANET,* pp. 383–85).

mean living. The dead do neither, and consequently the one who does not plea and praise is like them (see Psalms 6:5; 30:9; 88:10; 11; Isaiah 38:18f.). God is the one to be petitioned and praised. If not God, then someone or something takes his place to be exalted, but this is, for the Psalms, not life but death.

Psalm 22 is the LI par excellence. It expresses a sense of abandonment on a par with such poignant texts as Lamentations 5:20 and Isaiah 49:14. It starts with the question "why?" arising from the very heart of the one suffering torment. It is Job's question in the Bible and the question of every Job throughout history. "Why?" introduces the supplicant's complaint, incomprehension, distress, but also his or her protest. Its very recurrence in the same person's (or the collectivity's) cry for help already shows that there is no real end to the query. There are, to be sure, moments of relief, but they are always temporary. The petitioner of Psalm 22 breaks out in praise because his plea has been heard, but another Psalm of Lament takes up again the complaint. Life is lived between the two poles of lament and praise. This tension is brilliantly expressed by bringing the two together in the same psalm. Plea is accompanied by praise; praise, by plea. Plea without praise is despair, absence of hope; praise without plea is complacency, arrogance. Psalm 22:4–6 pit two of God's attitudes against each other; they clash, leaving man puzzled about their coexistence: God is hidden, yet he made himself known through his acts of deliverance to the psalmist's ancestors. Were it not for the divine past self-revelation, there would be no psalm at all, no lament, no asking why, only the silence of nothingness. Hans-J. Kraus's words go right to the point when he says, "It is only the God who reveals himself and is present with his people who can hide himself. Hiddenness is an aspect of his revelation."[6] The Psalms of Lament teach us how to live before such a God.

It is a teaching by implication. The LI is no wisdom text. There is no theorizing about human suffering, its causes, its worth or lack thereof, or its outcome. The tension between plea and praise is existential; there is no glorification of prudence, of *in medio virtus*. Sages, it is true, come to the same conclusion as regards the wise attitude regarding human life. They tell us that the happy person should shed tears, and the wretched should laugh. But this is a lesson taught in a dispassionate ethos. Psalm 22, by contrast, is pronounced in the throes of torment

6. Hans-J. Kraus, *Theology of the Psalms*, translated by Keith Crim (Minneapolis: Augsburg, 1986), p. 39.

and in the heat of a devouring passion to be heard, to be helped, to be saved.

Not a wisdom piece, Psalm 22 is no mystical text either. There is here no mystique of suffering. As Patrick Miller reminds us, the psalm "tells us that God is at cross-purposes with suffering, fully present in it, and at work to overcome it. The cruciform character of life is everywhere apparent. The resurrecting work of God is more difficult to see."[7]

The place of the lament in the theology of the First Testament is to be found in the context of deliverance, itself modeled on the archetype of the salvation from Egypt (see Exodus 1–15; cf. Deuteronomy 25:5–11). In both texts, the structure is the following: Prehistory, Distress, Call for Help, Hearkening, Leading Out, Leading Into, Response. For, as Westermann says, the lament has a history in Israel. It is related to the saving acts of God. Lament is "an event between man and God" (p. 261). In fact, it is the ultimate recourse of man, who appeals to the tribunal of God, now that all human and worldly tribunals have been found wanting. Accordingly, although the speaker in the LI is an individual, the lament presents a dialogical structure. As within the framework of the people's history, the three elements of the narrator, God, and the enemy are present in the LI in the form of a more personalized structure of an I, a thou, and foes, as we saw above. Those in the dialogue are the suppliant and God; the foes are in the background and spoken about. The defendant's petition is primarily that God be God, as he ever was toward the ancestors. (In this regard, Psalm 22 is echoed by many other psalms.) The poignancy of the lament has two sources: the evident suffering of the petitioner and the realization that there is indeed no other one to whom to go but to Yhwh. If he is disappointing in his response, reluctant to act, "sleeping," or, God forbid, incapable of responding, there will be no one else. He is the God of Israel, the only one Israel has.

It is clear that there is a struggle within the person uttering the lament between conflicting sentiments. On the one hand, God is God; there is no doubt that he is capable of saving his people. On the other hand, the very dereliction of the faithful individual, or of the faithful nation in a Lament of the People (LP), shows a strange impotence or even ill will on the part of this same God. He must be petitioned; he must be reminded of his Covenant and of his own power! As the suppliant remembers the past acts of justice and salvation of Yhwh, so too he

---

7. Patrick D. Miller, *Interpreting the Psalms* (Philadelphia: Fortress Press, 1986), p. 110.

must remind Yhwh himself of such acts in the past. Trust in Yhwh is grounded on memory. There is between yesterday and today the bridge of remembrance. That is how God is also the God of history.

The lament roots itself in history, in the history of salvation. But it also belongs to the liturgy, that is, both to this history reduced to its sacred core and to its ritual actualization of the past, its *Vergegenwärtigung*, its re-presentation, and to its prolepsis, its "preview" of the future. In the LI, the past is vivid, the seat of the present, the historic throne of Yhwh (Psalm 22:4); and the future is *hic et nunc,* so much so that the psalmist abruptly shifts from plea to praise. It is on that foundation that the LI expresses its faith in the fulfillment of the petition. Faith and assurance, the conviction of things not seen. For God is with those who suffer (Psalms 16:8; 23:4; 91:15), being himself a "suffering God," according to the provocative title of Terence Fretheim's book.[8]

God suffers, but dialectically he is also sovereign. That is why the lament is, to a certain extent, a complaint against God. The abandonment comes from him; the refusal to help is his; he is to blame for his deafness to the cry of the suppliant. "You have put me in the depths of the Pit, in the regions dark and deep. . . . You have caused my companions to shun me. . . . I suffer your terrors; I am desperate. Your wrath has swept over me, your assaults destroy me" (Psalm 88:6ff. NRSV). We are close to an outright accusation, again reminiscent of trial procedures. These accents recall the outbursts of rage or despair found in narrative accounts. Rebecca raises such complaints (Genesis 25:22; 27:46); so does Samson (Judges 15:18). More particularly, the prophet Jeremiah vents existential doubts about the meaning of existence before an incomprehensible and unfathomable God (cf. 20:18). By the voice of the same prophet, however, God's answer to the query squarely puts the onus collectively on the people: "'Why do you complain against me? You have all rebelled against me,' says the Lord. 'In vain I have struck down your children; they accepted no correction. . . . My people have forgotten me, days without number'" (Jeremiah 2:29ff. NRSV).[9]

But no one goes as far as Job does in poignancy and eloquence. Here

---

8. Terence Fretheim, *The Suffering God: An Old Testament Perspective* (Philadelphia: Fortress Press, 1984).

9. Regarding the kinship between Psalm 22 and Jeremiah, we can follow Carroll Stuhlmueller in noticing the following, striking verbal parallels: Psalm 22:6b and Jeremiah 49:15; Psalm 22:7a and Jeremiah 20:7b; Psalm 22:7b and Jeremiah 18:16 (cf. Lamentations 2:15); Psalm 22:9–10 and Jeremiah 1:5, 15:10, 20:14, and 17f. (cf. Isaiah 49:1). See his *Psalms 1: A Biblical-Theological Commentary* (Wilmington, DE: Michael Glazier, 1983), p. 147.

the lament reaches its climax and "the outermost limits of its function as supplication," according to Westermann. Job "clings to God against God. . . . Doubt about God, even the kind of despair that can no longer understand God, receives in the lament a language that binds it to God, even as it accuses him."[10]

Finally, and consistently from a biblical perspective, God himself responds with his own lament to the lament of the sufferer. We had an inkling of it in what precedes, particularly in Jeremiah. God responds to the question "why?" with a "why?" of his own. In Jeremiah 8:5 we read, "Why then has this people turned away in perpetual backsliding?" There is here the juxtaposition of God's wrath and God's grief (12:7–13; 15:5–9; 18:13–17). We can also think of the book of Hosea, whose style, says Hans-Walter Wolff, "vacillates between compassionate lament and bitter accusation. . . . It testifies to the fact that God is wrestling with himself."[11] The biblical spectrum of lament is surprisingly broad. It is a "history which ultimately reaches the point where God, as the God of judgment, suffers for his people."[12]

In the scriptures cited above, there is a definite emphasis on the community. God is justified in his wrath or in his complaining because his people "turned away in perpetual backsliding." Deuteronomic theology, for one, agrees with this comprehensive judgment. But clearly a tension will transpire when the problem of evil and suffering is individualized and the existential question "why?" is raised by one, but not necessarily by all. Such a tension is felt from the very outset of Psalm 22, when it opposes God's faithfulness and salvation toward the ancestors (v. 5) and the whole of Israel (v. 4), on the one hand, to the psalmist's predicament, on the other—forsaken as she or he is by God. It is thus to be expected that some critics would demur at this and read in the "I" of the Psalms a collective "I." Rudolph Smend, to cite one such example, was a defender of the collectivist theory on the basis of the Targums and traditional Jewish exegesis from the Middle Ages (as were Calvin and, later, de Wette). The expressions of trust in the Psalms of Lament could not come, he thought, from individuals.[13] But Hermann Gunkel showed that there are LI as well as LP, along with PI (narrative praise)

---

10. Westermann, *Praise and Lament in the Psalms*, p. 273.

11. Hans-Walter Wolff, "Hosea," *Dodekapropheten 1* (Neukirchen: Neukirchener Verlag, 1961), p. 151.

12. Westermann, *Praise and Lament in the Psalms*, p. 280.

13. Rudolph Smend, "Über das Ich der Psalmen," *Zeitschrift für alttestamentliche Wissenschaft* 8 (1888): 49–147.

and also hymns (liturgical collective praise). This conclusion entails a different *Sitz im Leben* for each form, and the problem of defining them with any accuracy is a vexing one.

Gunkel thought that the LI was originally cultic but that it evolved from the cult setting and could be sung far from the shrines.[14] Sigmund Mowinckel reacted strongly against this "spiritualization" theory. The LI belong with the official religious rites of repentance and purification.[15] Hans-J. Kraus, too, thinks that the *Sitz im Leben* is cultic. But the same year that Kraus was publishing his Psalm commentary in German, Rainer Albertz, a disciple of Westermann, protested that in most of the LI there is no reference to either the cult or the Temple.[16] He agrees instead with Erhard Gerstenberger, who comes to a different conclusion on the basis of a comparison with the Babylonian psalms. The latter are ritual, but they do not belong to the official cult. They are at home in casual ceremonies at the bedside of the sick person, for example. The liturgist is a "man of God" or a prophet, more or less independent from the cultic institution.[17] In the First Testament, the situation is similar. Albertz refers to healing sessions in 1 Kings 14; 17:17–24; 2 Kings 1; 4:8–37; 5; 8:7–15; and Isaiah 38, for example. If so, from such a perspective that does not restrict the scope of the cultic to the confines of the shrine, it is clear that the alternative is no longer cultic versus noncultic. "Cultic" must be differentiated.

Regarding the date of composition (in its final form as transmitted to us in the Hebrew Bible), the question again is an interpretive crux. Albertz does not believe that the Laments received their final form until after the exile (p. 24). But the parallels we listed above with other First Testament texts lead Carroll Stuhlmueller, among others, to the conclusion of a kinship, not just with Jeremiah and his disciples, "but also with an expanding group of the 'afflicted,' like Second Isaiah during the exile, as well as with Job and other late 'Davidic Psalms' (Psalms 69, 71, 139) after the exile."[18] This seems borne out by Westermann's remark

14. Hermann Gunkel and Joachim Begrich, *Einleitung in die Psalmen* (Göttingen: Vandenhoeck & Ruprecht, 1933), pp. 261–63.

15. Sigmund Mowinckel, *Psalmenstudien*, vol. 1 (Kristiania: Dybwad, 1921–24), p. 138.

16. Rainer Albertz, *Persönliche Frömmigkeit und officzielle Religion* (Stuttgart: Calwer Verlag, 1978).

17. Erhard S. Gerstenberger, "Der klagende Mensch," in *Probleme biblischer Theologie, Festschrift für Gerhard von Rad*, edited by Hans-Walter Wolff (Munich: C. Kaiser, 1971), pp. 64–72. See now also Gerstenberger, *Psalms, Part I, with an Introduction to Cultic Poetry* (Grand Rapids, MI: Eerdmans, 1988).

18. Stuhlmueller, *Psalms 1*, p. 147.

about Psalm 22:27. He speaks of "a universalism which became important with the exile and the preaching of the Second Isaiah."[19] I shall
return to the sociological problem below.

I have said that two key concepts undergird Psalm 22 as a representative of the LI in the psalter: the "poor" and his or her "foes." I now
intend to consider these two major elements of Psalm 22 in succession.

Verse 25 reads, "For he did not despise or abhor the affliction of the
afflicted (*'enuth 'ani*)," and verse 27, "The poor (*'anawim*) shall eat and
be satisfied; those who seek him shall praise the Lord." With the exception of Numbers 12:3 about the outstanding personality of Moses, the
term "poor" is absent from the narrative and prescriptive literary genres.
In contrast, it is found twelve times in the hymnic genre (plus five times
in the prophetic, and three times in the sapiential). Again in these contexts, there is no mystique of poverty. A measure of good news is announced to the *'anawim*, not because they are unhappy, but because
their unhappiness is coming to an end. They hope for an era of definitive justice, and the prophets promise them the fulfillment of their hope
(cf. Zephaniah 2:3). For Yhwh has a common cause with them (cf.
Amos). The situation in the Psalms is similar.

Now it has to be realized that such an idea of God's involvement in
the wretchedness of the poor, entailing the conception of plea and
praise as the two faces of one reality, on the one hand, and the calling
of the lamenters *ḥasidim* (pious ones), *ṣadikim* (righteous ones), *yeśarim*
(virtuous ones), on the other, runs counter to the official theology of the
Temple in Jerusalem. It is therefore doubtful whether Kraus is right
when he considers the names given to the lamenters (poor, wretched,
pious, just, righteous, etc.) as designating the crowd of pilgrims coming
to the Temple at the three annual festivals, and not as a party within
the people, as Anthonin Causse believed, following Alfred Rahlfs.[20]
Furthermore, it must be noted that Kraus speaks of these same people
as in legal need (persecution, indictment) and without legal standing or
influence (Psalm 82:3f), "underprivileged," outcast, alien. Hence, we
might say, despite Kraus's protest, that they form a social class. Can we
be more specific? We should perhaps look somewhere between the two
extremes. Those who lament use a formulaic language that seems to
belong to the repertoire of the Temple personnel (*pace* Westermann).

19. Claus Westermann, *The Living Psalms*, translated by J. R. Porter (Grand Rapids, MI: W. B.
Eerdmans, 1989), p. 90.

20. Anthonin Causse, *Du groupe ethnique à la communauté religieuse* (Paris: Alcan, 1927); Alfred
Rahlfs, *'Ani und 'Anaw in den Psalmen* (Göttingen, 1892).

But it is to be surmised, in tune with the opinions of Gerstenberger and Albertz reviewed earlier, that those who speak in the LI are pious laypeople and men of the cloth recruited among the lower clergy. Furthermore, we are probably right to imagine that there was a rather deep hiatus between the official ideology of the high clergy and the marginal but vigorous "sectarian" differing voices. At any rate, "God is the God of the helpless" is polemical. Were it not so, but a tenet of the official religion, there would be no enemies within the ranks of the establishment. "God of the helpless" contrasts, I said, with Deuteronomy and with Deuteronomistic theology. It also contrasts with the theology of Zion, with its insistence on God's rulership over the whole earth and the reflection of the divine glory in the king of the nation. There is here little room for a lament that is not communal, when the circumstances bring the people to cry unto the Lord for his intervention within the political realm.

It seems as though there was, on the part of the poor, a reinterpretation of the theology of Zion, in the sense that the One who is enthroned in Zion, *El 'Elyon,* is none other than the "God of the helpless" (Psalms 9:18; 10:17; 18:27; 25:9; 37:11; 69:32; 147:6; 149:4). Psalm 22:28–29 is the expression of such a claim. There the reader is surprised to find in the midst of a personal prayer the proclamation of the universal kingship of God: "All the ends of the earth shall remember and turn to the Lord; and all the families of the nations shall worship before him. For dominion belongs to the Lord, and he rules over the nations."

Much of this stance, it is true, is put to the test in the interpretation of verse 27 here. "The poor shall eat and be satisfied" is often understood as indicating that the poor, including the suppliant, are sharing liturgically in the sacrificial meal, thus showing that there is no sectarianism in this psalm. Artur Weiser, for example, thinks that the psalmist himself vows to bring to God a sacrifice within the circle of the pious and to invite the poor to the meal.[21] Similarly, A. A. Anderson recalls that the widows, orphans, and foreigners share in the tithes (Deuteronomy 14:29; 26:12) and in the offerings at the annual festivals (Deuteronomy 16:10f., 14). They are shown kindness according to the principle, "Share because you have already received" (cf. Psalm 142:7).[22] In the background is the idea that the offerer, the priest, and the altar,

21. Artur Weiser, *Die Psalmen übersetz und erklärt* (Göttingen: Vandenhoeck & Ruprecht, 1959), p. 158.
22. A. A. Anderson, *The New Century Bible Commentary: Psalms 1–72* (Grand Rapids, MI: W. B. Eerdmans, 1972), p. 193.

shared in consuming the sacrifice. Blood and fat for the altar, breast and one leg for the priest, the rest for the offerer to be eaten outside the Temple precincts (Leviticus 7:12–36).

But the hostility displayed earlier in the psalm by the enemies points in another direction. The poor would not be admitted to the liturgical meal. "The sick person was not allowed to come to the temple until he was healed," recalls Kraus. "We cannot separate socioeconomic and spiritual poverty," he adds.[23] But now God's will is stronger than men's prohibitions. The psalmist exclaims that "nothing" indeed "can separate" the poor "from the love of God." The poor will be fed, and not just with the crumbs that fall from the table, for they will be satisfied. In other words, the enemies will be confounded, and they will have to admit the afflicted to the forbidden table. They will thus become like Haman compelled to glorify Mordecai in the book of Esther.

Hence Psalm 22:27 ("The poor shall eat . . ."), which begins a probably added conclusion to the psalm (vv. 27–31), must be read with Stuhlmueller as saying that "other 'afflicted' outlaws are now summoned to participate in the liturgy: foreigners, the sick and diseased, and even the unborn."[24] All will come to the "table" and be fed. But where is that "table"? True, it could be the altar within the Temple precincts, but the psalmist may also have in mind a table that stands outside those precincts and that all the same constitutes access to the sacred ground defended earlier by the "bourgeois" as by "dogs" (v. 17). In the latter case, we again join ranks with Gerstenberger and Albertz.

It is strange that the antinomy present in the LI, and in Psalm 22 in particular, should be between the poor and their enemy, instead of between the poor and the rich. This has puzzled critics. Mowinckel, for example, equates the poor with the victims of magic, while others see in them a political party. Be that as it may, it is clear that in the background there is a prevailing notion of distributive justice according to which the just are automatically happy because they are blessed by God. Hence the sick one is seen as rejected, as punished. The notion is simplistic but consistent with Israelite realism. Before blessing and curse are spiritual concepts, they are actual situations. What is more, the Word in ancient Israel is a lot more performative than it would be in our conceptual languages. To bless and to curse, in particular, have a real power of their own. Illness may be the outcome of an "evil word."

23. Kraus, *Theology of the Psalms*, pp. 53 and 95.
24. Stuhlmueller, *Psalms 1*, p. 150.

Furthermore the psalms make us aware of a deeply divided society in which feelings are expressed with great intensity. The "enemies" are not inactive, they curse, they set "snares and snakes," they dig traps (Psalms 69:23–29; 109:6–20). They impudently reject the otherness of the poor in order to protect their own affluence as legitimate. Poverty must be a deserved evil, in order that their riches be also a deserved bliss. Therefore, we often do find the identification of the enemy with the rich, the well-to-do. These escape their bad conscience by rejecting all responsibility for others' suffering and for the wretchedness of those who suffer (cf. Luke 7:36–50). Kraus, following Mowinckel, says that the foes are more than human, they are somewhat mythic.[25]

We can recognize in Mowinckel's and Kraus's view their fundamental conviction regarding the cultic setting of the Psalms. Curses are also mythic and liturgical. Willy Schottroff, however, concludes from his analysis of curses in early Israel that the curses are by no means tied to the cult. They are used as means to exclude offenders from the clan or tribe. Later, however, the cultic connection becomes more pronounced.[26]

To understand this, we need only remember what transpires in the LP. The enemies of the nation are at war against God (for example, Psalms 2:8; 18:47; etc.). The LP, using a stereotyped terminology, emphasizes the universal authority of the kings in Jerusalem and the paradoxical, intolerable, oppression of the people of God. Hence the lament and petition in theses psalms. They ask, "Why?"—and more often than not conclude with a divine judgment (60:11–12). They ask, "How long?" (74:10; 79:5)—and come to acknowledge that the foes of the nation are scourges in the hand of God. But the hostility of the instruments of Yhwh goes regularly beyond the measure of the divine wrath. Hostile nations set themselves against the Creator and Lord of the peoples; from being God's allies, they become Yhwh's foes (8:3). It is often asked that God punish them as harshly as they have oppressed Israel. Guilt is shifted from Israel to those initially chosen to chastise her.

On the model of the LP, the situation is transferred to the LI. Parallels are drawn between the nation's enemies and the individual's foes; between the guilt of both and that both need repentance. As Israel must repent, so too must the suppliant Israelite. The complaint about the

25. Kraus, *Theology of the Psalms*, pp. 125ff.

26. Willy Schottroff, *Der altisraelitische Fluchspruch* (Neukirchen-Vluyn: Neukirchen Verlag, 1969).

enemy is the most developed part of the lament. Thirty-six psalms speak of an attempt against the life of the lamenter. Sometimes, the stress is on the hostile preparatory acts: the enemies surround, they encircle (Psalm 22:13, 14, 17). The foes are godless (14:1); they are powerful and rich, beyond the reach of God's judgment (73:3–5, 12); no opposition to them seems possible.

As seen above, the lamenter's predicament is compounded by the discovery of a grave hiatus between collective and personal history. There is a scandalous contrast between the "larger context" and the "intimate context." The two are out of tune with each other (Psalm 22:3–6). Therefore, the "enemies" feel that it is fair to say: How could the poor be part of us? Their wretchedness denies the efficacy of God's Covenant with us. They say, "where is *your* God?" (42:10; 79:10) and the possessive pronoun in the second person insists once again on the chasm between the individual's alleged private God and the official God of official religion.

But in the LI a new problem has arisen that was not present in the LP, namely, a doubt about the validity of the Covenant as far as the individual Israelite is concerned. The individual in the LI is worried about his or her status within the covenantal community. The point is to know whether the terms of the compact between God and the people are also applicable to his or her case. For, if so, according to one important aspect of the ancient Near Eastern treaty, both the partners are in a relation of "kinship." They are bound as "brothers," or as "father and son." This latter metaphor is especially important for us as it is invoked by the suppliant in Psalm 22:10f. as descriptive of the type of relationship discerned between God and him or her: "it was you who took me from the womb . . ." (NRSV; cf. the Hittite treaty formula: "into my sonship [says the suzerain to the vassal], I take thee").[27] Such a "blood" tie unites the parties against a common enemy: "My enemy is your enemy and my friend is your friend."[28] This whole concept sheds light on the psalm's problematic. The major role played by foes in the LI is better understood from the standpoint of an implicit plea that such enemies be also God's enemies, as indeed they are in the terms of the contract between God and his people.

Within this perspective, the prayer's emphasis on the first-person singular is crucial. God is *my* God, not just "our" God or the God of

---

27. See E. F. Weidner, *Boghazkoi-Studien* = fasc. 8–9 of the Mitteilungen der vorderasiatisch-aegyptischen Gesellschaft (Berlin, 1923), no. 2, obv. 22.

28. See J. Nougayrol, *Le palais royal d'Ugarit* (Paris: Klincksieck, 1956), vol. 4, pp. 36, 10ff.

the Ancestors. Conversely, it is not just our God who has forsaken me, but my God, the one whom I used to trust and who all the same remains in all circumstances my God. That is why lament and praise go together. "'My God' designate[s] the divinity to whom the individual supplicant and his family or clan group are intimately or even exclusively attached. The term indicates the 'personal God,' originally in small-scale family worship in a setting of primary-group rituals."[29]

The one who says "my God" wonders how it is possible to live on a collective level within the covenantal communion with God, while on an individual level feeling abandoned by God. Invoking the temporal axis, he asks, is there any relation between the redeemed past of the Ancestors and the unredeemed present of the individual? Is "their" wonderful Deliverer also "my" God? Does my wretchedness also reflect something of their blessedness? At first glance—which is the glance of the enemies—there occurs nothing of the sort. How could suffering and loss be part of deliverance and success? In fact, the solution of the dilemma is given by divine confirmation and deliverance of the sufferer. For the situation demanded no less than a theophany—left untold (see also Isaiah 41:8–13; 14–16; Jeremiah 15:19–21)—in order to reverse the terms of a demonstration upheld by official theology, a perfectly logical one at that.

But once the theophany vindicates the sufferer, one of two things must happen. Either the theophany also convinces the "theologians" and they repent, or they stick to their theology in the name of the authority granted them by the very God who showed himself to the lamenter. In the latter case, the official theologians fatefully persist in being the "enemies, dogs, lions, and buffaloes" that are after the one who, in contrast, is the just and the pious individual. Significantly, in the reuse of Psalm 22 by the Gospel, those who scorn and jeer are the chief priests, scribes, and elders: Matthew 27:39–44; Mark 15:29–32; Luke 23:35–37.

Kraus has conducted a thorough inquiry into the identity of the enemies of the individual.[30] They are evildoers, godless, persecutors. The *rašaʿim* say in their hearts, "I shall not be moved" (Psalm 10:6). They assert through their lies and malicious gossip that the innocent are guilty. They want the destruction of the defenseless and the poor, they

---

29. Gerstenberger, *Psalms, Part I*, p. 109. He indicates that the word *'eli* (my God) appears only eleven times in the Old Testament. He adds to this, "a personal prayer for small-group worship that took place within the general Israelite society" (ibid., p. 110).

30. Kraus, *Theology of the Psalms*, pp. 125ff.

ridicule their victims (Psalm 35). They spread slander (for example, 5:9; 27:12; etc.). They are respectable members of the community (4:2, emendation; 35:10). The situation is that of war (35:1). They are compared to ravenous beasts (22:12f., 17, 21–22; 35:17; etc.). Their victims are no match for them, for the just are weak (35:10), vulnerable, destroyed (22:24; 10:2, 9; etc.). As their sole recourse, they are "cast" upon Yhwh alone (22:10).

According to Kraus's study, the settings for the foes' misdeeds are two in number. First, at the court, where they accuse the victims of breaking the law. Second, in the sanctuary, where they appear as captious guardians of the institution of purification for those who are sick. As a matter of fact, in sickness, guilt is made manifest as its true cause and must be atoned for.[31] This indeed reveals a disturbing aspect of the practice of retributive justice in the precincts of the sanctuary.[32]

There are clearly parallels and contrasts between Psalm 22 and the book of Job. In both, we find a comparable consciousness of abandonment, although in Job there is a striking absence of praise. But Job is, let us recall, non-Israelite. He is not dealing with a God he can call *Eli* (Psalm 22:2), *Elohay* (22:3), or *Yhwh* (22:20, 24, 27, 28, 29). The problematic is different. Job raises the problem of unjust suffering in general; it is a universal problem. Psalm 22 does not raise the problem of unjust suffering. At no point does the lamenter claim innocence, nor does she or he put the lie to the accusers. But in both places we witness the struggle of the sufferer with an ideology of retribution. Like the enemies in Psalm 22, Job's "friends" are supporters of retributive justice. Another particularity of the psalm is its setting in the Temple, where difficult legal cases are judged (Deuteronomy 17:8–13). In the presence of enemies (Psalm 4), the accused describe their plight as an "archetypal affliction of God-forsakenness . . . in a mortal sickness," says Kraus.[33]

At any rate, with the private suffering of an individual, we are smack in the middle of the cosmic struggle for divine justice. As the psalmist is convinced of the ultimate victory of God, she or he wraps up the hymn with a proclamation of God's victory. But, before the psalmist can celebrate, she or he must acknowledge and assume the presence of evil both in the suppliant's personal life and in God's creation. This indeed is what brings the psalmist to lament rather than to dogma or

---

31. See ibid., pp. 131, 132.

32. See Klaus Seybold, *Das Gebet des Kranken im Alten Testament* (Stuttgart: Kohlhammer, 1973).

33. Hans-Joachim Kraus, *Psalmen 1–50* (Neukirchen-Vluyn: Neukirchen Verlag, 1978), p. 294.

ideology. True, many an aspect of existence and history can receive a valid and decisive explanation by causality. But when we come to the issue of evil, we remain in a quandary because it is the aporia par excellence. Any "definitive solution" to this query entails a crime: the innocent is treated as guilty, and the judges become ravenous beasts thirsty for the blood of the poor; they are the enemies of the lamenter.

Whether we can go much further in identifying the enemies in the LI is doubtful. It is clear that those who accuse and perhaps judge the defendants are not their peers. With E. Podechard, we can say with confidence, however, that they are "those in power" or "the officials"; we can compare Psalm 22:19 and 1 Kings 21:15f. (the story of Naboth).[34] Very unsettling information is provided, however, by the Middle Assyrian laws (*ANET,* p. 183, par. 40). In them, we find a stipulation that sheds light on Psalm 22:19. According to it, the condemned one's clothes are given to the prosecutor or to the one who arrested the culprit.[35] If this practice was also extant in Israel, it would be an enticement to many to unjustly surround a defendant and accuse him or her. In that case, as well, the powerful judges would not be the only "enemies." There are also those whom Gerstenberger calls "neighbors," thus adding more misery that seems typical of the sufferer's plight (Psalms 31:10–14; 38:11–14; 69:4–5; 8–13; Job 19:13–19; 30:1–15).[36] In Psalm 22:17–19, someone is condemned and exposed to public jeers (cf. Isaiah 53:3). He is tied up, persecuted by "bulls" (= powerful men; v. 13), and by a lion (= their leader; v. 14). He is about to be executed by the sword (v. 21f.).

All this, it seems to me, points in the direction of a deepening chasm between two types of population in Israel. Those divisions did not originate, as Morton Smith among others has shown, as a postexilic phenomenon. There is nothing surprising in having in the Temple of Jerusalem, before its destruction by the Babylonians, a trend of piety that would not conform with the official established ideology. After all, the heavy insistence of the LI on powerful enemies surrounding the lamenter, whom the latter would not even dream of confronting, clearly betrays a profound rift within people living in the same places and visiting the same courts and shrines.

That such foes are compared with dogs, wolves, lions, bulls, and sun-

---

34. E. Podechard, *Le Psautier: Traduction littérale et explication historique* (Lyon: Faculté catholique, 1949), pp. 104, 107.

35. Cf. A. A. Anderson, *The NCBC: Psalms,* p. 191.

36. Gerstenberger, *Psalms, Part I,* p. 111.

dry such beasts, while in other literary genres those animals designate hostile foreign nations, shows how seriously we must take the hatred and loathing dividing the two groups. Unless we do just that, the intercession prayer for the enemy on the part of the Suffering Servant (or, later, of Jesus on the cross) becomes a rhetorical exercise in self-control and magnanimity. But the enemy in the psalms is the antipode of the *hasid* (the pious). Both do not ultimately belong in the same community. An expression of Psalm 22 such as *qahal rab* (v. 26a) is perhaps somewhat ambiguous; less so already is "those who fear him" (v. 26b); and quite unequivocal are "the *'anawim*" (v. 27), or in other psalms the *qehal hasidim, sadikim, yesarim, 'ebionim*. The qualifiers are distinguishing identifiers.

In summary, the enemies in Psalm 22 are probably more than just personal foes of the psalmist. There may be with the expression "great assembly" a play on words in the sense that the lamenter is conscious of belonging to a "great assembly of the afflicted," different of course from the Great Assembly of official religion.[37] While the "enemies" claim that they represent the majority, this claim is challenged. They share indeed a majority ideology and they represent the mainstream in Israel's "great assembly." But the petitioner recalls that suffering is not the lot of a few. The disenfranchised also are "a great congregation." A similar situation obtains when we realize with Artur Weiser that the ever more yawning gap between the "pious" and the "wicked" in the psalms must be explained from the side of cultic ideology.[38] "Humble, poor, etc." come from the cultic vocabulary in relation to the divine majesty and from the often recurring situation of the people humiliated by the neighboring nations and in need of God's help. The extension of such vocabulary to the social sphere within the people is thus secondary. It springs from the certainty that those most in need of help are especially protected by God.

The chasm between the "haves" and the "have-nots" did not result in the constitution of two communities, however, a situation that would have been made possible if individualism had prevailed as such. As

---

37. In Psalm 107:32, for example, *biqehal 'am ubemoshab zekenim* designates the cultic community. Cf. Psalm 35:18; Exodus 16:3; Leviticus 4:13ff., 21; Numbers 10:7; 15:15; 17:12; 20:6; etc. Probably in the same vein, Psalm 22 speaks of "my brothers." The expression is unusual, but inconclusive; it appears again in the plural in 69:9 (in parallel with "sons of my mother"); 122:8 (general use); 133:1 ("how good it is for brothers to sit together"). For Hans-J. Kraus, the "brothers" are merely fellow worshipers.

38. Weiser, *Die Psalmen übersetz und erklärt*, p. 63.

there is in Psalm 22 no protest of innocence, there is also no political viewpoint expressed. Even at the time of the composition of the psalm we are not yet witnessing that kind of opposition between two parties. However, the enemy is a ferment contributing to the dissolution of the community. As Kraus says, "The subject is not the 'Hebrew individual' (L. Köhler), but 'the individual in Israel.'" This explains why the psalmist uses a body of stock formulas and thereby stresses his "participation in the tradition of Israel's prayer language" (Psalm: 22:3–5).[39]

It may, therefore, be that Rahlfs, Causse, and others after them erred by sheer exaggeration. It is only after the exile and in the then-prevailing circumstances that the Hasidim/Ebionim became a religious party. Not all the psalms need to be read as composed by those people, even when the term "hasidim" or its cognates are used (contra Causse). Before they were a party, the Hasidim were a class. Kraus's definition is initially correct: "the 'poor' are . . . those who appeal to Yhwh for mercy and for help in obtaining justice (Psalm 9:18; 10:2, 8–11; 18:27; 35:10; 74:19)."[40] Whether a religious and economic class, or a religious and political party, they were always the disenfranchised ones, demanding justice from the "establishment."

This is why I agree with Carroll Stuhlmueller, who sees in Psalm 22 a style of piety akin to nonliturgical manifestations of religious feelings in Israel's early history; what Roland de Vaux called the prereligion period of Israelite history. Stuhlmueller supposes that laments started to be gathered "out of religious services during the exile, without temple or sacred place."[41]

The very presence of the truly guilty party, of the arrogant godless ones, sufficed to make the Hasidim innocent victims. In short, there was no necessity of spelling out in great detail how the adversaries were wicked, or how the Hasidim were innocent. "This conception of the poor practically contains a legal claim upon Yhwh; and it was precisely this which later made it a self-designation of the pious before Yhwh."[42] For a long time, the two antagonists could remain without any kind of "electoral program." But the pious knew that the *reša'im* made *shalom*

39. Kraus, *Theology of the Psalms*, pp. 138, 139.

40. Ibid. p. 151. "'Poor' are those who are denied justice . . . who lack social status. . . . Paradoxically, the claim to rights is not based on what one 'has' but on what one does not have. . . . It is characteristic of the human situation before God, which finds its theological expression in the New Testament in the doctrine of justification" (ibid., pp. 152–53).

41. Stuhlmueller, *Psalms 1*, pp. 36, 38.

42. Gerhard von Rad, *Old Testament Theology*, vol. 1, translated by D. M. G. Stalker (New York: Harper & Row, 1962), p. 400.

impossible, were destroying *shalom* by their very attitude and fundamental options.

After the exile, however, the psalms, among other scriptures, were reread in the light of the new circumstances that then obtained. The vocabulary of wretchedness, persecution, and injustice, on the one hand, along with that of piety, righteousness, and faithfulness, on the other, was naturally reinterpreted as reflecting the new era of the readers. If need be, some editing occurred, which brought the texts up to date, as we find in Psalm 22 in the last verses of the psalm. Hence Kraus's declaration that "the 'poor' do not represent a religious party in Israel" (*Theology of the Psalms*, p. 153) must be taken with caution. The very fact that he feels obligated to put the word "poor" consistently within quotation marks is significant.

It is worth noting that Jesus' attitude of denunciation and condemnation was due, at least in part, to his opposition to "sinners" corresponding to the "wicked," the *reša'im*, in the psalter. It is the same inner strife in the time of the Gospel as in the time of the laments of the pious in the psalter. It is, therefore, with no surprise that we discover that Psalm 22 is a text frequently referred to by the New Testament. It plays a central role in the scene of Christ's Passion where we are told that Jesus uttered verse 2a on the cross. Maurice Goguel thinks that the tradition is authentic, for no one would imagine in the early Church that Jesus was abandoned by God.[43] Thus Psalm 22 becomes a prophecy followed by its fulfillment; in John 19:23f. we read, "This was to fulfill what the scripture says [in Psalm 22]." In fact, in the Gospel, Psalm 22 was seen as a promise accomplished by events in which three motifs of the psalm were incorporated:

1. the deriding of the sufferer (22:7 // Mark 15:29 and parallels);
2. scornful challenge (v. 8 // Matthew 27:43);
3. the dividing of the clothes and the casting of lots (22:18 // Mark 15:24 and parallels).

As Hartmut Gese points out, the New Testament offers this oldest understanding of Jesus' death by escalating death to the highest degree of suffering. God's rescue of Jesus from death brings about the King-

---

43. We find the same point in Kraus: "This cry belongs to the unforgettable remembrance of what had occurred" (*Theology of the Psalms*, p. 188).

dom of God. The Lord's supper "deals with the *todah* of the Risen One."[44]

In a similar vein, Hebrews 2:10–17 refers to Psalm 22:23 as a proof text for the kenosis and glorification of the Son of God. But there is here a totally new element: Christ says that he came to *doxazein* (glorify) God, and there is no doubt that he means this through his sacrifice. Psalm 22:23, "I will tell of your Name . . ." is now interpreted in a most radical way as predicated by the cross. John 17:1, 26 are unequivocal about it; verse 26 reads, "I made your name known to them . . ." Similarly, John 21:19: "He said this to indicate the kind of death by which he would glorify God." Thus, while Psalm 22 showed the shift from lament to praise through the removal of evil and suffering, now praise is through death, in death (John 2; 7; 12; 13; 17; and especially Philippians 2:8).

The early Church saw in Christ's suffering and death another aspect that is made clear, for example, in Matthew 8:17. After showing that Jesus cured all who were sick, the text adds, "This was to fulfill what had been spoken through the prophet Isaiah, 'He took our infirmities and bore our diseases.'" To affirm with the New Testament that Jesus took upon himself all suffering that befell people and individuals in Israel means that Christ identified himself with all his people's suffering, bearing it vicariously. Both faces of this understanding must be kept in mind when the disciples testify that they heard Jesus reciting, "My God, my God, why have you forsaken me?" By quoting Psalm 22 in the unique circumstance of the cross, Jesus, according to the Church's hermeneutic, not only taught the deep interpretation of the Hebrew text, he also provided the psalm with a unique, decisive, and ultimate meaning. This is a privileged hermeneutical example of a text's increased meaning from the time of its composition. True, from that initial moment on, the total meaning of the text was included within its words, as in a jewel case to be some time opened. The original lamenter was, to be sure, justified to complain to God about being abandoned. His or her experience was complete in itself as it reached the bottom of the abyss. But the psalmist did also share this terrible experience with the whole of the community and thus was able also to associate the whole congregation with his or her subsequent praise of God. In other words,

44. Hartmut Gese, "Psalm 22 and the New Testament," *Zeitschrift für Theologie und Kirche* 65 (1968): 22.

the suppliant's experience was brought to the level of a common, universal experience, and there an experience susceptible of being elevated to its ultimate expression and fulfillment. As Westermann writes, "Only because [the psalmist] had experienced God's remoteness and God's silence could he experience their reversal; and because he had experienced this reversal, he had to recount it. What he had to recount had to advance even further, for God has acted."[45]

The giant step universalizing the lament is made when Jesus adopts the words of Psalm 22 to describe the event on Calvary. With Jesus crucified, it becomes kerygmatically clear that from the outset of its history, Israel has been a crucified people and that the lamenter's words were in fact reflecting the profound identity of the whole community.

Furthermore, it also becomes clear that such ongoing suffering has not been for nought, that it has not been "marginalized" as just one dimension of Israel's being, rendered relative by other more "acceptable" dimensions. Israel's vicarious suffering has not been lost. In Christ's suffering, Israel's suffering receives its letters of mark, so to speak, letters that it did expect with trust and certainty all along. As the Epistle to the Hebrews says, "[Jesus] had to become like his brothers and sisters in every respect, so that he might be a merciful and faithful high priest in the service of God, to make a sacrifice of atonement for the sins of the people. Because he himself was tested by what he suffered, he is able to help those who are being tested" (2:17–18 NRSV).

That is how Israel's suffering becomes paradigmatic for human suffering.[46] Psalm 22 itself broadens the individual and national perspective to the universal by the addition of verses 27–31: "all the families of the nations shall worship before him. . . . To him, indeed, shall all who sleep in the earth . . . all who go down to the dust. . . . Future generations will be told about the Lord, and proclaim his deliverance to a people yet unborn, saying that he has done it" (NRSV). The invitation to the dead to praise God is clearly related to the psalmist's former predicament that he described as being no better than death itself. Similarly, the second part of the statement, including those yet unborn, alludes to the psalmist's earlier evocation of his birth, even of his embry-

45. Westermann, *The Living Psalms*, p. 91.

46. Jesus' "plight becomes a paradigm of the trouble of the lamenting petitioner; and his experience of personal agony, of God-forsakenness, and of the taunts and attacks of various kinds of enemies and evildoers gives us the cardinal example of how the dimensions of the lament express the realities of human experience" (Miller, *Interpreting the Psalms*, p. 63).

onic state when God was already his God (v. 11).[47] The inclusion of the dead in the chorus praising God is not necessarily a metaphor, for the "comparison" of the sick with the dead is more than a comparison (more than an "oriental exaggeration"). For the ancient Near Eastern literature, it is simply realism.

There is no consensus on the interpretation of the psalmist's declaration, however. For W. O. E. Oesterley, the dead will celebrate God in Sheol,[48] while for E. J. Kissane, the dead celebrate in the person of their descendants.[49] A. A. Anderson thinks of those who were close to death, as in Psalm 30:3, so that the verse here would mean "even those who were about to sleep in the Sheol will pay homage to him, and all those who were nearly gone down to the dust (of the underworld) will bend their knee before him."[50] Be that as it may, Weiser is certainly correct when he speaks here of the "eschatological fulfillment of the Kingdom of God."[51] Gerstenberger goes even further: "The last part (vv. 28–32) is eschatological if not apocalyptic in nature." These verses, he adds, "presuppose . . . late postexilic life and theology."[52]

Its absence of vindictiveness belongs to the psalm's eschatologization. In contrast with Psalms 2, 3, 5, 6, 7, 9, 10, and many others, there is here no request for vengeance. On the contrary, Weiser calls attention to the inclusive character of an expression used by the psalm in the thanksgiving part, such as "the children of Israel" (v. 24). These include the "enemies" as well.[53] It is the first time that the enemy is included in the supplication of the mediator (cf. Isaiah 53:12). "This," says Westermann, "is the clearest connection we can find between the Old and the New Testament. The Gospel accounts of the suffering and death of

---

47. In this way, it is made clear that for biblical anthropology, God's praise starts before birth and lasts beyond death. Human existence has a prehistory of its own and a posthistory.

48. W. O. E. Oesterley, *The Psalms Translated with Text-Critical and Exegetical Notes*, 2 vols. (London: SPCK, 1939), vol. 1, p. 181.

49. Edward J. Kissane, *The Book of Psalms* (Westminster, MD: Newman Press, 1953–54), vol. 1, p. 102.

50. Anderson, *The NCBC: Psalms*, p. 194.

51. Weiser, *Die Psalmen übersetz und erklärt*, p. 152.

52. Gerstenberger, *Psalms, Part I*, p. 112. This opinion is shared by Westermann. Regarding all those "who sleep in the earth," he says, "only in apocalypses do we meet anything like this" (*The Living Psalms*, p. 90).

53. Weiser, *Die Psalmen übersetz und erklärt*, p. 152. Similarly, we have the "posterity of Jacob/Israel" (v. 24), which goes back at least to Jeremiah. It is true that Anderson may be right when he puts this expression in parallel with "you who fear the Lord" and, thus, thinks that it refers "to the true Israel and not to the whole ethnic unit" (p. 192).

Jesus follow the Servant Songs point by point. In both the suffering is vicarious; in both the one who suffers is confirmed by God in and through death; in both he intercedes for his enemies; and, in both there is a community which believes that the suffering and dying was for them."[54]

This double "extravagance"[55] of the psalm opens it to its eschatological use by Jesus. Verses 28–32 are the exact counterpart of verses 2–3. Lament, praise, the assertion that wretchedness belongs within the covenantal relationship with God, and the vindication/glorification of such an assertion, of every aspect of human life, from before birth (v. 11f.) to after death (v. 32f.), and every aspect of the human response to God are found in this psalm. Hence, in its complexity, Psalm 22 is not only a LI (borrowing heavily from the LP) and a Thanksgiving Hymn in its second part, it is also a Royal Psalm celebrating the universal kingship of God.[56] As verse 28 says, ever larger circles of people shall praise, to the ends of the earth; even the dying and the dead, and those as yet unborn (v. 31; cf. Psalm 117).[57]

The theme of all nations recognizing God's kingship and praising him belongs to the larger context of the doctrine of divine creation. Interestingly, Psalm 22 alludes at least twice to God as Creator. It is the Creator God who is also the Redeemer/Healer. Here is another sign of the influence of Second Isaiah on Psalm 22. This theology allows the psalmist daringly to make the leap from his personal restoration to the cosmic meanings of such redemption (v. 28ff.), as we saw above. We return to it in these final remarks on Psalm 22 in order to make a further point.

Psalm 22 is a *prayer* from beginning to end. There is something misleading in imagining that the psalmist heard a reassuring oracle in the middle of his petition. Perhaps Begrich and Gunkel are correct in thinking that there was such an intervention, but there is nothing *ex opere operato* in such a priestly or prophetic response to the supplication. If there is a shift in tone between the former and the latter part of the psalm, as indeed there is, such a transformation remains within the con-

---

54. Westermann, *The Living Psalms*, p. 278.

55. The term is used in this context by P. D. Miller, *Interpreting the Psalms*, p. 107.

56. Westermann says that v. 28 is "a clear reminiscence of the psalms celebrating God's kingly rule, Psalm 93; 95–99" (*The Living Psalms*, p. 90). Along these same lines, Bentzen and Eaton had argued that Psalm 22 is a Royal Psalm with a symbolic humiliation and restoration of the king. See Aage Bentzen, *King and Messiah* (Naperville, IL: Allenson, 1955); John H. Eaton, *Kingship and the Psalms* (London: SCM Press, 1976).

57. Cf. from Ugarit: "Yea, to him all who sleep in the earth bow down."

fines of the plea. Here, I believe, is the limit of Westermann's division between plea and praise. Praise remains plea until the end. On the model of the LP, where the motif of divine victory over chaos is used to beg Yhwh to be as powerful with Israel's present enemies as he was in the beginning with the Ancestors and former generations, in the LI as well, God is begged to be the Redeemer he is and proved to be in the past (Psalm 22:5–6). "You answered me!" (v. 22c) is profoundly and decisively true, but only for the believer. It is an act of faith, a vote of trust in God, so to speak, a proleptic present of the indicative. Before it occurs factually and in history, it is already true liturgically and spiritually.[58] Already—not yet: the whole "Christian" faith is fully present in Psalm 22. Because of the absence of hiatus between the two poles, the Psalm is said by Christ on the cross as if it were for the very first time.

58. "We cannot overemphasize therefore the unmediated juxtaposition, in the Hebrew Bible, of the liturgical and hymnic affirmation of the omnipotence of God and the confession of the persistence of evil, a confession that is itself raised to the lyrical plane of the lamentation. The relation of the full sovereignty of God to the end of time only underscores the dissonance between the proclamation of omnipotence and the confession of the 'terror of history.'" Paul Ricoeur, "Fides Quaerens Intellectum: Antécédents bibliques?" *Archivio di Filosofia* 68 (1990): 38.

Lamentation as Prayer

PAUL RICOEUR

There are few texts whose subsequent trajectory has had such an effect on their original meaning as is the case with Psalm 22. The use of this verse by the crucified one, according to the evangelists Mark and Luke, and the incorporation of the whole Psalter into the liturgies of the synagogue and of Christian churches of different confessions—not to speak of their use within domestic or personal piety—bears witness to the astounding power of reactualization of these poems stemming from Hebrew piety.

The quite particular style of this actualization cannot fail to draw our attention to the side of the linguistic structure that allowed the psalms in general, and the one which we have chosen to consider, to perpetuate themselves with such an extraordinary vigor. As regards the "great cry" of Jesus on the cross, it is worth noting that it does not reduce to the "quotation" of one verse, as is the case for many other of the borrowings that the New Testament makes from the Hebrew Bible, especially to show that the ancient Scriptures were "fulfilled" in the Christ event. It is not a question of a linkage brought about by the narrator, but rather of a new actualization of the same words by the central character of the Passion narratives. The dying Jesus clothes his suffering in the words of the psalm, which he wears, so to speak, from the inside. The liturgical use of the Psalter over the millennia does not escape the rules of "quotation." It rests on the repetition of the same sort of language acts in a practice analogous to the communal or private worship that found its original expression in the prayers of the psalms.

Therefore it is the quite original mode of this actualizing perpetuation that invites us to seek within the poetic composition of the psalm one of the conditions of its reactualization in subsequent prayer.

The psalms are first of all poems that bring to the rank of speech, and writing, and finally of a text, fundamental moments of religious experience. Therefore it is from this original link between experience and language that we must begin. We may, certainly, speak of religious experience to characterize attitudes toward the divine as different as a feeling of absolute dependence, the experience of a boundless trust, the thrust of ultimate concern, and the consciousness of belonging to an economy of the gift that precedes every human movement of charity. Yet these feelings would remain unformed if they were not articulated in language. And in this regard, prayer is the most primitive and original act of language that gives form to religious experience. If, with William James, we distinguish among "varieties of religious experience," in each case it is different forms of prayer that give it a flesh of words. The prayer of lamentation will be, I shall say, a privileged form of such prayer. We might even risk saying that if there is a means by which religious experience lets itself be said beyond any theology, any speculation, it is through prayer.

It is true that the Bible knows other ways of "naming God." The Hebrew Scriptures divide themselves into the Torah, the Prophets, and the other writings. If, within the Torah, we distinguish narratives and laws, none of these writings, as such, consist in an address *to* God, which is what prayer does. God is the great "actant" whose deed is what the narratives recount. God is also the legislator who addresses human beings in the first person what the Law applies to the second person: "you shall not kill." As for the prophets, they speak in the first person in the name of another who, through their voice, also speaks in the first person and who addresses human beings called in the second person like the Law. As for the wisdom writings, the core of the group of "other writings," they speak of God rather than speaking to God, even if they sometimes do give wisdom the authority of a word of God or give the sages' question the form of a prayer addressed to God. In this respect, we shall see below that the *why?* of the psalms of lamentation is contiguous with the *why?* that wisdom turns toward God. But we shall also see the frontier that separates a why held within the bounds of prayer from a why that frees itself from this framework and enters into the space of gravitation of speculation concerning God. So long as interrogation remains included within the boundaries of an address to God, it conserves a more "existential" than speculative aspect, or, we might say, it continues to arise from the practice of worship, whether this be public or private.

Therefore if we want to distinguish prayer from the other ways in which God is "named" in the Bible, it is through the speech act consisting in a praying subject who says "I" in addressing himself to God as the supreme "thou." In this regard, if prayer alone does not distinguish monotheism from polytheism, it has a place only within a religion where the God to whom it is addressed is recognized, if not as a person, at least as not less than a person. In the Hebrew Bible, then for the writers of the New Testament, prayer is addressed to the one who, even before the faithful one addresses himself to him, has declared to the faithful: "Hear, O Israel, Yhwh our God is alone Yhwh."

The time has come to situate the genre of the prayer of lamentation within a general typology of Hebrew prayer. Like André LaCocque, I will adopt, without being overly concerned about its limits, the classification of the psalms established by Hermann Gunkel, and taken up and refined by Claus Westermann and Hans-Joachim Kraus.[1] It rests, as is well known, on the polar opposition between lament and praise and continues with the distinction between the individual lament and that of the people (the collective lament). In this way, Psalm 22 finds itself classified among the psalms of lamentation. This classification constitutes a useful guide to help us orient ourselves within the typology of the forms (*Gattungen*) of the psalms. Nevertheless, what is most important to me does not lie in the classification but in the disquieting, paradoxical, and almost scandalous character of the prayer of lamentation.

---

1. Hermann Gunkel's work, *Einleitung in die Psalmen* (1933) marks an important step in the exegesis of the psalms. The divisions he proposes are founded on (1) the tie to a specific occasion of devotion, principally the cultus; (2) the type of thoughts and sentiments expressed; and (3) the verbal structure. Claus Westermann adopts Gunkel's typology and refines it even further in *Lob und Klage in den Psalmen* (Vandehoek und Ruprecht, 1977). He superimposes on Gunkel's typology what might be seen as a kind of transversal structure consisting of the triad: You (God)—Me (the one praying)—the Other (the "enemies," in the case of the lament, the congregation of the "poor" and the "pious" in the case of the psalm of praise). Considering the psalms of lamentation from a diachronic point of view, Westermann insists on the repression of the lament to the profit of supplication and penitence under the influence of the theology of the prophets, and particularly of the Deuteronomist. This subsequent effacement brings to light another triad, one that we can still observe in Psalm 22, between lament (*Klage*), supplication (*Bitte*), and the vow of praise (*Lobegelübde*). Hans-Joachim Kraus, *Psalmen 1–50* (Neukirchen-Vluyn: Neukirchener Verlag, 1978), also relativizes Gunkel's distinctions. For example, to the question, *who* is lamenting? we have to reply that, within the type of culture to which the biblical writers belonged, the individual is never considered in isolation. Hence even the "enemies" of the individual are themselves members, that is, groups of individuals, within the community. Above all, the lament is almost always just one of two foci of a psalm considered as a whole, praise constituting the other focal point. Finally, critical reflection always insists that the theme and the form have to be taken into consideration together with each other.

Or, to put it a better way, of the "lamentation as prayer," taking up the apt title of a book by Ottmar Fuchs: *Die Klage als Gebet*.[2] In order to respect the striking character of this title, the terminology we must use is not indifferent. The translation of the German *Klage* by *lamentation* in French and by lament in English does not capture the provocative kinship in German between lament (*Klage*) and accusation (*Anklage*). Indeed, we shall soon have to confront the enigma of a lament that remains for all that caught up within an invocation, but which gives an interrogative form to its lament, which dares to speak of suffering as "being abandoned by God," and yet that leads by way of the poem to the edges of praise, thanks to a no less enigmatic reversal than the inaugural moment of the lament itself.

We speak of a path "by way of the poem." In fact, it is the form of the poem that we must interrogate to identify the linguistic and scriptural features that allowed the Psalter, as a whole, and Psalm 22 in particular, to be reinscribed and, as I said above, to be reactualized in new contexts.

Structure and Sense

A methodological comment is called for before we undertake our investigation. Owing to its structural character, this investigation seems to be oriented in an opposite direction from that of the historical-critical method, which is the basis for André LaCocque's approach. Instead of placing the accent on the *Sitz im Leben* of the psalms within the cultus or among other concrete practices, literary analysis sets out in quest of a suprahistorical invariant, capable of being removed from the historical conditions of its first appearance and of being reinvested in new life contexts.[3]

Without denying this difference in orientation, I would like already to emphasize the complementary character of these two methodologi-

2. I owe to Ottmar Fuchs, *Die Klage als Gebet. Eine theologische Besinnung am Beispiel des Psalms 22* (Munich: Kösel Verlag, 1982) not only the title of this chapter, but also the attention I pay in turn to the structural aspects of the poem. Fuchs expressly links these features to what he calls the textualization (*Vertextung*) of the feelings that are expressed. In turn, these features are responsible for the capacity of the verbal form to be reactualized in contemporary Jewish and Christian prayer—even after Auschwitz! This link between the quasi *zeitlos* character of the model and the generative power that the poem is held to develop within the practice of prayer constitutes the principal thesis that Fuchs proposes concerning a renewed theology of the practice of prayer.

3. André LaCocque summarizes the discussion opened by Gunkel concerning the localizing of the psalms of individual lament within the cultus and also speaks to the question of dating them. He also takes up the problems of identifying the protagonists with his discussion of the question of who were the "enemies" and the "poor."

cal approaches. In fact, only knowledge of the circumstances in which a text was produced and composed allow us, by means of comparison and contrast, to identify the features capable of contributing to what we can call the decontextualization of the message and its recontextualization in a different setting than the original setting.

All these features, we shall see, have to do with the textual status that the psalm gained. More precisely, it is as a written poem that the psalm, considered in terms of its final redactional state and its canonical setting, has come down to us, to the point of being able to be inserted once again today into our practice of prayer. This general feature of poetic textualization bears a special significance within the case of literary works like the psalms, which express feelings—especially when these feelings are of the order of suffering, distress, and dereliction as is the case with the psalms of lamentation. First of all, speech had to bring to articulated expression what might have remained only cries, tears, and sighs. Next, writing—writing composed in terms of the canons of Hebrew poetry—had to raise this speech to the rank of a text capable of being memorized, recited, and sung.[4] In this respect, the time is no longer when, owing to romantic taste, one praised the spontaneous expression of a religious soul in the psalms. What is surprising, however, is that the poetic composition should have attempted to fix and to preserve that emotional spontaneity, that it should have made it exemplary and communicable, in a way "outside its context."

It is the procedures responsible for this poetization of the lamentation that we need now to render more explicit. The first one occurs on the lexical plane, in the choice of words to speak of suffering. It consists in a concerted effacement of the singularizing marks of the suffering that is expressed. It is difficult to be precise whether the sufferer is ill, close to death, or who it is exactly that is persecuting him. Poetic language's tour de force is that it preserves enough concrete indications to keep the lament within the horizon of an individual experience and, thanks to a calculated indetermination, to raise the expression of suffering to the rank of a paradigm. This stylistic effect corroborates the

4. Kraus emphasizes the tension between the concrete character of situations of distress and the effect of verbal ritualization brought about by poetic expression. If the accusations and thoughts that afflict the supplicant present a certain precision, it is difficult to identify the individuals and groups designated as "enemies." In this sense, all the positions designated are empty places capable of being occupied by different individuals or groups. A comparable attention to the linguistic function can be found in John S. Kselman, "Why Have You Abandoned Me? A Rhetorical Study of Psalm 22," in *Art and Meaning in Biblical Literature*, edited by David J. A. Clines, David M. Gunn, and Alan J. Hauser (Sheffield: JSOT Press, 1982), pp. 172–98.

opinion of many exegetes for whom the poems we are reading serve as available formulations within a cultic setting for the expression of individual laments that vary among themselves. This interplay of singularization and generalization also affects the personality of the one praying as much as it does his suffering. Words such as "I," "my," "you," and "your" lose their deictic function, which is to designate one particular individual. In this regard, one of the most extreme effects of the poetic style is to transform the "I" into an empty place capable of being occupied in each case anew by a different reader or auditor who, following the poet, can say: "My God, my God" (see André LaCocque's comments regarding this possessive, above, pp. 198–99). This is why, we may say in passing, so many discussions concerning the personality of the one praying, in particular those provoked by the Scandinavian School and the upholders of the royal ideology theory, lose their pertinence as soon as we become attentive to the process of poetization affecting the position of the subject of the suffering. Here is a place to return to our earlier comment regarding method. To the degree that the historical-critical method sometimes allows us to identify the status of the presumed speaker of the lament, textual analysis in turn can account for the poetic gap that confers a kind of exemplarity on the sufferings of the suppliant.[5]

In the case of Psalm 22, this poetization of the expressions of suffering takes an extraordinary turn whence follows the whole theological problematic of the psalm of lamentation. Raised from singularity to exemplarity, suffering is moreover radicalized by the expression: "abandoned by God." Exegetes talk in this regard of the *Urleiden des Gottesverlassenheit*.[6] There is no clinical description of this suffering beyond comparison, which André LaCocque defines as the privation of shalom. This dimension of suffering is revealed only to the suppliant who places his distress before God. For him, to suffer before God is to suffer due to God's hand, it is to posit oneself as a victim wounded by God. One of the literary procedures used in the service of this universalization and this radicalization consists in the recourse to metaphors that, in a way, desingularize suffering even while taking a paroxystic turn. Drawing

5. Kraus, even while underscoring the *Scharfe Profile* of the suffering person of Psalm 22, shifts the accent to the "archtypal" side of the affliction he calls *Urleiden* (*Psalmen 1–50*, p. 324).

6. It is not just the generality, notes Kraus, but the radicality of suffering that is signified by the theme "abandoned by God." He even puts his commentary on Psalm 22 under the title: "Aus der Gottesverlassenheit errettet," (*Psalmen 1–50*, p. 320). Fuchs, for his part, proposes the expression, "Urleiden der Gottesverlassenheit."

especially on the bestiary of ferocity, the poet directly evokes the spiritual virulence of primordial suffering, that of having been abandoned by God. The same can be said about the expression "poor" in verse 25, whose historical roots and symbolic import are laid out by André La-Cocque. This stands in opposition to the theme of the "enemy," which poses a parallel problem of identification and generalization.[7] Yet it remains the case that the metaphorization operates in an opposite direction to the search for identity legitimately undertaken by the critical exegete.

The second poetic procedure has to do with the composition of the poem. More than the preceding one, it has to do with the textualization of the psalm. Critical exegesis has often emphasized that the psalm proposes in its final redaction—and perhaps in its oldest literary forms—the enigma of an apparently sudden and unjustified reversal from lament to praise. It is this reversal that we need to transpose even further from the structural to the spiritual, that is, the theological, plane. The exact moment of reversal has been situated differently by different authors. André LaCocque points to its anticipation in the "aversative clause" (the "but" of verse 3) that returns in verse 19. Those who translated verse 23b as "you have heard my lament" localize it precisely at this level.[8] Some see in it the mark of a "salvation oracle," eventually pronounced by a priest or a prophetic character in the form: "Do not be afraid . . . I am with you."[9] The discussion arising from this explanation is perfectly at home in a historical-critical investigation. But it loses its importance in a literary analysis that only takes into account those features that can be pinpointed at the level of the text itself and that, therefore, ignore the extratextual event that might have been the place for an oracular word pronounced in some cult setting. Yet the two approaches agree once again, if we take the absence of such an oracular saying for a feature of textuality. This absence then can be included among the procedures that desingularize the expression of suffering described above. Just as the poetic "I" is open to whoever says "I," the intratextual reversal is offered to every suppliant invited to trace out the pathway

7. LaCocque discusses at length the study Hans-J. Kraus devotes to the identification of the enemies of the individual in question and proposes his own solution to this problem.

8. For verse 21b Kraus adopts the translation: "You have heard me," and not "my poor soul" (as in the Jerusalem Bible). O. Fuchs also sees in verse 22b, which he translates as "Du has mir erhört," the core of the exemplary drama that structures Psalm 22. The climax of the lament and the qualifying seal indicative of a regained confidence coincide at this point.

9. See Joachim Begrich, "Das priesterlishe Heilsorakel," *Zeitschrift für alttestamentliche Wissenschaft* 52 (1934): 81–92.

from lament to praise. In this way, the poetic reversal indicated likewise becomes paradigmatic. Hence it is the task of literary analysis to show through what artifices it is constructed in and through the text. When we do this, we see that the whole dynamic of the text has to be considered from a more or less dramaturgical point of view.

As every exegete has noted,[10] this reversal is in a way anticipated in the paradoxical formulation of the lament. On the one side, the lament comes close to being an accusation; on the other side, it remains caught up within an invocation and held within the space of prayer, inasmuch as it is addressed to God. The paradox is heightened through what we can call the "questioning address." It is by asking "why?" that the *Urleiden* of being "abandoned by God" is addressed to God.

Next comes the role played, on the plane of poetic construction, by the two episodes of rememoration. First, there is the recalling of the acts of salvation coming from the national tradition (vv. 4–6), then comes the nostalgic evocation of maternal solicitude, when long ago the suppliant felt himself to be "cast on god" (vv. 10–12). There is, in other words, a double assimilation of historical and personal salvation in terms of an act of creation: the creation of a people, the creation of the wretched individual! This twofold rememoration produces two contrary effects. On the one hand, through an effect of contrast, today's suffering appears to be all the more intolerable. This effect is the predominant one. Nevertheless, on the other hand, it is not in vain that such a distant past should be evoked, a time when trust in God had not yet been attained. For in this way it is suggested that a regained trust must finally be anchored in the recalling of what is immemorial. No doubt this is why André LaCocque notes that "the lament belongs to the liturgy, that is, both to history reduced to its sacred core and its ritual actualization of the past . . . and to its prolepsis, its 'preview' of the future."

We need also to take into account the linking point that the supplication (*Bitte*, petition) properly speaking plays between lament and praise.[11] Westermann strongly emphasizes the triadic structure: la-

---

10. Hans-J. Kraus is particularly insistent about the paradox of a lament that is also an invocation. It is by way of this paradox, he says, that the Crucified "comes in by clothing himself with words of Psalms."

11. Cf. above, note 1 regarding Westermann's emphasis on this distinction. He also points out, in counterpoint to this, the prolonging of the lament in the "negative supplication": "But You, O YHWH, do not stay far from me." Fuchs takes great care to preserve the difference in signification between the lament and the supplication and takes as established Westermann's thesis that the reabsorption of the lament into the supplication characterizes the late psalms, where the audacity of the lament/accusation is repudiated.

ment—supplication—praise. It is this threefold structure, according to him, that undergoes a profound alteration in the late psalms, to the extent that the lament, taken as out of place in a theology where the accent is placed on penitence, tends to be reabsorbed into the supplication. The mediating role of supplication thus lies in the fact that, under the form of "negative supplication" ("do not be far from me"), it still prolongs the lament, whereas the force of the invocation, underlying the supplication, keeps the supplication on the way to refound trust in God.

Finally, ought we to attach any importance to the lexical and grammatical subtleties in which the poet sets the expression of praise in the last part of the psalm? The moment of praise is introduced as a "vow of praise" (*Lobegelübde*). What is more, the poet plays on the connection set up between the future of intention and the present imperative addressed to himself and to the refound community.

In sum, we can affirm that through his art of composition, the poet has succeeded both in preserving the surprise of the reversal from lament to praise and in constructing this latter as an effect of the overall progression of the poem. Finally, we must not just speak of a tension between lament and praise, but of an imbrication of the one within the other. The praise already announces itself in the initial invocation, and the lament is sustained, without being suppressed, in the closing praise. In this sense, we can say, with André LaCocque, that the transmutation to praise remains within the limits of the lament. "Here," he adds, "lies the limit of the division proposed by Westermann between lament and praise. The praise remains a lament right to the end."[12]

However, something important is still missing from our analysis of the literary structure of the poem, namely, taking into account the very polarity upon which the poem is constructed and the dynamism that this polarity imposes on its composition. This polarity bears a certain character of violence, resulting from the extreme contrast that the poem sets up between the expressions of two equally extreme emotions. "Life," observes André LaCocque, "is lived between the two poles of lamentation and praise." "It is clear," he adds, "that the suppliant is caught up in a struggle within himself between these two conflicting feelings." What we have characterized as the *Urleiden* of being "aban-

---

12. O. Fuchs emphasizes the dramatic character of the reversal brought about in the psalm. It is dramatic in the sense that this reversal affects the three protagonists distinguished by Westermann: God (you), the one praying (me), and the Other (the enemy,-friend). More precisely, it is the bonds between them that are dramatized. What Fuchs calls on this basis the dramaturgy of the psalm constitutes the "deep textual structure" that the author seeks to disengage before projecting it on the history of reception.

doned by God" is indeed extreme. It is extreme in relation to every one of the afflictions outlined by the poem. The literary procedure the poem uses to convey this extreme expression stems from hyperbole. To this hyperbole can be linked the literary procedures mentioned earlier: attenuation of the singularizing descriptions, metaphorization of the figures of the fiction, radicalization of the expressions of pain set within the proximity of death. All these features relate to hyperbole, the stylistic figure most appropriate for the expression of extremes. Between such hyperbole and the *Urleiden* of being "abandoned by God" there is a perfect congruence. If the *Urleiden* does not consist in any particular affliction, in no supplementary affliction, if it is the religious sense assigned by the poem to all excessive suffering, expressions that themselves are excessive are what fit best with it in order to express it. Yet the praise into which the lament is inverted consists in no less an extreme manifestation of feeling. From the abyss to the summit, we might say. Hence it is once again under the sign of the stylistic figure of hyperbole that we can place the expressions of praise—of the vow of praise—in Psalm 22. Thus the "enemies" denounced by the lament become, under the figure of the "poor," the friends of the rediscovered community. The excess of satisfaction ("the poor shall eat and be satisfied" v. 27) corresponds to the excess of the complaint.[13]

Interpreted in light of this hyperbolic rhetoric, two aspects of our psalm, found in verses 28–32, take on meaning in terms of the framework of the literary composition of the psalm in its final version. Exegetes, no doubt rightly, see in them the effects of a later adjustment inspired by the eschatological tendencies of the period in question. Yet, if these additions could be made without doing violence to the general movement of the psalm, was this not because they agreed with the hyperbolic turn of the praise already to be found there? André LaCocque speaks here, following P. D. Miller, of a double extravagance. He also emphasizes the universalizing function of these verses in regard to the

---

13. My comments on the hyperbolic character of the psalm go together with those of Ellen F. Davis, "Exploding the Limits: Form and Function in Psalm 22," *Journal for the Study of the Old Testament* 53 (1992): 93–105. She underscores the essentially surprising or "subversive" character of poetic language in general. Her exegesis of Psalm 22 highlights the ironic features (such as the evocation of the Most High "comfortably but precariously based on old praises become as dry and fragile as dust, even while the mouths of the faithful psalmists cry out for help" [p. 97]). In sum, there are two extravagances that the psalm brings together, that of the lament and that of the praise. To conclude, Davis sees the whole of the psalm as traversed by a process of "resymbolization," thanks to which the subject of the psalm as a whole consists in the "possibility of the efficacity and necessity of praising God *in extremis*" (p. 96).

individual and national perspective of the psalm. Moreover, the absence of any spirit of vengeance in these final verses confirms the eschatologization of the psalm. All the peoples, it is said, will join in the praise and even the dead will not be excluded from a jubilation that, to be universal, has to be total and endless. Nor does it seem necessary to seek here for a dogmatic teaching concerning the destiny of the dead—a teaching that hardly coheres with the general beliefs of the Hebrews—in this enlisting of the dead in a praise extended to the limits of the geography and the history of every people. For what other jubilation than one that includes all the peoples and that gathers together the living and the dead could be as high as the Abyss is deep into which the suppliant "abandoned by God" is thrown?

We need still to interpret this *Urleiden* insofar as it is a *theologoumenon,* insofar as it is a theme capable of taking on not just an anthropological but a theological meaning.

Toward What Theology?

It is usually said that the Psalms, unlike the wisdom writings (and also the instruction dispensed by the Torah and the proclamation of the prophets) makes no claim to any dogmatic teaching concerning the nature of God, Creation, the course of history, or, finally and above all, the origin of evil. This assertion is true up to a certain point. Certainly the reversal of the lament into the promise of praise is, as we have said, not motivated in the text of the psalm. And even if we allow the extratextual element of the prophetic oracle of the form "fear not" to intervene at some moment, this word itself would not be a dogmatic saying about God, but at most a word of comfort from God. In this sense, the whole poem unfolds within the confines of a presupposed existential relation ("my God! My God") whose crisis it presents. It has even been said that the psalm from one end to another is a poem of trust *in* God, a trust that is shaken then regained. Such trust, it is rightly added, is a movement of the heart, not of speculative reason. What the poem reconstructs is a movement of trust *in spite* of everything, a vow of praise *in spite of* . . .

This is all true. A psalm is not a wisdom writing. As André LaCocque puts it: "The LI is no wisdom text. There is theorizing about human suffering, its causes, its worth or lack thereof, or its outcome."

Having said this, it is appropriate to recall our earlier reflection concerning the expression "abandoned by God." It imposes a theological stamp on all suffering. All suffering is in this way designated not just as suffering before God, but, in truth, owing to God. It is at the level of this *Urleiden* that the questions "why?" and "how long?" arise. The expression "abandoned by God" is not limited to gathering up all suffering into one archetypal suffering, rather it turns them toward a question, making the psalm a "questioning lament." How, then, can we fail to deal with the content of this question as a *theologoumenon*, which is none other than the meaning and reason for this *Urleiden*?

If the questioning lament does not directly give rise to a theology, inasmuch as it also remains a prayer, and, like any prayer, is not part of any speculation, we can legitimately ask whether the expression "abandoned by God" does not rightly belong to a theological field privileged by the Hebrew Scriptures, and whether it does not receive from being included within it a significance that the genre of the psalm does not allow the psalm to make explicit.

Claus Westermann, in considering the "role of the lamentation in the theology of the Old Testament," turns directly to the theology of history unfolded in the Torah and the Prophets.[14] This theology of history, summed up in the well-known Credo of Deuteronomy 26 (according to von Rad) and the sequence laid out in Exodus 1–15, is built on the narrative of the acts of deliverance that bring an end to situations of distress. It is in this sense that the events include "verbal exchanges between God and human beings." The framework of distress, supplication, response ("God has heard . . ."), deliverance, cries of recognition constitutes both the underlying interconnections of a theology of history and the appropriate framework for two types of speech acts upon whose polarity the psalms are constructed: the lamentation and praise. André LaCocque confirms this: "the place of the lament in the theology of the First Testament is to be found within the context of deliverance, itself modeled on the archetype of the salvation from Egypt."

This way of framing the movements of the heart, brought to speech and writing by the psalm accounts for the structural features emphasized above: the reversal from lament to praise, the triad God—suppliant—enemies, the alteration of the individual lament into a lament of the people. Finally, and this final corollary is not last in importance, this encompassing theology suffices to suggest the theme of the divine inscrutability (*Verborgenheit Gottes*). Whether God abandons his people to its enemies or delivers them from them, his plans remain inexplicable

14. See Westermann, *Lob und Klage in den Psalmen*, Book 2, chap. 7.

and unfathomable. This is why the theology of history by itself is not sufficient to convey the Word of God and why it encourages a Word of God that the psalm alone articulates.

The framework of such a reflection is certainly appropriate. The only theology Israel produced is a theology of history, which, according to von Rad's still insightful account, is organized in terms of the two focal points of narration and prophecy. But, once we have determined this general framework, we need to be attentive to the diversity of ways this theology of history gives the cries of distress a place that is proportional to the place it gives to the theme of deliverance.

The prophets impressed on the theme of the believer abandoned by God an interpretation that can be taken as the dominant line of the Hebrew theology of history. Nevertheless, we must be careful not to take it as the exclusive interpretation of this theology.

This interpretation is linked to the important event constituted by the destruction of the Temple and the State, that of deportation and Exile. For a meditation on suffering, this event is clothed with a radically different significance than the one the tradition attached to the liberation from Egypt and the Exodus. "In those days," the cry of distress had been heard, praise could legitimately follow the lamentation of the people, if not of the individual. The present test is of a wholly different nature. The question was whether Yhwh had not been conquered along with his people, as the political theology of all the peoples of the ancient Near East would suggest. Thus what was called into question was the equation between Yhwh and his people. A cry of distress was raised in the direction of a God who seemed to have removed himself from history. The lack of a response to this cry constitutes the highest historical distress, the *Urleiden* at the scale of history.

We must not, therefore, confine ourselves to giving the framework of traditional history, where deliverance in fact answered the people's supplication, as the background of the dynamism that leads from the lament to praise. The lament has to be set within the context of an exile, where one does not know whether it will repeat the Exodus. It is the very credibility of the credo of Deuteronomy 26 and Exodus 1–15 that is struck by this terrifying text of Israel's essentially historical faith.[15]

It is on the basis of this crucial silence of the God of the Election and the Covenant that the Prophets composed—and to a certain extent,

15. See Hans Wildberger, "Die Neuinterpretation des Ezwählungsglaubens Israels in der Kreise der Exilzeit," in *Wort-Gebot-Glaube*, edited by Hans-Joachim Stoebe, Johann Stamm, and Ernst Jenni (Zurich: Zwingli Verlag, 1970), pp. 307–24.

imposed—an interpretation of the *theologoumenon* "abandoned by God," in terms of a proclamation by God himself of the abandoning of his people, in response to God's having been abandoned by his people, accused of constantly have transgressed the Law.

In a forcefully argued article, Lothar Perlitt presents a structure consisting of three moments: yes, the believers of Israel, like all believers in the ancient Near East, pleaded with their God not to forget them; yes, the particular message of Israel is the link established between lamentation and the theology of history at the moment when this latter is submitted to the test of possible failure; yet the most significant response to this moral peril is the theology of retribution already announced in Hosea 4:6, 6:5, and 13:6 and 9 (cf. André LaCocque's comments above, p. 291), and which finds accents of a hitherto unknown violence in Isaiah 1:3ff., 5:13–17 ("Therefore my people will be deported without understanding"), and 29:14b ("The wisdom of these wise men will fall short, the discernment of the discerning will be eclipsed"). Perlitt notes that this word is the same one as that which expresses being abandoned by God as found in Psalm 22:2. Even more serious, this revelation has been sealed: "I bind up this testimony, I seal this revelation" (8:16). It is reserved for a small circle: "I and the children Yhwh has given me, we are signs and portents in Israel" (8:18). A century after Isaiah, Jeremiah renews this accusatory violence: "You are a burden for Yhwh" (23:33). The abandoning of his people by its God is here presented in the guise of punishment for their sins. The most radical expression of this punitive vision of history is found, as is well known, in the chroniclers of the Deuteronimist school, whose concern it was to exonerate God at the price of indicting his people. Paradoxically, the theme of the inscrutability of God is weakened by this theory of retribution, inasmuch as the alleged unfathomable justice of God is henceforth seen in history understood in terms of punishment.

Nevertheless, if this theology of retribution were to have succeeded in exhausting and dissipating the mystery of divine inscrutability, then the expression of the people's lament and, even more so, that of the individual would have been swept out of, expurgated, from Hebraic literature. Psalm 22, along with other psalms, bears witness that this did not happen.

I would like now to propose several critical comments concerning the basis of this resistance of prayer as lamentation to the suppression that might have been inflicted upon it by overly zealous disciples of the greater biblical prosecutors.

First of all, on the side of the theology of history against the background of which the lament stands out, the last word was not said by the upholders of a punitive history. For an Isaiah, a Jeremiah, and even an Ezekiel, the withdrawal of God remains the setting for a struggle against occultation. This struggle is what is really at stake in their suffering. The Prophet admonishes his people only to conjure up, in the same breath, a people "returned to God" and a God who "once more turns his kindly face toward them. The preaching of a hidden God remains a struggle for manifestation. After Isaiah, says Lothar Perlitt, the withdrawal of God is suffered and struggled against. If this had not been the case, the message of Second Isaiah would have remained unheard: "Comfort, comfort my people . . ." (40:1), cries the new prophet. What is most astonishing in this regard is not that a prophecy of hope as such follow one of condemnation, but that the same accusation that was said to justify God's withdrawal is prolonged within the announcement of the end of tribulation. It is at the depths of rejection that salvation is expected (40:27–31). It is, we might dare to add, the breast of his own suffering that Yhwh offers once more for the salvation of his people (50:1–3). Perlitt proposes here the following formulation, which seems to sum up his whole essay: "The God who hides himself is the savior." And again, "There is no salvation except through the God who has hidden himself."[16] Here a theology of paradox, which von Rad shares with Karl Barth, takes up the theme of the *Verborgenheit Gottes.*[17]

In the second place, this theology of paradox, which calls for hope in the very depths of distress, is not the only reply that the Old Testament proposes to the punitive theology of the "prophets of misfortune." The poems of the Suffering Servant, linked to the theme of the "Servant of Yhwh," suggest a theology of history that is not limited to proclaiming that in God even anger gets changed into compassion, as if the reversal of lamentation into praise, on the side of the believer, were founded on an incomprehensible and unjustifiable reversal at the level of God's inscrutable plans. These poems also announce that the Servant of Yhwh—concerning whom we cannot say if this figure indicates an individual, a sect, or the people as a whole—will raise his own suffering

16. Lothar Perlitt, "Die Verborgenheit Gottes," in *Probleme biblischer Theologie,* edited by Hans Walter Wolff (Munich: Kaiser Verlag, 1971), p. 382.

17. See Gerhard von Rad, *Old Testament Theology,* vol. 2: *The Theology of Israel's Prophetic Traditions,* translated by D. M. G. Stalker (New York: Harper & Row, 1965), pp. 374–78. Karl Barth, *Church Dogmatics,* translated by T. H. L. Parker et al. (Edinburgh: T. & T. Clark, 1957), vol. 2, Part 1, 27, pp. 200–204.

to the rank of "suffering-for." In adding an active dimension to suffering per se, the Servant of Yhwh opens an absolutely new issue regarding the *Urleiden* of being abandoned by God. Suffering-for, suffering in the place of is what Emmanuel Levinas will call "substitution."[18]

Hence it seems reasonable to leave in a certain state of dispersion the multiple ways of living, professing, enduring the *Urleiden* of being abandoned by God that the Old Testament proposes. They are not all solidary with the proclamation that God has abandoned his people, because this people first abandoned its God, to the point of being absorbed into this proclamation. The pluralism that seems to impose itself in our interpretation of the *theologoumenon* "abandoned by God" seems to me finally to fit better with the goal of preserving the theme of divine inscrutability.

In the third place, to be added to this argument drawn from the variations in the Old Testament theology of history is the—to me, considerable—argument that underscores the simple fact that the Psalms of Lamentation preserved their individual identity alongside the Penitential Psalms, so highly valued by Christian, especially Protestant, piety, given the basis of the theology that Saint Paul built on the themes of sin, the righteousness of God, and salvation by faith. The Psalms of Lamentation have their place within the Psalter. They bear no trace whatsoever of a confession of guilt, nor of a protestation of innocence. In them we hear the cry of pure suffering.

What the Psalms of Lamentation preserve, in the first place, is the specificity of individual suffering, which no theology of history seems able to account for. The distinction between individual lamentation and that of the people finds a new legitimation here, despite the overlappings from one genre to the other, already mentioned above. Psalm 22 itself, observes André LaCocque, allows the tension to appear between faithfulness to the God of the ancestors and the personal dereliction of the psalmist. This latter is inscribed outside history and outside the theology of history. The Psalms of Lamentation are there to recall that the individual is fragile, exposed to illness and death, vulnerable to the attacks of others. In the final analysis, up to and including the disasters of history, it is the individual who suffers. Suffering requires a place for the first person that the anonymity of history cannot grant. No doubt this is the reason why the piety that Psalm 22 bears witness to includes

18. Emmanuel Levinas, *Otherwise than Being or Beyond Essence*, translated by Alphonso Lingis (Boston: Kluwer, 1991).

nonliturgical features (cf. André LaCocque's comments, p. 193). The only convergence that would subsist at this level would be between the Psalms of Lamentation and the Songs of the Suffering Servant. The question as to the priority of one over the other on both the historical and the theological planes remains open. But whatever the case may be as regards this problem of priority, the reader can interpret the singularity of the Psalms of Lamentation as an indication of a discrete resistance to the accusatory theology of the prophets. In preserving the "why" posed by suffering from any reduction to a penal theology, these psalms preserve the duality of the figures of evil: the evil of suffering, the evil of guilt. In so doing, they tip our meditation on the inscrutability of God in another direction than that of the prophecy of condemnation, namely, in the direction of wisdom. I have already said that the psalm as a form of prayer does not speculate. And it is within the prayer that the enigmatic reversal from lamentation to praise takes place. There is nothing more to be drawn from this observation. But we can now add to it a supplementary measure of interpretation, once we have made the detour of Isaiah and Ezekiel. Having heard from the mouth of the prophets that God had in fact and deliberately abandoned his people, it is permissible to return to the "why" of the psalm and hear it as a question to which the response of the prophets does not give a satisfactory response, to hear it as a question obstinately reopened beyond an explication that, in a certain way, does not leave intact the divine inscrutability.

It is then that the reader of the Bible, who is free to move within the space opened within the very closure of the canon, takes the step that leads from the Psalter to the Wisdom Writings. It is surely only through an act of reading, which is also an act of interpretation, that this reader passes from Psalm 22 to the Book of Job. Yet the canonical unity of the Bible allows precisely this equation, this synchronization, that places side by side two texts stemming from highly different settings and quite distant ages, and reflecting literary genres that are far removed from each other. In this way we are led, at the end of a long periplus, to reread the Psalms of Lamentation in the light of the controversies of the Book of Job. The "why" of Psalm 22 is then extracted, under the shock of this encounter, from the context of trust safeguarded by the "My God, my God" of invocation. In being so removed from its initial setting, the "why" of Psalm 22 is lifted up as a question expecting another answer than the one imposed by the prophets, a question that is left hanging. It would be the task of another study to inquire whether Job's final resignation preserves any features that might be common to the vow of praise that the psalm of lamentation changes into, or whether the silence within which this resignation is enveloped does not leave in suspense along with the theology of retribution even this vow of praise. The Book of Job, André LaCocque observes, presents "a striking absence of praise. But Job is, let us recall, not an Israelite. He is not dealing with a God he can call *Eli* (Psalm 22:2), *Elohay* (22:3), or *Yhwh* (22:20, 24, 27, 28, 29)." All that remains is that it is left to wisdom alone to discern within the very excess of the *Urleiden* the reply, on the human plane, of divine inscrutability.

A Millenary Heritage

To conclude, I want to return to the double trajectory referred to in the opening lines of this chapter. I want first to consider, as does André LaCocque, the reprise of Psalm 22 by the evangelist Mark in his narrative of the Crucifixion.

As we said in beginning, what seems formally to be a "quotation" has merely the appearance of being one. It is not the word of an Other that is recounted, as when the authors of New Testament writings make use of an Old Testament text detached from its context, either to make explicit the meaning of a new proclamation or to justify a new assertion by an ancient declaration taken as a prophecy of the new "fulfilled" era.

If the cry of Jesus can be said to "fulfill" the Old Testament, it is in a quite different sense. Instead the recounted event "clothes" itself in the words of the Old Testament. Hartmut Gese, from whom I have borrowed this powerful expression, adds that it is Psalm 22 as a whole that is actualized here.[19] Furthermore, he adds that the Passion narrative reveals a decisive influence of this psalm on several other occasions as well. If we recall that the terrifying declaration of Psalm 22:2 is not isolated within the Psalter (cf. Psalm 9:11; 16:10; 27:9; 37:28, 33; 38:22; 71:8, 12, 18; 94:14; 116:8), the "vestment" that clothes the cry of the crucified Jesus consists at the same time of a typical expression and a highly structured development. Therefore it is the whole movement of the psalm that is reactualized here. Gese even thinks he can discern in this movement the mark of an apocalyptic theology, according to which it would be within an act of deliverance affecting an individual threatened with death that the *Basileia tou theou*, the king-

19. Hartmut Gese, "Psalm 22 und das neue Testament," in *Vom Sinai zum Zion, Beiträge zur evangelischen Theologie* (Munich: Chr. Kaiser Verlag, 1974), pp. 180–201.

dom of God, signified by the conversion of the nations and the resurrection of the dead, would occur. In other words, it is individual piety that would assume an apocalyptic structure: "in the salvation of the pious man torn away from death is revealed God's eschatological lordship" (p. 192). Therefore it is not just this one verse "quoted" from Psalm 22 that is taken up by the evangelist Mark, but the theme of the breaking through of the Kingdom, thanks to the deliverance from death. Hence it is not surprising that the narrative of the Crucifixion includes so many references (Mark 15:24, 29) to particular details of Psalm 22, in particular the verse concerning the "enemies." The marvels and cosmic signs that accompany the event of death (the tearing of the veil of the Temple, the trembling of the earth, the resurrection of the dead) all stem from the same apocalyptic spirituality. And it is in light of this apocalyptic slant that we can understand that the centurion, "seeing that he had expired," could confess: "truly, this man was the Son of God." In this way, the centurion "fulfills" Psalm 22:28 and 30.

This reading of the Markan narrative should be of interest to the reader to the extent that, on the one hand, it rests on a profoundly innovative interpretation of the psalm, and, on the other hand, because the psalm is reinterpreted in such a way that the resources of meaning we had not yet realized are liberated. Here I rejoin André LaCocque when he says that "this is a privileged hermeneutical example of the text's increased meaning from the time of composition. True, from that initial moment on, the whole meaning of the text was included within its words, as in a jewel case to be opened one day. The original lamenter was, to be sure, justified to complain to God about being abandoned. His or her experience was complete in itself as it reached the bottom of the abyss" (p. 205).

At the same time, our insistence on considering the Psalms of Lamentation apart from the theology of history received from the Prophets is also justified. Even more so, the lamentation itself is justified as a prayer pleasing to God.

Having said this, we are not forbidden from retaining, within the very core of the eschatological perspective, those earlier interpretations that had already broken with the theology of punishment: the announcement of the great deliverance by Second Isaiah, the messianic themes, and especially the Songs of the Suffering Servant. The eschatology of Psalm 22 adds a new dimension to these important themes. In this regard, we can even say that Jesus taking up the cry of the suppliant from Psalm 22:2 bears witness to and seals the kinship between all these theological interpretations of the *Urleiden* of being abandoned by God.

At the end of this meditation the question arises of the contemporary significance of a "lamentation as prayer" for an age like our own marked by secularization and the Nietzschean proclamation of the "death of God." Can the suffering person of today still give the form of an invocation to his lamentation? Does not the *Urleiden* of today consist in the sense that there is no one any more to whom we can direct our lamentation? Did not the expression "abandoned by God" stop being a *theologoumenon* once it came to signify not the distance, the withdrawal, the inscrutability of God, but his nonexistence? Do believers have any answer to propose to this extreme challenge? How can they escape the alternative: either construct (or reconstruct) unbelievable proofs or profess an incommunicable fidism?

One narrow way remains open between these two precipices. It would be to ask believers, once again today, to let "lamentation as prayer" speak, with a force comparable to its initial energy. This is the avowal formulated by Ottmar Fuchs in his book that has so often inspired me. "The lamentation," he says in the *Vorwort* to his book, "is a type of prayer that has fallen into forgetfulness." Let us rehabilitate it, he concludes, within contemporary Christian spirituality. If we succeed in doing so, there is a possibility that the lamentation as prayer will again be heard and pronounced after Auschwitz . . .

Several conditions are imposed on this rehabilitation that means to be a reactualization. The first one is that the hyperbolic radicality of a lamentation that dares give a name to the *Urleiden* "abandoned by God" has to be preserved over against the empty nonsense of a prayer of supplication from which every trace of an accusation directed against God has been expunged. Exegetical practice that meets this condition will call for even greater attention to the polycentrism of the biblical text, including the figures of the divine and the modes of relations between the human and the divine. Over against the tendency to accentuate in a unilateral way the well-known scheme of the *Heilsgeschichte*, intertwining sin, the righteousness of God, penitence, and punishment or acquittal, the Psalms of Lamentation are the privileged witness of a resistance to every unilateral conception of biblical theology. Freed from the concern to justify God and renouncing every theodicy where human beings claim to prove God's innocence, the questioning prayer of lamentation expects nothing more than the compassion of a God concerning whom the one praying does not know how he can be both just and compassionate. This is why he has no choice but to cry: "why?"

A second condition goes with this first one concerning the telos of interpretation, a condition attached to exegetical practice itself. It follows from our attempt at structural analysis that the "historical" energy capable of being unfolded by the biblical poem proceeds from the *Überzeitlich* or "surpahistorical" quality that the textualization confers on the expression of affliction, raised in this way to the rank of a paradigm of suffering. If the lamentation as prayer is still capable of actualization, it is insofar as the exemplarity that it owes to the poetic form is a permanent source of transposition and new historization in previously unknown cultural conditions. We cannot be too attentive, for example, to the history of reception of the biblical prayer, both in and outside the liturgy of worship. In this regard, we must not expect any automatic transposition into the present of a model rendered as atemporal or transhistorical as we might like by literary analysis. Without the mediation of a chain of rereadings consisting of as many innovations, the ancient prayer will not be transposed into a contemporary prayer. A living tradition is always required between the invariant structures brought forth by an appropriate exegesis and the reactualization called for by practical theology. (I say this in part as a corrective to the analyses of Ottmar Fuchs which seem placed in the service of an overly optimistic expectation concerning the direct power of historization and actualization contained in the atemporal structure of the poem.)

The resumption of Psalm 22 by the Crucified attests first of all to the aspect of innovation that is attached to every new actualization of the Hebraic poem. To this we must add that the reprise of the biblical lament in the "great cry" of Christ on the cross can only become in turn a model for prayer if it gives rise to a continual innovation in the prayer of lamentation in verbal expressions that may be far removed from the literary form of the original psalm.

Another condition for the rehabilitation of the prayer of lamentation would be that what we might call its agonistic character has to be preserved. Looked at from the point of view of its end, the movement from lamentation to praise seems to unfold within a single "being-with-God." Looked at from its beginning, the prayer is a movement that starts from the silence of God and never loses its aspect of being a struggle for renewed trust. In this sense, the starting point remains contained within the end point, despite the reversal to regained trust. In other words, the *Verborgenheit Gottes* remains the existential and theological condition common to both the lamentation and the praise. The paradox of reversal from the one to the other is inseparable from this struggle whose outcome is never guaranteed. The divine inscrutability is not lessened by the conversion of the *Urleiden* into jubilation. We may even say that it is rendered all the more impenetrable as soon as it no longer signifies what it seemed spontaneously to imply, namely a rediscovered access to a divine presence without a dialectic of absence.

One last condition today's suppliant has to satisfy would perhaps be that he or she discover a secret kinship between what we can risk calling the suffering of God, as André LaCocque suggests in referring to a God who also laments. This goes with the call for a personal and communal practice of compassion in regard to our human brothers and sisters who often are not so much guilty as suffering.

The Song of Songs

The Shulamite

ANDRÉ LaCOCQUE

[There are] various methods . . . for making [an undesirable] book
innocuous. [1] Offending passages . . . [can be] made illegible. . . .
The next copyist would produce a text . . . which had gaps. [2]
Another way would be . . . to proceed to distort the text. [3] Best
of all, the whole passage would be erased and a new one which said
exactly the opposite put in its place.

Sigmund Freud[1]

The one whose "gentilice" is given only in chapter 7, namely the "Shulamite," is also called, among different terms of endearment, a šošanah
(lily), thus attributing to the central persona of the story the name of a
flower. As a matter of fact, the Song's imagery delights in natural descriptions (see, for example, 2:8–17; 7:11–13). This point underscores
the unusual character of the poem, for everywhere else in the Hebrew
Bible the role of nature, when at all highlighted, is secondary and subordinated to the function of carrying a religious message (cf. Jeremiah
1.11, "And the word of the Lord came to me saying, 'Jeremiah, what
do you see?' And I said, 'I see a rod of almond.' Then the Lord said to
me, 'You have seen well, for I am watching over my word to perform
it.'" See also Amos 8:1–2; etc.). In the Song, on the contrary, we find
enraptured descriptions of a series of plants (henna, rose, lily, fig tree,
vine in blossom, pine-tree, cedar, apple-tree, palm-tree); fruits (grapes,
nuts, pomegranates, dates, figs); products from the field (wheat, honey,
wine); and animals (gazelle, stag, turtledove, sheep, horse). These evo-
cations are, it appears, purely aesthetic, without need of being "author-

---

1. Quoted by Gayatri Chakravorty Spivak, Preface to Jacques Derrida, *Of Grammatology* (Baltimore: Johns Hopkins University Press, 1976), p. lxxvi.

ized" by a "superior" order. Nature is beautiful in and of itself. Such a discovery is unique in the Hebrew Scriptures.

The woman in love is *šošanah*, lily; she is also narcissus, garden, vine or vineyard, mare, dove, myrrh, ray of honey, wine, milk, in addition to other metaphoric terms of endearment like dawn, sun, moon. She truly represents the beauty of the entire universe. The lover, too, is a bag of myrrh between the two breasts of his beloved, he is a cluster of henna in blossom, an apple tree, a gazelle, a fawn—he is a king, a bullion of fine gold, he is Solomon "in all his glory."

This already provides a profound difference from the biblical narratives. For while Suzanna, the heroine in the *Additions to Daniel* also has a flower's name, and etymologically "Esther" reminds one of a bright celestial body, of a star, while Ruth, like Esther, makes use of perfumes and cosmetics, not dissimilar from those we encounter profusely in the Song, we do not find in these stories an affability for the things of nature, for when it exists at all, it is at the service of praising feminine beauty for its "usefulness" in fulfilling a sacred design (Suzanna, Judith, Esther and, by implication, Ruth). These heroines, in their turn, also *use* aesthetics to attain a historical and theological end. But not so in the Song. Here, the aesthetic is cultivated for its own sake, without embarrassment and without excuse.

This biblical book must thus be treated apart. My thesis here is that the poem's purpose is subversive—I will come back to this amply—while the tone is deceptively lyrical and pastoral. That is, the poet allegedly uses an innocent language of courtship while at the same time defying the customary institutions by presenting to the straight-laced, in the form of contrast and irony, a universe that is outright erotic. The author shuns any theological contrivance meant to render the message acceptable.

From the very first verse of the book, a problem poses itself: the poem is attributed to Solomon. We should not, however, take this indication literally. It is indeed remarkable that in the body of the song, Solomon is mentioned in the third person, or at times in the second-person singular. Yet we also recall texts like 1 Kings 5:12 (in the LXX, 4:32), which say that Solomon composed 1,005 songs and 3,000 proverbs. The great king established himself as the traditional patron of the literary genres of both wisdom and lyric poetry in Israel, and it is well known that "Providence is always on the side of the big battalions." On the other hand, if the poem is not Solomon's in person, some critics do consider the Solomonic era as the time of its creation. Such is the case, for instance, with a critic whom we will discuss below, M. H. Segal.[2] The atmosphere of the Song, he says, is the one of the period in question. One finds here an ideological humanism and also signs of a material comfort that are characteristic of that time. Even the extensive topography of the poem points in that direction. It is also important to emphasize the well-to-do position of the young woman; she has a beautiful house (1:17; 2:9; 3:4); she owns a shawl, a sign of wealth according to Isaiah 3:23 (cf. 5:7);[3] she wears jewels and her perfumes are precious (1:10, 12–14; 3:6; 5:5; etc.). What is more, in spite of the cliché that has made its way in all the world's literature, the various scenes do not always unfold in the countryside, and the heroine is not uniformly a country girl or a shepherdess (see Song 3 and 5).

Yet, all of this, which must undoubtedly be considered seriously, should not be overestimated. Rather than Solomonic, the Song exudes an atmosphere of the "Thousand and One Nights." It is fruitless, it seems to me, to attempt to date it by using clues that are historically imprecise. If Solomon is evoked in the Song, thus giving it a legendary flavor, it is not so much Solomon-the-Wise that the author is calling to the bar, as Solomon-the-Don-Juan. With his thousand wives (1 Kings 11:3), Solomon appears as one who has known love in all its forms, as the paragon of love. True, Solomon-the-Wise is not absent either, for, in the ancient Near East, questions relative to love and marriage are appealing topics for Wisdom. Strikingly, there are numerous linguistic parallels between the Song and the biblical Proverbs.[4] One might add that it is in the "New Wisdom" (Proverbs 1–9; Sirach; Wisdom of Solomon) that one finds the language of *eros*. There, Wisdom is personified and represented as a woman attracting men into her house (Proverbs 9:1–5; cf. 1:20f.; 8:1ff.). Wisdom, in fact, loves human beings and wants to be loved by them (Proverbs 4:6, 8; 8:17; Sirach 14:20–27; Wisdom of Solomon 8:2, 16; 6:12–16). Some readers of the Song have thus concluded that the book describes in a language that is symbolic, even alle-

---

2. M. H. Segal, "The Song of Songs," *Vetus Testamentum* 12 (1962): 470–90.

3. Note the psychological connotation of these enveloping images (house, shawl; etc; also elsewhere "a locked garden, a sealed fountain" 4:12, 15).

4. André M. Dubarle, "L'amour humain dans le Cantique des Cantiques," *Revue Biblique* 61 (1954): 67–90, draws a parallel between Proverbs 5:3 and Song 6:11; Proverbs 5:15–18 and Song 4:12; Proverbs 5:19 and Song 2:9, 4:5, 8:14; Proverbs 7:17 and Song 4:14; Proverbs 6:21, 27f., 34 and Song 8:6–7; Sirach 26:18 and Song 5:15, 6:10.

gorical, the "loves" between Wisdom and her initiates (see below).[5] This interpretation is quite old, as we just saw, but does not correspond to the original intent nor to the plain meaning of the Song. Wisdom stresses rather the negative aspect of *eros* (cf. Proverbs 7), or else the morality that must accompany it (Proverbs 5). In the Song, by contrast, *eros* is "de-moralized." The point is not always honored by modern scholars, as the following passage from Brevard Childs's conclusion to his "canonical" analysis of the Song testifies:

> The Song is wisdom's reflection on the joyful and mysterious na-
> ture of love between a man and a woman within the institution of
> marriage. The frequent assertion that the Song is a celebration of
> human love *per se* fails utterly to reckon with the canonical con-
> text. . . . Nowhere is human love in itself celebrated in wisdom lit-
> erature, nor in the whole Old Testament for that matter. Wisdom,
> not love, is divine, yet love between a man and his wife is an inex-
> tinguishable force within human experience, "strong as death,"
> which the sage seeks to understand (cf. Proverbs 5:15ff.).[6]

We cannot follow Childs in several of his affirmations. First of all, if it is indeed a question of the love between a woman and a man in the Song, to add, as he does, "within the institution of marriage" is not grounded upon any textual basis. A marriage is mentioned only in 3:6, which is an epithalamium for Solomon's wedding—in the context of a dream (cf. 3:1)! It serves no other purpose than to provide terms of comparison. On the contrary, the entire Song strums on the chord of "free love," neither recognized, nor institutionalized. It is clear that a declaration by the "fiancée" such as the one in 8:1–3 would make no sense if the couple were "legitimately" married.[7] We must insist strongly on this truly decisive point for the understanding of the poem.

On the other hand, Childs is statistically and objectively correct

---

5. Abravanel (who died in 1508) had already written, *'eyn derek lehagid ha-debarim ha-ruḥaniim ki'im behamšal ha-debarim ha-gupim* ("one can only express spiritual things metaphorically through sensible things"). He was the first to identify the fiancée in the Song with Wisdom. Among the modern critics defending the same thesis is Gottfried Kuhn, *Erklärung des Hohen Liedes* (Leipzig: A. Deichert, 1926). He perceives in the person of Solomon a type of person who seeks Wisdom. However, Kuhn also adopts the literal meaning of the book and observes, "so kann also jede reine Ehe im Hohen Liede zum Teil ihr Spiegelbild finden" (ibid., p. 60).

6. Brevard Childs, *Introduction to the Old Testament as Scripture* (Philadelphia: Fortress Press, 1979), p. 575.

7. Moreover, if the poem were a wedding song, its end would no longer make sense. In fact, 8:8–12 discusses what should be done when the girl will be of age to marry.

when he says that human love is never celebrated in the Bible for its own sake. Yet let us not exclude the possibility of the Song creating a precedent! Barring oneself from new avenues, as does Childs in this instance, may foreclose access to the meaning of the text. And, since in Childs's analysis the canon of the Scriptures is discussed, let us recall— as also do most commentaries and studies, although not always felicitously—Rabbi Aqiba's protest against the (habitual?) singing of the Song in "banquet places."[8] Much was at stake for Aqiba and his disciples. Their point was to go against the stream of a "profane" understanding and to impose in its stead an allegorical interpretation of the poem so as to give it access to the canon of Scriptures. Hence the Talmudic testimony by no means provides a proof of an original allegorical interpretation of the Song. On the contrary, R' Aqiba's hermeneutical method is too well known to allow the slightest hesitation in this regard. It is not just the Song that Aqiba read allegorically or to which he attributed spiritual values at the slightest stroke of a letter in the text. He read the whole Bible this way and his success with other traditional readers was not always assured. As regards the Song of Songs, it is without a doubt his reading that triumphed, however. The Targum, for instance, sees in the Song a historical allegory of the Exodus from Egypt. Along that line, the book was to be at a late date associated with the Passover feast. In that context, there is a saying in the marginal Talmudic treatise *Aboth de-Rabbi Nathan* 1.5 that, although difficult to understand, seems to imply that the books of "Proverbs, Song of Songs, and Qoheleth were put aside [as apocryphal?] because they were *mešalim* [(mere) proverbs? parables?]." They remained in this sort of quarantine until "the men of the Great Synagogue came and *pirᵉšu* [interpreted?] them." From this ambiguously phrased statement, we are probably justified in thinking that there existed, prior to the intervention of the "men of Hezekiah," different interpretations of these "Solomonic" documents.[9]

Harold Fisch is thus in the wrong regarding the comparison, which is often made, between the Song's allegorization on the one hand, and

8. *Tosephta Sanhedrin* 12.10; the same opinion is expressed anonymously in *Sanhedrin* 101a. Aqiba says, "The entire world is not worth the day the Song was given to Israel" (*Mishnah Yaddayim* 3.5). He also said, "Had the Torah not been given, the Song would have sufficed to guide the world," *Agadoth Shir,* edited by Schechter (1896), p. 5.

9. Concerning the Song, it is possible that the objection to its canonization came from a "puritan" inclination and that only its allegorical interpretation could reassure nervous moralists. It is quite clear that the spiritual narrowness of a bygone era cannot serve as an excuse for a modern imitation.

Homer's by the Stoics, on the other. Fisch's conclusion is that such a comparison does not hold, because "however far back we go, we cannot discern any traces of an earlier 'literal' interpretation of the Song such as we can with Homer."[10] But the discussion at the Council of Jamnia (end of first century CE) on the meaning of the Song would have been impossible had the allegorical interpretation been established once and for all or since its inception. We will also see a text from the Song whose Masoretic vocalization indicates that the book was not read allegorically by the Masoretes centuries after the Council of Jamnia (see 8:5).

The date of the (final) composition of the Song is also much disputed. I will not, in this limited study, go into all the arguments alleged in favor of one period over another. We saw earlier that there are arguments in favor of the Solomonic era. More reliable than the "atmospheric" surrounding of the poem, however, is the philological basis. Already the presence of Aramaisms alerts the reader, although this does not prove anything in itself. But M. H. Segal, whom I have already mentioned, has set up an impressive list of linguistic phenomena that prove the late composition of the poem as now written (as opposed to the time of its creation). He says, "Its language represents the latest stage of biblical Hebrew as current in the Hellenistic period before it passed into the dialect of the Mishnah and its allied literature."[11] It is this date that we will keep in mind, with Otto Eissfeldt, for example.

With Eissfeldt as well, we shall broach the essential problem of the identity of the biblical author. The German critic writes the following about the attribution of the poem to Solomon: he "was thought of as the king who was the most famous because of his splendor and his reputation for love."[12] Michael V. Fox too sees that "Solomon was the logical candidate for the authorship of this book because his name is mentioned in it and because he was famous both for the number of his wives and for his songs."[13] However, if Solomon is ostensibly but not actually the one who wrote the Song, who did? I am convinced that the author is a woman and I will try to demonstrate this. I am not the first one to propose this thesis, but my predecessors were often somewhat more

10. Harold Fisch, *Poetry with a Purpose* (Bloomington: Indiana University Press, 1988), p. 97.

11. "The Song of Songs," p. 478. Segal distinguishes the written composition from the oral formation of the Song, the latter of which he dates from the Solomonic era, as we saw earlier.

12. Otto Eissfeldt, *Einleitung in das Alte Testament*, Part 3 (Tübingen: J. C. B. Mohr, 1964), pp. 67, 487. He is thinking of the third century BCE. The term "appirion" (palanquin) in Song 3:9 probably comes from the Greek "phoreion," which has the same meaning.

13. Michael V. Fox, *The Song of Songs and the Ancient Egyptian Songs* (Madison: University of Wisconsin Press, 1985), p. 95.

timid than I choose to be. Thus, in 1963, A. S. Herbert took a pioneering step in this direction.[14] He wrote, "So finely and sensitively indeed has the poet portrayed the maiden's feelings, that we might even conjecture that the poet was a woman" (p. 468). Yet, in the remainder of his commentary, Herbert talks about the poet in the masculine. He has not taken his own idea seriously.[15] Likewise, H. Lusseau calls attention to the female authorship of the Papyrus Chester Beatty I "Songs of Love," as well as to the bas-reliefs of El Amarna where a woman conducts an orchestra. Still, he does not draw from this any potential consequences for the Song.[16] Rolf Rendtorff writes, as a matter of evidence, that "the Song is constructed a woman's song."[17] Roland Murphy also writes that "one is pressed to ask if the author may have been a woman, and surely she was, at least in part."[18] Before him, and with more energy, Andrew Greeley had insisted on the same point.[19]

Indeed, in the Song, the young woman does the talking. The majority of the discourses come from her and, if the lover speaks often and lengthily as well, it happens several times that his utterances quote the Shulamite. Such a situation is simply unique in the Bible, although it would not be the first ancient Near Eastern or biblical poetry composed by a woman. Samuel Kramer has shown that "the first love song" occurred in Sumer within the framework of the "sacred marriage" between the king and the fertility goddess in the person of a priestess.[20] In this poetic genre, it is the woman who speaks. "In the fertility liturgies," writes Daniel Lys, "the role of women is preeminent." There, the goddess is called spouse, mother, daughter.[21]

This concerns not Israel—at least not "Verus Israel"—although here as elsewhere in the ancient Near East, the woman is a specialist in love

14. A. S. Herbert, "The Song of Songs," in *Peake's Commentary on the Bible*, edited by M. Black and H. H. Rowley (London: Thomas Nelson and Sons, 1962), pp. 468–74.

15. The same author has a similar attitude concerning Song 6:12, which we will examine later.

16. H. Lusseau, "Le Cantique des Cantiques," in *Introduction à la Bible*, edited by A. Robert and A. Feuillet (Tournai: Desclé et Cie, 1957) vol. 1, pp. 655–66.

17. Rolf Rendtorff, *The Old Testament: An Introduction*, translated by John Bowden (Philadelphia: Fortress Press, 1986), p. 263.

18. Roland E. Murphy, *The Song of Songs* (Minneapolis: Fortress Press, 1990), p. 70. Murphy refers to Phyllis Trible, *God and the Rhetoric of Sexuality* (Philadelphia: Fortress Press, 1978), p. 145, and to Athalya Brenner, *The Israelite Woman: Social Role and Literary Type in Biblical Literature* (Sheffield: JSOT Press, 1985), pp. 46–50. See also Murphy, pp. 82, 91, etc.

19. See Andrew M. Greeley and Jacob Neusner, *The Bible and Us: A Priest and a Rabbi Read Scripture Together* (New York: Warner Books, 1990), pp. 34, 36, etc.

20. Samuel N. Kramer, *The Sacred Marriage Rite: Aspects of Faith, Myth, and Ritual in Ancient Sumer* (Bloomington: Indiana University Press, 1969).

21. Daniel Lys, *Le plus beau chant de la création* (Paris: Cerf, 1968), p. 48.

songs and war songs—the songs welcoming back the warriors after the battle in particular.[22] S. D. Goitein mentions 1 Samuel 18:6–7; Exodus 15:20; Judges 4:9; see also Psalm 68:12; Isaiah 37:22; Jeremiah 38:22. Albeit, belonging to another genre, we should also not forget to mention what is said about the Shunamite at the time of the prophet Elisha in 2 Kings 4:8–37; she may have served as a model for the author of the Song. Women also belong to wisdom guilds. One such wise woman came from Tekoa to give a lesson to King David (2 Samuel 14:13–14); another one is Abigail the Carmelite (1 Samuel 25:29–31).

Other poetic genres are women's fare as well. For example, the funeral song, which plays a very important role in traditional societies (see 1 Samuel 1:24; Jeremiah 9:16–19; Lamentations 1; 2; 4). Furthermore, just as at Mari on the Euphrates, the prophetic oracle in Israel is not the exclusive domain of men. Scripture gives us the name of four prophetesses. Miriam and Deborah are "bards," as Goitein pointedly says, and it is difficult to distinguish between oracle and poem as far as they are concerned (cf. Judges 5:12). Huldah and Noadiah belong to the period of classical prophecy (2 Kings 22:14–20, Nehemiah 6:14).

In spite of her exclusion from liturgy in the Temple of Jerusalem, a woman is not denied access into it. The story of Hannah, the future mother of Samuel, is a case in point.[23] Women form groups of singers or dancers (Judges 21:19–21; Jeremiah 31:3–4), a fact that explains why we find in the Song the designation "daughters of Jerusalem."[24]

22. See S. D. Goitein, "Women as Creators of Biblical Genres," translated by Michael Carasik, *Prooftexts* 8 (1988): 1–33.

23. But we ought to contrast it with a text like Deuteronomy 16:11, 14.

24. Concerning this, it is interesting to draw a parallel between the "daughters of Jerusalem" in the Song and the ancient Greek chorus, which, from the time of Aristotle, plays the role of spectator in the drama, represents the people, and defends the generally held opinions. This last point explains, in my view, the profound hiatus between this chorus—a possible result of the Hellenistic influence on the Song—and the Shulamite. One could say, following Søren Kierkegaard, in *Fear and Trembling*, that the "daughters of Jerusalem" represent what is general, while the lovers in the Song represent the particular. The latter alone relativizes what is proper according to the social mores of the time. The notion of a chorus in the Song may also explain in part the difficult text of 7:1 where effectively the versions speak of a double chorus (LXX, "like choruses"; Pesh.: "Like a chorus, and like a chorus of camps"; Vulgate: "nisi chorus castrorum"). Paul Joüon, *Le Cantique des Cantiques: Commentaire philologique et exégétique* (Paris: Beauchesne, 1909), ad loc., translates: "[rangées] comme un double choeur?" Denis Buzy, "Le Cantique des Cantiques traduit et commenté," in *La Sainte Bible*, vol. 6 (Paris: Letouzey et Ané, 1946), p. 347: "à la façon d'un choeur à deux parties." More decisive, in my opinion, is the study by Jack Sasson, "The Worship of the Golden Calf," in *Orient and Occident: Essays Presented to Cyrus Gordon*, edited by Harry A. Hoffner (Neukirchen-Vluyn: Neukirchener Verlag, 1973), pp. 151–59. He shows that the term *meholah* present in Song 7:1 designates an antiphonic song in two groups composed of women and musicians. As regards the Hellenistic influence on the Song, see note 12 above; one also thinks of love personified in Song 2:7; 3:5; 8:4, 7; etc.

In summary, it is not only possible but it is expected that a love song in the ancient Near East be written by a woman. If we come closer to the contents of the Song, furthermore, we may be surprised by the great freedom of the Shulamite. She is presented as taking the initiative most of the time. This is so unexpected in the biblical context in general that certain critics have thought of an influence coming from the Sangam poetry of the Tamils.[25] Others look toward Egypt—I believe, more felicitously. Michael Fox, for example, writes,

> [Ch.] Rabin surmises that the Song was written by someone who became acquainted with Indian love poetry. . . . But it is not necessary to turn to India to find parallels to the qualities in the Song that Rabin considers to be derived from Tamil love poetry. [For instance] the mention of spices originating in East Asia is not (contrary to Rabin) evidence for Indian influence . . . The names of two of the spices (*nerd* and *karkom*) were probably borrowed through the medium of Persian.[26]

In my opinion, the Egyptian influence on the Song is definitely established. There are too many traits common to both literatures to be ignored. I am thus willing to believe that the country on the Nile, with its more liberal conception of women in general, served as a model for the Song's poet—although we should not diminish the importance of the differences. It remains that certainly more stress should be laid than has been done in general on the feminine initiative demonstrated by folkloric poetry inside Israel. Such is the case in a text like Isaiah 27:2–6, where the personified vine speaks like a woman. The same is true of a Mishnaic tradition that is important for our purpose, *Mishnah Taanit* 4. 4. The maidens of Jerusalem dance in the vines; they ask the young men to turn their eyes upon them. The men's answer is also interesting: "Has anyone ever seen a young man speaking first to a maiden?"

Thus, it is after all not too surprising that the author of the Song be a woman. It is a woman's song from beginning to end and it puts the heroine center-stage. "All events are narrated from her point of view, though not always in her voice, whereas from the boy's angle of vision we know little besides how he sees her," says Michael Fox (*The Song of Songs*, p. 309). He adds that the apparent absence of the author is deceptive, for she stands everywhere "behind the scenes, communicating

25. Ch. Rabin, "The Song of Songs and Tamil Poetry," *Studies in Religion* 3 (1973): 205–19. Norman Gottwald, *Interpreter's Dictionary of the Bible*, vol. 4, art. "Song of Songs," also develops the idea of an Indian origin of certain objects in the Song.

26. Fox, *The Song of Songs*, p. xxvi, n. 6.

to us attitudes about the personae . . . and setting many of the norms by which we are to understand and evaluate the characters" (p. 258).

Before proceeding, I must respond to a possible objection. There exists, in fact, in the ancient literary world (I am referring for instance to the Japanese Nô theater) or in modern literature (for instance, D. H. Lawrence, *Lady Chatterley's Lover*, 1928), the possibility of a masculine author or actor playing the part of a woman. Consequently, we might think of the same fiction regarding the Song. But such a thing is absolutely impossible in Israel where any form of "travesty" (in the modern sense of the word) is regarded with horror. We would no longer be in the presence of subversion but of blasphemy pure and simple (cf. Deuteronomy 22:5).

One significant text is Song 8:12, "My vineyard, my very own, is for myself" (NRSV). According to Lys, it is the young man who speaks in verses 11–12, but he admits that it could be her (see Lys, *Le plus beau chant de la création*, p. 302). The latter reading is preferable. She says that her "vineyard" belongs to her, using the term *lepanay*, which is generally translated by "at my disposal" (Genesis 13:9; 20:15; 24:51; 34:10; 47:6; 1 Samuel 16:16; 2 Chronicles 14:6). The formula is already present in 1:6, in the mouth of the heroine. As André Robert says, *lepanay* can only stand in opposition to *le-noterim* ("the keepers," masculine, in the same verse).[27] Clearly, the Shulamite proclaims that her "vineyard" belongs to her, she takes care of it without the help of anyone.[28] In the Song, the Shulamite is always the one who says *'ani*, "me," or *napši* "my soul, me," or even *libbi* "my heart, me" (cf. v. 10 here). No exception is set by Song 8:12, where we see that, by contrast, Solomon does not allow the one he loves to keep her own vineyard, her body that is, but would rather have it kept by others in his harems. This is the continuation of the preceding argument (verses 6–7) according to which one cannot buy love; it is not a measurable quantity that could be "commercialized." Solomon views love in terms of one thousand and two hundred—let him keep this reckoning to himself! Let him have his "vineyard" kept by others if he so wishes, he will gain nothing by it.

The argument in Song 8:12 is directed first of all against those who are called the "brothers" of the Shulamite (1:6 and 8:8ff.). In this latter

27. A. Robert, R. Tournay, and A. Feuillet, *Le Cantique des Cantiques, traduction et commentaire* (Paris: Gabalda, 1963), p. 321.

28. Cf. Marvin H. Pope, *Song of Songs: A New Translation with Introduction and Commentary* (Garden City: Doubleday, 1977), p. 690: "If the female here asserts autonomy, this verse becomes the golden text for women's liberation."

text, the brothers speak of their duty to defend and see their sister married. In the Middle East, brothers play a major role in the engagement and wedding of their sister (Genesis 24:29, 50, 55, 60), as well as in the protection of her chastity (Genesis 34:6–17; 2 Samuel 13:20, 32). It should be noted that the term *ledabbér be-* in verse 8b (NRSV: "to speak for") means, among other things, "to ask in marriage" (1 Samuel 25:39). In verse 10 comes the young woman's response, something like: "If I am a wall for Solomon, it is not on account of a supposed immaturity on my part. In fact, I have towering breasts, and my chastity is in my keeping." Here, as in the entire poem, the Shulamite makes herself look dangerously like a loose woman. The parallel is striking with the attitude of several heroines, such as Ruth on the threshing floor, for example, or Tamar at the entrance to Enaim, or again Judith in Holophernes' tent. We should say here of the Shulamite what must be said of these heroines. What they all advocate is not the loosening of morals, still less so-called free love. The Shulamite is, indeed, a free woman, but her freedom consists in remaining unswervingly true to the one she loves. She is faithful to him outside matrimonial bonds and social demands. The Song is diametrically opposed to the bourgeois praises of feminine loyalty (cf. Deuteronomy 22:13–29), or of a woman as wife and mother (cf. Proverbs 31), for example. This time she is praised as lover, in contrast to antifeminist texts such as Qohelet 7:28 or Proverbs 9:13; 21:9, 19; 27:15. For, in the Song, the entire societal structure is put under fiery criticism. With respect to Song 8:6, Andrew Harper rightly perceives that there is here a reaction against marriage as:

> a mere matter of contract, and the price given for the bride a subject of pride, as it still is among Orientals. Immediately and inevitably this statement of the nature of love leads on to a condemnation of the common point of view in an arrow-like phrase, which having first transfixed the gorgeous and voluptuous Solomon, goes straight to the heart of the ordinary practice of the time.[29]

Let us note, by the way, that the reading of the poem as a subversive piece sheds light on the recurring exhortation "do not stir up nor awaken love until it please." Roland Murphy is no doubt right when he emphasizes that "Love is personified as a power, as in 8:6. . . . Love has

---

29. Andrew Harper, *The Song of Solomon, with Introduction and Notes* (Cambridge: Cambridge University Press, 1902), p. 58. Heinrich H. Grätz, *Schir Ha-Schirim oder das Salomonische Hohelied* (Breslau: W. Dacobson, 1885), sees in the oath by the gazelles and hinds an exhortation to the daughters of Jerusalem that no woman should sign a marriage contract against her will.

its own laws and is not to be achieved artificially."[30] But the question is, what contrary opinion is there that must be countered? I suggest that the allusion is to the customary exchange of (compensatory) presents between the two betrothing families. The exhortation is thus an internal commentary to the declaration in 8:7 that one cannot buy love.

To be sure, it is not superfluous at this point to recall that in the ancient Middle East, marriages are arranged independently of the consent or preferences of those primarily concerned. If love is to emerge between spouses, it is after the wedding. Genesis 24:67 is a case in point. *A contrario*, the case of Jacob and Rachel is unusual, but the young man is already living with his future father-in-law. Thus, the allusion in 8:7 to those who would buy love is not fantasy on the part of the author; that is exactly what she saw happening around her, and she defies the custom with a biting irony. Not only are the lovers in the Song unmarried, but, as says Harper, in response to Karl Budde[31] who thought otherwise, like many others, "what more immoral than to incite young people to seek for that which the 'good custom' of their people sought to render impossible for them?"[32]

Something else is important to remember: there is no law in the Bible or in ancient Judaism against polygamy. That the Song considers true love as an exclusive relationship between a man and a woman opens a wide perspective. Some have seen in the poem a sort of commentary on Genesis 2–3. There also, the myth presents us with one man and one woman. Phyllis Trible writes:

> the first couple lose their oneness through disobedience. Consequently, the woman's desire becomes the man's dominion. The second couple [the one of the Song] affirm their oneness through eroticism. Consequently, the man's desire becomes the woman's delight. Whatever else it may be, Canticles is a commentary on Genesis 2–3. Paradise Lost is Paradise Regained.[33]

Now, it is certainly true that Song of Songs is a celebration of the joy of living and of the joy of loving from which is absent, *mirabile dictu*, all sense of culpability. The guilt felt by the original couple when dis-

---

30. Murphy, *The Song of Songs*, p. 137. Cf. Israel Bettan, *The Five Scrolls: A Commentary on the Song of Songs* (Cincinnati: Union of American Hebrew Congregations, 1950), about Song 2:7.

31. Karl Budde, "Das Hohelied erklärt," in K. Budde, A. Bertholet, D. G. Wildeboer, *Die Fünf Megillot* (Tübingen: J. C. B. Mohr, 1898).

32. Harper, *The Song of Solomon*, p. 58.

33. Phyllis Trible, "Depatriarchalizing in Biblical Interpretation," *Journal of the American Academy of Religion* 41 (1973): 47.

covering nudity is here transcended by a ravishment before the *différ-ence*. But if so, instead of seeing in the Song with Karl Barth[34] and, later, Phyllis Trible, a complement to Genesis 2–3, we should instead perceive them as in mutual opposition.[35] It does not suffice to merely contrast Genesis 3:16 (*tešuqatêk*, your [fem.] desire shall be for your husband) and Song 7:10 (*tešuqato*, his desire is for me [fem.]), without further ado. Rather than just a contrasted complement, there is in the Song opposition to the letter of Genesis 3. The Song of Songs is icono-clastic, a point we shall return to below. It is only by distancing them-selves from the two texts that readers can conclude that these do not necessarily exclude each other, but are true alternatively.

This does not mean that Genesis is a religious text, while Song of Songs is a secular rejection of the former's point of view. Daniel Lys is certainly correct to conclude his beautiful analysis of the Song by saying that the literal and natural meaning of the book is theological. The poem demythicizes the sexual and refers it back in a veiled but powerful way to the existential experience of the union between God and Israel. To the extent that some texts on Mesopotamian hierogamy have influ-enced the poetess—at least her vocabulary[36]—a polemical stance is taken here against their spirit. Carnal love is here no mimetic duplica-tion of a primordial divine archetype. All utilitarianism, even religious, is excluded. Fertility is never contemplated in the Song as the justifica-tion of the coming together of the human couple, and this fact renders totally impossible the idea that the poem is the "legend" or the accom-panying script for a seasonal renewal celebration or—another tenacious

---

34. For Karl Barth, the Song *completes* the thought of Genesis 2. The feminine voice was im-plicit there and becomes explicit in Song 7:11. See his *Church Dogmatics*, vol. 3, Part 2, translated by Harold Knight et al. (Edinburgh: T. & T. Clark, 1960), p. 294.

35. See also Trible, *God and the Rhetoric of Sexuality*, pp. 144–65.

36. This theory is advanced particularly by H. Schmöckel, *Heilige Hochzeit und Hoheslied* (Wies-baden: Deutsche Morgendländische Gesellschaft, 1956); Theophile J. Meek, *The Song of Songs*, *Interpreter's Bible*, vol. 5, (Nashville: Abingdon, 1992), pp. 98–148; Helmer Ringgren, *Das Hohe Lied* (Göttingen: Vandenhoeck & Ruprecht, 1958); also M. H. Pope, *Song of Songs*, whose source of inspiration is the Canaanite literature from Ugarit. These authors think that the Song is in the Canon of Scriptures on account of a confusion or a deliberate annexation. The poem is a booklet about sacred hierogamy, a culminating point of the New Year celebration in Babylon. As there were "pagan" manifestations in Israel, it is not surprising to find a text such as the one we have here; it must have been well known in popular circles. It was freed of its most shocking elements by a Yahwistic editor and reinterpreted allegorically as celebrating the love between God and His People. To this, I would retort that the hierogamic texts center on fecundity, since the ritual has for object the renewal of the year and its abundance. We find nothing of the sort in the Song. Moreover, no one explains how a text revised by *bona fide* Yahwists does not contain any allusion to the God of Israel or to the *Heilsgeschichte*. We will come back to this later.

theory—for a marriage ceremony. For instance, some saw in the mutually voluptuous descriptions of the lovers *wasfs* of sorts, that is, poems which were in vogue among the Syrian peasants during a seven-day wedding ceremony.[37] But this theory, which seemed quite promising at the end of the nineteenth century, must be rejected. A confirmation of the Syrian structure has not been found in Palestine. Besides, the Song is too short for a ceremony lasting seven days.

Before pursuing our investigation of the literary method of subversion used in the Song, let us note how important this feature is in helping to establish the unity of authorship. As a matter of fact, it would be difficult to imagine a group of lyrical authors uniting their poetic efforts with the unique and common goal of extolling Eros and freedom from the "Establishment" in a language that remains surprisingly consistent throughout.

Othmar Keel points out the extent to which the Song stands apart from ordinary social structures. The institution, he notes, is simply ignored here and this explains, for instance, the absence of the father and of descendants, that is, of past and future.[38] Now the institution, familial or other, includes the ritual as well, a point that deserves to be looked at more closely. According to a widespread custom, the fiancée is transferred during the nuptial ceremony to her fiancé's family. The latter is called *beit-ʾab*, that is, literally, the "father's house." In the Song, however, the motif of this ritual passage to the "father's house" is replaced by the unexpected invitation, made by the fiancée to her fiancé, to enter her mother's house (3:4; 8:2).[39] Thus the roles are doubly reversed, the invitation is in the female's mouth, and the future kinship is with her mother. Furthermore, as said above, there is no mention in the Song of

37. Syrian *wasfs* from Qasim el-Chinn were collected by J.-C. Wetzstein, German Consul in Damascus in the nineteenth century. "Die syrische Dreschtafel," *Zeitscrift für Ethnologie* 5 (1873): 270–302. These are dithyrambic mutual descriptions of the betrothed. One finds there "the whole gamut of feelings . . . from boundless joy to bottomless depression" (Robert, Tournay, Feuillet, *Le Cantique des Cantiques, traduction et commentaire,* p. 421). The German critic Karl Budde was much influenced by Wetzstein in his 1898 commentary. But an enthusiasm of this sort must be strongly tempered for a variety of reasons. Michael Fox, for example (*The Song of Songs,* p. 232), remarks that there are *wasfs* in Egyptian love songs, but not in a nuptial context. By contrast, in the nuptial songs, there are none. (Thus these would be in accord with the Song as we read it, but not as Wetzstein and Budde read it.) Furthermore, Wesley J. Fuerst objects that Syrian customs from the nineteenth century hardly shed light on a situation in biblical times. See his *The Books of Ruth, Esther, Ecclesiastes, The Song of Songs, Lamentations: The Five Scrolls* (Cambridge: Cambridge University Pres, 1975), p. 166.

38. Othmar Keel, *Deine Blicke sind Tauben: zur Metaphorik des Hohen Liedes* (Stuttgart: Vlg. Katholisches Bibelwerk, 1984), p. 13.

39. See Genesis 24:67: Isaac takes his newly wed wife into his late *mother's* tent.

the girl's father—an omission all the more surprising since an unmarried girl was dependent on her father prior to becoming dependent on her husband.[40] Already from this point of view the poem stands out from customary and institutional framework. It does not set out to celebrate the social assent to the "conventional wedding" of a couple but to sing of "undisciplined" love. Paul Ricoeur writes:

> Eros is not institutional. It is an offense to reduce it to a compact, or to conjugal duty. . . . Eros' Law—which is not law any more— is the reciprocity of the gift. It is thus infra-juridical, para-juridical, supra-juridical. It belongs to the nature of its demonism to threaten the institution—any institution, including marriage.

Then, in a dense page, Ricoeur develops this point and shows its subversive character:

> It is an enigma that sexuality remains incompatible with the human trilogy: language-tool-institution. . . . Sexuality, it is true, mobilizes language; but it goes through it, upsets it, makes it sublime or silly, reduces it to fragments of murmur or invocation; language ceases to be mediation. Sexuality is Eros, not logos. . . . It is supra-instrumental as its instruments must go unnoticed. . . . Finally, whatever is said of its equilibrium in marriage, Eros is non-institutional.[41]

For the purpose of praising *eros*, the poetess dared adopt a language that prophets and some priests had traditionally used to describe metaphorically the intimate relations between God and people. Put in a nutshell, it is a language accepted into the religious realm by virtue of its figurative usage. That is why the allegorizing school has no trouble showing the impressive overlapping possible between the prophets' language and the Song's. André Robert, in particular, insists that the origi-

40. See Roland de Vaux, *Les Institutions de l'Ancien Testament*, vol. 1 (Paris: Cerf, 1958), p. 48. Cf. also R. Tournay in Robert, Tournay, Feuillet, *Le Cantique des Cantiques, traduction et commentaire*, p. 385. The mother is frequently mentioned in the Song: 1:6; 3:4; 6:9; 8:2, 5. Günther Krinetzki contrasts this use of the theme with Egyptian parallels where the mother serves as a useful intermediary in the development of the narrative. Here she is "Urbild des Mädchens hinsichtlich seiner Weiblichkeit." See his *Kommentar zum Hohenlied: Bildsprache und theologische Botschaft* (Frankfurt: Lang, 1981), p. 257, n. 231.

41. Paul Ricoeur, "Sexualité: la merveille, l'errance, l'énigme," *Histoire et vérité* (Paris: Seuil, 1955), pp. 209, 208. Cf. G. Gerleman, concerning Song 2:6: "The drama of love according to the Song is indifferent to customs and morality. What is more, the Song affirms with calm the priority of love over any social regulation and over any family blood relation (and even over any preliminary marriage condition)." *Ruth; das Hohelied* (Neukirchen-Vluyn: Neukirchener Verlag, 1965), p. 120.

nal intention of the Song is allegorical. He calls attention to the incontrovertible fact that biblical prophecy too mentions kings, shepherds, herds, vineyards, gardens, Lebanon, spring flowers, nocturnal awakenings. For Robert, these terms and expressions have in the Song the eschatological meaning they have in the works of the prophets. What is alluded to is God's restoration of his unfaithful people, and the resumption of their honeymoon, as it were. Israel and her land are God's beloved. The numerous topographical terms in the Song, it is stated, become clear when one perceives them as descriptive of Palestine during the Messianic times.

Along the same line, Robert *et alii* point out the Prophets' erotic language ever since Hosea. But that exegetical school remains silent about the fact that the Prophets took great pains to avoid explicit sexual allusions, for these were branded as Canaanite naturalistic idolatry. Furthermore, the Prophets provide the key to their metaphors, especially in the sensual realm. Yet in the Song we look in vain for this key—for the obvious reason that there is no door that it would open. Many of the passages obstinately resist any allegorization; the allegorizing school must then force them into prefabricated molds; about Song 8:5, for example, where we find the term *'orartika* ("I awakened you," in the mouth of the Shulamite). Marvin Pope writes, "The text as received would, in keeping with the allegory, represent Israel as arousing Yhwh under the apple tree where His mother conceived and bore him!" (Pope, *Song of Songs*, p. 663). The allegorizing school must consequently and against all evidence to the contrary, alter the traditional Masoretic vocalization of the text and put the discourse in the young man's mouth. In other words, the Masoretes undoubtedly did not read the poem allegorically. After this, it is rather difficult to allegorize in the name of the ancient hermeneutical tradition about the Song. Moreover we can apply to all allegoric interpretation the following judgment of Daniel Lys, echoing Rowley, "they utilize a key found outside the text to interpret the text."[42]

But then, if such is the case, we find ourselves in a highly paradoxical

---

42. Lys, *Le plus beau chant*, p. 39. H. H. Rowley too does not find anything in the Song "but what it appears to be, lovers' songs. . . . All of the other views find in the Song what they bring to it." See his "The Interpretation of the Song of Songs," in *The Servant of the Lord and Other Essays on the Old Testament* (London: Lutterworth, 1952), p. 233. For Michael V. Fox: "The equality of the lovers and the equality of their love, rather than the Song's earthly sensuality are what makes their union an inappropriate analogy for the bond between God and Israel" (*The Song of Songs*, p. 237).

hermeneutic situation. In fact, we are dealing with a limit-case in biblical hermeneutics. The "trajectory" of the text might be retraced as follows: first of all, we could say, the author of the Song de-metaphorizes
the language of the Prophets when describing the relationship between
Israel and God. In a fashion, the Song thus restores the language to its
first and original meaning, making that language once again available
to describe the love between a man and a woman. Second, the author
goes even further. In her poem she magnifies luxury, nature, courtship,
eroticism, all things which Prophets and Sages found objectionable
(here we can compare, with Othmar Keel, Proverbs 7:8 and Song 4:14;
1:13; Isaiah 3:16 and Song 4:9; Hosea 4:13 and Song 1:16f., for example). So, in summary, language has gone full circle, from literal sense
to metaphorical to nonfigurative again.

There occurred one more veering. What the original author of the
Song wrote with a subversive and liberating intent became forcibly rein-
tegrated into a "bourgeois" mentality through subsequent readings of
the text. To the *eros* of the poem was artificially opposed a disembodied
agapè. Because of this, the rebellious spirit of the work was tamed into
a mystical and dualistic hymn where the male character is no longer a
man and the female character is no longer a woman; they are asexual
personae. Jacques Winandy is possibly correct in saying that already the
final redactor, by means of some interpolations, muted the love song
into a sapiential piece describing Solomon's love of Wisdom.[43] At any
rate, the superscription "Song of Solomon" is quite suspect. Furthermore, the final verses of the Song may have been read at some point of
the text's transmission as providing an interpretative key to the whole
poem, in the sense of the female here being none else but Wisdom herself. We then can compare this phenomenon with a similar one at the
end of Qohelet. For Robert and Tournay, for instance, Song 8:13–14
are appendices identifying the Shulamite with Wisdom, thus slanting
the general theme of the poem.[44]

It is clear that the author wrote a song, a romance, which quickly
became an embarrassment for her fellow Jews (and, later, for Christians). However, it is well known that a handy principle of interpretation of something deemed scandalous by diehard conservatives is the
recourse to allegory. The text by Freud cited at the beginning this chapter says it well. It seems that the more a love scene is daring, the more

43. Jacques Winandy, *Le Cantique des Cantiques, poème d'amour mué en écrit de sagesse* (Paris:
Casterman, 1960).
44. Robert, Tournay, Feuillet, *Le Cantique,* pp. 351f.

it is likely to be interpreted mystically. Origen, says Jean Daniélou, had already set forth the rule that "the Scriptures cannot tell us anything unworthy of God, and so where something is unworthy of Him, it must be interpreted spiritually."[45] Thus, if "something unworthy of God" is found in the Song, a figurative interpretation is automatically imposed. Consequently, by virtue of the "domino principle," rather than of a female author, one thinks of a scribe, that is, precisely a representative of the conservative party. M. H. Segal speaks of a school of popular love poetry; Robert Pfeiffer, of professional poets; and so forth.[46]

The paradox is that if one wants to avoid the "indignity" of the literal text, one falls into yet a greater indignity. In the fourth century CE, Theodore of Mopsuestia in Sicily defended the literal meaning of the Song. His ideas were condemned by the Council of Constantinople in 553 and his works were destroyed. "Hide that breast that I must not see!"

One can easily imagine the sort of message a scribe would want to put forward, either about Wisdom, desirable like a beautiful woman, or about the thwarted yet gracefully continued love between God and his people. Shunning a poem that glorifies *eros* and, by its very genre, might even find its way to bars and whorehouses, the official representative of tradition and wisdom redirects the Song toward a more acceptable, but innocuous and lukewarm, understanding. Through allegory the erotic is only a rhetorical vehicle, while the tenor is sanctified by its aloofness and its spirituality.

True, if we reject the facile escape of allegoresis, all perils are not thereby avoided. For it is one thing to say that the poem is, indeed, a love song between a man and a woman, but it is another to detect what is the project of a book that is paradoxically more problematic. Michael Fox, for example, has a hard time finding out why the Song was written in the first place. Proceeding by elimination, he rejects the idea that it was composed to favor courtship, or marriage, profane or sacred, or even that it should be construed as a mortuary song (usually associated with the cult of Tammuz and Adonis).[47] He concludes that the poem

45. Jean Daniélou, *Origène* (Paris: La Table Ronde, 1948), p. 149. Daniélou refers to the work of Ferdinand Pratt, *Origène, le théologien et l'exégète* (Paris, 1907), p. 179. Yet let us note that there is no complaisance toward eroticism in the Song. Even in the ravished and reciprocal descriptions of the anatomy of the opposite sex, "their eyes neither pass over intimate parts of anatomy nor dwell on them" (5:14; 7:2–3 [1–2]), as R. Murphy quite rightly says (*The Song of Songs*, p. 102). This is why, moreover, the modern exegete must respect the ambivalence of the metaphors and must not smother it with a "clinical translation" (ibid., p. 102, n. 395).

46. M. H. Segal, *The Song of Songs*; Robert H. Pfeiffer, *Introduction to the Old Testament* (New York: Harper and Brothers, 1948, p. 711).

47. On the Song as funeral song, see Pope, *Song of Songs*, pp. 210–29.

was written for entertainment. Such a conclusion, however, constitutes a grave error which weakens an otherwise convincing book on the Egyptian parallels to the Song. Entertainment may be right as far as Egypt is concerned, but the critic transposes into Palestine a foreign *Sitz im Leben*. In so doing, he forgets that the two societies are in certain respects totally different, in particular and specifically with respect to the relations between men and women. It appears certain that in Egypt the relations between sexes before marriage were less controlled by social conventions than in Israel.[48] Egyptian love poetry could, therefore, adopt a more relaxed and uninhibited style. But not so in Israel. Imitating Egyptian love songs was certainly not self-evident. If there is dependence, it is intentionally defiant of national traditions. In fact, we might, in a more general manner, compare the cultural dependence in question to what happens in philology when one language "borrows" a term from another language. The term is eventually the same on either side, but the original semantic field has not moved over with the word into the receptive language, and the meanings here and there are now different. The Israelite poetess naturally turned her attention toward Egypt whose love literature expressed itself more freely. There was present in Egyptian literature a feminine aggressiveness the Jewess put to better use by turning it into a sort of sarcastic carnival of manners.[49] But the Israelite was not by a long shot thinking of amusing her public. She wanted to shock. "Solomon" is reduced to the risible dimensions of an Ahasuerus in the book of Esther. The family and familiar guardians of women's chastity, namely the "brothers" and the night watchmen in the Song, are largely outdone by events over which they have lost control. Those who consider the future marriage of their son or daughter as a commercial transaction are derided. The institution in general is swept aside and the event of love is glorified. But there is even more here.

We have seen above that the institution in the ancient Near East, familial or other, includes the cultic as well. Now it so happens that the defiance of our author reaches its summit when sacrosanct oath formulas are ironically parodied in the form of conjurations invoking wild animals. To this development we now turn. Our inquiry, however, must be prefaced by a general statement underlining the absolutely irreligious

48. Michael Fox says himself that in Israel premarital sexual relations were "anathema" for the masters of religion. He cites Sirach 42:9–13 (*The Song of Songs*, p. 314, n. 13).

49. My critique of Fox applies also to Othmar Keel's commentary on the Song of Songs, which draws heavily upon textual and iconographic parallels from the ancient Near East, especially Egypt. See his *The Song of Songs*, translated by Frederick Gaiser (Minneapolis: Fortress Press, 1994).

nature of the Song.[50] In the book of Esther we meet with a comparable situation, yet the Song goes even further. We do not find here any religious motif, any moral exhortation, any reminder of events of the *Heilsgeschichte,* any national theme, or any divine invocation (no prayer, not even a fast as in Esther). Carol Meyers summarizes this phenomenon in a brief but accurate judgment; the Song she says is "the most 'unbiblical' of all biblical books."[51]

Now we may return to the formulas of conjuration in the Song. These are "secular" oaths, a totally blasphemous utterance for the ancient world where it is taken for granted that an oath is sworn in the name of gods. Critics understandably are perplexed. Carl Siegfried went so far as to say that it is an exaggerated interpretation of Exodus 20:7 on the part of the biblical author.[52] For Robert Gordis as well, to cite another example, we have here both the shying away from the proper name of God and the substitution of harmless terms (like "darn" for "damn" in English, or "bleu" for "Dieu" in French). Thus, once again, what is originally and plainly irreverent is turned by eisegesis into an excess of religious respect. In the same vein are some critics' remarks that animals like bucks, goats, and gazelles are traditionally associated with the goddess Astarte. It is then said that in Israel there is a "remnant of the lyrical pagan world in its experience and interpretation."[53] Franz Delitzsch had already stressed the character of absolute freedom represented by the invoked animals, however.[54]

All of this is not unappealing and probably has a certain but limited accuracy. But the homophony between the poetess's selected terms, on the one hand, and customary religious expressions of oath, on the other, must be emphasized. Song 2:7, repeated in 3:5 (cf. 8:4; 5:8), says, "I

50. In this essay, "religious" and "theological" are *not* synonyms. Song of Songs is profoundly theological; see below.

51. Carol Meyers, *Discovering Eve* (New York: Oxford University Press, 1988), p. 177.

52. Carl Siegfried, *Prediger und Hoheslied* (Göttingen: Vandenhoeck & Ruprecht, 1898), p. 101. He refers to Socrates' expressions in the vernacular, such as "nè ton kuna," "by the Dog" or "by the Cabbage," "by the Goose" (Cf. Plato, *Apology* 22a; *Protagoras,* 482b). We have perhaps something similar in the following Sumerian poem cited by Robert Murphy: "Your right hand be placed in my private parts, your left shall support my head, and when you have neared your mouth to my mouth, when you hold my lip in your teeth, [then], thus you must swear me the oath!" (*The Song of Songs,* p. 53). Cf. Song 5:4, with regard to which another Sumerian text may be cited, "Dumuzi thrust a hand against the door [crying]: Make haste to open the house, Milady! Make haste to open the house!" (ibid., p. 50).

53. Keel, *The Song of Songs,* p. 100.

54. Franz Delitzsch, *Hoheslied* (Leipzig, 1875). All the same this interpretation is preferable to that of Karl Budde, for example, who says that the conjuration "by the gazelles" not to awaken love makes sense because gazelles are timid (*sic,* "Das Hohelied erklärt," p. 9).

adjure you, O daughters of Jerusalem, by the gazelles or the hinds of the field." The Hebrew has, "*bi-ṣebaot 'o be-'ayelot ha-sadeh.*" "*Ṣebaot*" is clearly the same word as in the well-known Yahwistic expression, "Yhwh Ṣebaot." As for "'*ayelot,*" it resembles both morphologically and etymologically, "'*el,*" or "'*eloah,*" God. Finally, "*sadeh*" is in assonance with "*šadday,*" so that "'*ayelot ha-sadeh*" evokes "'*el šadday,*" "God Almighty."[55] As for the verb in the first hemistich, "to adjure, to charge under oath," it is no less surprising here. The Koehler-Baumgartner dictionary indicates at *šbʿ* (swear, etc.):

> The preposition *be* [by] after *šbʿ* indicates the valuable thing that is pledged in case the oath is not kept: God swears by his life, Jeremiah 51:14; Amos 6:8. . . . With *be*, "by" names the god who is witness and sponsor of the oath: *b'élohim.* Genesis 21:23; 1 Samuel 10:15; Isaiah 65:16; Jeremiah 5:7. . . . Hifil [causative] with *be*, Genesis 24:3 ["by Yhwh, God of heaven and earth"]; 1 Kings 2:42 ["by Yhwh" (under death penalty)]: Nehemiah 13:25 [after inflicting corporal punishments, Nehemiah demands an oath by the name of God]; 2 Chronicles 36:13 ["by God"]; [and the texts of the Song that we are here discussing].[56]

One cannot imagine a more solemn and performative an oath.

It is hardly imaginable that listeners and later readers of the Song in Hebrew missed the allusion. The only issue is one of intent, or if one will, of tone. The general atmosphere of the poem answers this question. Just as "Solomon" is used ironically in the book as though the author were putting out her tongue at the "Establishment," so do the formulas of conjuration parody the religious language and make fun of it.[57] The same applies to the obvious comparison between "My beloved is mine and I am his" (2:16; 6:3; 7:10), and "I am your God and you are my people" in Leviticus 26:12 (Ezekiel 36:28; 37:27).

If we move on to another "crux interpretum," namely 2:17, my gen-

---

55. The LXX has: *en tais dunamesin kai en tais ischusesin tou agrou* (= Vetus Latina; cf. Targum: "by the Lord of the armies and the Power of the land of Israel"). For R. E. Murphy: "The reference to the gazelles and hinds seems to be an imitation of an invocation of God" (*The Song of Songs,* p. 137). Robert, Tournay, Feuillet: "The poet can evoke in this conjuratory formula the divine name *'elohei ṣebaot,* 'God of the armies,' by not mentioning it explicitly but by only suggesting it through a play of words with *'ayelot* and *ṣebaot*" (*Le Cantique,* p. 108).

56. Ludwig Koehler and Walter Baumgartner, *Lexicon in Veteris Testament: Libros* (Leiden: E. J. Brill, 1953), p. 943.

57. Another purpose, of course, consistent with the Song's general tone, was to celebrate nature and the freedom of the animals of the field.

eral understanding of the poem will allow us, I believe, to make sense of the text more accurately than by other hermeneutical methods. Verse 17b, to recall, speaks of the "beloved, comparable to a gazelle or a young stag *upon separate mountains [harey-bater]*." It is possible, of course, that by now the allusion, once clear to the original audience, escapes us irremediably. However, insofar as A. Robert, for example, is right to see in the text a reference to the language of Genesis 15 where Abraham is said to "cut in two" (*wa-yebatter*) the animals, whose halves (*bittero*, verse 10; cf. Jeremiah 34:18–19) face each other,[58] we are probably dealing here again with an irreverence on the part of the poetess. "The separate mountains" have now become by metaphor a woman's breasts![59] On the other hand, we have just seen that "gazelle and young stag" are terms that closely recall divine names. The image formed by the beloved on the breasts of his belle has replaced that of the God of the Covenant with Abraham the Patriarch. Furthermore, as is clear from parallel texts in the Song (4:6; 8:14) concerning the mountains, "holy geography" is here radically "de-moralized, de-sacralized." We are at the antipodes of spiritual allegory.

On the subject of "de-moralization," let us also note the process of "demythologization" involved in the central passage of Song 8:6. As is well known, it is the only segment of the poem where there is found a trace of the divine name; the last word of the verse is *šalhèbètyah*, composed, it appears, with the theophoric element *-yah* for Yhwh. Many commentators either follow the LXX (it read the suffix as a pronoun in the feminine singular, *autès*, a far cry from a religious reading; moreover it should be noted that the ancient commentators did not exploit the possible presence of the Name of God here),[60] or else they emend the text. But, here again the author may have been irreverent. All the more since there is in the nearby context of verse 7 an allusion to Canaanite divinities (Mot; Rèšèp) and to the mythology of Yamm/chaos (v. 7: "many waters," cf. Genesis 1; Isaiah 51:9–10; Psalm 76:12–14; Jonah

58. A. Robert, "on the mounts of the covenant" (*Le Cantique*, pp. 128f). The Targum refers to Mount Moriah and to Genesis 15:10. The *Midrash Rabba* also refers to this same Genesis text. Paul Joüon translates: "the mountains of the [victims] cut in two."

59. In Song 8:14, "*bater*" is replaced by "*besamim*" ("mountains of spices" NRSV) and it is clear that in both texts, the "mountains" in question represent the girl herself. G. Krinetzki thinks of "mons veneris," following Paul Haupt, *The Book of Canticles: A New Rhythmical Translation with Restoration of the Hebrew Text* (Chicago: University of Chicago Press, 1902). The same reading of 8:14 is proposed by Wilhelm Wittekindt, *Das Hohelied und seine Beziehungen zum Ištarkult* (Hanover: Orient Buchhandlung, 1926), ad loc.

60. Cf. Pope, *Song of Songs*, p. 672.

2:3, 5–6; etc., some twenty-eight times in Hebrew Scripture). I will return to this in my closing remarks.

One last text will suffice, I hope, to support my thesis. I am selecting it from among the most difficult in the poem. The verse in question is 6:12, a downright *crux interpretum*. Numerous theories have been advanced to resolve the problem posed by this text and I cannot review them all here. The Hebrew Masoretic text reads as follows (it is uttered by the Shulamite): "*lo' yada'ti napši samteni markebot 'ammi nadib.*" The French translation of the *TOB* says, "Je ne reconnais pas mon propre moi: il me rend timide, bien que fille de nobles gens!" ("I do not recognize my own self: he makes me timid, although I am daughter of noblemen!"). The text is difficult right from the first part of the verse. The LXX betrays its embarrassment: "My soul did not know it had made of me the chariots of Aminadab" (= Vulgate, Vetus Latinus, Arabic, etc., also twenty Hebrew mss.). The translation is as literal as it is problematic. The last words, in Hebrew *'ammi nadib*, have been understood by LXX and Vulgate to be a proper name, Aminadab, which is extant in biblical Hebrew and resembles closely another name, Abinadab, whence eliciting a certain confusion. In fact, in the LXX (as the following verses attest, 1 Samuel 7:1; 2 Samuel 6:3f.; 1 Chronicles 13:7) we always have Aminadab, with an *m*, even when the MT has Abinadab. What is this Abinadab/Aminadab/Ammi-nadib doing in the Song? First of all, honoring the spelling of the MT, we can invoke the biblical connection often made between *'am* (people) and *nadib* (noble); see Judges 5:9, Numbers 21:18; Psalm 47:10; 113:8; 1 Chronicles 29:9; etc. (= Aquila, Symmachos, Quinta, Peshita). This is what encourages Marvin Pope to translate: "Unawares I was set in the chariot with the prince" (that is, with the belle's beloved; *'ammi* is understood to be the preposition *'im*, with, and *napši* to be a substitute for the pronoun of the first person singular).[61] As for the Jewish tradition, it translates: "my generous people (prince)" and is thinking of Israel. Within a similar perspective, A. Robert understands 6:12 in the sense that Yhwh, following a spontaneous impulse, has placed himself at the head of his people. Such a position is shared by other French translators, like A. Crampon and J. Bonsirven, who want to set in apposition *nadib* and "my people": "I do not know . . . but love has thrown me on the chariots of my people, as a prince!"

On the other hand, the name *Aminadab* (also with *m* in the Hebrew)

61. Ibid., p. 552.

is well attested (Exodus 6:23; Numbers 1:7; 2:3; 7:12, 17; 10:14; Ruth 4:19f.: Aminadab is the great-grandfather of Boaz; 1 Chronicles 2:10; 6:7; it is the name of a Levite in 1 Chronicles 15:10f.). We can thus distinguish among the different *Aminadab/Abinadab:*

> 1. a son of Jesse (1 Samuel 16:8; 17:13; 1 Chronicles 2:13);
> 2. a son of Saul (1 Samuel 31:2; 1 Chronicles 8:33, 9:39, 10:2);
> 3. the one who housed the Ark before David transferred it to Jerusalem (1 Samuel 7:1; 2 Samuel 6:3f.; 1 Chronicles 13:7).

We shall keep in mind these texts for the development that follows.

Propositions of text emendation of 6.12 are obviously not lacking. Tur-Sinai suggests: "I do not know myself (so great is my joy); there, you will give me your myrrh, O daughter of noble parent" (conjecture: *šam teni morek bat 'ammi nadib*).[62] Vincenz Hamp proposes (from the mouth of the youth), "I no longer recognized myself; she placed me on the sumptuous vehicle of the princely train" (cf. 7:2; 3:6f.) (conjecture: "'*al markebot* [plural of majesty] . . . '*ammei.*" Or perhaps we should understand: *sim* + 2 accusative = to make something out of something = "he [she] made chariots out of me").[63] Andrew Harper reads *napšo* instead of *napši* and says that the term can signify desire (cf. Proverbs 23:2): "So taken, the words would mean that . . . suddenly, before she knew, her longing to see the plants brought her among the chariots of her noble people, that is, of noble people who were hers, that is, rulers of her land" (Harper, *The Song of Solomon, with Introduction and Notes,* p. 47).

In short, there is no consensus. The impasse is due, I would argue, to the bypassing of the subversive nature of the book, which must be the guideline for the interpretation of the different pericopes of the poem. When this principle is respected, the result is the following: (1) Verse 12 (like v. 11) is from the lips of the Shulamite (cf. LXX, "There, I shall give you my breasts"; the response to the lover began in v. 11; the same verbal construction continues in verses 11 and 12). (2) The terms "chariots" and "Abinadab/Aminadab/Ammi-nadib" refer to the books of Samuel. In 1 Samuel 6, the Ark of the Covenant is on a chariot, coming from among the Philistines. It came to be housed by Abinadab. In 2 Samuel 6, it returns on a chariot from Abinadab's house to Zion. In the 1 Samuel text that serves as reference for Song 6:12d, the central

---

62. N. H. Tur-Sinai, *Ha-lashôn weha-sépher,* vol. 2 (Jerusalem: Bialik Institute, 1950), pp. 385f.
63. Vincenz Hamp, "Zur Textkritik am Hohenlied," *Biblische Zeitschrift* 1 (1957): 207f.

word is "return." Now, we should note that in the verse that follows Song 6:12a (6:13, Hebrew 7:1: "Return, return, O Shulamite, return, return, that we may look upon you!"), the verb "return" appears four times—a possible allusion to the compass and, beyond, to prophetic vision of the return of exiles from all places, see Ezekiel 37. Furthermore, the parallel is striking with 1 Samuel 7:3 ("If you are returning to the Lord with all your heart . . ." [NRSV]), coming immediately after the mention of the Ark's transfer into the house of Abinadab. We should also draw a comparison with a prophetic text in which both themes of the Ark and the return to Yhwh are conjugated, namely Jeremiah 3:14–16 ("Return, O faithless children . . . they shall no more say: 'The Ark of the Covenant of the Lord!' . . . It shall not come to mind, or be remembered, or be missed" [NRSV]). It is quite clear that, in these texts which served the author of the Song as literary models, the "return" is charged with theological meaning. The issue is one of repentance and change of life. In the Song, however—this must be emphasized—the "return" of the Shulamite has totally lost this spiritual dimension.

The "chariots," in Hebrew, *markebot,* remind us of the famous *merkabah* (singular) in Ezekiel 1 and 10, or again of those (*rèkèb,* collective singular in Hebrew) of Elijah and Elisha (2 Kings 2:12; 13:14). Elijah, of course, "goes up to heaven" on a *rèkèb 'ēš* (chariot of fire; 2 Kings 2:11–12). In other words, ninth-century prophetic inspiration used to lift up men and mountains for the sakes of Elijah and Elisha; now, it is Eros that transports the Shulamite. Although she does not, like her models, become a "guru," she can, in their wake, declare "I no longer know myself" (*lo' yada'ti napši*)—for the phrase conveys a certain sense of intoxication, prophetic or erotic.

Once again, with this text of Song 6:12, it was simply impossible for anyone in Israel to miss the allusion to the Ark of Covenant. True, we are not dealing with an exact quotation from Samuel, but this makes the manner in which the Song reflects Samuel all the more significant. It is so in this sense that Song 6:12a strikes two chords at the same time; let us call one of them metaphorical and the other rhetorical. Metaphorically, the Shulamite is compared with the chariot that carried the Ark of Yhwh, or with those Prophets of old who were identified with the whole chariotry of Israel. The shepherd's love transforms the Shulamite into the (sacred) chariot that transported the Ark of the Covenant to and from the house of Abinadab. The latter's name is an opportunity for the author to use the other chord, a rhetorical one. Abinadab/Aminadab is spelled by her "Ammi-nadib," thus changing the meaning of the name, like Abram became Abraham. Abinadab, who housed the Ark at the time of Saul/David, is now *'ammi nadib*, "my noble people." Thus, the Shulamite appears to her lover as princely and awesome as was the chariot of the Ark, the most famous chariot in the history of Israel, the "merkabah" or Yhwh's throne. To this, she joins *'ammi* and *nadib*, that is Israel, the noble people—all this in an erotic evocation![64]

The transformation of *nadab* into *nadib* opens the door to another wordplay. We have seen that the following verse four times summons the Shulamite to "return." The text continues in 7:1 (Hebrew 7:2) with a new designation for the belle, namely *bat-nadib* ("fille de noble" [nobleman's daughter], says the *TOB*). With respect to this, we should evaluate the theological weight of the root *ndb* in Scripture. The Chronicler, in particular, insists strongly on this verbal root. Here, it can signify in the hitpael (reflexive mode) the voluntary engagement toward God; see especially 1 Chronicles 29 (in v. 24, we have both *'ammi* and *hitnaddéb;* while v. 17f. emphasize the importance of the root *šlm* at the basis of the name "Shulamite"). Indeed, for Chronicles, Israel is *nadib*, noble, and is committed to God (*hitnaddéb*), because they are a "theophoric" people, to cite R. Tournay (see note 68). This is why the chariots mentioned here and there are fearsome (in 1 Samuel 6, 70 men die; in 2 Samuel 6, the victim is Uzza). In Song 6:4 and 10, the Shulamite is "terrible as an army with banners."[65]

The text continues on its own impetus. After the "return" motif (brought about by the metaphor of the chariot), and before the designation of the belle as "nobleman's daughter" (an expression created by association with the name Aminadab), comes a dance motif (or quadrille, according to the *TOB*) in 6:13b [Hebrew 7:1b]. The motif per se is unexpected in this context. It gave rise at times to more or less far-fetched scholarly reconstructions. One of the least exaggerated suggestions is to see it referring to a war dance or a saber dance. Our reading simplifies the matter. When the Ark was transferred to Zion, we are

64. A. S. Herbert, "The Song of Songs," p. 473 (par. 410 b) has seen the parallel between Song 6:12 and 2 Samuel 6.3, but he cannot believe his own eyes. He adds, "But to suggest that the betrothed one be identified with God's Ark is hardly probable."

65. We agree with Carol Meyers, "Gender Imagery in the Song of Songs," *Hebrew Annual Review* 10 (1986): 209–23, noting the remarkable military imagery in the Song (cf. 4:4, "tower of David"; 7:4, the pools and towers are there for military usage as well; 8:9, surrounding walls). All of these images, borrowed from the masculine world, are applied to the woman. "It is here an unexpected reversal of conventional imagery," she says (ibid., p. 215).

told that David led the procession while "swirling with all his might" (2 Samuel 6:14). Several texts in Samuel must be cited along the same line (they all spring from Exodus 15:20), such as 1 Samuel 18:6; 21:12; 29:5 (cf. Jeremiah 31:4). Song 6:13b [7:1b] being built against that background, the theme of the dance became imperative here also. As M. Pope says, although *meḥolah* of Song 7:1 is absent in 2 Samuel 6, "the term would have been quite appropriate to the [Davidic] celebration."[66] As already seen above, the author does not borrow her references servilely. Her rule is to transform her sources, although never beyond recognition.

In the mention of *maḥanayim*, probably the place called Mahanayim or a wordplay on it, I perceive the influence of 1 Kings 4:14. There, one of the twelve prefects of Solomon named Ahinadab (the author of the Song probably confused him with Abinadab, mentioned precisely a few verses before [v. 11]), is given a place by the king at Mahanayim!

As a final point, let us stress that Song 7:1 is the first and only text where the maiden is called (twice) "the Shulamite." This designation deserves all our attention. We know of one Abishag the Shunamite (that is, coming from Shonem or Shunem) in 1 Kings 1. This "extremely beautiful" girl was brought to old king David (him again!) to share his bed and warm him up. We are also told that the poor creature remained a virgin in this rather sordid affair. We find her once more in 1 Kings 2:22 as a stake in court intrigue, where once again no one asks for her opinion.[67] Just as Abinadab ("my noble father," a patriarchal boasting) becomes Aminadab ("my people are noble and generous"), so does the *Shunamite* become the *Shulamite*.[68] But what a find. The Shulamite is the anti-Shunamite. The latter is as much a passive and reified woman as the other is like quicksilver, an active subject whose first-person pronoun dominates the poem. In the same way, the Shulamite is the anti-Solomon. Both figures are united by the common verbal root of their Hebrew names, "Shulamite" and "Shelomoh."[69] The

---

66. Pope, *Song of Songs*, p. 603.

67. Pope rightly suggests that Solomon did not remain indifferent to the charms of Abishag (ibid., p. 598). This is probably not foreign to his violent reaction to Adonyah's request.

68. See R. Tournay, "Les chariots d'Amminadab (Cant. vi.12): Israël, peuple théophore," *Vetus Testamentum* 9 (1959): 288–309.

69. There is a great deal of irony in feminizing the Great King. Solomon personifies without difficulty the universe of the phallus, like Ahasuerus in the book of Esther. But we shall not retain the theory that sees in the name Shulamite in the Song a Hebrew form of the Akkadian goddess Shulmânitu (like Mordecai recalls Marduk, and Esther Astarte). On the other hand, it is interesting to recall, and possibly stems originally from the Song of Songs, that the maiden who requests

deliberateness of this rapprochement is emphasized in Song 8:10 where the belle is "the one who encounters peace" (*shalom*).[70] Once again, the poetess plays on several strings at the same time, and with the same brilliance.

The conclusion to this textual analysis is valid for the entire book of Song of Songs. We are in a setting of total irreverence. The author ironically uses expressions that had become "sacred" in a Yahwistic context. The Song is not the booklet for a pagan hierogamy. Nor is it an allegory for the use of the straightlaced on the intimate relations between God and Israel (even less, of course, between Christ and the Church). It is an exaltation of *eros;* it speaks of free love, untamed and even, to a certain degree, clandestine (cf. Song 8:1–3), between a man and a woman. The language of the author is naturalistic and thus exposed to censorship by "men of the cloth," and parodylike, as it imitates in a mode of mockery the jargon of the fundamentalists.

Now, there are two ways to speak ironically of the world one rejects. Either one demonstrates that that world is in its essence but a fraud, or else one protests against what some have made of that world, fundamentally beautiful yet presently disfigured. The Song is painted against the background of the supreme value of love in Israel. It protests the substitution by "religionists" of a kind of misunderstood *agapè* for the *eros* which ties a man to a woman (cf. Genesis 2). This is why, in this book that is the least "biblical" of all the biblical books, the message hidden behind poetic aesthetics (not behind allegorical esoterism) is decidedly theological. Love, love "pure and simple," love faithful and wholly integrated, is a reflection of the covenant between the divine and the human. It is probably in this sense that we should read Song 8:6 where love is compared to "a flame of Yah[weh]." The expression is ambiguous. It can just indicate a superlative, but in the subversive language of the author, it indicates precisely that human love reflects divine love.[71] Andrew Greeley goes even further. He suggests that the female author is "speaking of the (always potent) male organ of Yhwh [the flame symbol represents the penis], but, as it were, appropriating it for herself."[72] In A. Herbert's very simple formulation (from which I re-

---

John the Baptist's head from Herod Antipas received from tradition the name of Salome, Solomon in the feminine!

70. This parallel is strongly emphasized by A. Harper, who thinks of an ironical reference to Solomon raising the siege from the "city" he could not invest.

71. Murphy, *The Song of Songs,* p. 104.

72. Greeley and Neusner, *The Bible and Us,* p. 35. As to the sex of the Song's author, Greeley says quite accurately, "Only in stories written by women are men treated as likable but irresponsible little boys."

move the term "sensuality," unfortunate in this context), "Natural love, freed from its sinful perversions . . . is recognized in the Bible to be the least inadequate type of the love of man for God and of God for man."[73] To sing it, there is no need to be a theologian. Sometimes even to be a "specialist in religious matters" becomes an obstacle, one is subject to blindness rather than perceptiveness. It is a miracle in itself that the Song of Songs is in the canon of the Holy Scriptures. When Rabbi Aqiba said, "all the Scriptures are holy, but the Song of Songs is the Holy of Holies,"[74] he had a point.[75]

73. A. Herbert, "The Song of Songs," p. 469, par. 406g. It is what inspires the First Epistle of John (4:8) with the only definition of God the Scriptures hold, "God is love." This "analogy of faith" must be seen with Kant: [it] "does not signify . . . an imperfect similarity of two things, but a perfect similarity of relations between two quite dissimilar things" (*Prolegomena* 58, quoted by Paul Ricoeur in "From 'I am who I am' to 'God is love'—An Essay in Biblical Hermeneutics"). Ricoeur adds that the formula of 1 John brings us to give a surplus of meaning to God and to love. By this statement "we think more about God and about love."

74. *Tosephta Sanhedrin* 12.10.

75. This essay on Song of Songs is only one aspect of a book-length study published as *She Wrote Romance: A Hermeneutical Essay on the Song of Songs* (Philadelphia: Trinity Press, 1998).

The Nuptial Metaphor

PAUL RICOEUR

To retrace the trajectory of the Song of Songs is an all the more legitimate undertaking in that it is inevitable. As has often been said, few texts in the history of interpretation have had as exuberant or as encumbering a fortune. For a superficial glance, this fortune may be confused with the rise and fall of allegorical explications of the Song. Today, however, the situation seems to be as follows. Once contemporary exegesis almost unanimously had adopted the explication, which, in contrast to allegorical, has been called "naturalistic," and that I would prefer to call (and shall henceforth speak of as) the erotic interpretation—according to which the Song is nothing more than an epithalamium, a carnal love song in dialogue form—then the allegorical explications, which endured for so long within both the Jewish and Christian traditions, found themselves divested of their ancient credibility and relegated to the prehistory of this erotic explication. Indeed, for many commentators, these allegorical interpretations are only referred to in their introductions as examples of the prescientific antecedents of an investigation of the text that owes everything to the historical-critical method, which was unknown to the initiators of allegorical interpretation and even resisted by the last advocates of this approach.

For my part, I would like to oppose a multiple, flowering history of reading, set within the framework of a theory of reception of the text, to this unilinear conception of the "trajectory" of explication of the Song of Songs. This is a history where not just ancient allegorical exegesis finds a place, but also modern scientific exegesis, and—why not?—even new theological interpretations, whether related or not to the older allegorical exegesis.

The Obvious Sense of the Text

Before characterizing this history for itself, I want first to render justice
to the exegetical method that is opposed to it, at least as a first approximation, as its polar opposite, before revealing their complementarity,
which I shall attempt to justify with great care. The historical-critical
method, with its three faces—the history of sources, the history of
composition, and the history of redaction—can be assimilated overall
to a history of the writing of the texts we now read. It is noteworthy, in
fact, that in the interpretation proposed here by André LaCocque, as in
most contemporary commentaries on the Song of Songs, the dominant
focus is that of the origin of the text, if we include under this heading
the questions of author, date, and cultural setting, along with the question, which is inseparable from this dominant question, of the nature of
the original audience. Thus André LaCocque, who does not venture
any conclusions regarding date and place, does give a great importance
to the hypothesis that the author was a woman, a hypothesis accredited
by numerous indications within the text. The poem, he says, is "a woman's song from beginning to end" (p. 243). This hypothesis is solidary
with the thesis toward which all his detailed explications point, namely
that this beautiful erotic poem would be equivalent to a plea in favor
of a free, socially unacceptable, and uninstitutionalized love—a plea,
moreover, based on a subversive intention directed against accepted
thinking, sometimes called "bourgeois" or the "establishment." If André
LaCocque tempers his radical thesis somewhat with the admission that
the freedom of this free woman "consists in remaining indefectibly
faithful to the one she loves," it is no less true that the principal accent
of his interpretation is placed not on the fidelity of this love so much
as on its expression "outside the bonds of marriage and outside social
strictures." This interpretation could enter into a fruitful discussion
with other interpretations arising from what I have called the history of
the reception of the text if it could be detached from the postulate—
which, by the way, it shares with the modern upholders of an allegorical
reading—that there exists one true meaning of the text, namely, the
one that was intended by its author, authors, or the last redactor, who
are held to have somehow inscribed this meaning in the text, from
which exegesis has subsequently to extract it, and, if possible, restore it
to its originary meaning. Hence the true meaning, the meaning intended by the author, and the original meaning are taken as equivalent
terms. And commentary thus consists in identifying this overall true,

intended, and original meaning. To identify it, the text has to be explicated in a detailed manner; that is, one has to demonstrate that the solution brought to local difficulties fits with the general meaning assigned the text, coherence becoming the principal epistemological criterion indicating the adequacy of any commentary.

It is striking that contemporary allegorizing commentators base themselves on the same postulates. (This was not the case for ancient typological and allegorical interpretations, as I shall show in the second section of my remarks.) Thus modern allegorists compete with the explications they call "naturalistic," with the same ambition to identify, to explicate in detail, the true, intended, and original meaning. And hence today's readers find themselves confronted with an alternative that in fact stems from the quasi unanimity among commentators, even those who favor what their opponents call "naturalistic" explication. I would like to show in the second part of my study that another outcome, built on ancient allegorical interpretation on the basis of a history of the reading and the reception of our text, is possible other than the one most modern commentators reserve for our text, an outcome that relocates these interpretations into another epistemological category than the one that is implied by the notion of true, intended, and original meaning, along with the postulates of identification and explication that go with it on the methodological plane.

However, before doing so, I would like to bring to light a few features of the text of the Song of Songs that, I believe, hold it open to a plurality of interpretations, among which allegorical readings, which are themselves multiple and even contrary to one another, would find a place. These features, let me say straightaway, do justify one part of André LaCocque's reading, namely that the Song of Songs can be read as an erotic poem, perhaps one written by a woman (after all, why not?), a poem with several voices that celebrates the love of a man and woman, apart from any reference to the institution of marriage or to the rules of kinship that ordinarily assign to the father and brother of the finacée a determined social role, in this way imposing a perspective of fertility and descendants on conjugal love. On the other hand, these features fit less well with the hypothesis of a subversive intention indicated by the ironic, nonreverential connotation of those expressions that many commentators have seen as opaque. My hesitation in this regard does not result from my mistrust of too much concern for a recourse to the intention of the presumed author, but from the fact that these connotations seem to me to be compatible with an interpretation that would place the principal accent instead on the metaphorical dimension of a poem dedicated to erotic love, which is raised by its literary structure beyond any exclusive social-cultural context. These features, which I am now going to consider, seem to me to have as their effect—I do not say, intention—precisely to decontexualize erotic love and to render it in this way accessible to a plurality of readings compatible with the obvious sense of the text as an erotic poem.

I propose reserving the phrase "nuptial bond" to designate this love that is rightly called free and faithful, it being understood that nuptial does not signify "matrimonial." And I shall take as indications of the nuptial as such all those metaphorical features that have to do with the erotic, even at the level of the obvious sense of the text. Note that I say "obvious sense" in order to remain on the textual plane, without having to refer in any way to the intention of the presumed author, hence without having to say anything about the "true" or original meaning. Perhaps the metaphorics constitutive of such expressions of erotic love is such that it blocks any inquiry into such an intentional, original, univocal meaning.

I would like to begin by bringing together those quite striking features of indetermination that have to with the identification of the characters, places, times, and even the emotions and actions, then next to put the accent on those features that characterize what we can call the "movements of love" and that remain relatively indifferent to their individual attribution to the people in question. Finally, remaining strictly on the literary plane, I want to underline the tendency of the whole metaphorical interplay unfolded by the poem to free itself from its proper referential, that is, sexual, function. All these features taken together constitute the indication of the nuptial in the erotic and, by implication, make possible and plausible a disentangling of the nuptial from the erotic and its new reinvestment in other variations of the amorous relation.

Concerning the phenomenon of indetermination, I shall base what I have to say on a remark made by many commentators concerning the difficulty of identifying the lover and the beloved of this poem.[1] Besides the fact that they never identify themselves nor are they called by a proper name, the term Shulamite in book 7 is not a proper name (cf. what André LaCocque has to say, p. 261). We have to admit that we

---

1. Daniel Lys, *Le plus beau chant de la création. Commentaire du Cantique des Cantiques* (Paris: Cerf, 1968), p. 16.

never know with certitude who is speaking, to whom, or where. We can even, without being ridiculed, imagine that there are three personages involved: a shepherd, a shepherdess, and the king, Solomon.[2] Is it a question, for example, in 1:6–8 of a shepherd and a shepherdess, or in 1:4 and 3:2 and 11 of a king and a woman who might be a towns-woman, or of a peasant in 1:12–14 and 7:6 and 13? What is more, the dialogue is rendered even more complex by internal explicit and implicit quotations. Nor is it sure that certain scenes are not dreamed or that they might consist of recounted dreams. After all, the appearance of Solomon in 3:7–11 seems to fit quite well with this indecisiveness concerning the boundary between dreaming and wakefulness. Does not the lover say in 5:2: "I am sleeping but my heart is awake. I hear my beloved who is knocking"? Is not the shepherd a king in his dreams, and why not in terms of the figure of Solomon? These features of indetermination are incontestably favorable to the freeing of the nuptial held in reserve within the erotic.

But should we not simply speak of overdetermination rather than of indetermination? Paul Beauchamp, for example, emphasizes the overlapping of generations in the shifting evocation of the characters.[3] If we consider the succession 1:6, 3:4, 3:11, 6:9, 8:1, 8:4, the figure of the mother returns again and again: the mother of the woman, on the one hand, referred to by the young woman in 1:6 and 3:4 (along with the "chamber of the one that conceived me"); that of the young man in 8:5 ("Under the apple tree, I awaken you, there where your mother conceived you, there where she conceived you, the one who engendered you"). Beauchamp observes, "there is no marriage, royal or otherwise, without the marriage of memories and without the couple being marked by the line of generations."[4] How can we not be struck by this coincidence between wakefulness and this access to embodied memory where innovations and rememoration overlap? (Note, too, that this insistent evocation of the mother makes all the more remarkable the absence of the father, so forcefully underscored by André LaCocque, contrary to the presence of the brothers who try to hold back the crazed lovers.)

2. G. Pouget and J. Guitton, *Le Cantique des Cantiques* (Paris: Gabalda, 1934). "We can assume that it was Jacobi who, in 1771, really inaugurated the strict interpretation of the Song of Songs as a drama" (Lys, *Le plus beau chant,* p. 35).

3. Paul Beauchamp, *L'un et l'autre Testament,* vol. 2, *Accomplir les Ecritures* (Paris: Seuil, 1991), p. 177.

4. Ibid.

All these indeterminations and overdeterminations would be incomprehensible if we did not strongly emphasize, as does Paul Beauchamp, the distance opened between the poem and narration. It is within a narrative perspective, not a poetic one, that the question "who?" would be pertinent, or that we would be authorized to speak of individualized characters. In truth, the lover and the beloved are not identifiable characters; by this, I mean the bearers of a narrative identity. In this respect, it is not out of bounds to suggest that the question "who," ordinarily linked to narrative identity, comes into the poem only to accentuate, in what is undoubtedly a rhetorical fashion, but one that is poetically significant, what Beauchamp calls the appearance of the origin: "who is coming up from the desert?" (3:6); "who arises like the dawn?" (6:10); "who is coming up from the desert leaning on her beloved?" (8:5). Is it not from the end of the world and the depth of time that love arises? But then no name corresponds to or answers the question "who?"[5]

The poetic and non-narrative character of the song is further confirmed by another kind of indetermination that affects the division into scenes. Is it a question of seven poems, as Buzy suggests, where the action in each case progresses from the admiring description of one of the lovers to their mutual possession of each other?[6] Or is it really a question of action in a narrative sense?[7] The reader will have a difficult time in situating exactly the alleged moment of consummation of the union in question, which, I repeat, is not recounted but rather sung. And is it not rightly said that a poem places its climax at the middle, not at the end, which authorizes its imminence or recent accomplishment within the void of a narrative present, occupied by the song alone?[8] In this respect, what we can continue to call a denouement— "Set me like a seal on your heart / Like a seal on your arm. / For love is strong as death, / Jealousy is unyielding like Sheol . . ." (8:6)—must not be treated like some sapiential epilogue added to a narrative conclusion: "Under the apple tree, I awakened you, there where your mother conceived you, there where the one conceived you who gave birth to you" (8:5). It is rather the sapiential crown given to what is from one end to

---

5. Ibid., pp. 184–91.

6. Cf., for example, the division into seven poems proposed by Denis Buzy, *Le Cantique des Cantiques* (Paris: Letouzey et Ané, 1949), or that into eight segments by Daniel Lys, or the division into two developments and ten sections distributed around a center ("eat, friends, drink" 5:1) of Paul Beauchamp, *L'un et l'autre Testament*, pp. 161ff.

7. Ibid., pp. 173–80.

8. As Beauchamp says, "In a way, love is in the song itself" (ibid., p. 164).

another a song and not in any way a narration, the covenant language ("set me like a seal on your heart, like a seal on your arm") serving to tie together the spontaneity of the song and the meditative point of the organlike sententious declaration.[9]

These reflections concerning completion, which the poem places in the center, lead us to a series of comments concerning the primacy of the "movements" of love over the individual identities of the lover and the beloved. I borrow this expression, "movements of love," from Origen, one of the initiators of allegorical interpretation.[10] This phrase from the most important of the witnesses to the allegorism of the Fathers of the Church should make us attentive to what in the Song of Songs has to do with love as a kind of "movement." For one thing, there are movements in space. Hardly has the beloved exclaimed in the Prologue: "Let him kiss me with the kisses of his mouth," then she adds, "draw me in your steps, let us run." Next there is an evocation of wandering like a vagabond "among the herds and their guardians." And a bit further on, she says, "He led me to the storeroom and the banner he placed upon me is love." Then she hears the beloved arrive, "leaping over the mountains, bounding over the hills." And the lover says to her, "Come then, my beloved, my lovely one, come." In a dream, the beloved "seeks the one that [my] heart loves." As the poem unfolds, we come to understand that this mobility, which is sometimes disconcerting to follow with its changes of tone, is the indication of a game, which is the play of desire itself, or rather of two desires intermingled. The texture of this desire is made up of movements away from each other, then back toward each other, and once again away. In this regard, the scene set at the gate, in chapter 5, is particularly troubling. The beloved knocks and asks to enter. He reaches through the opening of the gate and then, "I opened to my Beloved, but, turning his back, he had disappeared." And the chorus, a bit further on, mocks: "Where has your love gone, oh most beautiful of women? Where did your beloved turn away, should we look for him with you?" (6:1). And the chorus adds: "Return, return, Shulamite, return that we may look upon you!" (6:13). Then once again

9. Ibid., pp. 180–84.

10. His second *Homily on the Song of Songs* begins as follows: "All the movements of the soul (*motiones animae*), God, the author of all things, created for the good, but in practice it often happens that good objects lead us to sin because we use them badly. Now one of the movements of the soul is love. We use it rightly to love when we love wisdom and truth, but when our love lowers itself toward things less good, it is flesh and blood that we love. . . . You, therefore, who are spiritual, spiritually listen to the song of these words and learn to raise yourself to what is better as regards the movement of your soul as much as the embrace (*incendium*) of your natural love."

there is a departure: "Come, my beloved, let us go to the fields!" (7:12). This playing with distance sets off the moments of mutual possession, which the poem, let me repeat, does not describe, or show, but only evokes, in the strongest sense of this word: "His left arm is under my head and his right embraces me" (2:6 and 8:2). Or again: "My beloved is mine, and I am his. He pastures his flock among the lilies" (2:16; 6:3). Carnal love is perhaps consummated in 5:1 or 6:3, but this is not said in a descriptive mode. Rather it is sung. Hence we can ask whether the veritable consummation is not in the song itself. And if, as I suggested above, the true denouement is to be found in 8:6 ("set me like a seal on your heart, like a seal on your arm"), then what is important is not the carnal consummation, which is never described, never recounted, but the covenant vow, signified by the "seal," which is the soul of the nuptial, a soul that would have as its flesh the physical consummation that is merely sung. But when the nuptial is invested in the erotic, the flesh is soul and the soul is flesh.

If we follow this path, we discover other indications, both closer and farther from movement in space, that are close to the movements of love itself. This is the case with the oscillations between waking and sleep. And the movement from one pole to another is never linear or narrative. Four times, we read: "I adjure you, daughters of Jerusalem, by the gazelles, by the does of the fields, do not stir up, do not awaken my love, before he is ready" (2:7, 3:5, 5:8, 8:4). And the awakening in 8:5 ("Under the apple tree, I awaken you, there where your mother conceived you, there where the one conceived you who gave birth to you") is not properly speaking a narrative conclusion, inasmuch as, as has been said, the awakening in 8:5 and the seal in 8:6 belong to the same economy of desires mutually accepted and acknowledged and, in this sense, fulfilled. Similarly, the stages of wakefulness—"My beloved is mine and I am his. He pastures his flock among the lilies" (2:16)—easily falls into a kind of dreaming: "On my bed, at night, I sought him whom my heart loves" (3:1), if it does not turn frankly into a dream between 3:1 and 5:1, as some commentators, such as Daniel Lys, have suggested.[11] But these alternations between sleep and being awake, between dreaming and awakening, belong to the same dynamic of intersecting desires and to the interplay of distance that opens and closes.

Someone may object that not everything in the poem is "movement." Apart from the moments of repose, of possession, which we have said

11. Lys, *Le plus beau chant*, p. 79.

belong to the "movements" of love, to love as movement, the poem makes room for admiring descriptions of the body of the beloved and for that of the lover. This is true. And it does not suffice to reply that these pauses can be assimilated, on the linguistic level of the poem, to a stasis of desire. What we need to add to such a response is that the metaphors through which the marvels of the lovers' bodies are sung are themselves metaphors of movement borrowed from the extraordinary bestiary that the poem draws upon, along with the luxuriant flora of an almost Edenlike countryside.[12] This takes nothing away from the stasis of admiration: "You are beautiful, my beloved, and without flaw!" (4:7). However the poetic pause is all the more striking in that the poem leads without transition from the questing movement to the repose of admiration: "Come from Lebanon, my fiancée, come from Lebanon, make your entry" (4:8). In this way, the poem weaves the stasis of admiring description into the very movements of love, so as to heighten, so to speak, the energy, the power of embracing.

I would like to indicate finally in what way the literary form of the poem contributes to this subtle liberation of the nuptial with regard to the erotic within which it is rightly enmeshed. Above I indicated the importance of the metaphors in the admiring descriptions of the bodies but limited myself to pointing to their origin in the marvelous flora and fauna of Creation. We need to return to them now from the point of view of the effect of sublimation that interests us here. Robert Alter had the genial idea of placing his reflections on the Song of Songs under the title the "Garden of Metaphor," producing in this way his own second-degree metaphor.[13] After having pointed to the unusual frequency of comparisons and the abundance of grammatical expressions that convey these comparisons ("is like," "resembles a," etc.), he takes up the kind of liberation that occurs through the verbal play that consists in the weaving together of these metaphors in relation to their ultimate corporeal referent. The body is not just sowed with vegetal and animal allegories, to the point of becoming a body/landscape; the verbal play itself tends to dissociate the metaphorical network from its support in the body. Even if, as good Freudians, we can indeed give a sexual meaning to the "fountain that makes the gardens fertile" in 4:15, or the gar-

---

12. The beloved is said to be like a gazelle, a young stag (2:8). The hair of the female is beautiful like a troop of goats (4:2); her teeth, a troop of shorn ewes coming up from being washed; her breasts, "two fawns, twins of a gazelle, that feed among the lilies" (4:5); etc.

13. Robert Alter, *The Art of Biblical Poetry* (New York: Basic Books, 1986), chap. 8, "The Garden of Metaphor," pp. 185–203.

den itself in 4:16 and 5:1, or to the "hole in the gate" in 5:4, or even to the lilies among which the beloved "pastures his flock" in 6:3, or even, why not, to the navel in 7:2 or the "mountain of myrrh" in 4:6—the all-knowing naiveté of the psychoanalyst is always joyful when it is applied to poetry!—what is important is not the euphemism that preserves the sexual referent without directly naming it, but rather the inclusion of the body itself within the overall metaphorical play of the poem, thanks to the phenomenon that Alter rightly calls "double entendre." I do not mean to suggest, out of some hidden some apologetic purpose, that the sexual referent is thereby abolished, as sexual, but rather that it is placed on hold, precisely as a referent. The verbal play thereby becomes an autonomous source of pleasure.

This poetic sublimation at the very heart of the erotic removes the need for contortions meant to desexualize the referent. That it should be poetically displaced is sufficient. And it is in this way that the same metaphorical network, once freed of every realist attachment through the unique virtue of the song, is made available for other investments and disinvestments.

At the end of this series of comments, we can say that through these purely literary procedures of calculated indetermination and metaphorization, a certain distance of meaning is introduced between the nuptial as such and the sexual, without thereby setting the nuptial within the matrimonial orbit. It is even this equidistance preserved between sexual realism and matrimonial moralism that will allow what I am calling the nuptial as such to serve as the analogon for other configurations of love than that of erotic love.

Are these remarks compatible with André LaCocque's interpretation? The distinction I am making between nuptial and matrimonial confirms the dissociation he so strongly emphasizes between the plea for free and faithful love and the apology for the marriage bonds in Proverbs and, even more fundamentally, in the whole Mosaic legislation. (Still why qualify as "bourgeois" the praises of conjugal fidelity in Deuteronomy 22:13–29?) Nor do I have any difficulty in making a place for irony in a celebration of love that says a pox on every institutional dimension. If the nuptial has to be sung of as distinct from the matrimonial, why shouldn't irony, just like metaphor, be one rhetorical means of praise? Are not many metaphors, through their very exaggeration, charged with irony? I would have more hesitation about making the step from irony to derision, and even beyond this to subversion. Besides the reservations referred to above concerning the intentions assigned to the presumed author, derision and subversion seem to me to stem from the genre of pleading, which, unlike irony, does not fit well with that of free and joyous celebration. As for any subversive intention properly speaking, it seems to me to arise from a hypothesis about reading, a perfectly legitimate hypothesis to be sure, but one that is recognized as such as soon as its place in a history of the reception of the text is recognized. Indeed, I shall attempt to show at the end of the second section of this essay that it belongs to one precise epoch of reading, one that precisely values every sort of subversive reading.

It remains to say that André LaCocque gives exegetical arguments that tend to reduce the distance I have emphasized between what the reader contributes and the obvious sense of the text. I would like to draw on those arguments in particular, however, that lead to interpreting certain expressions whose opaqueness has often been remarked—does one not speak in their regard of a *crux interpretum?*—expressions with a irreverent if not subtly blasphemous sense. We need to linger over these arguments inasmuch as the interpretation of these difficult passages takes on the value of evidence as regards the alleged subversive intention. When the poem seems to take up for its own use expressions that the prophets apply to the "loving" relation between Yhwh and his people, this procedure is said to stem from the polemical and liberating strategy of the poem in demetaphorizing, or more exactly in detheologizing, the poet's language. Furthermore, the author's challenge reaches its peak when the sacrosanct formulas of oaths are ironically parodied as conjurations invoking wild animals. The same parody will be also found in oaths with a religious connotation. In the same way, the separated hills of biblical geography come to designate in an irreverent way the breasts of the beloved. "We are at the antipodes of a spiritualized allegory," says André LaCocque. His exegetical subtlety culminates in the exegesis of 6:16. With this text, it would have been quite simply impossible for anyone in Israel to miss the allusion to the Ark of the Covenant. Any theory of interpretation that does not recognize this doesn't deserve the name. "The Shulamite joins, in the eyes of her lover, the chariot of the Ark, the most famous chariot in the history of Israel, the *merkabah* or throne of Yhwh, with *Ammi*, that is, Israel, and *Nadib*, the noble people. All this in an erotic evocation!" I have no grounds— nor any competence—to challenge the properly exegetical argument. But it seems to me to lose much of its unilateral—and unilaterally subversive—character if we set it back within the overall metaphorical context of the poem. I will even risk asking, in staying as close as possible to André LaCocque's interpretation, why does a certain detheologization not belong to the rhetorical strategy placed in the service of the conquest of the nuptial dimension per se? To demetaphorize is still to metaphorize. And why can what has been demetaphorized not be remetaphorized on the basis of the general metaphorization of the nuptial, as I shall attempt to demonstrate in the third part of this essay.

It is this latter suggestion that I shall attempt to develop by taking a broader view of the relations of intertextuality that lead to the intersecting of the Song of Songs with other texts in the biblical canon.

Fragments of a History of Reading

I want now, however, to give a continuation to my initial proposition of a "multiple, flowering history of reading and more generally of the reception of the text." I want to say right away that the allegorical exegesis of modern interpreters is far from occupying the whole ground of readings, which, for lack of an appropriate vocabulary, have been called allegorical. The allegorical exegesis of the Greek fathers is unaware of any claim to compete with an exegesis based on the historical-critical method. This is why is necessary to place the allegorism of modern interpreters at the end of our history of reading and link it to the same epistemological category as that which characterizes what these interpreters call a "naturalist" interpretation, inasmuch as they share with the proponents of such an interpretation the claim to tell us the true meaning that was intended by the author.

A complete history of the reading of the Song of Songs would constitute a considerable undertaking, which is impossible within the brief compass of this essay. I will limit myself, therefore, to indicating four significant moments of this rich history.

1. Analogical Transference

What made allegorical interpretations plausible, acceptable, and plainly significant in the Patristic age was something other than an exhumation of a meaning inscribed in a text considered apart from any act of reading.[14]

14. Anne-Marie Pelletier, *Lecture du Cantique des Cantiques: de l'énigme du sens aux figures du lecteur* (Rome: Editrice Pontificio Istituto Biblico, 1989), contains a detailed presentation of the linguistic and hermeneutical presuppositions that preside over the contrast between an exegetical method that assimilates the search for meaning to that of a search for the origin and one that connects the destiny of meaning to a history of reading of the text. On the linguistic side, there is the distinction between a statement (or proposition), independent of any subjective commitment

Let us take the most simple case, that of citation or paraphrase, where the words, the sentences of the Song of Songs find themselves taken up into the framework of a discourse offered by other speakers or other writers. The new fact is the situation of the one who restates the text in reading, citing, or paraphrasing it. Another place for speaking than that of the text to be interpreted is presupposed as given, starting from which there takes place an exchange of meanings between the text that does the citing and the cited text. In this way are born interpretations that augment the meaning of the text, through a meaning that is, in a way, in front of the text, without necessarily claiming that this meaning preexisted in the text.[15] In this regard, the allegorical interpretations we shall refer to below have to be considered as amplified effects of reading, of the same nature as these implicit or explicit citations, where the duality of the text cited and the text that cites them remains visible. The restatement of the cited text in another situation for speaking produces a displacement, a transference, for which allegory constitutes just one special case, however considerable it may be. This displacement or transference stems from another epistemological category than the search for the true meaning, than an explication and the search for an adequation between this explication and the features that convey the obvious sense. We have to speak instead of a "use" of the text or, if one prefers, of a reuse. Citation and paraphrase constitute in this respect a simple case of reuse, the cited text conserving its identity, which is perfectly capable of being taken up into the new text. The first condition that this reuse depends on is the emergence of a new speech situa-

on the part of the reader, and an utterance, which is the act of the speaking subject understood in terms of his or her personal, historical, and communal setting. This distinction is warranted by the linguistic theory of Emile Benveniste and by the speech-act theory of J. L. Austin and John Searle. It is necessary for any treatment of a dialogical poem where the subjective involvement of the speakers is an integral part of the meaning of their words. On the hermeneutic side, there is the work of the theoreticians of the historicity of understanding (Hans-Georg Gadamer's *Wirkungsgeschichte*) and of the reception of the text (Hans-Robert Jauss). Pelletier draws the "methodological consequences" of these presuppositions for the study of the Song of Songs (ibid., pp. 124–42), namely, an initial displacement, shifting the supposed originary meaning of the text in the direction of the "forms of existence of the text in history" (ibid., p. 125); then a second displacement, operating within this very history of transmission, which leads the commentary that claims to be explanatory toward those usages of the text that bring into "play, as equal, the text and the subjects that appropriate it" (ibid., p. 127). I am all the more willing to build on the general theory of interpretation proposed and practiced by Pelletier in that I share the same linguistic and hermeneutic assumptions.

15. Cf. the formula used a number of times by Gregory the Great, whose history is recounted by Pier Cesare Bori, *L'interpretazione infinita: l'ermeneutica cristiana antica e le sue trasformazioni* (Bologna: Il Mulino, 1987): "Scripture progresses (*crescat*) along with those who read it."

tion in relation to the one that was the original setting of the biblical poem. Citation tends in a way to fill the gap between the new speech situation and the old one, through a process of assimilation of one meaning to another. Allegory will later be cited as the justification for this abolition of the initial gap. But it was not necessary that authors or communities as a whole had at their disposal an explicit theory of allegory before they could make a practical use of the kind of correspondence or analogy that the theory will spell out.

This was the case, it would seem with the form of interpretation defended by Rabbi Aquiba at the gathering at Jamnia, an interpretation that must have been current prior to him if it is true that Aquiba made use of it as an argument in favor of the canonicity of the Song of Songs. The beloved of the Song is there identified with Israel and its land, the lover with Yhwh. This will also be the case for those Christian interpretations where the beloved will be by turns identified with the Church taken as a whole, with baptized individuals, or with the mystical soul drawn in on itself, and the lover will be Christ or the God of love himself.

What cannot fail to strike us in this quick overview is the mobility in the identification of the partners in the amorous dialogue—better than mobility: the substitution. It is this capacity for substitution that decomposed into the positing of a gap and the overcoming of this gap. The love between Yhwh and his people, then the love between the Christ and his Church are celebrated from places for speaking that, as regards their utterance, are different than the one in which the original epithalamium was sung. These places can be the cultus, the liturgy, meditation, prayer, study. And it is through a second movement that these places for speaking are identified by an operation stemming from the use of the text and not first of all from its explication. This audacious transfer creates a new signification, which was not necessarily contained in the originary texts, even though it is capable of being inscribed in them in an enduring fashion within a tradition of reading. It is this process of identification that we can take as an extension of citation and paraphrase, where the citing text and the cited text remain distinct. This assimilation running all the way to identification is the fruit of a meditation on the profound kinship between the objects of love, or, as I shall say below, between its "movements." I am not saying that allegory, or what has been theorized as allegory, is the unique key to this abolition of distance, thanks to which Israel, then the baptized Christian, then the mystical soul come to occupy the place of the beloved in the Song of Songs, to the point of being able to sing as she does: "The king has brought me into his chambers." Anne-Marie Pelletier, for example, has shown that the use of analogy, or, to use a more neutral term, the use of correspondences, preceded a theory of allegory, in a work that has here served me as a guide, on the basis of long analyses which she proposes concerning the reuse of the Song of Songs within the framework of Christian liturgy, hymnody, and epistolary exchange.[16]

The case of liturgy is most enlightening as regards our inquiry. The liturgy makes use of a dialogical structure, where the participation of the worshippers is constitutive of the working of the liturgical action under the imprint of a convocation that generates a new "us." The practice of language within the liturgical framework has one specific intention, that of drawing near to a "mystery" that is as much enacted as said. Consequently, when the liturgy cites the texts of Scripture, the participants reassume the movement of involvement and commitment through the words and in the dialogue of the protagonists of the originary dialogue. In this way, the liturgy becomes a privileged place for the reproduction of the text.

The use of the Song of Songs in the baptismal liturgy, a usage attested by the catecheses of Cyril of Jerusalem and Ambrose, marvelously illustrates the double movement of gap and abolition of this gap referred to above. It is clear, first of all, that the ceremony of baptism constitutes as such a situation initially foreign to the biblical epithalamium. The institution of baptism sets up the initial gap starting from which the text of the Song of Songs is displaced into a new framework of utterance that no feature of the originary text allows us to anticipate. This gap is then filled thanks to the nuptial signification attached to Christian initiation, under the impulse of Saint Paul himself according to Ephesians 5:25 ("Husbands, love your wives as the Christ has loved the Church") and II Corinthians 11:2 ("For I promised you in marriage to one husband, like a pure virgin to present to Christ"). This nuptial initiation can be taken as a "mystery" that lacks a means of expression so long as it has not drawn upon the dialogical structure of the Song of Songs; not just its lexicon, its words, but its attitudes, its movements of approach and withdrawal, its thirst for being together and belonging to one another.

---

16. Re this whole second part, cf. Pelletier, "Le *Cantique des Cantiques* à l'âge patristique: lectures et usages," in *Lecture du Cantique des Cantiques*, pp. 143–287.

The exhortation that precedes the quotations of the Song of Songs within the liturgical framework clearly shows that these quotations are not meant to be an explication of the original meaning. The case seems rather to be something like the following. The liturgical gesture would remain mute without the aid of the words from the Song of Songs, reinterpreted by the very gesture that seeks and finds its expression in these words. In this way, an exchange is brought about between the rite and the poem. The rite opens the space of "sacramental mystery" to the poem, the poem gives the rite the rightness of an appropriate word. In this sense, it is not first the Song of Songs but rather the rite that one interprets in citing the Song of Songs. This latter is thus put in the position of an "interpretant" before being itself given over to interpretation. What is more, it is not just the rite that is interpreted by the words of the poem, but the faithful people themselves who recognize themselves in the gestures of the rite. Whence the place of exhortation in catechesis, the faithful being urged to put themselves in the place of the beloved so as to be able to speak the words of the Song of Songs.[17]

We can thus understand why the explicit or implicit quotations of the Song of Songs in hymns also find their final justification in the disposition of those who receive the text by quoting it. In truth, it is no longer a question of an explicit quotation, but rather of a genuine reuse, of a creation of new variations in those sung prayers that make up hymns. If we add that the hymn has not ceased to be a place of theological production, as we see, for example, even today in the recent revision of the Anglican Book of Prayer, we also will recognize that the hymn is one of the privileged places where we can catch sight of the augmentation of meaning at work in certain forms of the reception of the biblical text.

We also see then that the appropriation of the biblical text takes place in comparable ways within the frameworks of the liturgy and the hymn. A new speech situation becomes the source of a gap in relation to which the biblical epithalamium was first produced. In both cases, this gap is immediately overcome by the confession of a kinship between the two

---

17. Thus we read in Ambrose, in *De sacramentis*, IV.5: "Following this, you must approach the altar. You have begun to move forward. The angels are watching, they have seen you approaching. . . . Thus they have asked: 'Who is this who rises so white from the desert?'" "You have approach the altar. The Lord Jesus calls you or calls your soul or the Church, and says, 'Let him kiss me with the kisses of his mouth.'" Cited by Pelletier, *Lecture du Cantique des Cantiques*, p. 157, n. 33. Re the general relationship between theology and liturgy in the fathers, cf. Jean Daniélou, *Bible et liturgie* (Paris: Cerf, 1951). This work includes a whole chapter devoted to the Song of Songs (pp. 259–80).

figures of the amorous dialogue. This kinship between speech situations first applies to the thematic level—the wounds of love, seeking, mutual possession—then to the vocabulary itself (kissing, touching, embracing). It is not until we come to the way in which the Song of Songs takes pleasure in describing and praising the bodies of the lover and the beloved that we find a shortfall of details for the hymn in its demand for fullness and overflowingness. From this taking up of attitudes, themes, and words is born what we may call the analogical unity of the figures of the nuptial bond.

2. Origen: Between Typology and Allegory

We can now take the step that leads to commentaries properly speaking on the Song of Songs. We shall take this step with Origen, who, in succeeding Hyppolitus of Rome, can be taken to be the founder of the whole exegetical tradition, first Eastern then Western, that has been labeled as allegorical.[18] The distinction between "homilies" and "commentaries"[19] will allow us to understand this passage as commentary properly speaking in terms of two stages. It is remarkable that Origen should have presented his rereading of the Song of Songs by means of two such different literary genres. As we shall see, if the commentary seems to place its principal accent on the meaning attributed to the words spoken in the Song of Songs, its juxtaposition with the homily will help make us attentive to those attitudes of reading that in this second type of text might have gone overlooked.

Like the entry into the Holy of Holies, access to the Song of Songs is not direct. It comes at the end of a passage through an ascending sequence of Songs, whose liturgical list constitutes a kind of typological *hexameron*.[20] What I above called a situation marked by a gap here takes

18. For a detailed study of Origen's exegesis, cf. Jean Daniélou, ibid.; Henri de Lubac, *Histoire et esprit, l'intelligence de l'écriture d'après Origène* (Paris: Aubier, 1950); Lubac, *Exégèse médiévale, les quatre sens de l'Ecriture* (Paris: Aubier, 1959), vol. 1; H. Crouzel, *Origène et la connaissance mystique* (Paris: D.D.B., 1961).

19. We have access to his two homilies on the Song of Songs only in the Latin version by Jerome. According to Eusebius, of Origen's long commentary, which was made up of ten books, only one book remains in the partial translation we owe to Rufinius. Scholars have more confidence in Jerome's strict translation than in Rufinius's more free one. Re all this, cf. the Introduction by O. Rousseau to the translation of the homilies on the Song of Songs in *Sources chrétiennes* (Paris: Cerf, 1953), which I am using here.

20. This typological hexameron is made up of Exodus 15:1f. (the song of praise after the crossing of the Red Sea); Numbers 21:17–18 (the song at the well); Deuteronomy 32:1f. (Moses's song); Judges 5:2 (Deborah's song); 2 Samuel 22:2f. (David's song); and Isaiah 5:1f. (the song of the vineyard). Each of these provides the occasion for an allegorical interpretation similar to that of

on the form of a mystical ascension. In this way, the initial gap between two lovers is widened. It takes on the form of an opposition between spiritual and carnal love. And yet the dialogue between the Word and the soul wounded by the Word's arrow succeeds once again in being spoken by way of the movements of the Song of Songs. The union of the Church, understood as a body or as the members of a body, and its celestial spouse is recognizable through the nuptial dimension unfolded by the Song of Songs. In other words, the transcendence of spiritual love is compensated for by a similitude. Here is where, as a kind of mediation, the typological interpretation applied by Paul to the relationship between the two covenants (the economy of the Hebraic structure with its characters, events, and institutions) as a prefiguration of the Christian economy of salvation can be taken up. This gesture of typological reinscription brings into equilibrium the existential distance that separates the two modes of love and makes possible the assumption of the language of the Song of Songs into Christian discourse.[21] But we need to recognize that this third moment is not yet of the nature of a commentary. It is not the relating of one sense to another for a reader who is not implicated in this process. As in liturgical and hymnic uses, the homily is addressed to the believer in the second person.[22]

Origen was careful to respect the dramatic form of this play with

---

Pauline typology. Had Exodus not already provided the basic metaphor of liberation taken up into the baptismal liturgy? In a similar way, each of the songs borrowed from the Hebrew Bible marks a stage in the mystical journey.

21. I shall discuss below the question to what point Origen's allegorism remains within the limits of Pauline typology. It will suffice here to note that each step in his homily is addressed to the believing soul in the second person. "You must leave Egypt and, having left the land of Egypt, cross the Red Sea, in order to sing the first song, saying, 'Sing to the Lord because he has triumphed gloriously.'" And further along: "And when you shall have surpassed all of them, you shall rise even higher, so that you may, with a soul henceforth shining beautifully, also sing with the husband of the Song of Songs." "Sing with"—this indicates the foundational operation of language for an allegorical reading, governed by one underlying identification: "Recognize Christ in the husband, the spotless, unblemished wife, the Church," following the suggestion found in 1 Corinthians 1:21 and Ephesians 5:27.

22. Here is an example from Song of Songs 1:2, "Let him kiss me with the kisses of his mouth." The interpreter understands this as follows. In the time of Moses and the Prophets, the Word only *sent* its kisses; in Christ there is no distance in the kiss of the Word. As for the "aroma of your perfumes," which follows, the interpretation consists of a movement through a series of canonical texts, both Hebraic and Christian, that speak of smells, perfumes, and odors, and that point toward the words of praise: "Your name is perfume poured out." The chorus of maidens can thus receive the approbation of the lover: "This is why maidens love you and lure you on." The maidens reply: "We run after you in the fragrance of your perfume," a saying that brings in its wake 2 Timothy 4:7 and 1 Corinthians 9:24.

more than one character. The thread of this small drama turns out to be just as important as the spoken dialogues. It outlines the variations in distance and proximity, of approach and withdrawal along the way of mutual belonging. It is at the level of this dramatic dynamism that the transposition of the whole poem takes place, which alone allows one to reinterpret the very words (*verba*) of the Song of Songs in terms of all the diversity of their details.

It is not to be denied that words play an essential role in this interplay of assonances. Subsequent allegorism will be swallowed in this kind of exercise,[23] whose underlying conviction is that Scripture is a vast field of interrelated words, a unitary field, in which every word has a reason and where, as a consequence, every possible linkage or comparison between words is not just authorized but even called for. Here is where we come upon the moment where explicative commentary can break away from the control exercised by a similarity of speech situations, to become an arbitrary exercise, guided by the mere co-occurrence of the same words within a work that is taken to be indivisible and coherent.[24]

To this is added the conviction that the spiritual sense is the sense intended by the author, that is, in the last analysis by the Holy Spirit, who inspires this author. In this sense, the allegorical use of the Song of Songs is not aware of itself as an effect of reading, as the creation of new meaning through reinterpretation.

Finally, we must not underestimate that the initial gap, which we have situated at the origin of the assimilation of two kinds of love, is not stated in terms of a Platonic dualism of the sensible and the intelligible, but rather than in terms of the duality of Pauline typology. This latter, as Jean Daniélou and Henri de Lubac have shown, places into relation two historical economies, not two ontological levels, and requires the reality of the first term, without any reduction of it to appear-

23. Consider the example of what is said about the blackness of the beloved: "I am black and beautiful, O daughters of Jerusalem" (1:5). This blackness without the beauty would be the ugliness of sin, but penitence confers upon it that beauty that leads one to ask, "Who is coming up clothed in whiteness?" (8:5).

24. Discussing the "nard" ("my nard gave forth its fragrance"), Origen assures us, "The Holy Spirit did not have the intention (*non de nardo propositum*) to speak about nard. Nor does the Gospel speak of that perfume we can see with our eyes, but rather of a spiritual nard, a nard that is fragrant." The second Homily again rings all the biblical changes concerning nard: Matthew 26:6; Luke 7:37; Mark 14:5; up to 2 Corinthians 2:15, "For we are the aroma of Christ for those who are being saved." A contrast is also drawn with Psalm 38:5, "my wounds grow foul and fester because of my foolishness."

ance or illusion, at least if the "type" is really to function as the basis of meaning. Hence the spiritual sense is not substituted for the carnal sense. It is not substituted because it cannot be. Whereas for Platonic philosophers, the intelligible world has its own language, its own concepts, its own dialectic, within the setting of the Christian Church, the spiritual lacks a means of expression. This is why the language of the Song of Songs turns out to be irreplaceable. Without it, mystical experience would remain mute. This is why the "nuptial" is a necessary recourse for such experience. If, nevertheless, Origen, despite the typological basis of his allegorism, could give in to a tendency toward a Platonic kind of dualism, this was due to the fact that within the Song of Songs the carnal lacks a historical dimension that would clearly link it in an explicit way to the old covenant. It unfolds entirely within the dimension of the "sensible" from which Platonizing spiritualism drains its reality. Hence, what was once a restatement at the level of new situations of discourse, in particular that dramatic setting that displays the protagonists and their "movements" (of approach, withdrawal, union), becomes a substitution of meaning as soon as this interplay of correspondences frees itself from this setting and gives itself over to the explication of meaning for its own sake. Origen's homilies bear witness to this fragile equilibrium, already on the point of breaking, between, on the one hand, a complicity that takes place on the level of utterance, a level where new protagonists can take up an old place, and, on the other hand, a correspondence between words that in the final analysis will justify the substitution of one meaning for another.[25]

25. We have seen how in the Song of Songs description and praise of corporeal beauty interweave through a highly elaborate and refined metaphorical interplay. But whereas in the poem this interplay constantly moves from external analogies (tower, tree, bird, ewe) toward carnal intimacy, allegorical exegesis shifts the trajectory of these comparisons, thanks to the fact that the same words belong to other semantic networks capable of reorienting them toward the spiritual sphere. This is the case as regards the well-known declaration of the lover, "Ah you are beautiful, my love, you are beautiful, your eyes are doves" (1:15). Origen takes great care first to emphasize the variations in proximity whose importance we have already seen for the parallelism between utterances. "If the beloved is far from the lover, she is not beautiful; but she becomes so when she is united to the Word of God" (Homilies, 86). It is our aspiration to become the bride that allows the believing soul to take up the words of the Song of Songs, "your eyes are doves." "If you understand the law spiritually, your eyes are doves" (Homilies, 87). The whole metaphorics of eyes and seeing is brought into play here, reinforced by the particular one of the eyes of the dove—to have the eyes of a dove is to see aright, and the one who sees rightly deserves mercy (Psalm 107:42)—as well as that of the dove in the theophany of Matthew 3:16. Another example: the wound of love, "sustain me with apples because I am wounded with charity" (2:5) with the embrace that follows: "his left hand is under my head and his right hand embraces me." For Origen, the arrow that wounds can

It remains true, however, that the similitude of situations continues to govern the transference of meaning on the level of words.[26] Thus, if we are to follow Origen, we must, on the one hand, hold firmly to the initial equivalence between the bearers of gesture and meaning (husband = Christ; bride = the Church or ecclesial soul), and, on the other hand, admit that the whole of Scripture is a vast field of words open to comparisons and linkages without any constraint or limit on this process, from the moment that they are made appropriate to the primordial equivalence. This way of subordinating the comparisons and linking of words to the equivalence between positions of discourse constitutes the hermeneutical key to allegorical explication. Once this subordination is loosed, commentary breaks away from the homily.[27]

---

only be the one indicated by Isaiah 49:2 and 6, and Luke 24:32. Yet, here too, the transfer in meaning only holds if the hearer feels himself or herself wounded by this arrow. "If someone is wounded by our words, by the teaching of divine Scripture, and can say, 'I am wounded by charity,' this may perhaps apply to him. But why do I say 'perhaps'? Is it not clear?" As for the embrace, it unfolds its spiritual meaning only for someone who sets himself on its path. Whence the exhortation: "O would that the law of the Lord should entirely embrace you!" (Homilies, 96).

26. For example, the sleep of the beloved: "The Word of God still sleeps in unbelievers and in those whose heart is filled with doubt. It awakes in the saints. It sleeps in those who are tossed about by storms (Matthew 8:23f.), but it awakes at the cry of those who want to be saved by the awakened lover" (Homilies, 97). The same conjoining of attitudes and the same transfer on the plane of words occurs regarding the verse, "the voice of my beloved! Look he comes leaping upon the mountains, bounding over the hills" (2:8). Origen claims, "Here we are to understand the soul of the loved one, happy and perfect. . . . If you are a mountain, the Word of God leaps onto you; if you cannot be a mountain, but if you are a hill, inferior to a mountain, he steps over you. How lovely and appropriate (conventientia rebus) are these words!" (Homilies, 98). And just below, concerning 2:9: "Be an ecclesial mountain, the mountain of the house of God and the lover will come to you, like a gazelle or a young stag on the mountains of Bethel" (Homilies, 99). Only with the "windows" of 2:9 does the interpretation become clearly spiritual: "One of our senses is a window. Through it, the beloved looks at us. Each other sense will be another window through which the beloved regards us. Indeed, through what sense does the Word of God not regard us? What does it mean to look through these windows? And how does the lover look through them? The following example will show you. There where the lover does not look, we see death enter, as we read in Jeremiah, 'Death enters through your windows' (9:20). Whenever you look at a woman coveting her, death enters through your windows."

27. Did this already occur with Origen? It doesn't seem so. According to Pelletier, the Commentary is intended to answer the question, "how are we to read the Song of Songs?" as much as it is meant to explicate the poem (Lectures du Cantique des Cantiques, p. 265). The Song of Songs, it is said, is "strong food," suitable for the "perfected." "For whoever reads it apart from this understanding, the Song of Songs can only be an object of scandal" (ibid., p. 266). If the text is difficult, it is owing to the homonymy of words expressing the two kinds of love: spiritual love would be impoverished when it comes to words if carnal love did not provide its richness. But the transfer of meaning borrows its dynamism from the mystical ascension in virtue of which the text is significant only "at the height of one's capacities, that is, owing to the spiritual advancement of the one who is reading it" (ibid., p. 257).

3. Modern "Allegorical" Commentary

The preceding remarks help us to understand the change in epistemological status that takes place in contemporary allegorical commentaries. Indifferent to the conditions of restatement of the canonical text
that, within the ancient ecclesial tradition, allowed a Christian soul to
occupy the place of the beloved in the Song of Songs so as to sing her
epithalamium with her, the authors of these commentaries undertake
to hold themselves within a kind of nonobjective place, exactly like their
"naturalist" opponents. From this unmarked place, they claim to observe, within the depth of the text, the double meaning constitutive of
allegory. Thus it is no longer the Song of Songs that plays the role of
an interpretant in regard to an interpreted believing attitude. Instead it
has become the object of explication, the allegorical meaning being
taken to be the true meaning intended by the presumed author, himself
or herself inspired by the Holy Spirit. It is not surprising that the
weight of evidence is placed almost exclusively therefore on a comparison taking place on the level of the words of the text.

Let us consider the example of the scholarly commentaries by A.
Robert, R. Tournay, and A. Feuillet.[28] Their commitment to philological technique is undeniable, and the so-called method of parallels is
unfolded within the wide intrabiblical space marked out by the canon.

If it is true that it is a theory of reading the *Commentary* sets out here, it is in *Peri Archon*, book
IV, that we have to seek the principles of this reading. (Re the correlations between the *Peri Archon*
and the allegorical doctrine of the *Homilies* and the *Commentary*, cf. the works already cited by H.
Crozel and Jean Daniélou, as well as M. Harl, *Origène et la fonction révélatrice du Verbe incarné*
[Paris: Seuil, 1958].) There we find the materials drawn upon (whether Stoic or Platonic, etc.),
and, furthermore, the rule for their reuse in Origen's hermeneutic. I shall not take up this inquiry
in this essay. Allow me only to say that the theory of interpretation we find in the *Peri Archon*,
book IV, has to be evaluated in terms of the practice of interpretation for which the *Homilies* and
the *Commentary* provide the leading examples. It cannot be denied that his controversies with
Judaism and the Gnostics led the great Alexandrian to give a theoretical turn to the hermeneutical
question: the theory of the threefold meaning, set in parallel with the triad body/soul/spirit; the
role of obscurities and incongruities in the text commented upon; the assumption that these had
been planted in the text as stones one tripped over in order to encourage the reader to push still
further ahead; the link between understanding texts and the spiritual commitment of the reader.
However this polemical turn ought not to obscure the determining fact, namely, that the reader
worthy of the biblical text is a reader who has previously acquired a christological sense of the
whole of Scripture. If Origen could seem to exercise a mastery over the whole biblical text equal
to that of the Hellenistic rhetoricians, it was because he knew himself to be submissive to a requirement that preceded him. This was the *mysterium* that governed and warranted what seemed arbitrary, fantastic, even an aestheticizing complacence in the face of the obscure.

28. A. Robert and R. Tournay, with the assistance of A. Feuillet, *Le Cantique des Cantiques,
traduction et commentaire* (Paris: Gabalda, 1963).

These authors call the reuse of words or formulas from earlier Scripture, whether literally or as an equivalent, "anthologizing." The rule for this procedure is strict: "The only significant references are those in which identical terms or synonyms are used along with a context announcing an identical or positively analogical thought" (p. 10). In order to do them justice, we need to emphasize that these authors warn us against the abuse of unfounded comparisons, such as may be found, for example, in the work of another well-known allegorist, Father Joüon. We must, they say, seek the highest possible degree of "positive resemblance founded on a sufficient convergence of subjective evidence" (p. 12). We can speak in this regard, then, of a lexical intertextuality based on synonymity. Yet we would never get under way if we did not know what we were looking for, namely, a network of allusions to the major point of the sacred history culminating in the return from Exile. The love of the beloved, with its hesitations and reprises, describes the steps in the conversion of Israel as it awaits the salvation that will be the work of Yhwh. This working hypothesis finds confirmation in all of the features of the Song of Songs, there is not one that cannot be explained in light of the nuptial allegory of the prophets. For example, in reading 1:2–4, "let him kiss me with the kisses of his mouth . . . the king brought me into his chambers," R. Tournay does not hesitate to say that "the lover is the king. Nothing is more central to the biblical tradition than that Yhwh should be called king" (p. 65). Along the same lines, the bed chamber designates the temple. As for the beloved, she represents the personified nation. "There are numerous texts that speak of Yhwh's ongoing love for Israel despite its unfaithfulness" (p. 67). More precisely, "On the basis of the classical themes of the Old Testament, we have assumed that the presumed situation is that of the Exile. Israel, preserving its love for Yhwh, aspires to return to Palestine and to enjoy the possession of the one from whom it is separated. This is the starting point for exegeting the Song of Songs" (p. 68). This being the general orientation, it is the details that must confirm the anthologizing procedure.[29]

29. Thus, in the first poem (1:5, 2:7), when the young woman says, "I am black and yet beautiful, O daughters of Jerusalem," we are to understand that "it was the sufferings of the Exile that darkened the taint of the woman, without altering her beauty." Does the text speak of the mother ("The sons of my mother")? It must refer to the country of the ancestors of Abraham. The vine? It would be shocking if it meant the chastity of a woman. The expression refers to the land of Canaan and to the true religion, following a metaphor much used by Hosea, Isaiah, Jeremiah, and the Psalms: "the beloved's vine is Palestine" (ibid., p. 75). Is she unguarded? It has to be an allusion to the faults that led to the Exile. Where will the shepherd lead his flock? Again, into Palestine.

The most noteworthy of these details, to me, is having to assume, owing to the allegory, the theme of perfect mutuality in the loving exchange, at the limit of the prophetic formulas found in Hosea, Jeremiah, and the Deuteronomist. As much as the Prophets knew the alternation of "seeking and finding," does not Yhwh conceal himself in the presence of an imperfect penitence? Thus we can understand how in the Song the lover suddenly hides himself when the beloved, not yet fully disposed to love, gives the illusion of possessing the lover. Our commentators connect Song of Songs 5:5–6 with Isaiah 41:1, "a context that announces the return of Israel and that shows Yhwh ready to return to Palestine and reestablish the nation on the one condition that it faithfully seek him" (p. 205). They emphasize that these verses contain a "theological meaning," for which the Prophets, particularly Hosea and Jeremiah, give us the key. "The Shulamite cannot enter into possession of the lover because the disposition of her heart is not yet perfect" (ibid.). Nonetheless, because Yhwh becomes all the more pressing and the ardor of the beloved continues to grow, we can say that "it is clear that we are moving toward a denouement." What denouement? It is to be found in 8:5b: "Beneath the apple tree, I awoke you." "The meaning of this sentence is that the nation on the very land of Palestine is awakened by Yhwh and goes on to love him" (p. 297). "The certitude that God will bring about a total conversion" is thus made apparent. And once again this is based on Hosea, Jeremiah, Ezekiel, and Isaiah.

If the woman compares herself to a mare attached to Pharaoh's chariot? The condition of being a "mare of Yhwh" can only signify a state of humiliation according to Jeremiah 22:7–8 and Second Isaiah. What is more, we are meant to hear an implicit exhortation to wait with confidence the lifting of the yoke, that is, the return to Palestine. Does the lover speak of the breasts of his beloved? "One can ask whether the image of breasts does not symbolize the tribes of the North and the South" (ibid., p. 89). If so, "on my breasts" means "on my heart," that is, the "center of Israel." As for the "bed of green" in 1:16, it refers to Palestine covered with olive and fig trees, as celebrated in Deuteronomy 8:7–10 and in numerous other passages of the Old Testament. Similarly, when 3:1 says, "upon my bed at night," "this bed is Palestine" (ibid., p. 130). We understand how the woman can say of herself in 2:1, "I am the rose of Sharon, the lily of the valleys," if we admit that Israel and its land are embraced within a unique eschatological oath of union with Yhwh. Does the woman say, "He brought me to the storeroom" (2:4)? We are not to stop at the image of a nuptial chamber (or even less to ferret out an allusion to a sanctuary of Ishtar). The biblical texts that depict Palestine as a land of vineyards are sufficient to sustain the fundamental allegory. Nor are our authors shocked by the erotic appearance of 2:6, "his left hand . . ." However they do not follow Joüon who refers to the presence of Yhwh in his tabernacle. No, "there is nothing to be seen in this scene beyond the reciprocal demonstration of a passionate love" (ibid., p. 106). As for the difficult verse, "do not awake . . . before the hour" (used as a refrain in 3:5 and 8:4), the awakening in question is that spoken of in Isaiah 41:17; 42:1, and 43:1. It is a question, after the torpor of the Exile, of the awakening and return to Yhwh. When set with the prophetic context, especially that of the Exile and the postexilic period, this verse discreetly places us on guard against an imperfect repentance.

Beyond this, the parenetic accent found in 8:6–8 ("for love is strong like death") recalls Deuteronomy 6:6–8, which draws on Exodus 13:9 and evokes Jeremiah 31–33 where the intransigence and invincible force of love are proclaimed.[30] Therefore our exegetes are not surprised that the name of Yhwh should finally be pronounced, not in passing, as though "flame of Yhwh" (8:6) were an expression as banal as, say, God's thunder, but because on the basis of all that has preceded, the great protagonist of the quest for love can finally be named, as soon as the love between Yhwh and his people is finally consummated.

In the criticism that has been brought to bear on allegorical explication in the modern period, we need to distinguish, I believe, between what stems from the techniques of exegesis and what expresses a radical change in the usage of the biblical text, a change that also governs the position of those exegetes for whom the erotic interpretation has become the obvious explanation. Let us confine ourselves, therefore, for the moment, to the objections that have arisen on the same ground where modern allegorists have taken the risk of challenging those who uphold what these allegorists call a "naturalistic" explication of our text.

Usually, three vices are condemned.[31] First, the arbitrary aspect of the comparisons made between words or expressions. Second, the fastidious repetition of what looks like an a priori theory, whether it be the case of the thesis that discerns the figures of Yhwh and Israel beneath all the features of the lover and the beloved or the one that sees in them Christ and the Church. Finally, there is the arbitrary imposition of an allegorical meaning by the ecclesial magisterium. Once the situation of a Jewish or Christian reader is no longer directly connected with the initial linguistic setting, this kind of commentary finds itself extremely vulnerable to this kind of threefold critique. We could even say that it offers itself imprudently to this kind of criticism due to the very fact that it places itself on the ground of a search for the true meaning.

In this regard, the anthologizing method of Robert and Feuillet is particularly vulnerable to the first criticism, owing to its very concern to isolate words or verbal bits from their context, the Bible being dealt with as one vast store of expressions and words that the exegete may draw on based solely upon the rule that there be some semantic kinship to govern the anthologizing method. Those contextual connections that

30. Numerous texts in the Old Testament emphasize divine jealousy in any encounter with idols. "To say that love is as strong as death is therefore to emphasize how ready it is to claim its right, its claim wholly to possess its object and to defend it against any alien touch" (ibid., p. 301).

31. Cf. T. Todorov, *Symbolism et Interprétation* (Paris: Seuil, 1978); A. Compagnon, *La seconde main ou le travail de la citation* (Paris: Seuil, 1979).

resist this kind of skimming and comparisons, which such semantic kinship seems to authorize, are overlooked.

Once doubts are raised concerning the anthologizing method, it is difficult not to lend an attentive ear to the second accusation. Is it not because the selection of texts placed in parallel was guided by some prior external conviction that the allegorist is able to refer to, under the appearances of an a posteriori argument, the probability of these comparisons chosen ahead of time by such a prior principle of selection?

At the same time, the door is opened to the third charge, despite its perhaps overly suspicious look and its nasty thrust. Is it not because the magisteriat, in different, sometimes violent, ways has imposed an allegorical interpretation that the gap thereby opened between the official reading and the obvious, required one calls for the expedience of allegory, at any price—at the price, in particular of inventing slights of hand that in turn motivate an overabundance of subtlety in drawing semantic comparisons?[32]

Whatever the case may be, these objections, in my opinion, only apply to that one segment of the allegorical tradition where commentary that claims to be scientific has substituted itself for those usages of the biblical text where the actual position of the person stating or restating the biblical text is still conscious of itself. In this regard, the work of Anne-Marie Pelletier, by shifting back from modern commentaries to the liturgical, hymnic, and homiletic uses of the Song of Songs represents in a decisive way a complete reorientation in the argument. For anyone who wants to consider the whole trajectory of allegorical interpretations and not just the more or less artificial allegorism of modern commentators, the arguments just referred to then lose much of their force. In response to the first objection, it is possible to rediscover, at the origin of what seems to be the most arbitrary wordplay beginning with Origen, a gesture of obedience to an experience *princeps:* that of a pious Jew of the community of Israel, then, with Christianity, that of one baptized into this faith, and subsequently that of a mystic in quest of meaningful language. As for the second objection, we must remain attentive to the inventiveness that is never completely eliminated and that even often gives rise to commitment in the act of communal reading. Finally, as regards the third objection, which in fact is an accusation, we are not forbidden to salute the vow of confident adherence to

---

32. The arguments of modern critics concerning patristic interpretation are summarized and discussed in Pelletier, *Lectures du Cantique des Cantiques,* pp. 291–300.

an ongoing community of interpretation, up to and including submission to the external power of an ecclesial magisterium. This is why it still seems possible, even today, to go some distance with the Rabbinic and Patristic readings and to encounter in them the branches of a blossoming history of reading, within which we remain as the heirs of reading stances that continue to be available to us.

4. Abandoning Allegorical Interpretation: The Change in the Reader

In the preceding section, I have outlined the objections that are addressed to the claim of allegorical interpretation to serve as the explication of the true meaning of the Song of Songs, that is, of its original, intended meaning which is immanent in the text. However the disfavor that today affects allegorical interpretation today does not just apply to the methodological vices that an improved science might be able to correct. If, as we have said, following Pelletier, the oldest allegorical interpretations are rooted in *uses* of the Song of Songs, liturgical, hymnological, and homiletic uses, where the new sites of the use of words are still visible—baptism, for example—beginning from which the words of the Song are reuttered, then the reasons for the decline in these interpretations must equally be sought at the level of such usages and, more generally, on the plane of the conditions that prevailed during the times of the re-enunciation, the reuse of the Song of Songs in an allegorical style.

This decline can be attributed to quite heterogeneous factors. For example, an alleged misuse of the biblical sources allegorical interpretation draws on, or even an internal breakdown of the allegorical conception itself beginning already in the Patristic period, or, finally, to cultural changes, stretching from the Middle Ages to the contemporary period, which made untenable the reading stances adopted by the allegorizing exegetes.

I shall not dwell on the first of these possible motives for decline, inasmuch as it would force us to anticipate what will be said below about an eventual theological meaning grafted to the erotic interpretation. The argument, however, can be briefly stated as follows. Is the love relation between God and human beings that the rabbis and the Greek fathers assumed to be metaphorically projected by the Song of Songs really akin to the one celebrated by the Prophets: Hosea, Jeremiah, Isaiah, Ezekiel, and even the Deuteronimist? What is at issue here is the fusional and totally reciprocal character of the love celebrated by the Song of Songs. If I invoke this argument at this point, it is because it has been used by a number of exegetes against allegorical interpretations in general. The Prophets, these exegetes have observed, never risked speaking of a mutual love, a mutual possession between God and human beings, in that the reverence for the God of the Torah and the Covenant imposed a vertical distance at the very heart of the covenantal bond. This argument is extremely important. It puts a finger on the invisible line that separates an ethical religion from a mystical one. And it is in this sense that it outruns the properly exegetical plane to which we have so far confined ourselves. This is why I shall defer until my concluding section any detailed examination of this objection.

The second reason for abandoning the allegorical way has to do with the very conception of allegory, which I indicated above is itself only a systematic interpretation of the analogical linkage, lived out before being brought to reflective awareness, that Jews and Christians discerned between two levels of love. Indeed, we can ask whether the allegorism professed by Origen and all the interpreters who embraced his way was not secretly discordant in relation to the typological interpretation practiced, sometimes—it is true—under the label of allegory, by Paul and the Fathers, giving rise to confusions that endured for a long time. I shall not dwell on this objection, which we have already taken into account above.[33] Let me merely add here, from the perspective of a history of reading of the Song of Songs, that the mystical reading was carried out principally within a setting marked by asceticism, sometimes as practiced by laypeople, but most often it was that of clerics and monks. As was the case for Origen, access to the text of the Song of Songs was explicitly reserved to those who were already well advanced on the way of renouncing carnal life and its reading was strongly discouraged or forbidden for beginners in the spiritual life. Even if this asceticism was marked by specifically Christian features, it also borrowed from Platonic allegorism the dualism of the "sensible" and the "intelligible." However the influence of the monastic condition on reading seems to have governed that of interpretation by an allegorism freed from the constraints of a specifically Christian typology and given over to a Platonizing spirituality. In order to speak of the nuptial beauty of the mystery of faith, it was necessary first to empty the erotic of its nuptial quality per se, which was then fed into the Christian "mystery" in an exclusive fashion. To assume the place of the beloved meant first of all

---

33. Again I refer the reader to the works by Daniélou and de Lubac cited above.

to remove this image from its erotic setting. Whence the paradox that in order to function as an allegory, exegesis no longer had as a limit to its reach anything other than purely verbal associations, or, better, nonsexualized homonymies gleaned from throughout the biblical text. In this sense, the priority given to purely verbal analogies had as its origin the effacing of the nuptial analogy that was still felt on the level of the conditions of utterance and reutterance in older uses of the Song of Songs. Hence it is difficult not to feel this way of analogizing two heterogeneous kinds of love by means of words they have in common more as a displacement of meaning than as an increase in meaning.

But these faults of allegorical exegesis on the plane of the explication of meaning would not have become so obvious to us if we had not set aside the reading stances that made allegorical exegesis possible. In this way, we come to those changes in the reader that led to encompassing in one and the same disaffection Patristic exegesis and allegorism that claims to be scientific, to a point where we no longer know how to acknowledge the real merits of the former, except by way of the filter of scholarly allegorism.

Therefore it is to this change in the reader that we must now turn.

I recalled above the tie between the allegorical tradition and the monastic condition. The fundamental experience for which this condition provided the basic framework is no longer paradigmatic. If, for the ascetic and mystical tradition so strongly tied to the monastic condition, the nuptial signification was first of all spiritual, for we moderns it has become carnal, to the point that we no longer see any difference between the nuptial and the erotic than the Alexandrian did between the nuptial and the mystical.

I shall not attempt here a history of what I am calling the change in the reader. Nevertheless, I must say at least a few words about the role played by the Reformation, especially by Luther, in this history of reading. For one thing, in abolishing the difference between the monastic state and that of laypeople, the Lutheran Reformation broke apart the framework within which the reuttering of the Song of Songs by the baptized or by the Christian soul in quest of union with its Lord flourished. The Reformation call to live out one's faith within the setting of a worldly vocation—work and marriage—took away from monastic life its paradigmatic character and forbade seeing in it the privileged setting for the correct reading of the Song of Songs. For another, on the properly exegetical plane, the declaration that Scripture is its own interpreter had the consequence of discrediting allegorical interpretation in general, which was henceforth understood to be contingent and arbitrary. In this way, the properly exegetical argument links up with the anti-authoritarian one in such a way as to reinforce both of them, so that they become indiscernible from each other. In this sense, the Reformation paved the way for the three major objections of contemporary critics discussed above.

However, the Reformation in turn only constitutes one stage in the long change in the reader that leads to the kind of assumption that today distinguishes the naturalistic from the allegoristic reading. The major cultural factor, in this regard, was the evaluation of sexuality as a meaningful human relation. It is true that this favorable regard as concerns sexuality was never completely absent, even during those times when the monastic condition was held to be the model of perfection. Nonetheless, an accent of condescension—recall Paul saying that "it is better to marry than to burn"—always accompanied the esteem accorded to sexuality within the setting of Christian marriage. This esteem finds its most apt expression in discourse about conjugal chastity.

The evaluation of sexuality that I have in mind here has two distinctive features. First, there is what we can call a declaration of innocence as regards the value of sexuality per se. It is not that the idea of sin, guilt, or wrongdoing is excluded from this sphere, but the sexual act itself is declared innocent. The fault, if there be any, can only be henceforth assigned to the quality of relation to the other at play in the sexual relation: a lack of consent, reduction to the status of an object, exploitation, violence, etc. The second feature is the one that counts most for the history of reading of the Song of Songs. We do not find it difficult today to celebrate sexual pleasure for its own sake, without any reference to the matrimonial setting. In other words, we are ready to distinguish that mutual belonging to one another that is consummated in the erotic relation from the matrimonial institution, whether we continue to approve of the latter or not. The quotation André LaCocque cites from one of my earlier works takes this change into account. This was exactly the situation as regards the lovers in the Song of Songs. No allusion is made there to marriage or to fecundity. The glory of the nuptial bond unfolds apart from any reference to the matrimonial bond, without, it is true, excluding it or requiring it.

In my opinion, it is to this major cultural change that we must attribute the almost universal triumph of the erotic reading of the Song of Songs, which has become the dominant reading. Of course, this reading is largely traceable to changes that have occurred within the sphere of exegesis itself. But it would be naive to believe that the transformations that have taken place on the level of modern culture have had no effect on the history of reading. In fact, they belong to it in two ways. First, as I emphasized at the beginning of this essay, the search for the original meaning independent of any engagement on the part of the reader is not some atemporal, ahistorical attitude, but itself stems from a history of reading. Next, the triumph of the erotic sense, taken as self-evident, is itself a fact of reading, where the technical changes within the exegetical field and cultural changes affecting public discourse about sexuality reinforce each other.

May I add a final somewhat mischievous dig that the reading proposed in this volume by André LaCocque, which places the Shulamite among the "subversives," itself arises from a "subversive" reading that we might take as typically modern?

Toward a Theological Reading of the Song of Songs

The question of a possible theological meaning of the Song of Songs thus today arises within a new setting. On the one hand, we have been able, over the course of the first part of this essay, to amass a number of indications, provided by the text itself, that we can take as marks of a nuptial bond within the erotic, yet capable of being freed from this setting. On the other hand, at the end of the second part we find ourselves with a rule for reading, illustrated by the example of allegorical interpretation among the Patriarchs, according to which it is thanks to the reuse of the poem in new situations of discourse that the Song of Songs is led to say something *other* than what it literally says.

If we bring these two lines of analysis together, we may venture the hypothesis that the relocating of the nuptial bond in nonerotic figures of love can result from comparisons and intersections of different biblical texts, in the sense of new, originally unnoticed effects of reading. In other words, it is to the general phenomenon of intertextuality, as an effect of reading, rather than allegory, as allegedly immanent within Scripture, that we may appeal in order to generate theological readings of the Song of Songs, setting out, almost like sparks of new meaning, points of intersection among the texts that belong to the biblical canon. What is more, if allegorical interpretations can themselves be taken as effects of meaning, it then seems plausible to place them on the trajectory of a process of growth of interpretations that would begin on the plane of an intrabiblical reading. Before any reuse of these texts there would be the intersecting reading that takes places within the canon.

To give some indication of such a reading, I shall not begin with a confrontation between the Song of Songs and the prophetic texts, where the nuptial symbolism is applied to the relationship between the God of Israel and his people, even though this *locus theologicus* is where modern criticism that takes up allegorism has focused, as I indicated earlier. Instead, I would like to test my proposal of an intersecting reading through a comparison of texts stemming from different literary genres, where the creative aspect of the process of intersecting such texts will be more clearly visible. Thus I want to begin by turning to the cry of jubilation found in Genesis 2:23—"This at last is bone of my bone and flesh of my flesh; this one shall be called *ishshah,* for out of *ish* this one was taken."[34] Giving priority to this comparison is justified for several reasons. First, it safeguards the idea of a plurality of theological interpretations, which an overly exclusive concentration on the comparison of the Song of Songs and the texts usually cited from the prophetic cycle may hamper. The parallel of Genesis 2 invites us to make room for a theological interpretation that does not identify itself as an allegorical interpretation, at least in the usual sense of this term. In Genesis 2, human love is celebrated within the framework of a creation myth that ignores any separation of a spiritual from a carnal love and therefore does not suggest any analogy between them. Genesis 2:23 and the Song of Songs know just one love, the erotic love between a man and a woman.

How then is this comparison between Genesis 2:23 and the Song of Songs significant? To ask this question is to ask what augmentation in meaning each text receives from the other through such intersecting readings, like in the case of the production of a live metaphor that conjoins heterogeneous semantic fields.

In the first place, the verse from Genesis 2 carries with it the wealth of meaning that the man's cry of jubilation in discovering the woman owes to its setting within a myth of creation. Above, I risked, following Paul Beauchamp, speaking of a "return to the beginning" in regard to the return to the maternal home in Song of Songs 8:5 and the emphasis in 3:6, 6:10, and 8:5. Genesis makes explicit and amplifies to the extreme this sense of absolute beginning attached to love, by setting birth within a "history" of beginnings, a move totally foreign to the Song of

34. The connection between the Song of Songs and Genesis 2 is forcefully presented in Karl Barth, *Dogmatique* (Geneva: Labor et Fides, 1960), vol. 3:1, pp. 337–40; 3:3, pp. 317ff., and vol. 4, p. 225. See also Georges Casalis, Helmut Gollwitzer, and Roland de Pury, *Un chant d'amour insolite, Le Cantique des Cantiques* (D.D.B., 1984); Lys, *Le plus beau chant;* Beauchamp, *L'un et l'autre Testament,* vol. 2, *Accomplir les Ecritures,* pp. 115–37 ("L'homme, la femme, et le serpent").

Songs whose non-narrative character I have already underscored. What is more, the "history" that frames the cry of jubilation in Genesis 2:23 has to be read as the narrative of a sequence of absolute births: the animals, human solitude, the splitting of the human into two. Over the course of this history—which is therefore not that of a time before time, but rather of a time underlying history itself—the woman appears at the moment when the man, who is capable of naming all the animals, feels the distress of something lacking, the lack of a true partner: "but for the man there was not found a helper as his partner." The undivided one does not become two, however, except at the price of a rending for which he is not the author. The other only comes to him in the unawareness that is sleep. How can we fail here to think of the awakening of the woman by the man in Song of Songs 8:5: "Under the apple tree I awakened you . . ."? Paul Beauchamp has the following insight about this.[35] Before the creation of the woman, language is already there, but only as language as a mere set of labels assigned to living creatures. It is only with the appearance of the woman that language is born as "speech," or more precisely as sentences marked by deictic phrases ("this," an expression that is repeated, "this at last"). For the man's first discourse to be one of admiration, the woman is necessary. But, for all that, is the birth of discourse, contemporaneous with that of the woman, that of a poem? No, not at all, for, to the discourse that the man addresses to the woman, Song of Songs adds the reciprocity of speech between two lovers who are equal in their admiration for each other; even more, if we follow André LaCocque, a reciprocity whose initiative comes from the woman.

A second intersection between the poem and the myth is worth reflecting on. Both speak of an innocence of the erotic bond, considered apart from its social setting and the institution of marriage. Yet the myth and the poem speak in different ways of this innocence. In the myth, innocence is marked by the significance of a good creation: "Yhwh God said: 'It is not good that the man should be alone'" (2:18). In this way, the innocence of *eros* is clothed with divine approbation. It is a creaturely innocence, where creature indicates God's creation. It is true that breakdown is near. Indeed, if we replace the narrative of the creation of the woman within the broader framework of the complete "history" of beginnings, this birth and this discourse occur within a significant interval between a prohibition—"You shall not eat . . ." (Gene-

35. Ibid., p. 129.

sis 2:17)—and the act that transgresses it (Genesis 3). Yet this interval does not constitute a mere rapid narrative transition, but rather a key time within the "history" or origins, namely the one where the status of being a creature—a good creature—is sovereignly affirmed. The man's cry of jubilation sets the erotic bond beyond good and evil, for it exists prior to their distinction. May we not then say that the Song of Songs reopens this enclave of innocence and gives it the space that allows for the autonomy of the poem as a whole?[36]

The poem, in turn, when placed alongside the myth, confers on the interval of innocence the glory of a poetic pause.[37] Ought we then, in order to bind the poem of innocent love more closely to the myth a good creation, assign to the Song of Songs an eschatological significance, following Karl Barth, the innocence sung by the Song anticipating the Kingdom to come, like the eschatological banquet? This interpretation clearly stems from a theology that means to be systematic and that has to be received in this way. Its force is that of a coherent theological discourse, where the song of beginning and that of fulfillment frame the history that this theology calls the "history of salvation," marked by the Fall and the disgrace that goes with a mutilated love, as well as by the warnings and the promises of the Prophets. This interpretation is perfectly acceptable within the setting of a systematic theology whose central thread is a history of Salvation, itself centered on a Christology. But is it necessary to be systematic at this point, given the diversity of the biblical texts? In a more polycentric conception of the biblical writings, like the one I am advocating in my essays in this volume, it may

36. This suggestion finds full support in André LaCocque's analysis of the poem.

37. There is another feature common to Genesis 2 and the Song of Songs. If, like Daniel Lys, we make use of the categories of the sacred and the profane, principally in the perspective of a comparison with Oriental hierogamies, we see in the Song of Songs a reconciliation between the sexual and the sacred. This is a tie that is dissociated by those for whom the sexual is especially profane, even obscene, for whom only the process of allegorization can save our text and its canonical status. It is also dissociated by those for whom only the sacred dimension of love is saved by the allegory. The lesson of the Song of Songs is to "live the covenantal relation even in one's sex life" (*Le plus beau chant*, p. 52). Lys sees in the Song of Songs the result of a double demythologization, both of the divine, under the pressure of the theology of the Covenant, and of the human freed from its linkage to sacred hierogamies. "The best way to demythicize pagan *eros* is to describe human love not just in the manner of profane Egyptian songs, but also on the model of God's love for his people" (ibid., p. 53). The power of demythization seems here to be assigned to the theology of the Covenant, which allows Lys to write that sex becomes sacred when it "demystifies pagan love and reflects the Covenant" (ibid., p. 54). Without objecting to the comparison with the Prophets, which I shall return to below, it is worth noting that the Covenant is signified implicitly in the Song of Songs by the "seal" in 8:6. It remains true that the explicit sense of the Covenant with God requires the bringing together of the Song of Songs and the Prophets.

be preferable to allow each text to speak to the reader from its particular setting and to entrust the chorus of voices to the chance encounters that are one of the joys of reading. By assigning an eschatological status to the Song of Songs, symmetrical to the origin, we perhaps strip it of its most noteworthy feature, which is to sing of the innocence of love within the very heart of everyday life. Far from being diminished, the theological significance may even then be strengthened. The poem, re-read in light of Genesis 2:23 may suggest that creaturely innocence was not abolished by the Fall, but that it underlies even the history of evil, which the erotic relation never completely avoids. A theological way of reading the poem would then consist in proclaiming and celebrating the indestructibility at the base of the innocence of the creature, despite the history of evil and of victimization. This proclamation and celebration need not be placed at the end of time, it can be sung today. If we still want to speak of allegory in the broad sense of saying-other, or in another manner, this allegory is not born from a split between spirit and flesh but from a split, in some way on the same level, between two ways of speaking about innocence: that of the myth that recounts immemorial birth and that of the epithalamium that sings of an ongoing rebirth at the very heart of profane, everyday existence.

A last intersection between the poem and the myth is also intriguing. One may challenge the theological character of these two texts where God is not named or referred to. To this we can reply that it is the myth of creation as a whole that names God. Did we not refer above to the verse that says that "Yhwh God said, 'It is not good that the man should be alone . . .'"? This divine approbation authorizes us to say that love is innocent before God. But, someone may say, can God be the witness of a declaration for which he is not the intended audience? Perhaps we should answer, in an exploratory vein, that the origin has no need of being distinguished, named, or referred to insofar as it inhabits the creature? Man loves, beginning from God.[38] If so, when reread in light of Genesis, the Song of Songs becomes a religious text insofar as we can hear in it the word of a silent, unnamed God, who is not discerned owing to the force of attestation of a love caught up in itself.

This is confirmed by the truncated naming of Yhwh in the sapiential

---

38. "If we say that there is an allegory in these love poems, it is in a quite precise sense. Not because the words have to be decoded, but because the things of men signify those of God. They go together. In the sense that we have said that the first words of Adam to his wife are spoken beginning from God and in God, without naming him. This is where we have to begin" (Beauchamp, *L'un et l'autre Testament*, p. 186).

denouement of the Song of Songs,[39] which we can risk setting in parallel with that other, also sapiential denouement that says, "This is why a man leaves his father and his mother [even though there is not yet either a father or a mother during the time of Creation!] and clings to his wife and they become one flesh" (Genesis 2:24). Does not the seal of the Covenant in Song of Songs 8:6 have the same sapiential flavor? In both cases, we do not know who is speaking: the masterless voice of Wisdom? A hidden God? Or a discrete God who respects the incognito of intimacy, the privacy of one body with another body?

Armed in this way so as to arbitrate the struggle between the accord and disaccord among texts, we can also risk taking up again the discussion concerning the relation between the Song of Songs and the prophetic texts that celebrate in apparently erotic terms the love between the God of Israel and his people. The heterogeneity, even the apparent incompatibility, between these two series of texts constituted a strong argument on the part of the adversaries of allegorical explication. I shall not take up this argument using the terms of the older discussion, which for the opposed camps had as its stake the actual meaning of the Song of Songs, its original, intended meaning, which is immanent in the text. For the allegorists, the Song of Songs could have an allegorical meaning since the Prophets had already applied the nuptial metaphor to the relation between Yhwh and his people. The author of the Song of Songs must have had this same nuptial metaphor in mind, which she or he concealed under what appears to be a profane poem. To which the adversaries of such allegorical explication reply: (1) in the Prophets, Hosea, Ezekiel, Jeremiah, and for the Deuteronomist the metaphorical intention is clearly indicated by the context, which is not the case with the Song of Songs; (2) that the classification of the Song of Songs among the Wisdom writings ought to set us on guard against what may be an abusive mixing of genres; and (3) that the Prophets had in mind a covenantal bond that respects the distance and hierarchy between the partners and that, moreover, denied any sexual signification to the love between Yhwh and his people.

---

39. This poses a difficult problem for exegetes. As Paul Beauchamp says, regarding the syllable that says God in 8:6 (*shalhevet Yah*), "commentators are right to respect the discretion of the text. But to suppose that *Yah* coming here really says almost nothing is to make light of the poem" (*L'un et l'autre Testament*, p. 180). We can understand that the complete name of God should be absent from the epithalamium yet return in a truncated form in the passage from the lyrical to the sapiential. However, it is also true that this truncated name stems from the impertinence that André LaCocque points to. I have suggested that the alleged detheologization itself belongs to the metaphorical interplay that unfolds across the whole poem on the basis of many different rhetorical variations.

It seems to me, however, that if we approach the relation between the Song of Songs and the prophetic texts with the same kind of thinking that we applied to the relation between it and Genesis 2, we escape the preceding dilemma and its arguments. The question—at least for a hermeneutic centered on reading rather than on the writing of a text— is not whether the Prophets inspired the author of the Song of Songs, and whether he (or she!) intentionally reinscribed the Prophets' conjugal metaphor within the idiom of a popular song, even at the price of an eventual "detheologization" of the erotic metaphor found in the Prophets, and with the intention obviously marked by derision and provocation, as André LaCocque thinks. In other words, the question is not, at least here, that of some filiation at the level of the origin, hence of the writing of the text, even if this question has its legitimacy within the framework of a historical-critical inquiry into the composition of the Song of Songs. The question for me is, as in the case of Genesis 2, that of an intersecting reading that respects the difference in the setting of the texts under consideration. Following this pathway of intertextuality, many rich insights can be discovered.

First of all, the metaphorization at work takes place in two opposed directions, in a mirrorlike relation. For the Prophets, it is the love of God that is spoken through the nuptial metaphor. In the Song of Songs, the nuptial dimension of love first loses its erotic cloak thanks to those virtues of the poem discussed earlier, so as to reinsert them in new discourse situations, thanks to a shift in the place of utterance (the baptismal liturgy, for example). In this sense, bringing these texts near to one another gives birth to what we might call an intersecting metaphor: on the one side, the prophets "see" the love between God and his people "as" conjugal love; on the other side, the erotic love sung in the Song of Songs is "seen as like" the love of god for his creature, at least if we interpret it with reference to the Prophets' language. This "seeing as" is the organon of every metaphorical process, whether it works in one direction or the other.

Next, to speak of an intersecting metaphor is to give allegory a much broader field than that of Platonizing allegorism conceived of as the vertical transfer from the sensible to the intelligible, at the risk of abolishing, denying, even of defaming the sensible. The idea of an intersecting metaphor instead invites us to consider the different and original regions of love, each with its symbolic play. On the one side, the divine love is invested in the Covenant with Israel and later in the Christic bond, along with its absolutely original nuptial metaphorics; on the other, there is human love invested in the erotic bond and its equally original metaphorics, which transforms the body into something like a landscape. The double "seeing as" of intersecting metaphors then finds itself as the source of the "saying otherwise" constitutive of allegory. It is the power of love to be able to move in both senses along the ascending and descending spiral of metaphor, allowing in this way for every level of the emotional investment of love to signify, to intersignify every other level.

Finally, if we respect the different tonalities of the texts, we become attentive to the corrective action that they exercise on one another. And we need especially to emphasize here the recoil effect of the Song of Songs on the prophetic texts. If the prophetic reading of the Song of Songs—conjoined, it is true, with the exegesis of Genesis 2—brings out the so-to-speak sacred innocence of the erotic bond, the reinterpretation of the prophetic texts tends, in return, to inflect the Covenant relation in the direction of a mutual belonging of equal partners to each other. Regarding this point, the objection raised by the adversaries of every allegorical reading has to be taken into account. Prophecy is inscribed in an ethical sphere where every relation of familiarity, even that of a tender partnership, seems to be excluded. Therefore it is important to allow each series of texts its own setting. Here, the reverential love of the Yahwehist believer for his God; there, the mutual sharing of lovers placed on a plane of equality by their mutual exchange of desire and pleasure. The reinterpretation of the prophetic texts in light of the Song of Songs can only proceed owing to a veritable passage to the limit, even owing to a subtle subversion, in another sense than that intended by André LaCocque, at the end of which ethical religion moves toward mystical religion. Here, perhaps, we cross a frontier beyond which only a few fools for God will want to venture.

Returning one last time to our methodological considerations, it seems as though the objections raised against treating the allegorical sense as the literal sense lose their pertinence just as do those contrary arguments of the allegorists. (1) For an intersecting reading, it does not matter whether the allegorical meaning was intended by the authors of the Song of Songs, nor that the text itself give objective indications of such a reading. (2) The frontier between prophecy and wisdom also loses its pertinence inasmuch as an intersecting reading deliberately crosses it, in the very name of the principle of intertextuality at work within the canonical framework. (3) As for the shift in meaning of the Covenant between Yhwh and his people that results from the rapprochement with the Song of Songs, we have shown that it has to be reckoned among the meaning effects of an intersecting reading. More important than the arguments of the older quarrel is the freedom to move among the biblical writings that inspires an intersecting reading freed from the constraints of a concern for influences and filiations.

In this sense, an intersecting reading must come at the Song of Songs from both sides. Along the second way we shall encounter the New Testament texts that the historical-critical method tries to classify as certain (Revelation 3:20, John 20:18), likely (Revelation 12:1, 15:6, Ephesians 5:27), or simply possible (Revelation 22:17, John 3:29, 13:2). These texts, read in the Second Testament, would be in some manner symmetrical to those in the First Testament, playing freely with the nuptial symbolism. Let us therefore allow all these texts to project themselves on one another and let us gather those sparks of meaning that fly up at their points of friction. Why shouldn't we end this round of metaphors with the one that is most outlandish, the most impertinent, in every sense of the word: "the wife of the Lamb" (Revelation 21:9)? That this is a completely unexpected association is the least that one can say! Let us instead, with Paul Beauchamp, speak of hyperbole and condensation:[40] hyperbole through which "the sense is taken to its excess," condensation "through which the alimentary code of the Banquet (the slaughtered Lamb) and the code of sexual union (the wife) come together thanks to the hyperbolic collision."

If the places where we speak of love are so diverse, even dispersed, the figures of no one of them can be said to be superior to any other. They intersignify one another instead of arranging themselves in some hierarchy. May we not then suggest that what I have called the nuptial is the virtual or real point of intersection where these figures of love all cross? If such be the case, may we not then also say that the nuptial as such is an effect of reading, issuing from the intersecting of texts, only because it is the hidden root, the forgotten root of the great metaphorical interplay that makes all the figures of love refer to one another?

---

40. *L'un et l'autre Testament*, pp. 191–95 ("L'Epouse de l' Agneau").

Exodus 3:14

The Revelation of Revelations

ANDRÉ LaCOCQUE

In this essay on the Name of God revealed to Moses in Midian according to Exodus 3, we shall remain faithful to this volume's program of focusing on the trajectory of texts. This means that many a critical problem will be hardly touched upon or even mentioned. As a matter of principle, we shall also be content with transcribing the consonants of the Hebrew word Yhwh, thus respecting the Jewish prohibition to pronounce the Name out of fear of irreverence.[1]

Statistically, "Yhwh" appears 6,823 times in the Hebrew Bible. The question of the origins of this philologically strange formation, as well as of its religious roots is very moot. Numerous scholarly studies have been published, and most of them are intriguing and of profound interest. Suffice it here, however, to mention with the *TDOT*[2] that "the original home of Yhwh was in the south, in or among the mysterious mountains Sinai (Deuteronomy 33:2), Seir (Deuteronomy 33:2; Judges 5:4), Paran (Deuteronomy 33:2; Habakkuk 3:3), and Teman (Habakkuk 3:3)." From there, the Name "reached" Zion in the north, which is identified with *ṣaphôn* in the far north, the home of Ugaritic Baal (Psalm 48:2). As we shall see, this account corresponds to the reconstruction by the History-of-Religion school of pre-Israelite "Yahwism."

---

1. In the postexilic community, utterance of the Name became forbidden, except for its use by the High Priest on the Day of Atonement when it was impossible to misuse it, which indicates that the Name did not become taboo or secret. Henri Meschonic writes, It "is not a *name*—over which, as in polytheism one could, by magic have power. It is a *verb*. It has the power. And it is a promise. What is unaccomplished continues . . . to be accomplished." "Traduire le sacré," in *Corps écrit*, vol. 3 (Paris: PUF, 1982), p. 17.

2. *Theological Dictionary of the Old Testament,* edited by G. J. Botterweck and Helmer Ringgren (Grand Rapids, MI: W. B. Eerdmans, 1947–97), s.v. "YHWH," vol. 7, pp. 500–521; the quote is from page 520.

In the source P, at any rate, the revelation of the Name belongs to the Sinai-tradition (to the so-called *Ur-theophanie*). So much so that God can be designated simply as *zeh sinai* (Psalm 68:9; Judges 5:5). As Hartmut Gese has said, the Reed Sea events must have been interpreted very early on as an act of Yhwh. Hence, although the two traditions of Exodus and Sinai had their own independent developments,[3] they were all the same *materialiter* tied up together. Indeed, the Sinai tradition preceded the Exodus tradition and gave birth to it.[4] It is, indeed, the Sinai tradition that provides the ground for the association Yhwh-Israel. For obvious tactical reasons, it was felt necessary to have Moses first experience at Horeb the "revelation of revelations" that would be in time granted to the whole people in the desert. In summary, God's name-giving is connected: (1) with Mount Sinai (Exodus 20:2, 33:18f., 34:6f.); (2) with the Exodus from Egypt (Exodus, *passim*); and (3) with Moses' call (Exodus 3, 6). We shall return to these points in what follows.

Among the extrabiblical witnesses of the name "Yhwh," the oldest is the Mesha inscription from Edom (ninth century BCE), "I took the vessels of Yhwh and dragged them before Chemosh." Also noteworthy is the inscription of Kuntillat ʿAjrud (fifty kilometers from Kadesh Barnea) in Phoenician script. Gösta Ahlstrom concludes from this inscription, which he dates ca. 800 BCE, that the name Yhwh is of Edomite "origin." The inscription reads: "Yhwh of Teman and his Asherah."[5] Other scholars insist, however, on the biblical localization of the revelation to Moses among the Qenites and on the role of Jethro/Reuel in the early history of Hebrew Yahwism. They therefore conclude to a Midianite origin for the religion of Moses (cf. Exodus 2–3 and 18 in particular). Collective memory in Israel renders it probable that there was indeed among the Midianites a cult to Yhwh, but in all justice such a conclusion must not undermine the fundamental originality of the revelation transmitted by Moses, for here "the exclusivity of the relationship between Yhwh and Israel is constitutive, by which the concept of Israel as a confederation of tribes finds its very definition."[6]

---

3. This point is strongly argued by Gerhard von Rad, "The Form-Critical Problem of the Hexateuch," in *The Problem of the Hexateuch and Other Essays*, translated by E. W. Trueman (New York: McGraw-Hill, 1965), pp. 1–78.

4. Hartmut Gese, "Der Name Gottes im Alten Testament," in *Der Name Gottes*, edited by H. von Stietencron (Düsseldorf: Patmos, 1975), p. 35.

5. Gösta Ahlstrom, *Who Were the Israelites?* (Winona Lake, IN: Eisenbraun, 1986).

6. Gese, "Der Name Gottes," p. 80.

As a name distinguishes one from all others, it does not make much sense that the sole God have a name. It is not without surprise that we find God complying with the request of Moses for his Name in the amazing dialogue at the Burning Bush, just before the return of Moses to Egypt. As we said above, the context of Moses' commissioning is here crucial for the understanding of God's epiphany and the function of the Tetragrammaton in Israel's history. Until then, God had spoken to Moses using such expressions as "I" ('*anokhi*, Exodus 3:6, 7, 12) or "the God of your father, the God of Abraham, the God of Isaac, the God of Jacob" (3:6, cf. v. 15). But now, Moses raises a Near-Eastern, or more precisely in keeping with Moses' background, an "Egyptian" question about the name of the divinity. This ideological background is clearly set by the role of divine names in the ancient Near East, a point that cannot be overemphasized. Although there is not sufficient space here to deal with the issue in any depth, it will suffice to recall the theological legends of Moses' land of origin. They tell us about gods of the Egyptian pantheon vying for power. There is, for example, a dramatic dialogue between Ra and Isis centering on Ra as the victim of a fatal poisoning. Isis has the magical know-how to heal Ra, but to do so must pronounce a formula of incantation with the secret name of power of Ra, thus, by the same token, obtaining the upper hand over the god. This episode is typical of a conception that pervades magic religion; we find numerous examples of this in the section of *Ancient Near Eastern Texts Relating to the Old Testament* (*ANET*) titled, "The God and His Unknown Name of Power."[7] The Near-Eastern gods bear several general names by which they may be invoked, and these are, so to speak, "for general consumption." But gods also have a particular name inaccessible to the humans. This one, even when known by magic, must be avoided as much as possible. For example, "Ilani, Elim, Nathir, Astarot, Baalim, Elohim" all can be rendered simply by "the divine." William F. Albright stresses their plural form and concludes that they refer to the "totality of manifestations of a deity."[8] In practice, the (general) proper names of the divine are only used when no generic noun is fitting. For example: "The help of *Ra* (not just any god) comes from afar."

Within this magical-religious context, Moses appears as raising the question of God's identity in a less than innocent way. His hidden

7. James B. Pritchard, ed., *Ancient Near Eastern Texts Relating to the Old Testament* (*ANET*) (Princeton: Princeton University Press, 1950), pp. 12ff.

8. William F. Albright, *From the Stone Age to Christianity* (Baltimore: The Johns Hopkins University Press, 1962), p. 213.

agenda might well be to appropriate "the unknown name of power" of God for the sake of using it as a shield to protect himself from adversity in Egypt.[9] From this perspective, further developed in the whole context of the confrontation of Moses with the Egyptian magicians, the meaning or the bearing of *mah šemô* ("what is his name?") in verse 13 acquires its importance. In verse 11, the question was *mi 'anokhi*, "who am I?"; now in verse 13 it becomes *mah šemô*, "what is his name?" The shift from *mi* to *mah* must be stressed. *Mah šemô* is not simply "how is he called?" as Judges 13:17 attests. There the question is *mi šemèkha*, "what is your name?" and the interrogative pronoun is *mi*. Moses uses the interrogative *mah* as in 1 Samuel 29:3 (*mah ha-'ibrim*, "who are these Hebrews?" in the sense of "what are these Hebrews up to?"). The inquiry is the same as the one John and Peter were submitted to in Acts 4:7: "By what power or by what name did you do this?" At Qumran, *1 QapGen* gives an interpretation of Genesis 15:2 that goes in the same direction: the *mah titén li* of the MT is said to mean, "what is the point of giving me . . . ? To what end will you give me . . . ?" Hence, although it may be an exaggeration when Martin Buber thinks that *mah šimkha* or *mah šemô* never mean a simple "what is your/his name?"[10] it seems clear that, at least in certain circumstances and texts, there is a shade of nuance in *mah* with *šem* that renders the question equivocal. A case in point is Genesis 32:28. It would be difficult to argue that the mysterious wrestler does not know with whom he is fighting by the brook of Jabbok. When he is asked *mah šemèkha*, Jacob gives an answer that would look innocent enough, were it not for the angelic retort. He says "Jacob" but the numinous figure replies, "your name will not be called any longer Jacob but Israel" (v. 29; cf. 35:10), thus retrospectively charging the interrogative *mah* with its full "philosophical" potency.[11]

Furthermore, although it is evident that the ancient Israelites in their daily humdrum would not raise philosophical questions each time they asked a question with the interrogative pronoun *mah*, it remains uncontrovertible that Hebrew text after text attribute what to us may look like an extraordinary value to proper names, construing them as equivalent

9. See also Gerhard von Rad, *Moses* (London, 1960), p. 20: "[Moses] wants to put God to work for him . . . he is practicing magic." His question to God is thus equivocal, an "expression at the same time of man's need for God and of man's impudence in relation to God." See Günther Röder, *Urkunden zur Religion der alten Aegypten* (Jena: E. Diederichs, 1923), pp. 138–41.

10. Martin Buber, *Moses: The Revelation and the Covenant* (New York: Harper and Row, 1958), p. 55ff.

11. Other texts come to mind, see Proverbs 30:4; cf. Isaiah 42:8, 52:6, etc.

to the human or divine persons bearing them.[12] A new name would be a new god. *Mah šemô* therefore has a neutral ring to it that should not deceive us. The question is not to be understood simply as a request that God spell out his name, but it conveys the nuance of inquiring about its meaning. What is the secret implied within God's Name?

Maimonides is certainly right when he states that the revelation of "Yhwh" to Moses is no accreditation of Moses if it is a name that both Moses and the Hebrews already know. In that case, it is not even a revelation. But the same situation obtains if Moses comes with a name that they don't know (*Guide* I, 63). The issue must lie elsewhere. Nahum M. Sarna faces essentially the same quandary. The problem for Moses is that he must receive a mandate from the people. But according to the Exodus text Moses himself does not know God's Name, while assuming that the people do, so that, recognizing it, they will find in it a sign authenticating his mission.[13] In fact, says Sarna, the people are expected to be convinced of the divine mission of Moses by the power inherent in the Name, not by the utterance of an old or a new name. The very logic of Moses' question demands that from the outset Moses' request is for "a Name of power."[14]

For the Name itself is here revelatory, as its enormous importance throughout Scripture demonstrates (cf. Psalm 54:3 [LXX 54:1]; Psalm 20:2; Proverbs 18:10; Zechariah 4:9; Isaiah 45:3; etc.). There is, however, within the gracious response of God to Moses a negative aspect, a refusal to comply with the request (as it is formulated). Several scholars have forcefully insisted on that negativity. Some even see only that dimension in the paronomasia *'ehyeh 'ašer 'ehyeh*.[15] True, the paronomasis, by its very circularity and indeterminacy (like in the modern expression, "*que sera sera*"), makes sure that no magical power is deduced from it. *But God has a name;* he is personal and invocable; one can call upon his name, one can pray and address him as a "thou" (Psalm 99:6; 1 Kings

12. See below the development on the *Selbstvorstellungsformel*.

13. Nahum M. Sarna, *Exploring Exodus: The Heritage of Biblical Israel* (New York: Schocken, 1986), pp. 50f.

14. The divine revelation is of the *meaning* of the Name, not of the Name itself. Martin Buber, *Königtum Gottes* (Berlin, 1936), pp. 82f., 237, n. 30a; and Buber, *Moses* (Heidelberg 1952), p. 58.

15. Cf. B. Couroyer, *L'Exode* in *La Sainte Bible* de Jerusalem (1952), p. 34; André-Marie Dubarle, "La signification du nom YHWH," *Recherches en sciences religieuses et philosophie de la religion* (1951): 3–21; G. Lambert, "Que signifie le nom YHWH," *Nouvelle Revue Théologique* (1952): 697–905. Shoring up this thesis, three texts can be referred to in which God refuses to fulfill human desire to know his name: Genesis 32:30; Judges 13:18; in Exodus 33:18–34:9, God refuses to show his face to Moses.

18:24). What is rejected by God is his own demise, his own dismissal, his demotion to the rank of an idol.[16] But through revealing a Name that is, as we shall see further, a total and dynamic commitment to his people, God transcends the ambiguous request and the somewhat impure intention of Moses.

Hartmut Gese goes further than does Buber, "More important than the meaning of the Name is its function as name."[17] Gese translates *'ehyeh 'ašer 'ehyeh*, "ich erweise mich, als der ich mich erweisen werde," "ich bin, als der ich erweisen werde" (I show myself as the one who I shall show myself, I am as I shall show myself), and he insists on this "opening toward the future."[18] With this interpretation, the focus has shifted to the use of the root *hyh* in the linguistic formation of the Tetragrammaton. From the outset, it must be said that the problem raised by this versatile Hebrew verb is eminently difficult. Even, for the case in question, the connection of the form "*Yhwh*" with the stem *hyh* is problematic. Decisive in this respect is the weight of a persistent tradition, biblical and postbiblical, according to which the Name is in fact a verbal construction closely related to the root *hyh*.[19] For this account, the formula *'ehyeh 'ašer 'ehyeh* shows that a consensus associated the Name and its proclamation with the semantic field of the verb *hyh*. Furthermore, the phrase, by virtue of its paronomastic formulation, excludes from consideration the understanding of *hyh* here as a mere copula. It rather signals a dynamic action, something like "to be with, to become, to show oneself . . ." or even, when the verb retrieves its fundamental and full force, "to fall, to befall, to happen, to become (*cadere, evenire* . . .)."[20] Thus, a first conclusion to be drawn is that we should not indulge in any ontological abstraction about Being, a sense that the

---

16. As Terence Fretheim writes, there must be "a commandment specifically designed to protect the name of God . . . (Exodus 20:7; Deuteronomy 5:11). The concern here is expressed somewhat more fully in Leviticus 19:12. . . . God is concerned about God, about God's own future. . . . Giving the name opens up the possibility of, indeed admits a desire for, a certain intimacy in relationship. . . . Naming entails availability . . . historicality . . . vulnerability . . . [misuse and abuse, hence] the possibility of pain . . . the possibility of suffering." In *The Suffering of God* (Minneapolis: Fortress Press, 1984), pp. 99–100.

17. Gese, "Der Name Gottes," p. 81.

18. Ibid., p. 82.

19. In Mari, too, isolated verbs represented divine names; see Herbert B. Huffmon, "Yahweh and Mari . . . ," in *Near Eastern Studies in Honor of W. Albright* (Baltimore: The Johns Hopkins University Press, 1971). There are also two pre-Islamic examples, *yagut* "he helps" and *ya'tiq* "he protects."

20. See Paul Joüon, *Grammaire de l'hébreu biblique* (Rome: Institut Biblique Pontifical, 1947), par. 111h.

root may have acquired much later when Jewish reflection came under the influence of speculative thinking from the West. Leaving aside here this late development—a witness of which is found in the LXX "translating" Exodus 3:14 by *ho ôn*, the Being—a large semantic field of the verb *hyh*, one not conducive to speculative formulations, still remains open to our investigation.

G. S. Ogden presents us with a synoptic review of the various temporal uses of the verb *hyh*, ostensibly at the root of the verbal formation of *Yhwh*. His conclusions seem well grounded.[21] He distinguishes three kinds of use:

> 1. as a *copula* (cf. 1 Samuel 3:1: *debar-Yhwh hayah yaqar*, the word of Yhwh was rare);
> 2. as indicating *existence* (with the subject almost always nondefined, cf. 2 Kings 3:9: *we-lo' hayah mayim*, and there was no water);
> 3. as indicating *transition* from one sphere of existence to another, *becoming* (with the preposition *le-*; cf. 1 Samuel 10:12: *'al-kén hayta le-mašal*, therefore it became a proverb).[22]

Some scholars have suggested reading the *'ehyeh* and *Yahweh* of the MT as representing in fact hiphil (factitive, causative) forms, thus rendering the action expressed by those forms as I/the One who make(s) be, that is, the Creator. One must complete the formula with a complement object, either Moses or his people.[23] But there is, actually, no basis whatsoever in the Hebrew Bible or in the Versions for such an understanding; besides, the hiphil of *hyh* is nowhere to be found in the Hebrew Bible. Ogden, therefore, examines the uses of the qal (indicative) imperfect of the root and again distinguishes three levels:

> 1. as *copulative:* cf. Exodus 3:12 *'ehyeh 'imkha* (I shall be with thee), indicating a future setting;
> 2. as *existential:* a situation to occur in the future, or that will continue to be what it is now, cf. Zechariah 14:13: "a great panic *tihyeh* = shall fall";
> 3. as *transitional:* expecting a future alteration in present circumstances; or *frequentative*, cf. 1 Kings 5:28 (= LXX 5:14), *yi-*

---

21. G. S. Ogden, "Time, and the Verb *hyh* in OT Prose," *Vetus Testamentum* 21 (1971): 451–69.

22. Let us add here the astounding text of Deuteronomy 26:17–18, where the verb *hyh* is used, like in Exodus 3:14ff., with its full force. See also below, note 62.

23. So William F. Albright, David N. Freedman, and Frank M. Cross, among others. See especially Cross, *Canaanite Myth and Hebrew Epic* (Cambridge: Harvard University Press, 1973).

hyu = they used to be (by association with other verbs that revert to the simple perfect).

From this situation, Ogden concludes that *hyh* is used primarily with the function of a temporal indicator. This usage is present throughout the biblical material and, "even if . . . an acquired viewpoint," is close to the shades of meaning of the tenses in contemporary European languages.

This conclusion of Ogden is in general correct; it is however misleading as far as Exodus 3:14 is concerned. Clearly, *'ehyeh 'ašer 'ehyeh* is more than a simple overture to the future, although that aspect is present. Similarly, the meaning of existence, although also present in the Name, is not sufficient. The LXX witness is important as it shows that Exodus 3:14f. was understood, before the Masoretic reading, as representing a qal and not a hiphil form; but the rendition *ego eimi ho ôn*, I am the one being, misses too much of the fundamental meaning of the Hebrew expression, as a concession to Hellenistic ontology. August Dillmann tried to recover this aim by adding that God is "der Seiende" because he is active, living.[24] This note is struck with renewed strength by Nahum M. Sarna, for whom the name of God does emphasize his Being but not in opposition to nonbeing. God's Being means his active, dynamic Presence. "The Divine Personality can be known only to the extent that God chooses to reveal His Self, and it can be truly characterized only in terms of itself, and not by analogy with something else. This is the articulated counterpart of the spectacle of fire at the Burning Bush, fire that is self-generating and self-sustaining."[25] The intimate tie

24. August Dillmann, *Handbuch der alttestamentlichen Theologie* (Leipzig: S. Hirzel, 1895), p. 217. Cf. Paul van Imschoot, *Théologie de l'Ancien Testament*, vol. 1 (Tournai: Desclée & Co., 1954), p. 16; Sigmund Mowinckel, "'I am the acting God' ('The Name of the God of Moses')," *Hebrew Union College Annual* 32 (1961): 127; for Johannes Lindblom, "X *ašer* X" is a construction present elsewhere in the Old Testament (Genesis 15:7, 45:4; Leviticus 20:24; 1 Kings 13:14), and *"ehyeh ašer ehyeh"* is to be understood as *I am the one who is*. Lindblom refers to Jeremiah 35:9 (to be, to exist), but he is mistaken; the text of Jeremiah proves nothing of the sort. See his *Lectures on Philosophical Theology* (Ithaca: Cornell University Press, 1978). More interesting is this statement by the philosopher Immanuel Kant: "The divine knowledge of all things is nothing but the knowledge God has of Himself as an effective power" (quoted in ibid., p. 89), a statement that Kenneth Seeskin rephrases as, "The object owes its existence to the fact that God represents it to Himself," in *Jewish Philosophy in a Secular Age* (New York: SUNY Press, 1990), p. 84.

25. Sarna, *Exploring Exodus*, p. 52. Cf. van Imschoot, *Théologie de l'Ancien Testament*, vol. 1, "Dieu," pp. 16–17: The Name of God must buttress the people's trust in the declaration that God "is with you" (Exodus 3:9–12). It must be able to perform the deliverance from Egypt. Thus the Name means, "The One who efficiently manifests his existence." Cf. James Plastaras, *The God of Exodus* (Milwaukee: Bruce Publishing Co., 1966), p. 95: "the name YHWH 'defines' God in terms of active presence." Brevard Childs, *The Book of Exodus* (Philadelphia: Westminster, 1974), p. 88:

between the Tetragrammaton on the one hand and the divine action on the other indicates in what direction philological research should go. An agent is designated whose work is actualized in Israel's exodus from Egypt. Whatever may be the deep meaning of the Tetragrammaton, "Israel" is the name of the *Thou* in dialogue with the divine *I*.

Thus, the name Yhwh is clearly action-oriented and not conceptually devised. In other words, the Tetragrammaton cannot be reduced to a dogmatic-philosophical formula. Besides, "the word-play on the name of God (*'ehyeh-Yahweh*) confirms the connection between name and significance," as says Brevard Childs. He adds that the paronomasis does not indicate indefiniteness but actuality: I am really there; cf. Exodus 33:19. Moses' question expressed in Exodus 3:13 constitutes the prophet's last resistance before accepting his vocation. He now challenges the One who has revealed himself as the God of the forebears to announce a new program of action through *becoming different* from what he used to be and has been until now. If Moses goes back to Egypt and talks liberation to his fellow Israelites, such address must inaugurate a new mode of divine revelation to them. The people in Egypt will no doubt "seek to learn [God's] new relationship to them. Formerly, he related to them as the God of the Fathers. What will he be to Israel now?"[26]

Revelation of the Name by its very nature stresses exclusivity. Such divine exclusivity is in its turn the foundation for the recipient's exclusivity as the relation between the two is one of I-and-Thou. God's vis-à-vis receives a proper name *within the relationship* with a God who is not nameless. "Israel" is already descriptive of a transfigured reality— known formerly and at the surface of things as Jacob—that is present only in the face-to-face relation to God. The Name of God is echoed in the name of the human (Isaiah 45:3). The Face of God grants a face to man. That is why the revelation to Moses in Midian finds its *Sitz im Wort* within a *Botenspruch*, a prophetic commission addressed to him in the second-person singular, "to you." Thus, the divine first-person singular, "My Name" (v. 15), "*ehyeh*" (v. 14), "the remembrance of Me" (v. 15) is combined with the human second-person plural, "you will say . . . has sent me [Moses] to you [all]," etc. The sharpest paradox is that the only One who is really entitled to say "I," and who is the unique

"the God of Israel makes known his being in specific historical moments and confirms in his works his ultimate being by redeeming a covenant people."

26. Brevard Childs, *Introduction to the Old Testament as Scripture* (Philadelphia: Fortress Press, 1979), pp. 76, 75.

'ehyeh,[27] has a Name that includes a second person, a "you." A "you" that is revealed and enshrined in the Name itself, let us say in the *'aser* (what/who) that constitutes the place of fall and rebound of the divine "being"/"(be)falling"/"occurring"!

Hence the Name is *theophanic* and *performative;* it elicits recognition and worship as the recipients are not just made privy to a divine secret but are the objects of an act of salvation. *'ani hu' Yhwh* (it is I who am Yhwh) goes far beyond a rhetorical statement—it reveals the ultimate meaning of the redeeming event. Thus we see why the Name is no atemporal, ahistorical, abstract axiom about the divine aseity. God says *'ehyeh* and the unaccomplished tense helps us see the action as a process. It is not a question of divine essence, but it is a promissory statement that God, as it were, "stands and falls" with his people, and in the first place with Moses about to return to Egypt where a price is set upon his head.[28]

As Walther Zimmerli says, it is "a statement laden with significance."[29] Exodus 3:14 with its context about Moses' prophetic commission belongs to the source E. It is remarkable that also in the Priestly literary source (P) present in Exodus 6, the revelation of the Name is intimately connected with Moses' commission to announce to the people their liberation and redemption: "You shall know that I am Yhwh your God, who has freed you from the burdens of the Egyptians. . . . I am Yhwh" (v. 7f., see also 7:5, 14:4, 17f., 16:9, etc.). Such a performative function of the Name becomes especially clear if we translate the preposition *be* that introduces the *ground* for recognition by something like, "by the fact that I . . . in that I (freed you) . . ."[30] To know Yhwh is, as a matter of fact, "to recognize his beneficial deeds on Israel's behalf, especially the deed of the Exodus" (cf. Leviticus 23:43).[31]

---

27. A marvelous Hasidic story tells us about the refusal of a Master to open his door to his friend who had simply identified himself with a familiar "that's me!" (*'anokhi*). "Who can say of himself *'anokhi* but God?" said the Master—and the friend decided on the spot to return for further studies at the "yeshibah"!

28. Cf. Walther Eichrodt, *Theologie des Alten Testaments*, vol. 1 (Stuttgart: Ehrenfried Klotz, 1959), p. 93: "Ich bin wirklich und warhaftig da, bin bereit zu helfen und zu wirken, wie ich es von jeher war." Evode Beaucamp, *La Bible et le sens religieux de l'univers* (Paris: Cerf, 1959), p. 19: "Le Dieu du Sinaï ne s'est pas contenté d'ouvrir un dialogue avec ses créatures, il a pris en charge leur destin, les entraînant derrière lui en une marche haletante vers un terme de lui seul connu (cf. Is 45.2; 52.12; Ps 18.30)."

29. Walther Zimmerli, *I Am Yahweh* (Atlanta: John Knox, 1982), p. 19.

30. In a footnote on Exodus 20:2, *TOB* mentions the possible translation of this verse as follows, "C'est moi le Seigneur qui suis ton Dieu, pour t'avoir fait sortir du pays d'Egypte." Thus the tie with Exodus 3:14 is very strong.

31. Zimmerli, *I Am Yahweh*, p. 44.

Yhwh means savior (Exodus 34:6–7; Isaiah 43:11–13). Psalm 138:2 makes it abundantly clear that the Name of God is *promise*.[32] It promises a history of merciful guidance whose onset, namely the Exodus, constitutes both its beginning and its end, its apex and the figure of things to come at the *eschaton*, because the Event in question is paradigmatic *kat'exochên*.

This tension between the past and the future, between the known and the unknown, the experienced and the hoped for, agrees with the dual character of the Name of God. Its revelation is dialectically a revelation of God's hiddenness. Consistent with this dialectic, the promise conveyed by the Name is the obverse face of a coin whose reverse is chastisement. The Name is blessing and curse; it is beneficent and maleficent, like the image of the pillar of cloud that moved before the Israelite army in the desert and was both light and darkness (cf. Exodus 14:19ff.). The Name implies also punishment, both of Israel's enemies and of Israel themselves (Exodus 8:9, 9:14–16, 29, etc.). This second aspect, which must be seen within the context of polemics against the other gods (as in Exodus 20:2ff.), had to be mentioned here for the sake of completeness, although it is not emphasized in our focal text of Exodus 3:14 (but see Exodus 6:1, 6, etc.).

The revelation of the Name to Moses must not be considered in isolation from other texts that provide linguistic as well as ideological contexts to Exodus 3. Zimmerli in particular has studied in great detail the recurrent biblical formula "I am Yhwh." A veritable mine of information can be found in his book that bears this formula as its title, as well as in his studies on the book of Ezekiel, where this formula recurs often.[33] I acknowledge my debt to those works, particularly as regards the following development. The formula "I am Yhwh" whether in its simplest or expanded form is especially well illustrated in the Priestly literature (Ezekiel; P; H). The shortest statement is found in Leviticus 18:5, 21.[34] In Leviticus 18:2 (H) *ani Yhwh 'eloheikhem* (I am Yhwh your God) is followed by a paraenesis (vv. 3–5) and then by apodictic commandments (vv. 6ff.). But the formula appears at the conclusion of other pericopes found in Leviticus 18–26. It finds support, for example, in

---

32. The Hebrew of Psalm 138:2 says something like, "for you have made your [promissory] word well above your name."

33. Walther Zimmerli, *Ezekiel: A Commentary on the Book of Ezekiel* (Philadelphia: Fortress Press, 1979).

34. Texts where the formula can be found: Exodus 6:6–8, 7:5, 17, 8:18, 10:2, 12:12b, 14:4, 18:11, 16:12, 29:28–46, 31:13ff.; Leviticus 11:42–45; Numbers 3:12f., 10:8–10, 15:38–41; Deuteronomy 29:5; 1 Kings 20:13, 28; Jeremiah 24:7; Joel 2:27, 4:17.

the deed of Exodus (Leviticus 19:36), the promise of the land (25:38), the liberation from slavery (26:13), the separation from other peoples (20:24), etc.

In Ezekiel, the pure formula appears only in chapter 20. Elsewhere it has become a component in an extended statement demanding allegiance, "You will know that I am Yhwh." The latter is called by Zimmerli a "statement of recognition"; it comes in response to the self-introduction by God, or "*Selbstvorstellungsformel*" to use Zimmerli's term. In both Exodus 6 and Ezekiel 20, "Yhwh's name [is] an event of Yhwh's self- introduction."[35] It reveals something previously unknown (Ezekiel 20:5 = Exodus 6:7), eliciting "the recognition of Yhwh's self-revelation precisely in his name," cf. Ezekiel 20:44. That the formula is often set at the end of the discourse shows that it is a formula of legitimation. It is a causal phrase ("*for* I am Yhwh, your God"). Characteristically, in Ezekiel 20 the name entails a prescriptive consequence. After the promise comes the *commandment* (Ezekiel 20:7). Similarly, in Exodus 20:2 and 5, the formula frames the first two commandments in dual form, thus setting "the underlying foundation for the commandments themselves," says Zimmerli (p. 26). At this point of our study, it is highly significant that the *Selbstvorstellungsformel* is the basis of both the Holiness Code and the Decalogue. This is again the case when we turn to Psalm 50 and Psalm 81, that is, to the liturgical setting of the Ten Utterances.[36] In those Psalms, God is present himself in the mediation to the community as the one who commands (as in Exodus 19; 20; Deuteronomy 5). There is, says Zimmerli, a "tenacious cohesion of the formula . . . to the proclamation of maxims."[37]

Within the perspective of this connection between the divine Name and the prescriptive, the *Selbstvorstellungsformel* is set within the context of the interdiction of any divine figuration. At face value, such iconophobia might be interpreted as a deliberate divine incognito. But, on the contrary, the revelation of the Name is granted by an imageless God who desires to be accessible and known.[38] The situation as it now transpires, however, is paradoxical. All representations of the Living God

35. Zimmerli, *I Am Yahweh*, pp. 10f.

36. This setting is not necessarily original. On this issue, we refer the reader to our chapter on "Thou shalt not kill." In Psalm 50:18ff. can be found the sixth, seventh, and eighth commandments; in Psalm 81:10, the first commandment.

37. Zimmerli, *I Am Yahweh*, p. 28.

38. This "compensatory" aspect of the Name revelation for the lack of plastic representation did not escape the attention of Gerhard von Rad, *Old Testament Theology*, vol. 1 (New York: Harper and Row, 1962), p. 183; cf. Gese, "Der Name Gottes," p. 86.

are forbidden in Israel. Here the mediate relation in the third person through representation is replaced by the immediate relationship in the second person without mediation. But then the danger of trivializing the human relation with God has been substituted for the danger of objectifying the divine. Therefore the first two commandments excluding rivals and idols are followed by a third commandment regarding the proper dialogue with God as a Thou. For Anthony Phillips, this prescription is not against blasphemy—this would amount to suicide in the covenant community; nor can it be against false oaths, for the oath formula itself included a self-curse; nor can it concern syncretism, for this was already dealt with in the first commandment. There remains only *magic*,[39] a very substantial realm of reality in ancient Israel, the importance of which is stressed in our study on Psalm 22.[40] At any rate, the Decalogue, with its insistence on the honor due to God and the respect due to God's, as well as to man's human partner, may be understood as an explanation of the Name. There cannot be any separation in the revelation between the divine Self and the divine Will.

Above, I said that the *Sitz im Wort* of the revelation of the Name, as Childs also rightly insists, is provided by the context of the *Botenspruch*.[41] This situation is all the more remarkable in that the reverse is true in Isaiah, Jeremiah, and Ezekiel, where the *Botenspruch* is imbedded in the proclamation of the statement of recognition. This constitutes a marked difference with the Patriarchal revelations, where there was no commission to transmit a message. Clearly, the tradition of Exodus 3 has been influenced by classic prophetism and by the messenger formula. Within that context, Moses' question in Exodus 3 belongs to the well-known motif of the Prophets' reluctance at the time of their calling. The eventual tactic of luring God into revealing the bearing or meaning of his proper Name is motivated by the shift in the divine activity from relating to the Ancestors as the God of the Fathers (an activity oriented toward the fulfillment of the promise of family expansion and of land inheritance) to the activity of liberating the people from the Egyptian slavery and leading them to the Promised Land. As

39. Cf. Gerhard von Rad, *Deuteronomy*, translated by Dorothea Barton (Philadelphia: Westminster, 1966), p. 57; Josef Schreiner, *Die zehn Gebote im Leben des Gottesvolkes* (Munich: Kösel, 1966), pp. 82f. A. Phillips, *Ancient Israel's Criminal Law* (New York: Schocken, 1970), p. 57, calls attention to the special provision of Exodus 22:17 for the summary execution of a sorceress, for women in general were free from criminal liability.

40. Note that Gese opposes this restriction of the commandment's bearing to magic. He says that the prohibition envisages the entire cultic realm as Exodus 20:24 indicates.

41. Cf. Childs, *The Book of Exodus*, p. 56.

an illustration of this dramatic transition, the P source, for instance, presents the interesting feature of strictly compressing the formula's use within the story of Moses (never in Genesis, for example). This is particularly clear in texts such as Exodus 6:7 (cf. vv. 6–9 on the divine acts); 7:5, 14:4, 17f., 16:12, 29:43–46; Leviticus 23:43. "Yhwh's fundamental beneficial deed on Israel's behalf . . . is the leading out of Egypt. It is no accident that this act completely dominates the statements in Exodus 6:7 and 7:5."[42]

Along with the *Botenspruch* and the divine promise to act in history on Israel's behalf, two more elements also belong to the context of the *Selbstvorstellungsformel*, namely, the prescriptive in its apodictic form, and the cultic "priesterliches Heilsorakel."[43] These were brought together under the overarching category of "Sinai." As regards the latter, one aspect has already been highlighted: the Decalogue as a legal commentary on the divine Name. Now we must shift the emphasis to Sinai as an event, even as the symbolic event par excellence. Strikingly, the formula is closely knit with that event, the paradigm of all subsequent events of the *Heilsgeschichte*, meant, according to their accompanying interpretation, to provoke a *decision* from their audience. "The symbol gives rise to thought," says Paul Ricoeur. Sinai and its related symbols make one think of acknowledgment and commitment. Symbolic or referential events are at home within the priestly and the prophetic spheres; as they are also "in forensic situations where decisions are rendered possible by means of proofs."[44] On that basis, a critical choice must be made between two possibilities. Either one rejects the conviction and its evidence, or one *recognizes* that God is the Lord, Yhwh, the One who is up to his name.

The Holy War, for instance, is such a symbolic event; it eventuates in the recognition of Yhwh. The sign is announced by the prophet in anticipation of its outcome, thus making the latter "meaningful in relationship to a particular recognition process. . . . It gives the historical event caused by Yhwh the status of a decision-making sign directed at human recognition."[45] The same is true of the sign announced by the priest to individuals (cf. 1 Samuel 1). Both in the collective and the

---

42. Zimmerli, *I Am Yahweh*, p. 44.

43. Cf. Joachim Begrich, "Das priesterliche Heilsorakel," *Zeitschrift für die alttestamentliche Wissenschaft* 52 (1934): 81ff. Also, Yhwh is known as the one who sanctifies Israel by means of a sign to be kept, for example, the Sabbath (Exodus 31:12–17; Ezekiel 20:12, 20). The context remains one of divine deeds.

44. Zimmerli, *I Am Yahweh*, p. 77.

45. Ibid., p. 78.

individual contexts, there is reference to the fundamental paradigm of the divine promise made to Moses at Horeb, although there, by contrast, the communion with God is announced without prophetic or priestly intermediary but directly by God in person, without mediation, through the divine Name. The latter, far from being a deviation in the trajectory between the divine and the human, is to be understood as the very communication itself. Consequently, when Moses utters the Name in presence of the Hebrews in Egypt, he provides them with the kind of immediacy he himself has been privileged with. The I-thou relationship opened by the Name demands recognition on the basis of the proof-sign that the name itself constitutes.

The Burning Bush dialogue with Moses, bringing about the revelation of the Name, represents an entirely original event within a general context of proclamation followed by popular or individual recognition. Such statement of recognition stands in all circumstances within the context of proof-signs. In the interpersonal sphere, one finds such a context in trial proceedings about guilt and innocence on the basis of proofs; and in battles such proofs manifest Yhwh's lordship or the credentials of his envoys. But so far as the utterance of the Name is concerned, it itself contains all that needs to be shown and said; it is the sign and its interpretation, without mediation, without hiatus between sign and decoding, between event and meaning. The Name is theophanic and performative, I said. With his Name, God reveals his "most personal mystery. . . . The name encloses the unassailable mystery of his singularity and uniqueness."[46] That is why, as an appellative name, the grammatical proper person is not the third person as in the LXX rendition *ho ôn*, but either the first person, when God speaks, or the second person, when the human responds. More on this will be said below, but here we should note with what extreme care the biblical texts keep alive the primary appellative aspect of the Name, before allowing it to become predicative, namely, "Yhwh."[47] Thus, ostensibly avoiding any indirect reference to the divine Sender in the third-person singular, Moses is commissioned to tell the Hebrews in Egypt, "'*ehyeh* sent me" (Exodus 3:14b). More generally, the demand for recognition is phrased, "and you shall know that I am Yhwh," instead of the simple "know Yhwh," because in the recognition event, Yhwh himself is the subject, not the object.

A necessary conclusion is that, since the Name is itself a symbolic

---

46. Ibid., pp. 81, 83.
47. The distinction between the categories appellative and predicative comes from Paul Ricoeur.

event, its potency (*Wirkung*) is not dependent upon a correct etymological understanding of the root *hyh* and its actual forms in 'ehyeh and *Yahweh.* In fact, says Zimmerli, any attempt to understand the statement of recognition from the meaning of the name "Yhwh" misses the point because of "the mystery that cannot be reduced to a definition—and the irreversible direction of the process of self-introduction."[48] The recognition does not come from some conceptual reflection but from an encounter with Yhwh's self-manifestation. In contrast to the lack of mediation as far as Moses is concerned, the divine *Selbstvorstellung* is mediated to the people by God's emissary proclaiming either divine judgment or divine deeds calling for decision. Similarly, the knowledge/recognition of the lordship of God is no metaphysical knowledge. The Tetragrammaton is no invitation to speculate upon the aseity of God. It does not refer to a divine *causa sui;* on the contrary, it always takes place within very concrete happenings. And the human recognition, on the model of the divine action, "is not an inward, reflective, spiritual occurrence, but rather manifests itself in open, public prostration before Yhwh."[49] In the words of Hartmut Gese, "[God] does not reveal himself *in se,* but as Self."[50]

But it remains that the Name is specifically stated in reference to a shade of meaning conveyed by the Hebrew verb *hyh.* At least, it is that way that tradition has from time immemorial understood its message. "Yhwh," God-as-Agent points to a type of action that the root *hyh* was deemed appropriate to express. Can we come closer to the full meaning of that usage? I think we can. But before we draw any firmer conclusion in this respect, it must be remembered that Moses as the first recipient of the Tetragrammaton, or the Prophets and the priests as secondary recipients, are not merely the receivers of a gift granted by a Communicator. They themselves become part of the communication. Moses, as a prototype, is called to be "God for Aaron" and "for the Pharaoh" (Exodus 4:16; 7:1). The recognition statement thus includes Yhwh's emissaries because Yhwh acts through human vehicles. Witnesses are invited to recognize not only "*Yhwh hu'*" (he [only] is Yhwh), but also "that there has been a prophet among them" (Ezekiel 2:4f.; 33:33). It is thus to be expected that, within the revelation to Moses of the 'ehyeh 'ašer 'ehyeh Moses himself must be present. My contention is that, with

48. Zimmerli, *I Am Yahweh,* p. 153, n. 90; cf. Herbert Haag, *Was lehrt die literarische Untersuchung des Ezekiel-Textes?* (Freiburg: Paulusbrückerei, 1943), p. 35.
49. Zimmerli, *I Am Yahweh,* p. 67.
50. Gese: "er offenbart sich eben nicht an sich, sondern als Selbst" (p. 79).

the revelation of His Name as Yhwh, God tells of himself something like "With you Moses—and with Israel throughout history—I stand or fall!" The revelation is the proclamation that God has invested the whole of himself in his emissary's history. Even his judgment over, and his condemnation of, his people is to be seen from the perspective of God's personal commitment. For the judgment is here not just forensic, it is always close to the lament, "O my people, what have I done to you? In what have I wearied you? Answer me!" (Micah 6:3 NRSV). It is indeed highly paradoxical when exilic Prophets, Ezekiel in the first place, claim that the people will know "that I am Yhwh" when submitted to God's fury (Ezekiel 6:12–14; 12:15f.; 24:24). Ezekiel 23:49, for instance, shows that the Name does not convey only salvation (as in Exodus) but also judgment and condemnation; not only life but also death.[51] Especially noteworthy is Ezekiel 20:44, "and you shall know that I am Yhwh in that I am not dealing with you, for the sake of my Name, according to your evil ways." (The recognition formula occurs six times in Ezekiel 20.) The people's death remains penultimate, Israel shall rise from the dead (cf. Ezekiel 37).

However we define the meaning of the Tetragrammaton, the intimate communion of God and God's people must be emphasized. That is why the identity-formula 'ehyeh 'ašer 'ehyeh refers to a shared history between God and humanity, to a "becoming" of God with Israel, most especially through the liberation from thralldom in Egypt. To Moses in Midian, the God of the Ancestors who manifested himself thus far as El Shadday (Exodus 6:2) reveals his "becoming with," as it were,[52] indeed his "dependence upon" Israel's relationship with him.

Israel never felt capable of plumbing the depths of such an intimacy with its God. Such a mystery it could never comprehend. All the biblical literary genres testify to the fact that Israel, whether in its interpretation of the *Heilsgeschichte* or in its more "atemporal" deliberation, has the sole ambition of spelling out the Name of God.[53] Thus Israel's re-

51. Like the Torah, according to Ezekiel, which is not only good and brings about life, but is also "not good" and brings about death, cf. Ezekiel 20:25f.

52. "As it were" is important here. It indicates the approximation of the statement, incapable as we are to express in a satisfactory way the dialectical movement in God of his transcendence and immanence. Abraham Heschel said, "God remains transcendent in his immanence, and related in his transcendence." See his *The Prophets* (New York: Harper and Row, 1962), p. 486. Eberhard Jüngel, *God as the Mystery of the World* (Grand Rapids: Eerdmans, 1983), p. 328, writes, "He loves another one and thus is and remains himself."

53. For we all are little children, says Tennessee Williams (*Suddenly Last Summer*), playing with alphabet blocks and trying endlessly to spell out the Ineffable Name.

flection went in two parallel directions, the one toward human identity, established and fulfilled in the relationship with Yhwh; the other toward divine identity, no less established and fulfilled in the relationship with Israel. Understandably, the texts are a great deal more cautious and sober regarding the second direction of thought. They preclude any semblance of irreverence by magnifying, extolling, and blessing the Name of God. Praise is the proper human response to revelation, rather than speculation on how it is that God made himself dependent on the human to be Yhwh, as the human is dependent on the divine to be the imago Dei. To the extent that praise is also reflexive, it gave birth to the notion of *berit*, covenant, which Hosea, for instance, equates with matrimonial union.

Consequently, most philosophical speculations on the Divine are in need of a radical revision. The philosophical concepts of transcendence, omnipotence, infinitude must be considered *sub specie historiae*, instead of *sub specie aeternitatis et absoluti*. God's omnipotence is more the expression of Israel's prayer, hope, faith, and love than an objective statement of fact. So are also transcendence and eternity or any other divine "attribute" speculatively discovered within God. True, God *is* transcendent and eternal, but he is this and that "to the extent"—if such a parlance is fitting—that his love, care, and commitment transcend and overcome human godlessness. Another way to express this is through predicating the divine attributes with the qualification "eschatological." At the *eschaton*, God will be God (cf. Isaiah 11:9; Psalm 110:1; 1 Corinthians 15:24–28.). Meanwhile, God is in the process of establishing his lordship, his Kingdom on earth. *'ehyeh 'ašer 'ehyeh*, he says, and the unaccomplished form of the verb must be taken in all seriousness. I will be what I will be; I will become what I will become. There is here an uncannily taut drama concentrated in the relative pronoun *ašer* (what), for its content essentially depends on the quality of history that Moses and his people will pour into it.

Because God is God, he might have chosen for himself to be a Zeus, a Brahma, or a Baal. There is something of that theism conveyed in the name *Elohim* given to the Living God. Elohim creates heaven and earth by his word. Elohim demands the sacrifice of the beloved unique son Isaac. Elohim sits in heaven and laughs.[54] But Elohim chooses to be *Elohei* Abraham/Isaac/Jacob; and this genitival form of his name already indicates that he makes himself vulnerable through initiating a

54. Cf. Psalm 2.

relationship with someone else. God ties himself with the human. Elohim—a name derived from a common noun—is one aspect (or one attribute) of the Living God. The other aspect/attribute is conveyed by a name-of-invocation, Yhwh. God thus ceases to be the Unnameable, the inaccessible, the one *a se et per se*. He ceases to be impassible—if he ever was. Yhwh is "emotional," changing, affected. He repents (Genesis 6:6f.; Exodus 32:14; 1 Samuel 15:11, 35; Amos 7:3; etc.), and he laments (in Jeremiah 8:5, for instance, we read, "Why then has this people turned away in perpetual backsliding?" cf. 12:7–13, 15:5–9, 18:13–17). We can also think of the book of Hosea whose style, says Hans W. Wolff, "vacillates between compassionate lament and bitter accusation. . . . It testifies to the fact that God is wrestling with himself."[55] He can be cursed or blessed, ignored or praised. If justice triumphs, it is only because it is justice, by its intrinsic force, which is persuasive, not coercive. Justice triumphs in the prayer, faith, hope, and love, of those who seek justice. God is God only through the proclamation of his people: *Yhwh malakh!* (God reigns! cf. Psalm 93:1, 96:10, 97:1, 99:1, etc.). In this acclamation is redeemed the human abandonment of God reported in the myth of Genesis 2–3. God's risky wager, which he lost from the outset of creation, is now salvaged in Israel's liturgy celebrated in the Temple. Jon Levenson cites this incredibly compact Midrash on Isaiah 43:12:

> "So you are my witnesses, declares the Lord, and I am God." That is, if you are My witnesses I am God, and if you are not My witnesses, I am, as it were, not God.[56]

As we saw above, what prevents *'ehyeh* from being an ontological declaration about the divine essence is the first person in the present tense of the form. Paul Ricoeur speaks of "attestation of existence in the sense of efficiency."[57] The Name is "performative" and has a *Wirkungsgeschichte*. It is not in any kind of superdetermination that it performs, but on the contrary through its indeterminacy,[58] thus conveying a "surplus of meaning" that overwhelmed Moses in Midian and the people of Israel ever since. In this respect, the "appellative" aspect of the for-

---

55. Hans Walter Wolff, *Hosea* (Neukirchen-Vluyn: Neukirchener Verlag, 1967), p. 151.

56. *Sifre Deuteronomy* 346 (in Finkelstein ed.). Quoted by Jon Levenson, *Creation and the Persistence of Evil* (San Francisco: Harper and Row, 1988), p. 139.

57. Paul Ricoeur, "Sur l'exégèse de Gen 1.1–2.4a," in *Exégèse et herméneutique* (Paris: Seuil, 1971).

58. *Pace* Childs, in *The Book of Exodus*, who rejects the idea of "indefiniteness" in the paronomasis of Exodus 3:14.

mula is all important because the first person "is experienced by contrast (with a *you*). It is this condition of dialogue that is constitutive of *person*, for it implies that reciprocally *I* becomes *you* . . . *I* posits another person, the one who, being as he is, completely external to 'me,' becomes my echo to whom I say *you* and who says *you* to me."[59] This means that God and his vis-à-vis are, so to speak, in a syntagmatic relation, in a mutual contrast that defines both.[60] In the Talmud, *Abodah Zarah* 19a presents this moving insight: the Torah is given to the one who studies it in the name of Yhwh, "but in the end it will be called in his [the student's] name." In the end the student will see that the Torah is his own first person speaking and thus witness the fulfillment of the promise of Jeremiah 31:33.

But the "appellative" shifts to the "predicative" for the sake of narration. In the Psalms, for instance, God "is identified in 'who' clauses which may be a narrative reduced to a single sentence . . . 'who brought you out of the land of Egypt.' Psalm 136 . . . is a long chain of 'who' clauses . . . [indicating that God is] a participant in the story of the people."[61] Also in Deuteronomy 26 and in Second Isaiah, all the *Heils-geschichte*'s events are reduced to a single account of deliverance.[62]

Within Israel's consciousness, the Exodus inaugurates not only its history as a people (for the first time Israel is called an *'am*, a nation), but also the world's redemption. The exodus from Egypt is toward the Promised Land, the microcosm and "bridge-head" from where the whole of creation has started its transfiguration into the Kingdom of God. The Exodus is thus *the* event par excellence, the "V-Day" of history, the day when the world is changed into itself by eternity.

In the Greek mind, "the world is eternal. It can have no goal. It can only be. . . . In a general way, what is important for the Greek is neither

---

59. Emile Benveniste, *Problems in General Linguistics*, vol. 1, translated by M. E. Meek (Coral Gables: University of Miami Press, 1971), pp. 224f.

60. As says Jacques Derrida, "Whether He is Being or the master of beings, God himself is, and appears as what He is, within difference, that is to say, as difference within dissimulation." In *Writing and Difference*, translated by Alan Blass (Chicago: University of Chicago Press, 1978), p. 74.

61. Bernard Anderson, *Out of the Depths: The Psalms Speak for Us Today* (Philadelphia: Westminster, 1983), p. 142.

62. Deuteronomy 26:17f. is a late formulation but in its substance is called by Julius Wellhausen, "the beginning and abiding principle" of Israel's history. It reads, "Today it is YHWH whom you brought to declare that he becomes your God, that you will walk in his paths, keep his statutes and his commandments and his ordinances, that you will obey his voice. And YHWH brought you today to declare that you become his treasured people according to his promise, and to keep his commandments."

to become nor to own, neither to be able nor to will; it is to be."[63] José Faur adds: "Therefore physical phenomena cannot signify."[64] It is precisely here that the distinction between Athens and Jerusalem is the strongest, namely, on the problem of metaphysics. Whereas a Jew deeply influenced by Hellenism, such as Moses Mendelssohn, proposes the translation of Exodus 3.14, "I am the Being, who is eternal,"[65] Maimonides asks us to think of God as of an agent with a purpose, not as a being with an essence (*Guide* 1.54–58). God is what God does, he says.

If there still be any doubt regarding the dynamic *wirkung* of the Tetragrammaton, all such skepticism disappears when we turn to the traditional reading of Exodus 3, to its trajectory. *Hayah*, at the basis of the Name, means in the agadic tradition *to be with, to be like*.[66] In *Midrash Agadah*: "As you are (*howeh ata*) with me, so I am (*howeh 'ani*) with you." *Exodus Rabba* 3:6 reads: "*'ani še-hayiti 'ani hu' wa-'ani hu' la-'atid*—I who used to be the One is I who shall be the One (for the word *'ehyeh* occurs three times in the sacred text). Also the ninth century Saadia Gaon stresses God's eternity: "for he is the first and the last" (Isaiah 44:6; cf. Revelation 1:4, see 4:8). *Mekhilta Baḥodesh* 5 on Exodus 20:2 wonders, "Why are not the Ten Utterances [the Decalogue] at the beginning of the Torah? Because God wanted first to build trust by his gracious deeds towards Israel; then He said I shall rule over you, and they answered 'yes, indeed.' . . . So as not to give the nations of the world a chance to say that there were two Dominions, [Scripture says], 'I the Lord am your God'—I was in Egypt; I was at the sea; I was at Sinai; I was in the past; I will be in the future; I am in this world and I will be in the world-to-come!' as it is written" (the Mekhilta quotes Deuteronomy 32:39; Isaiah 46:4, 44:6, 41:4).

As can be expected, the situation is similar in the Targum. Of particular interest is the text of *Targum Onkelos* (in a version unknown but to Nahmanides), "I am like the one with whom I am." Exodus 3:14b in

63. Kostas Papaioannou, "Nature and History in the Greek Conception of the Cosmos," *Diogenes* 25 (1959): 5, 9.

64. José Faur, *Golden Doves with Silver Dots* (Bloomington: Indiana University Press, 1986), p. xxii.

65. Moses Mendelssohn, *Zweistromland* in *Gesammelte Schriften* (Leipzig: Brockhaus, 1843), p. 804.

66. Cf. in the patriarchal stories: "I will be with you" (Genesis 26:3, 24–28, 28:15, 31:3, 39:2, 3, 21, 31). The same situation obtains in David's covenant, cf. 2 Samuel 7 (passim). See also Qur'an 20:11–24.

Targum Yerushalmi I reads: "I who was, who am, and who shall be, sends me to you." In *Targum Yerushalmi II* (fragment):[67] "The one who says to the world . . . be! and it is; and who will say to it: be! and it is. . . . It is He who sent me to you." (This reading recalls the interpretation of W. F. Albright, D. N. Freedman, F. M. Cross, etc. cited above). Let us also mention the following remarks of Nahmanides: The miracle in not in the Name per se; "it is rather in the invocation of the Name. . . . In my opinion, the ancient Israelites had no doubt regarding the existence of the Creator. . . . God said (to Moses): 'This will you tell the children of Israel: *'ehyeh* sent me to you.' It was so that Moses invoke before them a name that is unique, alone, and so give them also a lesson of the oneness of God." The fourteenth-century *Zohar Wayyiqra*, t. III, fo. 11a says: "*Ehyeh*, it is the supreme occultation. . . . 'I, it is Myself.' . . . *'ašer 'ehyeh*, it is I who am about to reveal Myself. . . . *Ehyeh* is 'the mother become pregnant.' . . . *Yhwh* is the blossoming stage of the All."[68] Earlier, Rashi had paraphrased *'ehyeh 'ašer 'ehyeh* thus, "I shall be with them in this misery as I shall be with them in their slavery to other empires . . ."[69]

As for the early Church, it saw in the coming of Christ the fulfillment of the promise contained in the Name of God. The *factum externum* that brings about the statement of recognition is now the Word become flesh. 1 Corinthians 12:3b daringly states, "No one can say 'Jesus is *kurios*' (Lord) except by the Holy Spirit" (cf. 1 John 4:2f.: "every spirit that confesses that Jesus Christ has come in the flesh is from God"). Falling in parallel with *Targum Yerushalmi I* on Exodus 3:14b, mentioned above, Revelation 1:8 puts in God's mouth: "I am . . . the one who is, who was, and who is to come [*ho erchomenos*]," an idea already expressed in Isaiah 4:6, "the first and the last." We can find an echo of this in Philo who rendered Exodus 3:14, "I am he who *is*" and added in way of commentary, "No name at all can properly be used of Me, to Whom alone existence belongs" (*Vita Mosis* I.75).

---

67. A parallel to which is found in *Targum Neofiti*.

68. Master Eckart speaks of a "parturition of the self."

69. Rabbinic literature goes in the sense followed by Rashi. It is said that the discrepancy between *'ehyeh 'ašer 'ehyeh* in the first part of the verse 14 of Exodus 3 and *'ehyeh* in the second part finds its explanation as follows: *'ehyeh* means "I shall be with you in the servitude of Egypt," while *'ehyeh 'ašer 'ehyeh* means this *and* that God will be with them in further servitudes to come. Thus, to spare the Hebrews in Egypt, Moses was ordered to speak in the Name of only *'ehyeh* to conceal the other servitudes to come. (So Jacob b. Abina in the name of R. Huna of Sepphoris; *Exodus Rabba* 3:6.) Note this compassionate dealing with the people which amounts to a "teleological suspension of the ethical" à la Kierkegaard, says Jacob L. Halevi in *Judaism* 4 (1955): 13–28 and 8 (1959): 291–302.

In the Hebrew Scripture, the recognition of the Name is not only expected from Israel; it is also the eschatological goal of the divine revelation on Zion, "Be still and know that I am God [Yhwh]. I am exalted among the nations, I am exalted in the earth" (Psalm 46:11 [10]). Consistent with its claim to point to the eschatological fulfillment of the old promise, the New Testament saw this knowledge of the Living God spread over the whole world with the coming of Christ. Probably no other text surpasses in this respect in clarity and decisiveness the following reinterpretation from a Christological viewpoint of the recognition formula: John 17:6 reads, "I have made your Name known to those whom you gave me from the world . . . now they know . . . in truth that I came from you."

From Interpretation to Translation

PAUL RICOEUR

In my complement to André LaCocque's essay, I would like to begin from the difficulty attached to the act of translating the *'ehyeh 'ašer 'ehyeh* of Exodus 3:14. A long history of translation into languages other than Hebrew, beginning with Greek and Latin, separates us from the original text as well as from the way in which it was understood by its initial audience, and all the more so for that reason from the presumed intention of its author. What is more, because the LXX (Septuagint) translated 3:14 as *ego eimi ho ôn,* and the Latins by *sum qui sum,* Exodus 3:14 was to exercise on all of Western thought the influence whose breadth and depth I shall refer to below. The Greek translation has to be considered a veritable event in thinking. The semantic field of the Hebrew verb *hyh* found itself linked in an enduring manner to that of the Greek verb *einai,* then to the Latin verb *esse,* where these verbs bring into the field of translation a broad conceptual history, stemming principally from the philosophies of Plato and Aristotle, and therefore from modes of thought that antedate the translation of the LXX. This history of meaning continued on, interconnected with that of the Hebrew and Christian Bibles, through the Greek and Latin fathers, then by way of the age of Scholasticism and its giants (Bonaventure, Thomas Aquinas, Duns Scotus), to include even Descartes and the Cartesians, up to Kant and beyond; that is, until it reaches us, readers of the Bible, situated at the end of this tumultuous history of the relationship between God and Being.

We might deplore this encounter. Today some even try to unknot the bonds woven from it. But we cannot undo that this encounter occurred, nor that it contributed to the intellectual and spiritual identity of the Christian West. Adolf von Harnack's program of "dehellenizing Christianity," to cite just one example, would not make sense other than as a momentary break in this struggle where Athens stands over against Jerusalem. This is so true that contemporary efforts to translate, if not better, at least in another way, our well-known verse all bear the mark of this struggle with the Greek source of philosophy and fundamental theology. (I shall consider a few of these efforts at the end of this chapter.)

Let us draw an initial lesson from these opening remarks. There is no innocent translation; I mean one that could escape the history of reception of our text, a history that itself is immediately a history of interpretation. To translate is already to interpret. The scholarly work of exegetes such as Albright, Childs, Gese, Sarna, and Zimmerli (to cite just those most often mentioned by André LaCocque), and even LaCocque himself, do not escape this constraint. They all belong to this long history of reading and interpretation. This assertion, we need to be clear, is not equivalent to a criticism of scholarly exegesis. On the contrary, the struggle for another translation, for another interpretation, draws its force from this struggle with a multimillenary tradition. Modern exegetes are like us. They work and think at the end of a history. In this sense, the one thing that would be criticizable would be the naive claim of an exegesis that held itself to be without a history, as though it were possible to coincide, without the mediation of a tradition of reading, with the original signification of a text, even with the presumed intention of its author.

The Enigmas of the Text

Before taking up a few of the central moments in the so-called ontological reading of Exodus 3:14, I would like to emphasize certain features of our text, which, despite the quasi obsessive distrust of exegetes as regards what to them seems to be only a speculative abstraction, give rise to a perplexity of such a nature as to make, if not legitimate, at least plausible, the so-called ontological reading.

First of all, I want to emphasize the gap that seems to me to exist between, on the one hand, Exodus 3:14 and the group of biblical texts bearing generally on the quest for the Unknown Name and, on the other hand, those texts that gravitate around the expression "I [am] Yhwh."

As regards the former group, André LaCocque begins his essay by usefully recalling the history of the name Yhwh. When set against this background of the quest for the Unknown Name of Power, Moses' question, which is answered in Exodus 3:14, seems still to depend on the magical conception of the name that existed throughout the ancient Near East.[1] But what in fact is the answer? LaCocque quite rightly replies: In his answer, "God transcends the ambiguous request and somewhat impure intention of Moses" (p. 312). In what way does the answer escape the magical sphere of the question? What gap is suggested between the question and the answer "I am what I am"?

What comes into consideration here is the formula "I am Yhwh" or "I am Yhwh your God," which Zimmerli and LaCocque characterize as God's self-presentation, and the complementary formula of recognition on the part of the people: "You shall recognize that I [am] Yhwh."[2] Here self-presentation and recognition form an asymmetrical pair in which the one who presents himself holds the initiative, the recognition implying a "responsive" attitude. In this respect, it is noteworthy that in Leviticus 18 this formula frames as its introduction and conclusion a normative discourse. To the extent that the first commandment is the one that forbids any figurative representation of God, it is legitimate to expect that Exodus 3:14, when joined to this group of texts, will be drawn toward the side of ethics and of the *incognito* of the one who enjoins it. Nevertheless a significant gap seems to me to remain between Exodus 3:14 and all those formulas where the name Yhwh is set in the position of the divine "I" without the mediation of a copulative "is," which is rare if nonexistent in Hebrew.[3] This absence of a copulative

---

1. As André LaCocque points out, the texts collected in *ANET* set in relief the magical power attached to the "unknown Name" and conferred upon humans who succeed in figuring it out.

2. Walther Zimmerli, *Ich bin Yhwh, Geschichte und Altes Testament* (Tübingen, 1963); Karl Elliger, "Ich bin der Herr—Euer Gott," in *Kleineschriften zum Alten Testament,* edited by Hartmut Gese and O. Kaiser (Munich 1966), pp. 211–31; André-Marie Dubarle, "La signification du nom de Yahweh," *Revue de Sciences philosophiques et théologiques* 35 (1951): 3–21.

3. Cf. André Caquot, "Les énigmes d'un hémistiche biblique," in *Dieu et l'Etre. Exégèses d'Exode 3,14 et de Coran 20, 11–24* (Paris: Etudes Augustiniennes, 1978), pp. 17–26. Caquot notes that "the verb *hàyàh* can cease expressing the lexical notion of existence and take on the function of a simple copula by adding a temporal modality" (p. 18). (For example, see Genesis 29:17; 2 Samuel 15:34.) But he also adds, "It is useful to recall these few phrases drawn from passages where one often senses the influence or imitation of a more everyday language in order to appreciate the enigmatic response of God talking to Moses, but we cannot forget that this enigmatic character depends in great part on the fact that this expression has no parallel in biblical phraseology" (p. 19). From another perspective, Henri Cazelles, "Pour une exégèse de Exode 3,14, Texte et Contexte," *Dieu et l'Etre,* pp. 27–44, insists that "this verb in Hebrew is never a copula, but rather signifies an existence, an active presence" (pp. 29 and 33). Still, for Caquot, the principal point is:

"is," whose use is required in our languages, renders all the more surprising the *'ehyeh* by which Exodus 3:14 breaks with all the expressions of the form "I [am] Yhwh." The comparison between 3:14 and the formulas under consideration stops precisely at the threshold of this *'ehyeh*.

The grammatical enigma that the recourse to the semantic field of the verbal root *hyh* constitutes is accentuated even further in that the first *'ehyeh* is strangely redoubled into the form of an onomastasis that places the second *'ehyeh* in a predicative position. The enigma is, if I may put it this way, tripled by the reappearance of the same *'ehyeh* in the position of a subject in the first-person singular with a vocative value in Exodus 3:14b. It is this third appearance that will cause the greatest problem in the history of interpretation owing to the Greek translation *ho ôn*, already in 3:14a and again in 3:14b. The Vulgate, unlike the Greek, follows the Hebrew in the repetition of the first two *'ehyeh* as *sum* in 3:14a but continues on the model of the Greek in 3:14b: *qui est misit me ad vos.*

Our perplexity increases if it is true that the Tetragrammaton itself belongs to the semantic field of the same verb traditionally translated by "to be."

Here is where the translator runs into a wall.[4] As legitimate as it may be to emphasize in a commentary the opening toward the future and the mark of becoming and dynamism, to the same extent it remains

---

If the first *'ehyeh* has a predicative value as a declaration of identity, it is the second one that bears the more Hebraic than Greek connotations, that is, the dynamic idea of an actual presence. But, if the second *'ehyeh* is equally predicative, "we are in the presence of a tautology that comes down to a pure and simple refusal to answer. If the very 'being' is 'existential' here, God is content to remain discrete about the way in which he manifests himself in general or will manifest himself when the time comes, and the translation 'I will be what I will be' is at least as legitimate as 'I am what I am'" (p. 21). Finally, "if we give up seeing in *'ehyeh* the transcription of a theonymy or the adaptation of *yihyeh* to the first person, 'he is' equals YHWH, we may say that the divine declaration of Exodus 3:14a has its raison d'être in itself: God reveals his existence even while concealing his identity, and the first word of this declaration, *'ehyeh*, taking the place of the proper name Moses expects, becomes in what Moses must say to the Israelites, a pseudonym of God and figures in this way in the hemistich 14b" (p. 24).

4. Along with André LaCocque, I salute the contribution of G. S. Ogden to the grammatical and semantic discussion. In the same way, H. Cazelles in the article already cited takes as his guideline in the second part of his essay the progression from the question about identity through the phases of the call narrative. What is in question then is the name of the "sender." It remains that "in the present state of the text the desire to set in relief the verb 'being' is indicated by the fact that, from one sentence to the next, the first person in the form 'HYH, to the third person in the form YHWH, in a way conjugates the verb 'being'" (p. 33). The translation of August Dillmann, cited by André LaCocque, which uses *der Seiende*, although implying a nuance of activity and life, does not distance itself radically from the semantic field of the German *Sein*, a point I shall return to below.

doubtful that in a translation into a modern language one can do without the verb "being" or without verbal forms belonging to the same semantic field. The underlying issue of this discussion is twofold. It has to do, first of all, with the degree of polysemy that we grant to the verb "being." In this regard, we will not cease asking whether the Hebrew *'ehyeh* does not suggest an extension of meaning to the Greek *einai* and the Latin *esse* beyond the plurivocity explored by philosophy with its Greek and Latin origins. Beyond this semantic question, the second fundamental question is whether, in commentaries that explicate a translation, we must guard against "any ontological abstraction regarding being," as André LaCocque demands. The remainder of my remarks will consist in great part in a discussion of this warning. The paradox, as we shall see, is that the most audacious ontological considerations of the medieval thinkers stand in complete opposition to an "abstract" or "essential" conception of being, precisely under the impact of Exodus 3:14. In this sense, however ontological they may be, these philosophers agree with the refusal of any claim to intellectual mastery recommended by André LaCocque.

I would like now to explore another source of perplexity concerning the actual signification of Exodus 3:14. It results from the fact that our text takes place or arises within the course of a "call narrative."[5] Within this narrative framework, it fits closely with the formulas of commissioning, sending, and a mandate characteristic of the whole family of call narratives.[6] The question I want to ask is whether Exodus 3:14 does not overflow the narrative framework of a call narrative, just as it breaks with the formulas belonging to the family of statements that say "I [am]

5. In his study of the *Sitz im Leben* of the revelation of the Name, André LaCocque emphasizes, on the one hand, with Brevard Childs, the context of the *Botenspruch*, of the "formula of the messenger," followed by the motif of the prophet's reticence; on the other hand, with Joachim Begrich, he also underscores the importance of the prescriptive dimension conferred on the interpretation of the Name owing to this narrative's being set alongside that of the Sinai event. The expected acknowledgment has to be one marked by a highly ethical overtone.

6. Norman Habel, "The Form and Significance of the Call Narratives," *Zeitschrift für alttestamentliche Wissenschaft* (1965): 297–329, examines seven stylized narratives: the call of Gideon in Judges 6:11–17, of Moses in Exodus 3:1–12, of Jeremiah in Jeremiah 1:4–10, of Isaiah in Isaiah 6:1–13, of Ezekiel 1:1–3:15, and of Second Isaiah in Isaiah 40:1–11. From them he draws a *Gattungsstruktur* made up of six episodes: confrontation with God, introductory speeches, the mission properly speaking, objection of the one being sent, reassurance accompanied by an oath, the giving of a sign. In Exodus 3, the episode of the Burning Bush corresponds to the confrontation; the call "Moses, Moses" and the answer "Here I am" are the opening speeches; the "now go" of 3:10 is the call properly speaking, followed by the objections. It is to one of these objections that the "I am who I am" is the response. As for the word of reassurance, here it is repeated along with the crescendo of objections coming from Moses.

Yhwh." The call narrative (Exodus 3:1–4:7)[7] opens with the vision of the burning bush, to which is added the call coming from God: "Moses! Moses!" Moses responds: "Here I am!" This response already counts as the recognition of a presence that is all the more imperious in that it is marked by the spectacle of the bush that is burning yet is not consumed (3:3). The vocation story might have ended at this point. It goes on thanks to a narrative procedure that consists of a series of five objections raised by Moses despite his previous, apparently unequivocal reply. To the first objection "who am I to . . . ?" God responds: "I shall be with you." Is this reassurance not sufficient? No. Moses again objects: "But if [the children of Israel] ask what is his name [the name of God, of the God of the fathers who sends the prophet], what shall I answer them?" It is to this objection that the *'ehyeh 'ašer 'ehyeh* is the response. The place of this formula therefore is not unimportant. The Revelation of the Name—this is the title usually used for this fragment—is the reply to an objection that itself constitutes one segment of a call narrative. So it seems reasonable to take the formula in Exodus 3:14 as an emphatic expansion of the self-presentation of God, intended to reinforce the authority of the mandated prophet but reaffirming the authority of the sender. Yet, to obtain such an effect, was there really a need for such an accumulation of enigmas? I mean, as we have seen, the recourse to the semantic field of *hyh*, the use of the first person of the imperfect, the paronomasis linked to the doubling of the *'ehyeh*, and the repetition of the second *'ehyeh*, which transforms the predicative name into an appellative one, not to speak of the substitution of the name Yhwh for the third *'ehyeh*, which stands in the same grammatical position: "'Yhwh, the God of your fathers,' has sent me to you. 'This is the name I shall bear forever, by which future generations will call upon me'" (3:15).

It seems to me that our reading can legitimately oscillate between a minimizing and an amplifying reading of this chain of *'ehyeh*'s culminating in the Tetragrammaton. The minimizing reading is warranted by the narrative frame of Exodus 3:14 and dissuades the reader from over-estimating and hypostatizing the threefold *'ehyeh*, this accumulation only serving to authenticate the mandate by a kind of rhetorical emphasis. The ontological emphasis I shall speak of below would in this way be the combined effect of an exegetical misunderstanding, a misreading

---

7. Re the call of Moses, cf. Brevard S. Childs, "The Call of Moses," in his commentary on the book of Exodus. *The Book of Exodus: A Critical, Theological Commentary* (Philadelphia: Westminster, 1974), pp. 47–89.

of the sense of the Hebrew when it is translated into Greek and, especially, of the projecting into the text of interpretations accumulated over
the centuries through ontological speculation. Back to exegetical sobri-
ety! Let us look for the meaning of Exodus 3:14 only in its function,
and let us replace the so-called metaphysics of the Name where it belongs within the ethical orbit of the mandate.[8]

The amplifying reading begins from the fact that no other call narrative appeals to the rich semantic field to which belong the threefold
'ehyeh and the Tetragrammaton itself. Something is said in this way and
pointed to that exceeds the narrative framework of Exodus 3 and that
sets itself beyond the interplay of questions and answers that serves in
a way to screen this precious gift. Something is said about the mandate
itself, something that has the power to authenticate itself in another
manner than in terms of all those other formulas that do not contain
the enigma of this passage. And precisely because this formula exceeds
its context, its meaning outruns its function. This excess, this supplementary signified, creates an exceptional hermeneutical situation, namely, the
opening to a plurality of interpretations of the verb used here.

It is this hermeneutical situation that is reflected in the commentaries
and attempted translations within the Jewish tradition itself.[9] It is striking that expressions such as "being with"—not to speak of those that
find their origin elsewhere than in Exodus 3:14: "I was, I am, I shall
be"—do not break away from the verb "being," but rather explore its
resources, which would remain unexploited if Hebraic thought, followed by Christian thought, had not itself been transferred into the
space of Greek thought. Here is an occasion to repeat what was said
in my introduction to this essay: translation belongs to the history of
reading, itself governed by the "history of effects"—the *Wirkungsgeschichte*—of the words themselves.

8. André LaCocque seems to favor what I am calling a minimizing reading when he draws on
the force of the ethical commitment constitutive of the recognition that responds to the proclamation, along with the personal engagement of God, which is an integral part of his self-presentation.
The formula in Exodus 3:14 thus comes down to a "history shared by God and man." However,
he also agrees with Zimmerli in saying that, through his name, God reveals the "most personal
mystery. . . . The name includes the most personal . . . it includes the inaccessible mystery of his
singularity and its uniqueness." This is why I can only partly accept his assertion that "consequently, most philosophical speculations on the Divine are in need of a radical revision. The philosophical concepts of transcendence, omnipotence, and infinitude must be considered *sub specie
historiae*, instead of *sub specie aeternitatis et absoluti*." I recognize that he does not exclude philosophical speculation, but rather calls for a revision of its classical forms. I shall return to this question at the close of this essay.

9. See above, pp. 327–29.

It is impossible not to say something about the initial role exercised within this history of effects by the LXX translation, which introduced the use of the Greek verb *einai*, which was to be followed by the Latin *esse*. We need first to notice that this choice can claim the right of a translation/interpretation that, even if it was contingent, nonetheless bears the authority conferred upon it by an intellectual and spiritual fruitfulness whose effects are not yet exhausted. Next, let us observe that this choice was not unexpected. It happened at a moment when the Hellenization of Jewish culture was more advanced than has until recently been recognized.

In this regard, Philo constitutes an especially noteworthy witness. He, who has been called "the most eminent representative of Helle-nized Judaism,"[10] took the Greek translation of the LXX, where God designates himself with the words *ego eimi ho ôn*, to be inspired. This formulation, inspired on the one hand by the Hellenic conception of Being and on the other by the use of the masculine *ho ôn*, continued to evoke the personal God of Israel better than could the neuter *to on*, which was customary in the philosophical discourse of the day. Yet this did not prevent Philo's interpretation of *ego eimi ho ôn* from seeing itself as a prolongation of Platonism. Thus, in Mos. I:75, he says that the opposition that separates the God of Israel from the false gods redou-bles the opposition that separates "what is" from "what is not" and also what separates real being from mere opined existence. Whereas every-thing changes, God remains immutable. For God, existence is not sub-ject to *genesis*. We may find it surprising that, following the Plato of the *Timeaeus* and the Seventh Letter, Philo can hold that no proper name can designate God. "Reflections concerning the absence of a proper name for designating God could have been suggested to a Hellenized Jew, like Philo, by the fact that the Tetragrammaton does not appear in the Septuagint. Contrary to *'ehyeh 'ašer 'ehyeh*, *ego eimi ho ôn* does not constitute an explication of the Tetragrammaton. God reveals to Mo-ses, not his Name, but that he exists."[11] Philo will not be the only one to take the ineffable aspect of God to be a philosophical truth. Exodus 3:14 strengthens him in this conviction. "I am the one who is" is equiva-lent to "my nature is to be, not to be said." In this way, through a subtle intermixing of the Hebraic and the Hellenistic, the fusion between a

10. E. Starobinski and Alexandre Safran, "Exode 3,14 dans l'oeuvre de Philon d'Alexandrie," in *Dieu et l'Etre*, pp. 47–55.
11. Ibid., p. 50.

positive ontology and an ascetic suspension of the Name is announced, under the aegis of the verb *einai*.[12]

However, neither the authority of Philo, nor that of the Greek philosophers of late antiquity, would have sufficed to acclimatize the Greek *einai* to the biblical setting if the New Testament itself, written and published in Greek, had not served as a relay point between these two cultures, at least on the plane of the vocabulary for being. Here the Book of Revelation and the Gospel of John stand out as contributing to this fusion of vocabularies. We read in Revelation 1:4: *ho ôn kai ho ên kai ho eikhomenos*. "The one who is, and who was, and who is coming." There can be no doubt that this formula, repeated five times (in 1:4 and 8; 11:17; 16:51; and 4:8), is meant to retranslate Exodus 3:14.[13] And the Gospel of John states: "Before Abraham was, I am" (8:58).[14] These

---

12. An important further testimony worth adding is that some Greek philosophers in late antiquity made the infinitive *einai* the name of God. See C. J. Vogel, "Antike Seinsphilosophie und Christentum im Wandel der Jahrhunderte," in *Festgabe Joseph Lortz* (1958), vol. 1, pp. 527–48, and "*Ego sum qui sum* et sa signification pour une philosophie chrétienne," *Revue des Sciences Religieuses* 35 (1961): 337–55. Vogel shows that the identification between God and Being was Greek before it was Christian and that the translation of the LXX was probably inspired by Greek philosophy. The most noteworthy text in this respect is Plutarch, *De E apud Delphos*, 17–20, in *Dialogues Pythiques,* edited and translated by Falcelière (Paris: Belles Lettres, 1974). Pierre Hadot adds the testimony of a commentary on Plato's *Parmenides* (which he attributes to Porphyry) where the One of the first hypothesis is interpreted in terms of Plotinus's One, which is above Being. The interesting point is that the author of this commentary is willing to risk attributing to Plato himself the secret teaching according to which this One would be "neither Existing, nor Essence, nor Act, but rather acts, is itself *pure acting* such that it is itself the 'being' (*to einai*) that is before Existing." See Pierre Hadot, "Dieu comme acte d'être dans le néo-platonisme. A propos des théories de E. Gilson sur la métaphysique de l'Exode," in *Dieu et l'Etre*, p. 57. (This essay is reprinted in a slightly modified version in *E. Gilson et nous: le philosophe et son histoire* [Paris: Vrin, 1980], pp. 117–21). What is surprising about this text attributed to Porphyry is that the infinitive "being" is considered higher than every other substantive term, particularly every verbal tense implying a subject and a predicate. As Hadot comments, on the basis of the Greek syntax, "the Greek word that indicates the infinitive *aparemphaton* is opposed to the indicative. The indicative necessarily implies a subject—that is, a determined person and a determined number. The infinitive is nonindicative—that is, it abstracts itself from any person or number. It is without any relation to a subject or a multiplicity. It fits perfectly with the One. But at the same time it allows a certain representation of transcendental reality. Hence it appears as an infinite and absolute activity" (ibid., p. 61). And he concludes: "By way of the intermediary of Boetheus, it is quite likely once again Greek philosophy that exercised its influence on the constitution of the theology of Being" (ibid., p. 63).

13. In Revelation 4:8, the divine name is conjoined with the *trisagion* of Isaiah 6:3: "Holy, Holy / Lord, God Master of Everything. / He was / He is / and He is coming."

14. We should also cite 8:23–24; 8:28; 13:19; and 18:5. Cf. A. Feuillet, "Les *egô eimi* christologiques du Quatrième Evangile," *Recherches de Sciences Religieuses* 54 (1966): 5–22 and 213–40. In the first part of this article, Feuillet takes up the abbreviated from of *egô eimi*, in the second part, the developed forms: the way, the truth, the life, the light, the resurrection, the bread of life, the

uses of the verb *einai* are all the more significant in that they are extended from God to Christ. This christological use of the Greek *einai* (and subsequently of the Latin *esse*) will accompany us as we move through the Greek and Latin fathers to the Christian Middle Ages.

This impressive convergence of Philo, pagan theologians, and especially the Johannine school shows that the choice made by the LXX was in harmony with a tradition of translation from Hebrew to Greek that was widespread in the Hellenistic world. This linguistic decision in a way sets a seal on the encounter between two cultures, the Hebraic and the Greek, an encounter that, occurring by chance, became a destiny, by way of the secular work of conceptual interweaving.

But we need to understand that in occupying the place we have spoken of within the work of translating the Hebraic Bible, the Greek verb *einai* (followed by the Latin *esse*) did not bring with itself the universality of an unquestionable notion, but rather the equivocity of a notion of being, concerning which Aristotle had already said that it is "spoken in different ways" (*pollakhôs legetai*).[15] Owing to this insurmountable plurivocity, the Greek *einai* led to an incredible variety of interpretations in the history of the scholarly readings of Exodus 3:14, where the mere difference between Plato and Aristotle can convey some idea of their range. This is why the tormented history of the relations between Hellenism and Judaism, and between Hellenism and Christianity, will be marked by innumerable reworkings of the way in which the meaning of *einai* and *esse* is to be understood.

Allow me to recall a few of the stages of this history and to return once again to the Hebrew term that is the object of these translations. If it is true that the Greek *einai* and the Latin *esse* have always signified more than one thing, can the same thing not be said about the semantic field from which applies to the Hebrew *'ehyeh* and even to the Tetragrammaton? Who can say whether in the ears of the ancient Hebrews the declaration *'ehyeh 'ašer 'ehyeh* did not already have an enigmatic resonance? And if so, this resonance would already have at least a double sense: the enigma of a positive revelation giving rise to thought (about existence, efficacity, faithfulness, accompanying through history), and of a negative revelation dissociating the Name from those utilitarian and magical values concerning power that were ordinarily associated

---

gate, the vine, etc. See also E. Stauffer, "*egô*" in *Theologisches Wörterbuch zum Neuen Testaments, II*, pp. 342ff. (§B: *das christologische egô*).

15. Aristotle, *Metaphysics* E2: "Being properly speaking has different meanings" (*pollakhôs legetai*).

with it. And perhaps the even greater enigma of a revelation, in the usual sense of a theophany, or a nonrevelation, in the sense of a withdrawal into the incognito. Let us go even further. If we admit with Hans-Georg Gadamer that there are no specifically philosophical words, but only a philosophical use of words in particular contexts, why not assume that the biblical writer proceeded like the Greek philosophers and raised to a hitherto unheard-of level a verb that was as common in his language as the verb for being in Greek or Latin or contemporary languages? In other words, why not assume that Exodus 3:14 was ready from the very beginning to add a new region of significance to the rich polysemy of the verb being, explored in other terms by the Greeks and their Muslim, Jewish, and Christian heirs?

God and Being: Augustine and Pseudo-Dionysius

Today we are part of a radical questioning, framed in terms of the deliberately provocative label of ontotheology, of what from the Patristic period through Leibniz and Wolff remained a common conviction, namely, that the God of the Mosaic revelation and the Being of Greek philosophy are to be joined together, without being simply identified with each other, within the framework of making sense of faith. This conjunction stands as a founding event as regards a historical development that extends over more than fifteen hundred years. Therefore, before denouncing an unacceptable confusion in this encounter, or some scandalous perversion, it would be fairer to ask how such a broad and enduring consensus could have come about.

Two comments are necessary at the beginning of such a reflection.

First, none of the thinkers that we are going to refer to, however briefly, doubted that God himself pronounced the words in the declaration found in Exodus 3:14. None of them, as a result, confused philosophical speculation with what he understood, with the Church, to be a direct revelation of God. If they did not discuss the Greek translation based on the verb *einai* and the Latin translation based on *esse*, this was not because they understood these translations as the effect of an initial infiltration of Hellenism into the Hebraic field, but rather because they took them as an undiscussible exegetical given (even if minds as alert as Jerome, the translator of the Vulgate, or Augustine, the author of *On Christian Doctrine*, never confused the words of God with any human ones, even if they were in Hebrew, and even less if they were a translation from the Hebrew into Greek or Latin).

Second, none of the fathers, and none of the great Scholastics, ever thought that speculation on Being would reveal to human reason the secret of the divine essence in the intimacy of its innermost nature. When they said in unison that "Being is the name for God," they added in the same breath that Being is undefinable. And they said this in two different yet convergent ways. Instructed, on the one hand, by the philosophical spirituality of the neo-Platonists, from Plotinus himself and Porphyry to later thinkers such as Proclus and Damascius, they were accustomed to reading that the One, about which we can only say that it is "itself" (*autos*), transcends Being understood as the setting for intelligible ideas.[16] This apophatic tradition, according to which we cannot affirm anything about God, was never eclipsed, even during the age of Aristotelian scholasticism from the end of the twelfth through the thirteenth centuries. It was principally represented by the work of Dionysius the Areopagite (whom we now call the Pseudo-Dionysius), who, owing to the misunderstanding of who he was, when he actually lived, and his speculative framework, enjoyed, throughout the Middle Ages, an authority equal to that of Augustine.[17] Instructed, on the other hand, by the great tradition of analogy, they held that Being could be spoken of in affirmative statements, at the horizon of an elevation to the highest point of the most sublime titles and attributes encountered along the road of not just rational speculation but also spiritual purification.

These two ways, the apophatic and the analogical, mutually presupposed each other insofar as, on the one hand, what one negates is always something that one represents to oneself, even when it is a question of about the most sublime attributes of God, and, on the other hand, the elevation to the highest point of these titles and attributes by the way of eminence is equivalent to negating what we ordinarily affirm concerning such attributes. Apophatism and ontology thus ran along together side by side from the Patristic period to that of scholasticism. The great teachers saw no contradiction in saying that Being is what we think of as coming first—Avicenna, a Muslim, even called God "the first one"—and that it has no essence. To see this, we need only recall the saying of John Damascene, constantly repeated throughout the Middle Ages, about "an infinite ocean of ignorance." This ultimate *un-*

16. A well-known text of Plato's places the idea of the good "beyond essence" (*Republic* 509b).

17. See Jean Pépin, "Univers dyonisien et univers augustinien," in *Aspects de la dialectique* (Paris: Desclée de Brouwer), pp. 179–224, reprinted in *Les Deux approches du Christianisme* (Paris: Minuit), pp. 157–204. I shall cite this latter printing.

knowing was not to be abolished until Albert the Great and Thomas Aquinas claimed to raise speculative theology to the rank of a science.

These limits were never crossed by the thinkers I am now going to consider. As we shall see, for them speculative thought can, on the one hand, try to link up with the revelation of the Name; however, this latter remains part of a different order, as Pascal will subsequently recall. On the other hand, speculation on Being encounters its internal limit, either in the apophatism that stamps every affirmation with negation and points to something beyond Being or in the transcendence of Being itself that is the outcome of the affirmation of being in relation to any conceptual system.

Augustine

Let us consider for a moment Augustine, the Christian neo-Platonist whose authority would not be shaken even by the arrival in the West in the twelfth and thirteenth centuries of Aristotle.[18]

The Augustinian exegesis of Exodus 3:14, which may be found in numerous commentaries, is indivisibly philosophical and theological.[19] However, Augustine's originality lies not so much in the ontological interpretation of Exodus 3:14 inaugurated by the LXX, consecrated by Philo of Alexandria and transmitted by the Greek and the first Latin fathers. It lies rather in the continual inscription of this exegesis in an all-encompassing ontology, marked by a twofold neo-Platonic and Christian spirituality. This undividedness is explained by the nature of Augustine's thought, upon which we ought not retrospectively to project a concern, belonging to the medieval doctors of the twelfth and thirteenth century, for placing philosophical and theological discourse in a hierarchy. For one thing, Augustine does not conceive of Christian faith apart from a quest for intelligibility. For another, the Reason that he sees at work, during the period of his conversion, in the "books of the Platonists"—those of Plotinus and no doubt of Porphyry, transmitted and translated by the Bishop of Milan—is inseparable from a genuinely spiritual ascesis, consisting in a return to the origin, first of the soul, then of rational intelligence as such. In this way, neo-Platonic spirituality could appear to Augustine as naturally agreeing with Christian faith. As a result, he perceives no split between the *esse* of philosophy and the

18. See Etienne Gilson, *Introduction à l'étude de Saint Augustin* (Paris: Vrin, 1949).

19. E. Zumbrunn, "L'exégèse augustinienne de 'ego sum qui sum,'" in *Dieu et l'Etre*, pp. 141–63.

ego sum qui sum of Exodus 3:14a, inseparable from the *qui est* of 3:14b,[20] but rather a marvelous consonance. What does what Augustine names *vere esse*, true Being, or *ipsum esse*, which we translate as Being-itself, signify? Not an abstract concept, say the being common to everything that exists, but, in the words of Etienne Gilson, "the subsisting act of existing," as it is envisioned at the end of a gradual ascension. The starting point of this anabasis is the experience of change, taken to be a veritable ontological scandal. In this sense, the ascent, which is both spiritual and intellectual, across the decisive step of the apprehension of immutable truths, leads to the God of the Exodus, it being understood, by the philosopher as well as the exegete, by the thinker who makes an argument as well as by the believer who prays, that Being is synonymous with, first, the immutable, then the eternal, and finally the incorporeal.

Immutability stands at the top. The one who calls himself "who is" also calls himself "the one who does not change." This equivalence offers a magnificent example of the reciprocal action between textual interpretation and philosophical speculation, ending with the joining together of the understanding of faith and philosophical ascesis. As for eternity, which flows from immutability, it is exalted by its contrast with the painful experience of temporality, marked by the distention of the soul torn between the "it was" of memory, the "it will be" of expectation, and the "it is" of attention. For God, to be is to be unmovable, therefore eternal: "Think of God, and you shall find a 'he is' where no 'was' nor 'will be' has any place."[21] Immutability and eternity are the major implications of *ipsum esse*. Reason can comprehend this to the extent that it can establish through argumentation that change depends on immutable being. In this sense, we can speak of proofs. But we must immediately add two important qualifications. First, this argument does not enjoy the kind of autonomy claimed by Anselm's ontological argument in the *Proslogion*, which rests on a deduction of existence starting from essence. To say that God is Being is to give him the same name as the one God used to designate himself. In this respect, Augustine has no doubt that the *qui sum* of 3:14a and the *qui est* of 3:14b signify perfect

---

20. If the "*qui est*" of Exodus 3:14b is refereed to as often as is the "*ego sum qui sum*" of 14a, this is due to two reasons. First of all, *qui est* immediately counts as a name, without the complication created by the repetitions of *sum*; next, the *qui est* brings about the connection between the self-designation of God and its missionary extension, to which Augustine, for whom the call to conversion was inseparable from personal conversion, was particularly attentive.

21. See Gilson, *Introduction à l'étude de Saint Augustin*, p. 27. "What does it mean to say *ego sum qui sum*, if not 'I am eternal'? What does it mean to say *ego sum qui sum*, if not 'I cannot change'?" (ibid., p. 28).

immutability, which is also the meaning of the highest essence of the philosophers. Second, as a believer, Augustine confesses with no difficulty that he knows nothing of the profound nature of this immutable being. *Essentia* remains another name for *esse* (just as *sapientia* derives from *sapere*, to taste) and authorizes no intellectual intuition of *what* God is. The *qui est* gives no access to any *quid est. Someone is not something.*[22]

It remains true that, however weak it might be, ontological language is adequate for speaking about God, to the extent that Being is not a category of the mind, nor even a super category, but Existing itself, rejoined by an inner regard. It is to indicate this transcendence, which is both inward and outward, that in his later dialogues Augustine makes *esse* more specific as *ipsum esse* and even as *idipsum esse.*[23]

We cannot move on from Augustine without saying a word about the christological interpretation of Exodus 3:14. This interpretation is warranted by the Johannine theology of the Word, which I referred to above, and by the kinship between the sequence of *ego eimi* in John (especially John 8:58) and the *ego eimi* of Exodus. What is especially worth noting is the at first sight surprising fact that the christological interpretation does not fit with a spiritual ontology directed toward the immutable, the eternal, and the incorporeal. Was it possible that the entry into history of the Word of God through the incarnation—not to speak of the entry into history of the God of Israel signified by the event of the Exodus—should have no effect on the reading of Exodus 3:14a and b? Yet the contrast between the immutable and the changing, between the eternal and the transitory, and finally between being and the nothingness toward which the sinful creature inclines implies that nothing carnal or historical has any warrant for being associated with the heart of Being. Better to assume the paradox of an immutable God who *also* enters into history than to let that history enter into the Being of God in the very depths of his being.

Before turning to the medieval heritage of Augustine, we need also

22. "Therefore we are in the presence of a philosophical illumination integrated with a religious experience, one that we cannot hope to separate without falsifying Augustine's own testimony" (ibid., p. 308).

23. "Augustine did for Plotinus what Saint Thomas Aquinas was to do later for Aristotle: to submit to a rational revision, in the light of faith, a great philosophical interpretation of the universe. Each time this has happened, a Christian philosophy has been the result" (ibid., p. 310). And, in each case, Exodus 3:14 will be the somewhere along the way the thinker takes, sometimes as an incitation to think deeper, sometimes as a confirmation of an independent discovery, but always as a sign indicating the connection of philosophy and theology.

to say a few words concerning the disturbing couple formed by Augustine and Pseudo-Dionysius, who the Middle Ages cited together as equally worth consideration, in spite of everything that seems to separate them: "Augustine's complete ignorance of the age, the place, the language, the literary genre, and the preoccupations of Dionysius."[24] Yet it would not be an error to compare them regarding one essential point, their hierarchical conception of the universe. The idea of order, which forms the capstone of this conception, concerns our investigation as regards one essential point. The question is to what knowledge of God this traversal by degrees of the cosmic order leads. The knowledge of God procured through this idea of order consists in a fragile equilibrium between the "analogies" suggested by the highest realities and the "negations" that indicate the inadequacy of these analogies. In this sense, an affirmative (or cataphatic) theology and a negative (or apophatic) theology are held in a tensive relation by this interplay between approximation by the way of eminence—the best qualities of the beings that make up the universe being carried to the point of paroxysm—and denegation by the way of difference. By placing the One above Being, Plotinus and all the neo-Platonists who followed him invite us to subordinate the affirmative way to the apophatic way. And this is where Dionysius most clearly differs from Augustine. Whereas Augustine continues to call Being the highest term of the ascending quest, no doubt recalling his struggle against the Manicheans, who granted Being to evil, Dionysius speaks of a beyond Being and calls unknowing (*agnô-sia*) the least inadequate knowledge of God: "But the manner of knowing God most worthy of him is to know him in the mode of unknowing in a union that surpasses all intelligence." And again, "it is this perfect unknowing taken in the best sense of the word that constitutes the true knowledge of the one who surpasses all knowing."[25]

However it is not necessary to overemphasize the opposition of this affirmative and this apophatic theology. The way of eminence, marked by use of analogy, does not take place without the negation of lower-order attributes, and the apophatic way, with its battery of negations,

---

24. Jean Pépin notes that the neo-Platonism that Augustine depends on is that which is born from Plotinus and Porphyry, whereas Dionysius is more inspired by the later systematizations of Iamblicus and Proclus. "But," he adds, "it would be to grant too little consistency to neo-Platonism and to believe that it could thoroughly transform itself between the *Enneads* and the *Platonic Theology*. What is essential remains unchanged" (Pépin, "Univers dyonisien et univers augustinien," p. 157).

25. Quoted in ibid., p. 201.

distinguishes itself from a purely privative unknowing only if it continues to be a kind of overthrown affirmation.[26]

This reservation is of great importance if we are to make sense of subsequent interpretations of Exodus 3:14, particularly among the medieval thinkers. The name *qui est,* predicated of a subject ("I 'am'") is taken in turn, or even simultaneously, for a name that negates, that eliminates everything that is not worthy of the title Being—in other words, it is both a name for ignorance, for unknowing—and a name that affirms, that speaks positively of Being par excellence, Being itself, *esse ipsum.* There is finally more than just a nuance between these two readings. In the first of them, we can hear the Plotinian transcendence of the One over Being, understood as the place of intelligible ideas; in the second, the transcendence of Being over beings is affirmed. Someone will say that it all comes down to the same thing. Logically, perhaps; spiritually, no. The *via negativa* in the end has more affinity with a unitive mysticism than with demonstrative speculation. The *via eminenciae* bears witness to a greater perseverance in the service of understanding faith.

Having said this, may not these two readings be carried out without appealing to each other, despite the paradox there seems to be in "negating every quality of God at the same time that one attributes the highest one to him"?[27] But is this not the same paradox we sensed in reading Exodus 3:14, at least in its Latin version, common to Augustine, Dionysius, and the medieval thinkers? Does saying "who is" not affirm something about . . . Being, one might ask? Or does it mean the withdrawing of God beyond . . . everything that really is not?

No alternative other than that between apophatism and ontologism seems to have been opened by the Latin version of our Hebrew verse. The question was not raised whether this Hebrew verse allowed for other readings, and first of all for other translations, than those indicated by the history of the philosophical uses of the Greek *einai* and the Latin *esse.* Even less was the question posed whether such readings might stem from another history, from a non-Greek and non-Latin history of the verb "being," or whether such readings might not require a break with every possible signification of this verb.

If we jump to the end of the twelfth century and the thirteenth century, the golden age of Latin scholasticism, three things are striking.

26. Cf. ibid.
27. Ibid., p. 189.

First, progress in the affirmation of the intelligibility of Being tended to render superfluous the self-affirmation of the Being of God according to Exodus 3:14. Recourse to this verse tended to become an extrinsic confirmation, once *doctrina sacra* was raised to the rank of a science and once the divorce was consummated between theological speculation, governed by the *quaestio* and its logical order, and the hermeneutic interpretation of the biblical text, governed by its *lectio* and the order that the text imposes.

However—my second point—the most independent theological speculation, on the epistemological plane of argumentation, with regard to biblical interpretation continued to be intimately bound to this interpretation as regards its inquiry into the concept of Being, as though the question *quid est?* (what is God?) were still driven by the question *qui est?* (who is God?), where the personal pronoun attests to the deep kinship, for Christian understanding, between the *quaestio* and *lectio divina*. In this sense, the Christianization of Hellenism is secretly more powerful than the Hellenization of Christianity.[28]

Third point: medieval Christian thinkers did not fail to pose to the question of the relation between discourse about God as One and Simple and Trinitarian discourse. Here is where the philosophical-theological *qui est* returns in full force. Is it said concerning the essence of God, or rather concerning one person of the Trinity, by preference Christ the Word, or does it apply to all three persons in common?

Therefore, if medieval philosophy tended to marginalize the *ego sum qui sum* through its first aspect, through its second and especially its third one, philosophical-theological interpretation of our biblical verse continued, sometimes subterraneously, sometimes openly.

If these three features of medieval thought could conjointly characterize, without dissociating, works as complex and as different as those of Bonaventure, Albert the Great, Thomas Aquinas, and Duns Scotus, this was because none of these thinkers dared to take the step that so clearly sets Anselm of Canterbury apart from them. He was the only one to risk giving a *definition* that gathers up and summarizes what is essential about the divine essence: "a being than which nothing greater [or nothing better] can be conceived," and in sketching out an argument that will become the ontological argument with Descartes and the Cartesians, an argument that existence is necessarily part of God's es-

---

28. Cf. Claude Geffré, "Thomas d'Aquin ou la Christianisation de l'Hellénisme," *L'Etre et Dieu*, (Paris: Cerf, 1986), pp. 23–42.

sence.[29] It goes without saying that such an argument renders superfluous any recourse to the self-designation of God according to Exodus 3:14. And, in fact, the great scholastic thinkers indicated a great distrust of this short way and as regards the intellectual intuition on which the argument rests. They preferred the long and laborious way of proofs starting from sense experience and the fact of change, and, because of this, did not expect such proofs to lead beyond the assertion of a first cause. As for the nature of that author of all things, they were as restrained as were their predecessors, holding to the older dialectic between ontologism (God is Being) and apophatism (God is ineffable). This discretion is all the more noteworthy in that the pressure was so great, with the arrival of Aristotle in the West by way of the Arabs (Avicenna) and the Jews (Maimonides), to push even further the rational impulse of natural theology. I would like to say a few more words about this, without losing sight of Exodus 3:14.

29. We read in the Preface to the *Proslogium:* "I began to ask myself whether there might be found a single argument which would require no other for its proof than itself alone (*ad se probaendum*); and alone would suffice (*et solum ad astruendem*) to demonstrate that God truly exists (*quia Deus vere est*). Not just that God truly exists, but also that his is "the supreme (*summum*) good requiring nothing else, which all other things require for their existence and well-being; and whatever we believe regarding the divine Being." In *St. Anselm: Basic Writings,* translated by S. N. Deane (La Salle, IL: Open Court, 1962), p. 1. To whom is this argument addressed? To the fool who says in his heart that there is no God: "this very fool, when he hears of this being of which I speak—a being than which nothing greater can be conceived—understands what he hears, and what he understands in his understanding; although he does not understand it to exist" (p. 7). Here, undoubtedly for the first time, we find the meaning of the word "God" dealt with outside of a context of faith and moreover confined to the noetic plane and marked by the hypothesis of the plane of existence. This is the way along which will advance boldly Descartes and the Cartesians. But we would be wrong to attribute to Anselm a genuine ontological argument or a plainly self-sufficient argument. His argument is, in the first place, enveloped within an invocation in the second person that speaks of God in the third person, whose idea is a thing (*quid*), not someone (*qui*). What is more, faith is expected to understand—to recognize, if we follow Corbin's insightful translation of the Anselmian *intelligere*—what is already implicit in faith. What is it a question of "recognizing"? This: "that thou art *as* we believe; and that thou art *that* which we believe" (ibid., my emphases). The "knowledge" (or approximation) that is at stake here certainly has to do with being, but under the guise of a verb conjugated in the second person in harmony with the "thou" of the invocation. A secret link is thereby preserved between the "thou art" of the invocation and the *ego sum* of Exodus 3:14. The uncoupling of the argument in relation to faith can thus be better circumscribed. It becomes manifest in the phrase "you are something . . ." Anselm suggests that this passage from someone to something is in some way already an object of faith ("we believe that . . .") and that the understanding of faith consists in unfolding this *nexus* from someone to something, in recognizing it, but in such a way that this recognition becomes by itself a proof. Therefore, with Anselm, we are far from an argument that is so autonomous, so self-sufficient that it merits the name of proof. Cf. Jean-Luc Marion, "L'argument relève-t-il de l'ontologie?" in *L'Argomento ontologico,* edited by Marco M. Olivetti (Milan: CEDAM, 1990), pp. 13–18.

The reinterpretation of Aristotle in the sense that Gilson was to call a "metaphysics of Exodus"[30] had been prepared by a deepening of the debate between ontologism and apophatism, beginning near the end of the twelfth century. In an important article, Edouard Weber unfolds the double line of ontological interpretations of the Name in Exodus 3:14 and the application of this same interpretation to the persons of the Trinity.[31] He goes into great detail concerning Alexander of Hales, the first important teacher of the Franciscans in Paris, and Bonaventure, his disciple. To summarize, Exodus 3:14 gives the principal name of God. It philosophical equivalents are *esse, essentia, existentia*, terms that imply eternity, immutability, and aseity (in the sense of independence from everything else). Every other determination is reducible to Being. Here the lesson of Avicenna is taken up. Being is the first concept our thinking acquires. "By being (*esse*) one indicates the pure act of being (*ipsum purum actum entis*) for being (*esse*) is that which first befalls our thinking and this is that it is pure Act."[32] Have we for all that, however, taken possession in thought of the innermost nature of God? In no way. It is starting from traces, vestiges, that knowledge gets its first view of God. Being turns out to constitute the last step in a difficult journey. In this way, the impression of purely philosophical immediacy given by the Avicennian notion of being as the first thing conceived of is corrected. By distinguishing anteriority per se and in relation to us, an element of negativity is retained at the very heart of the knowledge of God as Being.

When Saint Thomas comes on the scene, the tradition was well established that *qui est* is the principal name of God.[33] It designates true being, that is, being that is eternal, immutable, simple, self-sufficient, and the cause and principle of every creature. Equally established was the subtle equilibrium between ontologism and apophatism. Whence the extreme distrust as regards the amalgamating of the name stemming from Exodus 3:14 and Anselm's argument based on intellectual evidence of God. John Damascene needs also to be recalled, celebrating

30. See Etienne Gilson, *The Spirit of Mediaeval Philosophy,* translated by A. H. C. Downes (New York: Charles Scribner's Sons, 1936), pp. 50–52.

31. Edouard Weber, "L'herméneutique christologique d'Exode 3,14 chez quelques maîtres parisiens du XIIIème siècle," in *Celui qui est, interprétations juives et chrétiennes d'Exode 3,14,* edited by Alain de Libera and Emilie Zumbrunn (Paris: Cerf, 1986), pp. 47–101.

32. Ibid., p. 74, n. 1.

33. Ibid., p. 74. See also E. Zumbrunn, "La 'Métaphysique de l'Exode' selon Thomas d'Aquin," in *Dieu et l'Etre,* pp. 245–73.

"the infinite and unlimited ocean of being." *The one who is* is the most proper name of God because it is the most indeterminate one. We only know *quod est*, not *quid est*, which remains concealed from us.

The first originality of Thomas Aquinas as regards our inquiry is that he pushed to an extreme the conceptual purification of the *ipsum esse*, to the point of identifying it with the pure Act of Being. In this regard, his citations of Exodus 3:14, from the period of the *Commentary on the Sentences* (1254) to his last writings, the *de Substantiis separatis* (1272), play much more than an ornamental role. The biblical verse brings its authority to the deepening of speculative thought. The pure Act of Being says more than perfection, or Good, or even One. Next, the principal attributes of the *ipsum esse* are reclassified as a function of the exigency for meaning proceeding from the pure Act of Being. The farthest that thinking can advance in this direction is to affirm that God is identical with his essence, as will be said in the *Contra Gentiles*. The proper name of God according to Exodus 3:14—that is, "the one who is"—receives its correct philosophical interpretation in the identity in God of being and essence. The divine *esse* itself constitutes the essence of God's nature. But this affirmation has its counterpart in the confession that this essence is for that very reason unconceptualizable.

From this inaccessibility of the intimate nature of God follows the fact that Thomas's well-known proofs—the "five ways"—only show God's existence, in response to the pure philosophical question "does God exist" (*an sit*)? This second aspect of Thomas's work must not be separated from the first one. The claim to give a purely rational proof of the existence of God is certainly a large one. And, in this regard the shift from Exodus 3:14 to Romans 1:20 is especially significant. But, to know that God is, is to know nothing about what he is. What is more, the sensible things from which the argument begins are too far removed from the divine nature for the analogical way to lead to the heart of divine existence.

That the question of existence is the product of a new philosophical method, where the *quaestio* takes pride of place over the *lectio*, is beyond doubt.[34] Never had a theologian posed the question whether God exists and whether his existence was demonstrable. And when Thomas cites Exodus 3:14 in the second question (Ad 3) of his *Summa*, it is as a kind of confirmation, not as his principal argument. Certainly, a theological

---

34. Cf. M. D. Chenu, *La Théologie comme Science au XIIIème siècle* (Paris: Vrin, 1957).

intention runs throughout his work, and in the first place a concern to explicate the first article of the Creed, but the epistemology of his rational proof is based on the very meaning of the *ipsum esse*. The first question posed concerning God shifts attention to the "existential" aspect of *esse*, as though the question of existence takes priority over that of the name. (We can discern one indication of this displacement in that the *Summa* more readily cites the *ego sum qui sum*, again with reference to Romans 1:20, than the *qui est*, which leads directly to the question of the name, hence of essence, however undefinable it may be.)[35]

Let us break off our inquiry into the ontological interpretation of Exodus 3:14. We have said enough to be able to pose the fundamental question: does this convergence without fusion between the biblical verse and the ontologism inherited from the Greeks—with its apophatic corrective—represent an intellectual aberration, as is often said today, sometimes by theologians, sometimes by philosophers?

Before responding, we need to be clear about the very nature of this encounter. One important witness in this regard is Etienne Gilson, the great French scholar of medieval philosophy. His variations on what he called the "metaphysics of Exodus" are very instructive in this regard. This contentious expression was formulated in his 1931 Gifford Lectures, published as *The Spirit of Medieval Philosophy*, along with the following reservation: "Of course we do not maintain that the text of Exodus is a revealed metaphysical definition of God; but if there is no metaphysics *in* Exodus there is a metaphysic *of* Exodus; and we shall see it developed in due course by the Fathers of the Church, whose indications on this point the medieval philosophers merely followed up and exploited" (pp. 433–34, n. 9). Already at this time Gilson notes that nothing in Greek philosophy could have led to a monotheism comparable to that of the Hebrews. Neither Plato nor Aristotle nor the Stoics nor the neo-Platonists posited the existence of a unique God, the author of all that is. They did not do so "because they lacked that clear idea of God which makes it impossible to admit more than one" (ibid., p. 47). Even with Aristotle there is no link established between the being as being of *Metaphysics* Γ 1003–31 and the pure act of thinking defined in *Physics* VIII and *Metaphysics* Δ. Without the book of Exodus,

---

35. "The earlier patriarchs were taught in a general way the omnipotence of the one God, but then Moses was more fully instructed concerning the simplicity of the divine Essence when it was said to him, as is written in Exodus 3:14: 'I am the one who is . . .'" (*Summa Theologica* IIa–IIae, qu. 174 a.6, cited by E. Zumbrunn, p. 264).

philosophers would have never reached the idea that Being is the proper name of God and that this name designates God's very essence. "Exodus lays down the principle from which Christian philosophy will be suspended" (ibid., p. 51). "There is but one God and this God is Being, that is the corner-stone of all Christian philosophy" (ibid.).

This text from 1931, of course, does not assert the complete fusion of the revealed word and the philosophical argument, but it does presuppose the conviction, transmitted to Augustine from the Greek fathers, that philosophy, in its neo-Platonic version, *naturally agrees* with Christian faith. From this follows that mixed concept of "Christian philosophy" that has given rise to so many polemics in France. Besides this, Gilson's text postulates that the convergence of a faith seeking understanding and philosophical speculation is not complete until the latter understands Being as the pure Act of Existing.[36]

Gilson was to return to this question shortly before his death in 1978 in a work that has been published posthumously under the title *Constantes philosophiques de l'Etre*.[37] This text takes up Heidegger's condemnation of the alleged confusion of God and Being. Gilson's reply is to say that the critique of classical ontology, inaugurated by Kant, was possible only because late scholasticism, followed by modern neoscholasticism, betrayed the identity between Being and pure Act of Existing, splitting essence from existence, a split that allowed for the highly suspect ontological argument of Anselm and Descartes.

However, forty years after his well-known statement about the "metaphysics of Exodus," Gilson is willing to admit that the rapprochement between the God of the Scriptures and the Being of philosophers remains historically contingent and speculatively fragile. This encounter is contingent in the sense that nothing in Greek thought points to a fusion of God and Being. Being for the Greeks never coincides with

---

36. Gilson cites this text from Duns Scotus: "O Lord our God, when Moses asked of Thee as a most true Doctor, by what name he should name Thee to the people of Israel; knowing well what mortal understanding could conceive of Thee and unveiling to him Thy ever blessed name, Thou didst reply: *Ego sum qui sum;* wherefore art Thou true Being, total Being. This I believe, but if it be in any wise possible this I would also know. Help me, O Lord, to seek out such knowledge of the true being that Thou art as may lie within the power of my natural reason, starting from that being which Thou Thyself has attributed to Thyself." And he goes on to say, "Nothing can surpass the weighty fullness of this text, since it lays down at once the true method of Christian philosophy, and the first truth whence all the others derive" (*The Spirit of Mediaeval Philosophy*, pp. 51–52).

37. Etienne Gilson, *Constantes philosophiques de l'Etre*, edited by J.-F. Courtine (Paris: Vrin, 1983).

a God. The gap between the gods of the Greek cults and the principles of metaphysics is a wide one.[38] This is why it is legitimate to ask how "God happened to fall into and to be identified with the Being of metaphysics" (p. 178), and "how Being entered into theology" (p. 179). This vocabulary with its connotation of an event—happen, fall, enter into— is surprising. The encounter that had earlier been said to be natural now appears as an improbable conjunction. It was only with the great medieval doctors that "an ontology that was profoundly theological and not distrustful of theology" (p. 187) could come about. And this remains an improbable success, given the different origins of the ideas of God and of Being. This is so true that given Heidegger's critique of Western metaphysics, we must in fact return to Parmenides to find a conception of Being that is sufficiently pure that its conjunction with the pure Act of Existing does not constitute a speculative monster.

That Parmenides' Being might be identical with God is the striking twist that Gilson gives to Judeo-Christian speculation. Nothing in the inheritance of Greek thought prevents this. But the initiative comes from thought about faith instructed by Exodus 3:14: "Henceforth it is Christians themselves who will be charged with demythologizing, with demythicizing political religion, up to and including philosophy itself" (p. 189). This mutual purification is the effect of Exodus 3:14 inasmuch as God himself claims his name to be "I am," *qui est*. Starting from here, philosophy only offers its language, its conceptuality, and attempts "an interpretation of its object [faith] in terms of the language of reason" (p. 191).

Historically contingent, the coincidence of the biblical God and the Being of philosophers also appears to be conceptually fragile. Pascal reminds us: between the God of the philosophers and the God of Abraham, Isaac, and Jacob, the difference remains insurmountable. As for us, after the contemporary critique of metaphysics, we find ourselves confronted with the nonphilosophical origin of God and his nonnecessity for philosophy. God remains someone we can pray to. Suddenly, the expressions *sum* and *qui est* stand out in their splendid isolation.

In this way, the encounter that was taken for granted by Augustine and, up to a certain point, by Bonaventure, Thomas, and Duns Scotus appears astonishing and problematic for the postmetaphysical spirit of our contemporaries. Indeed, we have to admit that if the convergence

---

38. "[With Aristotle] we see what came to pass. It was not God that entered into metaphysics, it was rather the metaphysician who sought for God in physics, in order to annex it to him, but he did so only after having made this god undergo a necessary purification" (ibid., p. 183).

between God and Being could have been called, as I did above, an event in thinking, this does not mean that another such event in thinking is not also possible, one where this convergence becomes undone, where it shifts from being plausible to being suspect.

The Trial of Ontotheology

We can take up this issue of a break in the equation of God and Being by starting from the ontological pole. According to Heidegger, the genuine thought of Being excludes Christian faith, inasmuch as this leads to a God who is not Being but a being, even if he turns out to be the highest being.[39] The ontological difference, as the primary, central, and final theme of philosophy distinguishes between Being and beings, including the highest being, God. Heidegger does condescend to reserve a domain for theology, which is that precisely of the highest being, intended by faith alone. In this sense, theology is at best a positive science, a historical science, owing to its connection with the events that mark out this reserved domain.[40] As for philosophy, it has once again to become Greek, thinking through to the end the demands of the idea of Being, which no longer encounters the God of faith. Hence the divorce is demanded by philosophy itself. For philosophy, Being, wholly other than being; for theology, a region of being, a historical science of a particular kind. As Christian, theology is essentially New Testament theology, with no speculative ambition.[41]

This relegating of theology to a reserved domain has found an echo among those theologians who are most distrustful concerning any form

39. Cf. D. Bourg, "La critique de la 'Metaphysique de l'Exode' par Heidegger et l'exégèse moderne," in *L'Etre et Dieu*, pp. 215–44.

40. Cf. Martin Heidegger, "Phenomenology and Theology," in *The Piety of Thinking: Essays by Martin Heidegger*, translated by James G. Hart and John C. Maraldo (Bloomington: Indiana University Press, 1976), pp. 3–71. A few other, brief indications are to be found in the first two volumes of his Nietzsche lectures, translated by David Farrell Krell (San Francisco: HarperCollins, 1991) and in *An Introduction to Metaphysics*, translated by Ralph Manheim (Garden City, NY: Anchor Books, 1961).

41. Gilson's affirmation that the thought of absolute being is fruit of medieval theology's speculation applied to Exodus 3:14 has been also challenged in the texts of C. J. de Vogel and Pierre Hadot, who claim that the Greeks were the first to have identified perfect being with the divine. This argument not only challenges Gilson's thesis that only Christian meditation on Exodus 3:14 could have led to the idea of God as pure act, it also raises questions about Heidegger's thesis that metaphysics has always confused Being and beings. What is more, even if it does stem from Porphyry and not meditation on Exodus 3:14, the apprehension of Being in its difference in relation to beings becomes still more radical in Saint Thomas, as I shall say in a moment. Cf. Bourg, "La critique de la 'Metaphysique de l'Exode' par Heidegger et l'exégèse moderne," p. 239.

of speculation. It even finds a partial justification in Saint Paul when, in Corinthians 1:18–20, he opposes the scandal of the Cross to the wisdom of human beings. But one tends to attenuate the continuation of this text that speaks of "wisdom for God." Must this latter be absolutely incommunicable? For me, the error of this radical position is that it rests upon a reduction of the whole history of metaphysics to its late scholastic version, which can indeed give rise to a confusion between *esse* and *ens* and thereby justify the definition of ontology as the science of *ens* as *ens*. However, Heidegger, ignores the constant pressure exercised on ontology by the thought of a One beyond Being, and by Dionysius's apophatism, which, we have seen, runs throughout medieval ontology. Even more important, Heidegger completely overlooks the care Thomas takes to situate the Act of Being above every being, making impossible any confusion between this Act of Being and the *ens commune,* that is, the general fact that every being has to be. Also overlooked is the fact that the divine name drawn from Exodus 3:14—*qui est*—remains inadequate for Thomas Aquinas to the sacred Tetragrammaton. In this sense, we ought not to speak of a fusion, much less of a confusion, between God and Being, but of a convergence that respects the misalignment between the philosophical and the biblical names. That it was faith that led to and sustained the effort to think through the elevation of Being above beings cannot be doubted. But this conjunction, which seems so astonishing to us today, proves at least negatively that genuine Thomist ontology does not correspond to the defaming criterion of ontotheology.

However, whatever may be said about the injustice of Heidegger's statements concerning the forgetting of Being by every metaphysician, including those who Gilson, it is true, a bit imprudently enrolled under the banner of "Christian philosophy," the dissociation between God and Being is perceived by most contemporary thinkers as a new event in thinking that annuls that earlier event that consisted in conjoining God and Being, and whose impact lasted for over fifteen hundred years. One reason contemporary thinkers take this dissociation between God and Being as having taken place definitively and irrevocably is that it seems to them to be a secondary effect of a more radical break that has taken place in Western culture, the one Nietzsche placed under the title "the death of God." This is held to be the actual event in thinking starting from which both believers and nonbelievers have to define themselves. Heidegger himself interprets the Nietzschean proclamation in the sense of the death of the "God of metaphysics," under whose banner, he holds, is to be placed all ontotheology. What he himself sees beyond this death is a thinking of Being that has jettisoned all biblical dross and been enriched by the kind of philosophizing poetry best illustrated by Hölderlin. A new sense of the divine may arise on the horizon of this thinking, but it will be in terms of a post-Christian thinking, strongly marked by a kind of neopaganism.

In short, the few positive evaluations of theology to be found here and there in Heidegger add up to a marginalization of our Judeo-Christian heritage, which is referred back to its Near Eastern place of origin and divested of any universalizing intention its marriage with Hellenism might have conferred on Hebraic thought or on newly born Christianity. In turn, this expulsion of Judaism and Christianity from the sphere of Western culture goes along with an acceleration in the process of secularization of this culture, despite Heidegger's own personal distaste for almost every aspect of this process. It is this marginalization—or better, this regionalization—of any Christian thought with a Jewish origin that must give the most to think about to theologians who take the divorce between God and Being to be an acquired fact and who, in the same breath, take the Nietzschean proclamation of the death of God to be the necessary starting point for a new way of thinking theologically.

In fact, for a number of Christian theologians, the question is how to think "after Nietzsche." Any new starting point has to be sought, they hold, in what differentiates the categories of Jewish thought from those of Hellenism. In this sense, they hold that the theme of manifestation must once again be submitted to that of redemption, with its strongly historical connotations, as much on the side of the proclaimed message as on that of the founding events. In the end, and above all else, the ambition of thinking must be substituted by the force of testimony and the ethical dimension of Revelation.

It is this ethical dimension that Emmanuel Levinas opposes with no concessions to the thought of Being, which he sees condemned not to celebrating some poetic *Ereignis,* as in Heidegger, but to totalizing experience, thereby missing the initial difference constituted by the appearance of the other person in my field of experience. The face of the other conveys to me directly and immediately the message of Sinai: you shall not kill me! The face teaches, and it does so directly in an ethical fashion, without passing through any prior positing of existence. Hence the face of others, as an ethical occurrence, can be the trace of the God of the Torah, which inaugurates my responsibility and commends the orphan, the widow, and the stranger to my care.

This breakthrough of an ethics without ontology, brought about by a Jewish thinker, has found many echoes among Christian thinkers. Different attempts have been made to ground a new kind of theological thinking on the categories of "love" and the "gift" under the sign of "God without Being." Jean-Luc Marion, the most brilliant of these new philosopher-theologians, for example, himself also begins from the Nietzschean proclamation of the death of God.[42] But he interprets it as a critique of the Names of God known so far, including the name Being. In this way, the field of "divine names," in the sense of Dionysius, is reopened. What conceptual atheism has demonstrated is merely the vanity of any conceptual determination of God. The theologian can see in it another version of idolatry, "conceptual idolatry." Marion's thesis here is that Being is one such concept and that, like every concept, it is a blasphemous "representation." In this way, he incorporates into his argument a criticism stemming from Heidegger of the screenlike role exercised by all representation. This critique of representation does not lead to a new thought of Being, however, but to a return to the Johannine tradition that the first name of God is love. Love has no need to say that it exists in order to affirm or communicate itself. It has no need to pass through a proposition. God exists, says, and understands that God first loved us.

The difficult point here is whether the Johannine proclamation that "God is love" leads to thought unless we make a detour through Exodus 3:14. Marion thinks this is possible if we renew an important current of patristic and even of medieval thought according to which the first name of God is the Good and not Being. "No one is good but God alone" we read in Luke 18:19 and Matthew 19:17. "For Dionysius and Bonaventure," writes Jean-Luc Marion, "the name of being has to give way before the unconditioned hyperbolic of the absolute gift" (*God Without Being*, p. 123). "To praise God with the name of charity, rather than that of being, is thus authorized by a biblical revelation, a patristic tradition, and the requirements of spirituality. . . . Love alone does not have to be, since it suffices that it be given" (p. 125). To submit God to the disjunction of being or not being, a human disjunction par excellence, is to submit God to a criterion of existence, to conditions of possibility, hence to a principle of reason over which we would retain mastery.

This attempt to think God apart from being poses a problem for theologians concerned to preserve a link with philosophy. For them, it

---

42. See Jean-Luc Marion, *God Without Being*, translated by Thomas A. Carlson (Chicago: University of Chicago Press, 1991). He gives a summary of his argument in "De la 'mort de Dieu' au noms divins: L'itinéraire théologique de la métaphysique," in *L'Etre et Dieu*, pp. 101–30.

is a question what kind of thinking love and the gift give rise to and whether they must renounce every possible signification of the verb being, whose polysemy is perhaps broader than has yet been explored by the philosophical hermeneutics of this verb. The logic of superabundance of love, opposed to the logic of equivalence of justice, certainly appeals to a logic of paradox, to a rhetoric of hyperbole. But it still needs to be shown that neither this logic nor this rhetoric contribute to reinforcing the current vogue for irrationalism. In short, it still needs to be shown that thinking in terms of love does not demand a new *sacrificium intellectus,* but rather another reason. In other words, can a theology of love resist better than the so much decried ontotheology Heidegger's verdict relegating all Christian (and by implication, Jewish) theology to the margins of Western thought? To put this a better way, would a theology of love that sets out to do without ontology be in a better position to conclude a new pact with Western reason, on the level, for example, of the criticism this latter exercises today as regards its own totalizing or foundational claims? This would be the case if, in rejoining philosophy in the midst of its crisis, the theology of love were to invent a new mode of inculturation into the Western sphere of thinking, a new pact capable of supporting the comparison with the one once formulated in support of the Judeo-Christian conjunction with Hellenistic neo-Platonism and then with medieval neo-Aristotelianism. Without this pact, declaring themselves totally foreign to Greek thought, identified globally with the metaphysics of being, do Jewish and Christian thought not "disenculture" themselves and consent to their marginalization?

To conclude, I would like to consider briefly three questions in response to what has happened to Exodus 3:14 during this post-Nietzschean adventure.

My first question: has the theology of love eclipsed the Hebraic *shema*—"Hear, O Israel: Yhwh our God is alone Yhwh"—which is theologically close to our verse? I do not think so. The efforts of Christian theology to dehellenize itself cannot take place apart from a certain rejudization of its ideas. In this sense, Christian theology has to move from the proposition "God is One" to the proposition that "God is Love." One way of doing so might be to show that the declaration of John's Gospel unfolds, through the resources of metaphor, dialectic, and narrativization, the proclamation of Exodus and Deuteronomy.[43]

---

43. See Paul Ricoeur, "D'un Testament à l'autre: essai d'herméneutique biblique (de 'Je sui celui qui sui' à 'Dieu est amour')," in *La mémoire et le temps: Mélanges offerts à Pierre Bonnard* (Geneva: Labor et Fides, 1991), pp. 299–309.

Second question: has the exegesis of Exodus 3:14 cut off, even on the level of textual meaning, every basis for a conjunction between the Hebraic *'ehyeh* and the Greek *einai* and the Latin *esse*? Again, I do not think so. To the reasons given in the first section of this essay, which tend to preserve the sapiential point of this declaration, which is unique in its form in the Bible, I would like to add a new reason drawn from the preceding discussion. Why not formulate the hypothesis that the Hebraic *'ehyeh* proposes a "gap in meaning" that enriches the already broad, albeit culturally limited, polysemy of the Greek verb *einai*, which was all that was available during the period of the LXX for translating Exodus 3:14? Being, Aristotle says, is said in many ways. Why not say that the Hebrews thought being in a new way?

My third question takes us back to where we began. If translation has to be taken as a particular case of reading, of reception, hence of the interpretation of a text, my question is as follows. Can we translate Exodus 3:14 without making any recourse to the verb being, even setting aside any thought about the polysemy of this verb, even when augmented by its Hebraic usage? I do not think so. The alternative translations that have been proposed are in fact paraphrases, even commentaries, that restore the cultural, spiritual, and theological context of this verse and, in this way, make explicit what I above called the gap in meaning produced by Exodus 3:14. This gap in meaning does force us to think in another way about the verb being, but it does not force us to eliminate it from our translation. This is what the paraphrasitc translations proposed by some modern Jewish thinkers writing in German lead me to conclude.[44] They have tried to draw from German verbal resources unknown to Latin and to languages that derive from Latin. Hermann Cohen led the way by using the expression *der Seiende* to underscore the shift from the neuter to the first person. But the expression *der Seiende* still belongs to the semantic field of *Sein* (and, in fact, the Greeks and the Latins had already anticipated such a move in saying *ho ôn* and *qui est*). Next Mendelssohn proposed what I have called a paraphrasitic translation. But he too did not really get away from a phil-

---

44. See R. Goetschel, "Exode 3,14 dans la pensée juive allemande de la Première moitié du XXème siècle," in *Celui qui est*, pp. 269–76. Rosenzweig, for example, took up Exodus 3:14 in an essay written in 1929 entitled "Der Ewige." Its subtitle, "Mendelssohn und der Gottesname," is indicative of its content (p. 270). (This essay was published in a collection of his writings entitled *Die Schrift* [Frankfurt, 1964].) Mendelssohn himself found an heir in Hermann Cohen, who would signal the renaissance in Jewish philosophy with the posthumous publication of his *Religion der Vernunft aus den Quellen des Judentums* (1919; reprinted, Wiesbaden, 1978).

osophical vocabulary when he wrote: *das ewige Wesen*. Franz Rosenzweig went the furthest in translating our verse as follows: *Ich werde dasein, als der ich dasein werde. . . . ICH BIN DA schikt mich zu euch.*[45] Hence, no longer eternal Being, nor even the existent (*der Seiende*), but the "existing" (*der Da-Seiende*) present to the Dasein of human beings.[46] We need to honor this struggle with words.[47] But it remains that the German words *Da-Sein* and *Werden* do not convey a complete break with the verb *Sein*, but rather another extension of its polysemy. In this way, one modern language attempts to draw near as possible to the enigmatic Hebrew formula. *'Ehyeh 'Ašer 'Ehyeh* continues to give rise to thought, at the bounds of every translation.[48]

45. Rosenzweig, *Die Schrift*, p. 37.

46. "It is clear," declares Rosenzweig, "that given their condition as slaves, the suffering Hebrews did not expect a lecture *ex cathedra* from Moses concerning the necessary existence of God. They had need, as did their hesitant leader, of an assurance that God was close to them. Unlike Moses who had this assurance from God's own mouth, they had need of some form confirming the divine origin of this assurance, through a clarification of the obscurity of the old divine name" (cited by Goetschel, "Exode 3,14 dans la pensée juive allemande de la Première moitié du XXème siècle," p. 272).

47. We need also to note the translation of the Hebrew *'ašer* by *als der*, which gives an explicative sense to the redoubling of the verb. "As the one who will always be there, so shall I be present in every time," comments Martin Buber, *Königtum Gottes* (Heidelberg, 1956), p. 69, cited by Goetschel, "Exode 3,14 dans la pensée juive allemande de la Première moitié du XXème siècle," p. 274.

48. In this way, we come to the most convincing translations of contemporary exegetes, in particular to that of Hartmut Gese, in "Der Name Gott im Alten Testament" (already cited by André LaCocque): "ich erweise mich als der ich mich erweisen werde" (I shall show myself in that I shall show myself, as the one who will show himself).

Genesis 44

An Ancestral Narrative: The Joseph Story

ANDRÉ LaCOCQUE

" . . . Please let your servant remain as a slave to my lord in place
of the boy"

Genesis 44:33

If modern sociologists of the Bible are to be trusted, Israel from the
outset was a revolutionary movement. It was born from an uprising
against the overlords of the Canaanite city-states. Interestingly, at the
other chronological extreme, the Hebrew Scriptures end up during the
Second Temple period with a whole strand of subversive literature.
Then again, some in Israel deemed it necessary to protest the authori-
tarianism of the establishment, this time their own.

Between those two termini, Israel's mind-set remained remarkably
consistent. True, after a relatively long period during which the ideal of
liberty from the tyranny of sacral kingship was kept alive, Israel in her
turn instituted kingship as a mode of government. But no sooner was
there a king in Israel than there was also a prophet to censure him.
Prophetic presence is a permanent thorn in the side of the establishment. The prophet is the watchdog making sure that the institution
remains just and humane, that is, a means to an end rather than an end
in itself.

Within that perspective, the story of the Patriarch Joseph is built
along two axes: familial and political. The narrative is multidimensional, displaying psychological, sociological, and folkloric, as well as
theological elements. In fact, the complex biographical relations between Jacob and Joseph, as well as between Joseph and his brothers,
provide a litmus test for the exercise of political power at a specific time
in Israel's history. At stake is that exercise of power and whether it is
consistent with the ideal of the nation as expressed in the records of

its pristine existential options. For Claus Westermann, a family story (Genesis 37; 42–45) becomes, in chapters 39–41, a political story. The former reflects nomadic Israel; the latter the time of Solomon (see chapters 37–38). The story of Joseph taken as a whole serves as a literary transition between the two eras. It shows God as tutelary and "on the move," at ease in the national development of the group, as he was at its clannish stage.

Clearly, Westermann's stance depends on the Joseph story belonging to J and on the consensual early date of that literary source. Such a premise is nowadays severely criticized, however. Furthermore, it is doubtful whether we may slice the narrative in layers. Chapters 39–41 (the "political story") are, for George Coats, for example, a mere digression.[1] It is preferable, I believe, to take our distance from several of Westermann's assumptions, such as: the attribution of the narrative to J; an early dating, in the time of David-Solomon;[2] the splicing of two different trends in the story. The narrative, barring chapter 39,[3] is more consistent than admitted by Westermann. But it is, as said above, multi-dimensional. On one level, its aim is political. On another level, however, we leave the political and step into the sociological and the psychological. A particular aspect of the father-and-son relationship transpires in the texts that demands assessment and evaluation. On that score, the reader is first surprised to discover how dispassionate the record is. The generational relations are simply reported with an apparent objectivity and moral indifference. This is not out of line with the patriarchal narratives in general, which are known for their condensed form and the "matter-of-factness" of their style. The rape of Dinah, for example, is reported in Genesis 34 with terseness and with a quasi absence of feeling. The soberness of the composition also reflects what appears to be a striking lack of human sentiment in Jacob, Dinah's father, unless this be understood as a silent condemnation of his sons' lack of control.[4] In this chapter dedicated to the narrative genre, I intend to address this aspect of kin relationships; the father-son relationship in particular.

The Joseph story is not history, although it is historylike. Actually, it

1. George Coats, *From Canaan to Egypt: Structural and Theological Context for the Joseph Story*, Catholic Biblical Quarterly Monograph Series 4 (Washington, DC, 1976).

2. See also Gerhard von Rad, *The Problem of the Hexateuch and Other Essays*, translated by E. W. Trueman (New York: McGraw-Hill, 1966), p. 295.

3. And, of course, chapter 38, which has been inserted in Joseph's story for specific reasons.

4. Even today it is not clear to interpreters what to do with this text. Cf. Meir Sternberg, *The Poetics of Biblical Narrative* (Bloomington: Indiana University Press, 1985) and the critical review by Naomi Segal in *Vetus Testamentum* 38 (1988): 243–49.

belongs to folklore. As is usual in a tale emanating from an ancestral society, there is here a remarkable tension between the stability of a traditional framework and the authorial freedom of the poet. The result is refreshingly creative and properly artistic. As Robert Alter writes, "the artist, in fact, might be defined as a person who thrives on realizing new possibilities within formal limitations."[5]

It is of utmost importance to realize that the tale reflects the culture within which it was born and at least in part expresses the worldview of that culture. The Joseph novella sets the story mainly in Egypt and the author displays some knowledge of that country and its customs. The problem for the critic, therefore, is to assess the depth of the poet's familiarity with the alleged setting and to what Egyptian period he might be referring. Donald Redford has thoroughly researched this issue.[6] His conclusions are that the Joseph novella is a late composition. Its picture of Egypt reflects the Saite period or later (seventh to fifth centuries BCE), a fact that seems to be confirmed, according to his computation, by the presence in the story of some fifty terms of exilic or postexilic provenance. Of particular importance is the realization that, in contrast with the other patriarchal stories, we have here a single author (albeit an uncannily versatile one), using not only literary devices like suspense and pathos, but also occasionally reviving older traditions (see, for example, chapter 39).[7] The virtually total absence of any echo in Israelite tradition to the Joseph story points in the same direction, for it certainly can be construed as an indication that the story was not in existence before the exile in Babylon.[8] Redford proposes a time of composition between 650 and 425, that is, a time when the Jewish diaspora was already important both in the East and the West. This is not to say that the novella necessarily emanated from outside Palestine, but only that its general ethos corresponds to the diaspora mentality.

The Joseph story displays all the characteristics of the *Diaspora-*

5. Robert Alter, *The Art of Biblical Poetry* (New York: Basic Books, 1985).

6. Donald B. Redford, *A Study of the Biblical Story of Joseph (Genesis 37–50)* (Leiden: Brill, 1970).

7. This chapter may be an interpolation in the tale, a solution favored by Redford but rejected by Claus Westermann, *Genesis 37–50: A Commentary*, translated by John J. Scullion (Minneapolis: Augsburg, 1986).

8. One must put aside, to be sure, the texts where "Joseph" is the eponymous ancestor of the Northern Kingdom, like Deuteronomy 27:12; 33:13, 16; Amos 5:15; 6:6; Ezekiel 37:16; 1 Chronicles 5:2. James Kugel writes, "Joseph's forcible removal from his homeland resonated with the Jews' own experience of captivity and exile in Babylon." For Kugel, ancient stories were read again at that time. However, Chronicles omits this story, perhaps because it is a story of exile. One must wait until the "intertestamental" literature for a "rehabilitation" of Joseph. James Kugel, *In Potiphar's House* (San Francisco: Harper, 1990), p. 18.

novelle, such as Esther, Daniel, or Judith, which all describe a tense situation in which the Jews find themselves in a foreign land. In Egypt, Joseph is a slave, thrown in a dungeon after being abused by his master's wife, or consigned to oblivion by fellow prisoners after their liberation. Even when his fortune turns for the better, Joseph must, like other heroes in this literary genre, bear two names, display two faces, have two agendas, don two sets of clothing, eat at two tables, hold two discourses, live at the edge of two worlds.[9] The unexpected upshot of such a predicament is that, despite these strictures, exiled Jews become prime ministers, viziers, or queens. Their choice to trust God as their only salvation eventuates in making them in their turn saviors—of Jews and non-Jews alike. That is why the Egyptians come to Joseph and acknowledge that he saved their lives (Genesis 47); similarly, in the book of Esther, we come across the surprising note that the inhabitants of Susa rejoiced with the Jews at the "enthronement" of Mordecai (8:15) and that many Persians even became Jews at that occasion (8:17). Bringing these texts together has the effect of shedding more light on the relative age of each one. Westermann, who dates the story of Joseph from the time of Solomon, notes the prosperity of the pagans "because of Joseph," and adds, "This occurs again only after the collapse of the state of Israel: 'But seek the welfare of the city where I have sent you in exile and pray to the Lord on its behalf' (Jeremiah 29:7)."[10]

As a *diasporanovelle,*[11] the Joseph story is postexilic. The litmus test for this chronology and provenance is the theology of the tale. In stark contrast with the preceding sagas on the Patriarchs that are collective creations (cf. Gunkel), the distinction is clear because, as mentioned above, a single author is responsible for the core of the story of Joseph. It is also worth noting that the novella displays no concern for God's Covenant or for his promise of progeny and land. The absence of the Tetragrammaton (except in chapter 39)[12] befits such a situation. Instead, "Elohim" is used, but only in direct discourses and never to intimate a divine intervention from behind the scene. The discretion of the

9. See Genesis 41:45; 42; 43:32; etc.

10. Westermann, *Genesis 37–50,* p. 69.

11. Such nomenclature is used with full consciousness of its relative worth. Dorothy Irvin is right to remind us that, to call a narrative "saga, a myth, an epic, a legend, a *novelle,* a *stammessage* . . . is apt to be somewhat arbitrary, because it is not clear which ancient characteristics deserve which modern labels." See "The Joseph and Moses Stories," in *Israelite and Judaean History,* edited by J. H. Hayes and J. M. Miller (Philadelphia: Westminster, 1977), p. 184.

12. The use of the Tetragrammaton here comes from editorial intervention in the story. Clearly, the aim was to link the Joseph story with the patriarchal sagas.

document matches what is found elsewhere in such novellas. It is indeed characteristic of that literary genre that it focuses on the events themselves, showing their effect on a person or a group. It tends to present the circumstances as due to chance or fate (cf. Ruth 2:3; Esther 6:1–9). Serendipity governs every turn of the plot. As writes E. K. Bennett, "the effect of the impact of the event upon the person or group of persons is to reveal qualities which were latent and may have been unsuspectedly present in them, the event being used as the acid which separates and reveals the various qualities in the person or persons under investigation."[13] This applies well to the evolving person of Joseph.

Dating the Joseph novella to the postexilic or the Second Temple period explains a number of features that would otherwise remain unsolved. During the exile in Babylon, a veritable watershed that separates its history into two distinct units, Israel's vision changed; life was considered in terms of less of a sacral aura. The collapse of the institutions that maintained and emphasized the sacred character of history and of everyday existence was deeply felt. Theology went through a profound transformation and became more nuanced, for the circumstances were not conducive to imagining epiphanic interventions of God in national history or individual routine. Rather God was to be discovered in events as Providence. Concomitantly, there occurred a downplaying of the particular Covenant with Israel alone.

As could be expected, such a revision entailed more openness toward non-Jews, even to the point of implying that at times they might be theologically more sophisticated than the Israelites themselves. This is clearly the case in the third century book of Jonah,[14] as well as in the somewhat later short stories of the first part of Daniel (chapters 1–6). The novella of Joseph is not that late, but here already the Egyptians are presented at times in a favorable light (see Genesis 41:38–40; 43:23), and there appears to be no reluctance in having Joseph marry an Egyptian princess, daughter of a "pagan" priest (Genesis 41:50). Egypt welcomes Joseph and, later, the whole of his clan. In Genesis 48:1–20, Jacob as grandfather of Ephraim and Manasseh adopts and legitimizes those children born from a foreign mother.[15] Furthermore, there is a

---

13. E. K. Bennett, *A History of the German Novelle from Goethe to Thomas Mann* (Cambridge: Cambridge University Press, 1934), see pp. 18–19.

14. On the late date of the book of Jonah, see André and Pierre-E. LaCocque, *Jonah, A Psycho-Religious Approach to the Prophet* (Columbia: University of South Carolina Press, 1990).

15. In the first century CE story of *Joseph and Aseneth*, Ephraim and Manasseh's births provoke a scandal.

definitely ironic twist in stating (in Genesis 42:32) that the Egyptians would not eat with Jews. We would expect to find the opposite statement and J. A. Soggin understands the text as reflecting the later Jewish dietary laws.[16] I believe that he is wrong on that point. The wording of Genesis 42:32 is one more element in a list pointing toward not only a late date for the novella but also to a possible goading of the Jerusalem "orthodoxy." It is, as a matter of fact, a startling feature in the story how negatively are judged Joseph's brothers and, most especially Judah, who is the prime actor in the selling of the young lad to slave merchants (Genesis 37:26f.). Thomas Römer emphasizes this aspect. He pointedly adds that the Egyptian marriage of Joseph (41:50–52) runs counter to the politics of Ezra (Ezra 10).[17]

Putting "Joseph" among other mature forms of short stories and novellas helps us better to appreciate the importance in those tales of the courtier's acts of salvation through wise government. Everyone under his/her jurisdiction is blessed, Jews first, but also Persians in the story of Esther, Ninevites in Jonah, Babylonian kings and people in Daniel, Egyptians in Joseph. W. L. Humphreys is right to point out that "human intentions and deeds are caught up in ever larger contexts of will and design."[18]

The young Joseph can be classified among those whom Susan Niditch calls the *underdogs*.[19] Put in a nutshell, the story is about someone who, although facing impossible odds, somehow succeeds in fulfilling great designs. In a way, this is a feature that "runs in the family." Before his son, Jacob had also experienced very modest beginnings as an expatriate offering his services for hire. He too had climbed up the social ladder "from rags to riches." But on that score there is already a great difference between father and son. Jacob's fate fitted the folkloric pattern according to which the underdog often becomes a trickster. He brings about a change or resolution of problem through trickery. And for a while, this is precisely what could have been expected from Joseph. The reader could surmise, from the dreams of the lad, that it was in his

16. J. A. Soggin, "Notes on the Joseph Story," in *Understanding Poets and Prophets: Essays in Honor of George Wishart Anderson,* edited by A. G. Auld (Sheffield: JSOT Press, 1993), pp. 336–49.

17. Thomas Römer, "Le cycle de Joseph," *Foi et Vie* 86, no. 3 (1987): 3–15.

18. W. Lee Humphreys, *Joseph and His Family: A Literary Study* (Columbia: University of South Carolina Press, 1988), p. 124; cf. p. 130.

19. Susan Niditch, *Underdogs and Tricksters: A Prelude to Biblical Folklore* (San Francisco: Harper and Row, 1987).

intention to somehow help the favorable spinning of the wheel of fortune. To our surprise, however, Joseph is no trickster. Rather, he is described as a sage. True, his actions are not always up to wisdom's expectation, but his attitude is all the same a middle-of-the-road prudent progression in life. "The trickster," says Niditch, "sees God face to face, whereas the wisdom hero receives his messages through symbolic dreams."[20] This well defines the contrasting characters of Jacob and Joseph. The latter, initially at least, reports incredibly offensive dreams to the very people from whom he should expect the worst. Such a naiveté on his part is probably to be understood as a total absence, not only of imagination—a grave flaw in a sage!—but also of self-assertion. In stark contrast with his father's natural guile, it does not occur to him that he could connive and work toward the realization of his dreams. It is precisely this absence of aggressiveness on his part that obliterates, in his eyes, any offense in his revelations. Why get angry at something no one has control over? Why would his father and brothers hold a grudge against him when he is not responsible for what he dreamed and has no intention to do anything to make the dreams come true? To him, they will come true by themselves, without effort on his part. His parents and siblings should not take umbrage at the issue. For Joseph is no trickster; if anything, he is simpleminded. His brothers, however, deeply resent this dubious aspect of quietism in their younger sibling. They are not of the same pacifistic type and they prove it. They have recourse to deceit and worse in order to counteract what they construe as a conspiracy. But, if Joseph is different from his father, how much more so are his brothers? The nuance is important, for, however deceitful they may be, none of them is made of the same stuff as their father. They connive like he did in his time, but they do not see God, face to face or otherwise. Their audacity lies in sinking to the depth of perversity, a far cry from Jacob's challenges to men and God alike.

In short, the plot of the story displays intricate moves by different actors to grab power. Some of them will shrink from nothing to take their destiny into their own hands—even if it means simultaneously taking away their brother's life. As for Joseph, he will continue to walk through existence as in a dream, until the brutal reality catches up with him and teaches him the lesson of his life. After that, his persona becomes very different. True, there are still some lingering remnants of

20. Ibid., p. 106.

passivity in Joseph in Egypt, but he too, he more than all the others combined, will eventually deal with power and accede to supreme authority.

Thus, the core of this family saga is about the seizure of power. Grabbing power may, of course, take various forms. But in this story it invariably amounts to becoming the favorite of a central power figure: father, slave master, or the Pharaoh of Egypt. As to the means to satisfy such ambitions, they span a whole gamut of possibilities, from bragging to murder, via envy, enslavement, deceit, parricidal cruelty, moral callousness, indifference to others' fundamental feelings, utter spiritual dryness, and other such manifestations of vice that provoke the eclipse of God, but also wisdom, determination, and steadfastness.

Reserving for a later development further reflections on the contrast between Joseph and his father Jacob, it may already be noted here that Joseph is never graced with a theophany. There is here no vision of an *axis mundi* bridging heaven and earth—to cite only one such experience of Jacob. In Genesis 28, Joseph's father peers, so to speak, into another realm; he crosses the boundary between heaven and earth and comes out from this rapture entirely transformed. Not so with Joseph. To him God is only more or less present, more or less absent, as it befits a man who himself is rather lukewarm and without any trace of extravagance in his behavior. That the absence here of theophany or even of direct divine discourse is not due to accident or to the stylistic preference of an author different from the one of the Jacob saga is demonstrated by Genesis 46. For here there is a theophany, but it is for Jacob's benefit, not for Joseph's, who, by way of contrast, is mentioned in the divine discourse as a mere instrument. He is to close the eyes of his father when the time comes. As Niditch rightly says, "a study in typology becomes a study in comparative theology."[21]

Theophany has made room for a more indirect divine revelation: the "visions of the night." Dreams play a major role in the story. Like angels in similar narratives, dreams represent amphibologically God's closeness—but as "through a glass darkly"—and God's remoteness—but at a short distance, as is the case in Wisdom literature in general. Here, dreams are acknowledged as bona fide vehicles of the divine will (see 40:8; 41:15–16, 25, 32). In contrast to this, however, such confidence in their mantic value is questioned by several texts expressing a definite skepticism (see Deuteronomy 13:2; Zechariah 10:2; Sirach 34:1–8).

21. Ibid., p. 148.

But, we need to recall, the tendency in the later writings is to deempha-
size direct divine dialogues with human beings. God's direct addresses
recede behind dreamed revelations (compare, for example, Jubilees 14:1
and Genesis 15:1). At that point, the Israelite approach falls in closer
parallel with the ancient Near Eastern literature where, indeed, the divine prefers to draw near through the oneiric medium. But the analogy
stops here, for, in contradistinction to the Egyptian literature, for instance, where dreams are presented as giving clear revelations, in the
story of Joseph they need an authorized interpretation (as is often the
case in the Bible, see Judges 7:13–14; Daniel 2:1ff.; Esther 11:5–11).[22]
In the present study, I am less interested in the forecasting quality of
dreams than in what their patterns reveal of the dreamer's character and
of his relations with others.

It is not superfluous at this point to insist again upon the initial passivity of Joseph. It is, as a matter of fact, a striking feature of the novella
that the events seem to carry the character Joseph more than he moves
them along. On this score as well, he is more a dreamer than an actor.
At some point of his life, however, his expertise in dream-making and
in dream-interpreting will propel him to the top of statesmanship. It is
exactly where the hinge point in the life of Joseph is set by the narrative.
Then, the quiet young man suddenly goes through a metamorphosis of
sorts and proves to be up to his task. True, the task is somewhat dictated
to him by Pharaoh's metaphors, but, beyond such "manipulation," it is
evident that the text wants to show the passage in the young man of
potentiality to actuality. There occurs an interesting evolution in Joseph
toward decision making and performance. The contrast is all the starker
with the early beginnings when options were so surprisingly circum-
stantial, the "hero" drifting, so to speak, at the will of a wheel of fortune
taking him up and down to resounding successes and dismal failures.
In the episode with Potiphar's wife, for example, Joseph displays not
only an absence of initiative, he opposes no resistance to the aggressiveness of the woman other than flight without honor if not without conscience. It is indeed no little achievement of this novella to treat the

22. To be noted is the use of the verb *ptr* and the noun *pitaron* to speak of the interpretation of
dreams. This only occurs in the Joseph story (40:8, 16, 22; 41:8, 12, 13, 15; 40:5, 8, 12, 18; 41:11)
and the book of Daniel (under the Aramaic form *pšr;* 2:4–7, 9, 16, 24–26, 30, 36, 45; 4:3f., 6, 15f.,
21; 5:7f., 12, 15–17, 26; 7:16). It is also the case in postbiblical Hebrew and Aramaic (cf. D. B.
Redford, *The Biblical Story of Joseph,* p. 58). Another parallel between Joseph and Daniel is the
remarkable feature, common to both, that what the Jewish interpreter reveals to the pagan mon-
arch is simply the latter's projection onto the screen of "his spirit" (Daniel 2:1, 3) of what he has
in "the heart" (Daniel 2:30). Thus the dream is thrown down from its magic pedestal.

central character, as well as more secondary ones, in a dynamic fashion, showing how their minds can change over the years and how youthful weaknesses can be transcended by mature options. These latter, surely, do not eradicate the past but they grant it an entirely new meaning (see Genesis 45:5ff., and especially the central text of 45:8).[23]

Transformation reveals former potentiality. Joseph could not have become a dynamic—and somewhat Machiavellian—statesman,[24] unless he already had such capacities. It is now made clear that he first repressed them and was hiding behind a debonair front. In hindsight, the possibility exists that Joseph's dreaming of dreams was not as passive as we intimated earlier. To be sure, the young Joseph's attitude was one of sheer denial of liability regarding his visions of self-aggrandizement, but retrospectively, from the way he chooses to treat his brothers when they come down to Egypt, we are led to conclude that here is a man perfectly able to control his own feelings, or to deny them altogether, and to give priority to other inner drives deemed more important. Among these no doubt are the will for status, for power. Thus later, the natural emotions at the sight of his siblings and at hearing what they have to say about his father and his younger brother, whom he hardly or never knew before, are not allowed to interfere with his plans for revenge. He sticks no matter what to his intended manipulation of these unjust fools. The influence of Wisdom literature is again clear here. The glorification of the sage's self-control is a familiar motif, and the tales of the wise courtier delight in showing that their hero's wit plunges into confusion those who had connived against him. Suffice it to recall the stories of Esther or of Ahikar.

It is within that perspective that we must read Genesis 47. Morally this chapter is shocking. But it is apparently acceptable, from the Wisdom point of view, to spoil the whole of Egypt to fill the coffers of Pharaoh and thus give a patent proof of Joseph's total commitment to the person of his lord.[25] Furthermore, the chapter is clearly etiological. It provides a flattering explanation to Israelites, astounded as they must

23. The evolution of characters in the course of the narrative is a particularity of the novella, in contrast with the "short story," for instance, where the characters are at the end as they were at the start. Cf. Humphreys, *Joseph and His Family: A Literary Study*, pp. 184f.: Joseph becomes an exemplary courtier, a theme that belongs to Wisdom literature.

24. See the terrible development in Genesis 47:13ff.

25. Frank Crüsemann defends the thesis that the Joseph narrative was written in the Solomonic time to exalt kingship as a form of government. The lesson of the story is that kingship is the only condition for national reconciliation. In Genesis 47, its use of coercion is the only way to avoid

have been by what they saw happening in neighboring Egypt, of the subservience of its inhabitants to the all-powerful Pharaoh, the sole owner of both land and souls. In so doing, the story killed two birds with one stone. It brought about smiles in the audience of freedom-loving Israelites, and it credited an ancestor of theirs with keeping alive both Israelites and Egyptians at the time of the story. Besides, did not the latter acknowledge their indebtedness to the Pharaoh's sage vizier?[26] As we will see, it befits the novella genre to present the hero as a providential person not only for his or her own people but also for the host nation in the midst of which the action transpires.

For the story of Joseph is a salvation story. It is also a taut drama between father and son, brother and siblings, the equivalent of which would be hard to find in the ancient world—although the narrative structure as such is not without several parallels. As intimated above, the narrative unwinds on both the familial and the political levels. It is on both levels as well that salvation will occur. First, following the order and intention of the story, the familial is envisaged. Genesis 37 sets the stage by stating that Jacob irrationally prefers Joseph over all his other sons. In the image of this first and primordial paradox, the whole story is filled with taut ambiguities and woven with extremes that uneasily coexist. The father's reaction to his son's bragging is itself a mixture of reprobation and pride. He chides Joseph but we learn that he also cher-

---

famine (cf. 41:34ff.). The long-term policy (*Vorratspolitik*) is what legitimizes Joseph's power. It is a life-saver (45:5, 11; 50:21). *Der Widerstand gegen das Königtum: Die antiköniglichen Texte des Alten Testaments und der Kampf um den frühen israelitischen Staat* (Newukirchen-Vluyn: Neukirchener Verlag, 1978), p. 148; Crüsemann's thesis is made clear in the very title of this section of the book (p. 143): "The Story of Joseph-Legitimation of an Administrative Rulership and of a Royal Policy of Taxation." In that connection, we can recall the very harsh conditions prevailing in Jerusalem in the sixth century "Restoration."

26. Genesis 47:25: "you saved our lives!" 47:1–12 and 13–26 offer a counterpoint. While Egypt is enslaved to Pharaoh in order to survive, the Hebrews' welfare is taken care of by the Pharaoh (and we know that they will become slaves in Egypt). All this is fraught with irony. "The family of the one who came to Egypt as a slave has become an independent community that owns land, while the native Egyptians have become landless slaves (47:13–27)." In Thomas W. Mann, *The Book of the Torah* (Atlanta: John Knox Press, 1988), p. 76. Crüsemann (*Der Widerstand gegen das Königtum*, p. 149) does not seem sensitive to the irony in the text. He draws a parallel with the text of 1 Samuel 8:17, a correlation that itself does not lack irony! In fact, the Egyptians become Pharaoh's slaves in the crudest sense of the word. We should contrast this with chapter 50 where the brothers proclaim themselves the slaves of Joseph. But the term is rejected in all its connotations, *because Joseph is not God* (50:19). Does this not mean by implication that Pharaoh was claiming a divinity that belongs only to Yhwh? Genesis 47 and 50 do not stand in parallel, but in contrast (*pace* Crüsemann).

ishes his son's blusters in his heart (37:11). As for Joseph, he feels little inclination toward his brothers, but he goes out of his way (Genesis 37:14b, 17) to inquire about their well-being (37:13, 16 . . .). These other sons of Jacob are first presented as a mixture of viciousness, cruelty, blood-thirstiness, and later on of straightforwardness, simplicity, self-forgetfulness. Tension is maintained from start to finish in the novella because, after being sold as a slave to slave traders, everyone thinks that Joseph is dead when in fact he is alive and well. There is irony, even dark humor, in that Jacob mourns the lad when he really need not weep but rejoice.

It is clear to any reader of the novella that the relationship between father and son is highly unhealthy and outrageously unjust. Jacob projects on his sons the Manichean split he discovers within himself. One child is all good and the others are all bad.[27] Until the end, the personality of Jacob remains a battlefield where the best and the worst cleave indecisively to each other in a mortal embrace. Jacob is the man of equivocation. Here we come as close to his soul as we did in the episode at the Brook of Jabbok (Genesis 32).

Similarly, there is irony in the roller-coasterlike destiny of Joseph, who started in life with the conviction of being immune from the ills that generically plague the rest of humanity. He is tossed from success to dismal dereliction, from general oblivion to fame, from there again to the pit, and eventually to consummate elevation. Fittingly, even God's presence and action become here highly ambiguous. True, we are told at times that "the Lord was with Joseph" (39:2, 21), but such declarations are conspicuously rare and all in one chapter, so that the suspicion of the reader is aroused that we are probably dealing with pious additions to an otherwise purposefully "secular" tale.[28] These sensational ups and downs in Joseph's life, such descents and ascents, humiliations and glorifications are, generally speaking, characteristic of myth. Much of the power of the story resides in the deeply rooted human empathy that the reader feels vis-à-vis a man described without complacency by the author, but one who goes through the vicissitudes of life as through the purifying crucible of initiatory rites of passage.

The story stresses that God's presence to Joseph is mediated by the

---

27. See the terrible accusation addressed to ten of his sons by Jacob in Genesis 42:36, "You are making me childless!" This reminds Westermann (*Genesis 37–50*, p. 113) of the oracles of woe by some prophets, for example, Hosea 9:12).

28. See below my remarks on Genesis 39. Gerhard von Rad (*The Problem*, p. 295) says that there are no signs of interest in anything theological or pertaining to the *Heilsgeschichte*.

Patriarch Jacob/Israel. In the absence of his father, Joseph in Egypt lives with only a dimmed and faint divine presence. Only when Jacob is about to come down to Egypt to join his son is there a multiplication of references to God on the part of Joseph (45:4–8; 50:15–20). E. M. McGuire has pinpointed that indissolubility of the persons of God and father for Joseph. He writes, Joseph "consistently and graciously defers to both father and God in questions of authority, precedence, and definitive interpretations."[29]

In that respect, the theological statements in Genesis 39:1–5 display a strictly authorial point of view. Before it can be said with this chapter that "the Lord was with Joseph"—a declaration that, strictly speaking, belongs to the denouement—it is important to follow Joseph into the general oblivion of which he is the victim (40:23). If chapter 39 were not an authorial intervention in the narrative, the motif of providential governance at this point of the story would be anticlimactic. Joseph, we are shown, was forgotten, not just by one individual, the Pharaoh's cupbearer, but by all, including God for all practical purposes.

The paradox is that there is one who has not forgotten him, namely his father (37:11 and passim). It is only through that human medium that the divine remembrance is also secured. Joseph in the pit where his brothers threw him, or Joseph in the Egyptian solitary confinement where he is consigned to oblivion, holds to life only by one thread, the other end of which is in his father's hands. Whether they know it or not does not change the fact. In the story of Joseph, God speaks exclusively through the channel of the father/son relationship. It is the key to the novella. Statistically, there are no less than ninety-two occurrences of the word "father" in the chapters 37–50 of Genesis. Nowhere else in the Old Testament do we find such a focus on fatherhood.

As in the relation of male and female according to earlier chapters of Genesis, father and son are here only one organic reality contemplated from two different vantage points. As the "human" is one flesh seen either from the side of masculinity/convexity, or from the side of femininity/concavity, so paternity-descent are two aspects of the same relation. In the novella, Jacob is envisaged strictly in his role as the father of Joseph (or of Benjamin, Joseph's alter ego; more on this below); and Joseph is throughout the son of Jacob/Israel. Were it not for this particularity, the story would make very little sense. The deepest creative am-

29. E. M. McGuire, "A Tale of Son and Father," in *Images of Man and God: Old Testament Short Stories in Literary Focus*, edited by Burke O. Long (Sheffield: Almond Press, 1981), p. 19.

biguity in the tale obtains through the physical separation between father and son, while spiritually (and psychologically) communion between the two is what triumphs over all odds.

It is remarkable that, in partly dealing with a similar topic, the Greek myth of Oedipus brings us to the other extreme in this type of relation. Oedipus is the murderer of his father, who is in the first place the murderer of his son (and the relations between mother and son or son and mother do not fare much better). In Genesis 37–50, on the contrary, there is no Joseph without Jacob—not only from the generational point of view—and there is no Jacob/Israel without Joseph. True, between father and son, the story also acknowledges a process, albeit a provisional one, of distancing. As is typical of adolescence, this occurs when Joseph is seventeen (37:2). But the separation, although combining the temporal and the spatial axes, is only temporary; it is transcended by at least one of the two partners refusing to consider the distance as decisive and final.

From the beginning, there is the relationship father-son, son-father. One reality that can only be put asunder when both cut the cord and break the unity. On the contrary, when this is not permitted to occur, the being, common to both, falls victim of the "death" of Joseph. Jacob goes through "negative-being," as the mourning rites (37:34) signify. They display all the signs of death of the mourner herself or himself. One throws dust on one's head, as an acknowledgment of our return to the dust of the earth, and one dons rags, tokens of disaffection for life and its vanities. Jacob refuses to be comforted and declares, "I am going down to the Sheol to the son of my grief" (37:35).

But, in the story, there is an important peripeteia: Joseph is not dead, so neither is Jacob. One of them goes up toward more and more being, toward plus-being, and therefore the other's going down to negative-being by sympathy is untimely and ironical. Symbolically, the story juxtaposes in stark contrast the abundance in Egypt, thanks to Joseph's wisdom, and the famine that hits Canaan, now that Joseph is gone and that Jacob is the shadow of himself. (Only when he is sure that Joseph lives, does "the spirit of Jacob revive" [45:27] and abundance is within reach [45:18–20]).

That is why, even when the text focuses on Joseph in Egypt and seems to forget about Canaan where Jacob resides, the father is never absent from the background. The elevation of Joseph as well as his earlier humiliations must be read with Jacob/Israel in mind. Joseph's sufferings were his at Haran (Genesis 29–31). And it belongs to the artistic tension in the composition that the son's glorification is not shared by his father for a long time—he does not even know about his son's continued existence. But as soon as Joseph feels that the relationship with his family can be restored, he rushes into a highly revealing statement regarding his father: "And now," he says to his brothers, "you see with your own eyes, and so does my brother Benjamin . . . and you'll tell my father . . . all you have seen" (45:12–13). As McGuire writes, "As significant as the brothers' knowledge of him may be, that knowledge seems to have largely the function of bringing Jacob into Joseph's presence so that the father may at last truly see and hear his lost son."[30] Jacob's response to Joseph's invitation is perfectly fitting, "I shall go and see him before I die" (45:28). That declaration announces the denouement as it celebrates the restoration of the equilibrium in the shared being of father and son. Then Jacob/Israel once again speaks of his death, but in a totally different spirit. "Bounteousness of my son Joseph alive! I'll go and see him before I die" (45:28), and, after the realization of his desire, "This time I can die now that I have seen your face, for you *are* alive!" (46:30).

The father's exclamation rings as an echo of the son's illogical but so meaningful cry, "I am Joseph! Is my father alive?" (45:3), a question that makes little sense after the dialogue with Judah and that is set in contrast with 43:7, 27f., for instance, for Judah's eloquence had been precisely based on the heart-wrenching evocation of the father Jacob, whose "life" [or, "soul," *nephes*] is bound up in his [Benjamin's] life [*nephes*]" (44:30). But Joseph's inquiry makes sense within the referential framework of his intimate and almost symbiotic relation with the father. This point, we just saw, is again emphasized by Judah speaking of the ties between Jacob and Benjamin.

Benjamin, also born from Rachel like Joseph, is almost completely identified in the story with Joseph. This is an important feature, as it shows another alternative in the father-and-son relationship whereby the son does not go away from the father, or else only for a short span of time. (Here again is a possibility not contemplated by the Oedipus myth.) Within this perspective, Benjamin is Joseph not betrayed and not sold into slavery by his brothers; he is Joseph at home with the father and spared of all tribulations and adventures of an "independent"

---

30. Ibid., p. 16.

life. The father, we are told, dotes on Benjamin as he did on Joseph. Each of the two sons in turn "fills the horizon" of Jacob, so that he seems to have no other children than those he begot through Rachel. With a cruelty that only age and despair excuse, he tells his other children, "My son [Benjamin] shall not go down with you. Now that his brother is dead, he is the only one left" (42:38), a declaration curiously and perhaps pathologically repeated by Judah in his speech to the vizier Joseph (44:20). Thus Joseph's desire to see his brother Benjamin amounts to the contemplation of himself as not-betrayed, not-rejected, not-murdered by his fratricidal brothers. And Judah, in his address, fully confirms Joseph's intuition. The sameness between Joseph and Benjamin is uncanny. The symbiotic attachment of Jacob to the one and the other makes them interchangeable twins.

That is why Joseph places Benjamin above all of the other brothers at the banquet table. In the person of Benjamin also is accomplished the initial dream of leadership (37:5ff.). His receiving "five times as much as all of them" (together?) in 43:34 parallels the prostration of all before Joseph in 43:28. There is nothing random in the fact that the royal cup of Joseph is "found" in Benjamin's sack (44:12). Benjamin, of course, is innocent as Joseph was innocent while found "guilty" by his brothers in Canaan. Similarly, Benjamin is threatened with slavery as Joseph was sold as a slave before him. The parallel is so evident that Judah readily draws it in 44:16ff. The royal cup, furthermore, has passed from Joseph to his alter ego. Symbolically, the sign is ambiguous, for it includes Benjamin and excludes the other brothers.

As a foil of sorts to young Benjamin, Simeon, the second eldest[31] is put by Joseph in prison, as he himself had been in the Egyptian dungeon. Thus, Simeon as well is put in the position of "sameness" with his brother. He too becomes Joseph's alter ego. The difference with Benjamin, however, is that he is Joseph-humiliated, Joseph-betrayed. Benjamin and Simeon are the antipodes between which the whole life of Joseph is wavering. Halfway, so to speak, between the one and the other are the rest of the brothers participating in the royal banquet organized by Joseph. They too are included within the aura of Joseph's personality but with an ironic twist: the brothers are extremely uncomfortable, unsure whether the meal marks the end of their torments or the end of their lives (43:33).

31. Dorothy F. Zeligs may be right in suggesting that if Joseph keeps Simeon as a hostage rather than the elder brother, Reuben, it is because of the intercession of the latter on behalf of Joseph in Canaan. *Psychoanalysis and the Bible: A Study in Depth of Seven Leaders* (New York: Bloch, 1974), p. 81.

Pharaoh also is another contrasting persona in Joseph's web of relationships. Joseph describes himself as a father to Pharaoh (45:8). But it is a sham relationship. Egypt is, to Israel or to Joseph, a false substitute, in fact an obstacle, a usurper. Joseph brings Egypt to total dependence on Pharaoh (47), thus taking an anticipatory vengeance, it seems, on the future slavery of the Hebrews in Egypt. It is ultimately not to the Egyptians that he is called to be brother and father but to his own family. As he says at the end of the story, all the preceding events have led to bringing his family to a land of plenty and to installing his father in Goshen (50:20). There, "Joseph *nourished* his father, his brothers, all the family, according to their little ones" (47:12; and see 50:21).

The word "nourish" is stressed in the passage above for, in contrast to what happens in the Oedipus myth, the father-and-son relationship is here not a question of fate but rather of opportunity. The accent in the Hebrew tale is not on a deterministic distribution of roles that makes Jacob forever the father of Joseph, and of Joseph forever the son of Jacob. What is, on the contrary, emphasized is the dynamism of their relationship and the reversibility of their roles. As seen above, Joseph is the "father" of Pharaoh (45:8) as much as Pharaoh is to him a father-figure while he is deprived of the presence of Jacob. It is thus to be expected that, being father to Pharaoh, Joseph should be father also to Jacob. He is father of his father, and he demonstrates that much not only in nourishing him, as the texts insist, but even more importantly in being charged with the mission to carry his bones out of Egypt (50:5, see also the following verses; contrast with 49:29). As the parent carries the child, so Joseph, as another Aeneas, brings his father to ultimate fulfillment. Jacob depends on Joseph as Joseph used to depend on Jacob. As Shmuel Trigano writes,

> Here a fundamental concept of the Hebrew thinking comes to life, according to which the world is in a constitutive relationship of descent and generation. A word does not begin, as for the Greek, on the "tabula rasa" of abstraction; for any word has parents before it. The thinker . . . is essentially the son of his father and mother (even when he ignores or hides it), and he prolongs, willy-nilly, a text that had begun a long time before him.[32]

The theme of Jacob's bones stresses the transitoriness of the Hebrew stay in Egypt as Israel understood it. But as regards the father-son rela-

---

32. Shmuel Trigano, *La demeure oubliée: Genèse religieuse du politique* (Paris: Lieu Commun, 1984), p. 39, n. 9.

tion, it also reveals a dialectic of life and death that needs to be emphasized here: The presence of the son spells out the imminence and un-
avoidability of death for the father. The new generation pushes out the
old. The insistence of the texts on the necessity to move the Patriarch's
bones from Egypt and transfer them to the Promised Land shows that
it is no trivial or romantic detail. Jacob comes down to Egypt on the
condition of not staying in Egypt. It was necessary for the perpetuation
of the Covenant between God and Israel that the father and son be
reunited (even if it be in Egypt), but that reunion as strangers in a
strange land is a new stepping-stone toward further achievements. At
the same time, the dialectical relationship of father and son demands
that, in return for his "dependence" on Joseph, Jacob requests his son's
filial loyalty (47:29–31). Such a reversibility of roles is again movingly
emphasized in the description of Joseph bowing before Jacob (48:11–
12), as Jacob bowed before Joseph (47:31; cf. 43:28), so that no one can
tell who is more important than the other.

The story of Joseph explores as well another plane of family relationships. Sibling rivalry evidently plays a major role. It is, however, noteworthy that the brothers' hatred toward Joseph comes in the tale after
the statement that the brothers' relationship with their father was already twisted. We can understand what Joseph reports to his father at
the beginning of the novella in a more positive light than is usually
conceded. Joseph, we are told, "brought an evil report of them to their
father" (37:2). True, the deed raises suspicion in the reader's mind. It
might well be a despicable initiative on the part of Joseph, acting as a
"stool pigeon" in a detective story. We feel no natural empathy for that
kind of character, however useful their spying may be to justice. It is
legitimate to understand Joseph's initiative as embittering the relationship between his father and his siblings through a demonstration of his
own contrasting faithfulness and worthiness. This would fit his portrait
as something of a brat, and this reading is certainly correct. Joseph may
simply have been outraged by their contempt for Jacob. This reading
seems confirmed by the following verse, which says, "Now Israel loved
Joseph more than his [other] sons."[33] Furthermore, it is highly remarkable that there is a total absence of competition between Joseph and one
of his brothers, namely, Benjamin. Here, no envy, no jealousy, mars a
relationship that reflects all the more negatively on the warfare with
"the gang of ten."

---

33. Interestingly, *Midrash Rabba* on Song of Songs 8:6 applies the text to Genesis 37:3, 11: the
love strong like death refers to the love of Jacob for Joseph, and jealousy strong like hell applies to
the envy of the brothers.

Thus, in this astute story of familial turpitude, there is a factual reflection on evil and its appalling perpetuation from generation to generation. But the interpretations of this phenomenon are multifarious. Already the fact of Joseph telling his dreams to his father and siblings is open to several explanations. First, telling the dreams through haughtiness and spite to whoever cares to listen may be one way to play for the hand of the father; it may be a ploy for confirming him in his preference and his injustice. Jacob must be right, for he has bet on a winner; the dreams say so.[34] Thus the visions may appear "dictated" by the father's projection on Joseph of his desire for grandiosity. Hearing Joseph's report, Jacob only feigns to be upset, in fact keeping the event in his memory, probably with a secret desire to see the dreams come true (Genesis 37:11).

But another understanding leaves open the possibility that Joseph is in fact calling for help. He needs reassurance, and he tells the dream with the desire that his father and elder brothers will forestall a destiny that he dreads rather than welcomes.[35] Furthermore, there is a gradation in the two dreams he shares with others. In the first one, the metonymy remains strictly impersonal. The sheaves are tied by Jacob's sons, and one of them, Joseph's, stands upright (note the phallic symbolism and the implicit acknowledgment of his superiority by the other males around him). To be sure, the meaning of the allegory is clear, and one cannot blame the brothers for interpreting it the way they do. Only, if indeed it is on Joseph's part a call for help, they badly miss the point as their hatred increases toward someone they, no less than their father, have boxed into a preconceived role. Soon, the family's conspiracy not to let Joseph be Joseph will become a conspiracy not to let him be. Jealousy, envy, hatred, hostility (37:4, 11) on the one hand, and doting and spoiling love on the other (37:3), conspire in wrapping Joseph in smothering bonds—murder is in the air.

34. Alfred Adler writes, "No child likes to be the smallest, the one whom one does not trust. . . . Such knowledge stimulates a child to prove that he can do everything. His striving for power becomes markedly accentuated and we find the youngest very usually a man who has developed a desire to overcome all others, satisfied only with the very best." In *Understanding Human Nature* (New York: Fawcett World Library, 1954), p. 123.

35. Adler's concept of birth order is useful for understanding the psychology of Joseph. Adler repeatedly refers to our story as one of the best illustrations of his theories in that respect. About Joseph's frustration of being the favorite, for instance, he writes, "History as well as experience demonstrates that happiness does not consist in being the first or best. To teach a child such a principle makes him one-sided; above all it robs him of his chance of being a good fellow man" (ibid., p. 124). Besides, it is to be noted that Joseph combines in his person the problems of both the youngest and the eldest child! He is, allegedly, the last child of his father, and he is the first child of his mother (his brother Benjamin, by the same mother, is born a long time after Joseph.)

This side of the story above all is Oedipal. In avenging themselves on the person of their younger brother, the siblings murder the father. The blow their crime deals to Jacob leaves no doubt in that respect.[36] With the alleged death of his son, Jacob cannot see anything good remaining in the world, only the evil side of reality. His attitude vis-à-vis the surviving sons is more distant than ever, more distrustful, more suspicious. Murder never comes to its full realization in that family, but all the same, the members kill each other, however quietly. There is among them a sadism of sorts that is to become eventually still more disconcerting when Joseph, under the guise of probing how much his brothers have changed, plays cat and mouse with them.

Another "gap" in the story[37] must be mentioned, one which constitutes a prologue to the story's sequel. Between the moment Joseph is sold as a slave, when he is seventeen (see Genesis 37:2), and the time of his confrontation with his brothers in Egypt, some twenty years elapse (Genesis 41:46, 47). During all these years, Joseph apparently makes no attempt at letting his family know that he is safe and sound, not even when he occupies the second highest position in Egypt. This is certainly one of the most disturbing silences of the whole story. Is it perhaps a sign of relief on the part of Joseph, who feels that for the first time he can be himself? Or are we to interpret it as a sign that Joseph blamed his parents as much as his siblings for what happened to him in Canaan? Traditional Jewish literature has seen the problem and has tried to solve it. The intertestamental *Testament of the Twelve Patriarchs* says that Joseph acted out of respect for his brothers whom he would not denounce (*Testament of Joseph* 10:6; 11:2; 15:3; 17:1). Later, being honored by Potiphar, he rejoiced to have forgotten his father's house, especially as he was no longer the object of envy. But God was displeased with this, adds the Midrash (*Genesis Rabba* 87:3–4), which exonerates Joseph for having delayed so much the reconciliation with his brothers. An angel (Gabriel?) prevented him from doing so forthwith by accusing them of intending to kill him.[38]

All this is not very convincing. One feature in the text may, however,

---

36. Westermann draws a parallel here with the story of Abel and Cain. The latter turns his hatred against the one who is preferred rather than against the One who prefers. This, "shows a profound understanding of the human condition" (p. 37). All the more so, let us add, as God is in fact the one who is murdered by proxy.

37. On the device of "gapping" in biblical stories, see Sternberg, *The Poetics of Biblical Narrative.*

38. Cf. *Yelamdenu* 28 in *Beith ha-Midrash,* edited by Adolf Jellinek (Jerusalem: Bamberger and Vahrman, 1938), vol. 4, pp. 79–90.

prove more revealing, namely, how Joseph called his sons in Egypt. He must have been moved by powerful emotions, for their names seem to express vindication over the odds created by his relatives (41:51–52). The firstborn of his sons he names Menasheh and explains, "God has made me forget [put aside] all my toils and all my father's house" (Genesis 41:51). The second son's name is not any more considerate as regards his family in Canaan or for his past. He calls the lad Ephraim, "For God has made me fructify in the land [meant to] afflict me." Thus, Joseph betrays sentiments that he never expressed and which the narrator never volunteered.[39]

If so, Joseph's silences shed an unexpected light on his habitual attitude of obedience to authorities (all, of course, being fatherly figures). It is not that Joseph's submissiveness be necessarily a convenient expedient. For it may rather be his way not to offend anyone for whom he feels natural respect and allegiance. The rest of the story shows at any rate that it is not lack of backbone on his part, nor, we can venture, a display of obsequiousness. Simply, Joseph is too much of a good son, of a good servant, of a good law-abiding citizen, to be really helpful to anyone (and first of all to himself). He has not yet discovered the virtue of disobedience, the creative side of negativity. When he realizes it— as indeed he does—he tends naturally to go overboard. He becomes unnecessarily cruel toward people as he blames himself for not having better loved when there was still time.

We must remember that the identity of Joseph is strictly narrative and is exhausted in the narrative. In contrast with Abraham, for example, Joseph exists in his experience and only there. I believe it is one of the reasons why he unduly prolongs to the point of excess the testing of his brothers—a test that includes, among other extravagances, giving five times more food to Benjamin than to the others, an echo of the situation when Joseph was by far preferred by his father over the rest of his siblings. In Joseph's mind, it is a test to see how the others will react this time; but it is also a revelation of his solitude; he tries to make someone share his viewpoint. What is he secretly desiring? Is it that the others once again retaliate against the one who has been so blatantly elevated over them? Or is it that the story—which, in fact, is his story—be made different this time? Either way, there is some advantage for Joseph. There could be the removal of his feeling of guilt as he can-

---

39. Joseph's words and deeds must speak for themselves. He is generally seen from the circle of those around him. He himself gives an impression of insensitivity.

not escape the thought that perhaps he has brought upon himself his own fate—history repeating itself with another victim would, of course, reassure him—or else the brothers will not harm the one who has been singled out from their midst, thus demonstrating that their minds have changed. The continuation of the story goes in the latter direction. But Joseph is not yet convinced—what role does his nonassuaged guilt play in this?—and he intensifies the experiment as well as the dark irony of the whole situation. "The narrator's intention in the test is to increase the tension of the story to its breaking point. . . . [Joseph] plays their anxiety to the hilt."[40]

But there is in the midst of that particular episode a dramatic peripeteia. At mid-course, Joseph shifts gear; he switches from retaliation, and his dealings with his brothers become acts of forgiveness. Instead of death, Joseph gives them life; not just survival, but a good life with food in a time of famine; with space for themselves and their cattle in a time of dearth and forced exile; with respect and honor in a time of understandable xenophobia in Egypt. Twenty-some years of envy, hatred, vengeful dreams; a score of years with tears, mourning, grudge-bearing, mistrust, bitterness are erased in one instant. Joseph has risen to consciousness and conscience. Melanie Klein speaks appropriately of a "drive to repair,"[41] that inspires in some rare moments actions that defeat determinism. Joseph himself undergoes remorse and repentance. Then he can accept the possibility that his brothers have also repented. He realizes that he must give credence to a deep change in them; they are no longer those who sold him as a slave and would have him killed some twenty years earlier. In this respect, the textual insistence on the theme of the famine in Canaan and the contrasted banqueting in Egypt accentuates a frightful detail in the narrative description of the callousness reached earlier by the murderous brothers. Right after throwing Joseph into a dry cistern, the culprits, we are told, sat down around the pit to eat (Genesis 37:25) while their victim was "beseeching them" (42:21). They repressed with food any remorse they may have felt in their throats. They stuffed their stomachs and also their ears. Reuben seems to have been the only one moved by some remnants of humaneness (37:21, 29–30). His intervention belongs to the literary device of foiling the others' insensitivity.

40. Coats, *From Canaan to Egypt*, p. 37.

41. Melanie Klein, "Love, Guilt, and Reparation," in *Love, Hate, and Reparation*, by Klein and Joan Riviere (New York: W. W. Norton, 1964), pp. 57–119. See also, "Some Theoretical Conclusions Regarding the Emotional Life of the Infant," in Klein, *Envy and Gratitude and Other Works 1946–63* (New York: Dell, 1975), pp. 61–93.

Later on in the narrative, however, Reuben is replaced by Judah. The latter's discourse in Genesis 44 is one of the most moving as well as being the most artistically composed in the whole of the Bible. It is also the longest discourse in the book of Genesis. In many respects, it constitutes a climax to the story. Judah bases his whole argumentation on the legitimacy of the father's preference for one son over all others and on the symbiosis of sorts that exists between them both (44:30). It is the responsibility of the other sons to protect this intimacy between Jacob and Benjamin. All the more so since the other sons have been instrumental in bringing about an exacerbation of such a relation: Benjamin replaces in the father's eyes a former favorite, now dead, "torn to pieces." In that respect, "God has found out their guilt" (44:16).

Thus, although in Judah's discourse there is "not a single sentence about God,"[42] we are witnessing a conversion. It is particularly clear in 44:33f., when Judah substitutes himself for Benjamin, a veritable reversal of the brothers' attempt in chapter 37 to prevent Joseph from taking their place before the father. "The Bible speaks for the first time of vicarious suffering (vv. 18–34)."[43] True, we are perhaps for the first time made conscious of this notion of substitution,[44] but it is far from being just a peculiarity in Judah's speech, as the motif is interwoven throughout the whole story. Here, the substitution is for Joseph as much as for Benjamin. For Judah now volunteers to become a slave in Egypt, the very condition into which he and his brothers have put Joseph in the past. Joseph's ascension has left the place of thralldom empty, as it were, that Judah is ready to fill in his stead.

The door is now open on the possibility for Joseph to exclaim, "God sent me here before you to preserve life" (45:5) or "to preserve for you a remnant in the land, and to keep alive for you many survivors" (45:7). Strangely, the vocabulary belongs to late prophecy and to its expectation of salvation after the catastrophe of exile, either announced or already experienced. One thinks of texts such as Isaiah 10:20; 15:9; 37:32 [= 2 Kings 19:31]; Ezra 9:14. Von Rad writes, with reference to Genesis 50:19–21, "God's hand . . . directs all the confusion of human guilt ultimately toward a gracious goal."[45] Let us at this point take note of this

42. Westermann, *Genesis 37–50*, p. 137.

43. Ibid.

44. Unless we reckon as an example of substitution the fact that Jacob is the one who is ultimately tested by Joseph testing his brothers. "The old deceiver is deceived again, and by . . . his favorite son. . . . Jacob must be willing to risk the life of Benjamin, who is in fact his son, his only son, the one he loves (42:36, cf. 22:2). In order for the family to survive, Jacob must be willing to risk the life of Benjamin" (ibid., p. 71).

45. Quoted by Westermann, ibid., p. 143.

feat, to which we must return below: the story of Joseph contains already at this stage the seeds of its subsequent hermeneutic development. The "trajectory" starts here, within the text itself.

Before this episode of redemption, however, the brothers have been consistently presented as less than admirable. Not a trivial feat when we recall that they are the ancestors of the tribes of Israel. Their display of meanness and mediocrity of feelings is not without temporary reprieves, though, which is another way for the author to go on striking a note of ambiguity. For another side of reality is that these men are ill-treated, although they do all the dirty work and take care of the family's subsistence. Their father's attitude says clearly that whatever they do, they will never rise up to his expectation. They are his sons by accident, as if they embodied repeated attempts at perfection until their younger brother Joseph finally came along. This one, in contrast, need not do anything.[46] He *is* perfect in his father's eyes. No competition with him is possible. In short, Jacob has by lack of insight set up hatred among his children. Now, it is certainly no accident if the author charges the character Jacob with yet one more failure on the familial plane. After all, he is also the one who deceived his own father, tricked his own brother, manipulated his father-in-law, humiliated one of his wives. Jacob is at times without complacency described as a borderline personality. Melanie Klein would say that he "thinks from a paranoid/schizoid position."[47]

Were we, however, to stop here, our reading would be misleading. It would give the wrong impression that the story has been created for making a psychological point or for illustrating human pettiness and cheapness. Such is not the case. The story must be read "intertextually." Set within its close and more remote context, the Joseph novella once more calls attention to the nature of the covenantal relations between God and humans and between "brothers" inside the covenantal community. When we take the *Sitz im Worte* seriously, the characters of the story acquire a dimension that transcends the psychological. Speaking

46. While his brothers are in the fields, Joseph parades at home dressed like a prince (Genesis 37:3). Alfred Adler's following remark is well taken: Often the youngest child "looks for a field of activity remote from that of the other members of the family—in which, I believe, he gives a sign of a hidden cowardice. If the family is commercial, for instance, the youngest inclines to art or poetry; if scientific, he wants to be a salesman." In *Problems of Neurosis: A Book of Case Histories,* edited by Philip Mairet (New York: Harper and Row, 1964), p. 107; see also *Social Interest: A Challenge to Mankind* (New York: Capricorn Books, 1964), p. 239.

47. See Melanie Klein, "Notes on Some Schizoid Mechanisms" (1946), in *Envy and Gratitude and Other Works 1946–63,* pp. 1–24.

of Jacob, for example, we must realize that with him we are always, to quote Robert Alter, at "the intersection of incompatibles—the relative and the absolute, human imperfection and divine perfection, the brawling chaos of historical experience and God's promise to fulfill a design in history. The biblical outlook is informed, I think, by a sense of stubborn contradiction, of a profound and ineradicable untidiness in the nature of things."[48] The story of Jacob, Joseph, and the brothers does not remain at the sordid level of paternal injustice, of fratricide and parricide, of narcissism and obsequiousness. It so happens that Jacob's preference for one of his sons mirrors God's election of a particular people from all the nations.[49] Joseph indeed represents that uniqueness, that difference that others passionately deny to him because of his "sameness." Within such a perspective, even the persecution of the elect becomes providential, "so it was not you that sent me here, but God. . . . And now be not grieved, nor angry with yourselves, that you sold me here, for God did send me before you to preserve life" (Genesis 45:8, 5). Unmistakably, the apex of the Joseph story is his statement to his brothers—a declaration that sounds as a cry of triumph of someone conscious of his moral superiority—"You meant evil against me, but God meant it for good" (Genesis 50:20; cf. 45:8). The Joseph novella is a comedy. It ends happily.

Such is the conclusion of our inquiry. It takes us back to our starting point. A trivial story of envy and jealousy becomes a parable of Jewish destiny in the world. A notion of election and providence, of vocation and divine direction, as well as of human mediocrity and divine transcendence, permeates the narrative and gives it its ultimate dimension that leaves far behind its other qualities of entertainment or as portrait of mores. Thus, from the axis of a family saga, we pass over to the axis of a political intrigue. For Frank Crüsemann, in the words of Claus Westermann, who reports his position, "The conflict in the family itself also exhibits a political aspect in the question of whether a brother should lord it over his brothers."[50] This assertion falls in line with

---

48. Robert Alter, *The Art of Biblical Narrative* (New York: Basic Books, 1981), p. 154.

49. This is a point already discerned by Sigmund Freud. He writes: "the superiority which the people of Israel claimed for themselves. If one is the declared favourite of the dreaded father, one need not be surprised at the jealousy of one's brothers and sisters, and the Jewish legend of Joseph and his brethren shows very well where this jealousy can lead." *Moses and Monotheism* (London: The Hogarth Press, 1964), p. 106.

50. Westermann, *Genesis 37–50*, p. 21, referring to Frank Crüsemann, *Der Widerstand gegen das Königtum*, pp. 146–49. See already Westermann, *Die Josepherzählung der Genesis* (Stuttgart, 1966). But Crüsemann wrongly believes that such a problematic belongs only to one period of history,

Coats's opinion that it is a question here of "a political legend" about the proper use of power.[51]

With great mastery, the author of the novella shows in the adventures of an individual the necessary evolution from the patriarchal use of authority to the monarchical use of power. In the first case, there is no justification in the promotion of one over all. But when times of distress come, the clan turns its hopes toward another societal structure where power is centralized in the hands of one person. Only there "life is preserved," only there are "remnants and survivors." The narrative presents two worlds set on a collision course; the clash occurs in the person of one who is able to emerge from his former setting and to blossom in the next. But then a new danger arises, the misuse of power. The true warrant against it is here clearly expressed in 39:2 (cf. v. 21), which reads, "Yhwh was with Joseph so that he prospered." A paraphrase of this occurs again at the end of the story (45:5–8; 50:17–21). The warrant is God's election.

God is with Joseph, but the composition says little about it. As emphasized above, the "God-talk" here falls in line with the absence of religiosity in the *Diasporanovelle*. This, however, is somewhat deceptive. As in Esther, "God's saving rule . . . is concealed in profound worldliness," says von Rad.[52] Stressed is the fact that Joseph finds himself, despite every obstacle, every attempt at repressing him within his family, or at the hands of slave traders, in Potiphar's house, in prison, or at the court of Pharaoh—and also in spite of his own narcissistic and sadistic impulses. He transcends his mediocrity, and everyone around him is transfigured in the process.[53] Now, the impersonal mode of the initial dreams at the onset of the story makes sense entirely. It was theologically fitting that Joseph be passive (a general trait of his personality before maturity). He does not do anything by himself but rather reports that something is in process so that his sheaf stands while the other sheaves bow. Like so often in biblical novellas, the impersonal mode alludes to divine power. True, by contrast, a later parallel, the book of Esther, teaches us that passivity is no prerequisite to divine action. It remains that in the case of Joseph, this human flaw becomes, along with

---

namely the Solomonic era. We know as a certainty, on the contrary, that the postexilic community reflected on kingship and the Davidic dynasty (cf. I and II Chronicles, *passim*).

51. G. W. Coats, *From Canaan to Egypt*.

52. Gerhard von Rad, *Das erste Buch Mose, Genesis* (Göttingen: Vandenhoeck & Rupert, 1956), p. 438.

53. A fact symbolized here by the settlement of the whole family, now united, in a country of abundance, a paradise of sorts in that time of general famine.

all the other human "incongruities" (Robert Alter), a free margin for the exercise of God's power and direction.

Thus, also on the level of power, the Joseph novella is a story of salvation, as I said above. The two dimensions of the familial and the political are here closely intertwined, if only because of the deep influence on the narrative of a sapiential worldview, according to which success on both scores is the upshot of the right ethical attitude. The turning point in Joseph's fortune is reached with his refusal to commit adultery and treason.[54]

The Joseph novella has been traditionally read as preparatory to the Egyptian captivity and the Exodus. But it is also a chastening of kingship, for the sages were not willing to condone autocracy even though they recognized King Solomon as their patron. "Joseph" is the Wisdom tradition's response to the "Solomonic" weakness of kings with women, already exemplified by David. Joseph, as the perfect courtier, evolves in kingly settings, and the parallel is thus made easier with a royal referent. The composition of the novella is postexilic—whatever may have been its more remote origins—and thus has a synoptic vision of kingship. It is a *Diasporanovelle,* written at a time when one could look at the exile in Babylon in hindsight as constituting the end of an era. The story reflects a picture of the dispersion of the Jews. It is no accident that the scene is staged in Egypt, at the court of a pagan all-powerful king in a foreign country that remains forever in Israel's collective memory a "house of bondage," a "land of darkness." But there, even there, Jewish rightness, honesty, fortitude—all virtues highly praised by the sages— lead to being granted extraordinary gifts, *charismata.* Among them, mantic wisdom is the highest. It enables one to read into the future and, thus, to act accordingly, that is, with an awesome power. Joseph is a sage, and as such he is successful.[55]

On that score particularly, the "trajectory" of this text takes us to the

54. This aspect of the Joseph story occupies a space of choice in Jewish tradition. There are two contradictory trends, however; one stressing that Joseph was not even tempted (cf. *Testament of Joseph* in the *Testament of the Twelve Patriarchs*): his natural handsomeness was anyway so striking that all women felt attracted to him (also in *Midrash Tanḥumah*). This, incidently, was the cause of Jacob's preference for him. Joseph, moreover, had knowledge of the Ten Commandments, long before they were given by Moses. By contrast, other traditional voices charge Joseph with impropriety. Rabbi Johanan, reports James Kugel, "sees Joseph as something of a willing participant, a man who has given in to temptation" (*In Potiphar's House,* p. 95). In fact, they continue, Joseph was willing, until Potiphar seized his garment; then he changed his mind (see Kugel, *In Potiphar's House,* p. 96). Philo accuses Joseph of availing himself of his fellow slave women (see ibid., p. 46).

55. One will notice here the striking parallel with the Platonic conviction expressed, for example, in *The Republic.* Politics should be left to philosophers. Wisdom is not only theoretical but practical, not only speculative but political.

exiled Daniel allegedly living in sixth-century Babylon.[56] He too, in the image of Joseph, acknowledges that God only is wise, that wisdom belongs to Him (Daniel 2:20–23, compare with Genesis 40:8; 41:16). God gives wisdom to whom he pleases (Daniel 2.20), particularly to those who keep faithful to his will (chapter 1), resist idolatry (chapters 2–6), remain steadfast in their praxis (chapter 6). Such wisdom gives insight into the meaning of the present and into the orientation of the future, sure means for the gifted one to raise to the highest positions in the empire and the world.

Furthermore, if indeed the Joseph narrative has been reworked as a *Diasporanovelle* after the exile,[57] another purpose in its composition emerges. The Diaspora "provides for" ("nourishes") the mother community in Palestine (see Genesis 45:11, also 50:21); the Diaspora is the preservation of life for Israel (45:5). Within that perspective, the textual precision "in the land" (*be-qèrèb ha-'areṣ*, 45:6) becomes highly significant. *Ha-'areṣ* should not be translated "in the world," although such a reading would contribute to the understanding of the text's view as embracing more than the immediate area generally envisaged by this story. In a first reading, "in the Land" is indicative of where the eyes of the exiles are directed. Physically in Egypt, the Israelites' hearts are still or already in the Promised Land. On that score again, the book of Esther prolongs the lines sketched by the Joseph story.

That such a felicitous relationship between the Dispersion and the Home-land come after tensions of all kinds is no surprise. "Peace" has never been an easy state with the Diaspora; no less than a theophany is needed to convince Jacob/Israel to go down to Egypt (cf. 37:35; 39:1; 45:13)—besides, the Community at home is known for being rather moody and even quarrelsome (45:24)! The present development on the relation with the mother country is summed up with the expressed conviction that the Dispersion is temporary only. The "descent" into Egypt is only one chapter in Israel's history, a contingency transcended by the permanence of the Promised Land (cf. 46:1–4).

---

56. See my *Daniel in His Time* (Columbia: University of South Carolina Press, 1988). We might also think of certain traits in the story of David. Cf. 1 Samuel 18:12, 14, 28 regarding the rise of David. Westermann is, however, right when he says, "The points of contact between the story of David in 1 Samuel 16 and the Joseph story are striking; but no one would think of mutual dependence" (*Genesis 37–50*, p. 28).

57. Let us note that such a scenario runs counter to the one imagined by Walter Dietrich, *Die Josepherzählung* (Neukirchen-Vluyn: Neukirchener Verlag, 1989), according to which an original Joseph novelette was later reworked as history. It gives an image of monarchy that is idealistic (cf. Genesis 37:8). In the process, the novella was moralized.

To return to the subsequent development of our story in Daniel, this hero like Joseph definitely displays dimensions of manticism. The milieu in which both evolve is itself permeated with mantic wisdom. Like Moses and Aaron, who will outwit Egyptian soothsayers and magicians (Exodus 7ff.), Joseph surpasses experts of that same group in clairvoyance, and Daniel beats the Chaldeans at their own game. The tales of Joseph, of Mordecai, of Daniel (especially in chapters 1–6) belong to "the successful story of a wise courtier."[58] Another example of this is also provided by the extracanonical tale of Ahikar (in *Syriac* 5–7:23).[59] The prevailing structure is in four parts: (*a*) a person of lower status is called before a person of higher status; (*b*) the purpose of this meeting is to answer/solve a problem; (*c*) the problem is presented and the servant solves the problem; (*d*) he is richly rewarded.[60] Daniel as the ideal wise courtier at a foreign court is a new Joseph. Fidelity to God is the key to wisdom and success. Daniel, even more than his model, is pious, surrounded by the divine power, and enlightened by angelic interpretation. As regards the competitors, the Joseph and Daniel stories say in a narrative form what Isaiah says in the oracular (44:25f.): God is the one who makes diviners mad, turns wise men backward and makes their knowledge foolish.

By contrast with the latter, the truth heralded by Joseph/Daniel is convincing by nature and truly irresistible. The potentates of this world themselves must bow. It is probably a mistake to overemphasize in our

58. See W. L. Humphreys, "The Motif of the Wise Courtier in the Old Testament," Th.D. Dissertation, Union Theological Seminary, 1970; Susan Niditch and Robert Doran, "The Success Story of the Wise Courtier: A Formal Approach," *Journal of Biblical Literature* 96 (1977): 179–93.

59. In R. H. Charles, ed., *Apocrypha and Pseudepigrapha of the Old Testament in English* (Oxford: Clarendon Press, 1913), vol. 2, pp. 750–67.

60. The structure proposed by J. R. King, "The Joseph Story and Divine Politics: A Comparative Study of a Biographic Formula From the Ancient Near East," *Journal of Biblical Literature* 106 (1987): 577–94, works well for the Joseph story but not for the Daniel legends (except perhaps the possible background of some of them. I am referring to the Nabonidus narrative [see *ANET* 308–15] that inspired Daniel 4). King's structure "starts from an *Initial Situation*, in which the protagonist has some status and prestige. A *threat* to the equilibrium of the setting develops, one beyond the control of the hero. When the threat materializes (*Threat Realized*), he flees into *Exile*. There he gains the patronage of a person of power, and has *Success in Exile* because of his own abilities. He then faces an *Exilic Agon*, but overcomes it (*Exilic Victory*) and has redoubled success. However, he desires to return to his original setting, but to do so must see that the *Threat* has been *Overcome*. He is granted a *Return and Reconciliation* with his initial setting. The story concludes with an *Epilogue* in which the hero manages his affairs" (pp. 580–81). King detects the same pattern in the stories of Sinuhe, Idrimi, Hattusilis, Esarhaddon, and Nabonidus. He also selects four figures of the Bible and sees Jacob's story as presenting "the Initial Situation. Joseph's the Threat and the beginning of the Exile, Moses' contains the Exilic Agon and the start of the Return, and David's the culmination of the Reconciliation and the Administrative Epilogue" (p. 594).

stories the absence of hostility between foreigners and Jews in Egypt or in Babylon. For the optimism expressed here is not about human potential but about a transcendent truth and its indisputable nature. It does not need to be pushed down the throats of people. In that respect, the Maccabean successes in the second century, for instance, are but "a little help" (Daniel 11:34). The sage is calm and confident. If threatened with death, he quietly continues his devotions in his room three times a day (Daniel 6:10).

The influence of Wisdom on the Joseph story appears to me undeniable (*pace* D. Redford, *The Biblical Story of Joseph*), but there is a chasm between such Wisdom and the skepticism of a book like Qohelet, for example. There is here no despair in not understanding God's ways, for these are mysterious only to the ill-intentioned. The ideal set by Wisdom before the Diaspora is prosperity. The author of 1 Maccabees 2:53 cites Joseph's promotion to the supreme position in Egypt and attributes this to his keeping up the Commandments. Most other texts of the Intertestament see his wisdom as the instrument of his achievements. The Joseph story knew a great success in that literature. Wisdom of Solomon 10:13f., for instance, has this beautiful text,

> It was she [Wisdom] who would not abandon a righteous man sold into slavery, but rescued him from sin; she descended into the dungeon with him, and when he was in chains she did not leave him, until she brought him imperial sovereignty and authority over his masters; she gave the lie to those who found fault with him and she bestowed on him everlasting honor. (translated by David Winston)[61]

Wisdom of Solomon is within a trajectory already outlined by Psalm 105. An excerpt deserves being quoted (vv. 16f.),

> When he [God] summoned famine against the land, and broke every staff of bread, he sent a man ahead of them, Joseph, who was sold as a slave. His feet were hurt with fetters, his neck was put in a collar of iron; until what he had said came to pass, the word of the Lord kept testing him.... (Pharaoh) made him lord of his house, ruler of all his possessions, to bind his officials at will, and make wise his elders.

61. David Winston, *The Wisdom of Solomon* (Garden City: Doubleday, 1979), p. 211.

Joseph is thus close to being seen as a "suffering servant," an uncanny reading that did not escape the Fathers of the Church, who saw in Joseph the prefiguration of Christ and his passion. Franz Delitzsch's recalling of Pascal's interpretation is a later echo of the view of the Fathers, "Jesus Christ is prefigured in Joseph, his father's favorite, sent by the father to his brothers, the guiltless one sold by his brothers for twenty pieces of silver and so become their Lord. . . . Such is the Church's vital portrayal of the Joseph story from time immemorial."[62]

It is clear that this later development is already present *in ovo* in the Genesis version of the tale. The successful Joseph is also the one whose "death" at the hands of his brothers, of Potiphar's wife, of Potiphar himself, and of the Pharaoh's butler has granted continued life to his relatives and to all the Egyptians. We should not equate Joseph with the Suffering Servant figure, but the kinship between them is real. When Joseph forgives his brothers, he "clearly acknowledges the whole paradoxical purpose of his 'death' as God's way of preserving the family."[63]

The final success of Joseph may be seen from different points of view. From one standpoint, the story's happy end announces that the age of suffering is over. This is symbolized by Joseph's early passion leading to power and to the restoration of the clan. It parallels the prophetic threat of punishment fulfilled with the exile in Babylon and opening up a future of peace. Prosperity is for the righteous; it is taken for granted that the chosen people have learned their lesson during the national chastisement and that nothing really bad can happen after that; they have reached the land of Goshen.

It will take all the energy of a Second Zechariah to deflate the illusion. The following essay in this volume will deal with a Zechariah text that represents a very different vision of history. The days of wrath announced by Zechariah and other postexilic prophets indeed came with a vengeance. Hence, Wisdom in the Daniel book had to assimilate on a much deeper level the Suffering Servant ideology. Daniel 10–11 is an interpretation/actualization of that Isaianic tradition. Furthermore, the

---

62. Franz Delitzsch, *Kommentar* (1852), quoted by Westermann, *Genesis 37–50*, p. 18.

63. D. A. Seybold, "Paradox and Symmetry in the Joseph Narrative," in *Literary Interpretations of Biblical Narratives*, edited by K. R. R. Gros Louis, J. S. Ackerman, and T. S. Warshaw (Nashville: Abingdon, 1974), p. 71. Cf. Hartmut Gese, "the life of a community in a land can only be established by a grave [cf. Genesis 23, Machpelah]. . . . In Genesis 50 we read about how the great funeral of Jacob . . . was performed in reverse analogy to the Exodus. All the Egyptian court and the army of chariots and horsemen accompanied the deceased to the Holy Land." In *Essays on Biblical Theology*, translated by Keith Crim (Minneapolis: Augsburg, 1981), p. 37.

Servant furnished a model for the conception of the righteous that became so important in the second century BCE and throughout the intertestamental period.[64] But by then the distance with the story of Joseph seems considerable.

This point will serve as a transition to a second point of view and to the New Testament upshot of Joseph's story. There is, of course, something of a structural parallel between the Jesus of the Gospel, and the Joseph of Genesis. Joseph thrown in a pit/grave before a subsequent elevation to the royal throne is an apt metaphor in the early Christian kerygma. Along the same line, Alfred Jeremias (apparently influenced by Thomas Mann) saw in the scene of Joseph in the pit an allusion to Tammuz going into the underworld.[65] There is also in both stories what W. L. Humphreys calls a "supreme irony" as God turns evil into good, thus creating a tension between human intention and divine providence.[66] Joseph's "kenosis" is followed by a resurrection of sorts, and so also is his father's descent to "hell" vindicated by his son's life. All the same, a profound transformation of the Joseph story has occurred through the New Testament's synthesis of the theme of the Suffering Servant laying down his life for the sake of heaven and the Wisdom tradition assuring the ethical man of his eventual "prosperity" (the term is already present in Isaiah 53:10 and thus constitutes a bridgehead toward a confluence with Wisdom).

But the kinship between Christ and Joseph is not without its dangers. Paul for one must react against the Corinthian church's tendency to pass over the "Cross" and celebrate the Eucharist in a triumphant spirit. Then, Christ's passion is shortchanged, a kind of rite of passage, an unavoidable unpleasant moment to go through before the victory of Easter.

The Joseph story as told in the book of Genesis points undeniably in that direction. The sapiential influence on the narrative stresses the "successful courtier" side. If, for some, the higher they rise, the deeper they fall, for Joseph on the contrary, the deeper he falls, the higher he rises. And this is the lesson of the novella. It is, as said above, a comedy. So could also a misconstrued Gospel be read. On that score, one admires the wisdom of Mark ending his Gospel on an unparalleled sober

64. See G. W. E. Nickelsburg and M. E. Stone, *Faith and Piety in Early Judaism* (Philadelphia: Fortress), 1983.

65. A. Jeremias, *The Old Testament in the Light of the Ancient East*, translated by C. L. Beaumont (New York: Williams and Norgate, 1911), vol. 2, p. 278.

66. Cf. Humphreys, *Joseph and His Family*, p. 187.

note. The "felix culpa" of certain liturgies is closer to the Joseph legend than to the Jesus of Mark's gospel.

Another parallel between "Joseph" and "Jesus" is provided by the notion, common to the Genesis story and to the early Church, that ethical standards are known and must be upheld by nonbelievers. The general ethos prevailing in the Joseph novella finds its correspondence in New Testament statements such as Romans 2:14f.; 13:3; 1 Corinthians 5:1; 10:32; Philippians 4:8; and 1 Thessalonians 4:12. Romans 12:16ff., for example, could be read as a free commentary of Genesis 42ff. For the Apostle, in conformity with the Wisdom hero, the Christian is given a *charisma* along with the Holy Spirit (1 Corinthians 7:7; 12:7, 11); it can be described as wisdom (Colossians 1:9; Ephesians 1:8). But here again the transformation of the old material is striking. Paul does not mean that the gift of wisdom would lead to the adoption of an ethical norm of moderation, self-control, and shrewdness. Still less does he imply that "reason" (Romans 12:1) is the secret of success. For what constitutes the apex of obedience and of intelligence for Paul is summarized in the expression *mimesis tou Christou* (1 Corinthians 11:1, etc.). The paraenesis of both Jesus and Paul are the result of the confluence of traditional wisdom (cf. Matthew 6:19ff.) with the accomplishment of all sapience in the sacrifice of Christ; so that, concurrently with the fact that a natural ethic stems from Wisdom, the latter is "repeatedly shattered by eschatology (cf. Matthew 10:26)."[67] For the disciple's prudence is not with a view to any ulterior motive. Prudence, soberness, moderation, and all the virtues enumerated in the Epistles are just examples or aspects of the *imitatio Christi.*

---

67. See W. Schrage, "Ethics in the New Testament" *Interpreter's Dictionary of the Bible, Supplementary Volume* (Nashville: Abingdon, 1962), p. 282.

Zechariah 12:10

"Et aspicient ad me quem confixerunt"

ANDRÉ LaCOCQUE

Zechariah 12:10 is notoriously difficult to understand. In what follows, I shall attempt to retrace the trajectory of which this verse, and this pericope as a whole, are but a segment. A first step in the right direction is taken when parallels are noted between the Zechariah text and its model in Second Isaiah. Indeed, as I shall demonstrate, our pericope is a Midrashic expansion of Second Isaiah's development of "the suffering servant of Yhwh." We shall see, however, that we must go even farther back to trace the origin of Zechariah's theme in the book of Judges and even beyond. For the backdrop of Zechariah 12:10 is the quasi annihilation of the tribe of Benjamin by the other tribes (cf. the closing chapters of the book of Judges). Whether the Second Isaiah text also found its inspiration in the story of Benjamin is a moot question; Second Zechariah undoubtedly did.

The retrospective movement of exploring the background of Zechariah 12:10 must be completed by a prospective study of what the theme became in leading up to its utilization by the New Testament, for no other part of the Hebrew Bible was more influential on the writing of the early Church than Second Zechariah. No theme of the prophetic book was found more meaningful than the one of the Martyr of chapter 12.

As our purpose is to follow the evolution of the theme present in our verse, it is important to situate the prophetic book in terms of its time and circumstances. The problem is particularly difficult. Scholars waiver between the extremes of the eighth and the second centuries BCE! In my own commentary on Zechariah, however, I have concluded from a critical review of the external and internal evidence that chapters

9–14 were written in the first half of the fifth century.[1] Two characteristics are particularly decisive: the apocalyptic dimension of the book and its anthological reuse of older prophetic oracles.[2]

In this study, the "apocalyptic" character of Second Zechariah will be our main focus, but the anthological feature is a suitable place to begin. The loan sources are revealing for the chronology of Second Zechariah and, more specifically, the dependence upon Second Isaiah is verifiable at the level of vocabulary and ideas. For example, Isaiah 42 and 45:21–25 influenced Zechariah 9:12; Zechariah 12:1 was formed on the basis of Isaiah 42:5; Zechariah 12:2 on Isaiah 51:22, 17; Zechariah 12:10–13:1 on Isaiah 53:5 and 44:3; and Zechariah 13:7–9 on Isaiah 51:9. Perhaps more impressive still is the pattern displayed by the book of Second Zechariah, which sequentially reviews the four songs of the Servant:

> Zechariah 9:9–10 // Isaiah 42:1ff. (first song)
> Zechariah 11:4ff. // Isaiah 49:1ff. (second song)
> Zechariah 12:30–13:1 // Isaiah 50:4ff. (third song)
> Zechariah 13:7–9 // Isaiah 52:13–53:12 (fourth song)

The pioneering scholarship of Bernhard Duhm regarding the songs in Second Isaiah thus receives a strong confirmation.

In chapter 9, Zechariah, consistent with his method of reusing former oracles by reversing their original meaning, had made the Servant king over the whole earth. The one "poor and riding on an ass, a colt the foal of an ass" is also "justified and saved"; indeed, "your king comes to you." By contrast, the salvation of Judah and Jerusalem in chapter 12 is wrought, not by a king's might, but by the Servant's death. We have thus returned to the original intention of the exilic prophet. In chapter 9, it was a question of free poetic expansion of an older oracle. Here, the literary genre is of the Midrashic type.

The Slave of the Lord motif serves as a close ideological context to Zechariah 12. It shows in what direction to look for a correct interpretation of verse 10. The phrase "the one they have pierced" is a commentary on the suffering Servant as well as an eschatologization of that fig-

---

1. S. Amsler, A. LaCocque, R. Vuilleumier, *Aggée, Zacharie, Malachie* (Neuchâtel-Paris: Delachaux et Niestlé, 1981); see the Introduction to Second Zechariah, pp. 129–45.

2. Adolphe Lods says that "in general these chapters display the same spirit as in Jewish apocalypses." See his *Histoire de la Littérature Hébraïque et Juive* (Paris: Payot, 1950), p. 772. This is a significant statement coming as it does from a scholar who dates Second Zechariah before the exile.

ure. Furthermore, being the first full commentary on the famous oracle of the exilic prophet, it is of special interest to see how—only a few decades after its inception—the figure of the Servant was interpreted. For instance, we will not be indifferent to the transformation that the personage underwent in the subsequent tradition of Zechariah 12:10, whereby the Servant acquired a collective meaning.

But I anticipate. It is more important at this point to emphasize the continuation of the Isaianic model beyond the literary unit of Zechariah 12:10–13:1, precisely into 13:7–9. In the latter pericope, the one called by Yhwh, "my shepherd . . . the man close to me" is identified with the "pierced one" of 12:10.

> "Awake, O sword, against my shepherd,
> against the man close to me,"
> says the Lord of Hosts . . .

Thus a parallel is drawn between the martyr of chapter 12 and the good shepherd, prophet-servant of Yhwh in chapter 13. On the other hand, 13:7–9 presents a theme at all points similar to the one of chapter 11. This is so to such an extent that Heinrich Ewald thought that originally 11:17 was followed immediately by 13:7–8. Be that as it may, there is now in the extant text the insert of 12:1–13:6 reporting a victorious battle against the Nations but not without the violent death of a (collective?) character who is "pierced" by the sword. His suffering and death respond to the mishaps of the prophet in chapter 11 ("Be a shepherd of the flock doomed to slaughter"). In both cases, the model figure is the Second Isaiah's Servant. By contrast, there is the wicked shepherd of 11:16–17 ("The worthless shepherd who deserts the flock"). He is a Shepherd and a Servant in reverse. While, according to Heinrich Ewald, 13:7–9 originally continued the malediction wording on the deceiving shepherd, now at any rate these verses have become a prophecy of woe against the good shepherd (on the model of the suffering Servant). Otto Procksch and Ernst Sellin agree with this reading: 13:7–8 refers to the good shepherd who has been killed, and they refer to 12:10–11.[3]

The situation is thus the following: Both the Servant in Isaiah and the Shepherd in Zechariah are "pierced" (*ḥalol* in Isaiah 53:5; *daqor* in Zechariah 12:10). Both die following the will of God (Isaiah 53:10;

3. Otto Procksch, *Die kleinen prophetischen Schriften nach dem Exil* (Stuttgart, 1916); Ernst Sellin, *Das Zwölfprophetenbuch* (Leipzig, 1930); Heinrich Ewald, *Die Propheten des Alten Bundes*, vol. II (Stuttgart, 1841).

Zechariah 13:7), although they are innocent (Isaiah 53:9; Zechariah 11; 12:10; 13:7). Their self-sacrifice is not useless, however, for it stirs the people to repentance (Isaiah 53; Zechariah 12:8).

It is of particular interest to realize how deeply the theme of the suffering Servant influenced the (underground) literature of the oppressed or disenfranchised during the Second Temple period. As a matter of fact, it would be shortsightedness to believe that the New Testament's understanding of Isaiah 52–53 is one of a kind. Such a misconception is consistent with a certain Jewish reading of these prophetic chapters (see the Targum on Isaiah 52f.), but the stance there is polemical and clearly anti-Christian. Third Isaiah already developed the theme along the line of vicarious suffering (in 61:1–3; 63:17; 65:8ff.). These texts, of course, constitute the very first developments, perhaps composed by Second Isaiah's disciples.[4]

In chronological order, the next one to use the theme of vicarious suffering is Second Zechariah. Then comes perhaps First Enoch, but here the matter is particularly complex. Another milestone on the way to the New Testament literature, Daniel 11:33–35 and 12:3, is a Midrash of the Servant Songs.[5] A further landmark is provided by Wisdom of Solomon 2:12–20; 3; 5 (cp., for example, Daniel 11:32, 35; 12:3, and Wisdom of Solomon 2:13; 3:6, 7).

Third Isaiah, Second Zechariah, (First Enoch), Daniel, Wisdom of Solomon, the New Testament: all of these sources are feeding streams parallel to "main stream Judaism" (as it came to be known by the end of the first century CE). It is not inconsequential that along the line that runs from Third Isaiah to the New Testament literature, Qumran has transmitted the text of Isaiah 53:11 with the Servant "seeing the light" [*yir'eh 'or* instead of *yir'eh* of the MT]. For this is for the community of Qumran the special reward reserved for the children of light (cf. the *Manual of Discipline* from Qumran [IQS], 4:2–8; 11:3). More impor-

---

4. Cf. Sigmund Mowinckel, *He That Cometh* (Oxford: Blackwell, 1959), pp. 188–89; John McKenzie, *Second Isaiah, Anchor Bible*, vol. 20 (Garden City, NJ: Doubleday, 1959), pp. xxxviii–xlii; Georg Fohrer, *Introduction to the Old Testament* (Nashville: Abingdon, 1965), pp. 377ff. Fohrer finds six songs (not four as did B. Duhm in 1892). Five are autobiographic, the sixth one, Isaiah 52:13–53:12 has been composed by someone else about the Prophet himself.

5. H. L. Ginsberg, "The Oldest Interpretation of the Suffering Servant," *Vetus Testamentum* 3 (1953): 400–404, advances the thesis that in chapters 10–12 of Daniel we have "the oldest interpretation of the suffering servant" (plainly collective). We just saw that it is not the oldest one. Cf. my commentary, *The Book of Daniel* (London: SPCK; Atlanta: John Knox Press, 1976), pp. 230–43.

tant perhaps is the Qumran text of 4 QWarRule 5:1–5 that speaks of Messiah's killing, where it is not clear whether this a subjective or objective genitive.[6]

In Zechariah 11, the good shepherd is not triumphant but, to the contrary, undergoes a tragic death, although it spells out salvation for his flock—in parallel with the Second Song of the Servant in Isaiah. The good shepherd is rejected like the Servant in Isaiah 49:4. His mission is, however, universal (cf. Zechariah 11:10, 14 and Isaiah 49:6b). And indeed he himself is but an emanation of his people (Zechariah 10), so that there is here again tension between the individual and the collective dimension of the figure. In him, it is to be surmised, a certain party in Jerusalem recognized themselves. Being disenfranchised, they identified with the Suffering Servant of old. In their own eyes they alone were the true Israel.[7]

We must say more about these utopians in the fifth century BCE. As reflected in Second Zechariah, their socioreligious belonging to "Israel" became problematic because they were but a faction within that collectivity. Their eschatological vision was nationalistic and concerned the whole of "Israel," but the center of their preoccupation is the beacon of salvation, which is here called "Judah" (Zechariah 12:1). For the first and only time in the Bible, "Jerusalem" and "Judah" are not only distinguished from one another but pitted one against the other. Clearly the name "Judah" is to be taken with the restrictive meaning of "provincials" in opposition to the city-dwellers of Jerusalem. The distinction is more symbolic than concrete, but it differentiates two socioeconomical layers in the population. Even their geographical distance from, or their proximity to, the Temple of Jerusalem was construed as religiously important.[8] The situation that thus obtains is close to the great divide, in the New Testament times, between Jerusalemites and Galileans, Pharisees

6. See, for instance, L. H. Schiffman, *Reclaiming the Dead Sea Scrolls: The History of Judaism, the Background of Christianity, the Lost Library of Qumran* (Philadelphia: The Jewish Publication Society, 1994), esp. p. 346.

7. Some time later, after the fiasco of Bar Kochba's Messianic claim, the theme of the dying Servant served as a backdrop for the speculations on a Messiah ben Yoseph destined to die on the battlefield *before* the coming of the Messiah ben David.

8. In Rabbinic literature one finds an echo of the rivalry between the inhabitants of Jerusalem and those of the provinces. For instance, after the destruction by the Romans of the city of Bethar, following the revolt of Bar Kochba, it is said that Bethar deserved that chastisement for rejoicing at the destruction of Jerusalem (but that grim joy was grounded on the ill-treatment of Bethar by Jerusalem's people), cf. *j. Taan* 4:8, 69a; *LamR* 2:2.

In today's Israel, the "ultraorthodox" Jews swarm around the Western Wall of Jerusalem.

and Am ha-aretz.[9] Judah and Jerusalem are mutually opposed until there comes a reconciliation through the bloodshed of "the one whom they have pierced."

The tension sketched by Second Zechariah is specifically between "the chiefs of Judah" on the one hand and the "house/dynasty of David" on the other. Or again between the "tents of Judah" and "the burghers of Jerusalem." The Nations are involved in the struggle that opposes the two camps, thus giving the battle occurring at Jerusalem a cosmic dimension on the spatial axis, while on the temporal axis, the war is eschatological, occurring "in that Day." Zechariah's scheme is meant to resolve in one stroke two problems that plague the post-Restoration era: the hostility of Nations toward Jerusalem, and the internecine rivalry between the Temple party and the opposition party in Jerusalem.[10] Indeed, the reconciliation of "Jerusalem" and "Judah" will happen at the expense of and on the battlefield against the Nations (v. 5). "Judah" will be the instrument of renovation for Jerusalem (v. 6) after being itself at the benefice of salvation (v. 7).

Such a salvific action of "Judah" will prove humbling for "the burghers of Jerusalem" and "the house of David." They will relinquish all arrogance vis-à-vis the "provincials" ("Judah"), for they will recognize in the Judean martyrdom during the eschatological war the very condition of their salvation (v. 10). Moreover, their attitude will know a total reversal, they will mourn for "the one whom they pierced," "like one mourns for an only son . . . for a firstborn" (v. 10). Everyone in the party in power—where we are to understand those living in the shadow of the Temple—will participate (v. 12); of particular importance is that there are eleven sections of the people involved in the bereavement (the word "apart" is used eleven times). They weep over the twelfth member who was killed in the war.

The ostensible setting of this "preapocalyptic oracle," as Paul Hanson says, is clearly the New Year festival as described in Psalms 46; 48; 76; and perhaps 74.[11] Zion is under attack by demonic forces but is saved by God's intervention. Prophets of the classic period have eschatologized the liturgical theme, as can be seen in Isaiah 17:12–14; 29:1–8;

---

9. See also 1 Maccabees 1:11, where a faction of the people concludes an alliance with the "Gentiles."

10. The formulation of Matthew 2:10 is appropriate also for the situation transpiring in Second Zechariah times.

11. Paul Hanson, *The Dawn of Apocalyptic: The Historical and Sociological Roots of Jewish Apocalyptic Eschatology* (Philadelphia: Fortress Press, 1975).

Ezekiel 38–39; Joel 3. As for Zechariah, he keeps up this eschatological dimension but, as usual, he concomitantly revives the mythological strain of the Hymn to the Warrior God, as can be seen in the pericope of 12:1 through 13:6.

12:1–3: Onslaught of the Nations.

12:4: Yhwh counterattacks.

12:5–9: Deliverance of Jerusalem.

12:10–14: The "celebration of victory" is replaced by "a great mourning," and the characteristic "*teru'ah*" by "bitterness."

13.1: Similarly the "fecundity restored" through the outpouring of water is replaced by a ritual purification through the "opening of a fountain" for "the house of David and the burghers of Jerusalem" (cf. Ezekiel 36:25), no doubt on account of the violent death inflicted to "the one whom they have pierced."

13:2–6: Again one other traditional motif, the putting to death of the enemies who blocked the fertility in the land (cf. 10:3b–11:3), is here replaced by the motif of the suppression of idols and false prophets (cf. 10:2).

Generically, the Hymn to the Warrior God places itself on a cosmic and suprahistorical plane. It is useless to try to identify the protagonist Nations. Not that the characters in the drama should be reduced to symbols or principles of good and evil, however. The recourse to a cosmic and metahistorical worldview does not betray a dualistic contempt for history; it is the result of two converging sets of necessity. First, the visionary is simply unable to specify who the ultimate adversaries of Israel will be. In the same vein and for the same reason, Ezekiel spoke of Gog and those of Magog (chapter 38). These symbolic representatives of the Nations will be under judgment "in that Day" (38:10). Furthermore, the final events are suggested rather than described by Ezekiel. They have here and in Second Zechariah a character of absolute nonrepetitiveness, something that can hardly be conveyed by a historical event belonging to human annals. But, all the same, one of the two antagonists is well known. It is identical to itself from the beginning of history. Its name is Israel or Zion. Facing that named reality, the opponents are strikingly nameless, though they are "legion." Their origins are varied, but their goal remains constant: to destroy Zion. Constant also is the faith of Israel that they will always be unable to succeed. This hope, which permeates an important cluster of texts in Hebrew

Scripture, reappears in the *War of the Sons of Light* document in the Qumran (cf. 1 QM 12:10–15 // 19:1–8).

Now, if the Hymn had too precisely identified the enemy, with Egypt for example, the question would be whether the events described are only penultimate; Assyria, or Babylonia, Amaleq or Moab, the Arameans or the Edomites, being held in reserve for other, truly eschatological, ultimate events. It was therefore necessary to use general terms, provided that their inclusiveness embrace all possibilities, such as "all the nations/peoples" as we find in Zechariah 12.

This latter text presents us with a highly surprising situation. The theme of the Nations opposing Israel is traditional enough. But it is here compounded by a hostility, or at the very least a polarization, between Judah and Jerusalem. In that respect, verse 2 is notoriously difficult. Are we to understand—with Paul Hanson, for example—that Judah is first among the Nations laying siege to Jerusalem (cf. 14:14)? In this case, the sequence would be the following: Judah attacks Jerusalem; the city's apostates are punished; then Judah turns against the foes of Jerusalem. The model is provided by God's shifting camp from stirring up the Nations against His people, then punishing them because of their onslaught, as, for example, in Isaiah 10:5ff.; 29:1–8; Jeremiah 25:8–14; Ezekiel 38:1–23.

Such a radical reading is perhaps not necessary, as we shall see, but it remains that the distinction between "Judah" and "Jerusalem" is well established and that verse 2 is purposely ambiguous. Not surprisingly, some scholars bypass the ambivalence of the text by considering one element or another of verse 2 as a gloss.[12] This solution is unwarranted by the Versions that display great confusion and thus inadvertently reveal that they faced the same Hebrew text and unsuccessfully attempted to solve the problem one way or the other. The LXX reads, "and in Judah will be the siege against Jerusalem." The Vulgate understood that Judah will take sides with the Nations against Jerusalem, "sed et Juda erit in obsidione contra Jerusalem." The Targum and the Jewish tradition in general concur, but it is assumed that the antagonistic role of Judah is forced upon it by the Nations. Magne Saebö, along a similar line, thinks that Judah's participation in the siege is to be forgiven by God on account of the acknowledgment by Judah's leaders that God

---

12. See, for example, H. M. Lutz: "Eine Jerusalem-Glosse (v. 5) wird durch eine Juda-Glosse (v. 6) korrigiert!" In *Jahwe, Jerusalem, und die Völker* (Neukirchen-Vluyn: Neukirchener Verlag, 1968), p. 14.

manifests his favor to Jerusalem so that the City will be strengthened at its own place.[13]

In fact, the translation of the second verse should go in the direction that the siege of Jerusalem will be also the siege of Judah (which Jerusalem shunned before the eschatological war). Karl Marti has shown, on the textual basis of Ezekiel 4:3, that *yihyeh ba-maṣor* does not mean, "to take part in the siege," but "to be besieged."[14] This understanding is also found in M. L. Malbim (a nineteenth-century Jewish commentator), Friedrich Horst,[15] and Benedict Otzen.[16] Malbim sees here the indication of a series of catastrophes that will successively reach Judah before also hitting Jerusalem. Horst supplies the repetition of the word *maṣor* that fell, he says, by haplography, "the siege will be also of Judah like the siege of Jerusalem."

In summary, the Zechariah text is set against the backdrop of the chasm between Jerusalem and Judah. The ideological divergence, however, will be transcended by history. The fate of one camp is the fate of the other. The eschatological onslaught on the part of the Nations will swirl over both enemy brothers and unite them in a common tragedy; it is also together that the divine intervention will redeem them. Retrospectively, the arrogance of "Jerusalem" is groundless and sinful. "Judah" is not a liability to the People of God. "Jerusalem" also needs to be rescued by God from utter destruction. It will not be spared by the judgment/punishment. The paradoxical thesis of Zechariah is that salvation does not come from (the heads and burghers of) Jerusalem (despite Isaiah 2:3 or Micah 4:2). There is a considerable qualitative shift announced here by the prophet who, to make his point, is compelled to go back in time to a period when Jerusalem was not the "theological" center it became with the united monarchy. That flashback in history allows the "provincials" in Zechariah 12 to call themselves by archaic names such as "the clans/the tents/the house of Judah." In fact, those expressions, using terms such as *mišpaḥah* and *bayit* (particularly in 12:12–14), send us back to the time in the desert after the exodus from Egypt, when Israel was the youthful fiancée of God (cf. Hosea 2:14–16). The same typology is used later by the seceding northern tribes

---

13. Magne Saebö, *Sacharja 9–14, Untersuchungen von Text und Form* (Neukirchen-Vluyn: Neukirchener Verlag, 1969), p. 270.

14. Karl Marti, *Das Dodekapropheton* (Tübingen, 1904).

15. Friedrich Horst, *Die 12 kleinen Propheten* (Tübingen: Mohr, 1964), ad loc.

16. Benedict Otzen, *Studien über Deuterosacharja* (Copenhagen, 1964), p. 26.

after the death of Solomon (1 Kings 12:16: "to your tents, O Israel; see to your own house, David!") and eventually by the Covenanters at Qumran (cf. esp. 1 QM 3:16ff; 4:10; 1 QSa 1:15).

The sequence in verses 7–9 makes sense from that perspective. The "tents" of Judah, not only chronologically but spiritually, precede the "house" of David. Salvation is for Judah and this hierarchy corrigent conception prevails among the party in power at Jerusalem. The time will come when the presently disenfranchised of "Judah" will be vindicated. They will be saved "first" and this means that the others will benefit from their salvation. Sequentiality becomes instrumentality. It is in "the one they have pierced" that there is *also* salvation for the inhabitants of Jerusalem. Once this score is put straight, the rest follows suit. The shield of Jerusalemites will be the Lord himself, in contrast to the socioreligious establishment. As a consequence, the most shaky amongst them will be like David himself, and as for David's house, it will be like God, like the angel of the Lord preceding them in their march ahead. The allusion here is to 2 Samuel 5 where the Jebusites are equated with the lame and the blind, before David takes the City and brings into it the Ark of the presence of God (2 Samuel 6). When this condition is fulfilled, God, says the prophet, will really apply himself to the destruction of "all the nations that come against Jerusalem" (Zechariah 12:9), but not before. Clearly, the Restoration is still to come, pending the fulfillment of certain conditions; the proclamation of the unconditional theocracy by the ideologists of Jerusalem is unreliable.

Zechariah 12:10 is a *crux interpretum*. The fact is all the more vexing in that the verse is conspicuously the heart of the whole development. Its understanding is key to the thoughts of Zechariah. A first obstacle is grammatical; the phraseology here is awkward. *We-hibbitu 'elay 'et 'aser daqaru* is fraught with difficulties. It is true that a *lectio facilior* is provided by Kennicott mss. 38, Rossi mss. 13, Ginsburg mss. 6, etc. It is adopted by Heinrich Ewald and August Dillmann,[17] although not present in any of the Versions (cf. however John 19:37 in the New Testament, but John's reading may be apologetic).[18] The variant reads the third-person singular instead of the first, hence, *'elayw* instead of *'elay*. Hanson adopts this reading and translates it as: "so that they may look

---

17. August Dillmann, *Handbuch der Alttestamentlischen Theologie*, edited by R. Kittel (Leipzig, 1895), p. 543.

18. Not surprisingly, the early Christian texts see Christ in the "pierced one": Matthew 24:30; Revelation 1:7; cf. *Barnabus* 7:6–12; *Trypho* 40.

upon the one whom they have pierced and mourn over him."[19] But, here as always, the *lectio difficilior* is to be preferred. Besides, as Paul Lamarche says, this lesson is shored up by a text to which we referred above, namely Zechariah 11:13, "there already Yhwh identifies himself with His representative."[20] Lamarche also quotes Jewish traditional sayings on God's suffering in the persons of His children.[21] Another argument in favor of the *lectio difficilior* is that "to look upon" God is textually well attested. It is an attitude of prayer and supplication that is spoken of in Isaiah 22:11 and Psalm 34:6, for instance.

But the rest of the Zechariahan sentence constitutes such an unexpected rebound that it leaves the reader puzzled by the audacity of the author. The meaning seems to be, "they (the Jerusalemites) will look upon Me on account of the one they have pierced, and lo, in killing him they were killing Me." This "death of God theology" reading finds a confirmation in the mention in verse 11 of Hadad-Rimmon, the dying and rising Baal of the Canaanites. I shall return to this point.

The Hebrew verb *daqor* means "to pierce with a weapon." The term is found in Numbers 25:8; Judges 9:54; 1 Samuel 31:4; Zechariah 13:3. Marcel Delcor in 1951 proposed an understanding for this passage that I hold as generally correct.[22] The model text, says Delcor, is Ezekiel 36:16–28. Here it is said that Israel caused the land to be defiled with a feminine impurity, *niddah;* a word found again in Zechariah 13:1. So, says Ezekiel, God has poured upon (same verb in Zechariah 12:10) Israel His anger on account of their idols (in Zechariah, idolatry is carried over through the mention of Hadad-Rimmon in 12:11; cf. 13:2). After God scattered His people among the nations, they profaned His holy name. Now, the term used by Ezekiel to express the idea of profanation is *halol*, which in the present emphatic mode (piel) means "to profane, to defile"[23] but, in the indicative (qal) and sometimes also in the piel, means "to pierce."[24] An interesting text using *halol* with that latter meaning is Jeremiah 51:4, where *halol* is the pendant of the verb *daqor*!

---

19. Hanson, *The Dawn of Apocalyptic*, pp. 356 and 357.

20. Paul Lamarche, *Zacharie IX–XIV. Structure littéraire et messianisme* (Paris: Gabalda, 1961).

21. Cf., for example, the Rabbinic developments on the burning bush in *Exodus Rabba* 2:5 (Vilna ed.).

22. Marcel Delcor: "Un Problème de critique textuelle et d'exégèse, Zach. XII, 10, et aspicient ad me quem confixerunt," *Revue Biblique* 58 (1951): 189–99.

23. Cf. Leviticus 18:21; 19:22; 30:3; Malechi 1:12; and especially Isaiah 53:5.

24. In fact, there are two roots to *halol; halol₁* means "to profane" and *halol₂* means "to pierce." Zechariah has, consciously or not, confused the two.

Delcor thinks that Zechariah understood the text of Ezekiel 36 with the meaning "to pierce" (also adopted by Jeremiah 31:4; 37:10; Lamentations 4:9). Besides, the Versions A, S, θ, have *ekentesan* or *exekentesan*—to prod, to sting—while the Vetus Latina has *insultaverunt*.[25] Philologically speaking, we find a striking parallel case with the Hebrew root *naqob* that literally also means "to pierce" (2 Kings 18:21) and figuratively "to blaspheme" (cf. Leviticus 24:11, 16).

As a model text for Zechariah 12, Ezekiel 36 sheds light also upon other aspects common to the two texts. In both, it is a question of God's Spirit (Delcor is wrong in interpreting the Hebrew term *ruaḥ* as meaning here "disposition"). More decisive still is the parallel offered by Ezekiel 36:27 to the problematic *'et 'ašer*. Ezekiel's phrasing also is awkward. The meaning however is clear: "I shall cause you to walk in my laws," and the construction *'et 'ašer teleku* shows how the Zechariahan text should be understood as "they will look upon me because of the one they have pierced"[26] (the equivocation favoring the identification of God with his representative notwithstanding). Zechariah has thus read his illustrious exilic predecessor in a nonfigurative sense;[27] *ḥalol* for him conveys the violence of a deicide. What will happen in the eschatological times amounts to the ultimate blasphemy (*ḥalol₁*), that is, to putting God to death (*ḥalol₂*).

Zechariah's concept is perhaps the most audacious in the whole Hebrew Bible. We must realize, however, that the prophet is here using a typical cultic language, the pericope being non-narrative and still less speculative. Hence, in the light of such prophetic daring, we can pass judgment upon the modern-day "death of God theology." Had it chastened its language and patterned it after the cultic discourse, it would not have passed away like a worn-out fad. The liturgical and the speculative seldom coincide, for the ritual belongs to *mythos* rather than to *logos*. Zechariah does not come with a "death of God theology," but with a "death of God mythopoeic discourse." All the terms in Zechariah 12:10 have their setting in life in the royal liturgy of Jerusalem. Otzen shares the same opinion.[28] He sees in the expression "the one whom

---

25. The LXX has misread the verb and reversed the order of the consonants: *raqod*—to dance before someone (here, in derision)!

26. It is worth noticing that Redaq (Rabbi David Qimchi) reads *'al 'asher*, that is, "on account of," on the basis of the Targum which has here *'al de-*.

27. *Pace* M. Delcor, who speaks here of a "metaphorical sense"!

28. Otzen, *Studien über Deuterosacharja*, p. 178.

they have pierced" a quotation from the Israelite royal liturgy. There, the king is ritually pierced and passes through a rite of expiation, an echo of which is found in Zechariah 12:10. Furthermore, the drama is completed during the festival by a rite of purification, as is found also in Zechariah 13:1 (which, as we saw, belongs to one pericope with 12:10).

We probably should go one step further and retrace the influence on Zechariah 12 of the Canaanite background of the royal festival at Zion. A biblical invitation to do so is conveyed by texts such as Isaiah 51:9 and Job 26:13, which speak of the chaos monster Rehab being "pierced through." On the Canaanite side, Flemming F. Hvidberg calls attention to the fact that the god of rain and vegetation had been identified, already at Ugarit, with the Aramean and Babylonian god Hadad-Rimmon[29] (see 2 Kings 5:18).[30] Subsequently, Hadad was conceived of as a fertility god passing through the cycle of death and rebirth. The rites of lamentation in the liturgy for the death of Baal were also addressed to Hadad-Rimmon. It may even happen, says Hvidberg, that "the passage Zech. 12:9–14 somehow is based on an old (written?) tradition in which the term 'they have pierced' referred to the killing of a deity."[31] He calls upon Ugarit I A B col. I, 26, "I pierce thee!" It may be that the words "firstborn" and "only son" in Zechariah 12 originally designated the god.[32]

In the Zechariah text, the cultic language is historicized. In verse 12, the backdrop is reminiscent of the historical death of King Josiah "in the valley of Megiddo" (2 Kings 23:29; 2 Chronicles 35:22).[33] Now, Hugo Gressmann has suggested in his study on the Isaianic Songs of the Servant that the tragic death of Josiah in 609 at the hand of Pharaoh Necho gave birth to the expectation of a *Josia redivivus* (Gressmann refers to Jeremiah 30:18–21; Zechariah 12:9ff; the Songs of the Servant).[34] Be that as it may, Zechariah 12 has combined the themes of

29. Flemming F. Hvidberg, *Weeping and Laughter in the Old Testament* (Leiden: Brill, 1962), pp. 118–19. See M. Dietrich, O. Loretz, and J. Sanmartin, *Die keilalphabetische Texte aus Ugarit,* 1.5.vi.11–25 and 1.5.vi.31–1.6.i.8.

30. Cf. Arvid S. Kapelrud, *Baal in the Ras Shamra Texts* (Copenhagen, 1952), pp. 50, 52.

31. Hvidberg, *Weeping and Laughter,* p. 119.

32. Cf. B. Otzen, *Studien über Deuterosacharja,* p. 177 (hesitatingly).

33. Judges 5:19 speaks of "by the waters of Megiddo."

34. Hugo Gressmann, *Der Messias* (Göttingen: Vandenhoeck and Ruprecht, 1929), pp. 329–36. The question remains, however, whether the reference in the text is to Josiah. Gressmann himself stresses the future tense in the oracle both in Zechariah and in Isaiah 53 (cf. p. 336). Second Isaiah has created a new conception of the Messiah, that is, a "Messiah of the Exile," as the Israelites in exile "needed a Messiah who would first go through fight and suffering before reaching a glorious

Josiah's death with the Servant's suffering; on that score Gressmann is certainly right.

The process of historicization among Israel's prophets, particularly Zechariah, is a warning against overstressing the prophet's borrowing from myth. Similarly, Hosea 6:1–3 had used a language impregnated with the jargon of fertility myths. For instance, Hosea 6:2 alludes to the myth of the ritual murder of Baal. The prophet of the eighth century uses these popular categories to better express his thoughts without, of course, giving credence to the myth. The same applies here to Zechariah 12. The prophet is willing to use mythological concepts or the liturgical language of the Royal Festival of Zion, but he shows that he is precisely aware of the influence of the former upon the latter. He nonetheless makes use of the mythopoeic because that language is particularly equipped to convey a message of ultimate realities, historical and metahistorical, spatial and metaspatial. There is no condoning thereby by the prophet of the contents of the festival. If there were any doubt, it suffices to notice in the text the far-reaching shift from the person of the king to the people of Judah, who now become the center of attention. Using the royal liturgy style, Zechariah says that the substitutive sacrifice of the "pierced one"—collective—is acknowledged by the Jerusalem burghers, who thus identify themselves with the speakers in the first-person plural of Isaiah 52:13–53:12.

In other words, Judah has become for the prophet a royal character. Gressmann had already said that the one pierced through was doubtlessly (*ohne Zweifel;* see *Der Messias,* p. 330) a king, for the whole land weeps upon his death and calls that King-Messiah back to life through the bereavement ritual "as a dead Messiah is an inner contradiction." Gressmann's conclusion is essentially correct, although he takes too many shortcuts to reach it. In reality, it is not a king but the people of Judah that are slaughtered. Through that sacrifice, the martyrs acquire a royal dignity on the model of the humiliated king in myth and ritual of the ancient Near East. Through its identification with the King of the New Year Festival, Judah sacrificed is ennobled (made kingly), and *qua* collectivity, its self-offering elicits a process of democratization of

---

victory" (p. 338). This conception solidified among the successors of Second Isaiah, especially Third Isaiah and Second Zechariah. Let us note that Abravanel (fifteenth–sixteenth centuries) already defends this interpretation of Isaiah 53 as referring to the death of King Josiah, slain by Pharaoh Necho "on account of the sins of the Israelites." Cf. A. Neubauer and S. R. Driver, *The Fifty Third Chapter of Isaiah According to the Jewish Interpreters* (New York: KTAV, 1969), pp. 153–97.

the ritual (already conspicuous in Lamentations 3 or Ezekiel 37). As Harald Riesenfeld writes,

> It is thus to be considered that there is no exaggeration in subsuming that the cultic drama itself was interpreted as reflecting, by analogy with the role played there by the king, the fate of the people, so to speak sinking into death and coming back to life.[35]

In chapter 10, verse 4, the prophet showed that Yhwh Tsebaoth made of "the house of Judah his goodly horse in the battle." "From it [that is, from Judah][36] shall come out the cornerstone, from it the peg, from it the battle bow, from it all the potentates."[37] God rejects those in power (v. 3a) and picks the new leaders from the midst of the flock itself, that is, from the disenfranchised who now become at last free and independent (cf. Jeremiah 30:18–21). The democratization process follows the archaic model of the League of the Twelve Tribes (cf. Judges 20:2; 1 Samuel 14:38; Isaiah 19:13). A parallel is provided by Isaiah 60–62, the product of a similar socioeconomical milieu.

By bringing together Zechariah 12:10 and 10:4, we come closer to the Messianic dimension of "Judah." In 10:4, as a matter of fact, the trilogy of "cornerstone, peg, and battle bow" is probably a triple Messianic designation.[38] The Targum translates cornerstone by kingship and tent-peg by "messiahship." It is thus possible that we should see in the expression "the chiefs of Judah" (12:5, 6) a hendiadys. But if so, and in consequence of the democratization process, the Messiah has become collective. We are presented with a collective Messianism that finds its fulfillment in vicarious suffering. I am reminded of an earlier text, Isaiah 57:1, where there is a shift from singular to plural to singular again.[39] The "just" goes through martyrdom. The Isaianic text and in general the Songs of the Servant in Second Isaiah are a moving harbinger to Zechariah 12.

But now Zechariah sees the suffering of the just as inflicted, at least

---

35. Harald Riesenfeld, *The Resurrection in Ezekiel xxxvii and in the Dura-Europos Paintings* (Uppsala: Uppsala University Aarsckrift, 1948), p. 15.

36. "From him," says the Hebrew. With the Peshitta, it is to be understood as designating the house of Judah that is here personalized.

37. Here, as in Isaiah 60:17, the meaning of this word is positive (as shown by the context, cf. v. 3), although amphibologically it recalls the oppression exercised by those temporarily in power at Jerusalem (cf. 9:8).

38. Cf. W. Neil, *Interpreter's Dictionary of the Bible* (Nashville: Abingdon, 1962), vol. 4, s. v. "Zechariah," esp. p. 946.

39. *Ha-ḥadiq 'abad . . . we-'anśey ḥesed ne'esapim . . . ne'esap ha-ṣadiq.*

in part, by the "establishment" in Jerusalem. "Judah" is martyred and "Jerusalem" is the one who "does not understand," as says Isaiah 57:1, at least initially. That incomprehension is an outright participation in the "taking away of the righteous" (ibid.; see also the Psalms of Lament). And, as the prophet adopts here a mythopoeic language, "Jerusalem" takes rank among the chaotic forces unleashed ritually during the Royal Festival of Zion, against Yhwh and His anointed (Psalm 2). In the same way that, in the cult, the attempt against the latter is described as deicidal, so also at the *eschaton* when the "burghers" of Jerusalem "pierce" the "provincials" of Judah, they "kill" God.[40] As in the case of the martyrdom of the Isaianic Servant, it is the repentance of the witnesses/actors[41] that transforms failure into victory and death into life.[42] Here also the repentance and mourning over the one who lost "his" life by substitution, enthrones "him" as Messiah. The Suffering Servant had been bruised, humiliated, and put to death by the hand of Babylon. The "pierced one" as well is martyred by the Nations. However, in both cases, the true culpability falls on the prophet's people. The blindness of the "burghers of Jerusalem" led them to the flagrant injustice of confusing "Judah" and the Nations together. Their arrogance victimized/sacrificed their very brothers who eventually are to give up their lives for Jerusalem. Such a scandal and folly is on a par with the ultimate gravity of the event which the prophet considers as the last in history.

This, the Jewish tradition did not fail to see. It read Zechariah 12:10 (as well as Isaiah 53; Psalm 22:31; Psalm 69; etc.) messianically despite the "failure" of the Messiah in those texts. But for the Rabbis it is a question of the Messiah ben Yoseph (so the Targum, Redaq, Ibn Ezra, the *Meṣudoth Zion*). There indeed arose in Rabbinic Judaism a tradition about a pre-Messiah of sorts whose fate it was to be killed before Jerusalem's walls. His death is the harbinger of the coming of the victorious Messiah ben David. Whence comes such a figure is a moot question. Charles C. Torrey thought its origin was to be traced back to Isaiah 53 and thus preceded Christianity by several centuries.[43] True, traces of the

40. The words burghers, pierce, provincials, and kill are within quotation marks because they are all metaphorical.

41. The witnesses are actors, if only through their initial condemnation, contempt, and scorn of the Servant.

42. For Gressmann (*Der Messias*, p. 331), in both texts of Isaiah 53 and Zechariah 12, the life of the Messiah depends upon Israel's repentance. Furthermore, "the Psalm of repentance is the waking call to the dead."

43. Charles C. Torrey: "The Messiah, Son of Ephraim," *Journal of Biblical Literature* 66 (1947): 253–77.

doctrine are found in the Targum, the Talmud, and the Midrash, but Torrey was certainly wrong regarding the date of conception. None of the extant Jewish sources that speak of the Messiah ben Yoseph antedate the revolt of Bar Kochba in the second century CE.[44] The figure of a dying Messiah came certainly in response to the death of the guerilla fighter whom Rabbi Aqiba saluted as Messiah. In a way, therefore, the messianic reading of Zechariah 12 by Jewish tradition is an anachronism. But it is remarkable that within the concept of a double Messiah, the Messiah ben Yoseph is representative of the North, as the Messiah ben David is of the South (cf. Joshua 18:5).[45] Now, this conjunction of the North and the South happens to be one of the tenets of Second Zechariah's oracles. The sequence is also important, the Northern "Messiah" precedes the Southern Jerusalemite. It is not irrelevant that in Zechariah 12 the "only son" or "the firstborn son"[46] of verse 10 represents a collectivity identified as "Judah," while in Jeremiah 31:9 the "firstborn" is precisely Ephraim in the North!

The loss of such a precious life will be mourned "as the mourning of Hadad-Rimmon in the valley of Megiddon" (v. 11). The Targum sees here a double allusion, to the death of the Northern King Ahab in 853 (1 Kings 22:35) and to that of the Southern King Josiah in 609 at Megiddo (2 Kings 23:29). The Targum reading, "like the mourning for Ahab ben Omri who was killed by Hadad-Rimmon ben Tabrimmon," is probably misleading; the name of the Aramean king is not given in 1 Kings 22. Besides, as Joyce Baldwin points out, the mourning is not over an alleged victim of Hadad-Rimmon, but over Hadad-Rimmon himself.[47] But the Targumic evocation of 609 is right. I shall return to this point. Before I do so, however, a short summary of the findings so far will probably be helpful.

The oppressed ones of "Judah," meaning those opposing the "establishment of Jerusalem"—so that paradoxically "Judah" also includes the

---

44. The idea is expressed in 4 Esdras 7:28–31; 12:32–34; 2 Baruch 29:30, 40; 1 Enoch 90:30. Rabbi Dosa ben Harkinos (or, ben Hyrcanos, second century CE) in *Sukkoth* 52a, explains that in Zechariah 12:10 the Son of Ephraim dies because the people were unfaithful to him. *Psipta Rabbati* 36:2 calls him "the true Messiah, Ephraim." This text establishes a parallel with the "only son" or "firstborn son" of God (= Israel) in Egypt, thus orienting the reader toward an identification of the "pierced one" with the people.

45. Sigmund Mowinckel writes: "It might be thought that it arose among the Samaritans as a counterpart of the Jewish Messiah of the house of David, but that it was occasionally accepted in Jewish circles, partly because it could claim support from the interpretation of certain passages of scripture, partly because the Jews could regard the Messiah ben Joseph as one of the forerunners of the Messiah, like 'Taxo' of the house of Levi" (*He That Cometh*, p. 290).

46. On this, see Exodus 4:22; 1 Chronicles 5:1, etc.

47. Joyce G. Baldwin, *Haggai, Zechariah, Malachi* (London: Tyndale, 1972), ad loc.

Ephraimites in the North—are to be the victims of Nations and share the same fate with Jerusalem, for the siege against one is also the siege against the other. But Judah's slaughter is as regards Jerusalem a sacrifice of expiation for their blindness. Victims of Jerusalem's arrogance, the Judahites vicariously die in their stead, and the latter will acknowledge their guilt (that makes them the real murderers: *'et 'ašer daqeru*). As for the slaughtered ones, reality will overcome the fiction. For, despite all appearances (as in the case of the Servant of the Lord in Isaiah 52–53), the collective martyr is royal and messianic. He fulfills the Anointed One's vocation of judgment over the Nations and of redemption of Zion. God stands on his side, so that the Anointed One's death is simultaneously a deicide. Identity between the messenger and the one who sent him is strongly affirmed (cf. Zechariah 11:13). The mourning rites by the same token are unparalleled. They may remind one of the loss of King Josiah in 609, although to express his thoughts the prophet has recourse to mythopoeic language. He speaks of a mysterious Hadad-Rimmon who died at Megiddo, which he spells in a unique way "Megiddon." To this problem I now turn.

We have seen above that Hadad-Rimmon must be identified, as does Hvidberg among others, with the Canaanite god Baal who goes through death, before he returns to life, and is mourned ritually with dramatic popular lamentations. Along the same line, the text of the Septuagint on Zechariah 12:11 might well take us into the background on which the MT was built.[48] It has "Rimmon" in lieu of "Hadad-Rimmon." Now Rimmon is the name of the rock where, according to Judges 20:43–47, the Benjaminites pursued by the other tribes of Israel took refuge. This chapter of Judges is one of the bloodiest pages in Hebrew literature. It tells us about the awful massacre of one of the tribes by the other ones. The operation that started by being limited reprisals against Benjamin for its nonparticipation in the war against Gibeah soon got out of control (Judges 20:19–20). The whole tribe would have been annihilated were it not for a last minute realization by the avengers of the extent of the disaster (Judges 21). The eleven tribes then restored the tribe of Benjamin with "great weeping" (21:2). Peace was concluded at the rock of Rimmon (21:13).

Later on in history, at the time of the early monarchy in Israel, the text of 1 Samuel 14:2 tells us that by Gibeah—where the whole affair

---

48. A. van Hoonacker, *Les Douze petits prophètes* (Paris, 1908), called attention to the perspective opened by LXX here.

had started—King Saul "tarried . . . under a pomegranate tree in Migron." The text adds that "there were with him about 600 men," precisely the number of Benjaminites that escaped the fury of their brethren at the rock of Rimmon according to Judges. To Judges 20 and 1 Samuel 14:2 there are thus striking common elements. The Samuel text even continues by mentioning sharp rocks in the region of Gibeah (14:4) where Jonathan and his armor-bearer hid and from where they came forth to slaughter the Philistines (14:11–14).

It might well be that in Zechariah 12:11 a confusion crept in between *Migron* and *Megiddon,* two words which in Hebrew vary by only one consonant, the *r* of Migron and the *d* of Megiddon looking closely alike in any manuscript.

The phenomenon is far from unique. While Habakkuk 2:15 in the MT, for instance, has *m'oryhm,* 1 QpHab 11.3 has *mo'dyhm* and, in the Pesher, both spellings are used: *shame* and *festivals!* One may also, with some scholars, see in the "Shulamite" of Song of Songs another spelling for the "Shunamite" in 2 Samuel and 1 Kings. Further examples are provided in note 49 below regarding Luke 24:32 and Genesis 10:4. More convincing yet is that *Migron* in the MT has *mageddô(n)* in some Greek versions. For example, in Isaiah 10:28, the Hebrew has *migron,* but the Codex Alexandinus of the LXX reads *mageddô* and Theodotion reads *mageddôn;* that is, in both cases megiddo.

The spelling "Megidôn" can be found in a few texts of the LXX, probably under the influence of our Hebrew text. There is even a "Magedôn" in Judges 1:27 (Codex Alexandinus) and 2 Chronicles 35:22, hence the "Harmagedôn" of Revelation 16:16 (see below). In the Hebrew text of Zechariah 12:11, "Megiddôn" may be just an error in reading the *Vorlage,* but it may also be conscious.[49] If so, the morphological shift corresponds to a symbolic transformation of (the rock) Rimmon into the divine name Hadad-Rimmon by association of two sets

49. Jewish traditional literature already at the level of the Masoretic transmission of the *qeré u-ketib* variants within the texts (see, for example, Job 13:15), gives abundant examples of such voluntary confusions of consonants. Psalm 80:14 is thus read either *mi-ya'ar* (from the forest, hence a fierce boar), or *mi-ye'or* (from the river, hence a peaceful hippopotamus)! In the background of Luke 24:32, there has been a confusion between "heavy" (*yqyd*) and "burning" (*yqir*) according to Matthew Black, *An Aramaic Approach to the Gospels and Acts* (Oxford: Clarendon Press, 1954), p. 188. *'apiryon* in Song of Songs 3:9 is to be emended, say some scholars (following Winckler, *Altorientalische Forschungen,* vol. 1 [Leipzig: Verlag Eduard Pfeiffer, 1893]) into *'ap'don* = palace in Aram (from the Persian): cf. Daniel 11:45: *'apadana'.* The same applies to Genesis 10:4 where *dodanim* is to be read *rodanim,* that is, inhabitants of Rhodos island. Of course, examples of alliterations are numerous; cf. Isaiah 29:3: *weṣanti . . . muṣab . . . meṣurot.*

of mourning rites, one for the tribe of Benjamin's decimation and the other for the fall of King Josiah at Megiddo. This at any rate would explain the strange spelling of "Megiddon."

Of particular interest for us, of course, is the parallel thus set with the genocidal and fratricidal slaughter of a tribe by its confederates. In Zechariah 12, Judah dies at the hand and on behalf of Jerusalem. We can even at this point speculate that, if the original text of Zechariah 12:10 looked closer to the model drafted above, the collective meaning of "the pierced one" was by the same token explicit—so that many of the later exegetical controversies on this text could have been avoided!

When we turn to the New Testament use of the Zechariahan text, we find several passages of particular interest to us. To start with the strange spelling of "Megiddo" already encountered, it is repeated in a compounded way by Revelation 16:16, where, as we saw, it becomes "Harmageddon" (for "har-Megiddon"), that is, "mountain of Megiddo." This is all the more puzzling as Megiddo lies in the plain of Yizreel and there is no mountain within a ten-kilometer radius. Hence, normally, one finds the expression "the valley of Megiddô(n)" (Zechariah 12:11; 2 Chronicles 35:22). Moreover, that Megiddo is mentioned at all in an apocalyptic context can only be explained by reference to Zechariah 12:11. All other attempts to explain the problem pale in comparison.[50] Megiddo becomes a mountain here in spite of topography by adaptation to the eschatological perspective (cf. Ezekiel 38:8; 39:2ff.). At any rate, Revelation 16:16 alludes to the typology embodied in 2 Kings 23 (2 Chronicles 35), regarding the death of the saintly King Josiah, and in Zechariah 12:11, itself against the backdrop provided by Judges 20–21. John of Patmos eschatologizes the theme further by having recourse to Ezekiel 38–39 (Gog-Magog). The earlier motif of the fighting Nations has become one of "spirits of demons" (16:14).[51] The war is on the "Great Day," and Christ comes to defeat the enemy.

As seen above, the early Church saw in the "pierced one" Christ himself. This is the interpretation in Revelation 1:7 where the Zechariahan martyr is combined with the Danielic "son of man."[52] Those who pierced Christ are now "all the tribes of the earth" (corresponding to

---

50. Cf. Pierre Prigent, *L'Apocalypse de Saint Jean* (Neuchâtel: Delachaux et Niestlé, 1981), p. 249 n. 21, for a discussion of those, mostly far-fetched, hypotheses.

51. An interesting reversal of the process distinguished by Hermann Gunkel from *Götterkampf-mythus* to *Völkerkampfmythus*!

52. The conflation of Old Testament texts by Revelation is a common feature. In Revelation 16:16, we just saw Zechariah 12:11 combined with Ezekiel 38–39.

the Nations and Jerusalem in Zechariah), and they will mourn over him when they realize what they did to him. Let us stress the highly unusual expression "the tribes of the earth" that is found only here and in the parallel text of Matthew 24:30 to which we shall turn below. The term "tribes" instead of the expected "nations" is doubtless reminiscent of the tribal situation depicted by Zechariah 12, especially in the restored text of verses 10–11 as I suggested above.

While the text of John 19:37 seems less interesting for our study (the crucified body of Jesus is pierced by a soldier's spear in accordance, says John, with the Zechariah text), Matthew 24:30 is more striking. As an apocalyptic text, it falls perfectly in line with Revelation 1:7. Krister Stendahl thinks of an ancient tradition originating either in a *logion* attributed to Christ or in the most ancient traditional corpus of christological predication.[53]

Be that as it may, Matthew and Revelation, in terms of the trajectory of text receptions and interpretations, show the point where the parabolic line comes to a head. Such a conclusion required a double movement, of individualization of the "pierced one" and his identification with Jesus of Nazareth on the one hand, and of universalization of the guilty party which must eventually confess their sins and repent in order to be universally saved by the substitutive expiatory Victim, on the other hand.

The "death of God" was not for nought after all.

53. Krister Stendahl, *The School of St. Matthew* (Philadelphia: Fortress Press, 1968), p. 214.

Index of Passages

Index

CPSIA information can be obtained
at www.ICGtesting.com
Printed in the USA
LVHW111400280520
656833LV00002B/377